S THE
AMURAI,
THE MOUNTIE, AND
THE COWBOY

*Should
America Adopt
the Gun Controls
of Other
Democracies?*

DAVID B. KOPEL

A Cato Institute Book

Prometheus Books
Buffalo, New York

Published 1992 by Prometheus Books

96 95 94 93 92   5 4 3 2 1

Library of Congress Cataloging-in-Publication Data

The samurai, the mountie, and the cowboy : should America adopt the gun controls of other democracies? / by David B. Kopel.
    p.   cm.
"A Cato Institute book."
Includes bibliographical references and index.
ISBN 0-87975-756-6 (cloth : acid free)
    1. Gun control—Cross-cultural studies. 2. Gun control—United States.
I. Title.
HV7435.K66   1992
363.3'3'0973—dc20
        92-353
        CIP

Printed in the United States of America on acid-free paper.

Dedicated to the memory of my grandparents

Cornelius and Bess Blanke

Acknowledgments

Thanks to Roy Anderson, Bob Badland, Hanspeter Baumann, Paul Blackman, David Bordua, A. D. Castberg, Jerry Crossett, Stephen D'Andrilli, Charles Forsyth, Fred Gibbs, Mort Greenglass, Colin Greenwood, Brian Hughes, Richard Hummel, Chris Little, Richard A. J. Munday, Leah Murch, F. W. Noftall, Mark J. J. Offenbach, R. W. Oldin, Dick Paik, Noel Perrin, Ian Ramsey, Jean Skinner, Che Spector, Jan Stevenson, B. A. Sutcliffe, Takaki Tokuoka, Ray Traband, and R. A. Watt for their insights and thoughtful criticisms. Special thanks to my wife, Deirdre, for her support during this book's six-year gestational period.

"A system must be suited to the habits and genius of the people it is to govern, and must grow out of them."*

—Charles Pinckney

*From a speech by Charles Pinckney, a delegate to the Constitutional Convention. Pinckney was supporting a Constitutional ban on granting of titles of nobility. Advocates of nobility, such as Alexander Hamilton, had argued that the system of honorary titles worked well in Britain, and should be adopted in the United States. Quoted in James Madison, *Notes of Debates in the Federal Convention of 1787* (New York: W. W. Norton, 1987; first published in 1840 as vols. 2–3 of *The Papers of James Madison*), p. 185 (June 25, 1787). As recommended by Pinckney, the Constitution declares: "No title of nobility shall be granted by the United States." United States Constitution, Article I, Sec. 9.

Contents

1

Introduction

One of the core arguments for American gun control is the following rationale:

1. The United States is the only modern democracy that does not impose strict gun controls.

2. The United States suffers a much higher crime rate than those democracies that impose strict gun controls.

3. Therefore, adopting strict gun controls like other democracies would lower the American crime rate.

Virtually every advocate for strong American gun laws adopts this reasoning. Sarah Brady, chairperson of Handgun Control, Inc., states: "We are the only civilized nation in the world without a good gun law and we are the most violent in the West." Presidents who want gun control, attorneys general, congressmen, academics, medical researchers, and newspaper and magazine writers all promise that adopting the stringent gun laws of foreign countries will dramatically lower the American crime rate.[1] When restrictive American gun laws are upheld in court, judges often cite as justification the strict laws abroad.[2] The anti-gun lobbies agree that foreign gun laws would work in the United States,[3] and so do the police lobbies that have aligned themselves with the gun-control movement. The International Association of Chiefs of Police, in conjunction with the Fraternal Order of Police and Handgun Control, Inc., promises: "Gun laws can, do, and will work, contrary to the claims of the National Rifle Association. Other democratic nations clearly prove that." They reassure skeptical gun owners: "The rights of hunters and sportsmen are well preserved in those nations as well."[4]

That promise of reduction in crime, with no detriment to the sportsman, was made in a 1988 debate on gun control, repeating a promise made by President Lyndon Johnson in 1968 in his plea to the nation for gun control.[5] Indeed, the promise may be traced back to the turn of the century; as long as modern America has been trying to control guns, it has looked abroad for justification.[6]

As gun controllers line up their citations of foreign countries that control guns, suppress crime, and protect the sportsman, gun advocates pull out their counterexample of Switzerland, where everyone has a gun, and almost no one commits crime. Robert Sherrill, author of one of the most trenchant exposés of American gun culture, observes that no Congressional hearing on gun control

> would have been complete . . . without the appearance of a witness to claim that England has one of the toughest gun laws in the world and one of the lowest murder rates, and therefore we should outlaw guns. No hearing would have been complete without the appearance of a witness to claim that in Switzerland every adult male is issued a rifle and ammunition to keep at home and Switzerland has an extremely low crime rate, and therefore every American male should be issued a gun.[7]

The pro-gun and the anti-gun sides shout at one another, each trying to justify its own policies by citing the laws of other countries. The two sides never achieve any resolution, because neither side bothers with more than a superficial glance at the realities of gun ownership in the other countries. Gun controllers imagine a utopia in England, where rational gun laws are enforced fairly, crime is virtually nonexistent, and the sportsman thrives, accepting moderate controls. Gun owners imagine a utopia in Switzerland, where the government gives everyone an assault rifle, and there is virtually no violent crime. Each side wishes America could be more like its favorite foreign country.

One of the reasons that the foreign control aspect of the American gun-control struggle has remained stuck on the same point for the entire twentieth century is that American academics have failed to provide useful guidance. Outside of some statutory compilations by the Library of Congress, there is barely any American research on the subject of foreign gun control.[8] As a result, Americans have little idea what the actual laws in foreign countries are, and no understanding at all about how those laws

are administered, how they have affected crime rates, and—most importantly—how the gun controls fit into the rest of the society's culture.

This book is an effort to remedy that lack of research. First we will
examine the firearms laws of Japan, the one major democracy that enforces
a near prohibition on guns. Then our discussion will turn to several British
Commonwealth democracies, where gun laws are stricter than in America:
Great Britain, Canada, Australia, New Zealand, and Jamaica. Switzerland,
the democracy where everyone is armed, will be scrutinized to determine
to what extent, if any, it supports the claims of the American gun lobbies.
Each chapter analyzes not only the particular laws of a nation, but also
the historical, legal, and cultural context of the laws; evidence regarding
the efficacy of gun controls in reducing gun crime and gun suicide; and,
most importantly, the role of the nation's firearms laws in defining the
relationship between the people and their government.

Having studied foreign gun cultures, we will then analyze selected aspects of America's gun history to understand how the American experience
compares to that of other nations and to suggest in part why America's
firearm policies have diverged so sharply from the rest of the world's. Finally,
we will try to synthesize the foreign and American experiences in an effort
to fashion a gun-control policy that can work in the United States.

NOTES

1. **For the press:** "Starting with a Bang," (Baltimore) *Evening Sun,* January 4, 1991,
p. A8 ("It may take years, but make no mistake, the time will come when the United States
will adopt laws similar to those in European nations—laws which virtually ban handguns
altogether and which place the most stringent restrictions on ownership of *any* kind of firearm.
There is no other answer."); "1990: The Bloodiest Year Yet?" *Newsweek,* July 16, 1990,
p. 24; "Murder America," *Newsweek,* July 9, 1990, p. 7; "The Sale and Ownership of Handguns,"
(Greensboro, N.C.) *Carolina Peacemaker,* September 20, 1990 ("The ease with which
Americans can buy handguns has helped to make us the modern nation with the highest
murder rate in the world."); "Gun Training is the Answer," (Oxnard) *Press-Courier,* reprinted
in *Los Angeles Daily Journal,* September 12, 1990 (High American homicide rate compared
to Canada and Japan is "due, in large measure, to the wide availability of firearms in the
United States"); Julia Trotman, "New Support for Gun Control," *Newsweek,* August 15,
1988, p. 26 ("the nation's handgun death toll—9,014 in 1985, compared with eight for all
of Britain"); Tom Wicker, "Violence and Hypocrisy," *New York Times,* July 9, 1990, p.
A17; "Topics: Small Bangs, Big Bucks," *New York Times,* January 5, 1982, p. A14, col.1
("[T]he United States is the only industrial democracy without effective gun control laws.");
Volsky, "Guns in Florida: This Week It Suddenly Becomes a Lot Easier to Be Legal,"
New York Times, September 27, 1987; "Gun Control Around the World: How Other Nations
Achieve It," *Chicago Tribune,* December 29, 1980, p. VI:6 (Associated Press story); "Curb
the Handgun Madness," *Miami Herald,* March 6, 1981; "Canada Curbs Guns," *Toledo Blade,*
April 14, 1980 ("U.S. lawmakers would do well to examine closely what Canada has done

in an effort to limit the carnage."); "Delaying Gun Sales Will Stop Criminals," *USA Today*, May 26, 1987, p. 12A (comparative firearms murder rates in other democracies; praise for Canadian gun controls); Yoakum, "The British Prefer Baseball Bats," *USA Today*, October 10, 1983; Richard Strout (TRB), "A Scary Lesson in Gun Control," *Philadelphia Inquirer*, February 8, 1979 ("more killing in New York overnight than in Tokyo all year"); Henry Fairlie, quoted in Richard Strout (TRB), "Gun Control and the Death of Bobby Kennedy," in *TRB: Views and Perspectives on the Presidency* (New York: Macmillan, 1979), p. 329; Garry Wills, "John Lennon's War," *Chicago Sun Times*, December 12, 1980; Garry Wills, "Gun Rules . . . or worldwide gun control?" *Philadelphia Inquirer*, May 17, 1981, p. 8-E; "Gun Toting: A Fashion Needing Change," *Science News* 93 (June 29, 1968), p. 614.

Politicians and government commissions: President Johnson's address to the nation reprinted in *Congressional Record*, June 24, 1968: H5371-72 ("In other countries which have sensible laws, the hunter and the sportsman thrive."); Michael Dukakis, "Targeting Gun Crime," *Boston Herald*, August 30, 1990 (Quoting gun-control advocate Joseph Biden, chairperson of the U.S. Senate Judiciary Committee, that the United States is "the most murderous industrialized nation in the world" and attributing the fact to lax American gun-control laws). Former Massachusetts Congressman Robert Drinan writes: "Alone among the Western nations the United States permits the unrestricted availability of handguns, and alone it suffers an astronomical crime rate," Robert Drinan, "Gun Control: The Good Outweighs the Evil," *Civil Liberties Review* (A.C.L.U., June 1976). Also, "Drinan Proposes International Gun Control," (Lowell, Mass.) *The Sun*, May 22, 1981, p. 15; Senator Edward Kennedy, "Need for Gun Control Legislation," *Current History* 71 (July-August 1976), p. 26; Senator Howard Metzenbaum, *Congressional Record*, February 4, 1987, p. S792 ("The American homicide rate is far higher than virtually every other modern industrialized country."); former Attorney General Ramsey Clark, *Crime in America: Observations on Its Nature, Causes, and Control* (New York: Simon and Schuster, 1970), p. 85; New York senatorial candidate Mark Green, *Winning Back America* (New York: Bantam, 1982), p. 222 (per 100,000 population, there are 9.7 annual murders in the United States, 1.6 in Japan, 1.3 in Britain, and 1.3 in West Germany); Maryland Congresswoman Constance Morella, *Congressional Record*, September 15, 1988, pp. H7645-46 (citing Justice Powell's contrast of British and U.S. handgun homicide rates); former Maryland Senator Millard Tydings, quoted in Richard Hofstadter, "America as a Gun Culture," *American Heritage*, October 1970, p. 4; New York State Assemblyman Steven Sanders, letter to Stephen D'Andrilli, Guardian Group International, September 27, 1990 ("It is not a statistical accident that virtually every other democracy and industrialized nation long ago imposed stringent restrictions on gun ownership and those nations have only a fraction of the violent crime compared with the United States."); Patrick T. Murphy, public guardian of Cook County, "We Need Fewer Guns, More Individual Responsibility," *Chicago Tribune*, September 21, 1990 (America is the only society "that arms its hooligans. Other societies realize that giving guns to a thug is not unlike throwing a burning match on gasoline.").

For academics: Catherine F. Sproule and Deborah J. Kennett, "Killing with Guns in the USA and Canada 1977-1983: Further Evidence for the Effectiveness of Gun Control," *Canadian Journal of Criminology* (July 1989): 245-51; John Gunn, *Violence* (New York: Praeger, 1973), pp. 152-54; A. Kotz and H. Hair, *Firearms, Violence, and Civil Disorders* (Menlo Park, Calif.: Stanford Research Institute, 1968); Donald T. Lunde, *Murder and Madness* (San Francisco: San Francisco Book Company, 1976), pp. 41-42 (strict handgun laws and low murder rate in England); Charles R. Fenwick, "Crime and Justice in Japan: Implications for the United States," *International Journal of Comparative and Applied*

Criminal Justice 6 (Spring 1982), p. 70 (Japanese example proves that the United States should tighten its gun laws); Carl Bakal, *The Right to Bear Arms* (New York: McGraw-Hill, 1966); Richard Hofstadter and Michael Wallace (eds.), *American Violence: A Documentary History* (New York: Knopf, 1970), pp. 24–25 (Alone among industrial societies, America clings to the "unrestricted availability of guns."); Richard Hofstadter, "America as a Gun Culture," *American Heritage,* October 1970; Arthur M. Schlesinger, Jr., *The Crisis of Confidence: Ideas, Power and Violence in America Today* (New York: Bantam, 1969), p. 15.

The syllogism is quite prevalent in undergraduate sociology and criminology textbooks. Frank E. Hagan, *Introduction to Criminology* (Chicago: Nelson-Hall, 1986), p. 181; Lewis Yablonsky, *Criminology: Crime and Criminality* (New York: Harper & Row, 1990), p. 213 ("The homicide rate per capita is reported to be 35 times higher than the rate in Germany or in England, yet a substantial proportion of the American population appears to support the view that everyone should be entitled to own a gun."), p. 215 (citing the *New England Journal of Medicine* Seattle/Vancouver article); John E. Conklin, *Criminology,* 3d ed. (New York: Macmillan, 1989), p. 323 (strict gun laws in Japan help explain the low Japanese crime rate), and p. 115, citing approvingly for the efficacy of Canadian gun control, Stanley Meisler, "The Mounties Went Forth," *Boston Globe,* June 20, 1981, p. 3; Henry W. Mannle and J. David Hirschel, *Fundamentals of Criminology* (Englewood Cliffs, N.J.: Prentice-Hall, 1988), p. 112; William Tonso, "Social Problems and Sagecraft," in Donald B. Kates, Jr., ed., *Firearms and Violence: Issues of Public Policy* (Cambridge, Mass.: Ballinger, 1984), pp. 74–75 n.8, citing as examples, Amitai Etzioni, "Violence," in R. Merton and R. Nisbet, eds., *Contemporary Social Problems* (1971), p. 740; Empey, "American Society and Criminal Justice Reform," in A. Blumberg, ed., *Perspectives on Criminal Behavior* (1974), pp. 295–96; A. Shostak, ed., *Modern Social Reforms* (1974), p. 291; M. Bassis, R. Gelles, and A. Levine, *Social Problems* (1982), p. 477; R. Stark, *Social Problems* (1975), p. 226; M. Haskell and L. Yablonsky, *Crime and Delinquency* (1978), pp. 340–41; and D. Light and S. Keller, *Sociology* (1982), p. 254.

For **medical researchers:** J. H. Sloan, A. L. Kellerman, D. I. Reay, J. A. Fenis, T. Koepsell, F. P. Rivara, C. Rice, L. Gray, and J. Logerfo, "Handgun Regulations, Crime, Assaults, and Homicide: A Tale of Two Cities," *New England Journal of Medicine* 319 (November 10, 1988): 1256–62; Lois A. Fingerhut and Joel C. Kleinman, "International and Interstate Comparisons of Homicide Among Young Males," *Journal of the American Medical Association* 263 (June 27, 1990): 3292–95; Gary J. Ordog, "Socioeconomic Aspects of Gunshot Wounds," in Gary J. Ordog, ed., *Management of Gunshot Wounds* (New York: Elsevier, 1988), pp. 456–57.

2. *Siccardi v. State,* 50 N.J. 545, 284 A.2d 533, 573 (1971) (quoting California Supreme Court Justice Stanley Mosk's approbation of British gun control); *State v. Dawson,* 272 N.C. 535, 159 S.E.2d 1, 9 (1968) (historical English controls on the carrying of firearms as legal justification for American controls).

See also Justice Lewis F. Powell, Jr., "Capital Punishment," *Harvard Law Review* 102 (March 1989), p. 1044 (praise for English gun laws, and denial that Second Amendment confers a right to own handguns). The article is discussed in chapter 3.

3. For anti-gun lobbies, see National Coalition to Ban Handguns [renamed the Coalition to Stop Gun Violence], "20 Questions and Answers" (no date, unpaginated) (handgun murder rate in the United States 100 times higher than in England and Wales, 200 times higher than in Japan); Handgun Control, Inc., "Handgun Facts," (contrasting handgun death rate in the United States with Britain, Canada, Australia, Japan, Switzerland, Sweden, and Israel); Handgun Control, Inc., 1984 fundraising letter for "Safe Streets Petition Campaign," p.

2 ("Experience in other countries demonstrates conclusively that handgun laws do work effectively. . . . More handguns are available here than in any nation on Earth—some 60 *million!* The result: Each and every year more than 20,000 of our friends, neighbors, loved ones, and children are killed by handguns."); Michael K. Beard, National Coalition to Ban Handguns, "Showdown with the Gun Gang at Gun Control Corral," *Business & Society Review* 23 (Fall 1977), p. 71; Michael K. Beard, Coalition to Stop Gun Violence, "Oprah Winfrey Show," show no. 1034, August 30, 1990, Harpo productions transcript ("We have more guns than any other society in the world, and we have more deaths."); Pete Shields, then-Chairman of Handgun Control, Inc.: Japan has a low murder rate "because *they* control guns—above all, handguns—and we don't. . . . Once we sharply reduce the private possession of handguns, violent crime in this country will start to be cut dramatically" (quoted in Richard Harris, "A Reporter at Large: Handguns," *New Yorker,* July 26, 1976, p. 54).

4. Quotation from advertisement for International Association of Chiefs of Police and the Fraternal Order of Police, *Washington Post,* September 7, 1988.

See also, "Seven Ways to Reduce Crime and Violence," *The Police Chief,* May 1988 (magazine of the International Association of Chiefs of Police): "Do gun laws work? The experiences of other democratic nations that rationally manage firearms say clearly and convincingly 'yes.' A simple look at the homicide rates between American cities and cities of similar size and demographic and geographic characteristics in other nations shows beyond any doubt that America's inability to deal effectively with firearms, particularly handguns, manifests itself in a disgracefully high level of violence that diminishes the quality of life for decent, peaceful, law-abiding citizens.

"The gun lobby quickly dismisses these comparisons with feeble explanations of how America is different. We are different. We kill, maim, and cripple people at record rates. We should be ashamed of this situation."

Former San Jose Police Chief Joseph McNamara, a strong supporter of Handgun Control, Inc., writes, "[I]n countries like Japan, England, Australia, Israel, and Sweden, disproportionately fewer people are killed by handguns. These countries have laws that restrict their citizens from buying handguns they do not need. . . . When we look at other countries . . . [it] is clear that the lack of a rational national policy on firearms results in needless tragic shootings." Joseph D. McNamara, "Developing a Rational, National Firearms Policy," *The Police Chief,* March 1988, p. 29. Former Minneapolis Chief Anthony Bouza, another ally of Handgun Control, Inc., when addressing the Canadian Association of Chiefs of Police urged them to oppose loosening of Canadian gun controls, and blamed the high American violent crime rate on America's 70 million handguns. Michael Tenszen, "Keep Handgun Ban, U.S. Police Official Warns Canadians," (Toronto) *Globe and Mail,* August 27, 1986.

5. President Johnson's address to the nation reprinted in *Congressional Record,* June 24, 1968: H5371-72. "In other countries which have sensible laws, the hunter and the sportsman thrive."

6. In the debate preceding the Sullivan Law, the first major American gun-control law affecting citizens entitled to full civil rights, one newspaper letter to the editor recommended that New York copy Japan, "where intending purchasers of revolvers must first obtain police permits, and sales must be reported to the police" and civilian handgun possession was therefore "virtually nil." Albert L. Wyman, "Sale of Firearms," *New York Times,* August 19, 1910, p. 8, col. 5.

In the Congressional hearings over the 1934 National Firearms Act, Representative Lewis stated "it would be very helpful to me in reaching a judgment in supporting this bill to find just what restrictions a law-abiding citizen of Great Britain and these other countries is willing to accept. . . ." Attorney General Cummings obliged the Congressman by submitting a statement that greatly overstated the extent of British controls. "Statement of Hon. Homer

S. Cummings, Attorney General of the United States," before House Ways and Means Committee, hearings on the National Firearms Act, H.R. 9066, 73d Cong., 2d sess., April 16, 1934 (Washington, D.C.: Government Printing Office, 1934), pp. 17–18, 28. (The testimony is described in more detail in chapter 3.)

See also Baumes Crime Commission, 1929 Annual Report, quoted in Robert Sherrill, *The Saturday Night Special* (New York: Penguin, 1975), pp. 19–20; Lee Kennett and James L. Anderson, *The Gun in America: The Origins of a National Dilemma* (New York: Westport Press, 1975), p. 199 (a witness at 1922 House of Representative committee hearing claimed that England's low crime rate resulted from the absence of firearms).

7. Sherrill, p. 176.

8. Library of Congress, *Gun Control Laws in Foreign Countries,* rev. ed. (Washington, D.C.: Library of Congress, 1976); Library of Congress, *Gun Control Laws in Foreign Countries,* rev. ed. (Washington, D.C.: Library of Congress, 1981); Library of Congress, *Firearms Regulations in Various Foreign Countries* (Washington, D.C.: Library of Congress, 1990).

2

Japan: No Guns, No Gun Crime

"The squeaky wheel gets the grease."

—American proverb

"The nail that sticks out will be pounded down."

—Japanese proverb

"No one shall possess a firearm or firearms or a sword or swords." That is the basic rule of weapons possession in Japan,[1] where gun control is the most stringent in the democratic world, gun ownership is minuscule, and gun crime is virtually nonexistent.

GUN POSSESSION

Although Americans usually think of Japan in terms of complete gun prohibition, the government does allow a small amount of civilian gun ownership. While handguns and rifles are illegal, sportsmen are permitted to possess shotguns for hunting and for skeet and trap shooting, but only after submitting to a lengthy licensing procedure.[2] Without a license, no one may own or operate or even hold a firearm.

The licensing procedure is rigorous. Prospective gun owners must first attend classes and pass a written test,[3] followed by shooting-range classes

20

and a shooting test. After a safety exam, applicants take a simple "mental test" at a local hospital. They then produce for the police a medical certificate attesting that they are mentally healthy and not addicted to drugs.[4]

The police investigate each applicant's background and relatives, ensuring that both are crime free. Membership in aggressive political or activist groups disqualifies an applicant.[5] The police have unlimited discretion to deny a license to any person for whom "there is reasonable cause to suspect may be dangerous to other persons' lives or properties or to the public peace."[6]

Gun owners are required to store their weapons in a locker, and give the police a map of the apartment showing the location of the locker. Ammunition must be kept in a separate locked safe. The licenses also allow the holder to buy a few thousand rounds of ammunition, with each transaction being registered.[7]

In Japan, civilians can never own handguns. Small calibre rifles were once legal, but in 1971 the government forbade all transfers of rifles. Current rifle license-holders may continue to own them, but their heirs must turn them in to the police when the license-holder dies.[8] The number of remaining rifle licenses totals 27,000.[9] Even shotguns and air rifles, the two legal types of firearm, are becoming rarer and rarer, as few people find it worthwhile to pass through a burdensome gun-licensing process. The number of licensed shotguns and air rifles declined from 652,000 in 1981 to 493,373 in 1989.[10]

Although there is no mandatory minimum penalty for unlicensed firearm possession in Japan, 81 percent of sentences for illegal firearm or sword possession are imprisonment for a year or more, perhaps because most gun crimes are perpetrated by professional criminals.[11] The maximum penalty for an illegal handgun is ten years in prison and a one million yen fine (roughly eight thousand U.S. dollars).

GUN-RELATED CRIME

Gun crime does exist in Japan, but in very low numbers. Shotguns and air rifles, both legal for citizens to own, were involved in thirty crimes in 1989.[12] With no legal civilian handgun possession, Japan experiences an average of less than 200 annual violent crimes committed with a handgun, of which almost all were perpetrated by *Bóryokudan,* organized crime groups.[13] Most gun crimes involve only unlicensed possession, and not the commission of another crime. Including the possession cases, there are about 600 handgun crimes a year and 900 long-gun crimes.[14]

In the years following World War II, former soldiers were the major source of illegal guns. Today, illegal guns are usually smuggled from overseas (especially from the Philippines and the United States) by organized crime gangs that also import pornography, drugs, and illegal immigrants.[15] A small number of craftsmen specialize in converting toy and model guns into working handguns for criminals.[16] The gangster appetite for guns, and their success in procuring weapons is said by the police to be increasing.[17] Of weapons confiscated from gangsters, guns accounted for only 6 percent in 1960, and 39 percent in 1988.[18] On the other hand, the number of real handguns confiscated by the police has fallen from 1,338 in 1985 to 875 in 1989. The number of converted toy handguns seized has fallen from a high of 569 in 1985 to 128 in 1989.[19]

Because gun crime still exists in tiny numbers the police make gun licenses increasingly difficult to obtain. The test and all-day lecture are held once a month. The lecture almost always requires that the licensee take a full day off from work—not a highly regarded activity by Japanese employers. An annual gun inspection is scheduled at the convenience of the police, and also requires time off from work. Licenses must be renewed every three years, with another all-day safety lecture and examination at police headquarters.[20]

Because licensed gun owners commit almost none of the gun crime, and because guns licensed in Japan are almost never stolen and used in crime, it might be said that the Japanese police have found an appropriate level of stringency for enforcement of the gun laws. On the other hand, it could be argued that the heavy controls on licensed users have little to do with controlling the illicit smuggling that is the source of guns used in the commission of crimes.

Tokyo is the safest major city in the world. Only 59,000 licensed gun owners live in Tokyo.[21] Per one million inhabitants, Tokyo has 40 reported muggings a year; New York City has 11,000.[22] The handgun murder rate is at least 200 times higher in America than Japan.[23] The official homicide rate in Japan in 1988 was 1.2 homicide cases per 100,000 population, while in America it was 8.4.[24]

Robbery is almost as rare as murder. Indeed, armed robbery and murder are both so rare that they usually make the national news, regardless of where they occur.[25] Japan's robbery rate is 1.4 per 100,000 inhabitants. The reported American rate is 220.9.[26] The gap between the American and the Japanese crime rate is not quite so wide, however, as the official statistics indicate. First, many Japanese robberies are perpetrated by *yakuza* (gangsters), and the victims do not report the crime for fear of retribution.[27] And second, the inclusion of many self-defense homicides makes the official American homicide rate seem significantly worse than it really is.[28]

Whatever the statistics, the Japanese are among the most secure people of any industrial democracy. People walk anywhere at night, and carry large sums of cash.[29] Small children ride subways by themselves.[30] A shopper can put a bag of groceries down outside a store, and return half an hour later to find the bag still there.[31]

Japan has severe gun laws, and little crime. Does the former help cause the latter? Yes. Should America think about a gun law like Japan's? Some American writers favor prohibitions even more complete than Japan's.[32] Before copying the Japanese laws, however, it makes sense to examine Japan's gun laws within the context of Japan's social order and crime control.

A POLICE STATE

Illegal gun possession, like illegal drug possession, is a consensual offense. There is no victim to complain to the police. Accordingly, in order to find illegal guns, the Japanese police are given broad search and seizure powers. The basic firearms law permits a policeman to search a person's belongings if the officer judges a person "sufficiently suspectable to carry or bring a firearm, a sword or a cutlery" or if the person "is likely to endanger life or body of other persons by judging reasonably from his abnormal behavior or any other surrounding circumstances."[33] Once a weapon is found, the policeman may confiscate it.[34] Even if the confiscation is later admitted to be an error, the firearm is sometimes not returned.

In practice, the special law for weapons searches is not necessary, since the police routinely search at will. They ask suspicious characters to show them what is in their purse or sack.[35] In rare cases where a policeman's search (for a gun or any other contraband) is ruled illegal, it hardly matters; for the Japanese courts permit the use of illegally seized evidence.[36] Legal rules aside, the Japanese, whether they be criminals or ordinary citizens, are much more willing than their American counterparts to consent to searches and to answer questions from the police.[37]

The most important element of police power is not authority to search, but authority in the community. In modern Japan, the police are considered the new samurai, full of *Nihon damashii* (Japanese spirit).[38] Like school teachers, Japanese policemen rate high in public esteem, especially in the countryside. They are community leaders and role models who teach voluntary judo, *kendo* (Japanese fencing with sticks), and calligraphy classes for children and adults.[39] Although Japan is almost completely gun-free and crime-free, the police have a great deal of work.

Policemen in Every Neighborhood

Fifteen thousand *kōban* or "police boxes" are located throughout the nation.[40] Citizens go to the twenty-four-hour-a-day boxes for street directions, to complain about day-to-day problems such as noisy neighbors, or to ask advice on how to raise children.[41] About 90 percent of *kōban* put out their own small newspapers, with information about crime and accidents, "stories about good deeds by children, and opinions of residents."[42]

In a typical *kōban,* one officer supervises three patrolmen: one patrols the beat, one is stationed outside the box, and one processes paperwork inside.[43] Nine thousand of the police boxes, mostly in rural areas, house officers and their families.[44] Police-box officers solve 74.6 percent of all criminal cases solved.[45]

Police officers not in the boxes also stay close to the community. The patrol officer is called *omawari-san,* "Mr. Walk-about." Policeman generally travel by foot or bicycle. American-style motorized patrol—criticized for separating police officers from their beat—is rare.[46]

Keeping an Eye on Guns, and Everything Else

"Home visit is one of the most important duties of officers assigned to police boxes," explains the Japanese National Police Agency. In twice-a-year visits, officers fill out Residence Information Cards about who lives where and which family member to contact in case of emergency, what relation people in the house have to each other, what kind of work they do, if they work late, how much money they have, and what kind of cars they own.[47] The police also check on all gun licensees, to make sure that no gun has been stolen or misused, that the gun is securely stored, and that the licensees are emotionally stable.[48]

The close surveillance of gun owners and householders comports with the police tradition of keeping close tabs on many private activities.[49] The nation's official year-end police report includes statistics like "Background and Motives for Girls' Sexual Misconduct."[50] Another statistic tabulated is "Misconduct of Juveniles by Type." In 1989, "Smoking" accounted for 43.0 percent of the cases, "Roaming until midnight" for 28.4 percent, and "Unsound companionship" for 4.4 percent.[51] The police reports even note how many coffee shops are open at midnight.[52] That the police keep records on sex is simply a reflection of their keeping an eye on everything, including guns. Every person is the subject of a police dossier.[53]

The police also include in their reports the section "Labor Movements under Changing Economic Circumstances," which notes selected labor demands and interunion negotiations.[54] A Hokkaido University professor states, "The police consider all antigovernment political activity as sub-versive."[55] Attempting to subvert the dominant paradigm is a quick road to ruin in Japan. One American writer suggests environmental activism in Japan is weak because Japan's conformist society labels all dissenters as violent extremists.[56]

Almost everyone accepts the paradigm that the police should be respected. Because the police are so esteemed, the Japanese people cooperate with their police more than Americans do.[57] In American police academies, only 20 percent of officers-in-training believe they will not receive sufficient community support; after two years on the beat, 60 percent believe "it is difficult to persuade people to give patrolmen the information they need."[58]

Cooperation with the police also extends to obeying the laws, which almost every Japanese believes in. The Japanese people, and even the large majority of Japanese criminals, voluntarily obey the gun controls. No gun control law in America has remotely approached the near-unanimous level of Japanese citizen compliance.[59]

There is no right to bear arms in Japan. In practical terms, there is no right to privacy against police searches. Other Western-style rights designed to protect citizens from a police state are either nonexistent or feeble in Japan. For example, after arrest, a suspect may be detained without bail for up to twenty-eight days before the prosecutor must bring the suspect before a judge.[60]

Even after the twenty-eight-day period is completed, detention in a Japanese police station may continue on a variety of pretexts, such as preventing the defendant from destroying evidence. Rearrest on another charge (*bekken taihō*) is a common police tactic for starting the suspect on another twenty-eight-day interrogation process. Some defendants may be held for several months without ever being brought before a judge.[61]

Criminal defense lawyers are the only people who are allowed to visit a suspect in custody, and those meetings are strictly limited. In the months while a suspect is held prisoner, defense counsel may see clients for one to five meetings lasting about fifteen minutes each. Even that access will be denied if it hampers the police investigation. While under detention, suspects can be interrogated twelve hours a day, allowed to bathe only every fifth day, and may be prohibited from standing up, lying down, or leaning against the wall of their jail cells.[62] Amnesty International calls the Japanese police custody system a "flagrant violation of United Nations human rights principles."[63]

In general, suspects are not allowed to read confessions before they sign them, and suspects commonly complain that their confession was altered after signature. Explaining the high confession rate, a Tokyo police sergeant notes, "It is no use to protest against power."[64] The police use confession as their main investigative technique, and when that fails, they can become frustrated and angry. The Tokyo Bar Associations state that the police routinely "engage in torture or illegal treatment." The Tokyo Bar is particularly critical of the judiciary for its near-total disinterest in coercion during the confession process. "Even in cases where suspects claimed to have been tortured and their bodies bore physical traces to back their claims, courts have still accepted their confessions."[65]

Partly as a result of coercive practices, and partly as a result of the Japanese sense of shame, the confession rate is 95 percent.[66]

Suspects who insist on standing trial have no right to a jury.[67] Judges defer to prosecutorial judgment, and the trial conviction rate is 99.91 percent.[68]

American police officers are capable of abusing innocent suspects, too. Yet the American criminal justice system creates a system of checks and balances that makes police abuse more difficult. An independent judiciary and a strong force of defense lawyers check the power of the police and the prosecutors.[69] The American criminal justice system, like the American political system, expects that justice will arise out of the conflict between various independent authorities. In Japan, the legal system is, in effect, an omnipotent and unitary state authority. All law enforcement administrators in Japan are appointed by the National Police Agency and receive their funding from the NPA. Hence, the police are insulated from complaints of politicians or other citizens.[70] There is hardly any check on the power of the state, save its own conscience.

Japanese suspects who do not confess are merely prolonging the inevitable. Yet the extraction of a confession does not mean that more abuse is on the way. While the criminal justice system is single-minded in its determination to secure a confession, once the confession has been made, the defendant has taken the major step toward reintegration into the community. As in Britain, the police do not treat criminals as outcasts. One officer explains that even rapists or murders "may be disturbed and they need to be handled with care—otherwise they will feel isolated if put into prison. Everybody has the potential of committing a crime, and the authorities should make sure that a person who comes out from prison is able to live independently."[71] Prosecutors exercise broad discretionary powers to drop a case, or to divert the offender to alternative treatment. The system favors alternative treatments, so most defendants receive no prison time or only short sentences—provided they acknowledge their membership in and submission to the community by confessing as the police demand.[72]

To an American, especially an American concerned about civil liberties, the breadth of Japanese police powers is horrifying. The Japanese, of course, do not think so, and the Japanese police state yields tangible benefits.[73] Broad powers, professionalism, and community support combine to help Tokyo police solve 97.1 percent of murders, and 78.5 percent of robberies. In America, the police clear 70 percent of murders, but only 25.6 percent of robberies.[74] Overall, the Japanese police are three times as efficient at matching guilty persons to criminal offenses.[75]

Whether a Japanese-style police system could ever work in America, where citizens are far more conscious of their "rights" is another question. What does the analysis of police powers have to do with gun controls? Japanese gun controls exist in a society where there is little need for guns for self-defense. Police powers make it difficult for owners of illegal guns to hide them. Most importantly, the Japanese criminal justice system is based on the government possessing the inherent authority to do whatever it wishes. In a society where almost everyone accepts nearly limitless, unchecked government power, people do not wish to own guns to resist oppression or to protect themselves in case the criminal justice system fails.

Extensive police authority is one reason the Japanese gun-control system works. Another reason is that Japan has no cultural history of gun ownership by civilians.

HISTORY

Historian Richard Hofstadter rejected the idea that America's violent past might explain its present cultural attachment to the gun. He pointed out that Japan also had a violent past, but has managed to tame its passions and evolve to a more pacific, weapon-free state.[76] But the Japanese past, while violent, laid no cultural foundation for a gun culture. Weapons always were, and remain today, the mark of the rulers, not the ruled.

Masters of Gun Manufacture

Guns arrived in Japan along with the first trading ships from Portugal in 1542 or 1543. Confident of the superiority of Japanese civilization, the Japanese dubbed the Western visitors *namban*, "southern barbarians."[77]

The Portuguese had landed on Tanegashima Island, outside Kyushu. One day the Portuguese trader Mendez Pinto took Totitaka, Lord of Tanegashima, for a walk during which the trader shot a duck. The Lord of Tanegashima made immediate arrangements to take shooting lessons, and within a month he bought Portuguese guns, or *Tanegashima* as the Japanese soon called them.[78]

The *Tanegashima* caught on quickly among Japan's feuding warlords.

The novelty of the guns was the main reason that the Portuguese were treated well.[79] Lord Oda Nobunaga noted that "guns have become all the rage . . . but I intend to make the spear the weapon to rely on in battle." Nobunaga worried about how long it took to prepare a gun shot—fifteen minutes—and how weak the projectile was. The Portuguese guns, among the best of their era, were matchlocks (ignited by a match), and Japan's rainy weather made the gun's ignition system unreliable.[80]

At the battle of Uedahara in 1548, Lord Takeda Harunobu brought not only his usual samurai warriors (with the traditional two swords apiece), his peasant soldiers (one sword and a bow), but also his secret weapons— fifty soldiers with matchlocks. Unfortunately, Lord Harunobu started the battle in the traditional way, by ceremonially introducing himself. Combat began immediately after the ceremonies. The other side, which brought no guns and did not have to spend time igniting the matchlocks, triumphed quickly. Military history remembers that Harunobu's opponents won "because they did not have any guns."[81]

Despite the initial problems, the Japanese rapidly improved firearms technology. They invented a device to make matchlocks fire in the rain (the Europeans never figured out how to do this), refined the matchlock trigger and spring, developed a serial firing technique, and increased the matchlock's calibre. They also dispensed with pre-battle introductions.[82] Superior quality guns were produced; during the 1904 Russo-Japanese war, sixteenth-century matchlocks were converted to modern bolt-action and performed admirably.[83]

The Arabs, the Indians, and the Chinese had all acquired firearms long before the Japanese. But only the Japanese mastered large-scale domestic manufacture.[84] The Japanese triumph was to be expected. Japan had accomplished mass production (of miniature wooden pagodas) in the mid-700s, a thousand years before the West.[85]

During the centuries before the Portuguese arrived, Japan had become the world's leading arms manufacturer and exporter. The whole Far East bought Japanese swords, which were of superb quality. In 1483, China bought 67,000 Japanese swords.[86] A twentieth-century film depicts a machine-gun barrel being sliced in half by a sword made by the fifteenth-century master Kanemoto II.[87] Master swordsmiths like Kanemoto understood how to forge the edge of a sword to perfection, making it much harder than the rest of the blade. Europeans swordsmiths never perfected edge-hardening, and European swords were never as sharp.[88]

By 1560, only seventeen years after being introduced in Japan, firearms were being used effectively in large battles. That year, a bullet killed a general who was wearing full armor.[89] In 1567, Lord Takeda Harunobu declared, "Hereafter, guns will be the most important arms."[90] He was right.

Less than three decades after Japan saw its first gun, there were more guns in Japan than any other nation on the planet. Several Japanese feudal lords had more guns than the whole British army.[91]

It was Lord Oda Nobunaga, an early critic of the Portuguese matchlocks, whose army truly mastered the new firearms technology.[92] At Nagashino in 1575, three thousand of Nobunaga's conscript peasants with muskets hid behind wooden posts and devastated the enemy's cavalry charge. There was no honor to such fighting, but it worked.[93] Feudal wars between armies of samurai knights had ravaged Japan for centuries. Nobunaga and his peasant army equipped with matchlocks conquered most of Japan, and helped bring the feudal wars to an end.[94] (The rise of peasant armies with guns had also contributed to the decline of armored knights and feudal wars in Europe.[95])

Guns dramatically changed the nature of war. In earlier times, after the introductions, fighters would pair off, to go at each other in single combat—a method of fighting apt to let individual heroism shine. Armored, highly trained samurai had the advantage. But with guns, the unskilled could be deployed en masse, and could destroy the armored knights with ease.[96] Understandably, the noble *bushi* class thought firearms undignified. Even Lord Nobunaga personally refused to use guns, and continued to include samurai warriors in his armies. The warriors who became heroes were still those who used swords or spears.[97]

The Sword Hunt

Yet every day that Japan grew more pre-eminent in firearms manufacture and warfare, Japan moved closer to day when firearms would disappear from society. The engineer of Japan's greatest armed victories, and of the abolition of arms in Japan, would be a peasant named Hidéyoshi.

Starting out as a groom for Lord Nobunaga, Hidéyoshi rose through the ranks to take control of the army after Nobunaga's death. A brilliant strategist, Hidéyoshi finished the job that Nobunaga began, and reunified Japan's feudal states under a strong central government.[98] He assumed the aristocratic name Toyotomi.[99]

Having conquered the Japanese, Hidéyoshi meant to keep them under control. On August 29, 1588, he announced "the Sword Hunt" (*taikō no katanagari*) and banned possession of swords and firearms by anyone other than the noble classes. He decreed:

> The people in the various provinces are strictly forbidden to have in their possession any swords, short swords, bows, spears, firearms, or other arms. *The possession of unnecessary implements makes difficult the collection*

of taxes and tends to foment uprisings. . . . Therefore the heads of provinces, official agents, and deputies are ordered to collect all the weapons mentioned above and turn them over to the government.[100] (emphasis added)

Although the intent of Hidéyoshi's decree was plain, the Sword Hunt was presented to the masses under the pretext that all the swords would be melted down to supply nails and bolts for a temple containing a huge statue of the Buddha. The statue would have been twice the size of the Statue of Liberty.[101] The Western missionaries' Jesuit Annual Letter reported that Hidéyoshi "is depriving the people of their arms under the pretext of devotion to religion."[102] Once the swords and guns were collected, Hidéyoshi had them melted into a statue of himself. Historian Stephen Turnbull writes:

Hidéyoshi's resources were such that the edict was carried out to the letter. The growing social mobility of peasants was thus flung suddenly into reverse. The *ikki,* the warrior-monks, became figures of the past . . . Hidéyoshi had deprived the peasants of their weapons. Iéyasu [the next ruler] now began to deprive them of their self-respect. If a peasant offended a samurai he might be cut down on the spot by the samurai's sword.[103]

The inferior status of the peasantry having been affirmed by civil disarmament, the samurai enjoyed *kiri-sute gomen,* permission to kill and depart. Any disrespectful member of the lower class could be executed by a samurai's sword.[104]

Hidéyoshi forbade peasants to leave their land without their superior's permission and required that warriors, peasants, and merchants all remain in their current post.[105] After Hidéyoshi died, Iéyasu founded the Tokugawa Shōgunate, which would rule Japan for the next two-and-a-half centuries. Peasants were assigned to a "five-man group," headed by landholders who were responsible for the group's behavior. The groups arranged marriages, resolved disputes, maintained religious orthodoxy, and enforced the rules against peasants possessing firearms or swords. The weapons laws clarified and stabilized class distinctions. Samurai had swords; peasants did not.[106]

Having created a huge standing army, Hidéyoshi had set out in 1592 to conquer the civilized world, as far as he knew: China, Korea, and the Philippines. He was defeated in Korea by Chinese troops and Korean "turtle ships" (armored vessels that disrupted supply lines). Hidéyoshi tried again in 1597, but died the next year, and the expedition was withdrawn.[107] For the next 250 years, Japan adopted the policy of *sakoku;* it abandoned military aggression, turned inward, and shut off the outside world.

The total abolition of firearms never took place by a formal decree.

Hidéyoshi had taken the first step, by disarming the peasants. In 1607, the Tokugawa Shōgunate took the second step by dictating that all gun and powder production take place in Nagahama.[108] Permission from the central government was required to engage in the business.[109] In theory, the gunsmiths could fill any orders they received, as long as they obtained permission from the *Teppo Bugyo* (commissioner of guns). In practice, almost no orders, except those by the government, were permitted.[110]

The gunsmiths, starving for lack of business, slipped out of Nagahama. Some went to work for Lord Tokitaka's heirs on Tanegashima Island, where guns had first arrived in Japan. In 1609, the government ordered the gunsmiths back to Nagahama. This time, they would receive an annual pension, regardless of whether they produced guns, as long as they stayed put and let the government keep an eye on them.[111]

The pensions were low, and the work ethic was still strong. Many gunsmiths turned to sword production. The government compensated the other smiths by paying increasingly high prices for small gun orders. By 1625, the government monopoly was secure. There were four master gunsmith families, and forty families of ordinary gunsmiths under them. The government ordered 387 matchlocks a year, and cut orders even further in 1706.[112] Eventually, the number of gunsmiths dwindled to fifteen families, who supported themselves with government repair orders.[113]

Historian Noel Perrin offers five reasons why Japan renounced the gun while Europe did not, despite the fierce resistance to guns by the European aristocracy. First, the samurai warrior nobility, which hated guns, amounted to 6 to 10 percent of the population—unlike in Europe, where the noble class never exceeded 1 percent. The nobility simply counted for more in Japan.[114]

Second, Japan was so hard to invade, and the Japanese were such formidable fighters, that swords and bows sufficed for national defense.[115] The aristocracy of Europe never enjoyed the luxury of not worrying about war. European monarchs, such as England's Henry VIII, had tried to disarm their peasantry, but their desire to prevent poaching by commoners was often superseded by the need to have subjects armed for defense of the realm in war.[116]

While England had less to fear from invasion than did France or the rest of the Continent, the threat was still real. The Straits of Dover are only twenty miles wide. But a hundred miles separate Japan from Korea; five hundred divide Japan and China.

Third, writes Perrin, swords were what the Japanese truly valued. Guns depreciated the importance of swords, so a policy of protecting swords by eliminating guns was bound to be popular, at least with the classes who carried swords. Hailed as "the soul of the samurai," the sword was the physical embodiment of aristocratic honor and of the soul itself.[117] All nations have viewed swords as works of art, but none so intensely as Japan. In 1582, Lord Akechi Mitsuhide found himself besieged in his castle. As his forces crumbled, Lord Mitsuhide sent a message to his opponent: "My castle is burning and soon I shall die. I have many excellent swords which I have treasured all my life. . . . I will die happy, if you can stop your attack for a short while, so that I can have the swords sent out and presented to you."[118] When gun manufacture was still legal, and the government decided to honor the four leading gunsmiths, it gave them swords.[119] The cult of the sword persisted into World War II, when Japanese officers lugged traditional, cumbersome swords into Southeast Asian jungles.[120]

Even today, the sword is a common source of Japanese metaphor. Self-indulgent behavior is called "the rust of my body"—identifying one's body with a sword.[121] In the United States, guns provide dozens of common phrases, such as "son of a gun" or "keep your powder dry."[122]

The fourth reason Perrin cites for Japan's success in eliminating guns was a general reaction against outside influence, particularly Christianity. Although the firearms made in Japan were the world's best, they remained a symbol of Western technology. Hidéyoshi, who had conquered Japan with the gun, began the persecution of Christian missionaries, for he knew how missionaries had paved the way for Spanish rule in the Philippines. Eventually the missionaries were expelled, and the half-million Japanese Christians harassed. By 1640, Christianity survived underground only in a few Kyushu communities.[123] To prevent the influx of Christianity, foreigners were forced out.

The Japanese were forbidden to travel abroad. Those who did live elsewhere, such as the sizeable trading communities in Southeast Asia, were cut off.[124] Even today, Japanese who have worked or studied abroad are sometimes handicapped in competition for corporate jobs.[125]

Finally, writes Perrin, in a society where aesthetics were prized, swords were valued because they were graceful to use in combat. As he notes, in a modern movie, a sword fight may come close to ballet. A gun fight does not.[126]

A Japanese of proper breeding was expected to maintain certain body postures: to keep his hands and his knees together (symbolizing concentration of body will and power), and not put his elbows out at awkward angles. These rules still apply at the tea ceremony. A sword-fighter can obey these rules. A gun-fighter cannot.[127] And gun combat requires "cowardly" fighting from a distance, rather than face to face.

While the West was, by the time of the Japanese gun control, beginning to make a distinction between the practical and the beautiful (for example, designing weapons without regard for aesthetics), Japan made no such distinction. If a weapon was not beautiful, it was useless.[128] Technological progress was not a concern. Japanese scholars made important advances in mathematics, but never considered applying their discoveries to practical engineering. Plant breeders created handsome gardens, but never turned their knowledge to agriculture.[129]

Sociologist William Tonso adds one more reason that Japan would see no need for guns: there was not a great deal of big game to hunt.[130]

The abolition of firearms and abandonment of military aggression were just one element of the *sakoku* policy of isolation from the world and exaltation of "Japaneseness." The policy worked. Edwin O. Reischauer, America's leading historian of Japan, writes: "The brawling, bellicose Japanese people of the sixteenth century gradually were transformed into an extremely orderly, even docile people. . . . Nowhere in the world was proper decorum more rigorously observed by all classes, and nowhere else was physical violence less in evidence in ordinary life."[131] When Commodore Perry and his "Black Ships" arrived in 1853, Japan was backward only in technology. An officer in Commodore Perry's fleet reported, "These people seemed scarcely to know the use of firearms."[132] Japan had built a more harmonious, peaceful society than any Western nation had achieved before or since.[133]

True, the Japanese paid a price for their order. Freedom was an alien concept. Interclass, social, and geographic mobility were extinguished. Indeed, as Turnbull points out, Hidéyoshi's hunt for swords and firearms marked the end of social freedom in Japan. The abolition of firearms probably would not have succeeded if Japan had a free economy or a free political system. Yet most of the Western world of 1600–1850 was no model of freedom either. If the Japanese sacrificed a certain degree of economic and personal freedom, they also spared themselves the bloody conflicts that engulfed the Western world.

Too Much Too Fast: The Rush to Militarism

For centuries Japan had lived happily without guns, militarism, violence, or foreign influence. But Commodore Perry's arrival shook Japan profoundly. The Japanese realized that, however harmonious their society, they were centuries behind the West technologically, and, like China, in imminent danger of colonization. The government tried to strengthen itself by adopting Western military technology and sending missions abroad to learn about the West.[134]

Many centuries before, the Japanese had recognized the superiority of China's Confucian culture to primitive Japanese ways, and had successfully assimilated many Chinese practices. The experience of assimilating foreign learning into Japanese culture helped nineteenth-century Japan undertake the process of readily learning from the West.[135] Indeed, the shock of Western technological superiority was so great that for a time Western institutions were considered superior to Japanese ones. The formerly insular Tokugawa Shōgunate fell in 1867. Feudal lords were replaced by civil servants. The Meiji Restoration began.

In 1876, the government forbade the samurai to wear their two swords. The next year, forty thousand discontented conservative samurai rose up in the Satsuma Rebellion led by the *Shimpuren* ("God-wind League"). They rejected the chance to use imported muskets, fought with swords instead, and were crushed by the conscript peasant army using guns.[136]

Under Hidéyoshi, the peasant class lost its political power, and with it the privilege of owning arms. When the aristocracy lost its own political power during the Meiji period, it, too, lost its right to bear arms. As will be discussed in chapter 3, a similar process is occurring in modern England, where the aristocracy's political influence fades in tandem with its former right to bear arms.

The new Japanese government embarked on a rapid industrialization program, including development of a self-sufficient munitions industry.[137] Japan quickly changed from a feudal society to one which, by the early twentieth century, awarded rank mostly on education. It was considerably more meritocratic than British society of the time.[138] Reischauer notes the downside of the education, too: Japan pioneered the modern totalitarian technique of instilling national obedience and uniformity through a carefully controlled education system.[139]

During the early twentieth century, the gun controls were slightly relaxed. Tokyo and other major ports were allowed to have five gun shops each; other prefectures three. Revolver sales were allowed with a police permit, and registration of every transaction was required. Nevertheless, the ownership of revolvers was "practically nil" according to one American diplomat.[140]

Reischauer argues that the Japanese culture of the late nineteenth and early twentieth centuries did not particularly predispose the people to militarism and authoritarianism, at least not more than other national cultures did to their own people.[141] The Japanese historian Hidehiro Sonoda notes that Japan quickly assimilated Western military technology, but lacked the historical experience to keep the armed forces under control.[142] In any case, the Japanese (again) rapidly mastered state-of-the-art arms manufacture. Japan broke the Western monopoly on arms technology, and in the service of imperialism, set off to dominate east Asia.[143]

In the 1920s and 1930s, the military increasingly came to control civilian life. Sonoda explains: "The army and the navy were vast organizations with a monopoly on physical violence. There was no force in Japan that could offer any resistance."[144] The 1930s degenerated into a horrible period of government by assassination, as military factions attempted to destroy each other, and as militarists murdered opponents of war.[145] Despite the strict gun laws, the frequency of assassination far exceeded anything seen in Europe or North America this century. Even today, assassinations still occur.[146]

Peasants and workers enthusiastically accepted indoctrination about Japan's past military glory. Especially for rural peasants, conscription into the military offered escape from a life of drudgery.[147] As the Japanese military machine grew, it began to lead the country back into the policy of conquest that had been abandoned after Hidéyoshi's death in the late 1500s. Hidéyoshi had been defeated in Korea, but the new militarists conquered the peninsula for Japan. The military plunged into China, miring itself (as the French, Americans, and Soviets would do later) in an unwinnable war against a popularly supported and well-armed Asian guerilla force.[148]

The late 1930s and early 1940s saw Japan's military might grow as its expansionism in the Pacific exploded with unchecked force. As the tide turned in favor of the Allies in Europe, significant defeats on land and sea found Japan's empire imploding toward the mainland.

When the war turned against Japan, and the expected Allied invasion looked more and more imminent, the dominant Japanese war hawks prepared the final defense of their homeland. Twenty-eight million men and women began training as part of a civil defense force that would carry out a never-surrender guerrilla defense, from the cities to the forests to the mountains.[149] While there is little doubt that the Japanese civilians would have fought with all their heart had not the atomic destruction of Hiroshima and Nagasaki ended the war before an invasion, it is questionable how effective the civilian guerrillas would have been, given a culture that had fostered neither familiarity with arms nor individual initiative.

Reform

World War II, begun with such high hopes, ended in the first and only conquest of Japan. The soldiers who had left home as heroes were spat upon.[150] War and militarism were perceived as an unmitigated horror, and the army was abolished.[151]

Under the occupation forces of General Douglas MacArthur, America set out to transform Japan into a democratic society. Reischauer writes that the "wisest feature" of MacArthur's occupation was that "instead of attempting to transplant American democratic institutions to Japan, it based its reforms on the past democratic achievements of the Japanese," including the partial evolution of British-style parliamentary democracy around the turn of the century.[152] The democratic transformation succeeded, explains Reischauer, because the American goals coincided with what the Japanese people themselves wanted, and because the people already possessed the qualities, such as a high level of education, enabling them to reach those goals.[153]

Not all American reforms took root. American forces abolished the strict pre-war family system. "But the individualistic urge," writes Hidehiro Sonoda, "was not very strong among the Japanese; so, although the law may have changed considerably, the reality of family life was very much the same."[154] Despite the Japanese Constitution's bar on discrimination based on social relations or family origin, the law imposed a harsher penalty on homicides when the victim was "a lineal ascendant" of the murderer.[155]

Likewise, the Japanese Constitution, in stronger terms than its American counterpart, guarantees social equality for women, creates a right to counsel, prohibits prolonged detention, outlaws courtroom use of confessions extracted under duress, and bars convictions based solely on confession.[156] Today, every one of these provisions is routinely violated; action in accordance with those constitutional commands is the exception rather than the rule.

The written American Constitution is interpreted like a business contract: the most important element of interpretation is what the words themselves say.[157] Litigants insist on their written constitutional rights with the same intensity that businesspeople insist on literal adherence to the written terms of a contract. Political philosophy discusses the "social contract," as if autonomous individuals agreed to form a society under certain conditions. In contrast, the Japanese Constitution—while containing formal, rigid, American-style written guarantees—has been interpreted like a Japanese contract: regardless of what is written, the "agreement" can evolve as the needs of the parties change. Strict insistence on adherence to written provisions of a contract or a Constitution would disrupt the consensus. The idea of a social contract between the government and the governed would seem absurd because both are part of the same organic entity.

Thus, the American debate over the right to bear arms takes place in an argument over whether the Constitution's particular written references to a "well-regulated militia" and "the right of the people" recognize a right of individual citizens or merely a "collective" right that can never be violated because it belongs to no one. There is no Japanese debate on firearms, though, because the Japanese policy is based on a widely held social consensus. Under Hidéyoshi and the Tokugawa Shōgunate, strict gun control succeeded in Japan because it fit with the cultural needs of Japanese society. Today, the gun-control policy continues to succeed because it continues to match the basic character of Japanese society.

THE PREFERENCE FOR PATERNALISM

The Japanese historian Ike observes in modern Japan a "preference for paternalism."[158] Part of this preference can be traced to Japan's feudal past. In Europe, feudalism grew out the legal background of Roman law. The emphasis on feudal rights provided the groundwork for the eventual development of democratic institutions. In Japan, however, feudalism arose from Chinese Confucianism, with its emphasis on ethical loyalty. Hence, feudalism became legalistic in the West and moralistic (and more absolutist) in Japan.[159]

Feudalism survived in at least some forms until the mid-nineteenth century. Professor Reischauer finds vestiges of feudalism even today in the strong relationships of employers and employees, in the emphasis on loyalty, and in the belief (until after World War II) that military men were more virtuous than other people.[160]

An American historian writes: "Never conquered by or directly confronted with external forms of political rule (except for the MacArthur occupation), they remained unaware of the relative, fallible nature of authority. Authority was a 'given,' taken for granted as an unalienable part of the natural order."[161] A Tokyo University historian describes "an assumption that the state is a prior and self-justifying entity, sufficient in itself. This results in a belief that . . . the state should take precedence over the goals of other individuals and associations."[162] Psychiatrist Takeo Doi observes that Japanese mothers encourage their children to passivity and dependence, whereas American mothers are more apt to encourage individualism or aggression. Doi argues that the efforts of adult Japanese to recapture the feeling of oneness with the mother partly explain the Japanese preference for intimate, submissive relationships with their workplace superiors.[163]

The differing meanings of the phrase "rule of law" highlight the contrast between American and Japanese views of authority. In America, observes Noriho Urabe, "rule of law" expresses the subordination of government to the law. In Japan, the "rule of law" refers to the people's obligation to obey the government, and is thus "an ideology to legitimize domination."[164]

The contrast between the individualist American and the communal Japanese ethos is manifested in everything from behavior at sporting events to industrial labor organization. American professors who teach in Japan are initially dismayed about how reluctant Japanese students are to participate in classroom discussion. They fear standing out from their fellows.[165] Younger students are subject to two- or three-day suspensions for acting up in even a minor way.[166] Notably, the Japanese word for "different," *chigaau,* also means "wrong."[167]

The political structure is also unified. Most legislation, having been shaped to achieve consensus, is passed unanimously by the Diet (the Japanese Parliament).[168] Only recently has a party other than the Liberal Democratic Party come to control any part of the legislature.

The structure of the police system itself is more hierarchical in Japan. There is no such thing as an American-style autonomous police union.[169]

Physical mobility, like social mobility, is more attuned to social needs than to individual desires. Sonoda points out that even today, while Japan is the leading producer of automobiles, Japan's road network is primitive. He contrasts the railroad, "orderly and punctual, running smartly along its gleaming tracks," and "controlled by government agencies," with the automobile, directed by "the whim of the individual."[170]

The submission to paternalist state authority has its analogue in family life. A recent study ranked Japan lowest among developed nations in the status and equality of women. Japan received the lowest possible marks for the number of working professional women.[171] "On Japanese television, there are, by and large, two kinds of women. The happy ones wear frilly aprons and sing while they iron. The troubled ones work as nurses or secretaries, but neglect their children and spend time in bars consorting with men who want to take advantage of them," observes an American journalist.[172] Birth control pills are banned by the Ministry of Health.[173] Only a small percentage of the police force is female, and many women officers are relegated to traffic patrol or other duties less prestigious than kōban (police-box) work.[174] Female officers do not carry guns, and are forbidden to work after 10:30 P.M. They are expected to marry at about age twenty-five, and to leave police work.[175] The U.S. divorce rate is twice as high as Japan's—an indication of both greater female freedom and looser social controls on the family.[176]

In short, the individual's desires are "absorbed in the interest of the collectivity to which he belongs," whether that collectivity be the nation, the school, or the family.[177] There is no theory of "social contract," and no theory that individuals preexist society and have rights superior to society.[178] The strongest sanctions are not American-style punishments, but exclusion from the community.[179] When Japanese parents punish their children, they do not make the children stay inside the house, as American parents do. Punishment for a Japanese child means being put outside. The sublimation of individual desires to the greater good, the pressure to conform, and internalized willingness to do so are much stronger in Japan than in America.[180]

While the West relies on guilt for social control, Japan relies on shame, suggests Ruth Benedict's The Chrysanthemum and the Sword.[181] As the head of Tokyo's police department explains, "A man who commits a crime will bring dishonor to his family and his village, so he will think twice about disgracing them."[182] When a pollster asked the Japanese what advice they would give a relative who committed a crime, the overwhelming majority said they would advise him to turn himself in.[183] If a school child runs into trouble with the police, the school principal may have to apologize or even resign.[184]

More than gun control, more than the lack of criminal procedural safeguards, more than the authority of the police, it is the pervasive social controls of Japan that best explain the low crime rate. Other nations, such as the former Soviet Union, have had severe gun control, less criminal justice safeguards, and more unconstrained police forces than Japan. But the Soviets' crime rate was high while Japan's is minuscule because Japan has the socially accepted and internalized restraints on individual behavior that the Soviets lacked. While social controls fell and crime rose everywhere in the English-speaking world in the 1960s, social controls remained and crime fell in Japan. Japan's worst crime years came in the late 1940s, when social controls, extant before the war, collapsed.[185]

More than the people of any other democracy, the Japanese accept the authority of their police and trust their government. In this cultural context, it is easy to see why gun control has succeeded in Japan—the people accept gun control with the same readiness that they accept other government controls. Further, they have little incentive to disobey gun controls, since they have hardly any cultural heritage of gun ownership.

AN UNARMED GOVERNMENT

The Japanese government promotes a social climate for gun control by the good example of disarming itself. The police have little interest in using or glamorizing guns. When the National Police Agency was created in the late nineteenth century, many members were ex-samurai who were unemployed because of the abolition of feudalism. They of course believed that guns were for cowards, and that real men fought with the martial arts. Indeed, the Japanese police only took up firearms when commanded to do so in 1946 by General MacArthur. Two years later, when the American occupation forces noticed that few police officers had obeyed the order to arm, the Americans supplied the police with guns and ammunition.[186]

The police have only .38 special revolvers, not the high-power or high-capacity .45 and 9 mm. handguns often toted by the American police.[187] No officer would ever carry a second, smaller handgun as a back-up, as many American police do. Policeman may not add individual touches—such as pearl handles or unusual holster—to dress up their gun. While American police are often required to carry guns while off duty, and are always granted the privilege if they wish (even when retired), Japanese police not on active duty must leave their guns at the station. Unlike in the United States, desk-bound police administrators, traffic police, most plainclothes detectives, and even the riot police do not carry guns.[188]

Instead of using guns, the police rely on their black belts in judo or their police sticks. Indeed, police recruit training spends sixty hours on firearms compared to ninety hours on judo, and another ninety on *kendo* (fencing with sticks). After police school, few officers show any interest in further firearms training, while continued judo and *kendo* practice is frequent. Annual police martial arts contests are important events. Sixty percent of officers rank in one of the top judo brackets. Beer bellies are nonexistent. In contrast, many American policemen, if confronted with deadly assault, often have no combat technique to use except gunfire.[189] The American police's heavy reliance on guns serves, intentionally or not, to legitimize a similar attitude in the rest of the population.

The official Japanese police culture discourages use or glamorization of guns. One poster on police walls orders: "Don't take it out of the holster, don't put your finger on the trigger, don't point it at people."[190] Shooting at a fleeing felon is unlawful under any circumstance. Police and civilians can both be punished for any act of self-defense in which the harm caused was greater than the harm averted.[191] (American law allows anyone to use deadly force to meet threats such as rape or robbery, even if there is no reasonable fear that the rapist or robber will kill the victim.) In an average year, the entire Tokyo police force only fires a half-dozen or so shots.[192]

The police being disarmed, criminals reciprocate. Although guns are available on the black market, there is little use of guns in crime. The riot police leave their guns at the station, and the masses of angry students who confront the riot police also eschew modern weapons. The two sides instead study medieval military tactics, using mass formations of humans as battering rams or as shields. For a short time in the early 1970s, some demonstrators broke the informal rules by resorting to Molotov cocktails and homemade pistols similar to zip guns. The riot police augmented their armor, but continued to eschew firearms. In 1972, the radical students resumed adherence to the old code, and the firearms vanished.[193]

Comparative criminologist David Bayley, a proponent of stricter American gun controls, suggests that American police attitudes toward guns makes it impossible for gun control to be achieved. As long as the police are armed, writes Bayley, they send the implicit message that armed confrontations with civilians are the norm, and that shootings of police officers, while sad, are nothing extraordinary.[194] (It might be added that about 15 percent of shootings of American officers are perpetrated with guns snatched from an officer.) Moreover, while American officers on street patrol in high-crime areas do have a unique need for defensive armament, other criminal justice officials do not. As long as desk-bound American police administrators carry guns at work and at home, as long as police budgets continue to satiate demands for high-tech weaponry, it will be difficult to convince ordinary civilians that guns are not useful or necessary for self-defense.

The model of governmental disarmament is repeated at the broadest levels of Japanese society. The military is small. Japan's rejection of militarism sets another good example for both gun control and for nonviolence in general. The lack of involvement in foreign war, in earlier centuries and today, may be an important factor in Japan's culture of conformity and noncriminality. Criminologists Dane Archer and Rosemary Gartner analyzed homicide rates in combatant and noncombatant nations for the years immediately following World War I and World War II.[195] Archer and Gartner found a significant correlation between a nation's involvement in a war and a subsequent rise in homicide rates. Victorious nations and nations with high casualties suffered the greatest homicide increases.

Other criminologists who have noticed a correlation between war and homicide have suggested a number of mechanisms for the correlation: returning veterans might be prone to violence; defeated nations might lose social cohesion; postwar unemployment could increase crime. None of the testable hypotheses, though, were consistent with the data. Only one explanation was left: state sponsorship of violence legitimates individual violence. The "legitimation of violence" hypothesis is impossible to prove or disprove, but it fits with the worldwide data. Of course not every nation involved in war suffers a higher homicide rate. Britain after World War I and America after World War II enjoyed large drops in homicide. But on the whole, war and civilian homicide appear to correlate.

A HOMOGENEOUS SOCIETY

There is something else special about the people who live in Japan that helps explain their low crime rate. Ninety-seven percent of them are Japanese.[196]

Japanese social dynamics differ from the rest of the world's. Having lived together for several thousand years without significant immigration, the Japanese have developed a homogeneous and unified society. Of all the countries to enjoy a high civilization in premodern times, Japan was the most isolated.[197] The writing system is more complex than any other, and the language has no close relatives. Accordingly, Japan faces a bigger international language barrier than any other major nation.

Beginning with the Tokugawa Shōgunate, when overseas Japanese in trading communities in Southeast Asia were forbidden to return home, Japanese who adapted to foreign ways have been shunned. Today, a Japanese who has spent too much time abroad is considered *gaijin kusai* (smells like a foreigner), and may have trouble rising to the top of his firm.[198]

Japan's largest ethnic minority, the Koreans, amounts to less than one-half of one percent of the total population.[199] Koreans, like all non-Japanese, can never become Japanese citizens, even though they speak only Japanese, and their families have been born and lived in Japan for many generations.[200] When Japan, under severe American pressure, admitted one hundred Vietnamese boat people, a leading publication called them "the sword of an alien culture pointed at Japan."[201] A Tokyo apartment-rental guide lists which apartments are available to foreigners. In a typical page of sixty-six apartment building listings, only three apartments permitted non-Japanese.[202] The unfamiliarity with non-Japanese ways also leads the popular culture in Japan to endorse a brand of anti-Semitism that could not be taken seriously in any Western democracy.[203] The concept of *nihonjinron* (that the Japanese are physically different from and better than the rest of the human race) is sometimes escalated to fantastic proportions.[204]

As will be discussed in more detail in the following chapters, immigration sometimes correlates with crime. Immigrants are not inherently criminal, but crime is often associated with people at the bottom of the economic and social ladder who face difficulties and discrimination.

By shutting out immigrants and foreign culture, Japan has maintained its unified system of common social controls. Japan has also shut out people who might become criminals, albeit at the price of also shutting out many more people who could add diversity and innovation to Japanese society.

ECONOMICS

By maintaining ethnic homogeneity, Japan has maintained conformity and harmony. Similarly, Japan's efforts to maintain relative economic equality have prevented the development of the gaping differences in wealth that are sometimes associated with criminality in the West. Tokyo and New York City both have strict gun-control laws. But Tokyo does not present the Dickensian picture of New York City, where the wealthy ride in limousines and the poor sleep on grates. Japan suffers little of the grinding urban poverty so closely associated with crime in the United States. In the Tokyo train station, a commuter does not encounter the village of the homeless that one must step over every day at New York City's Grand Central Station.[205] Japanese income gaps are relatively small at all levels; the pay ratio of corporate executives to new employees averages seven to one in Japan, and thirty-seven to one in America.[206] Several researchers have suggested a correlation between income inequality and crime.[207]

Tokyo does have its Ikebukuro section, which a *New York Times* reporter described as a "teeming district of bars, cheap eating places, porno shops, Turkish baths that serve as a cover for prostitution, and two dozen love hotels where rooms can be rented by the hour." In contrast to New York City's Times Square, Ikebukuro has almost no violent crime.[208]

Finally, social policy in most nations is often influenced by corporations, all the more so in Japan. In America, firearms manufacture has always had a significant role in the economy. Mass production of firearms was America's breakthrough into the Industrial Revolution, and the nation's first major manufactured export. To say the least, guns do not rate highly in Japanese industrial policy. Japan is not entering the contest to produce super-durable guns made from plastic polymers and high-quality metal. Japan has only one handgun factory. The manufacturer's main business is heavy electrical apparatus; the guns are just a courtesy for the government. Factory spokesmen will not even reveal where the factory is.[209]

SUICIDE

The Japanese experience does not seem to support the hypothesis that fewer guns mean fewer suicides. While the Japanese gun suicide rate is one-fiftieth of that found in the United States, the overall suicide rate is nearly twice as high as America's.[210]

Disproportionately, Japanese suicide victims, like their American counterparts, are older males. American gun-control advocates argue that in America, more males die from suicide because males are more likely to choose a gun as a suicide weapon. Yet in Japan, disarmed males are still more likely to die in a suicide attempt. It is true, though, that the male-to-female suicide ratio is less disproportionate in Japan. In America, for every one female suicide there are 3.5 male suicides. The Japanese ratio is 2 males for every female suicide.[211]

American control advocates also point to guns as a cause of a high teenage suicide rate. Yet teenage suicide is 30 percent more frequent in Japan. Every day in Japan, two Japanese under twenty years of age kill themselves.[212]

Japan also suffers from double or multiple suicides, *shinju.* Parents bent on suicide take their children with them, in *oyako-shinju,* at the rate of one per day. In fact, 17 percent of all Japanese officially defined as homicide victims are children killed by suicidal parents.[213] One reason that the official Japanese homicide rate is so much lower than the official American rate is that if a Japanese woman slits her children's throats and then kills herself, police statistics sometimes record it as a family suicide, rather than a sensational murder. Thus, Japan's tight family structures, which keep the overall crime rate low, are not unalloyed blessings.

Of the many reasons suggested by researchers for the high Japanese suicide rate, one of the most startling is weapons control. Japanese scholars Mamon Iga and Kichinosuke Tatai argue that one reason Japan has a suicide problem is that people have little sympathy for suicide victims. Iga and Tatai suggest that the lack of sympathy (and hence the lack of social will to deal with a high suicide rate) is based on the Japanese feelings of insecurity and consequent lack of empathy. They trace the lack of empathy to a "dread of power." That dread is caused in part by the awareness that a person cannot count on others for help against violence or against authority. In addition, say Iga and Tatai, the dread of power stems from the people being forbidden to possess swords or firearms for self-defense.[214]

Stated another way, firearms prohibition is part of a culture that subordinates the individual to society. When individuals find themselves not fitting in to social expectations, self-destruction may often seem appropriate, since in a conflict between the individual and society, society is, by definition, always right. It is interesting to note that the overall violent death rates (counting both murders and suicides) in many of the developed countries are approximately the same. America has a high murder rate, but a relatively low suicide rate. Japan and Switzerland have very low murder rates, but suicide rates twice the American level. Seymour Martin Lipset notes the high suicide rates in Japan and western European countries and speculates that "psychopaths there turn it on themselves."[215]

CONCLUSION

The idea that Japanese gun laws should serve as model for America is not uncommon. Some Americans propose laws even more severe than Japan's.[216] Oftentimes the suggestion comes as an offhand remark in an newspaper editorial, but even when the suggestion is advanced by scholars, the reasoning may be unpersuasive.

For example, L. Craig Parker, an American expert on the Japanese police, proposes that the United States adopt Japanese gun control and also other Japanese strategies, such as a National Police Agency. Parker's brief discussion of guns, however, simply recites statistics showing that Japan has fewer guns and less gun crime. His only evidence that gun control would actually reduce crime in America is a study by Dr. Leonard Berkowitz arguing that guns cause aggression. Actually, what the studies by Berkowitz and others showed was that people acted more aggressively toward other people if the other person was associated with weapons; for example, motorists reacted more aggressively to other vehicles slow to accelerate when a red light turned green if the slow car had a rude bumper sticker and a rifle in a gun rack.[217]

Summing up the perspective of many gun prohibitionists, one Japanese newspaper reporter writes, "It strikes me as clear that there is a distinct correlation between gun-control laws and the rate of violent crime. The fewer the guns, the less the violence."[218] But the claim that fewer guns correlate with less violence is overly simplistic and plainly wrong. America experienced falling crime and homicide rates in the 1940s, 1950s, and early 1980s, all periods during which per capita gun ownership, especially handgun ownership, rose.[219] And Japan, with its severe gun control, suffers no less murder than Switzerland, one of the most gun-intensive societies on earth.[220]

Japan's gun control does play an important role in the low Japanese crime rate, but not because of some simple relation between numbers of guns and levels of crime. Japan's gun control is one inseparable part of a vast mosaic of social control. Gun control underscores the pervasive cultural theme that the individual is subordinate to society and to the government. The same theme is reflected in the absence of protection against government searches and prosecutions. The Japanese police are the most powerful on earth, partly because of the lack of legal constraints and particularly because of their social authority.

Powerful social authorities, beginning with the father and reaching up to the state, create a strict climate for obeying both the criminal laws and the gun-control laws. The voluntary disarmament of the Japanese government reinforces this climate. Ethnic homogeneity and economic equality remove some of the causes of criminality.

Simply put, the Japanese are among the most law-abiding people on earth, and far more law-abiding than Americans. America's *nongun* robbery rate is over seventy times Japan's, an indication that something more significant than gun policy is involved in the differing crime rates between our two nations.[221] Neither Japanese nor American prisoners have guns, but homicide by prisoners and attacks on guards occur frequently in American prisons, and almost never in Japanese prisons.[222] Another indication that social standards matter more than gun laws is that Japanese-Americans, who have access to firearms, have a lower violent crime rate than do Japanese in Japan.[223]

As a general matter, gun control does not take a great deal of police time to enforce because the Japanese voluntarily comply. There was and is little need for individual self-defense guns.

Even if gun control were resisted, it would be relatively easy to enforce in Japan. Police freedom to search and seize would help, and so would Japan's status as an island, which makes control of illegal imports such as drugs or guns easier than in the United States.[224] The civilian stock of guns was always small; hence, civil disarmament was easy to enforce. Today, the police set records when in a year they confiscate 1,767 handguns from gangsters.[225] It is not uncommon for that many illegal handguns to be seized by the police in a single American city in one year. Some Japanese tour groups in Hawaii take their customers to local gun clubs to do something that the customers have never done before: see, hold, and shoot a real gun.[226]

None of the reasons that have made the near prohibition of guns succeed in Japan applies to the United States. The existing American gun stock may be over 200 million (about one-third being handguns). Even if all guns vanished from America, re-supply by illegal imports smuggled over its vast borders would be easy.

Without abrogating the Bill of Rights, America could not give its police and prosecutors extensive Japanese-style powers to enforce severe gun laws effectively. Unlike the Japanese, Americans are not already secure from crime, and are therefore less likely to surrender their personal means of defense. Most importantly, America has no tradition like Japan's of civil disarmament, of submission to authority, or of trust in the government. The extensive network of social controls, which is the foundation for Japanese gun control, does not exist in the United States.

All of this is not to say that America should not or cannot adopt a better gun-control policy than it currently has. The point is that the Japanese system of gun controls cannot be separated from its Japanese cultural context. While the Japanese history of gun control is interesting to study, it cannot provide us with guidelines for a gun policy in a radically different culture such as that which exists in the United States.

NOTES

1. Article 3, "Law Controlling Possession, Etc. of Fire-Arms and Sword," Law No. 6, March 10, 1958, EHS Law Bulletin Series, No. 3920 (1978). Many thanks to Mr. Takaki Tokuoka for providing me with this English translation of Japanese law.

2. Article 4. As a technical matter, members of international shooting teams may own handguns, but all the members of such teams belong to the police or the military. David H. Bayley, *Forces of Order: Police Behavior in Japan and the United States* (Berkeley: University of California Press, 1976), p. 23. Airguns are also permitted with a license. Airguns use compressed air, rather than explosive powder, as their propellant, and hence are not firearms. Airguns fire small pellets or BBs, usually in .177 caliber. The discussion of guns

in the following chapters generally does not refer to airguns, unless they are specifically noted. Almost all airguns in Japan are air rifles.

3. The test covers maintenance and inspection of the hunting gun, methods of loading and unloading cartridges, shooting from various positions, and target practice for stationary and moving objects. The hunting license is valid for three years. Library of Congress, *Gun Control Laws in Foreign Countries* (Washington, D.C.: Library of Congress, 1981), p. 130 [hereinafter "Library of Congress (1981)"].

4. Hunting licenses require completion of a second series of lectures and a safety course given by the Public Safety Commission. Art. 5(3). Hunting licenses are valid only for the upcoming hunting season, a three-month period beginning on November 14. Gun licenses themselves are valid for three years. Permit fees for hunting rifles and hunting licenses cost 17,000 yen (over two hundred American dollars based on the February 1992 exchange rate of one yen = $\frac{4}{5}$ of one cent). Article 29. For a gun license, the safety course costs 3,000 yen, the skill examination 7,500, and the license fee 4,500. Takaki Tokuoka, letter to author.

5. Isao Yamazaki, letter to Jerry Crossett, December 1989; Jerry Crossett, letter to author, January 1990.

6. Article 5, para. 1, item 6; and para. 3.

7. Library of Congress (1981), p. 131; Jerry Crossett, letter to author, pp. 1-2.

8. *Japan Times*, May 20, 1971. Hunters who have used shotguns for more than ten years may still be granted rifle licenses. High-ranking target competitors, who demonstrate expertise with low-powered airguns, are also allowed to use rifles, only for competition.

9. National Police Agency, Japanese Government, *White Paper on Police 1986* (excerpt), trans. Police Association (Tokyo: Police Association, 1986), p. 79.

10. National Police Agency, Japanese Government, *White Paper on Police 1990* (excerpt), trans. Police Association (Tokyo: Police Association, 1990), p. 80.

11. Art. 31-2. For defendants sentenced to prison for firearms possession and who are not members of organized criminal gangs, the average term is 31.5 months. This compares to 38.5 months for rape, and 42.3 months for causing bodily injury that leads to death. Elmer H. Johnson, "Yakuza (Criminal Gangs) in Japan: Characteristics and Management in Prison," paper delivered at Academy of Criminal Justice Sciences, Denver, March 1989, p. 28, table 1, citing Ministry of Justice, *Annual Report of Statistics on Corrections for 1987* (Tokyo: Ministry of Justice, 1988), tables 15-24. (The paper is reprinted in *CJ International* 7, no. 1 (January-February 1991): 11-18.

12. *White Paper on Police 1990*, p. 80. The 1990 *White Paper* does not break down the crimes by category. In 1985, there were 35 crimes with shotguns or air rifles, of which 10 were homicides. *White Paper on Police 1986*, p. 80.

13. The Japanese police report details the total number of cleared crimes involving handguns, rather than the total number of offenses. In 1989, there were 157 crimes involving handguns cleared, of which 150 were associated with *Bōryokudan*. *White Paper on Police 1990*, p. 80. Because (as detailed below) the rate of solving violent crime is so high, the estimate of no more than 200 handgun crimes a year seems plausible.

In 1987, Japan experienced 39 total firearms deaths, about 46 percent related to *Bōryokudan*. A. Didrick Castberg, *Japanese Criminal Justice* (New York: Praeger, 1990), p. 12, citing *White Paper on Police 1988*, p. 28; *White Paper on Police 1986*, p. 81.

The organized crime families occasionally engage in public assassinations and shootouts with each other. David E. Kaplan and Alec Dubro, *Yakuza* (Reading, Mass.: Addison-Wesley, 1986), pp. 127-28.

14. Bayley, p. 168. There are about 8,000 cases involving illegal possession of swords. Ibid.

15. Kaplan and Dubro, p. 208; "Arms Smuggling to Japan Halted," *New York Times,*

March 26, 1976, p. 8. The police have also halted arms shipments from France and Italy. Kaplan and Dubro, p. 222.

A handgun smuggled into Japan may command ten times its original U.S. retail price. Ammunition may sell for five to twelve dollars a round. Kaplan and Dubro, pp. 254–55. A new law was put into effect on March 1, 1992, making it a crime to conspire to smuggle handguns into Japan. The police are now empowered to investigate Japanese who purchase guns while overseas. "Tough Weapons Laws to Be Enforced," *Japan Times* (weekly international edition), December 2, 1991, p. 2.

16. Johnson, pp. 4–5, 9; Norman Pearlstine, "A Disarming People: Japan's Assassins Have a High Failure Rate, Thanks to Extremely Strict Gun Control Laws," *Wall Street Journal,* September 12, 1975, p. 28, col. 1.

17. Kaplan and Dubro, p. 274.

18. Johnson, p. 5.

19. *White Paper on Police 1990,* p. 44.

20. Yamazaki.

21. "MPD Now Checking Owners of Firearms," *Mainichi Daily News,* April 1, 1979.

22. "Tokyo Police," "60 Minutes," September 17, 1978 (transcript), p. 1.

23. National Coalition to Ban Handguns, *20 Questions and Answers about Gun Control* (no date), citing Congressional Record, February 22, 1973. Also, Pete Shields, *Guns Don't Die—People Do* (New York: Arbor House, 1981), p. 28 (in 1974, there were 11,124 Americans murdered with handguns, and 37 Japanese; a 300:1 ratio).

24. National Police Agency, Government of Japan, *White Paper on Police 1990* (excerpt) (Tokyo: National Police Agency, 1991), p. 28.

25. Castberg, p. 13.

26. *White Paper on Police 1990,* p. 28.

27. "In the Land of the Rising Gun," *The Economist,* August 26, 1989, p. 23; Gary Cook, letter to NRA, December 27, 1988. Once a crime in Japan are reported, the data are collected by the National Police Agency in a uniform manner. In the United States, the Uniform Crime Reports published by the FBI are anything but. Craig Parker, *The Japanese Police System Today: An American Perspective* (Tokyo and New York: Kodansha International, 1984), pp. 16–17, 100–101.

28. The American rates of defensive gun use and defensive homicide are discussed in chapter 11.

29. Ezra F. Vogel, *Japan as Number 1* (New York: Harper & Row, 1979), p. 17.

30. Juan Williams, "Japan: The Price of Safe Streets," *Washington Post,* October 13, 1991, p. C1.

31. William Bohnaker, *The Hollow Doll: A Little Black Box of Japanese Shocks* (New York: Ballantine, 1990), p. 50.

32. For example, Hendrik Hertzberg, "Gub Control," *The New Republic,* April 10, 1989 (suggesting a ban on all guns). For more, see note 216.

33. Article 24-2.

34. Ibid.

35. "Tokyo Police," p. 12. As a technical matter, citizens do not have to show the policeman what is in their bag.

36. *Japan* v. *Hashimoto,* 32 Keishū 1672 (Sup. Ct., 1st P.B. Sept. 7, 1978).

37. Vogel, p. 216.

38. Bayley, p. 72.

39. *White Paper on Police 1990,* p. 47; Parker, p. 49; Yamazaki. *Kendō* combatants generally use four-foot bamboo staves. Bayley, p. 73.

40. *White Paper on Police 1990,* p. 46.

41. In rural areas, the police boxes are called *chūzaisho*. Tharp, "For Japanese Police, the Hours Are Long, but Respect Is Great," *Wall Street Journal*, August 30, 1979, p. 1; Parker, p. 33.

42. *White Paper on Police 1986*, p. 56; *White Paper on Police 1990*, p. 47; Parker, p. 87.

43. Parker, p. 36. Technically, police boxes are called *hashutsujo*, but the *kōban* term persists.

44. *White Paper on Police 1986*, pp. 51, 126; Parker, p. 89.

45. *White Paper on Police 1986*, p. 52.

46. Parker, p. 69. For example, in Aichi Prefecture, an area of 2,000 square miles with a population of 7 million, the police have only 1,328 autos, and 1,347 motorcycles (which are used almost entirely for traffic work). Castberg, p. 38.

47. *White Paper on Police 1986*, p. 53; Parker p. 35; Yamazaki; Bayley, p. 84; Murray Sayle, "Where Law Is the True Order," *C.J. International* 7, no. 3 (May-June 1991, p. 5. In recent years, time pressures have reduced the frequency of home visits for some police districts.

48. "Japan to Check Gun Owners Before Economic Summit Talks," *St. Louis Post-Dispatch*, May 13, 1986; "Tokyo Police," p. 11.

49. During the Meiji Period at the end of the nineteenth century, the police were frankly acknowledged as instruments of surveillance and political control. One police bureau chief at the time boasted: "There would be no household in Japan into which the eyes of the police would not see and the ears would not hear." Sugai, "The Japanese Police System," in R. Ward, ed., *Five Studies in Japanese Politics* (Ann Arbor: University of Michigan Press, Center for Japanese Studies, 1957), Occasional Papers, no. 7, p. 4, quoted in Parker, p. 33.

50. *White Paper on Police 1986*, p. 70.

51. *White Paper on Police 1990*, p. 64. The police not only enforce the laws against pornography, they determine the legal standard for pornography. (The current standard forbids the showing of pubic hair.) Williams, "Japan: The Price of Safe Streets."

52. *White Paper on Police 1990*, p. 78. In 1989, there were 21,817.

53. Rep. William G. Bray, "Guns and Gun Laws—Fact and Fancy," *Congressional Record*, July 18, 1968; Yamazaki.

54. *White Paper on Police 1986*, p. 117.

55. Parker, pp. 194–95.

56. Michael Cross, "Japan Wakes Up to the Environment," *New Scientist*, June 23, 1988, p. 39; Maggie Sazuki, "Environmental Groups in Japan Lack National Cohesion," *Japan Times* (weekly international edition), November 15, 1991, p. 12 ("It is not socially acceptable, and usually not as effective, to challenge authority in Japan, as it is, for example, in the United States.").

57. Japanese police statistics credit third persons with solving only 3 percent of crime, but this number does not account for situations where third-person tips did not lead to the solution, but still made an important difference. American police officers and prosecutors frequently face situations where the solution to a crime is clear, but the unwillingness of victims or witnesses to testify makes conviction impossible. *White Paper on Police 1986*, p. 47.

58. Joseph McNamara, "Uncertainties in Police Work: The Relevance of Police Recruits' Background and Training," in David Bordua, ed., *The Police: Six Sociological Essays* (New York: Wiley, 1967), p. 221.

59. American noncompliance with gun laws is discussed in chapter 10, at p. 393.

60. Parker, p. 111. Technically, detentions are only allowed for three days, followed

by two ten-day extensions approved by a judge, followed by a special five-day extension; but defense attorneys rarely oppose the extension request, for fear of offending the prosecutor. Bail is denied if it would interfere with interrogation.

61. The Joint Committee of the Three Tokyo Bar Associations for the Study of the Daiyö-Kangoku (Substitute Prisons) System, *Torture and Unlawful or Unjust Treatment of Detainees in Daiyö-Kangoku* (Substitute Prisons) *in Japan* (August 1989), pp. 5–6.

62. *Baba* v. *Japan* (Sapporo High Court, 1950) (defense counsel had 20 minutes of access on third day, and 30 minutes each on ninth and tenth days of detention; amount of access was reasonable), discussed in Castberg, pp. 76–77; Tim Jackson, "The Tokyo Chainsaw Massacre," *New Republic,* September 11, 1989, p. 21; Mayer, "Japan, Behind the Myth of Japanese Justice," *American Lawyer,* July/August 1985; Parker, pp. 112–13; Bayley, pp. 151–52.

63. "News and Notes," *C.J. International* (Criminal Justice International), 6, no. 5, September–October 1990, p. 24.

64. Parker, p. 110.

65. Joint Committee, pp. 3–7. The Bar Association report is discussed in Margaret Shapiro, "Police Violence: Flip Side of Japan's Low Crime Rate," *Washington Post,* April 30, 1990, p. 17. See also Igarashi Futaba, "Forced to Confess," in Gaven McCormack and Yoshiro Sugimoto, eds., *Democracy in Contemporary Japan* (Armonk, N.Y.: M. E. Sharpe, 1986), pp. 195–214.

66. Walter Ames, *Police and Community in Japan* (Berkeley: University of California Press, 1981), p. 136.

67. Trial by jury was created in by Law No. 20, 1928, and suspended by Law No. 88, 1943. Even during the years the Jury Trial Law was in force, the right to jury trial was seldom exercised. Juries did not render a verdict on guilt, but only offered answers to factual questions put by the court, answers which were not binding on the court. Juries operated by majority vote, rather than unanimously. Nakayama, pp. 182–83; Castberg, p. 3, citing Kenzo Takayanagi, "A Century of Innovation: The Development of Japanese Law, 1868–1961," in von Mehren, ed., *Law in Japan: Legal Order in Changing Society* (Cambridge: Harvard University, 1963), pp. 171–72.

68. Joint Committee, p. 3.

69. Another check on the American police is the often-aggressive American press. For example, when an American state executes a prisoner, press coverage is intense, and persons who advocate sparing the prisoner's life have ready access to a public forum. In Japan, the police never announce executions. The carrying-out of capital sentences remains a secret until the year-end police reports. Williams, "Japan: The Price of Safe Streets."

Freedom of speech in general is quite constricted in Japan, at least by American standards. For example, political candidates may not campaign door-to-door, may not publish a campaign newspaper, face sharp restrictions on the contents of all written campaign materials, and may have only one campaign headquarters. Masahiro Usaki, "Restrictions on Political Campaigns in Japan," *Law & Contemporary Problems* 53 (Spring 1990), pp. 139–41. The ban on canvassing was upheld by the Supreme Court in 35 Keishū 205 (June 1981).

70. Williams, "Japan: The Price of Safe Streets."

71. Parker, p. 91.

72. Johnson, pp. 14–15; Parker, p. 107. Only 3 percent of convictions result in jail terms, and of those, 87 percent are for less than three years. Moreover, two-thirds of all jail sentences are suspended. John Haley, "Unsheathing the Sword: Law Without Sanctions," *Journal of Japanese Studies* 8, no. 2 (1982): 265–81.

73. While police powers are still extraordinary, there are signs of gradual change. Many policemen note the emergence of "rights consciousness," particularly among the young, as

one of the most significant developments in the last generation. A Tokyo policeman complains: "They used to treat us like members of the family and invite us in for coffee and/or tea; today that would be unthinkable." Parker, p. 65. In one instance, a crowd of people even threw stones at a police station after an officer was accused of corruption. "Japanese Protest Cops," *New York Newsday,* October 5, 1990, p. 12.

74. *White Paper on Police 1990,* p. 132.

75. Bayley, p. 148.

76. Richard Hofstadter, "America as a Gun Culture," *American Heritage,* October 1970, p. 82.

77. Edwin O. Reischauer, *Japan: The Story of a Nation* (New York: Knopf, 1970), p. 87.

78. Noel Perrin, *Giving Up the Gun: Japan's Reversion to the Sword, 1543–1879* (Boston: David R. Godine, 1979), p. 6, citing Seiho Arima, *Kaho no Kigen to Sono Denryu* (The Origins of Firearms and Their Early Transmission) (Tokyo: Yoshikawa Kobunkan, 1962), pp. 615–33.

79. Charles R. Boxer, *The Christian Century in Japan* (Berkeley: University of California Press, 1951), p. 28.

80. Perrin, pp. 14–16, citing for the quote Walter Dening, *The Life of Toyotomi Hideyoshi,* 3d ed. (Kobe and London: J. L. Thompson, 1930), p. 74.

81. Perrin, pp. 17–18, citing for the quote Professor Kiyondo Sato, letter to Noel Perrin.

82. Colonel Arcadi Gluckman, *United States Muskets, Rifles and Carbines* (Buffalo: Otto Ulbrich, 1948), p. 28; Perrin, p. 17.

83. Perrin, p. 67.

84. Ibid., p. 8.

85. Ibid., p. 10 n.20.

86. Boxer, p. 68; Warner and Draeger, p. 11; Perrin, p. 10.

87. Perrin, pp. 11–12, citing Inami Hakusui, *Nippon-To, the Japanese Sword* (Tokyo: Cosmo, 1948), p. 118.

88. Perrin, p. 12.

89. Stephen R. Turnbull, *The Samurai: A Military History* (New York: Macmillan, 1977), p. 144; Perrin, p. 8, citing A. L. Sadler, *The Maker of Modern Japan: The Life of Tokugawa Ieyasu* (London: G. Allen and Unwin, 1937), p. 53.

90. Perrin, p. 17, citing Delmar M. Brown, "The Impact of Firearms on Japanese Warfare," *Far Eastern Quarterly* (now the *Journal of Asian Studies*), 7 (1947–48), p. 239.

91. Ibid., p. 25.

92. Tadao Umesao, with Shuzo Koyama, Naoki Tani, Takeshi Moriya, Hidehiro Sonoda, and Toshinao Yoneyama, eds., *Seventy-seven Keys to the Civilization of Japan* (Union City, Calif.: Heian International, 1985), p. 106. [Citations hereafter refer to the author of the individual chapter under discussion, plus the book's name, i.e., "Sonoda, *Seventy-seven Keys.*"]

93. Gordon Warner and Donn F. Draeger, *Japanese Swordsmanship: Technique and Practice* (Tokyo: Weatherhill, 1982), pp. 34–35.

94. Umesao, *Seventy-seven Keys,* p. 112.

95. Robert L. O'Connell, *Of Arms and Men: A History of War, Weapons, and Aggression* (Oxford: Oxford University Press, 1989), pp. 108–23.

96. Perrin, pp. 24–25.

97. Perrin, p. 25, citing for Lord Oda Nobunaga, Dening, p. 177; for battle heroes, Dening, p. 206, and Turnbull, p. 171.

98. Reischauer, p. 76.

99. Ibid.

100. Turnbull, *The Samurai,* p. 190. In the seventh century, the Taika dynasty had attempted to disarm its enemies by rounding up swords and bows under the guise of collecting weapons for the army. The attempt failed because the central government could not enforce its will throughout the nation. Warner and Draeger, p. 6. General MacArthur staged one final sword hunt in 1945-46, attempting to obliterate the last vestiges of feudalism. Bayley, p. 169.

101. Warner and Draeger, p. 36; Perrin, pp. 25-26.

102. James Murdoch, *A History of Japan,* vol. II (New York: Greenbery, 1926), p. 369; Perrin, p. 27.

103. Turnbull, p. 190.

104. Warner and Draeger, pp. 68-69.

105. George Storry, *A History of Modern Japan* (Baltimore: Penguin, 1960), pp. 53-54.

106. Barrington Moore, Jr., *Social Origins of Dictatorship and Democracy: Lord and Peasant in the Making of the Modern World* (Boston: Beacon Press, 1966), pp. 232, 261-62.

107. Reischauer, p. 77; Warner and Draeger, p. 37.

108. Perrin, pp. 47, 58.

109. Ibid., p. 58.

110. Ibid., p. 62. *Teppo* literally means "musket."

111. Ibid., citing Arima, p. 670.

112. Ibid., pp. 62-63, citing Arima, pp. 671, 676-77.

113. Ibid., pp. 64-65, citing Arima, p. 677.

114. Perrin, pp. 33, 35. Also, Bartholomew, pp. 25-26; Reischauer, p. 85.

115. Perrin, p. 35.

116. Chapter 3 elaborates the issue.

117. Inazo Nitobe, *Bushido: The Soul of Japan,* rev. ed. (Tokyo: Charles E. Tuttle Company, 1969) (1st ed., 1905), pp. 131-37.

118. Perrin, pp. 38-39, citing for the Mitsuhide story Hakusui, *Nippon-To,* p. xvii; Warner and Draeger, p. 46. The Samurai carried two swords, a long one and a dagger. Seward, p. 49.

119. Perrin, p. 39, citing Arima, p. 667.

120. Reischauer, p. 53. Many swords, though, were sacrificed to provide steel for the military during the war.

121. Ruth Benedict, *The Chrysanthemum and the Sword* (Boston: Houghton Mifflin, 1946), p. 296.

122. Chapter 10 offers more examples of gun phrases in the American idiom.

123. Reischauer, p. 88; Bohnaker, pp. 38-39.

124. Reischauer, p. 89.

125. Parker, p. 20.

126. Perrin, p. 42.

127. Ibid., p. 43.

128. Ibid., pp. 37-39.

129. Umesao, *Seventy-seven Keys,* p. 162.

130. William Tonso, *Gun and Society: The Social and Existential Roots of the American Attachment to Firearms* (Lanham, Md.: University Press of America, 1982), p. 146. There is some deer and boar. Umesao, *Seventy-Seven Keys,* p. 10.

131. Reischauer, p. 90.

132. John Rodgers, Lieutenant Commander, Letter to James C. Dobin, Secretary of State, February 15, 1855, in Allan B. Cole, ed., *Yankee Surveyors in the Shogun's Seas: Records of the United States Surveying Expedition to the North Pacific Ocean, 1853-1856* (Princeton: Princeton University Press, 1947), p. 43.

133. Reischauer, p. 134.

134. Ibid., p. 115.

135. Ibid., p. 133.

136. Jack Seward, *Hara-Kiri: Japanese Ritual Suicide* (Rutland, Vt., and Tokyo: Charles E. Tuttle, 1968), p. 96; Reischauer, p. 122; Perrin, pp. 72–73, citing E. W. Clement, "The Saga and Satsuma Rebellions," *The Asian Studies Journal* 50 (1922): 23–24, and Murdoch, vol. II, p. 658; E. Herbert Norman, *Soldier and Peasant in Japan: The Origins of Conscription* (New York: International Secretarial Institute of Pacific Relations, 1943), pp. 34, 44–45, citing John R. Black, *Young Japan,* vol. I (London: 1880), p. 138, and A. H. Mounsey, *The Satsuma Rebellion: An Episode of Modern Japanese History* (London: 1879), pp. 60–61, 231–32.

137. Reischauer, p. 123.

138. Ibid., p. 127.

139. Ibid.

140. E. G. Babbitt, American Vice Counsel General for Yokohama, quoted in Albert L. Wyman, "Sale of Firearms," *New York Times,* August 19, 1910, p. 8, col. 5.

141. Reischauer, pp. 182–83.

142. Sonoda, in *Seventy-seven Keys,* p. 200.

143. O'Connell, p. 237.

144. Sonoda, in *Seventy-seven Keys,* p. 200.

145. Hugo Byars, *Government by Assassination* (New York: Alfred A. Knopf, 1942).

146. On January 18, 1990, the mayor of Nagasaki was shot and seriously injured by a right-wing extremist angered by the mayor's admission of Japan's fault in causing World War II. *White Paper on Police 1990,* p. 110.

147. Reischauer, p. 187.

148. Ibid., p. 207.

149. Bohnaker, p. 84. Civilian firearms being scarce, women were given spears made from sharpened bamboo sticks. William Chapman, *Inventing Japan: An Unconventional Account of Postwar Years* (New York: Prentice-Hall, 1991), p. 2.

150. Reischauer, p. 223.

151. Obviously General MacArthur started the process, but independent Japan has showed little interest in rearming.

152. Reischauer, pp. 226–27.

153. Ibid., p. 245.

154. Sonoda, in *Seventy-seven Keys,* p. 224. Today, family structures are weaker, because of "the steady infiltration of individualistic notions" and economic prosperity, which has made close family-unity less essential. Ibid.

155. Penal Code, Article 205. The law was upheld in *Matsui* v. *Japan,* 28 Keishū 329 (Supreme Court, 1974), because the law regarding lineal ascendants only added one year to the minimum sentence. Castberg, pp. 82–83.

156. *Constitution of Japan and Criminal Statutes,* compiled by the Ministry of Justice (Tokyo: 1958): "[T]here shall be no discrimination in political, economic or social relations because of race, creed, sex, social status or family origin." Article 14. "Marriage shall be based only on the mutual consent of both sexes and it shall be maintained through mutual cooperation with the equal rights of husband and wife as a basis." Article 24, section 1. "No person shall be arrested or detained without being at once informed of the charges against him or without the immediate privilege of counsel; nor shall he be detained without adequate cause; and upon demand of any person such cause must be immediately shown in open court in his presence and in the presence of his counsel." Article 34. "No person shall be compelled to testify against himself." Article 38, section 1. "Confession made under

compulsion, torture or threat, or after prolonged arrest or detention shall not be admitted into evidence." Article 38, section 2. "No person shall be convicted or punished in cases where the only evidence against him is his own confession." Article 38, section 3.

157. Similarly, Japanese penal statutes are written with far less exactitude and detail of elements of the offense than American statutes on the same subject. Japanese defendants are much less likely than their American counterparts to raise claims that they cannot be convicted because of technical defects or loopholes in the statutory definition of a crime. Castberg, p. 7.

158. Nobutaka Ike, *Japanese Politics: Patron-Client Democracy,* 2d ed. (New York: Knopf, 1972).

159. Reischauer, p. 52.

160. Ibid., p. 53.

161. J. Victor Koschmann, "Soft Rule and Expressive Protest," in J. Victor Koschmann, ed., *Authority and the Individual in Japan* (Tokyo: University of Tokyo Press, 1978), p. 7, quoted in Parker, p. 32.

162. Matsumoto, "The Roots of Political Disillusionment: 'Public and Private' in Japan," in Koschmann, ed., p. 38, quoted in Parker, p. 32. Compared to Americans, a much larger percentage of Japanese believe themselves helpless to influence government actions. Chapman, p. 144.

163. Takeo Doi, *The Anatomy of Dependence* (Tokyo: Kodansha, 1973).

164. Noriho Urabe, "Rule of Law and Due Process: A Comparative View of the United States and Japan," *Law and Contemporary Problems* 53 (1990), p. 69.

165. Parker, p. 20. For example, cheering at baseball games is officially organized so that thousands of people utter the same shouts at the same time.

166. Ibid., p. 103.

167. Bohnaker, p. 42.

168. Vogel, pp. 118–19.

169. Parker, pp. 11–12. Professor Parker, in his research on the Japanese police, notes that once he obtained approval from the police administration, policemen at all levels cooperated readily with him. In America, says Parker, a researcher looking at the police would need approval from both the administration and the police union; even then, cooperation by the individual rank-and-file would not be guaranteed.

170. Sonoda, in *Seventy-seven Keys,* p. 212.

171. Mary Ganz, "Japanese Wives Remain Behind in Status, Equality," *Rocky Mountain News,* July 30, 1988, p. 66 (originally published in the *San Francisco Examiner*). In 1985, Japan enacted the "Equal Employment Opportunity Law" in response to international criticism of Japan's failure to integrate women into the workforce. The law is precatory, and enforceable by neither the government nor by private lawsuit. One of the reasons that even a law so weak was not enacted until 1985 was that Japanese women themselves, including younger ones, had little desire to change their traditional pattern of only working for a few years before marrying and taking charge of a household full-time. Loraine Parkinson, "Japan's Equal Employment Opportunity Law: An Alternative Approach to Social Change," *Columbia Law Review* 89 (April 1989): 604–60.

172. Susan Chira, "Working Women Find Slow Progress in Japan," *New York Times,* December 4, 1988.

173. Bohnaker, p. 28.

174. Parker, p. 61, citing Foreign Press Center, *Japan: A Pocket Guide* (Tokyo: Foreign Press Center, 1979).

175. Castberg, p. 30.

176. Parker, p. 99. The relative unavailability of Japanese divorce may partly explain the higher suicide rate.

177. Takeyoshi Kawashima, "The Status of the Individual and the Notion of Law, Right, and Social Order in Japan," in Charles A. Moore, ed., *The Japanese Mind: Essentials of Japanese Philosophy and Culture* (Honolulu: East-West Center Press, 1967), p. 264.

178. Kawashima, pp. 262–87.

179. Bayley, p. 155.

180. James Q. Wilson and Richard J. Herrnstein, *Crime and Human Nature* (New York: Simon and Schuster, 1985), pp. 452–57.

181. Benedict, pp. 222–27.

182. "Tokyo Police," pp. 10–11.

183. Vogel, p. 206.

184. Ibid., p. 218.

185. Ibid., p. 18, Chapman, pp. 9–10, 48. Anthropologist Joy Hendry attributes the current low Japanese crime rate to the effect of group controls such as shame. Joy Hendry, *Understanding Japanese Society* (London: Routledge, 1989).

186. Bayley, pp. 164, 180.

187. The primary arms are Smith & Wesson or Nambu .38s. Detectives sometimes carry .22s. Castberg, p. 38.

188. Bayley, pp. 11, 37, 64, 162–70; Castberg, p. 38.

189. Bayley, p. 163; Castberg, pp. 30–31.

190. Parker, p. 75.

191. Bayley, p. 164; Penal Code, Article 37.

192. "Tokyo Police," p. 10. Tokyo police fired their revolvers four times in all of 1984. "The World's Largest City is Also the Safest," *Washington Post,* April 20, 1975.

193. Bayley, pp. 174–75. The Japanese policy by which all players follow certain rules to keep their conflicts within bounds is also manifested in police raids on *Yakuza* (organized crime) headquarters. The *Yakuza* will frequently have received advance warning of the raid, and the highest bosses and the most valuable contraband will be long gone by the time the police arrive. Nevertheless, "so the police can save face, the gangsters generally leave behind a few guns for the officers to confiscate." Kaplan and Dubro, p. 162.

194. Bayley, p. 170.

195. Dane Archer and Rosemary Gartner, "Violent Acts and Violent Times: The Effect of Wars on Postwar Homicide Rates," in Dane Archer and Rosemary Gartner, eds., *Violence and Crime in Cross-National Perspective* (New Haven: Yale University Press, 1984), pp. 63–97.

196. Harold R. Kerbo and Mariko Inoue, "Japanese Social Structure and White Collar Crime: Recruit Cosmos and Beyond." Paper presented at the annual meeting of the American Society of Criminology, Reno, Nev., November 1990, p. 20.

197. Reischauer, p. 6.

198. Vogel, p. 243.

199. Parker, p. 19.

200. Joint Committee, p. 52. About three-fourths of the Korean population in Japan has been arrested at one time or another for not carrying their Alien Registration cards.

201. Quoted in Nicholas Lemann, "Why Can't We Be More Like Japan?" *Washington Post,* May 1, 1985, p. A17.

202. Charles Peters, "Tilting at Windmills," *The Washington Monthly,* September 1989, p. 6.

203. Many bookstores have "Jewish corners" for titles such as *The Jewish Plot to Take Over the World, Japan—Blueprint of Jewish Conspiracy,* and *The Protocols of the Elders of Zion.* Masami Uno, Japan's leading anti-Semitic ideologist, boasts over 650,000 sales for his last two books. They blame the rise of the yen on a Jewish conspiracy whose ultimate

goal is to destroy the Japanese economy, and then import black and Hispanic workers who will steal Japanese jobs and rape Japanese women. According to Uno, America is a "Jewish nation" run by Jews such as George Shultz, and Casper Weinberger and by Jewish families such as the Mellons, Du Ponts, Morgans, and Rockefellers. Uno tells tales of other Jewish conspirators such as Commodore Perry, Christopher Columbus, Vladimir Ilyich Lenin, Franklin Roosevelt, and Sheik Ahmad Zaki Yamani. Needless to say, no one on Uno's list is Jewish. *Yomiuri,* Japan's leading newspaper, treats Uno's theory that Jews are behind the revaluation of the yen as credible.

Anti-Semitism is hardly an evil known only to Japan. Still, the widespread popularity of such an extreme variant of anti-Semitism in Japan says much about Japan's cultural insularity. Clifford Goldstein, "Anti-Semitism in Japan," *Liberty* (March/April 1989): 21–23.

204. Among the claims of *nihonjinron* are that the Japanese have intestines longer than other people, that their brains work differently, and that they can communicate without speaking. Such beliefs are surprisingly common, and even at the most educated levels of society, there is a firm, and somewhat fascist, belief that the Japanese race is special. Peter N. Dale, *The Myth of Japanese Uniqueness* (New York: St. Martin's Press, 1986).

205. Parker, pp. 21–22.

206. Kerbo and Inoue, p. 20. Japanese in the bottom 10 percent income bracket received twice as much of their nation's income as did America's bottom 10 percent. Chapman, p. 201. One scholar describes the Japanese as "equality minded rather than liberty minded." Yasuhiro Okudaira, "40 Years of the Constitution and its Various Influences," *Law and Contemporary Problems* 53 (Winter 1990), p. 29.

207. W. Avison and P. Loring, "Population Diversity and Cross-National Homicide: The Effects of Inequality and Heterogeneity," *Criminology* 24 (1986): 733–49; H. Krahn, T. Hartnagel, and J. Gettrell, "Income Inequality and Homicide Rates: Cross National Data and Criminological Theories," *Criminology* 24 (1986): 269–95.

208. Kamm, "In Tokyo, A Raucous Honky-Tonk Area That Has No Crime," *New York Times,* July 22, 1981, p. A3.

209. Halloran, "Japan's Tight Controls Keep Guns at a Minimum," *New York Times,* September 12, 1975. Long-gun production for the limited domestic market and the export market is much more extensive. Browning, one of the world's largest gun manufacturers, assembles rifles and shotguns in Japan. Dave Tinker, "Downrange," *Gun Tests* (September 1990), p. 2. Japan also produces and exports SKB shotguns and Charles Daly shotguns. "Gas-Operated Semi-automatic Shotguns: Can One Shotgun Do the Job of Several?" *Gun Tests* (May 1991), pp. 14–16. Weatherby shotguns are made by SKB, whose name is a play on its home city of Sakaba.

Because airguns can only be possessed by adults who are highly motivated to overcome numerous licensing obstacles, Japanese airgun manufacturers have concentrated on producing expensive, high-quality guns for the adult market. Larry Hannusch, "Sharp Air Rifles— Proudly Made in Japan," *American Airgunner,* January-February 1991, p. 37.

Japan also has a thriving industry manufacturing highly realistic toy guns. Duncan Long, *The Terrifying Three: Uzi, Ingram, and Intratec Weapons Families* (Boulder, Colo.: Paladin, 1989), pp. 107–108.

210. World Health Organization, *World Health Statistics, 1984* (Geneva: WHO, 1984), pp. 183, 189; United States Bureau of the Census, *Statistical Abstract of the United States, 1989* (Washington, D.C.: Government Printing Office, 1989), p. 820.

211. Bureau of the Census, *Statistical Abstract of the United States, 1988* (Washington, D.C.: Government Printing Office, 1987), pp. 802–803. *White Paper on Police 1986,* p. 53. In 1985, the suicide rate per 100,000 was 19.5 overall; 26.3 for males, and 12.9 for females. *White Paper 1986,* p. 53. The ratio of male to female suicides: United States: 3.55:1; Japan:

1.98:1; England and Wales: 2.07:1; Canada: 3.51:1; Australia: 3.25: 1. Calculations based on *Statistical Abstract,* p. 803. If gun control does lower the male suicide rate relative to the female rate, the effect only seems to appear in countries with the strictest laws.

212. Parker, p. 149.

213. S. Jameson. "Parent-Child Suicides Frequent in Japan," *Hartford Courant,* March 28, 1981. *Shinju* literally means "inside the heart," figuratively, "revealing-the-heart death." Seward, p. 73.

214. Mamoru Iga and Kichinosuke Totai, "Characteristics of Suicide and Attitudes toward Suicides in Japan," in Norman L. Farberow, ed., *Suicide in Different Cultures* (Baltimore: University Park Press, 1975), p. 273.

215. David Rosenbaum, "The Symptoms Surround Us, But What is the Malady?" *New York Times,* April 5, 1981, p. IV:1, col. 5.

216. For example, Hendrik Hertzberg, "Gub Control," *The New Republic* (suggesting total prohibition on all guns); Richard Strout (TRB), "A Scary Lesson in Gun Control," *Philadelphia Inquirer,* February 8, 1979; New York senatorial candidate Mark Green, *Winning Back America* (1982), p. 222; Patrick V. Murphy, former New York City Police Commissioner, former head of National Police Foundation, speech to annual Police Medal of Honor Luncheon, Denver Hilton Hotel, April 16, 1974 ("The time has come for us to disarm the individual citizen."); James Ridgeway, "The Kind of Gun Control We Need," *The New Republic,* June 22, 1968, p. 11 ("Put simply, private citizens should be disarmed."); "The Gun Culture," *The New York Times,* September 24, 1975, p. 44 (". . . remove the guns from the hands and shoulders of people who are not in the law enforcement business."); Ramsey Clark, former United States attorney general, "Playboy Interview," *Playboy,* August 1969, p. 70 ("I think we should work for the day when there are no guns at all, at least in urban areas—even for the police on normal duty.").

217. Gary Kleck and David Bordua, "The Assumptions of Gun Control," in Donald B. Kates, ed., *Firearms and Violence: Issues of Public Policy* (Cambridge, Mass.: Ballinger, 1984), pp. 26–31.

Chapter 8 of the present volume discusses Berkowitz's "weapons effect" in more detail.

218. Yasushi Hari, quoted in Shields, p. 65.

219. Gary Kleck, "The Relationship Between Gun Ownership Levels and Rates of Violence in the United States," in *Firearms and Violence,* pp. 99–132.

220. Carol B. Kalish, "International Crime Rates," Bureau of Justice, *Statistics Special Report,* May 1988, p. 3, citing Interpol, *International Crime Statistics,* vols. 1983-84. The rate was 1.1 per 100,000 population in both countries.

One United States government advisory commission, in a 1973 report, while conceding that cultural factors may have something to do with Japan's lesser crime, argued that gun-related crime in Japan declined every year since 1964, when the controls were enacted in their current form. National Advisory Commission on Criminal Justice Standards and Goals, in *A National Strategy to Reduce Crime* (January 1973), p. 141. But the selection of 1964 was highly artificial. Near-absolute gun prohibition had existed for over three centuries, and the current system of controls was put in place during the American occupation, and formally codified in 1958. There was no reason to pick 1964 as the year that gun control went into effect.

221. The "over 70" figure is derived by starting with Kalish's Bureau of Justice Statistics data showing the reported robbery rates for the United States to be 205.4 persons per 100,000, and Japan's to be 1.8. Kalish, p. 8, table 10. Of all American reported robberies, about 67 percent do not involve a gun. The "over 70" figure makes the conservative assumption that hardly any of Japan's robberies are by gun.

222. Bureau of Justice Statistics, Department of Justice, *Sourcebook of Criminal Justice*

Statistics 1986 (Washington, D.C., 1987), p. 398 (10-24 American jail inmates per year die from injury inflicted by another person); Castberg, p. 109.

223. B. Bruce-Briggs, "The Great American Gun War," *The Public Interest* 45 (Fall 1976), p. 56.

Of course to the extent that Japanese-Americans own guns at a lower rate than other Americans, that could explain the lower Japanese-American gun-related crime rate. It should be noted though, that the Japanese-American violent crime rate is lower for the whole spectrum of violent crimes, not just crimes involving guns.

For the strength of social controls among Japanese-American immigrants, see generally Johan Thorsten Sellin, *Culture Conflict and Crime,* A Report of the Subcommittee on Delinquency of the Committee on Personality and Culture (New York: Social Science Research Council, 1938), S.S.R.C. Bulletin no. 41, pp. 73, 106 (attributing low juvenile delinquency rates among Japanese immigrants to importance of upholding family honor and "strength of the moral fabric" in families).

224. Parker, p. 168.

225. *White Paper on Police 1986,* p. 45.

226. Kaplan and Dubro, p. 232. At the Hawaii Gun Club alone, 14,000 Japanese a year go shooting. Rasmussen, "The Hawaii Gun Club," *Guns,* September 1987, p. 34.

3

Great Britain: The Queen's Peace

"One axiom I heard a lot when I was there: 'We're subjects. You're citizens.' "[1]

No country is more frequently cited as a model for American gun control than Great Britain—appropriately so given the common heritage of the two nations. The vision of a civilized society with few guns and fewer murders powerfully appeals to American gun-control advocates. Former U.S. Supreme Court Justice Lewis Powell notes that in England there were only 662 homicides in 1986, and only 8 percent of those with firearms. "Private ownership of guns is strictly controlled in other Western democracies," states Powell. "In Great Britain, for example, gun owners must apply for a special license and satisfy the authorities that their possession of firearms will not endanger public safety . . . [F]irearms dealers are strictly regulated and subject to record-keeping requirements."[2]

Sometimes the exacting controls in Great Britain are offered as legal justifications for American gun controls. In the mid-1960s, New Jersey enacted laws that remain the most stringent state-level gun controls in the United States.[3] The Supreme Court of New Jersey rejected a constitutional challenge to the controls; the court reasoned that the American right to bear arms derived from the British right to bear arms, and that in modern times, the British right had vanished: "[F]or all practical purposes the average citizen cannot lawfully obtain firearms in Great Britain at the present time."[4] Likewise, the North Carolina Supreme Court, in turning aside an argument that the Second Amendment protected an individual right to carry firearms, relied on English legal history as precedent.[5]

The New Jersey and North Carolina courts obtained their information about guns in England almost entirely from an article published in a leading American law review.[6] That 1966 article from the *Northwestern University Law Review* remains a linchpin of the legal argument for gun control, since it is one of the very few articles published in a top-twenty American law review to conclude that the right to bear arms is *not* an individual right.[7]

Unfortunately, that article was wildly wrong in its assertion that the average Briton could not lawfully obtain a gun. When the article was written, a Briton could walk into a store and five minutes later walk out with an armload of shotguns. Even today, shotguns are available to almost any Briton without a criminal record; and rifle and handgun permits are available for target shooting.[8]

Just as American courts searching for justification of American gun control have misunderstood Britain, so have American politicians. The U.S. National Firearms Act of 1934 (taxing the transfer of automatic firearms) was justified in part on the grounds that gun laws in England were already so severe that, according to the attorney general of the United States, "the use and possession of every kind of firearm, and of the ammunition therefor" required police permission and registration. In fact, at the time, an escapee from a British mental institution could stroll into a gun store, purchase two dozen shotguns with which to perpetrate a massacre, and stroll away with weapons and ammunition after paying the cashier, no questions asked. There would be no need for police permission, and no registration.[9]

The misinformed vision of Britain as an almost completely disarmed society is found not only in academia and the courts, but also in the popular press. For example, one *Los Angeles Times* story claimed that there were only 30,000 shotguns and 9,000 handguns in all of the British Isles.[10] Actually, there are approximately two million legal shotguns in England and Wales, and several hundred thousand handguns.[11] As of 1988, "shotgun certificates" were owned by 881,600 persons.[12] One hundred and fifty-five thousand Britons possessed a "firearms certificate," entitling them to own a rifle or handgun.[13] Overall, about one in twenty-five households admits to owning a gun.[14]

Of course while Britain numbers its guns in the low millions, the American count is in the hundreds of millions. Half of America's households contain a gun.[15] And while in the past two decades America has become an even more well-armed society, the number of persons legally owning rifles or handguns in Britain has declined by a third as the police have implemented a policy of making firearms permits less and less obtainable.[16]

In short, gun-ownership statistics in Britain seem to show that guns remain available in moderate numbers for sporting uses. As Justice Powell notes, Britain's gun-crime problem is very small. Does Britain then offer the United States a model for reasonable gun laws? Although Japanese-style gun prohibition might be unsuited for America, perhaps controls along the British model would work.

THE GOVERNMENT DISARMS SOME OF THE PEOPLE SOME OF THE TIME

Nineteenth-century U.S. Supreme Court Justice Joseph Story called the American right to bear arms "the palladium of the liberties of the republic" that served as the ultimate guarantor of all other rights.[17] He distinguished the British right, which he thought "more nominal than real."[18] Justice Story's point was to contrast the weak British right with the strong American right. Yet twentieth-century American gun-control advocates repeat Justice Story's quote, inverting the meaning. They reason that since the American right is a descendant of the British right, evidence that shows weakness of the British right also shows weakness of the American right. If the British right was merely "nominal," then the American right must also be nominal.[19]

But both Justice Story and modern gun-control advocates misunderstood the British right to bear arms. In fact, although the British right was often under attack, it was of much more than a nominal concern to the English monarchy, the aristocracy, and the people. Understanding the evolution of the Britain's right to bear arms is an essential first step in the evaluation of British gun control.

Weapons laws began long before guns were invented. In 1181, King Henry II's Statute of Assize of Arms ordered the surrender of coats of mail and breastplates owned by Jews. While Jews, being ineligible for the aristocracy, were forbidden aristocratic armor, all freemen were required to bear arms, befitting their rank, for national defense. The Assize required every freeman to "bear these arms in his [Henry II's] service according to his order and in allegiance to the lord King and his realm." The Assize was based on the old Saxon tradition of the *fyrd*, in which every male aged sixteen to sixty bore arms to defend the nation.[20]

Complaining about an increase in crime, King Edward I enacted the Statute of Winchester, which required "every man," not just freemen, to have arms. The types of arms required to be owned by the poorest people were gisarmes (a type of pole-ax), knives, and bows. Other anti-crime measures in the statute ordered local citizens to apprehend fleeing criminals, and established night watches.[21]

The Statute of Northampton, enacted in 1328 by King Edward III, prohibited any person "great or small" from going armed in a public place.[22] Jules Jusserand, a Pulitzer Prize–winning historian, found that "honest folk alone conformed to the law, thus facilitating matters for the others."[23] Accordingly, the common law courts moderated the statute by interpreting it to apply only to those who went armed in a manner "terrifying the good people of the land."[24]

Highwaymen armed with concealable weapons did terrify the people. Henry VIII barred anyone with an annual income of less than £300 from owning a handgun or a crossbow, the two weapons used by most robbers.[25] At the same time, the king ordered his subjects to possess longbows, to practice with them, and to provide longbows for their children; he complained that interest in handguns and crossbows was diverting people from longbow practice.[26]

Weapons-control laws such as the Statute of Northampton or Henry VIII's laws are sometimes cited by American commentators to show that the English right to bear arms was "more nominal than real."[27] Yet the mere existence of a restrictive statute, especially a statute that is widely disobeyed and generally disapproved, does not prove the nonexistence of a right. A future historian who points to the Alien and Sedition Acts as proof that the American right to free speech was "more nominal than real," would mislead his readers.[28]

Even under the statutes, British subjects were not precluded from armed home defense with long guns. A few years before Henry VIII's coronation, and a century later in 1603, the courts announced that "a man's home is his castle," being therefore "for his defense against injury and violence as for his repose."[29] The self-defense "castle doctrine" would later become a philosophical cornerstone of the American concepts of the right to privacy and the right to freedom from searches without probable cause.[30]

Moreover, draconian weapons control was made impossible by the need for an armed citizenry for national security. The monarchy might be uncomfortable with men of low degree having firearms or bows that could be used for poaching, but those same men at arms were necessary for national defense. Wars with France forced Henry VIII to lower the property qualification for handguns and crossbows, and eventually to repeal the statute entirely.[31] The king now wished "his loving subjects practiced and exercised in the feat of shooting handguns and hackbuts [sic, arquebus]."[32] After the war ended, the handgun and crossbow law was reenacted,[33] and then finally repealed for good in 1557, thanks to another war with France.[34]

By the late sixteenth century, gun ownership had become mandatory for all adult males—for anti-crime purposes, and for the defense of the realm. Arms were necessary so that all citizens could join in the *hutesium et clamor* (hue and cry) to pursue fleeing criminals.[35] Death was the usual judicial punishment for felons; pursuing citizens were allowed to use deadly force if necessary (since it mattered little if the felon died during the chase or a few weeks later in gaol).[36]

All able-bodied men from the age of sixteen to sixty were legally bound to join the hue and cry, and to participate in what came to be called, around 1590, "the militia." Although all men were required to serve, it was common for a county to choose a group of men to receive intensive militia drill in "trained bands." In either the general militia or the specialized trained bands, the men at arms were freeholders, craftsmen, or other middle-class citizens, under the command of upper-class men of the community.[37] The duty of subjects to bear arms for the common defense, as their financial means allowed, traced its roots back to feudalism. Because middle-class militiamen operated under the orders of well-to-do gentlemen officers, notions of hierarchy and due deference were reinforced.[38]

The seventeenth century was one of continual struggle between the king, the Parliament, and the rest of society, over who should have the ultimate power of force in Great Britain. As historian Lois G. Schwoerer details in her book *"No Standing Armies!" The Antimilitary Ideology in Seventeenth-Century England,* England was dominated by the contest for control of the militia and the army. The struggle led at first to civil war, and eventually to the formal recognition of a British subject's right to bear arms. This crucial century was studied intensely by the creators of the American republic.

From the Royalist perspective, the king of England had the authority to raise and maintain a standing army of professional soldiers. If necessary, the king could command that the soldiers be billeted in his subjects' houses, at his subjects' expense. The militia (the armed body of the people) was also to be under the king's command.

The competing view was best articulated by James Harrington's 1656 treatise *The Commonwealth of Oceana.* Harrington, speaking for both radical libertarians and for country squires, expressed the conventional wisdom of the opponents of a standing army. Widely read even a century later, Harrington also expressed what became the conventional wisdom of the founders of the American republic: A free society rests upon the foundation of small farmers who own their own land. The virtuous yeoman farmer, bringing his own arms to duty in a popular militia, is the best security of a free state. Unlike a standing army, a militia would never tyrannize its native land. Indeed, a militia could overthrow a despot. And unlike hired mercenaries or professional soldiers, the militiaman had his own country to fight for, and was therefore the best defense of a free state against foreign invasion.[39]

In general terms, the Parliament usually represented the views of the rural, landed aristocracy that was opposing monarchical efforts to centralize state power in London. In the "country versus court" battle, many of the small landholders, tenant farmers, and artisans sided with the faction of rural aristocracy opposed to central control from London. Although most people viewed militia service as a great annoyance, and did what they could to avoid it, militiamen had no particular objection to serving under the command of the "better men" of their county when militia duty was inescapable. While the middle class often saw the militia as an inconvenient obligation, there was a great fear of the king's standing army, since the army was often composed of the dregs of society and did more to terrify and abuse British towns than to protect them.

In 1642, Parliament asserted for itself the right to regulate the militia. "By God, not for an hour!" the king thundered back.[40] King Charles I recognized that whoever controlled the militia controlled the state. "Kingly power is but a shadow," without command of the militia, he noted. He considered the militia question the "fittest subject for a King's Quarrel," and challenged the Parliament's unprecedented usurpation of the power of the sword.[41]

A crisis of government ensued. In 1642, a Royalist army marched on London, but retreated without a shot when faced down by a twenty-thousand-man militia loyal to Parliament. John Milton wrote the poem "When the Assault was Intended to the City" in tribute.[42] Civil war began that year, with the militia issue being as important as any other question.[43]

After two decades of conflict, monarchy triumphed, and in 1660 the Restoration placed the English people once again under the authority of a monarchy. Shortly thereafter, the king ordered gunsmiths to report all gun sales, and banned imports.[44] By the Militia Act of 1662, a Parliament loyal to King Charles II confirmed the king's sole authority over the militia. The act authorized the king's agents "to search for and seize all arms in the custody or possession of any person or persons who the said lieutenants or any two or more of their deputies shall judge dangerous to the peace of the kingdom."[45]

The militia itself, though, was not supine. During the king's reign, the militia disobeyed orders to suppress Dissenters (Protestants who did not submit to the Anglican Church) and deserted at the first possible opportunity.[46] When Parliament later grew bolder, Sir Henry Capel, of the House of Commons, explained why Parliament felt free to defy Charles II: "Our security is the militia: that will defend us and never conquer us." It was clear that the militia would fight foreign invaders, but was much less willing than the standing army to obey royal orders to attack fellow Englishmen (particularly when those fellows were neighbors, or supporters of a popular cause).[47]

Under Charles II, Parliament initiated the most draconian gun-control program England had ever known. The 1671 Game Act forbade 95 percent of the population (persons not owning lands worth £100 in annual rentals) from hunting, and barred non-hunters from owning guns. The law further authorized daytime searches of any home suspected of holding an illegal gun.[48]

The strict laws failed. After the Catholic James II succeeded Charles II in 1685, he observed that "a great many persons not qualified by law" kept weapons in their homes. The new king commanded "strict search to be made for such muskets or guns and to seize and safely keep them till further order."[49] The king attempted to build up his standing army, with Catholic officers in charge. By neglecting the militia, he hoped it would wither as a threat to his power. But again, the courts resisted. A 1686 judicial decision recognized the right of the people to "ride armed for their Security."[50]

In the Glorious Revolution of 1688–1689, King James II was driven out of the country by the professional army of William of Orange, a Protestant from the Netherlands. James's standing army deserted at the first opportunity, and not a single life was lost. The new King William and his Queen Mary established the system of limited monarchy, operating under an informal constitution.[51] In response to the abuses of absolute monarchs, the 1689 Bill of Rights guaranteed British subjects certain rights. The first part of the statute listed the abuses of Charles II and James II:

. . .

5. By raising and keeping a standing army within this kingdom in time of peace, without the consent of parliament, and quartering soldiers contrary to law.

6. By causing several good subjects, being protestants, to be disarmed at the same time when papists were both armed and employed contrary to law.[52]

The second part of the Bill of Rights created laws to prevent recurrence of the abuses. It affirmed that the right to bear arms (like other rights) was not being created or granted by government, but had always been a traditional right of Englishmen:

And thereupon the said Lords Spiritual and Temporal and Commons . . . do in the first place (as their ancestors in like case have usually done) for the vindicating and asserting their ancient rights and liberties declare:

6. That the raising or keeping a standing army within the kingdom in time of peace, unless it be with consent of parliament, is against the law.

7. The subjects which are protestants may have arms for their defence suitable to their conditions as and allowed by law.[53]

Since a militia composed of all (Protestant) citizens was to be armed, and since standing armies were prohibited, the Bill of Rights implicitly created a right of popular rebellion, which acted as a guarantee of the other rights.[54]

The consensus view in the seventeenth century was that the militia had saved the nation. Historian Thomas Macaulay concluded that Britain's Parliament survived—while continental parliaments declined—because the British monarchy's power was dependent on the consent of the militia.[55] Macaulay's views echoed those of Sir John Fortescue, whose 1476 book *Governance of England* traced the development of a limited monarchy under law in Britain, in contrast to the absolute monarchy in France, to the fact that the British peasants were armed, and that Britain therefore did not have to rely on mercenaries for defense.[56] Sir John Dalrymple, the seventeenth-century statesman, held the same view.[57] Later histories agreed. *Cato's Letters,* written by John Trenchard and Thomas Gordon in the 1720s and reprinted many times in the following decades, vigorously condemned the idea of a standing army, and of the participation of army officers in Parliament.[58]

Britain's great expositor of the common law, Sir William Blackstone, called the right to bear arms the "fifth auxiliary right of the subject," which would allow Britons to vindicate all the other rights.[59] He explained that "in cases of national oppression, the nation has very justifiably risen as one man, to vindicate the original contract subsisting between the king and his people."[60]

Twentieth-century historian Edmund Morgan argues that the traditional historical understanding of the militia as a popular guarantor of liberty is a mistake.[61] In *Inventing the People: The Rise of Popular Sovereignty in England and America,* Morgan traces the philosophical transition from the fiction of the "divine right of kings" to what Morgan terms the fiction of popular sovereignty. Morgan explains how rural aristocrats, through the mechanism of Parliament, challenged and defeated the principle that national sovereignty and power were embodied in a monarch who ruled by appointment from God. To undermine the intellectual foundation of monarchical supremacy, the landed aristocracy supported the fiction that the people, acting through the Parliament and the militia, were the true sovereign in Britain.

Morgan sets out to debunk the fiction of popular sovereignty. He points out that the apotheosis of the militia was a tactic by the rural aristocracy to delegitimize the standing army, which was loyal to the London monarchy. Morgan persuasively argues that the rural aristocracy claimed to be ruling in the name of the people; but in practice as the aristocracy gained more and more power, the people gained little real influence over the government.

Morgan's critique of the militia itself, the theoretical foundation of popular sovereignty, is less convincing. The American and British militias, he writes, were useless against professional armies. Hence, the idea that the militia was the foundation of a free state was, like the idea of popular sovereignty, only a fiction. Unfortunately, Morgan's survey of military history is incomplete. He notes the various times when militias failed in battle; the popular idea that a militia, being more virtuous than a professional army, was invincible was indeed a myth. But Morgan's conclusion that the popular militia was a nullity is equally mythical: he does not acknowledge the decisive role played by state militias in the American War for Independence.[62]

The British militia never defeated a professional army in formal combat. Nevertheless, Morgan's dismissal of the British militias as utterly impotent seems at odds with the experience of Britain in the seventeenth century. Defeating a standing army in head-on battle was not the only use for the militia. The very existence of the militia denied the monarchy a monopoly on force. Limited financial resources meant that the standing army rarely amounted to more than a few thousand troops. Without the militia's consent, control of the nation was impossible. If the militias were nothing but a mere wisp of military force, monarchs would not have made such a concerted effort to control and disarm them.

The Glorious Revolution settled the question over who would hold the ultimate power in Great Britain. When King William asked Parliament for a standing army in 1697, he was at first rebuffed, and then permitted a small army. The seventeenth century established the rule that Great Britain would follow, with some exceptions, for the next two centuries: Britain would adhere to Harrington's precepts, and defend itself with a powerful navy, rather than a large standing army.[63] At home, the British people would be armed, and the government would not be. When professional police forces were established a century and a half later, they conformed to the verdict of the Glorious Revolution, and were unarmed. As the twentieth century opened, the British people were free to keep and bear any firearms they chose.

American scholars, aware that the American Bill of Rights derives in part from the English Bill of Rights, sometimes argue that the English right to bear arms was only a "collective" right, and not an individual one. Hence, the American right to bear arms is not an individual right.

The theory is that the British right was applied only to a single group (Protestants) and only for collective purposes such as national defense.

In fact, the Parliament that ratified the English Bill of Rights rejected drafts that would have limited the right to situations "necessary for the publick Safety" or "for their common defense."[64] (Likewise, the U.S. Senate in ratifying the Second Amendment rejected a change that would have narrowed it to bearing arms "for the common defense."[65]) The exclusion of Catholics (thought to be subversive) from the British Bill of Rights carried little practical significance. They amounted to less than 2 percent of the population; and even a Catholic was allowed by a separate statute to keep firearms "for the Defence of his House or Person."[66]

The Americans who drafted the Second Amendment to the United States Constitution were keenly aware of the history of Britain in the previous century.[67] They had their own experiences of being oppressed by standing armies of Redcoats and Hessians. Accordingly, the Second Amendment, as well as other sections of the Constitution, were drafted with the aim of preventing oppression by a standing army.[68]

The amendment dealing with the "well-regulated militia" was deliberately placed next to the amendment that forbade the quartering of soldiers in civilian homes.[69] Other provisions of the Constitution looked to keep a standing army under firm popular control.[70]

Gun-control advocates, citing the clear hostility of the framers to standing armies, argue that the Second Amendment guarantees no individual right; the Second Amendment embodies only the "collective right" to belong to the militia, or the "states right" to have a militia. The capstone to such an argument is often the quote from Elbridge Gerry (Massachusetts Congressman, and member of the Constitutional Convention) that the purpose of the Second Amendment was "to prevent the establishment of a standing army, the bane of liberty."[71]

The proponents of the "collective rights" interpretation of the Second Amendment (meaning no right can be asserted by any person) often stop at this point, without considering the implication of what Elbridge Gerry, Thomas Jefferson, James Madison, and the rest intended by their hostility to standing armies. The central concern of the Second Amendment was the central concern of Great Britain in the seventeenth century. Who would hold the ultimate power of the sword in "a free State"? The historical experience of Britain, as Americans saw it, showed that a people could best maintain their freedom if they depended for security on all ordinary citizens having their own weapons and being trained in their use. Hence the first part of the Second Amendment: "A well-regulated Militia, being necessary to the security of a free State." A free state was to be secured—as it had been in Great Britain—by individual citizens with their own firearms who, as the militia, could resist a tyranny imposed by a standing army.[72]

To suggest that Elbridge Gerry, or any other framer, would have acceded to Congressional disarmament of ordinary American citizens is to turn English and American history upside down. Congressional disarmament of American citizens would have destroyed the militia, since the militia was composed of ordinary citizens with their own arms. As the United States Supreme Court explained, "The Militia comprised all males physically capable of acting in concert for the common defense. . . . Ordinarily when called for service these men were expected to appear bearing arms supplied by themselves and of the kind in common use at the time."[73]

The Glorious Revolution had secured an Englishman's right to bear arms as a legal matter. Nevertheless, as a practical matter the right to bear arms in Britain began to suffer. The rural aristocracy accepted the right of the people to bear arms to overthrow a monarch, but had little use for peasants hunting game on aristocrats' property. The Black Act of 1722 created fifty new capital offenses, mostly dealing with poaching and related trespass, and with the unauthorized carrying of arms.[74] And nonlegal factors were contributing to a long-term decline in gun possession. By the eighteenth century, wild deer had been pushed out of most of the country, finding refuge only in the deserted moors in Devon and Scotland. With reduced large-game hunting, rifle use dwindled. Indeed, starting with the French and Indian War in 1754, England found itself in three decades of conflict in North America; but the Board of Ordnance had trouble finding craftsmen to turn out large quantities of rifle barrels.[75] Moreover, once the Glorious Revolution settled the issue of who would run the country, most of England's fighting was done overseas. There was little threat of invasion, and rarely a perceived need for revolution. The militia fell into disuse and decay.[76]

During the one period when revolution seemed possible, the government acted swiftly to impose arms control. After the French Revolution and the more than two decades of disorder that followed, the British aristocracy worried that it, too, might be vulnerable.[77] In Yorkshire in the early nineteenth century, the Luddites rampaged and smashed the machines of the Industrial Revolution; the government mobilized more troops than are currently deployed in Northern Ireland.[78] During the years after Wellington's 1815 victory over Napoleon at Waterloo, real income for urban workers sank lower and lower. Historian S. G. Checkland notes that some agitators urged overthrow of the government. "But the mass of workers, though prepared to protest, could not be persuaded from their almost pathetic legality." At St. Peter's Fields in Manchester, a crowd of sixty thousand assembled peaceably on August 16, 1819. They demonstrated for abolition of the corn laws (which barred grain imports) and reform of Parliament. When the crowd refused an order to disperse, the Fifteenth Hussars cavalry charged. As the regular army and the militia pressed forward, the crowd stampeded away in panic. Eleven people were killed and over six hundred injured. The massacre at St. Peter's Square was dubbed Peterloo, a local version of the Battle of Waterloo.[79]

Parliament responded with the Six Acts, which banned seditious libel and seditious meetings, and outlawed drilling and training in the use of arms. The Seizure of Arms Act of 1820 authorized magistrates to confiscate arms that might be used by revolutionaries, and to conduct searches in private houses.[80] The Duke of Wellington hoped the measures would prevent, "the universal revolution which seems to menace us all."[81] The Seizure of Arms Act expired by its own terms in two years, and for all practical purposes gun control disappeared from Britain for over half a century. But Peterloo would not be the last time that an English-speaking government would kill peaceful demonstrators and then drastically restrict the right of the people to bear arms.

MODERN GUN CONTROL

The modern push for gun control began in 1883 when Parliament considered and rejected a bill to ban the unreasonable carrying of a concealed firearm. Both political and nonpolitical crime were minor problems; the national crime rate was stable, near its all-time nadir.[82] Burglary, though, remained high in London, because of the proximity of desperately poor people to the wealthy. In the late 1860s, the London *Lloyd's Newspaper* had blamed a crime wave on "foreign refuse" with their guns and knives. "The revolver's appearance . . . we owe to the importation of reckless characters from America. . . . The Fenian [Irish-American] desperadoes have sown weapons of violence in our poorer districts."[83] After a pair of armed burglaries in the London suburbs in 1883, press hysteria about armed criminals ensued, and the police were authorized to carry revolvers. The authorities were concerned about the availability to criminals of cheap German revolvers.[84] Possibly another factor causing concern about guns was the development of mass-circulation newspapers and their reporting of crime. Advancing firearms technology also increased fears; the recently invented repeating breechloaders seemed a dangerous new type of high-firepower weapon, unlike the seemingly more benign firearms of the past.[85]

At the turn of the century, the only significant firearms law was the 1870 Gun License Act, which required a prospective buyer to purchase a ten-shilling gun license at the local post office. The bill was strictly a revenue measure. There was no background check, and as criminologist Colin Greenwood writes, "[a]nyone, be he convicted criminal, lunatic, drunkard or child, could legally acquire any type of firearm. . . ."[86]

In 1900, the British prime minister (Robert Arthur Talbot Gascoyne-Cecil, the Marquess of Salisbury) said he would "laud the day when there is a rifle in every cottage in England." Led by the Duke of Norfolk and the mayors of London and Liverpool, a number of gentlemen formed a cooperative association that year to promote the creation of rifle clubs for working men.[87] But within a century, the right to bear arms in Britain would be well on the road to extinction, for reasons that would have little to do with gun ownership itself.

During the reign of King Edward VII (1901-1910), hunting reached an apex of national popularity, as historian David Cannadine details.[88] Obese and flaccid, the king still wished to be a sportsman, and he took up hunting as his favorite hobby. Oftentimes the victims were semi-tame birds, released from captivity just in time to be shot; little skill was needed to slaughter them.

The "shooting party" became a favorite recreation of the early twentieth-century aristocracy. The invention of smokeless gunpowder and breechloading firearms had made shooting easier; railways and automobiles made it convenient for weekend guests to assemble at an estate.

Edward's successor, King George V (1910-1936), also was an obsessive hunter. One day, he personally killed over a thousand birds. Like Edward VII, King George led big-game-hunting expeditions around the globe.

Cannadine speculates that the aristocracy and the monarchy celebrated conspicuous and grotesque consumption through hunting as a way of affirming the virility of flabby males.[89] The hunting sprees turned out to be the last fling of opulence and carefree celebration before World War I shattered the smug confidence of the early twentieth century. Concludes Cannadine, "it was an ominous foretaste of the even greater slaughter which was soon to come, not on the grouse moors of Scotland, but on the battle fields of Flanders."[90]

But as the century dawned, the concept that guns were evil, or that severe gun controls were desirable, had little support. Strong pistol controls were rejected by a two-to-one margin in the House of Commons in 1895. Parliament did enact the Pistols Act of 1903, which forbade pistol sales to minors and felons and ordered that sales be made only to buyers with a gun license (obtainable at the post office, the only requirement being payment of a fee) or to those who intended to keep the pistol solely in their house.[91] The bill attracted only slight opposition, and it had no discernible statistical effect on crime or accidents. Firearms suicides did fall, but the decline was more than matched by an increase in suicide by poisons and knives.[92] The bill defined pistols as guns having a barrel of nine inches or less, and thus pistols with nine-and-a-half inch barrels were soon popular. The importance of the act itself was much less in substantive effect than in setting the precedent for control of weapons by a democratic British government.[93]

Observers in other Commonwealth nations thought the Pistols act ineffective. New Zealand, worried about labor insurrection, watched how poorly the act was working, and enacted much stricter controls.

In Britain the rising militance of the working class was beginning to make the aristocracy doubt whether the people could be trusted with arms. The next set of British gun-control initiatives reflected fears of anarchists and other subversives. When American journalist Lincoln Steffens visited London in 1910, he met leaders of Parliament who interpreted the current bitter labor strikes as a harbinger of impending revolution.[94]

As the coronation of George V approached that year, one American newspaper, the *Boston Advertiser,* warned about the difficulty of protecting the coronation march (the Royal Progress) "so long as there is a generous scattering of automatic pistols among the 70,000 aliens in the Whitechapel district." The paper warned about aliens in the United States and Britain with their "automatic pistols." Explained the *Boston Advertiser,* "the automatic pistol is a far more dangerous thing than the bomb." An "automatic pistol" was defined as "a quick-firing revolver." The paper wanted a ban on carrying any concealed gun, plus gun registration and restrictions on ammunition sales, all to the goal of "disarming alien criminals."[95]

What was the "automatic pistol"/"quick-firing revolver" that so concerned the newspaper? Around 1900, the British company of Webley-Fosberry introduced an "automatic revolver." It fired with the same principle as a semi-automatic pistol, but held the ammunition in a cylinder, like a revolver. It was an inferior gun. If not gripped tightly, it would misfire, and dirt and dust made the gun fail. Although the gun's most deadly feature was, supposedly, its rapid-fire capability, rapid firing also made it malfunction.[96] The automatic revolver more dangerous than the bomb, was, like the "undetectable" plastic gun and the teflon "cop-killer" bullet, simply one more weapon that existed nowhere on earth except in the imaginations of the press and gun prohibitionists.[97]

Whatever the actual dangers of the automatic revolver, immigrants scared authorities on both sides of the Atlantic. Crime by Jewish and Italian immigrants spurred New York State to enact the Sullivan Law in 1911 to license handgun purchases. Yet Britain resisted stricter laws.

In December 1910, three London policemen investigating a burglary at a Houndsditch jewelry shop were murdered by rifle fire. A furious search began for the Russian anarchist believed responsible: "Peter the Painter," otherwise known as Peter Straume from Riga. The police uncovered one cache of arms in London: a pistol, 150 bullets, and some dangerous chemicals. The discovery led to front-page newspaper stories about (nonexistent) anarchist arsenals all over the East End of London.

The police caught up with London's anarchist network on January 3, 1911, at 100 Sidney Street. The police threw stones through the windows, and the anarchists inside responded with rifle fire. Seven hundred and fifty policemen, supplemented by a Scots Guardsman unit, besieged Sidney Street. Winston Churchill, the home secretary, arrived on the scene as the police were firing artillery and preparing to deploy mines. Banner headlines throughout the British Empire were already detailing the dramatic police confrontation with the anarchist nest. Churchill, accompanied by a police inspector and a Scots Guardsman with a hunting gun, strode up to the door of 100 Sidney Street; the inspector kicked the door down. Inside were the dead bodies of two anarchists. "Peter the Painter" was nowhere in sight.[98] London's three-man anarchist network was destroyed. The "Siege of Sidney Street" turned out to have been vastly overplayed by both the police and the press.

While the Siege of Sidney Street convinced New Zealand to tighten its own gun laws, the British Parliament rejected new controls. Parliament turned down the Aliens (Prevention of Crime) Bill, that would have barred aliens from possessing firearms without permission of the local chief officer of police.[99]

In Great Britain, as in the rest of the English-speaking world, the "Great War" of 1914–1918 led to great increases in national government powers. The Great War also bred the Bolshevik Revolution in Russia. Armies of the new Soviet state swept into Poland, and more and more workers of the world joined strikes called by radical labor leaders who predicted the overthrow of capitalism. Many communists and other radicals thought the revolution was at hand; all over the English-speaking world governments feared the end.

The reaction was fierce. In America, Attorney General A. Mitchell Palmer launched the "Palmer raids." Aliens were deported without hearings, and American citizens were searched and arrested without warrants and held without bail. While America was torn by strikes and race riots, Canada witnessed the government assault on peaceful demonstrators at the Winnipeg General Strike of 1919.

In Britain, Defense of the Realm Regulations during the war had required a license to buy pistols, rifles, or ammunition at retail. There was concern about what would happen when the war ended and the controls expired. A secret government committee on arms traffic warned of danger from two sources: the "[s]avage or semi-civilized tribesmen in outlying parts of the British Empire" who might obtain surplus war arms, and "the anarchist or 'intellectual' malcontent of the great cities, whose weapon is the bomb and the automatic pistol."[100] At a January 17, 1919, cabinet meeting, the chief of the imperial general staff raised the threat of "Red Revolution and blood and war at home and abroad." He suggested that the government make sure of its arms. The next month, the prime minister was asking which parts of the army would remain loyal. The cabinet discussed arming university men, stockbrokers, and clerks to fight any revolution. Walter Long urged the government to license the bearing of arms.[101]

Sir Eric Geddes, minister of transport, predicted "a revolutionary outbreak in Glasgow, Liverpool, or London in the early spring, when a definite attempt may be made to seize the reins of government." "It is not inconceivable," Geddes warned, "that a dramatic and successful coup d'etat in some large center of population might win the support of the unthinking mass of labor. . . ." The home secretary noted the "Bolshevik" uprising in Winnipeg, Canada. Using the Irish gun licensing system as a model, the cabinet made plans to disarm enemies of the state, and prepare arms for distribution if necessary "to friends of the Government."[102]

Although popular revolution was the motive, the home secretary presented the government's 1920 gun bill to Parliament as strictly a measure "to prevent criminals and persons of that description from being able to have revolvers and to use them." In fact, the problem of criminal, nonpolitical misuse of firearms remained minuscule.[103]

Nevertheless, the public was ready for new gun controls. The Great War that had opened with imperial élan had degenerated into carnage and produced a general revulsion against firearms.

British gun control entered the modern era with the Firearms Act of 1920, which allowed sale of pistols and rifles only to those who showed "good reason" for receiving a police permit.[104] Shotguns and airguns remained exempt from control. Additional regulations restricted firearms sales, and prohibited carrying in certain areas.[105]

In Great Britain, the Bolshevik and anarchist threat of 1919 faded quickly, but it was soon replaced by another perceived danger: gangsterism. Sawed-off shotguns and automatic weapons were the favorite firearms of American gangsters in the 1930s; 1936 legislation—similar to the National Firearms Act recently enacted in the United States—limited their sale. The government's rationale for the ban was that the guns were crime-related guns in the United States, and that there was no legitimate reason for civilians to own such guns.[106] Starting in 1936, the police began adding to firearms (rifle and handgun) licenses the requirement that the guns be stored securely.[107] Shotguns not being licensed, there was no such requirement for them.

After the fall of Dunkirk, Britain found itself short of arms for island defense. The Home Guard had to drill with canes, umbrellas, spears, pikes, and clubs. When citizens could find a gun, it was generally a sporting shotgun—ill-suited for military use because of its short range and bulky ammunition. British government advertisements in U.S. newspapers and magazines asked Americans to "Send a Gun to Defend a British Home— British civilians, faced with threat of invasion, desperately need arms for the defense of their homes." The ads pleaded for "Pistols, Rifles, Revolvers, Shotguns, and Binoculars from American civilians who wish to answer the call and aid in defense of British homes."[108] Pro-Allied organizations in the United States collected weapons; the National Rifle Association shipped seven thousand guns to Britain, which also purchased surplus World War I Enfield rifles from America's Department of War.[109] Prime Minister Winston Churchill's book *Their Finest Hour* recalls the arrival of the loads of guns. Churchill personally supervised the deliveries to ensure that they were sent on fast ships and distributed first to Home Guard members in coastal zones. Churchill thought that the American donations were "entirely on a different level from anything we have transported across the Atlantic except for the Canadian division itself." Churchill warned his First Lord that "the loss of these rifles and field-guns would be a disaster of the first order." *Their Finest Hour* recalled: "When the ships from America approached our shores with their priceless arms special trains were waiting in all the ports to receive their cargoes. The Home Guard in every county, in every town, in every village, sat up all through the night to receive them. . . . By the end of July we were an armed nation . . . a lot of our men and some women had weapons in their hands."[110] America's role as the "arsenal of democracy" during World War II was not confined to government contractors; individual Americans donating their private arms had helped secure Britain against Nazi invasion.

Before the war, the British government had refused to allow domestic manufacture of the Thompson submachine gun because it was "a gangster gun."[111] When the war broke out, large numbers of American-made Thompsons were shipped to Britain, where they were dubbed "tommie guns."[112]

After WW II, Britain, like other European countries, was inundated with surplus military weapons. Many private citizens seem to have held on to them, not for day-to-day use, but for an "emergency." Guns that had been donated by American civilians were collected from the Home Guard and destroyed by the British government.[113]

As in most of the Western world, the late 1960s was a time of rising crime and civil disorder. In 1965, capital punishment was abolished.[114] Gun crime did not seem to be a problem. Scotland Yard stated "with some confidence" that the objectives of eliminating "the improper and careless custody and use of firearms . . . and making it difficult for criminals to obtain them . . . are effectively achieved."[115] In June 1966, Home Secretary Roy Jenkins told Parliament that after consulting with the chief constables and the Home Office, he had concluded that shotgun controls were not worth the trouble. Yet six weeks later, Jenkins announced that new shotgun controls were necessary, because shotguns were too easily available to criminals.[116]

In the meantime, three policemen at Shephard's Bush had been murdered with illegal revolvers. Popular outcry for capital punishment was fervent, and Jenkins, an abolitionist, responded by announcing new shotgun controls, in an attempt to divert attention from the noose.[117] The practical utility of shotgun controls as a response to crimes with revolvers was not clear.

The government began drafting the legislation that became the Criminal Justice Act of 1967. The new act required a license for the purchase of shotguns and further regulated short shotguns.[118] Like the Gun Control Act of 1968 in the United States, Britain's 1967 Act was part of a comprehensive crime package that included elements disapproved by civil libertarians.[119] The British act abolished the necessity for unanimous jury verdicts in criminal trials, eliminated the requirement for a full hearing of evidence at committal hearings, and restricted press coverage of those hearings.[120]

Under the 1967 system, which is for the most part still in force, a person wishing to obtain his first shotgun would obtain a "shotgun certificate." The local police could reject an applicant if they believed that his "possession of a shotgun would endanger public safety." The police were required to grant the certificate unless the applicant had a particular defect in his background, such as a criminal record or history of mental illness.[121] An applicant was required to supply a countersignatory, a person who would attest to the accuracy of the information in the application. During an investigation period that could last several weeks, the police might visit the applicant's home.[122] About 98 percent of all applications are granted.[123]

Once the £12 shotgun certificate was granted, the law allowed a citizen to purchase as many shotguns as he wished.[124] Private transfers among certificate holders were legal and uncontrolled.[125]

As will be detailed below, the regulation of shotgun certificates has been made stricter. The rules for most other guns, on the other hand, remain as they were codified in the 1967 Act, which essentially restated the 1920 law for rifles and handguns. [In Britain, a "firearm" is a rifle or a handgun. A shotgun is not a firearm. The usage in this chapter only conforms to the British usage. In other nations (and all other chapters), a "firearm" means a rifle, handgun, or shotgun.]

Obtaining a "firearms certificate," for possession of a rifle or handgun, requires the applicant to demonstrate he has "a good reason" for owning the gun.[126] Self-defense is not considered a good reason, although it had been in the earlier decades of gun control.[127] Because self-defense is not a justification for owning any weapon, even nonlethal chemical defenses, such as Mace, are illegal.[128]

In practice, being a certified member of an approved target-shooting club is the only way one can now legally obtain a pistol.[129] Unlike the shotgun certificate under the 1967 system, the firearms certificate specifies the exact type and number of rifles or pistols the holder may possess.[130] If the holder wishes to buy another rifle or handgun, he must receive approval for a variation to the certificate.

Private transfers of firearms must be noted on the certificate and recorded by the police. For both firearms and shotguns, private transfers are legal only between people who possess the appropriate certificate.[131] The firearms certificate may also specify how much and what calibre ammunition the licensee may own.[132]

Rifles and pistols stored in the home must be locked in "a secure place."[133] The storage rule for rifles and pistols is enforced stringently. Although the law, even today, does not require guns to be locked in a safe, the police have compelled gun owners to purchase safes—or even two, the second one for separate storage of ammunition. A man buying a low-powered, £5 rimfire rifle may have to spend £100 on a safe. A person with five handguns may be ordered to add a £1,000 electronic security system. The net effect of the heavy security costs is to reduce legal gun ownership by the less wealthy classes, as in the days of Charles I.[134]

Nevertheless, a pistol is eight times more likely to be stolen than a shotgun, even though a pistol must be locked in a case, and a shotgun could be hung on a mantelpiece (until 1989).[135] Although the number of burglaries and thefts had more than doubled since 1970, the number of stolen rifles and pistols has stayed constant.[136] This might seem a vindication of the safe-storage rule, except that there was no safe-storage rule for shotguns until 1989, and shotgun thefts also did not increase.

A certificate for rifle purchase often includes territorial conditions specifying exactly where the person may hunt.[137] Recently, police guidelines have revised the suggested intensity of enforcement of territorial conditions, because enforcing them took so much time.[138]

Violation of the gun laws is often based on the principle of strict liability. Even if a person had a reasonable, good-faith reason to believe he was in compliance with the law, any violation is grounds for criminal conviction, regardless of intent.[139]

While applicants for firearms certificates may appeal police denials, the courts are generally deferential to police decisions. Hearsay evidence is admissible against the applicant.[140] An appellant does not have a right to present evidence in his own behalf.[141]

The laws on unlicensed guns are enforced strictly. Sentences of one to two years in prison for possession of an unlicensed sawed-off shotgun are not uncommon, even in cases where the prosecution agrees that the defendant had no criminal purpose, and the defendant had previously been an exemplary citizen.[142]

A TOY OF THE LANDED GENTRY

In the last two centuries shotguns have been and continue to be subject to less regulation than rifles and handguns.[143] Not only is the licensing system less stringent,[144] the rules about carrying are more relaxed. A person who carries a rifle or handgun in a public place without lawful authority is guilty of illegal carrying of a firearm, regardless of whether the gun is loaded. Yet carrying a shotgun in a public place is unlawful only if the gun is loaded.[145] In contrast, Americans, Canadians, Australians, New Zealanders, Jamaicans, and Swiss make almost no legal distinction between a long gun that is a rifle and a long gun that is a shotgun.

Britain's relatively lenient treatment of shotguns seems all the stranger given the greater potential lethality of shotguns. Small caliber rifles are among the least deadly firearms in existence. In contrast, shotgun blasts at close range are usually fatal; the shotgun fires a large slug, or from six to more than sixty pellets, with one trigger squeeze. A single shotgun pellet, because it may be of a diameter equal to a small handgun bullet, can inflict nearly as much damage as a small handgun bullet and a shotgun can fire many such pellets at once.[146] Wound ballistics experts concur that at short range, a shotgun is by far the deadliest weapon.[147]

A Scotland Yard official explains that the British "think the shotgun is a toy of the landed gentry."[148] Because the shotgun is closely associated with bird shooting, there is, according to one British gun author, "a curious mental reluctance to appreciate that it can be used to kill a human."[149] The author points out that the rifle has "a close association with warfare in the public eye," and is considered "a totally lethal property, irrespective of its calibre or its ammunition."[150]

The British treat all rifles by their looks (military) rather than by their characteristics (less dangerous than the more leniently regulated shotgun). While Canada, Australia, and the United States do not stigmatize all rifles as military killing machines, rifles that look like military models have come under strong attack. As in Britain, the assumption seems to be that something associated with military use (even if just by appearance) must be more dangerous than something associated with hunting. That assumption is wrong. Many hunting weapons are designed to kill 600-pound animals with a single shot from a third of a mile away, while military rifles are deliberately designed to wound humans (not to kill them) at shorter range. (The reason is that a wounded soldier consumes his side's resources in medical care.)[151] While the AR-15 Sporter and the semi-automatic Kalashnikov rifle may look horrible, they are far less lethal than a standard hunting rifle such as Springfield bolt action .30-'06.* At one hundred yards, a bullet from the .30-'06 "sporting" rifle carries 2,347 foot-pounds of energy. The energy from the "deadly" Kalashnikov is only half that—1,162 foot-pounds. Additionally, military-type bullets (with a full metal jacket) are more likely to pass through the body, whereas hunting bullets are designed to deform within the body, to not exit, and to transfer all their kinetic energy to the target. As a result, wounds from hunting bullets are more severe than wounds from military-type bullets.[152]

The unique British attitude toward rifles is rooted in Britain's history. The sporting rifle has been ignored since the sixteenth century, partly because of the relative paucity of big game.[153] Until the 1940s, the British regarded roe deer as pests, rather than as interesting game.[154]

The British who do their sport hunting with shotguns are a relatively elite group compared to their American counterparts. British shooters boast of having the world's highest standards as sportsmen and as safe shooters, a virtue they attribute to their "calm and phlegmatic" nature.[155] They criticize the "ignorance and lack of self-control" of American hunters.[156]

In truth, gun ownership and hunting in Britain are not the exclusive preserve of the aristocracy. Skilled and semi-skilled workers own more guns than do the upper classes, although the upper classes have a higher per capita rate of ownership. Statistics aside, the popular perception remains, however, that the kind of people who own guns are the kind of people who do not have to work for a living.[157] The perception is understandable since for much of Britain's history, the upper classes tried to keep gun ownership to themselves. They especially tried to maintain hunting as their exclusive privilege.

As in Continental Europe, but quite unlike in the United States, the history of legal hunting in Britain is a tale of aristocratic amusement. In 1610, King James I called for laws to require that hunting arms "be used by none but gentlemen, and that in a gentlemen-like fashion. For it is not fit that clowns should have these sports."[158] The red-legged partridge, a common game animal in Britain today, was introduced from the Continent to game farms by the Marquis of Hertford and the Earl of Rochdale in the late eighteenth century.[159]

Elements of the aristocratic heritage remain. A London gentleman may

---

*.30-'06 is a caliber common for big-game hunting.

be measured and fitted for a shotgun, just as with a suit. But the richest and the poorest Americans buy the same mass-produced guns at the same hardware and sporting goods stores.[160] The large majority of American hunting takes place on public lands. In Britain, most land suitable for fishing or hunting is privately owned, and rented on a per day basis (if the hunter does not have a friend who owns land). A British gun book explains that "[n]ot every sportsman has his own shoot or ground and many rely on invitations or prefer to buy days on game shoots." Ducks and geese are the only animals huntable on public land. Grouse, pheasant, and partridge shooting is entirely private.[161]

Because the aristocracy has always owned most of the nation's open land, the association of the aristocracy with "shooting" was natural.[162] In earlier days, the unequal distribution of land motivated the aristocracy to disarm the lower classes to prevent poaching. The effort at disarmament was never entirely successful; national security needs and the lower classes' own political clout made sure of that. Still, the aristocratic hold on the land did prevent the growth of a strong tradition of recreational hunting among the middle and lower classes. The last century, however, has seen a democratization of hunting. Lord Swansea, chairman of the British Shooting Sports Council, explains:

> Game shooting nowadays is by no means the preserve of the aristocracy. The social revolution which we have undergone in the last forty years has led to the break-up of many large estates; while galloping inflation has forced many landowners to abandon rearing game at their own expense to entertain their friends, and instead to cover their expenses by forming syndicates from those who are prepared to contribute, often from wealthy business-men of a class which our grandfathers would never have had in their houses.[163]

Because the popular perception is that hunting is an aristocratic activity, as political power has slipped from the aristocracy, two tokens of aristocracy—hunting and gun ownership—have come under increasingly fierce attack from other classes. The Labour party believes that hunting is not a legitimate reason for gun ownership.[164] In August 1987, when a man named Michael Ryan went berserk in a small market town, Labour seized the opportunity to deal with "the toy of the landed gentry."

THE GUN LOBBY RESISTS

The 1967 British gun law had paved the way for more comprehensive controls a few years later, or so Edward Heath's Conservative government thought. In 1973, a British government Green Paper proposed a host of new controls.[165] The British shooting lobbies, however, mobilized and the Green Paper was withdrawn.[166] Law professor Richard Harding, Australia's leading academic advocate of gun control, later criticized the Green Paper as "statistically defective . . . scientifically quite useless."[167] Harding was looking at whether the proposed laws would reduce gun crime, gun suicide, or other gun misuse. The proponents of the Green Paper, on the other hand, did not care whether more gun control would reduce gun misuse. An earlier (and secret) draft of the Green Paper had stated that "a reduction in the number of firearms in private hands is a desirable end in itself."[168] As *Police Review* magazine noted: "There is an easily identifiable police attitude towards the possession of guns by members of the public. Every possible difficulty should be put in their way."[169]

Some parts of the Green Paper were enforced as law anyway, by police fiat. One Green Paper item would have required prospective rifle hunters to receive written invitation from the owner of the land where they would shoot, and then take the letter to the police; the police would investigate the safety of the hunt and other factors before granting permission. Several chief constables adopted this proposal and others from the Green Paper as "force policy" and enforced them as if they were law.[170] In the ensuing decades, the police used their discretionary powers to achieve, at least partially, the Green Paper goal of reducing the number of rifles and handguns in private hands. Although the shotgun ownership level, over which the police had little control, rose, the number of holders of firearms licenses (rifles and handguns) fell by over 20 percent from 1968 to 1980, remaining steady since then.[171]

Weapons-control advocates won some small legislative victories in the early 1980s. The Firearms Act of 1982 introduced restrictive licensing for imitation firearms that could be converted to fire live ammunition.[172] The original proposal had been to implement the 1973 Green Paper's outright ban on realistic imitation or toy firearms. The sponsor of the new law against imitation firearms promised that it would help stem "the rising tide of crime and terrorism"—although there had never been a crime or terrorist act committed with a converted imitation weapon.[173] A new Crossbows Act outlawed purchase by persons under seventeen. Some Britons favor putting bows under a licensing system identical to that for guns.[174]

But while the police used their discretion to reduce the possession of rifles and handguns, shotgun purchases continued in ever-greater numbers. The police had no discretion to refuse a shotgun certificate without demonstrating that the applicant was unqualified. Certificate in hand, a person could obtain an unlimited number of shotguns, without providing any reason to the government, receiving any further permission, or even telling the police. Complained a spokesman of the Police Federation (the police union), "The present legislation is farcical; it amounts to virtually no control at all. We have pressed the government three times to tighten the controls and to bring them into line with other firearms laws, but we have been turned down on each occasion."[175] Opposition politicians like John Cartwright, a Social Democrat M.P., also found that "[s]hotguns are too easily available. . . ."[176]

Although James Jardine, chairman of the Police Federation of England, told American audiences "the presumption is for people not to have guns," he was accurate only for rifles and handguns, over which the police had discretionary licensing control. Jardine complained about a "farmers' and sporting lobby," which impeded shotgun controls.[177] The Police Federation blamed "the powerful gun lobby" for blocking new legislation.[178] One member of Parliament was even said to have lost his seat because of his support for the 1973 Home Office Green Paper. Gun owners took credit for winning other close races as well.[179]

The largest component of the pro-gun forces is the British Association for Shooting and Conservation with a membership of approximately 100,000, and a full-time staff of fifty-five.[180] The BASC and a number of smaller firearms organizations are confederated in the British Shooting Sports Council, which acts as the formal voice of the what the press calls "the gun lobby."[181] The BSSC has one full-time staff person, and is chaired by Lord Swansea, a member of the House of Lords.[182] Relations between shooters' groups and the Home Office (equivalent to the United States Department of Justice) are polite, but wary.[183]

After two decades of success in blocking new gun controls, the British gun lobby was confronted in 1987 by the strongest, most broadly supported push for more gun control that Britain had ever seen. The result of that push and the gun lobby's reaction illustrate important elements of what makes Britain's gun culture special.

THE HUNGERFORD MASSACRE

On the morning of August 19, 1987, a licensed gun owner named Michael Ryan dressed up like "Rambo." At the Savernake Forest he shot a woman thirteen times with a handgun. After killing a filling station attendant, he drove to his home in the small market town of Hungerford, where he killed his mother and his dog. In the next hour, he went into town and slaughtered fifteen people, seven with his handgun, and eight with his Chinese-made semi-automatic Kalashnikov rifle. Ryan disappeared for a few hours, reappeared at 4:00 P.M. in a school, and killed himself three hours later.[184]

A few days later, another mass murder took place at Bristol, this one with a shotgun.[185]

The media's reaction, especially the print media's, was intense. The tabloid press ran editorials instructing the public how to spot potential mass murderers—advising suspicion of anyone who is a loner, who lives alone, who lives with his mother, or who is a bit quiet.[186] The tabloid press and the respectable press both pushed heavily for stringent gun laws.[187] Pressure also mounted for tighter censorship of violent television.

The Thatcher government's Home Office began work on a new set of gun-control proposals. Ann Taylor, spokesperson for Home Affairs for the opposition Labour party, worried, "I think the Home Secretary is under a lot of pressure from the gun lobby and what I'm afraid of is that the gun lobby may start to gather force and gain strength just as it has done in the United States."[188]

Initially, the Conservative (Tory) government focused its proposals mainly on semi-automatic guns. The Home Office suggested banning all semi-automatic rifles, banning shotguns with barrels less than twenty-four inches (which were already strictly regulated), placing pump-action and semi-automatic shotguns under the same controls as rifles and handguns, and imposing safe-storage requirements on shotgun owners.[189] The London police, meanwhile, unilaterally limited applications and renewals for certificates for rifles to bolt-action only, thereby banning new semi-automatic and pump-action rifles.[190]

For the Police Federation, the time had come to reintroduce the Green Paper proposals that had been rejected in 1973.[191] At that time it had urged that all shotguns be brought under the same strict controls as rifles and pistols.[192] The Labour party took a similar line, suggesting that shotguns be available only to people who demonstrated a particular need, such as farmers or target shooters, and that shotgun certificates allow the possession of only one shotgun.[193]

The Thatcher government had not previously been hospitable to broad new controls. In 1980, Home Minister Leon Brittan had stated that the new restrictions on shotguns would be useless, since even more severe restrictions had failed to stop the use of pistols in robberies.[194] At the start of the Hungerford debate, Home Office Minister Douglas Hogg rejected the police and Labour proposals. He told Parliament that if a "good reason" requirement were imposed for shotguns, Britain would "face massive non-compliance . . . very large numbers of guns will simply disappear. The effect would be to make gun control less effective."[195]

Rebuffed by the Tory government, the Police Federation began working with the Labour opposition. Labour Deputy Leader Roy Hattersley then struck an agreement with Tory Home Secretary Douglas Hurd: if the new gun law included more restrictions on the shotgun (the "toy of the landed gentry"), Labour would not oppose the government bill. The government accepted.[196]

Two days after the Hungerford massacre, Lord Swansea, of the British Shooting Sports Council, wrote to the Home Office, offering to assist the government. The Home Office declined the offer of dialogue, and went on to write its own bill.

Once the government proposal was publicly announced, the Home Office showed little interest in technical or other suggestions offered by the BSSC. Hoping to gain some concessions by acceding to much of the government plan, the British Shooting Sports Council offered its response. The BSSC reluctantly agreed that Kalashnikovs and all other semi-automatic rifles deemed not appropriate for target shooting could be banned. It asked the government (in vain) not to ban semi-automatics that were recognized as high-quality target guns, such as the M1A. The council also endorsed the safe-storage requirement, the ban on "short" shotguns, and a ban on electric stun guns.[197]

Incredibly (by American standards), the BSSC had this reaction to the concerns that people were buying shotguns for self-defense: "This, if it is a fact, is an alarming trend and reflects sadly on our society."[198] One hunting lobby official condemned "the growing number of weapons being held in urban areas" for reasons having nothing to do with sport.[199] The major hunting lobby, The British Association for Shooting and Conservation, defended not the right to bear arms, but only, in its words, "the freedom to possess and use sporting arms."[200] While offering major concessions on many issues, the gun lobby did squarely oppose any new restriction on the purchase of shotguns with small magazines (small ammunition capacity).

The contrast in approach of the British and American gun lobbies is instructive. After the January 1989 massacre in Stockton, California, the National Rifle Association, the Citizens Committee for the Right to Keep and Bear Arms, Gun Owners of America, and other groups blitzed their membership with urgent letters, imploring them to write to Congress and the president. The lobbies almost immediately adopted a "no compromise" position, insisting that further gun controls would have no effect except to infringe the rights of law-abiding citizens. Gun prohibitionists within the administration, such as drug "czar" William Bennett, were fiercely condemned. Unlike the British gun lobby, the American lobby mobilized a tremendous surge of grassroots activism, which gave it the political clout to influence the president before the administration introduced any legislation. As a result, the Bush administration gun bill, introduced in May 1989, was relatively weak; and as the grassroots clout of the gun lobby increased during the rest of the year, the administration lost interest even in its own relatively mild bill, and no gun-control legislation was enacted by Congress.

The British lobbies, moving into combat mode much later in the day, exercised less influence. Only when the British government gun bills began moving through Parliament were the British lobbies fully engaged. Originally the government had planned to confiscate banned weapons and pay nothing. A parliamentary committee, however, refused to schedule a meeting to consider the government bill until the government partly conceded on the compensation issue. As a result, the government has reimbursed gun owners 50 percent of the gun's purchase price or £150, whichever is less.

On most major issues besides compensation, the gun lobby lost. Semi-automatic centerfire rifles,* which had been legally owned for nearly a century, are now completely banned.[201] Pump-action rifles are banned as well, since it was argued that these guns could be substituted for semi-automatics. Practical rifle shooting, the fastest-growing sport in Britain, vanished.[202]

Shotguns that can hold more than two shells at once now require a "firearms license," the same as rifles and handguns.[203] All shotguns must now be registered. Shotgun sales between private parties must be reported to the police, and buyers of shot shells must produce a "shotgun certificate." Applicants for a shotgun certificate must obtain a "countersignature" by a person who has known the applicant for two years and is "a member of Parliament, justice of the peace, minister of religion, doctor, lawyer, established civil servant, bank officer or person of similar standing."[204] Most important, an applicant for a shotgun certificate must demonstrate to the police that he has a "good reason" for wanting a gun. Again, self-defense is not a good reason. (As a technical matter, the police have the burden of showing that the applicant does *not* have a good reason. In practice, the police have already been requiring that applicants prove they have a good reason, such as membership in a shooting organization.)[205]

One victory for gun owners was the establishment of a Firearms Consultative Committee to offer advice regarding gun laws. Gun owners see the committee as a partial shield against Home Office or police misapplication of the law.[206] In the United States and Australia, the gun-control movement complains about differing legal standards in different states. In Britain, it is the gun lobby that complains about the haphazard system imposed by the chief constables in the nation's mostly independent police districts. The gun lobby argues that although national laws are uniform, police interpretation varies widely.[207]

---

*Centerfire rifles fire ammunition whose primer is seated in the center of the cartridge. Most modern guns fire centerfire ammunition, except for some low-power .22 calibre rimfire guns.

While Great Britain suffered its version of the Stockton massacre, the nation also witnessed its own version of the Bernhard Goetz subway shooting. In March 1987, Eric Butler, a fifty-six-year-old executive with British Petroleum Chemicals, was attacked early one evening on the subway. Two men came after Butler, as one witness described: "strangling him and smashing his head against the door; his face was red and his eyes were popping out." No passenger on the subway did a thing to help him. "My air supply was being cut off," Mr. Butler later testified, "my eyes became blurred and I feared for my life." Concealed inside Mr. Butler's walking stick was a three-foot blade. Butler unsheathed the blade. "I lunged at the man wildly with my swordstick. I resorted to it as my last means of defense." He stabbed an attacker in the stomach.

The attackers were charged with unlawful wounding. Butler was tried and convicted of carrying an offensive weapon. The court gave Butler a suspended sentence, but denounced the "breach of the law which has become so prevalent in London in recent months that one has to look for a deterrent." A former Labour M.P. took up Butler's cause and raised funds to more than cover Butler's legal expenses.[208]

Apparently bladed weapons are supplanting guns as an urban self-defense weapon. Britain may be discovering that gun control is not much good without knife control. Scotland Yard recently carried out an amnesty program for illegal knives. The campaign was aimed not at criminals, but at people who carried knives for self-protection, or to appear "macho."[209] The Conservative government banned the sale of martial arts weapons, and the carrying of knives or sharp objects in public places.[210] After Eric Butler's defense of his life on the subway with a swordstick, these weapons were banned as well.[211]

THE MOMENTUM OF GUN CONTROL

Many Americans support handgun control because they hope it will end the demand for controls on long guns, particularly conventional hunting or target long guns.[212] Some U.S. politicians offer to broker a "reasonable" set of gun controls, such as a national waiting period, which will end the political battle over gun control. In light of the British experience, neither approach is realistic. While gun crime in Britain has increased markedly in the last three decades, it is still at a very low level. In a typical year, perhaps eight people may die of handgun wounds, and that figure includes suicides. In 1988, the number of homicides involving any type of firearm was only thirty-six, a number that New York City far exceeds in a typical month.[213] Yet as long as guns exist, there will always be at least occasional instances of gun misuse. The Hungerford Massacre was the first and only time a centerfire semi-automatic rifle was used in a homicide in Britain. It led to the confiscation of every centerfire semi-automatic.

Homicides with shotguns are rare in Great Britain, but when they occur, they are extensively publicized.[214] If a single well-publicized gun crime is enough to do away with centerfire rifles, a few more publicized shotgun homicides may have a similar effect. Already 76 percent of the population supports banning all guns.[215]

Firearms crime inevitably attracts media attention that becomes the basis for further tightening of controls. In the fall of 1989, a person who had been rejected for membership in a firearms club stole a handgun from the locked trunk of a club member and shot a Manchester policeman. A probationary member of a different firearms club, learning that he had a fatal disease, killed one club member, stole a gun from the club, and shot a personal enemy. The home secretary, at the urging of the Manchester Police Department, issued a new set of restrictions on firearms clubs, the most severe being that members would no longer be able to bring guests to the firing range to shoot a firearm.[216] The practical effect of the new restrictions may be to end the entry of new members into many firearms clubs.[217]

Some citizens who accept the proposition that there is no such thing as a legitimate self-defense weapon are turning to the guard dogs.[218] Unfortunately, dogs, unlike guns and knives, have a will of their own and sometimes attack on their own volition. The number of people injured by dogs has been rising, and the press is calling for bans on Rottweilers, Dobermans, and other "devil dogs."[219] Under 1991 legislation, all pit bulls must be neutered or euthanized. The British experience seems to indicate that a ban on one method of self-defense leads to the substitution of new methods, and to new prohibitions. (Interestingly, opponents of the government's dog registration proposals seem to have substantially more political clout than the opponents of gun control.[220])

The police leadership has made it clear that it views civilian gun ownership as something that should be abolished. One method of abolition is to prevent the entry of new generations into the world of shooting sports. Hence, it is illegal for a parent to give even an airgun (or other gun) as a gift to his thirteen-year-old child.[221] Now that shotgun purchasers, like rifle and handgun purchasers, must prove to the police a "good reason" for acquiring a gun, it may be that shotgun ownership will follow the same pattern of decline that rifle and handgun ownership have, as the police stringently enforce and invent gun regulations. Since 1989, the first year the new laws were in effect, the number of shotgun certificates has declined by 17 percent, reversing an annual 2 percent growth rate. Firearms (handgun and rifle) certificates also declined.[222]

If a future government presses for more gun restrictions, it will have the enthusiastic support of an increasingly powerful lobby—the animal rights movement. Britain's leading anti-hunting group, the League Against Cruel Sports, points to the "hundreds" of people killed by guns and "thousands" of guns used in robberies and demands a ban on all guns.[223]

If American gun controllers follow the lead of their British counterparts, they will not go out of business after the enactment of "moderate" compromise legislation. American anti-gun lobbyists who advocate "moderate" gun controls often propose those controls as a way-station to prohibition.[224]

Thus, the resistance of many American gun owners to even the mildest gun laws becomes more understandable. Great Britain began with a wide-open permit system for pistol purchases, and moved to a restrictive and pervasive regulation of all gun ownership in less than a century. Whether or not moderate gun controls in America would be a good idea, it may be difficult to enact them as long as American gun owners fear a British-style slide down the slippery slope.

EFFECTS OF BRITISH GUN CONTROLS AND SOCIAL CONTROLS

While it is too soon to evaluate the effects of the latest round of British gun controls, it is at this point possible to evaluate previous controls. Police time taken up by gun-law administration has ballooned. As of 1969, British officers spent about twenty man-years annually in administrative work relating to gun licenses and registration.[225] Today, police time spent on gun-law administration and enforcement takes up 250 man-years annually, and police time spent on enforcement takes a similar amount.[226] While the resources spent on firearms administration is not a large percentage of all police resources, the resource allocation issue is still significant; the question is whether the resources might have been better allocated to other anti-crime measures.

No one has produced any evidence that the many police hours spent implementing British gun-registration requirements have reduced crime. Interviews by Colin Greenwood with scores of police officers and his review of hundreds of firearms crime cases did not reveal a single instance in which registration aided the solution or prevention of a crime.[227]

Regarding the gun laws' overall impact on gun misuse, while the discussion that follows does offer some tentative conclusions about the efficacy of British gun control, the lack of criminological data makes it difficult to draw clear statistical conclusions. Only since the early 1970s have detailed gun-crime statistics been kept.[228] Moreover, there is almost no academic analysis of the British gun-crime situation. Roger Lorton, a police officer who wrote a 1991 LL.B. dissertation on British gun laws, began his research expecting to "be following a trail of authoritative works on the subject . . . [including] copious amounts of statistical analysis. What I actually found was an almost total lack of published writings on the subject other than articles in magazines aimed at those groups of people who actually use firearms."[229]

The academic gun debate in the United States is carried out in publications such as the *Yale Law Journal* and the *Journal of the American Medical Association*. The American government funds gun-control studies by top-ranking scholars such as law professor Franklin Zimring or sociology professor James Wright. In Canada, too, the important journals carry the pro and con of gun control, and the government sometimes hires professional criminologists to produce detailed firearms policy analysis.

But in Britain, there is essentially no research. The only British author of a serious book analyzing gun control is former police superintendent Colin Greenwood. Other than by compiling gun-crime statistics, the British government has never produced a useful contribution to the gun debate. The academic community in Britain has apparently decided that the gun-control issue does not deserve research effort.

The following analysis, while interesting to non-British readers, may be of little relevance to Britain itself, for the British government and British gun owners have both supported increasingly stringent gun controls without demanding any evidence that the existing controls have done any good. What evidence there is suggests that British controls may have reduced homicide, increased burglary, and had little influence on other crimes.

The number of illegally owned guns shows no signs of shrinking. Since 1948, the number of illegal, never-registered weapons voluntarily surrendered to London's Metropolitan Police has remained stable, fluctuating between 1,000 and 1,600 a year; the stability suggests that the supply of illegal weapons has not diminished.[230] While there are only 50,000 pistol licenses extant, over 300,000 illegal handguns have been surrendered nationwide since the end of World War II—another indication of a large reservoir of illegal guns.[231] Late 1970s estimates put the number of illegal guns at two million, compared with two and a half million that are legally owned.[232]

One attempt to estimate the number of illegal guns looks at the number of illegal guns voluntarily surrendered each year. The study (which notes that unless there is a special amnesty in effect, most illegal guns are surrendered by a relative upon the death of the owner) analyzes the number of annual surrenders rate in relation to the variations over time in the number of deaths. If one assumes that the current controls are highly effective (that there are no new guns being added to the illegal pool, and that all heirs always surrender all guns), then the approximate number of illegal handguns is 400,000 and the number of illegal long guns is 800,000. About 80,000 of the handguns are in the London Metropolitan area. If one assumes that only half of all heirs surrender the ancestor's gun, then the number of illegal guns approximate with other estimates of two million or more.[233]

"Fifty years of very strict controls on pistols have left a vast pool of illegal weapons," writes Greenwood.[234] He notes that domestic sales of handguns in the years before the 1920 Firearms Act imposed controls were about 30,000 per year and that most handgun owners did not register when the 1920 law went into effect. Greenwood speculates that most of the pre-1920 guns are still unregistered, still in private hands, and still operable.[235]

Now that shotguns have been brought under a registration system, illegal, unregistered ownership of these guns also appears to be on the rise. About 200,000 pump-action and semi-automatic shotguns were sold between 1978 and 1988, and at least 100,000 such guns were in private possession before then. But only 100,000 pump-action or semi-automatic shotguns have been registered, out of the total pool of 300,000. In other words, the disobedience rate to the new shotgun registration laws appears to be approximately 67 percent.[236] The English tradition of hiding guns from the government does, after all, date back at least to King Charles I in 1642.[237]

Whatever the exact numbers, an underground gun market remains intact and is more than sufficient for criminal demand. Besides the supply of illegal British guns, the black market relies on illegal imports from the United States and Belgium.[238] A handgun can be rented for use in a crime for about £100; if the gun is fired, the renter forfeits his £100 deposit and keeps the gun.[239] British criminals' demand for guns is small, and apparently can be satisfied by the existing black market.

For the last several decades, gun crime, and overall crime, in Britain has been growing worse.[240] The firearms crime rate rose dramatically in the 1960s, just as it did almost everywhere else in the Western world, with or without gun controls. In particular, the robbery and armed robbery rates soared, beginning in the late 1950s and accelerating in the 1960s.[241] Despite the 1967 extension of gun control, the criminal misuse of firearms skyrocketed over 450 percent in the 1970s.[242] Of course it is possible that firearms crime would have increased even more had there not been gun controls, and it should be remembered that the increases of the 1950s and after, while sharp, started from a very low base.

In general, the rise in firearms crime has paralleled an overall crime increase. Harding's study of British crime in the late 1970s found gun use in crime to be increasing at the same rate as crime in general.[243] Although handguns were subject to the most stringent controls, they remained the criminal's weapon of choice.[244]

Even if controls have not impacted the criminal weapons pool, it is possible that they have affected patterns of weapon use in crime. Shootings of police officers were the impetus for the 1967 controls. The number of police officers shot at every year has stayed about the same, even though overall crime has risen.[245] Perhaps the 1967 law can claim credit for preventing an increase in police murders.

Have gun controls protected ordinary citizens? From the 1950s to the 1970s, the British murder rate tripled, while the percentage of firearms or explosives used in murder stayed constant, at about 8 to 10 percent.[246] Indeed, the percentage is approximately the same as it was at the turn of the century, when there were no gun controls.[247]

Britain's murder rate is quite low compared to the U.S. rate. In 1981, there were only 179 homicides in London, compared with 1,557 in metropolitan Los Angeles, and 1,733 in New York City.[248] Although controls themselves may not have had much direct impact on their stated goal—depriving professional criminals of guns—it is possible that gun controls have indirectly reduced homicide. As bureaucratic obstacles to lawful gun possession, the controls may have reduced the overall rate of gun ownership by law-abiding citizens. Moreover, controls may have helped create a cultural climate hostile to gun ownership, which has then further reduced the presence of guns. If simply cutting the number of guns among law-abiding citizens reduces homicides, then Britain's controls may be said to have saved lives.

Support for this hypothesis is found in the fact that while attempted murder and serious wounding have risen sharply since 1974, total homicide has not.[249] The fact could suggest that many potential murderers for some reason could not or did not obtain a gun, and used another weapon instead, and the other weapon was less lethal. Add to this the fact that the large majority of guns in Britain are shotguns, which are extremely lethal at close range. Almost any personal weapon that might be substituted for a shotgun would be less deadly.

American critics of gun control have argued that handgun-only controls would probably increase the American death rate. Some potential murderers would use knives instead (about as lethal as small handguns); other potential murderers would use shotguns (much deadlier).

When strict handgun control was in place but not augmented with shotgun control—the British policy from 1921 to 1967—a large rise in the British homicide rate occurred.

In recent decades British gun control may have prevented some Britons from killing each other, but these controls do not seem to have prevented the British from killing themselves. Gun control apparently has had the same effect on suicide in Britain as it did in Canada. Since 1890 the percentage of British suicides involving guns has fallen by half. In modern times, firearms account for only 6 percent of British male suicides and just .4 percent of female suicides.[250] Yet the suicide rate has remained constant.[251] The overall rate today is nine suicides per 100,000 population per year, about the same as the United States, and about the same as the rate of suicide at the turn of the century, when there were no controls. People contemplating suicide have apparently substituted other means of self-destruction.

On the other hand, it might be argued that without the gun controls, the overall suicide rate would have increased, rather than staying constant. This hypothesis cannot be disproven, although it is inconsistent with the Canadian evidence, which shows gun control to lead to the substitution of other, equally deadly methods of suicide.

Only for one category of violent crime, namely, burglary, does the British rate exceed the American rate.[252] Burglary is a more socially destructive crime in Britain because most British burglars attack houses when a victim is present. A 1982 survey found 59 percent of attempted burglaries take place against an occupied home, compared to just 13 percent in the United States.[253] Fear of being shot convinces most American burglars to strike empty targets.[254]

While a serious burglary problem may be one of the costs of Britain's gun control, a lower armed robbery rate may be the benefit. The overall robbery rate is worsening; it is now up to 80 percent of the U.S. level. In the early 1950s the Bank of England moved its currency to affiliated banks on large flatbed trucks. Two men, neither of them armed, accompanied the trucks from bank to bank.[255] In 1954 in London, only four criminals used a firearm in a robbery, while 272 did in 1969. In 1979, London had 756 armed robberies.[256] In 1987 in London, a firearm was used in 1,693 robberies, and shots were fired in 79 of those. Fourteen security guards, four police officers, and three private citizens were injured.[257] Armed robbery seems to be mostly a London problem, with over half of all of Great Britain's armed robberies taking place in that city.[258]

Robbery and armed robbery have increased at about the same relative rate, with robbery by gun remaining at about 8 to 9 percent of total robberies.[259] In contrast, guns figure in about 17 percent of American robberies—twice as many.[260]

If British gun laws have made some robbers switch from guns to knives or to no weapon, the laws have probably saved lives, although it may also have increased injuries and victimization of the weak, since the availability of firearms as a robbery tool shifts robbers away from "soft," cash-poor targets like elderly pedestrians, and directs them instead to harder, richer targets, such as stores. In any case, it is not certain that Britain's gun controls have affected armed robbery rates, since incidents of that crime have soared as controls have grown tighter, and, at least for criminals who can find the black market, guns are readily available.

It should be emphasized that the armed crime rate remains far below the United States' levels. In England and Wales in 1986, there were 9,363 incidents of gun use in a crime; "criminal damage" accounted for 4,140 incidents, while more serious crimes accounted for the rest.[261] The most disturbing feature about armed crime in Britain is not its absolute level, but rather its rapid growth, starting from a very low base.

One explanation for the increase in gun crime would be that the pool of illegal weapons has increased, or has become easier for more criminals to find. Yet the statistics on illegal weapons show no evidence of an increase. What seems to be changing is the increased willingness of criminals to carry guns.

Some commentators attribute the shift to criminal gun use to Britain's abolition of the death penalty.[262] Police Federation Chairman James Jardine, whose calls for stricter gun control have finally been heeded, states: "There is no doubt in our minds that the abolition of capital punishment encouraged ruthless criminals to carry guns."[263] Other commentators suggest that criminal armament is a response to increased police armament, a theory that will be discussed in more detail momentarily.[264]

The micro picture of gun control in Britain might indicate that controls have reduced homicide in the last two decades, have had no tangible effect on robbery, and have increased burglary of occupied residences. The larger picture is summarized by Greenwood: "[O]ne is forced to the rather startling conclusion that the use of firearms in crime was very much less when there were no controls of any sort and when anyone, convicted criminal or lunatic, could buy any type of firearm without restriction."[265] Britain's gun (and nongun) crime rate was almost nil at the turn of the twentieth century, before controls were even enacted. For example, from 1878 to 1891, the average number of London burglaries in which the burglar fired a shot doubled—from two a year to four.[266] From 1911 to 1913, London averaged forty-one serious felonies a year.[267]

Over the last century, Britain has reduced its overall number of guns, and gone from no gun laws to severe gun laws. In that same period, gun crime has grown exponentially. It would be overly simplistic to draw a correlation between Britain's adoption of strict gun laws and its increase in gun crime, even though stricter guns laws have usually been followed by increased armed crime. Likewise, it would be overly simplistic to correlate Britain's present gun laws with its low homicide rate. The most important difference between 1900 Britain (almost no crime) and 1990 Britain (much higher gun crime) is not the increase in gun controls, but the decrease in social controls.

What is going wrong in Britain in the final decade of the twentieth century is not only a change in criminal attitudes about guns, but a decay in the entire social fabric. Sociologist Charles Murray observes the rapid growth of a British underclass, whose members and their families have no involvement in the job market, ever, and who subsist by government transfer payments and by crime. He notes that the British nonviolent crime rate is already equal to the American rate.[268]

For both crime and suicide, the most significant factor may be what criminologist James Q. Wilson calls "the investment in impulse control." Wilson argues that the development of bourgeois Victorian morality during the nineteenth century may have been the main cause of the dramatic declines in Britain's crime rate.[269] The current rise in the crime rate, especially in the late 1950s and 1960s, accompanied a weakening of internally accepted social controls.[270] Another historian attributes the low turn-of-the-century crime rate to "the 'civilizing' effects of religion, education, and environmental reform."[271] Although weaker than at the turn of the century, the self-control of the British people remains considerably greater than that of their American cousins.[272]

Wilson's hypothesis is consistent with the evidence about crime in medieval England detailed by James Given in *Society and Homicide in Thirteenth Century England*. According to Given, the English of that period—who carried knives but had no guns—slew each other at a far higher rate than Americans do today. Considered a rough and dangerous place to travel, thirteenth-century Britain had a crime rate higher than New York City does today.[273] Noting that many low-crime societies have had high rates of knife carrying or of intrafamily violence (factors sometimes blamed for medieval Britain's high homicide rate), Given instead attributes the high homicide rate of that period to changing social structures. He contends that the changes were produced by the "ever larger numbers of people who were pushed into a marginal position in society" and by the bringing of members of the old local communities into ever more frequent contact with people who were not from that community and with whom often uneasy relations obtained."[274] Given explains that the rapid development of the economy raised living standards, but marginalized many people, particularly peasants who could not afford plows or draft animals. The poorer peasants committed most of the century's homicides and robberies. The entire society was moving from the "intensely local" world of the early Middle Ages, to the "larger regional units of the high Middle Ages." Dispute resolution mechanisms had "required small, tightly knit communities to be effective," but those communities no longer existed.[275]

The British practice of carrying knives for cutting bread "possibly rendered fatal many quarrels that otherwise would have resulted in bruises," Given says. The prevalence of weapons, however, was not the root cause of British homicide. Many rural African societies today encourage the carrying of sharp weapons, yet their homicide rate is nowhere near medieval England's.[276] Likewise, the "prodigious" drinking of English beer was an important factor in quarrels and murders in Britain, but many other societies, including modern Switzerland, have high rates of alcoholism, but much lower murder rates.[277]

Culture matters more than statutes about guns. After New York City enacted strict gun controls in 1911, it suffered a much higher firearms crime rate than did London, where significant controls had not yet been enacted.[278] Today as well, Great Britain suffers less violent crime of all types (except burglary) than does the United States. The difference in crime rates seems best explained by internal social controls.

Certainly another factor is external control, particularly the deterrent effect of Britain's police. About 14 percent of all London robberies end in a conviction; only 10 percent of Chicago robberies even lead to an arrest.[279] For every five hundred serious American crimes, only twenty adults and five juveniles are sent to prison.[280] Until the mid-1950s, Britain executed half of its murderers (a rate never approached in the United States), and today a life sentence for murder is mandatory.[281]

Methadone maintenance programs have helped Britain keep heroin addicts out of the robbery game. And of course Britain only has 2,000 or so addicts, less than 1 percent of the American total.[282]

Moreover, America is simply a more violent, crime-prone society than Great Britain, with or without gun control. When neither Britain nor America had gun control, the ratio of American to British murders was even higher than it is now.[283] As noted above, New York with gun control has had far more crime than London, with or without controls. Europeans of the late eighteenth and early nineteenth centuries blamed the high American crime rate on America's broad freedoms (of which widespread gun ownership was only one), which the Europeans saw as license.[284] Both the American and the British police began unarmed; but the American police soon had to arm themselves because Americans were more violent toward and less respectful of the police.[285] Even disregarding gun crimes, America is much more crime-prone than Britain. Sixty-two percent of American homicides involve a gun, but only 17 percent of robberies and 7 to 8 percent of rapes.[286] Writes Greenwood:

> There are also more robberies [in America] involving knives and more in which the only weapon was the hands or feet of the assailant. If it is suggested that easier availability of firearms is the cause of firearms robberies, is it also suggested that knives are less readily available in England than they are in the U.S.A., or that American criminals have more hands and feet than their British counterparts?[287]

As the British Office of Health Economics once noted, "one reason often given for American homicide is the easy availability of firearms . . . [but] the strong correlation with racial and linked socio-economic variables suggests that the underlying determinants of the homicide rate relate to particular cultural factors."[288]

One of the most important of the "particular cultural factors" is America's legacy of racial discrimination. American blacks have an annual homicide rate per 100,000 of 34.4; Hispanics a rate of 19.9; and non-Hispanic whites (who own more guns per capita) a rate of 3.3.[289] Like the displaced peasants of the thirteenth century, some American groups find themselves missing out on the economy's forward progress and live in large urban communities where traditional dispute resolution methods no longer function effectively. Homicide, robbery, and other crime are the result. It may be that the availability of guns makes crime more dangerous, but it would not be realistic to blame guns as a significant cause of American criminal violence.

COULD BRITISH-STYLE GUN LAWS BE ENFORCED IN THE UNITED STATES?

Although Britain's 1967 gun act was stricter than any federal law seriously contemplated in the United States, the police and government claimed that guns were too accessible. If effective gun control has been difficult in Britain, similar controls would seem nearly impossible to effect in America. Before Britain tightly restricted handguns, there were only 1 percent as many handguns per capita as in the United States.[290] Big game being long since crowded from most of the country, rifle possession was rarer, too. Today, Americans are about ten times as likely to have a gun in the house as Britons.[291] In the mid-1970s, when America's gun stock was scores of millions less than today, the superintendent of Scotland Yard opined that America had too many guns for control to be plausible.[292]

As an island with a large police force in relation to the size of its overall population, Britain, much like Japan, has had a relatively easy time stopping illegal imports.[293] Since World War II, Britain has not been in a long-lasting war, a common source of illegal weapons acquisition.[294]

Because the number of handgun owners was already low, the fact that many of them disobeyed the 1920 registration law was relatively unimportant. Most other citizens complied with the gun laws and have not attempted to purchase guns outside the system. There being little need for self-defense against crime, there seemed little need to violate the restrictive gun laws. Two anti-gun American scholars suggest that Americans will not disarm until the government first reduces the crime rate.[295] Americans already disobey many of the existing gun controls; it is difficult to believe that they would obey even stricter ones.[296]

Notably, Britain does not share America's history of massive disobedience to commodity bans.[297] One of the largest British illegal gun amnesties, in 1964, brought in 25,000 illegal weapons; American gun amnesties almost never break the three-digit barrier.[298]

The British police are mostly unarmed and thereby set a climate for voluntary civilian disarmament. Starting with the 1967 Shephard's Bush murders, however, a growing minority of police officers have begun to patrol armed. Armed robberies and police armament closely correlate.[299]

Violent crime and police armament remain rarer than in the United States. Even in Britain's robbery capital, London, only about 15 percent of the police carry guns. The only police who are permanently armed are special security forces for "diplomatic, royalty and ministerial protection."[300] After the Hungerford massacre the police were criticized for taking so long to get armed officers to the scene. The Police Foundation and the Hungerford coroner called the deaths "the price we all had to pay for the maintenance of a largely unarmed police force."[301]

The patrolmen who are given guns are more lightly armed than almost all of their American counterparts. Patrol officers do not routinely carry backup guns. The primary guns are only Smith and Wesson Model 10 revolvers loaded with .38 special +P ammunition. They must be carried concealed. Bobbies have no powerful Colt .45s on display. They do not carry the same gun from day to day. At the end of every shift, their duty gun goes back into the police safe.[302] All officers must follow the policy in the Association of Chief Police Officers' *Manual of Guidance*. The guidance, although officially secret, is "very largely consistent with Colin Greenwood's *Police Tactics in Armed Operations*" and emphasizes extreme caution in police use of deadly force.[303] In 1987, only five Britons were shot dead by the police, and even this number was seen as alarmingly high.[304] Even if all civilian guns in the United States vanished, it is doubtful that American police would become as nonviolent as their British counterparts.

The police, being mostly disarmed, make civilian acceptance of gun controls more palatable. A British police superintendent who says people should not have guns has credibility in Britain because he himself is disarmed. High-ranking police administrators almost never carry guns.[305] American chiefs, sporting large, expensive handguns, are less credible as advocates of a disarmed populace.

Instead of needing to compel submission, the British police have historically been able to rely "upon the benign, nonaggressive image of the unarmed British Bobby."[306] The police authority has been achieved "by presenting an image of vulnerability, instead of the invincibility of their

Continental or American counterparts."[307] That the Bobbies today sometimes need weapons reflects of the general decline in social controls that is also associated with the rapid growth of the British underclass.

Because of the breakdown in the social consensus, police tensions with minorities and the rest of the populace are at alarmingly high levels compared to the recent past.[308] Perhaps increased crime and decreased trust in the populace will lead Britain into a second period of outright gun prohibition. The second prohibition, like the first one, over three hundred years ago, may be offered under the pretext of controlling hunting.

It should be emphasized that while the British social fabric is unravelling, relations between police and civilians remain much friendlier than in most of the United States. The society still enjoys enough cohesion that the British police rarely use handcuffs. The official manual instructs police never to allow their fellow citizen—defendant though he may be—to be humiliated by having the press photograph him in handcuffs. If necessary, the arresting officer should place his "raincoat over the cuffs to conceal the unpleasant truth."[309] According to one anthropologist:

> [T]he past century, the English policeman has been for his peers not only an object of respect but also a model of the ideal male character, self-controlled, possessing more strength than he has to call into use except in the gravest emergency. . . .[310]

The British policeman, like the Royal Canadian Mounted Policeman, has been a highly regarded symbol of masculine power carefully controlled by government authority. No one would claim that the American policeman—or any other appointed government official—plays the role of "ideal male character." American policemen may be just as virtuous as their Canadian or British counterparts; they certainly are called upon to display grace under pressure more often. Yet in America's individualistic, anti-authoritarian culture, the police have never been, and likely never will be, the preeminent male ideal.

THE PEARL OF GREAT PRICE: CIVIL LIBERTIES

The late Richard Hofstadter, one of America's greatest historians and a critic of America's "gun culture," condemned the "pathetic stubbornness" of Americans who cling to the notion that the right to bear arms protects liberty; for, wrote Hofstadter, "in some democracies in which citizens are better protected than in ours, such as England and the Scandinavian countries, our arms control policies would be considered laughable."[311]

It is true that the freedoms guaranteed in the American Second Amendment are subject to a host of restrictions in Britain considered reasonable and moderate by the government and most of the people. Likewise, the freedoms guaranteed in the First Amendment, particularly freedom of speech and the right to assemble, are also subject to a number of qualifications in Britain. The British government frequently bans books on national security grounds.[312] In addition, England's libel laws tend to favor those who bring suit against a free press.[313]

Prior restraint of speech in the United States is allowed only in the most urgent of circumstances.[314] In England, the government may apply for a prior restraint of speech *ex parte,* asking a court to censor a newspaper without the newspaper even having notice or the opportunity to present an argument.[315] The prohibition of such prior restraints was one of the primary goals of the authors of America's First Amendment.

Free speech in Great Britain is also constrained by the Official Secrets Act, which outlaws the unauthorized receipt of information from any government agency, and allows the government to forbid publication of any "secret" it pleases. Notably, the Official Secrets Act was enacted in 1911, the same year Britain was suffering from anti-foreign, anti-gun national security hysteria.[316] The act was expanded in 1920 and again in 1989—times when gun controls were also expanded.[317] While the American government carries the burden of proving that a document was appropriately classified as secret, the British citizen carries the burden of proving that a document should not be secret.[318] Altogether, America's Freedom of Information Act makes American government files more open to public scrutiny than the files of any other government in the world. British laws create a chilling effect, so that the press is afraid to publish even when a daring civil servant does leak information.[319]

In the fall of 1988, the same time that Prime Minister Thatcher pushed through the new restrictions on guns and seized property (firearms) without just compensation, her government enacted other laws constricting civil liberties. She forbade television stations to broadcast in-person statements which the government construed as supportive of a legal political party, Sinn Fein (the political arm of the Irish Republican Army).[320] The ban even applied to rebroadcasts of archive films taped many decades ago.[321] A confidential British Broadcasting Corporation memo announced the government's intention to keep journalists from broadcasting statements by U.S. Senator Edward Kennedy.[322]

While the First Amendment protects the rights of even repulsive organizations like the American Nazis to speak and demonstrate, it is illegal in Britain to so much as publicly express racist views.[323] The Obscene Publications Act and the Misuse of Drugs Act have been used as justification for the police to seize masterpieces such as William S. Burroughs's *Junky,* Hunter Thompson's *Fear and Loathing in Las Vegas,* and Tom Wolfe's *The Electric Kool-Aid Acid Test.*[324] British courts have never recognized a right to assemble or to demonstrate.[325]

Two civil libertarians gloomily summarize: "As our allies become more open, Britain grows yet more secretive and censorious. Perhaps the real British vice is passivity, a willingness to tolerate constraints which others would find unbearable."[326] The British press voluntarily submits to self-censorship unimaginable in America. A joint press/government committee sends "D-notices" to editors, requesting self-censorship on specified national security subjects. The press almost always obeys.[327] The BBC banned Paul McCartney's anthem "Give Ireland Back to the Irish," and a song by another group urging the release from prison of the Guildford Four.*[328] During the American-led war against Iraq, John Lennon's anthem "Give Peace a Chance" was ubiquitous on the American airwaves, and banned by the BBC.

The submissiveness of the media on national security issues is another manifestation of the British attitude of self-control—an attitude that keeps crime lower than in America, but also makes Britain less free.

National security concerns do more than prevent British citizens from learning about their government. The Security Service Act of 1989 provides: "No entry on or interference with property shall be unlawful if it is authorized by a warrant issued by the secretary of state." Upon an order from the secretary of state, theft, damage to property, arson, procuring information for blackmail, and leaving planted evidence are not crimes.[329] In the United States, no official of the executive branch can authorize such actions. Only a court could authorize a government breaking and entering and only if the government presented particular proof of necessity.

Security continues to eat away at other traditional rights of British subjects. In Northern Ireland the jury has been "suspended" for political violence cases; judges in the Diplock courts hear the cases instead. Confessions are admitted without corroboration and are often obtained through coercive tactics. Convictions may be based solely on the testimony of "supergrasses" (police informers).[330]

The British justice system's response to Irish Republican Army terrorism in Britain has been particularly disturbing. In 1974, terrorists bombed pubs in Birmingham, killing twenty-one people. Home Secretary Roy Jenkins (author of the 1967 shotgun controls) introduced the "Prevention of Ter-

---

*The Guildford Four were convicted of perpetrating an IRA bombing; after many years in prison, they were set free because of admissions that the police had fabricated evidence and had extracted confessions by beating them.

rorism (Temporary Provisions) Bill." Approved without objection in Parliament, the bill was supposed to expire in one year, but has been renewed every year since. Under the bill, the police may stop and search without warrant any person suspected of terrorism. They may arrest any person they "reasonably suspect" supports an illegal organization or has participated in terrorist activity. An arrested person may be detained up to forty-eight hours and then for five more days upon the authority of the secretary of state. Of the 6,246 people detained between 1974 and 1986, 87 percent were never charged with any offense. Many detainees reported that they were intimidated during detention and prevented from contacting their families. The bill also makes it illegal even to organize a private or public meeting addressed by a member of a proscribed organization, or to wear clothes indicating support of such an organization.[331]

The bill allows the secretary of state to issue an "exclusion order" barring a person from ever entering a particular part of the United Kingdom, such as Northern Ireland or Wales. Persons subject to this form of internal exile have no right to know the evidence against them, to cross-examine or confront their accusers, or even to have a formal public hearing.[332]

What America calls "domestic tranquility" Britain calls "the Queen's Peace."[333] The different phrasing reflects the British assumption that the government is not simply an arbiter between individuals, but an independent power, sufficient unto itself with the authority to take whatever steps it needs to protect its own interest in peace. As a result, many rights that are fundamental in America are less than secure in Britain. The "rights of Englishmen" were an important basis for the American Bill of Rights. Those rights, and not only the right to bear arms, have flourished in America and withered in Britain.

The grand jury, which was an ancient common law institution, as was civilian gun ownership, was abolished in 1933.[334] Civil jury trials have been abolished for all cases except libel, and criminal jury trials are rare. Today, over 90 percent of all jury trials in the world take place in the United States. Even when a British subject does receive a jury trial, *voir dire* (examination of potential jurors by the lawyers) is far more restricted than in the United States.[335]

While America has the *Miranda* rules, Britain allows police to interrogate suspects who have asked that interrogation stop, and allows the police to keep defense lawyers away from suspects under interrogation for limited periods.[356] The "Fruit of the Poisonous Tree" doctrine in America bars use of evidence derived from leads developed in a coerced confession. Britain allows use of such evidence.[337]

Further, defense trial lawyers (barristers) often serve as prosecutors on other cases. The clubby, collegial relationship between prosecution and defense counsel discourages defense counsel from aggressive defense of clients.[338] Four out of five defendants pleading innocent do not even meet their barrister until the first day of trial.[339]

Even the standard of proof beyond a reasonable doubt—the cornerstone of a fair system of justice—has been eroded. Suspected terrorists now carry the burden of proving their innocence.[340]

It is not difficult for the police to obtain legal authorization to search wherever they want. Wiretaps do not need judicial approval.[341] In any case, formal legal constraints are irrelevant. A study of police searches by London's Metropolitan Police showed that a large percentage of stops and searches were not supported by reasonable suspicion, and that the police did not care whether their searches comported with formal legal standards.[342] One reason the police do not need to care about legality is that Britain lacks an exclusionary rule to deter illegal police acquisition of evidence.[343] Indeed, it is unlawful in a British court to point out the fact that a police wiretap was illegal.[344]

Upon instructions of police administrators, officers in several jurisdictions have begun compiling Japanese-style dossiers on individuals in their locality. Reports contain unsubstantiated gossip and noncriminal information, such as the fact that a woman is three months pregnant and living with her parents.[345]

When the government cuts back on civil liberties, it couches its actions in the reasonable language of "balancing." The Police Act, authorizing incommunicado detention, was promoted as a "balance" between police powers and individual rights.[346] Likewise, Home Secretary Douglas Hurd justified the 1988 gun controls as "a better balance between the interests of the genuine sportsman and the safety of the public as a whole."[347] The gun lobby's concession that guns are only for sport, and not for defense, helps the government tip the balance against the gun owner. If guns make no positive contribution to personal or public safety, the public's concerns about safety must override the gun owners' interest in sports.

Yet although the government praises "balancing," the lack of checks and balances within the government itself endangers liberties. Any American law, including a restriction on liberty, must be passed by the legislature and signed by the executive, enforced by the executive, and upheld by the courts. The independence of the legislature, executive, and judicial branches is a deliberate formula for government gridlock, for it ensures that government cannot speak with a single voice.

In contrast, the British Parliament is supreme. An act of Parliament that is clearly expressed cannot be questioned on constitutional grounds by any British court.[348] A majority in Parliament means control of the entire government. The party leader (the prime minister) and that person's close advisors have a much easier time turning their unchecked will into law than do their counterparts in the United States, Australia, or Canada.[349] The British system does not mean legislative supremacy, but rather executive supremacy, since the leader of the dominant party in Parliament faces no effective opposition or check.[350]

In the seventeenth century, as Parliament took control of the militia away from the king, it exalted itself as the "epitome" of the nation, insisting "there can be nothing against the arbitrary Supremacy of Parliaments." Indeed, it was commonly said that "Parliament can do no wrong."[351] The fiction of a monarch as an infallible national sovereign was replaced with the fiction of an equally absolute and perfect Parliament. Virtually no one in the debates surrounding the creation of the American government, or in the two centuries of that government's existence, has ever asserted that any branch of government deserved absolute power. The "checks and balances" of the American Constitution reflect the explicit choice that government was itself something that needed to be controlled, both by the internal checks of three coequal branches of government and by the external check of an armed people who could resist tyranny.[352]

The right to bear arms is simply one thread in the tapestry of civil liberties. When the government pulls on any thread, other threads are dislodged, too. To enforce the gun-control laws, the police have been given broad search and seizure powers. Sections 46 through 50 of the 1968 Firearms Act authorized the police to search individuals and vehicles without warrants, to require the handing-over of weapons for inspection, and to arrest without a warrant in most cases.[353] (A warrant is still required for a home search.[354]) The principle of warrantless searches for firearms was expanded to include searches for "offensive weapons" by the Police and Criminal Evidence Bill of 1984. Since "offensive weapons" are never defined, the police have nearly unlimited authority to search and seize. African combs, bunches of keys, and tools have been considered offensive weapons. In one case reported by the National Council of Civil Liberties, a workman carrying tools to his car was asked "Would you use this tool to defend yourself if attacked?" Had the workman given an affirmative answer that he would, he might well have been subject to arrest for the felony of carrying an offensive weapon.[355] The principle of warrantless arrests is now a general practice in British law, even for minor offenses.[356]

Some civil liberties have partly withstood potential encroachments by the gun laws. In 1772, the Game Act effectively abolished the right to trial by jury for accused poachers.[357] Yet two centuries later, the right to jury trial remains more or less intact, at least for serious felonies.

Today the practice that police may inspect private homes without a warrant is being established by the "safe keeping" provisions of the gun laws. In many jurisdictions the police will not issue or renew a firearms or shotgun certificate without an in-home visit to ensure that the police standards for safe storage are being met. The police have no legal authority to require such home inspections, yet when a homeowner refuses the police entry, the certificate application or renewal will be denied.[358] The 1989 extension of the safe-storage law to shotguns—a reasonable concept in itself—has increased by several hundred thousand the number of British homes entry to which the police consider within their authority to enter without a warrant.

The gun-control laws have helped promote the idea that the police create the law, rather than merely enforce laws enacted by Parliament. Police departments have told hunters, incorrectly, that restrictions on hunting with semi-automatic weapons also apply to hunting with pump-action guns.[359] Although it is not legally necessary for shooters to have written permission to hunt on a particular piece of land, police have been stopping shooters, demanding written proof, and threatening to confiscate guns from persons who cannot produce the proof.[360] The police have, again without legal authority, refused to accept sporting purposes as "good reason" for owning shotguns capable of holding more than two shells.[361]

Without legal authority, many chief constables have decided to enforce existing gun laws "to reduce to an absolute minimum the number of firearms, including shotguns, in hands of members of the public."[362] Without legal authority, the police have begun to phase out firearms collections by refusing new applications.[363] Gun-licensing fees have been repeatedly raised far above the actual cost of administering the licensing system, and have been used as a mechanism to discourage gun ownership.[364]

One of the reasons that liberties of all types are so much stronger in America than in Britain is that American civil liberties organizations have so much more political strength and are so much more militant than the British one. America is the only country with a civil liberties lobby (ACLU) that makes so much of a difference.

Likewise, America's National Rifle Association (NRA) is considered, by friend and foe alike, the strongest gun lobby in the world. Yet Britain does not even have a gun organization that informs members of legislator's votes, or which employs a full-time lobbyist.

The British lobbies accuse their American cousins of going to extremes. The National Council on Civil Liberties favors suppression of racist speech, and has even refused to represent racist clients on other issues.[365] Just as the British NCCL thinks that Americans take free speech too far, British gun organizations criticize the laxity of American gun laws.[366] When the Home Office imposed severe restrictions on gun clubs, the chief executive of Britain's National Rifle Association affirmed his assent by simply noting that "the Government saw a need."[367]

Civil liberties in Britain lack not only the sword of strong citizens' groups, but also the shield of a written constitution. The preservation of civil liberties endures only so long as parliamentary majorities respect unwritten traditions. A civil liberties leader in the House of Lords explains why a written constitution matters:

> Human rights are built into American life by the Constitution, and protected by a court, the Supreme Court of the USA. Not so in my country. "Human rights" is not a term of art in English law. Civil liberties—yes, our courts understand them and protect them. We rely on the common law: but the common law has no constitutional protection against the inroads of the legislature. Judges are, in terms of power, subordinate to parliament. Mr. Justice Brennan's approach to human rights is the pearl of great price that we have lost in the rough seas that prevail outside the world of a written constitution.[368]

The differing constitutional policies of America and Britain, and the differing fate of the right to bear arms in the two nations, can be traced in part to the revolutionary times that gave birth to the formal recognition of the right to bear arms in each nation.

The Second Amendment was written just a few years after an armed America fought a long and violent insurrection that overthrew what many Americans considered an imperial dictatorship. The closest the British people ever came to successfully overthrowing a government was the century of instability preceding the Glorious Revolution of 1688–1689. And the resultant statutory "Bill of Rights" was as close as Britain ever came to a strong written constitution protecting a right to bear arms.[369]

The Glorious Revolution of 1688–1689—also called the "Bloodless Revolution"—amounted to King James II's standing army deserting at the approach of King William's standing army. The resultant Bill of Rights enacted by Parliament in 1689 has turned out to be of little value in protecting even a small core of a "right" to own guns in Britain. The appeal that an American makes to the Bill of Rights, on the other hand, is an appeal to the highest law, and a claim of entitlement. American gun owners (and about 90 percent of the American public) believe that they have a right to bear arms.

Professor John Dunn of Cambridge finds that the language of British civil liberties "has more the flavor of moral criticism . . . than confident appeal to existing or positive constitutional law."[370] Most British gun owners make no claim of right, but simply ask for respect for their traditional privilege to own sporting arms.

Dunn further notes, "the far greater salience of conflicts of class interest in British politics greatly accentuates the externality and conceptual instability of political defenses of civil liberties."[371] Perceived class interests, of course, are part of the Labour party's motivation for attacking shotguns, the "toy of the landed gentry."

British legal culture is not as extreme as Japan's with respect to subverting individual desires to national imperatives. But neither do Britons enjoy the robust rights consciousness of Americans. "One axiom I heard a lot when I was there," one American writer remembers, was "We're subjects. You're citizens."[372]

British constitutional scholar and former Member of Parliament L. S. Amery contrasts the British and American systems of government: In the American system, the individual citizen is the "starting point and motive power of the political process." Government is delegated authority by the people, and it remains subordinate to the people.[373] Indeed, the Constitution and the Bill of Rights were intended to keep the government inferior to the people in terms of ultimate physical force. As James Madison's friend Tench Coxe explained, the federal government could never successfully tyrannize America, for: "[T]he unlimited power of the sword is not in the hands of either the federal or state government, but where I trust in God it will ever remain, in the hands of the American people."[374]

In Britain, on the other hand, the people and the government possess what Amery calls "independent and original authority." Legislation is initiated by the government, and the purpose of Parliament is to provide a forum for the people to reject a governmental action. Amery describes the British system "of democracy by consent and not by delegation, of government of the people, for the people, with, but not by, the people."[375]

CONCLUSION

British gun laws are strict, and British violent crime rates are low. Many Americans assume that these two facts are causally linked; however, there is little evidence that they are. British gun control has historically been concerned with political subversion, not with ordinary crime. Britain's years of lowest gun crime came during an era when gun controls were nonexistent. Increasingly stringent gun controls have been followed by increasing gun crime (although again there is no strong proof of a causal effect). The supply of black-market handguns—after almost a century of strict controls—remains more than sufficient to fulfill criminal demand. Regulations of gun acquisition by law-abiding citizens has had little net impact on crime prevention except perhaps to reduce homicide and to increase sharply the burglary of occupied homes. Internalized social controls, rather than gun controls, seem to better explain the low crime rate, because changes in social controls more closely parallel the changes in the crime rate. In recent times, as the government has taken on ever more responsibility to control individual behavior, the British people have been found to be less and less responsible.

The experiment that began early this century with simple pistol regulations may lead to the near-extinction of gun ownership by the end of the century. The willing acceptance of moderate controls by British gun owners has not forestalled increasingly severe controls. Instead, strict control on "bad" guns supposedly made for killing (rifles and handguns in the British view) has become a model for control on "good" guns supposedly made for sport (shotguns). Sportsmen who condoned "reasonable" handgun controls in the hopes that their sporting shotguns would remain safe have been proven disastrously wrong.

British gun control occurs in a context of diminished civil liberties and greater government authority that many Americans would find unacceptable. The results of the British experiment with gun control provide little evidence in favor of stricter American controls. Instead, they offer a caution to proponents of moderate control who expect that their proposals will not lead to stringent control and prohibition.

NOTES

1. American writer James Atlas, "Censorship in Britain," *Rocky Mountain News,* March 5, 1989, p. 57.

2. Nancy Blodgett, "Powell: What Right to Own Guns?" *ABA Journal,* October 1, 1988, p. 30. Justice Powell's speech to the American Bar Association was elaborated in a *Harvard Law Review* article:

"A comparison of our crime statistics with those in other countries is striking. The murder rate per 100,000 persons in Canada in 1980 was 2.1; in the United States 10.5—five times higher. Similarly in 1986, our murder rate was over six times as high as the murder rate in England and Wales. Possible reasons for the disparity between our murder rate and that of other nations include the comparative newness of our country, the growing use of illegal drugs, and almost certainly the availability of handguns. Firearms consistently account for some sixty percent of the murders committed in the United States. The comparable figure from England and Wales is approximately eight percent.

"My understanding is that private ownership of handguns is strictly controlled in other Western democracies. In Great Britain, for example, gun owners must apply for a special license and satisfy the authorities that their possession of firearms will not endanger public safety. Firearm dealers are strictly regulated and subject to record keeping requirements. The British government now is considering even stricter controls in the wake of a shooting incident in which sixteen people were killed by a lone gunman." (footnotes omitted.)

Lewis F. Powell, "Capital Punishment," *Harvard Law Review* 109 (March 1989), p. 1044.

3. New Jersey Revised Statutes Annotated § 2A: 151-1, *et seq.* (West 1966).

4. *Burton* v. *Sills,* 53 N.J. 86, 248 A.2d 521, 526 (1968). See also, *Siccardi* v. *State,* 50 N.J. 545, 284 A.2d 533, 573 (1971) (quoting California Supreme Court Justice Mosk's approbation of British gun control).

5. *State* v. *Dawson,* 272 N.C. 535, 159 S.E.2d 1, 9 (1968). The *Dawson* court's language regarding the Second Amendment was entirely unnecessary, since the case involved Ku Klux Klan members going armed to terrorize the people, an act that had always been illegal at common law, and which was no more within the protection of the Second Amendment than was armed robbery.

6. Peter Buck Feller and Karl L. Gotting, "The Second Amendment: A Second Look," *Northwestern University Law Review* 61 (1966): 46–70.

7. For the Second Amendment, see chapter 9.

8. Colin Greenwood, *Firearms Control: A Study of Armed Crime and Firearms Control in England and Wales* (London: Routledge and Kegan Paul, 1971), pp. 208–209. Greenwood wrote his study while a Cropwood research fellow at the Institute of Criminology, University of Cambridge. It is the only scholarly book devoted to British gun control in practice in the twentieth century. Colin Greenwood formerly served as a chief inspector and as superintendent of West Yorkshire Constabulary, retiring in 1979. A specialist in firearms training, he authored *Police Tactics in Armed Operations,* whose guidelines are currently mandatory force policy for the British police. P. A. J. Waddington, *Arming an Unarmed Police: Policy and Practice in the Metropolitan Police* (London: Police Foundation, 1988), pp. 11–16. Greenwood's tactics training manual emphasizes safety and caution, trying to contain the gunman, rather than shooting it out. Colin Greenwood, *Police Tactics in Armed Operations* (Boulder, Colo.: Paladin Press, 1979). See also, Colin Greenwood, *Tactics in the Police Use of Firearms* (Todmorden, Lancashire: H. Leah, 1969).

9. The statement of the attorney general is contained in "Statement of Hon. Homer S. Cummings, Attorney General of the United States," before United States House of Representatives Ways and Means Committee, hearings on the National Firearms Act, H.R. 9066, 73d Cong., 2d sess., April 16, 1934 (Washington, D.C.: Government Printing Office, 1934), p. 28. Cummings's mistake derived from his misunderstanding of British law. Cummings was referring to Britain's Firearm Act 1920, which did place strict controls on rifles and pistols. The act imposed no controls on shotguns. In British terminology, a "firearm" is a rifle or pistol; while in America, a "firearm" can also be a shotgun. In this chapter, and this chapter only, the word "firearm" is used in the British sense. "Firearm" means a handgun or a rifle. A shotgun, in Britain, is a gun, but is not a firearm.

The National Firearms Act is codified at 26 U.S.C. § 5801-et seq.

10. William Tuohy, "British Gun Laws Could Become Tougher," *Los Angeles Times,* November 7, 1981, p. 1.

11. Joseph Magaddino and Colin Greenwood, "Comparative Cross-Cultural Statistics," in Donald B. Kates, Jr., ed., *Restricting Handguns: The Liberal Skeptics Speak Out* (Croton-on-Hudson, N.Y.: North River Press, 1979), pp. 47–48; Colin Greenwood, "Firearms Security: Law or Education," *Australian Shooters Journal,* January 1989, p. 39. [Hereinafter, "Greenwood, *Firearms Security.*"] See also, notes 232–35 and accompanying text.

12. Home Office, Statistical Department, "Statistics on the Operation of the Firearms Act 1968, England and Wales 1988," *Home Office Statistical Bulletin* issue 18/89, May 23, 1989 (Croydon: Government Statistical Service), p. 2 [hereinafter, "Statistics on the Operation of the Firearms Act, 1988"]; Sapsted, "Control of Shotguns Farcical, Say Police," *The Times,* July 10, 1987, p. 23.

13. "Statistics on the Operation of the Firearms Act, 1988"; Home Office, "Firearms Act 1968: Proposals for Reform," Cm. 261 (London: Her Majesty's Stationary Office,

December 1987), p. 4; Michael Yardley and Jan A. Stevenson, eds., *Report on the Firearms (Amendment) Bill*, 2d ed. (London: Piedmont, 1988), pp. 21–22 [hereinafter Yardley and Stevenson]; Greenwood, "Firearms Security," p. 39. According to the report, the number of certificate holders has declined from 209,946 in 1969, as a result of police efforts to cut the number of certificate holders.

14. Forty-seven households per thousand admitted to a pollster that they owned a gun. Martin Killias, "Gun Ownership and Violent Crime: The Swiss Experience in International Perspective," *Security Journal* 1, no. 3 (1990), p. 171. Killias's British figures are likely too low, since people with illegal or unregistered guns (a substantial percentage in Britain, as the discussion below will detail) are unlikely to admit to complete strangers that they are committing a crime.

15. Ibid., p. 171 table 1, found 48 percent of American households admitting to gun ownership. Killias's results are consistent with surveys by Gallup, Harris, and others. Again, the polling figures are probably too low since people who own illegal guns (i.e., many residents of New York City and Chicago) are not likely to confess to a stranger on the telephone. Killias's work is discussed in more detail in chapter 8.

16. Colin Greenwood, "The British Experience," in *Gun Control Examined,* collection of papers presented at conference on Gun Control, Melbourne University, August 27–28, 1988, p. 29.

17. Joseph Story, *Commentaries on the Constitution of the United States* (Boston: Hilliard, Gray, and Company, 1833; reprinted 1987, Carolina Academic Press, Durham, North Carolina), § 1001.

18. Joseph Story, *Commentaries on the Constitution,* vol. 3 (New York: Da Capo, 1970), p. 747, § 1891:

"A similar provision in favour of protestants (for to them it is confined) is to be found in the bills of rights of 1688, it being declared, 'that the subjects which are protestants, may have arms for their defence suitable to their condition, and as allowed by law.' But under various pretences the effect of this provision has been greatly narrowed; it is at present in England more nominal than real, as a defensive privilege."

19. E.g., George Newton and Franklin Zimring, *Firearms and Violence in American Life: A Staff Report Submitted to the National Commission on the Causes and Prevention of Violence* (Washington, D.C.: Government Printing Office, 1968), p. 255.

20. Statute of Assize of Arms, Henry II, art. 3 (1181); Robert W. Coakley and Stetson Conn, *The War of the American Revolution* (Washington, D.C.: Center of Military History, United States Army, 1975), p. 2.

21. 13 Edward I, chapter 6 (1285).

22. 2 Edward III, chapter 3 (1328): "That no Man great or fmall, of what Condition foever he be, except the King's Servants in his Prefence, and his Minifters . . . and alfo upon a Cry made for Arms to keep the Peace . . . go nor ride armed by Night nor by Day, in Fairs, Markets, nor in the Prefence of the Justices or other Minifters, nor in no Part elfewhere. . . ."

23. Jules J. Jusserand, *A Literary History of the English People from the Origins to the Renaissance* (New York: G. P. Putnam's Sons, 1985, first published 1906), p. 270.

24. 4 Blackstone, *Commentaries* *149; *Sir John Knight's Case,* 87 English Reports 75 and 90 English Reports 330 (King's Bench 1687) (the case is reported twice, by different reporters who summarized the legal arguments and the court's decision).

[Because Blackstone's *Commentaries* has been republished dozens of times, the standard of legal citation is to cite to the "star edition," an early edition of the treatise. Thus, later editions of Blackstone, with their individual pagination, often also include a parallel page number showing the "star edition" page. Further citations to Blackstone in this chapter are to the star edition, unless otherwise noted.]

25. 6 Henry VIII, chapter 13.

26. 3 Henry VIII, chapter 3; 6 Henry VIII, chapter 13.

27. See, for example, *United States* v. *Tot,* 131 F.2d 261, 266 (3d Cir. 1942), *reversed on other grounds,* 319 U.S. 463 (1943).

28. The Alien and Sedition Laws were enacted during the administration of President John Adams, and forbade writings which would bring the government "into contempt or disrepute," as well as other criticisms of the government. U.S. Statutes at Large, Vol. I, pp. 566, 570, 577, 596 ff.

29. "[M]es la maison dun e'a luy sa castel & sa defence, & ou il proprm't doit demeur', &c." [But a man's house is his castle and his defense, and where he has an absolute right to stay.] T. 14 Hen. VII (1499) reported in 21 Henry VII 39 pl. 50 (K.B. 1506).

"Que la meason de chescun est a luy come son castle & fortres si b'n'p' son defe'ce encou'ter iniurie & viole'ce, come put son repose." [That the house of everyone is to him as his castle and fortress, as well for his defense against injury and violence as for his repose.] *Semayne's Case,* 5 Coke Rep. 91a, 91b, 77 English Rep. 194, 195 (1603).

30. The modern right of privacy is rooted in the castle doctrine. "The common law has always recognized a man's house as his castle, impregnable. . . ." Samuel D. Warren and Louis D. Brandeis, "The Right to Privacy," *Harvard Law Review* 4 (1890), p. 220. See also William Cuddihy and B. Carmon Hardy, "A Man's House Was Not His Castle: Origins of the Fourth Amendment to the United States Constitution," *William and Mary Quarterly* 3d series, 37 (1980): 371–400.

The arguments of Boston lawyer James Otis in 1761 against the Writs of Assistance (searches by British customs officials with neither probable cause nor a particularized warrant) are usually considered the foundation of the American Fourth Amendment, which protects "The right of the people to be secure in their persons, houses, papers, and effects" from unreasonable and warrantless searches. Otis began his speech by referring to the castle doctrine: "This writ is against fundamental principles of law. The privilege of the House. A man who is quiet, is as secure in his house, as a prince in his castle—notwithstanding all his debts and civil processes of any kind." Otis later returned to the theme: "A man's house is his castle, and while he is quiet, he is as well guarded as a prince in his castle." James Otis's Speech Against the Writs of Assistance, February 24, 1761, C. F. Adams, ed., *The Works of John Adams,* vol. II, p. 521 ff., reprinted in Henry Steele Commager, ed., *Documents of American History,* 5th ed. (New York: Appleton-Century-Crofts, 1949), pp. 45–46.

31. 14 Henry VIII, chapter 7 (property qualification reduced from 300 to 100 pounds); P. Hughes and Larkin, *Tudor Royal Proclamations,* vol. I (1969), p. 372 (gun law repealed in 1539).

32. *Tudor Royal Proclamations,* vol. III, p. 261, quoted in Noel Perrin, *Giving Up the Gun: Japan's Reversion to the Sword, 1543–1879* (Boston: David R. Godine, 1979), p. 59.

33. "The Bill for Cross-bows and Hand-guns," 33 Henry VIII, chapter 6 (1541):

That no perfon . . . except he or they in their own right . . . to his or their own ufes . . . have lands, tenements, fees, annuities or offices, to the yearly value of one hundred pounds . . . fhall fhoot in any crofs-bow, hand-gun, hagbut or demi-hake, or ufe to keep in his or their houfes or elfewhere, any crofs-bow, hand-guns, hagbut or demi-hake. . . ."

One of Henry's main aims was to promote ". . . the good and laudable exercise of the longe bowe, whiche always heretofore hathe bene the suertie, savegarde and contynuall defence of this Realme of Englande."

34. Perrin, pp. 59, 62.

35. Any person who witnessed a felony could raise the hue and cry. Frederick Pollock and Frederic W. Maitland, *The History of English Law before the Time of Edward I,* 2d ed. (Cambridge: Cambridge University Press, 1911; 1st pub. Cambridge, 1895), vol. II, chapter IX, § 3, pp. 578–80; Blackstone, IV, pp. *293–94; Statute of Winchester, 13 Edward I, chapter 1 and 4; Bradley Chapin, *Criminal Justice in Colonial America, 1606-1660* (Athens: University of Georgia Press, 1983), p. 31, citing Michael Dalton, *The Country Justice, Containing the Practise of Justices of the Peace out of Their Sessions* (London: 1619), p. 65, and Ferdinando Pulton, *De Pace Regis Regni Viz A Treatise declaring which be the great and generall offences of The Realme, and the chiefe impediments of the peace of The King and The Kingdom* (London: 1609), pp. 152–56.

36. Duncan Chappell and Linda P. Graham, *Police Use of Deadly Force: Canadian Perspectives* (Toronto: Centre of Criminology, 1981), pp. 42–43, citing McDonald, "Use of Force by Police to Effect Lawful Arrest," 9 *Criminal Law Quarterly* 435 (1967); Binder and Scharf, "Deadly Force in Law Enforcement," *Crime and Delinquency* 1 (1982); James Fyfe, "Observations on Police Use of Deadly Force," in James Fyfe, ed., *Readings on Police Use of Deadly Force* (Washington, D.C.: Police Foundation, 1982).

37. Joyce Malcolm, "The Right of the People to Keep and Bear Arms: The Common Law Tradition," in Donald B. Kates, Jr., ed., *Firearms and Violence: Issues of Public Policy* (Cambridge, Mass.: Ballinger, 1984), pp. 391–92, citing R. Burn, *The Justice of the Peace and Parish Officer,* 2 (London: 1775), pp. 16–20; Frederic W. Maitland, *The Constitutional History of England* (1968) (1st ed. Cambridge, 1908), pp. 276–77; J. Morril, *Cheshire, 1630–1660* (1974), p. 26; G. Trevelyan, *England Under the Stuarts* (1928), pp. 187–88. Malcolm's essay first appeared as Malcolm, "The Right to Keep and Bear Arms: The Common Law Tradition," *Hastings Constitutional Law Quarterly* 10 (1983): 285.

38. Lois G. Schwoerer, *"No Standing Armies!" The Antimilitary Ideology in Seventeenth-Century England* (Baltimore: Johns Hopkins, 1974), pp. 15–16.

39. James Harrington, *The Commonwealth of Oceana* (1656), reprinted in J. G. A. Pollock, ed., *The Political Works of James Harrington* (Cambridge: Cambridge University Press, 1977).

40. David Hardy, *Origins and Development of the Second Amendment* (Chino Valley, Ariz.: Blacksmith, 1986), p. 25.

41. Schwoerer, p. 38.

42. The poem was Milton's only contribution to the militia debate. Contrary to the claims of some of his biographers, Milton never wrote any tracts on the militia. Schwoerer, p. 40.

43. Schwoerer, pp. 41.

44. Joyce Malcolm, *Disarmed: The Loss of the Right to Bear Arms in Restoration England,* reprinted from Mary Ingraham Bunting Institute of Radcliffe College (1980), p. 11, citing Privy Council 2/55/71, Privy Council 2/55/187, and Privy Council 2/55/189; Joyce Malcolm, "The Right to Keep and Bear Arms: The Common Law Tradition," *Hastings Constitutional Law Quarterly* 10 (1983), pp. 299–300.

45. 14 Charles II, chapter 3 (1662).

46. J. H. Plumb, *The Growth of Political Stability in England 1675-1725* (London: Macmillan, 1977), p. 17; John R. Western, *The English Militia in the Eighteenth Century: The Story of a Political Issue* (London: Routledge and Kegan Paul, 1965), pp. 49, 54.

47. Plumb, p. 20, citing Grey, *Debates* (1763), p. i, 218; Western, pp. 58–61.

48. 22 & 23 Charles II, chapter 25 (1671); Malcolm, "The Right of the People," p. 404. As Blackstone later observed, game laws are sometimes enacted "for prevention of popular

insurrection and resistance to the government, by disarming the bulk of the people . . . [a] reason often meant rather than allowed by the makers of forest and game laws." Blackstone, I, p. *412.

49. Earl of Sunderland, Letter to Earl of Burlington, December 6, 1686, reprinted in *Calendar of State Papers, Domestic Series, James II,* vol II (January 1686–May 1687), p. 314, cited in David I. Caplan, "The Right of the Individual to Bear Arms: A Recent Judicial Trend," *Detroit College of Law Review* 1982 (Winter 1982), p. 798; Malcolm, pp. 21–22 and n.57.

50. *Rex* v. *Knight,* Comb. 38, 39, 87 English Reports 75 (King's Bench, 1686).

51. Some Constitutional traditions are unwritten, while others, such as the 1689 Bill of Rights, are enacted as statutes. No Constitution exists in the American sense of an integrated document that is superior to legislative enactments.

52. Bill of Rights of 1689, 1 William and Mary, sess. 2, chapter 2.

53. Ibid.

54. Plumb, p. 64. The floor debates in the House of Commons revealed a strong sense of grievance against the kings for having done "an abominable thing to disarm the nation, and set up a standing army." Phillip Hardwicke, *Miscellaneous State Papers from 1501 to 1726,* vol. II (London: 1778), pp. 401–17, discussed and quoted in Hardy, pp. 36–37.

55. Macaulay thought the "the security without which every other would have been insufficient" was "the power of the sword. . . . The legal check was secondary and auxiliary to what the community held in its own hands." Thomas B. Macaulay, *Critical and Historical Essays, Contributed to the Edinburgh Review,* 5 vols. (Leipzig: 1850), vol. I, pp. 154, 162, discussed in Malcolm, *Disarmed,* p. 1.

56. Sir John Fortescue, *The Governance of England: The Difference between an Absolute and a Limited Monarchy,* rev. ed. (1885), pp. 114–15:

"Thai [the French peasants] gon crokyd, and ben feble, not able to fight, nor to defend the realm; nor thai haue wepen, nor money to bie thaim wepen withall. But verely thai liven in the most extreme pouertie and miserie, and yet dwellyn thai in on the most fertile reaume of the worlde. Werthurgh the French kynge hath not men of his owne reaume able to defende it, except his nobles, wich beyren non such imposicions, and ther fore thai ben right likely of their bodies; bi wiich cause the said kynge is compellid to make his armeys and retinues for the defence of his lande of straungers, as Scottes, Spaynardes, Arrogoners, men of Almeyn [Germans], and of other nacions, or ellis all his enymes myght ouerrenne hym; for he hath no defence of his owne except his castels and fortresses. Lo, this is the fruit of jus reale. Yf the reaume of Englonde, wich is an Ile, and therfor mey not lyghtly geyte succore of other landes, were rulid under such a lawe, and under such a prince, it wolde then be a pray to all other nacions that wolde conquer, robbe or deuouir it. . . ."

Quoted in Hardy, p. 22.

57. "Historian Reviews English Common Law Background to U.S. Second Amendment," *Gun Week,* May 8, 1981, p. 3.

58. Schwoerer, pp. 190–91. The Declaration of Independence and the Virginia Declaration of Rights both contained paraphrases from *Cato's Letters.* George Mason, *The Papers of George Mason,* ed. Robert A. Rutland (Chapel Hill: University of North Carolina Press, 1970), vol. I, pp. 277–80. Compare, for example, Cato's "All men are born free; liberty is a Gift which they receive from God himself," with the Virginia Declaration of Rights: "That all men are born equally free and independent. . . ."

See also J. Trenchard and W. Moyle, *An Argument Showing That a Standing Army Is Inconsistent with a Free Government and Absolutely Destructive to the Constitution of the English Monarchy* (London, 1677), p. 7 ("the Sword and Sovereignty always march hand in hand").

59. "The fifth and last auxiliary right of the subject, that I shall at present mention, is that of having arms for their defence, suitable to their condition and degree, and such as are allowed by law. Which is also declared by the same statute 1 W. & M. st. 2 c. 2. and is indeed a public allowance, under due restrictions, of the natural right of resistance and self-preservation, when the sanctions of society and laws are found insufficient to restrain the violence of oppression." William Blackstone, *Commentaries on the Laws of England,* I (Chicago: University of Chicago Press, 1979) (facsimile of First Edition of 1765-1769), p. 139.

60. Blackstone, IV, p. *82.

61. Edmund S. Morgan, *Inventing the People: The Rise of Popular Sovereignty in England and America* (New York: W. W. Norton, 1989).

62. The militia in the War for Independence is discussed in chapter 9.

63. Indeed, the accusation that an enemy politician supported a standing army was a potent charge. Douglas Edward Leach, *Roots of Conflict: British Armed Forces and Colonial Americans, 1677-1763* (Chapel Hill: University of North Carolina Press, 1986), p. 4.

As Blackstone put it: "In a land of liberty, it is extremely dangerous to make a distinct order of the profession of arms. . . . Nothing then . . . ought to be more guarded against in a free state than making the military power . . . a body too distinct from the people." Blackstone, I, pp. *408, 414.

64. Malcolm, "Right to Bear Arms," pp. 408, citing *Anonymous Account of the Convention Proceedings, 1688,* folio 8, Rawlinson MSD1079, Bodleian Library, Oxford; and 10 *House of Commons Journal,* 1688-93, pp. 21-22.

65. Senate Committee on the Judiciary, Subcommittee on the Constitution, *The Right to Keep and Bear Arms,* 97th Congress, 2d session, Senate Document 2807 (Washington, D.C.: Government Printing Office, 1982), p. 6. The senators in part may have wished to avoid the implication that a large standing army was acceptable for nondefensive, overseas war.

66. J. R. Jones, *The Revolution of 1688 in England* (New York: W. W. Norton, 1972), p. 77 n.2 (2%); Malcolm, "Right to Bear Arms," pp. 394, 410; 1 William and Mary, chapter 15 (1689).

67. See, for example, Caroline Robbins, *The Eighteenth-Century Commonwealthmen: Studies in the Transmission, Development and Circumstance of English Liberal Thought From the Restoration of Charles II Until the War with the Thirteen Colonies* (Cambridge, Massachusetts: 1959).

68. For example, Joseph Story's *Commentaries* traced the Third Amendment directly to abuses by Charles I, and a violation of the principle "that a man's house shall be his own castle, privileged against all civil and military intrusion." Story, § 1003.

The Declaration of Independence had complained that King George III had "affected to render to military independent of, and superior to the civil power."

69. "No Soldier shall, in time of peace be quartered in any house, without the consent of the Owner, nor in time of war, but in a manner to be prescribed by law." Amendment III.

It should be noted that the term "regulated" meant, in the 18th century, "properly disciplined." *Oxford English Dictionary* vol. 7, (1933), p. 416. The term "discipline," in relation to arms, meant "training in the practice of arms." *Oxford English Dictionary,* vol. 3 (1933), p. 416. Therefore, a "well-regulated militia" meant a militia trained in the use of arms. See also the discussion of "well-regulated" in chapter 9.

70. Congress, not the executive, had the sole authority to create an army and to declare war. Army appropriations were limited to a term of two years. Article I, § 8.

Further, persons holding military appointments were forbidden to serve in Congress. "[N]o person holding any Office under the United States, shall be a Member of either House during his Continuance in Office." Article I, section 6. Parliament in 1659 had debated the idea that anyone holding a paying office, especially someone in the army, suffered a conflict of interest, and should be barred from the legislature as "placemen." The bar on placemen was first articulated by the Levellers, during the English Civil War. Schwoerer, pp. 69–70.

An earlier draft of the Second Amendment exempted persons "religiously scrupulous" from bearing arms in the militia. The first known proposal for conscientious objectors being exempted from military duty had been offered by the Levellers. Schwoerer, pp. 53–54. Congress dropped the religious exemption, for fear that Congress could declare huge numbers of men religiously scrupulous, and thereby decimate the militia.

71. For example, Irving Brant's study of the Bill of Rights devotes less than a page and a half to dismissing the Second Amendment and concluding it confers no individual right. Brant's entire discussion of the Congressional debate on the proposed amendment is the one-sentence quote from Gerry. Irving Brant, *The Bill of Rights, Its Origin and Meaning* (New York: Bobbs-Merrill, 1965), pp. 486–87. Other sources relying on Gerry to prove that the Second Amendment protects no individual right are Feller and Gotting, pp. 61–62, and United States Department of Justice, "Memorandum," reprinted in Hearing before Subcommittee No. 5 of the House Committee on the Judiciary, 90th Cong., 1st. sess., p. 248 (1967); Senate Report No. 1097 (April 29, 1968), printed in *U.S. Code Congressional and Administrative News,* vol. II, p. 2169 (1968).

Gerry's remarks are reprinted in Gales and Seaton, *History of Debates in Congress,* vol. I (1 Annals of Congress, 1834), p. 778; Thomas Lloyd, *The Congressional Register; or, History of the Proceedings and Debates of the First House of Representatives,* vol. II (1789 and 1790), p. 219; Bernard Schwartz, *The Bill of Rights: A Documentary History,* vol. II (New York: McGraw Hill, 1971), pp. 1107–8. The original source is *Annals of Congress,* vol. I (1789), pp. 749–50.

72. For more discussion on the original meaning of the Second Amendment, see Sanford Levinson, "The Embarrassing Second Amendment," *Yale Law Journal* 99 (December 1989): 637–59; Donald B. Kates, Jr., "Handgun Prohibition and the Original Understanding of the Second Amendment," *Michigan Law Review* 82 (1983): 203–73; Senate Subcommittee on the Judiciary, Subcommittee on the Constitution, *The Right to Keep and Bear Arms,* 97th Congress, 2d sess., Senate Doc. 2807 (Washington, D.C.: Government Printing Office, February 1982) [This document is out of print. Reprints are available from the Second Amendment Foundation, in Bellevue, Washington]. For the minority argument that the amendment protects only the National Guard, see Roy Weatherup, "Standing Armies and Armed Citizens: An Historical Analysis of the Second Amendment," *Hastings Constitutional Law Quarterly* 2 (1975): 961–1001. For more on the Second Amendment see chapter 9.

73. *United States* v. *Miller,* 307 U.S. 174, 179 (1939).

74. For the Black Act and other poaching laws, see Douglas Hay, Peter Linebaugh, John G. Rule, E. P. Thompson, Cal Winslow, *Albion's Fatal Tree: Crime and Society in Eighteenth-Century England* (London: Allen Lane, 1975).

It would not be entirely accurate, though, to think of poaching solely in terms of poor people supplementing their diet. True, the poor did poach extensively, since they considered wild game not to belong to anyone. Gentlemen also poached, and so did organized gangs which sold the meat to innkeepers who resold it to the well-off. Clive Emsley, *Crime and Society in England 1750–1900* (London: Longman, 1987), p. 3.

75. William R. Tonso, *Guns and Society: The Social and Existential Roots of the American Attachment to Firearms* (Lanham, Md.: University Press of America, 1982), p. 119 citing Howard Blackmore, *Hunting Weapons* (London: Barrie and Jenkins), p. 276.

This is not to say that Britain never produced any more great gunsmiths. In the 1830s and following decades, Joseph Whitworth greatly improved the mass production of rifles, and became the world's most distinguished tool-maker. Eric Mottram, *Blood on the Nash Ambassador* (London: Hutchinson Radius, 1989), pp. 12–13.

76. Robert W. Coakley and Stetson Conn, *The War of the American Revolution* (Washington, D.C.: Center of Military History, United States Army, 1975), p. 11.

77. S. G. Checkland, *The Rise of Industrial Society in England 1815–1885* (New York: St. Martin's Press, 1964), pp. 325–28.

78. Luddism, which began in Nottinghamshire in 1811, was a movement in which rural textile workers secretly smashed textile frames. For Luddism in general, see Frank Darvall, *Popular Disturbances and Public Disorders in Regency England* (New York: A. M. Kelley, 1969); Robert W. Reid, *Land of Lost Content: The Luddite Revolt, 1812* (London: Heinemann, 1986).

79. Checkland, p. 328.

80. The Seizure of Arms Act, 1820, 1 George IV, chapter 47. The act applied only in two cities and eleven counties that were thought most vulnerable to sedition.

81. Greenwood, *Firearms Control*, p. 14; Lee Kennett and James LaVerne Anderson, *The Gun in America: The Origins of a National Dilemma* (Westport, Conn.: Greenwood Press, 1975), pp. 31–32.

82. The homicide rate per 100,000 was about 1.5 in the 1860s, declining in a fairly stable pattern to less than 1.0 in the early twentieth century. Emsley, p. 36.

83. Quoted in Wilber Miller, *Cops and Bobbies: Police Authority in New York and London 1830–1870* (Chicago: University of Chicago Press, 1977), pp. 114–15.

84. Emsley, pp. 91–92, 131. Scotland Yard Chief Constable Frederick Porter Wensley wrote that in the Whitechapel district of London in the 1880s and 1890s, "There was an enormous amount of robbery with violence. . . . Many of the offenders carried guns and knives, which they did not hesitate to use." Quoted in Daniel P. King, "Firearms and Crime," *The Criminologist* 8, no. 28 (Spring 1973), p. 58 n.8. Wensley's assertion is in conflict with criminal statistics collected by the British police.

85. Greenwood, *Firearms Control*, p. 18. Breechloaders load from the rear of the gun, as opposed to from the muzzle. Therefore, they are usually much quicker to reload. All modern guns are breechloaders.

86. Greenwood, *Firearms Control*, p. 25. The bill was repealed in 1967, as part of a comprehensive revision of gun laws.

There were a few gun controls of little general interest during the mid-nineteenth century. For example, section 4 of the Vagrancy Act criminalized possession of an offensive weapon with intent to commit a felony.

87. Jan A. Stevenson, "Firearms Legislation in Great Britain," *Handgunner*, March-April 1988, pp. 7, 9; Yardley and Stevenson, p. 41.

88. David Cannadine, *The Pleasures of the Past* (New York: W. W. Norton, 1989), pp. 233–36. David Cannadine, *The Decline and Fall of the British Aristocracy* (New Haven: Yale University Press, 1990), pp. 364–66.

89. Cannadine, *The Pleasures of the Past*, pp. 235–36.

90. Ibid., p. 236.

91. 3 Edward VII, chapter 18 (1903).

92. Greenwood, *Firearms Control*, p. 31. As discussed below, the homicide rate rose after the Pistols Act became law, but it is impossible to attribute the rise to the law with any certainty. The effect of gun control on national suicide rates is discussed more thoroughly in the chapters on Japan and Canada.

93. Roger Andrew Lorton, "Firearms Control in England and Wales: A Review of the Legislation; Its Hopes, Aspirations and Achievements" (LL.B. dissertation, Birmingham Polytechnic, 1991), p. 12.

94. Charles Tilly, "Collective Violence in European Perspective," in Hugh Graham and Ted Robert Gurr, eds., *The History of Violence in America* (Washington, D.C.: Government Printing Office, 1969) (report of the Commission on the Causes and Prevention of Violence in America), pp. 4, 7.

95. *Boston Advertiser,* reprinted in J. W. G., "The Menace of the Pistol," 2 *American Institute of Criminal Law* 23 (1911), p. 93.

96. R. A. Steindler, *The Firearms Dictionary* (Harrisburg, Pa.: Stackpole, 1970), p. 198.

97. The "plastic gun" that generated concern in the late 1980s was the Glock pistol, which included both plastic and metal components. The metal component weighed more than a pound, and made an outline of the pistol easily visible to metal detectors and x-ray screens. Phillip McGuire, an official with the Bureau of Alcohol, Tobacco and Firearms, who would later take a job with Handgun Control, Inc., testified before Congress: "[T]here is still no evidence that we hold that a firearm intrinsically capable of passing undetected through conventional x-ray and metal detector systems exists or is feasible under any current technology immediately available to us." Testimony of Phillip C. McGuire, associate director, Office of Law Enforcement, Bureau of Alcohol, Tobacco and Firearms, before the Senate Committee on Judiciary, Subcommittee on the Constitution, July 28, 1987. At that same hearing, Raymond A. Salazar, director of civil aviation security for the Federal Aviation Administration, testified: "[W]e are aware of no current 'non-metal' firearm which is not reasonably detectable by present technology and methods in use at our airports today."

High-density, "cop-killer" bullets are also known as KTW bullets, after the initials of the three persons involved in law enforcement who invented them for use in SWAT teams. The bullets had not been available for sale to the general public since the 1960s, even though NBC television discovered them in 1982 and announced that they were a tremendous threat to police lives. The teflon coating on some bullets does nothing to make the bullet penetrate body armor any better.

98. George Dangerfield, *The Strange Death of Liberal England 1910–1914* (New York: Perigree/Putnam, 1980; 1st ed. 1935), pp. 89–91.

99. Greenwood, *Firearms Control,* p. 33.

100. *Report of the Committee on the Control of Firearms* (London, 1918), p. 2; Stevenson, p. 10; Greenwood, *Firearms Control,* p. 38. The Blackwell Committee was chaired by Sir Ernley Blackwell, Under Secretary of State for the Home Department. The committee met in secret and never published a public report. The secretary, F. J. Dryhurst, was formerly Commissioner of the Prison Service. Other members represented the Metropolitan Police, the County and Borough Police Forces, the Board of Customs, Board of Trade, the War Office, and the Irish Office.

101. Greenwood, "The British Experience," p. 31.

102. Yardley and Stevenson, pp. 42–44; Stevenson, p. 9, citing Sir Eric Geddes, Public Records Office CAB 25/20.

103. Stevenson, pp. 9–10.

104. Firearms Act, 1920, 10 & 11 George V, chapter 43.

105. Greenwood, *Firearms Control,* pp. 34–35.

106. United Kingdom, *Hansard Parliamentary Debates* (Commons), vol. 312 (May 11, 1936), cols. 167–68. The laws were consolidated in the Firearms Act, 1937, 1 Edward VIII & 1 George VI, chapter 12.

In 1934, a government taskforce, the Bodkin Committee, evaluated the efficacy of gun controls. The committee collected statistics on misuse of the guns that were not currently regulated (shotguns and airguns) and collected no statistics on the guns under control (rifles and handguns). The committee concluded that there was no persuasive case for decontrol of any guns. United Kingdom, Parliament, *Report of the Departmental Committee on the Statutory Definition and Classification of Firearms and Ammunition,* Cmd. 4758 (London: Her Majesty's Stationery Office, December 1934). [The abbreviation "Cmd." stands for "Command Paper." The abbreviation is not spelled out because the particular form of the abbreviation signifies which of the five command paper series the document belongs to.]

In later years, the Bodkin Committee report was cited as validating the efficacy of the 1920 controls. *Report of the Departmental Committee on the Statutory Definition and Classification of Firearms and Ammunition,* Cmd. 4758, December 1934. United Kingdom, Parliament, *The Control of Firearms in Great Britain: A Consultative Document,* Command 5297, Green Paper (London: Her Majesty's Stationery Office, May 1973), p. 3 (misciting Bodkin); Jane Fiddick, "Control of Firearms," Background Paper no. 207, House of Commons Library Research Division, January 20, 1988, p. 2 (misciting Bodkin); Stevenson, p. 17.

107. "The firearms and ammunition to which this certificate relates must at all times when not in actual use be kept in a secure place with a view to preventing access to them by unauthorized persons." Breach of the provision is now punishable by a fine of up to 2,000 pounds and six months in jail. Greenwood, "Firearms Security," p. 39.

In one case, a person traveling from a range to his home left ammunition in a locked car for an hour. When the ammunition was stolen, the man was convicted of not keeping the ammunition in a secure place. *Marsh* v. *Chief Constable of Avon and Somerset, Independent,* May 8, 1987, discussed in Fiddick, p. 8.

108. Advertisement, *American Rifleman,* November 1940. The full ad:

SEND A GUN TO DEFEND A BRITISH HOME.

British civilians, faced with the threat of invasion, desperately need arms for the defense of their homes. The American Committee for Defense of British Homes has organized to collect gifts of pistols, rifles, revolvers, shotguns, binoculars from American civilians who wish to answer the call and aid in the defense of British homes. These arms are being shipped, with the consent of the British Government, to Civilian Committee for Protection of Homes, Birmingham, England[.] The members of which are Wickham Steed, Edward Hulton, and Lord Davies. You can aid by sending any arms or binoculars you can spare to American Committee for the Defense of British Homes, C. Suydan Cutting, *Chairman* Room 100, 10 Warren Street, New York, N.Y.

Also, Duncan Long, *Streetsweepers: The Complete Book of Combat Shotguns* (Boulder, Colo.: Paladin, 1987), p. 6 (availability of shotguns).

109. Yardley and Stevenson, p. 69; Edwards, "The Disarmament of Great Britain," *American Rifleman,* January 1988, pp. 36–37; Neal Knox, "Britain's Crime Rate Soars," *Gun Week,* December 30, 1966, p. 4.

The firm of Greenwald and Haughton, under contract from the United States government, offered to buy "all automatic pistols from .22 cal. to .45 cal." and all revolvers of size .38 or larger to give to an allied nation in order "to perforate a parasite." Advertisements in *The American Rifleman,* August 1943, p. 50; February 1944, p. 50.

110. Winston S. Churchill, *The Second World War,* vol. II, "Their Finest Hour" (Boston: Houghton Mifflin, 1949), pp. 237–38. Approximately one million guns were eventually donated.

111. Home Secretary Sir John Simon had explained the ban by calling the Thompson "the weapon we are informed is used by gangsters on the other side of the water." United Kingdom, *Hansard Parliamentary Debates* (Commons), vol. 312 (May 11, 1936), col. 168.

112. Representative William G. Bray, "Guns and Gun Laws—Fact and Fancy," *Con-*

gressional Record, July 18, 1968; Duncan Long, *Assault Pistols, Rifles and Submachineguns* (Boulder, Colo.: Paladin, 1986), pp. 35, 43.

113. London Public Records Office, H.O. 45, 21888; Bray; Tonso, p. 125.

114. The Murder (Abolition of Death Penalty) Act 1965, 1965, chapter 71. The act still allowed the death penalty for high treason and for piracy with violence.

115. Commissioner of Police of the Metropolis (Scotland Yard), letter to *Harvard Law Review,* November 9, 1966, quoted in Stanley Mosk, "Gun Control Legislation: Valid and Necessary," *New York Law Forum* 14, no. 4 (Winter 1968), p. 709, n.54.

116. Stevenson, p. 19.

117. Barry Bruce-Briggs, "The Great American Gun War," *The Public Interest* 45 (Fall 1976): 60–61; Greenwood, "Does Legislation Reduce Armed Crime?"; *Daily Telegraph,* September 13, 1966, quoted in Yardley and Stevenson, pp. 58–59. Jenkins noted that "criminal use of shotguns is increasing rapidly, still more rapidly than that of other weapons." The increase in shotgun crimes involved mostly poaching or property damage, rather than armed robberies or murders.

118. Criminal Justice Act 1967, Part V. The 1967 law was consolidated with previous firearms laws into the Firearms Act, 1968, 16 & 17 Elizabeth II, Chapter 27.

119. 18 United States Code § 921 et seq.

120. Yardley and Stevenson, p. 59. See pages 98–106 for more on the relationship between gun controls and other erosions of civil liberties.

121. Firearms Act 1968, § 28; Sapsted, "Control of shotguns farcical, say police," *The Times,* July 10, 1987.

122. "£ and no questions asked," *The Mail* (London), September 2, 1984. Some police forces, such as West Midlands or Merseyside, conduct thorough investigations and require personal interviews even for renewals; others, such as North Wales, move more rapidly. "Police Lack Resources to Make Checks for Licenses," (London) *Sunday Times,* August 23, 1987, p. 14.

123. "Statistics on the Operations of the Firearms Act 1968 England and Wales 1988," p. 3.

124. Firearms Act 1968, § 2; "Ninja gun gangs are invading Britain—MP," *London Standard,* May 29, 1986, p. 15.

125. Firearms Act 1968, § 2; Home Office, *Firearms: What You Need to Know About the Law* (1984), p. 2.

126. Firearms Act 1968, § 27(1); Imitation firearms require a license if they are "readily convertible" into firing mode. Firearms Act 1982, chapter 31, § 1. Automatic weapons, which fire continuously with one trigger squeeze, are completely illegal. Ibid.

British felons sentenced to a term of three or more years are permanently barred from owning firearms (rifles and pistols). People sentenced to terms of three months to three years face a five-year prohibition. Firearms Act 1968, § 21; Tony Jackson, *Legitimate Pursuit: The Case for the Sporting Gun* (Southampton: Ashford Press, 1988) (published in association with the British Association for Shooting and Conservation), p. 40. Americans convicted of a violent felony are usually barred from gun possession for the rest of their lives.

A "handgun" includes a revolver that is propelled by carbon dioxide. Firearms Act 1968, §§ 1(1), 57(4).

The maximum penalty for possession of an unlicensed firearm is three years in prison. Firearms Act 1968, § 51(1)(2) and Schedule 6, Part I.

127. *Greenly* v. *Lawrence,* [1949] 1 All England Law Reports 241, 47 L.G.R. 87, 65 Times Law Reports 86, 113 Justice of the Peace 120 (King's Bench Division, 1949) (upholding lower court's reversal of denial of application to renew firearms certificate for re-

volver possessed for self-defense); Fiddick, p. 3; Green Paper, p. 15; Godfrey Sandys-Winch, *Gun Law,* 5th ed. (London: Shaw and Sons, 1990), p. 30. The certificate costs 33 pounds.

128. Firearms Act (1968), § 5(b): "any weapon of whatever description designed or adapted for the discharge of any noxious liquid, gas or other thing." *Regina* v. *Bradish, Law Society's Gazette* 86, no. 45 (December 13, 1989), p. 35 (CS gas canister); *Flack* v. *Baldry* [1988] 1 All England Law Reports 673, 87 Criminal Appeal Reports 130 (electric stun device).

129. Cowper, "Massacre in a Market Town," *New York Law Journal,* October 5, 1987, p. 2.

130. Firearms Act 1968, § 27(2); Firearms (Amendment) Act 1988 §§ 9, 21(5); Sandys-Winch, p. 31; Greenwood, "Does Legislation Reduce Armed Crime?"

131. Firearms Act 1968; Jackson, p. 40.

132. Firearms Act 1968, § 27(2).

133. Firearms Rules 1989, Rule 3(4) and Schedule I, Part II; Jackson, p. 42.

134. Lorton, p. 143; Greenwood, "Firearms Security," p. 40.

135. Yardley and Stevenson, p. 19; Jackson, pp. 42–43; Greenwood, "Firearms Security," pp. 39–40.

136. Yardley and Stevenson, p. 29.

137. Cadmus, "Territorial Conditions," *Guns Review,* January 1979, p. 38.

138. "Police Lack Resources to Make Checks for Licenses," (London) *Sunday Times,* August 23, 1987, p. 14; Colin Greenwood, letter to author, November 24, 1989; Brian Hughes, Director for Firearms and External Services, British Association for Shooting and Conservation, Member of Firearms Consultative Committee, letter to author, November 27, 1989.

139. *Regina* v. *Bradish,* [1990] All England Law Reports 460, 1990 2 Weekly Law Reports 223, 90 Criminal Appeal Reports 271, 154 Justice of the Peace 21 (1989) (no defense that defendant did not know nor reasonably should have know that canister he possessed contained CS gas); *Regina* v. *Hussain,* [1981] 2 All England Law Reports, [1981] 1 Weekly Law Reports 416, 72 Criminal Appeal Reports 143, 146 Justice of the Peace 23 (1980) (defendant possessed an 8-inch metal tube with a striker pin activated by a spring, capable of firing .32 cartridges; he did not know it was a firearm); *Regina* v. *Howells* [1977] Queen's Bench 614, [1977] 3 All England Law Reports 417, [1977] 2 Weekly Law Reports 716, 65 Criminal Appeal Reports 86, 141 Justice of the Peace 641 (1977) (defendant bought modern replica of antique revolver, which he thought to be genuine, and hence exempt from Firearms Act; whether defendant's mistake was honest and reasonable was irrelevant to his criminal liability).

Not all gun laws are based on strict liability. A person may prove his innocence of possessing a convertible imitation firearm by proving that he did not know the firearm was readily convertible. Firearms Act 1982, § 1(5).

140. *Kavanagh* v. *Chief Constable of Devon and Cornwall,* [1974] Queen's Bench 624, [1974] 2 All England Law Reports 697, [1974] 2 Weekly Law Reports 762, 138 Justice of the Peace 618 (Court of Appeal, Civil Division, 1974) (firearms dealer registration).

141. Peter H. Burton, "Firearms Licensing," *Law Society's Guardian Gazette* 87, no. 19 (May 23, 1990), p. 27.

142. *Regina* v. *McRae,* 9 Criminal Appeal Reports (S) 308, [1987] Criminal Law Report 65 (18 months; defendant had taken sawed-off shotgun from friends of his former wife who had threatened him; defendant buried gun, and dug it up when threats were made against him); *Regina* v. *Cook,* 9 Criminal Appeal Reports (S) 71 (1987) (15 months, sawed-off shotgun); *Regina* v. *Jeffries,* 9 Criminal Appeal Report (S) 497 (1987) (sawed-off shotgun, 4-year sentence reduced to 2); *Regina* v. *Lee,* 8 Criminal Appeal Reports (S) 469 (1986) (sawed-off shotgun, 30-month sentence reduced to 12); *Regina* v. *Gibbons,* 6 Criminal Appeal Reports (S) 341 (1984) (sawed-off shotgun, 2 years); *Regina* v. *Fegan,* 78 Criminal Appeal

Reports 189 (Northern Ireland, 1971) (2 years, handgun); *Note of Appeal Against Sentence (Summary) Wagstaff* v. *Wilson,* 1989 S.C.C.R. 322 (High Court of Justiciary, 1989) (shotgun, £500 fine for defendant whose sole income was social security).

143. One reason that shotguns may be considered the gun of the gentry is that it was illegal for many years for persons with an income under £100 to possess shot, although the prohibition was widely flouted. "An Act against the Shooting of Hail Shot," 2 & 3 Edward VI, chapter 14 (1549), repealed by 6 & 7 William III, chapter 13 (1695).

144. The police may add extra conditions, in addition to those specified by law, to a rifle or handgun certificate, but may not do so to a shotgun certificate. Firearms Act 1968, § 28(2)(a); Firearms Rules 1989, Rules 4(4), 5 and Schedule 2, Part II.

145. Firearms Act 1968, § 19. The carrying of the rifle or handgun must be in conjunction with carrying of matching ammunition. Ibid.

146. Tony Lesce, *The Shotgun in Combat* (Boulder, Colo.: Paladin, 1984).

147. "At close range, the shotgun is the most formidable and destructive of all arms. . . . Unlike bullets, shotgun pellets rarely exit the body. Therefore, the kinetic energy of wounding in shotguns is usually equal to the striking energy . . . all the kinetic energy is transferred to the body as wounding effects." Vincent J. M. DiMaio, *Gunshot Wounds: Practical Aspects of Firearms, Ballistics, and Forensic Techniques* (New York: Elsevier, 1985), pp. 182–83.

"The wound created when the charge of a standard shotgun strikes a victim within a range of 6 meters is characterized by tissue destruction not unlike that caused by high-velocity missiles. Massive soft-tissue loss, bone and vessel disruption, and a high infection rate result." Gary Ordog, "Wound Ballistics" in Gary J. Ordog, ed., *Management of Gunshot Wounds* (New York: Elsevier, 1988), p. 45.

"Shotgun injuries have not been compared with other bullet wounds of the abdomen as they are a thing apart . . . [A]t close range, they are as deadly as a cannon." R. Taylor, "Gunshot Wounds of the Abdomen," *Annals of Surgery* 177 (1973), pp. 174–75.

148. "British Gun Laws Could Become Tougher," p. 1. Sporting clays, a variant of trap and skeet shooting, has grown quite popular with the middle class in recent years, perhaps because the shooters are trying to "recapture some of the atmosphere in aristocratic country life." Hunnicutt, "Sporting Clays: The Newest Shotgun Challenge," *American Rifleman,* January 1988, pp. 26, 28.

149. Jackson, p. 14.

150. Ibid.

151. Because wounding the other side is now the preferred goal, international law bars the use of hollow-point bullets in warfare. Round-nosed bullets are better for wounding and not killing since they may enter and exit in a straight, narrow path. Chapters 3 (notes 176–77 and accompanying text) and 5 discuss the controversial hollow-point bullet in more detail.

152. DiMaio, p. 145.

153. Jackson, p. 19.

154. Ibid., p. 36. The larger red deer of the Scottish Highlands has been considered desirable game for over 150 years. Colin Greenwood, letter to author, November 24, 1989; Lord Swansea, letter to author, December 21, 1989. Technically, deer are not included within the legal British definition of "game." Sandys-Winch, p. 66.

155. Jackson, p. 15.

156. Ibid., p. 26.

157. Colin Greenwood, letter to author, November 24, 1989.

158. Proceedings in Parliament 1610, I, p. 51, quoted in Morgan, p. 23.

159. Jackson, pp. 27–28.

160. Kennett and Anderson, p. 107.

161. Jackson, p. 75; Lord Swansea, letter to author, December 21, 1989.
Even today, "Shooting by the Royal Family and Her Majesty's gamekeepers" is exempt from the licensing requirements. G.L.A. 1860, § 5.

162. "Hunting" in Britain refers only to the pursuit of foxes, deer, otter, hare, or mink (originally imported from North America) with hounds. Oscar Wilde described the sport as "the unspeakable in full pursuit of the uneatable." "Shooting" refers to bird hunting and to target sports. "Stalking" refers to humans (without dogs) searching for animals to shoot. In American English, "hunting" is the equivalent of British English's "stalking." British-style "hunting" (with hounds) hardly exists in the United States. See generally, James Barrington, Executive Director, League Against Cruel Sports, "The Sport of Kings," *Animals' Voice* 2, no. 6 (December 1989), p. 49.

163. Lord Swansea, Letter to author, December 21, 1989. There is still some social status involved in gun sports. The best college clubs, such as Carlton and Brooks, have many more shooters per capita than the general population. T. H. Pear, *English Social Differences* 255 (London: George Allen and Unwin, 1978), p. 255, cited in Tonso, p. 116.

164. Jackson, p. 84. Labour would also outlaw hunting with hounds. K. L. Slee, "The Animal Welfare Debate," *New Zealand Wildlife* (Summer 1989), p. 32.

165. *The Control of Firearms in Great Britain: A Consultative Document,* Green Paper, Command 5297 (London: Her Majesty's Stationery Office, May 1973) [hereinafter "Green Paper"]. The committee was chaired by Sir John McKay, chief inspector of Constabulary for England and Wales. Other members were from the police, the Home Office, and the Scottish Office, although their identity has never been revealed. Stevenson, p. 21.

166. In 1973, members of Parliament sent 1,174 suggestions for improvement in the proposed bill to the Home Office, and 4,573 members of the public wrote to the Home Office to oppose all or part of the bill. Lorton, pp. 52, 57.

167. Richard Harding, "Firearms Use in Crime," *Criminal Law Review* 18 (1979), p. 772.

168. Colin Greenwood, "The Sun Sets on British Gun Owners," *American Rifleman,* May 1989, p. 26.

169. *Police Review,* October 8, 1982, quoted in Stevenson, p. 21.

170. Green Paper, p. 25; Yardley and Stevenson, p. 62. The abolition of gun collecting as a legitimate reason for gun ownership was also implemented without legal authority. See below.

171. On December 31, 1968, there were 216,300 firearms (rifle and handgun) certificates on file. In 1988, there were 155,000. In 1968 there were 715,500 shotgun certificates, and in 1988 there were 882,000. Home Office, "Statistics on the Operation of the Firearms Act 1968, England and Wales, 1988" (Croydon: Government Statistical Service, 1989), table 1 & 3.

172. Firearms Act 1982, Elizabeth II, 1982, chapter 31; "Carry on Squirting," *New Law Journal* 133 (1983), p. 989.

173. Green Paper, pp. 38–39; Yardley and Stevenson, p. 65; Stevenson, p. 23.

174. "New Animals Laws Success 'Helped By TV Series,'" Oregon University News Services Ltd., July 14, 1987, available in NEXIS.

175. Sapsted; Tuohy, p. 1.

176. "Ninja gun gangs are invading Britain—MP," *London Standard,* May 29, 1986, p. 15.

177. "New Zealand Eases Firearms Restrictions," *Gun Week,* September 7, 1984.

178. Sapsted.

179. Harding, p. 765 n.7. The winning candidate, a Liberal, became one of the most

trenchant opponents of more controls. See also, Schneider, "British Anti-Gunners Still Pushing, Still Misleading," *Gun Week,* January 6, 1982, p. 4.

180. Jackson, p. 53; "Lucky Iain Bags a Stag," *Sporting Gun,* November 1889, p. 5 (100,000th member); Hughes letter. The British Association for Shooting and Conservation was until 1981 known as the Wildfowlers Association of Great Britain and Ireland; some critics contend that the BASC places the interests of bird hunters ahead of the interests of other shooters or stalkers. "WAGBI: The Face Behind BASC's Mask," *Guns Review,* September 1990, p. 660.

181. The phrase "gun lobby" in Britain is an epithet applied by the press. Americans are used to having a lobby to support their favorite cause—as in the "public employees lobby" or the "pro-choice lobby" or the "farm lobby." In Britain, where citizen activism is not such an honored tradition, the phrase "gun lobby" creates a negative connotation. For simplicity of usage, the chapter uses the common term "gun lobby," but without making any judgment about the social value of the lobby.

Members of the BSSC are the National Rifle Association (no relation to the U.S. group with the same name), concerned with competitive shooting of center-fire rifles and pistols; the National Small-Bore Rifle Association, concerned with small-bore competitive shooting; the Clay Pigeon Shooting Association; the National Pistol Association, which is gradually taking control of pistol shooting from the NRA and NSRA; the U.K. Practical Shooting Association, concerned with practical or action rifle and pistol shooting; the Muzzle Loaders Association of Great Britain; the BASC, concerned with game shooting; the British Field Sports Society, concerned with all outdoor field sports, including hunting and fishing; the Gun Trade Association, for all registered gun dealers; and the Shooting Sports Trust, a gun dealer organization devoted mainly to fighting more gun control. Lord Swansea, letter of December 21, 1989.

182. "A license to kill," *The Mail* (London), September 2, 1984.

183. Greenwood, "Does Legislation Reduce Armed Crime?"; Hughes letter; Lord Swansea, letter of December 21, 1989.

184. Malcolm P. I. Weller, "The Anatomy of Violence—Part I," *New Law Journal* 137, no. 6322 (September 11, 1987), p. 858; Cowper; Greenwood, "The British Experience," p. 33; Greenwood, "The Sun Sets," p. 27.

185. Jackson, p. 48.

186. Woody Haut, "Hysteria, the Free Market, and the Hungerford Massacre," *Rolling Stock,* no. 14 (1987), p. 15.

187. Jackson, pp. 92, 99, quoting *Daily Telegraph, Daily Mirror, Daily Express, Yorkshire Evening Press.*

The British press, like the American press, had difficulty telling the difference between automatics and semi-automatics, and failed to realize that automatics were already banned. E.g., "Gun Law," *New Law Journal* 137, no. 6320 (August 28, 1987), p. 799 ("M1 carbine or other automatics"). The press was not, however, monolithic. Auberon Waugh wrote:

"One trouble with government by crackdown, as Douglas Hurd's measures against sporting shotguns showed, is that it leaves us with a welter of fatuous and oppressive legislation on the statute books long after the original frenzy has subsided. Another is that it gives an already unruly police force conceited ideas about its status and function in society."

Auberon Waugh, *Daily Telegraph,* May 27, 1990, quoted in Lorton, p. 76.

188. Raines, "A Second Mass Killing in Britain Raises Call for Tighter Gun Laws," *New York Times,* October 16, 1987.

189. "Firearms Act 1968: Proposals for Reform" (1987); Greenwood, "The Sun Sets," p. 68.

190. "After Hungerford," *New Law Journal* 137, no. 6321 (September 4, 1987), p. 823. The ban was upheld in *Regina* v. *Commissioner of Police for the Metropolis ex parte Swann,* CO/1540/87 (Transcript: Martin Walsh Cherer) (Queen's Bench Division, Crown Office List, February 15, 1988).

191. Jackson, p. 48. Among the proposals revived from the Green Paper were a ban on self-loading and pump-action firearms, greater police discretion over shotgun licensees, and ammunition controls on shotguns. Green Paper, pp. 13, 20, 28.

192. Jackson, pp. 48–49.

193. Ibid., p. 49.

194. Ibid., p. 79; Colin Greenwood, letter to author, November 24, 1989.

195. House of Commons Debate 120, c. 67, quoted in Fiddick, p. 21.

196. Greenwood, "The Sun Sets," p. 68. Interestingly, in 1975 Secretary Hurd had been fined five pounds for possessing two shotguns without a certificate. Jackson, p. 97, quoting Auberon Waugh, *Sunday Telegraph.* For analysis placing the 1988 act in the context of the British government's historical efforts to maintain a monopoly on force, see R. A. I. Munday, "The Monopoly of Power," paper presented at the annual meeting of the American Society of Criminology, San Francisco, Calif., November 23, 1991.

197. British Shooting Sports Council, press release, November 18, 1987, quoted in Fiddick, p. 26; Greenwood, "The Sun Sets," p. 68; Lord Swansea, letter of December 21, 1989.

198. Jackson, p. 74.

199. Ibid., p. 83, quoting John Hopkinson, Director of British Field Sports Society.

200. Advertisement, *Sporting Gun,* November 1989, p. 35.

201. Opponents of the ban had argued for a special exemption for disabled people, since semi-automatics have low recoil, and are hence easier for persons with less upper body strength to shoot. One pro-control lord replied that a handicapped person "would probably have a harder job to hold on to the rifle than an able bodied person if someone wanted to steal it." Lord Atlee worried about the possibility of "a disabled person who was also mentally unstable." House of Lords, *Official Report,* October 19, 1988, cols. 1134, 1131.

202. Capt. Bruce Breckenridge, "A Shooting Sport is Dead," *Australian Gunsports,* Summer 1990, p. 60.

203. Firearms (Amendment) Act 1988 § 2(1) and (2). Semi-automatic shotguns constitute about one-tenth of all British shotguns. Yardley and Stevenson, p. 15.

204. Firearms Rules 1989, Rules 3(2), 4(1)-(3), 5, 6, 7; Schedule 1, Schedule 2, Part I, all cited in Sandys-Winch, p. 29. See also George Wallace, Firearms Officer BASC, "Countersignatory Rears Ugly Head," *Shooting Times and Country Magazine,* October 12–18, 1989, p. 8. A somewhat weaker countersignature requirement had already been in force for shotguns. Fiddick, p. 10. That requirement had been imposed by the police without statutory authority. A 1984 Police/Home Office working party found the countersignature useless, and advised abolition. Cadmus, "Conspiracy to Disarm," *Guns Review* 4 December 1991, p. 926.

205. Cadmus, "Good Reason Abuse," *Guns Review,* November 1989: 862–63; Greenwood, "The Sun Sets," p. 69. A police decision regarding good reason will not be overturned by the courts unless it is arbitrary and capricious. *Hutcgusib* v. *Chief Constable of Grampian,* 1977 S.L.T. 98 (Sheriff Ct.). Home Office guidance states that the good reason language for shotguns "does NOT require the applicant to make out a good case for being granted a certificate but rather extends the chief officer's ground for refusing one." *Firearms Law— Guidance to Police,* para. 7.6, quoted in Lorton, p. 72.

206. Greenwood, "The Sun Sets," p. 69.

207. Jackson, p. 84.

208. Frances Cowper, "London's Parallel to the Goetz Case," *New York Law Journal,* October 30, 1987, p. 2.

209. Seumus Milne, "No Police Questions in Knives Amnesty," *The Guardian,* February 10, 1988, p. 2.

210. Criminal Justice Act 1988, 1988 chapter 33, § 139; Gilbert A. Lewthwaite, "Britain's Conservative Party Hopes to Outlaw Knife-carrying in Anti-crime Drive," *The Sun,* October 8, 1987, p. 25. See also Gail Tabor, "British Justice 'A Travesty,' Arizona Won't Visit Again," *Arizona Republic,* November 10, 1991, pp. B1, B6. (American female tourist given suspended prison sentence for using a penknife against men who attacked her in subway; possession of penknife not illegal, but intent to use penknife for self-defense creates illegal "possession of an offensive weapon.")

211. Criminal Justice Act 1988 (Offensive Weapons) Order 1988 (barring sale or transfer of swordsticks and of martial arts weapons).

212. One pollster asked if respondents agreed that "[r]equiring all handgun owners to be licensed is a good idea because it will defuse the pressure for total gun control." Seventeen percent strongly agreed; 30 percent agreed; 24 percent disagreed; 9 percent strongly disagreed; and 24 percent were unsure. Cambridge Research Associates, *An Analysis of Public Attitudes Towards Gun Control* (prepared for The Center for the Study and Prevention of Handgun Violence, June 1978), p. B17.

213. Firearms account for about 8 percent of British homicides (and about 65 percent of American ones). Statistical Department, Home Office, "Notifiable Offenses Recorded by the Police in England and Wales," *Home Office Statistics Bulletin* (Issue 20/89), June 21, 1989, pp. 5-6; Jackson, pp. 92-93, quoting Lin Jenkins, "Hurd's Gun Law," *Daily Telegraph,* September 23, 1987.

214. E.g., "Rampage Leaves 1 Dead, 14 Hurt in British Town," *Rocky Mountain News* (Associated Press), May 1, 1989, p. 33; "British Gunman Kills 1, Injures 14," *USA Today,* May 1, 1989, p. 4A. (The man used a shotgun.)

215. Gallup Poll from 1988 discussed in R. A. I. Munday, "On Liberty" (unpublished essay).

216. Home Office, "Gun Clubs: Home Secretary Plans New Controls" (press release), November 14, 1989; Cadmus, "From All Sides at Once," *Guns Review,* January 1991, p. 36. The restrictions apply to new clubs, which must be authorized by the Home Office.

217. Cadmus, "From All Sides At Once," *Guns Review,* January 1991, p. 36.

218. "International Briefs," *Animals' Agenda,* December 1989, p. 29.

219. Brian MacArthur, "Editors Take the Lead over Dangerous Dogs," (London) *Sunday Times,* May 6, 1990. One British columnist calls mainstream society "hysterical" and "pompous" for its habit of "happily raving about shotguns and rottweilers and drugs." Libby Purvis, "We Grown-ups Just Hate the Young to Party," *The Sunday Express,* October 22, 1989, p. 15.

220. "Thatcher's Majority Going to the Dogs: Pooch Registration Proposal Unleashed Opposition in Britain," *Rocky Mountain News,* October 31, 1990, p. 21 (Associated Press).

221. Firearms Act 1968, § 24.

222. Cadmus, "A War of Attrition," *Guns Review,* November 1990, p. 803; "Bleeding to Death," *Guns Review,* January 1992, p. 11.

223. Jackson, p. 94.

224. With the 1989 advent of the "assault rifle" as a major gun-control issue, the National Coalition to Ban Handguns changed its name to the Coalition to Stop Gun Violence. In 1977, an official with the National Coalition to Ban Handguns had been asked why her group did not attempt to ban all guns. She responded, "We didn't go after the long gun

because we don't want all those hunters on our back." Alan Gottlieb, *The Gun Grabbers* (Bellevue, Wash.: Bobbs Merrill, 1986), p. 68.

Handgun Control, Inc., Founding Chair Pete Shields explained his strategy for prohibition: "The first problem is to slow down the number of handguns being produced and sold in this country. The second problem is to get handguns registered. The final problem is to make possession of all handguns and all handgun ammunition—except for the military, police, licensed security guards, licensed sporting clubs, and licensed gun collectors—totally illegal." Richard Harris, "A Reporter at Large: Handguns," *New Yorker,* July 26, 1976, p. 58.

Handgun Control, Inc., has opposed change in the laws in Chicago and Washington, D.C., which prohibit the lawful acquisition of handguns. District of Columbia Code §§ 6-2132(4) and 6-2372. The group claims, however, that it does not support handgun prohibition; and in fact, the group does not at present actively campaign for national prohibition.

Pete Shields's book promises "our organization, Handgun Control, Inc., does not propose further controls on rifles and shotguns. Rifle and shotguns are not the problem; they are not *concealable.*" Pete Shields, *Guns Don't Die—People Do* (New York: Priam, 1981), pp. 47–48. But when long-gun restrictions became politically viable, Handgun Control, Inc., led a nationwide campaign to outlaw semi-automatic rifles and shotguns, even though such guns are difficult to conceal. The group has also successfully lobbied California to place a fifteen-day waiting period and police background check on transfers of traditional hunting rifles and shotguns.

Former New York City Police Commissioner Patrick Murphy explained that his goal of complete civilian disarmament cannot be accomplished all at once: ". . . it will be a gradual thing, to reduce the number of guns in the hands of criminals when private citizens will see the wisdom of a national policy of disarmament of the citizens." Patrick Murphy, Congressional Hearings on the "Saturday Night Special," *Congressional Record,* S. 2507, September 1971. In 1976, Massachusetts voters defeated a proposal to confiscate all handguns. One advocate of gun prohibition thought the all-at-once strategy a mistake: "In 1976, we went for everything. We weren't content to go step-by-step and take what we could get." Sheriff John Buckley, Middlesex County, Massachusetts, speech to United States Conference of Mayors, Washington, D.C., September 13, 1979, quoted in "USCM Conference Revealing," NRA/ICA, *Reports from Washington* 6, no. 14 (October 22, 1979), p. 6.

Gun registration in itself may seem innocuous. But when President Carter advocated national gun registration, and at the same time nominated a director of the Law Enforcement Assistance Administration who said "We seek a disarmed populace," it should not have been surprising that the National Rifle Association was able to convince millions of gun owners to petition Congress to reject the nominee and defund the registration program. The nominee was Norval Morris, who presented his disarmament strategy in Norval Morris and Gordon Hawkins, *The Honest Politician's Guide to Crime Control* (Chicago: University of Chicago Press, 1970), p. 69. Morris also suggested: "We require portable and discriminatory monitors capable of secretly searching anyone passing through a door or along a pathway to ascertain if he carries a concealed gun. There are surely no 1984 fears in this. There can be no right of privacy in regard to armament." Ibid. See chapter 2, note 216, for more American advocacy of complete gun prohibition.

225. Greenwood, *Firearms Control,* pp. 227–29. Greenwood calculated 36,000 man-hours for the police, and 19,000 for the clerks. The conversion of man-hours into man-years assumes that an average police officer or clerk works something less than 2,000 hours per year.

226. Lord Swansea, House of Lords debate, discussed in Peter H. Burton, "Firearms Licensing," *Law Society's Guardian Gazette* 87, no. 19 (May 23, 1990), p. 27. Issuing a

firearms certificate takes approximately 145 minutes of police time. A shotgun certificate used to take 45 minutes, but this time may well increase now that shotgun applicants must be investigated to see if they have a "good reason" for wanting a gun. Fiddick, pp. 5–6, 11. Much of the police time spent on enforcement involves use of a gun in a crime, and would therefore have to be expended even if there were no gun controls.

227. Greenwood, *Firearms Control,* pp. 246–47. A review of New York City newspapers for a fifteen-year period found no case in which a firearm traced by serial number was even relevant to the prosecution. Alan S. Krug, *Does Firearms Registration Work? A Statistical Analysis of New York State and New York City Crime Data* (Riverside, Conn.: National Shooting Sports Foundation, 1968), p. 28.

As will be detailed in subsequent chapters, a police review of registration in the Australian state of Victoria also indicated that registration is of no value. New Zealand's police successfully urged their government to abolish gun registration, because it wasted their time.

228. Lorton, pp. 80–81.

229. Ibid., p. i. Happily, the lack of research regarding the history of the right to bear arms in Great Britain will be remedied by the forthcoming publication of American scholar Joyce Malcolm's "Arms for Their Defense: The Orgin of an Anglo-American Right."

230. Greenwood, *Firearms Control,* pp. 236–37.

231. Burton; Yardley and Stevenson, p. 74.

232. Currah, "The Rush for Fake Guns in Britain," *San Francisco Chronicle and Examiner,* July 15, 1979; Dobson and House, *Sunday Telegraph,* December 17, 1978; Birch, "An Englishman's View of Gun Control," *Guns and Ammo,* December 1981, pp. 31, 32 (citing discussion with police sergeant). Others argue that the amount of illegal weapons exceeds the amount of legal ones. Yardley and Stevenson, p. 26.

233. Yardley and Stevenson, pp. 28–89.

234. Greenwood, *Firearms Control,* p. 242.

235. Colin Greenwood, "Armed Crime—A Declaration of War," *Security Gazette,* June 1983.

236. Cadmus, "A War of Attrition," *Guns Review,* November 1990, p. 804.

237. Malcolm, "The Right of the People," p. 294.

238. About 15,000 British guns are stolen annually. Home Office Ministers have repeatedly said that there is little evidence that legally registered guns are ever used in crime. Lord Swansea, letter to author, February 22, 1988, p. 3.

239. "The Rush for Fake Guns." Decades ago, a former Scotland Yard superintendent stated that illegal handguns could be purchased in London for the equivalent of twelve U.S. dollars. R. Fabian, *London After Dark* (1954), p. 116, cited in David T. Hardy and John Stompoly, "Of Arms and the Law," *Chicago-Kent Law Review* 51 (1974), p. 100.

240. Jackson, p. 44; Greenwood, "Armed Crime." The incidence of criminal misuse of guns increased from 1,734 in 1971 to 8,067 in 1981. "British Police Take Up Arms," *The Sun* (Baltimore), April 7, 1983. The statistics, supplied by the Home Office, may exaggerate the seriousness of gun crime, since they include relatively less serious offenses, as well as violent felonies. About two-thirds of the incidents involve children playing with low-powered airguns, the breaking of windows, or a similarly low threat type of offense. Greenwood, "Armed Crime."

241. Greenwood, *Firearms Control,* p. 160.

242. See note 240 for raw figures. During the same period, criminal misuse in the United States rose 36 percent.

243. Harding, "Firearms Use in Crime," p. 765.

244. Handguns are employed three times as often as sawed-off shotguns, and slightly

more often than shotguns as a whole. Home Office, Criminal Statistics 1986, 53, tables 3.5, 3.7, cited in, Yardley and Stevenson, p. 14. As in the United States, rifles are hardly ever used in crime.

245. Greenwood, *Firearms Control*, p. 244.

246. Gurr, p. 31. "Murder Rate Doubles over Past Fifteen Years," *New Scientist*, January 8, 1976. Also, "London Killings Increase," *Los Angeles Times*, June 2, 1980.

247. In 1902, there were 181 murders, 21 by gun (12 percent). In 1904, after the enactment of the Pistols Act, there were 208 murders, 15 by gun (7 percent). Greenwood, *Firearms Control*, p. 31.

248. Downie, "Britain, With Tight Gun Control, Is Exasperated by Laxness in U.S.," *Washington Post*, April 5, 1981, p. A17.

249. Lorton, p. 85.

250. Erwin Stengel, *Suicide and Attempted Suicide* (London: Harmondsworth, 1970), p. 38 (1965 data).

251. Greenwood, *Firearms Control*, p. 178. As of 1984, the rate for England and Wales was 8.5 per 100,000 population. The male rate was 11.8, and the female rate 5.7. Bureau of the Census, *Statistical Abstract of the United States, 1988* (Washington, D.C.: Government Printing Office, 1987), pp. 802–803.

252. In 1983, for example, there were 1,338 burglaries per 100,000 population in the United States, and 1,640 in England and Wales. Carol Kalish, *International Crime Rates*, Bureau of Justice Statistics Special Report, May 1988, p. 9, table 11.

In 1987, there were an estimated 1,030,460 robberies and 5,623,160 burglaries in the United States. The British government estimates that Britain had 177,000 robberies, and 1,180,000 burglaries that year. Bureau of Justice Statistics, *Criminal Victimization in the United States, 1987* (Washington, D.C.: Government Printing Office, 1989); Pat Mayhew, David Elliot, and Lizanne Dowds, *The 1988 British Crime Survey* (Home Office Research Study No. 111) (London: Her Majesty's Stationery Office, 1989), p. 15.

253. Pat Mayhew, *Residential Burglary: A Comparison of the United States, Canada and England and Wales*, National Institute of Justice (Washington, D.C.: Government Printing Office, 1987) (citing 1982 British Crime Survey); United States Bureau of Justice Statistics, *Household Burglary* (Washington, D.C.: Government Printing Office, January 1985), p. 4.

It should be emphasized that there a number of differences between the British Crime Survey and the American statistics which make direct comparison difficult. Sampling procedures, recall periods, questionnaire organization, question wording, and differences in the victim populations·all contribute to differences in the data sets. Nevertheless, while it would be a mistake to place too much emphasis on small statistical differences, it seems reasonable to conclude that the British burglary rate is at least as high as the American rate, and that British burglars are much more likely to strike an occupied home.

In the Republic of Ireland, where gun control is also severe, burglars have little reluctance about attacking an occupied residence. Claire Nee and Maxwell Taylor, "Residential Burglary in the Republic of Ireland: Some Support of the Situational Approach," in Mike Tomlinson, Tony Varley, and Ciaran McCullagh, eds., *Whose Law and Order? Aspects of Crime and Social Control in Irish Society* (Belfast: Sociological Association of Ireland, 1988): 143–54.

254. Gary Kleck, "Crime Control Through the Private Use of Armed Force," *Social Problems* 35, no. 1 (February 1988), pp. 12, 15–16. Kleck finds a burglar's chance of being shot is about equal to his chance of being arrested. In a survey of felony convicts in state prisons, 73 percent of the convicts who had committed a burglary or violent crime agreed "one reason burglars avoid houses when people are at home is that they fear being shot." Ibid., p. 16, citing Inter-university Consortium for Political and Social Research, *Codebook*

for ICPSR Study 8437. Armed Criminals in America: A Survey of Incarcerated Felons (Ann Arbor, Mich.: ICPSR, 1986). Surveys of burglars in suburban Philadelphia revealed that the burglars avoided late-night burglaries because of the chance of being shot. George Rengert and John Wasilchick, *Suburban Burglary: A Time and a Place for Everything* (Springfield, Ill.: Charles C. Thomas, 1985), pp. 30, 62.

Relatively few burglars are fatally wounded by home-owners, but the low death rate hardly proves that guns are not a deterrent. Deterred burglars avoid homes which might contain an armed victim. The burglars who get shot are the unlucky few who have made a terrible miscalculation.

255. Colin Greenwood, "An Anecdotal Analysis of Gun Laws and Crime," *American Rifleman,* May 1989, p. 27.

256. Tendler, "Police Stay Ahead of Gun Raids," *The Times,* July 10, 1987, p. 24; Downie, p. A17 (750 armed robberies in London in 1981); Greenwood, *Firearms Control,* p. 162; Greenwood, "Does Legislation Reduce Armed Crime?"; Greenwood, "An Anecdotal Analysis," citing, F. H. McClintock and Evelyn Gibson, *Robbery in London.*

257. Greenwood, "An Anecdotal Analysis," citing Report of the Commissioner of Police for London.

258. In England and Wales overall, there were 2,651 armed robberies in 1986. Yardley and Stevenson, pp. 19, 22. Pistols were used in 1,196 of the robberies, and shotguns in 727.

259. Home Office, "Notifiable Offenses Recorded by the Police in England and Wales, First Quarter 1989; Notifiable offices in which Firearms Were Reported to Have Been Used— 1988," *Statistical Bulletin,* issue 20/89 (Croydon: Government Statistical Service, June 21, 1989), p. 6.

260. In America, the use of a gun by a robber is associated, understandably, with a higher rate of victim death. Thus, the higher rate of U.S. armed robbery partly explains the higher U.S. homicide rate. But while the armed robber is more likely to kill, the armed robber is less likely to injure his victim. Perhaps the explanation is that victims who resist are more likely to be fatally shot; but most victims, intimidated by the gun, do not resist at all, and hence are not injured. The 17 percent figure is based on estimated total robberies, not reported robberies.

261. Yardley and Stevenson, table 3.7.

262. Stead, p. 161 ("before abolition, professional criminals largely eschewed carrying guns . . . [today] criminals have ways of acquiring firearms and in recent years have used them more and more often."). Greenwood suggests that now that the death penalty has been abolished in Britain, robbers are no longer so concerned about a felony-murder conviction.

263. "Abroad, Too, Fear Grips the Cities," *U.S. News & World Report,* February 23, 1981, p. 65.

264. Paddy Hillyard and Janie Percy-Smith, *The Coercive State: The Decline of Democracy in Britain* (London: Fontana, 1988), p. 241.

265. Greenwood, *Firearms Control,* p. 243.

266. Greenwood, "Does Legislation Reduce Armed Crime?"

267. Ibid.

268. Charles Murray, "The British Underclass," *The Public Interest* 99 (Spring 1990): 4-28.

Another non-gun crime which has waxed as social controls have waned is rape. Rape is a crime for which gun availability is mostly irrelevant. Perpetrators rarely use guns, because superior male strength usually suffices. By 1989, British women were so afraid of attack that the Home Office had issued "Ten Commandments" for men to help women feel safe, including "Don't chat to a woman alone at a bus stop" and "Don't give a woman admiring looks." Vivienne Clarke, "Help Women Feel Safe, Men Urged," *Evening Press,* October 26, 1989, p. 1.

269. James Q. Wilson, *Thinking About Crime,* rev. ed. (New York: Basic Books, 1983), pp. 228, 240. Also, Ben C. Roberts, "On the Origins and Resolution of English Working-Class Protest," in Hugh Graham and Ted Robert Gurr, eds., *Violence in America,* Report of the National Commission on the Causes and Prevention of Violence (Washington, D.C.: Government Printing Office, 1969), p. 216 (period from 1783 to 1867 was called "an age of improvement." Reduced crime and greater civility due to economic growth, political reform, moral suasion, and institutional developments).

270. There is currently an increasing problem of violence by drunken affluent young people, especially on weekends in prosperous southern counties. "The Affluent Young Need Better Examples," *The Times,* June 13, 1988, reprinted in "Press Briefing," *Insight* (July 4, 1988), p. 38.

271. V. A. C. Gattrell, "The Decline of Theft and Violence in Victorian and Edwardian England," in V. A. C. Gattrell, Bruce Lenman, and Geoffrey Parker, eds., *Crime and the Law Since 1850* (London: Europa, 1980), p. 300.

272. "[I]n English culture the preferred forms of discipline are all *internalized;* they are forms of *self*-discipline, *self*-control. They depend on all those institutions and process which establish the internal self-regulating mechanisms of control: guilt, conscience, obedience and super-ego." Stuart Hall, Chas Critcher, Tony Jefferson, John Clarke, Brian Roberts, *Policing the Crisis: Mugging, the State, and Law and Order* (New York: Holmes and Meier, 1978), p. 144.

273. James Given, *Society and Homicide in 13th Century England* (Palo Alto, Calif.: Stanford University Press, 1977); Ted Robert Gurr, "Historical Trends in Violent Crime: Europe and the United States," in Ted Robert Gurr, ed., *Violence in America: The History of Crime* (vol. 1 in *Violence in America*) (Newbury Park: Sage, 1989), p. 28. [The 1989 Gurr book *Violence in America* is entirely different from the 1969 book of the same name, cited at note 269.] Kent County, one of the more murderous regions, had a homicide rate of 23 per 100,000 population—over ten times the current British rate, and twice the modern American rate. "One can only assume," writes Gurr, that had the thirteenth-century British "been equipped with firearms rather than knives and rustic tools . . . they would have killed one another with even greater frequency." Ibid., p. 29. On the other hand, if potential victims had been protected by firearms, one might expect that potential killers would be less inclined to attack. The self-defense effect might be particularly powerful in preventing husbands from using their superior physical strength to assault their wives and children.

In Elizabethan times, the homicide rate declined, but was still far higher than today. In that period, handguns called "pocket dags" first came into use; about 7 percent of homicides involved firearms. Ibid.

274. Given, p. 200.

275. Ibid., pp. 210–12. The German sociologist Ferdinand Tönnies dubbed the contrast between rural, local community and modern impersonal society *Gemeinschaft* (community) versus *Gesellschaft* (association).

276. Given, pp. 188–91. The comparison of medieval English and rural African homicide rates is obviously limited by the difficulty in compiling accurate crime statistics in societies with limited record-keeping.

277. Ibid., 192–93.

In the next century, England suffered another sharp rise in violent crime. Historian B. A. Hanawalt attributes the increase to the numerous civil and foreign wars in which England was engaged. B. A. Hanawalt, *Crime and Conflict in English Communities, 1300–*

1348 (Cambridge, Mass.: Harvard University Press, 1979), discussed in Dane Archer and Rosemary Gartner, "Violent Acts and Violent Times: The Effect of Wars on Postwar Homicide Rates," in Dane Archer and Rosemary Gartner, eds., *Violence and Crime in Cross-National Perspective* (New Haven: Yale University Press, 1984), p. 66.

278. Gurr, p. 82. Some commentators argue that New York City's crime problem is merely a racial problem, since blacks and Hispanics perpetrate a high percentage of the violent crime. But in the 1910s, when New York City's crime rate was already far worse than London's, blacks composed only 1.5 percent of New York City's population.

279. Chicago figure from Franklin Zimring and James Zuehl, "Victim Injury and Death in Urban Robbery: A Chicago Study," *Journal of Legal Studies* 15 (1986), p. 26. London figure from *Criminal Statistics, England And Wales, 1976*, p. 195. There were 800 convictions at Magistrates Court for 5,522 robberies. The figure is for adults only.

From 1963 to 1983, the U.S. robbery clearance rate fell from 39 percent to 26 percent; aggravated assault clearance from 76 percent to 61 percent; and rape from 69 percent to 52 percent. Overall violent crime clearance declined from 62 percent to 46 percent. Paul Blackman, *Firearms and Violence, 1983/84* (Washington, D.C.: National Rifle Association, 1985), p. 43. Blackman attributes the decline to judicial restrictions on the police; but since the trend continued during the years of the Burger Court—when rules governing police behavior were becoming less restrictive—blaming the Warren Court may not be the answer. As detailed in the concluding chapter, studies show that Constitutional protections for American suspects are not a significant impediment in criminal prosecutions.

280. Blackman, *Firearms and Violence, 1983/84*, p. 43. According to Bureau of Justice Statistics survey of eleven states, only 34 percent of defendants convicted of violent felonies received more than a year in jail; 31 percent were sentenced to a year or less, and 36 percent did not go to jail. "Crime Data Show Low Jailing Rate," *New York Times*, January 19, 1988 (officials cautioned that the eleven-state figure might not be accurate for the nation as a whole).

281. James Q. Wilson, *Thinking About Crime*, p. 187. Other evidence suggests, however, that in the eighteenth century, only a couple hundred criminals were executed annually, despite the frequent imposition of the death sentence. Royal pardons and transportation to Australia mitigated much of the law's harshness. Douglas Hay, "Crime and Punishment in Eighteenth and Nineteenth Century England," *Crime & Justice* 2 (1980): 45, 48–49.

Today, a life sentence really means a sentence of indeterminate length. The average person convicted of murder will actually serve 10.5 years in prison.

282. Wilson, *Thinking About Crime*, pp. 209–10.

283. Between 1802 and 1818, the murder conviction ratio of New Orleans versus London and Middlesex was 27:1. In a similar fourteen-year period, there were 34 murder convictions in Pennsylvania, and only 20 in all of Scotland. Daniel B. Davis, *Homicide in American Fiction, 1798–1860* (Ithaca, N.Y.: Cornell University Press, 1957), p. 242 n.1, citing Edwin Livingstone, *A System for the Penal Law for the State of Louisiana* (Philadelphia, 1830), p. 30 (for New Orleans, London, and Middlesex); and William Bradford, *An Enquiry into How Far the Punishment of Death is Necessary in Pennsylvania* (Philadelphia, 1793) (for Pennsylvania and Scotland); Gurr, p. 31. From 1749 until 1771, there were an average of four murder convictions annually in London and Middlesex. Emsley, p. 36.

284. Davis, p. 242.

285. Frank Morn, "Firearms Use and the Police," in *Firearms and Violence*, p. 513.

286. Department of Justice, Bureau of Justice Statistics, *Criminal Victimization in the United States, 1987* (Washington, D.C.: Government Printing Office, 1989), p. 64. The 17 percent figure is for all robberies, based on national surveys. For robberies reported to the

police, the gun-use rate is about one-third. *Crime in the U.S., 1988* (Washington, D.C.: Government Printing Office, 1989), p. 21. The rape estimate is less exact, since the FBI does not collect weapons data for rape.

287. Greenwood, "Comparative Cross-Cultural Statistics," p. 37.

Of course Greenwood's view is a minority one in Britain. The country still enforces its firearms laws, despite Greenwood's argument of their inutility. An American critic of Greenwood rhetorically asks what would happen if the gun density in America and Britain were reversed. Fields, "Handgun Laws Work; Handguns Don't," *Washington Post*, December 21, 1980, p. C2. One suspects that the American murder and robbery rates would still be far above the British rates. As the statistics cited above indicate, America would still have 83 percent of its current robberies, even if every firearmed robber gave up robbery completely.

Greenwood's work has won the respect of at least one influential anti-gun scholar. Australia's Professor Richard Harding favorably cites Greenwood's articles, and agreed with Greenwood that no further shotgun restrictions beyond the 1967 controls were needed. Harding, "Firearms Use in Crime," p. 765.

288. Quoted in Donald B. Kates, Jr., "Gun Control: Can It Work?" *National Review*, May 15, 1981, pp. 541–42.

289. Blackman, *Firearms and Violence, 1983/84*, p. 18 (using FBI statistics).

290. Donald B. Kates, Jr., "Against Civil Disarmament," *Harper's*, September 1978, p. 2.

291. Killias, p. 171.

292. Bruce-Briggs, p. 55.

293. Tuohy, p. 1 (citing Scotland Yard spokesman); Hillyard and Percy-Smith, pp. 236–37.

294. After the Falklands War, several hundred captured Browning automatic rifles were smuggled home by soldiers and sold in pubs.

295. David McDowall and Colin Loftin, "Collective Security and Fatal Firearm Accidents," *Criminology* 23 (1985), pp. 401, 411. More recently, Britons have been buying inoperable replicas of pistols and revolvers, to frighten away burglars. "The Rush for Fake Guns."

296. For American disobedience to gun controls, see chapter 5 at note 210 and chapter 10.

297. Donald B. Kates, Jr., and Mark Benenson, "Handgun Prohibition and Homicide," in *Restricting Handguns*, p. 98.

298. Frances Gibb, "Thatcher Pledge to Consider an Amnesty on Guns," *The Times*, July 10, 1987; Yardley and Stevenson, p. 29. Many of the surrendered 1964 guns were airguns.

The Firearms Act (1920) led to the surrender of 39,000 firearms. Breckenridge, p. 60. A 1935 amnesty yielded 8,469 firearms. A 1946 amnesty brought in 75,000, and a 1961 amnesty yielded 70,000. Lorton, pp. 20, 22.

American amnesties tend to bring large numbers of guns only when cash payments are added as an incentive.

299. P. A. J. Waddington, *Arming an Unarmed Police: Policy and Practice in the Metropolitan Police* (London: Police Foundation, 1988), p. 51. The two correlated .79 in London, and .97 outside of London.

300. Waddington, p. 4, citing for London Police Hoare, "The Pattern of Experience in the Use of Firearms by Criminals and the Police Response," unpublished M.S. thesis, Cranfield Institute of Technology (1980).

301. Waddington, p. 111. The massacre was also the price paid for prohibiting civilians from carrying defensive weapons.

302. Waddington, pp. 17, 87, 108. Officers assigned to guard airports against terrorists carry Heckler and Koch MP5 submachine guns, to the dismay of many advocates of civil disarmament, including the Labour party. Ibid., pp. 21, 101, citing as protestors R. W. Gould and M. J. Waldren, *London's Armed Police* (London: Arms and Armour, 1986).

303. Waddington, p. 6, citing Colin Greenwood, *Police Tactics in Armed Operations* (Boulder, Colo.: Paladin Press, 1979).

304. Ewing and Gearty, p. 18.

305. Hardly any police above the rank of sergeant have guns. Waddington, p. 62.

306. Waddington, p. 1.

307. Ibid., p. 2.

308. One commentator notes the "sullen hostility between police and public that has increased alarmingly in Britain." Susan Crossland, "Police Paranoia Dulls the Blue Lamp," *The Sunday Times,* May 27, 1990, p. C5, col. 2. The percentage of people "satisfied" with the British police has declined from 75 percent in 1981 to 58 percent in 1990. R. C. Longworth, "Perjury, Abuse of Prisoners Lead to Criticism of British Police," *Criminal Justice International,* September 1990, p. 19 (reprint from *Chicago Tribune*).

309. Stead, p. 162; D. Smith and J. Gray, *Police and People in London,* pp. 241–42 (Report of the Policy Studies Institutes, 1985), quoted in Beynon, "The Ideal Civic Condition, Part I," *Criminal Law Review* (1986), p. 581 n.2.

310. Garviz Gorer, *Exploring English Character* (New York: Criteria Books, 1955), pp. 310–11. The quote retains a good deal of validity today. Parviz Saney, *Crime and Culture in America: A Comparative Perspective* (New York: Greenwood Press, 1986), p. 159.

311. Richard Hofstadter, "America as a Gun Culture," *American Heritage* (October 1970), p. 4.

312. For other recent flare-ups of media/government conflict, see "U.S. TV Broadcasts Banned BBC Data," *New York Times,* November 18, 1987; Julian Baum, "British Security Forces News Media to Turn in Tapes," *Christian Science Monitor,* March 25, 1988, p. 9 (BBC reporters forced to turn over videotapes of anti-British violence to the police).

313. Thus, many libel plaintiffs choose to litigate in Britain for tactical reasons. Canada is also a site for forum-shopping American libel plaintiffs. "Moving Abroad," *ABA Journal,* September 1989, pp. 38–39.

314. As the U.S. Supreme Court has stated, "liberty of the press . . . has meant, principally although not exclusively, immunity from previous restraints or censorship." *Near* v. *Minnesota,* 283 U.S. 697, 716 (1931). See also *New York Times* v. *United States,* 403 U.S. 713 (1971).

315. Duncan Campbell, "The Thatcher Government vs. the British Press," *Columbia Journalism Review,* May/June 1989, p. 36. Campbell is associate editor of *New Statesman and Society* magazine.

316. See the discussion of the Siege of Sidney Street, above at note 98 and accompanying text. The period was also marked by a mostly unfounded German spy hysteria. K. D. Ewing and G. A. Gearty, *Freedom Under Thatcher: Civil Liberties in Modern Britain* (Oxford: Clarendon Press, 1990), p. 137.

317. Official Secrets Act 1911, 1 & 2 George V, chapter 2; Official Secrets Act 1920; "Britons in Peril of Losing Rights," *Rocky Mountain News,* November 21, 1988.

318. Terence DeQuesne and Edward Goodman, *Britain An Unfree Country* (London: Heterodox, 1986), p. 24.

319. Hillyard and Percy-Smith, pp. 118–19.

320. Campbell, p. 35.

321. For example, the ban applies to footage of Eamon de Valera, former president and Taoiseach of the Republic of Ireland, filmed during the early 1920s when de Valera was leading the Irish war of liberation against Britain. Ewing and Gearty, p. 246.

322. Labour Member of Parliament Ken Livingstone denounced the plan to "prevent access to radio and TV by those who are critical of government policy in Ireland." On

the other hand, South African President P. W. Botha applauded the move, and suggested that South Africa emulate the British plan. Campbell, p. 35.

323. DuQuesne and Goodman, p. 119.

324. Ibid., pp. 143, 165. Gay literature has been seized by customs authorities, even though its sale is legal in Britain. Ewing and Gearty, p. 255.

325. Ewing and Gearty, pp. 85-86.

326. DuQuesne and Goodman, p. 33.

327. Ewing and Gearty, p. 165.

328. Ibid., p. 248, citing *Independent,* November 11, 1988; February 13, 1989.

329. Security Service Act 1989, § 3(1); Campbell, p. 37.

330. Barry James, "Justice in England Undergoes Stress," *Los Angeles Times,* April 7, 1985 (United Press International).

331. Hillyard and Percy-Smith, pp. 257-58, 272; Ewing and Gearty, p. 216. The Irish Bishops' Commission for Prisoners distributes a leaflet to Irish emigrants to Britain, warning young people that if arrested, they should expect "rough, accusational anti-Irish treatment" and should be prepared for "disorientation resulting from solitary confinement . . . and lack of contact with anyone except the police." The leaflet advises Irish to "sign nothing" without first consulting a lawyer. Mary Holland, "Ireland Laments Her Innocents Imprisoned Abroad," *Observer,* October 22, 1989, p. 2.

332. Hillyard and Percy-Smith, p. 273. *Regina* v. *Secretary of States for the Home Department, ex parte Stitt,* reported in *The Times,* February 3, 1987 (Divisional Court ruling that requiring reasons for exclusion "would be fraught with difficulty and danger"), quoted in Ewing and Gearty, p. 217.

333. Likewise, American criminal cases are prosecuted in the name of the people, while British cases are prosecuted in the name of the monarch; one nation is the "United States," the other the "United Kingdom." The head of state in one country is "Mr. President," and in the other, "Your Highness." And the British anthem "God Save the Queen" became in America, "My country tis of thee, sweet land liberty, of thee I sing."

The monarch, of course, no longer exercises political power in the United Kingdom. Nevertheless, the monarchy symbolizes the distinction between the sovereign and the subject.

When police authorities protested the home secretary's issuance of CS gas and plastic bullets to local police forces, and pointed out that the central government had no authority to force police departments to employ dangerous weapons against their will, the court ruled for the central government on the theory of the Crown's "prerogative power to keep the peace," which allowed the home secretary to "do all reasonably necessary to preserve the peace of the realm." *Regina* v. *Secretary of State for the Home Department, ex parte Northumbria Police Authority* [1988] 2 W.L.R. 590.

334. Philip John Stead, *The Police of Britain* (New York: Macmillan, 1985), p. 147.

335. Stead, p. 150. Although the prosecution can dismiss as many potential jurors as it wishes, the defense's peremptory challenges are limited to three. Hillyard and Percy Smith, p. 157.

336. Police and Criminal Evidence Act 1984, 1984 chapter 60, § 58(1); Ewing and Gearty, pp. 38-39.

337. Ibid., p. 45.

338. Stephen Gillers, "The Prosecution and Defense Functions: Do They Promote Justice?" *The Record* 626 (1987), pp. 661-63.

339. James, "Justice in England Undergoes Stress."

340. At the same time Prime Minister Thatcher was abolishing the presumption of innocence and confiscating guns, she also fired civil servants for refusing to quit a legal union.

341. DuQuesne and Goodman, p. 26, citing Interception of Communications Act, July 25, 1985. American wiretaps authorize only the recording of conversations regarding the subject of the tap. British wiretappers are required to record all conversations on the tapped line. Ewing and Gearty, p. 70.

342. David Smith and Jeremy Gray, *Police and People in London—The Police In Action* (London: Policy Studies Institute, vol. 4, November 1983), discussed in DuQuesne and Goodman, pp. 80–81.

343. *Kuruma Son of Kaniu* v. *Regina*, 1 All England Reports 236, 239 (1955) ("the test to be applied . . . is whether it is relevant to the matters at issue. If it is, it is admissible and the court is not concerned with how the evidence was obtained").

344. Interception of Communications Act; Ewing and Gearty, p. 81. The only judicial forum for discussion of a tap's legality is in a prosecution against the illegal wire-tapper, an extremely rare event.

345. DuQuesne and Goodman, p. 96.

346. Ibid., p. 27.

347. Douglas Hurd, home secretary, Speech to Police Superintendent's Association Conference, Torquay, September 22, 1987, reprinted in Fiddick, p. 19. Also: "[A] substantial shift in the balance of firearms law to meet the needs of public safety. This cannot be done unreasonably at the expense of the sporting interest. A proper balance must be struck between the two." Douglas Hurd, *Hansard* 1987/88, 120, October 21, 1987, col. 783. The 1973 proposals for more severe controls were presented as a "balance between the interests of the majority and the claims of those who are entitled to use firearms." Green Paper, p. iii.

348. *Webb* v. *Outrim* [1907] Appeal Cases 81 (Privy Council).

349. Ewing and Gearty, p. 15.

350. "The real power struggle is behind the scenes, in the informal advisory bodies with access to Secretaries of State, in the Cabinet committees, in the meetings of Ministers with their powerful back-benchers, and in the informal cabals that focus energies on future policy. A bill before the House signals the end of the real battle and the start of a squabble over detail." Ewing and Gearty, p. 6.

351. Schwoerer, pp. 46–49. As one British scholar wrote, in rejecting the American assertion that there should be no taxation without representation, "a supreme and uncontrollable power must exist somewhere in every state." James Macpherson, *The Rights of Great Britain Asserted Against the Claims of America* (London: 1776), quoted in Jack P. Greene, *Peripheries and Center: Constitutional Development in the Extended Polities of the British Empire and the United States 1607–1788* (New York: W. W. Norton, 1990), p. 130.

Supreme Court Justice William Paterson, a signer of the United States Constitution, contrasted the English system of government, where "the authority of Parliament runs without limits," to the American government, where "the Constitution is the sun of the political system, around which all Legislative, Executive, and Judicial bodies must revolve." *Vanhorne's Lesee* v. *Dorrance*, 2 U.S. (2 Dall.) 304, 308 (1795).

352. *Myers* v. *United States*, 272 U.S. 52 (Brandeis, J., dissenting). For the Second Amendment and the Militia clauses of the body of the Constitution as a deliberate check on tyranny, see chapter 9. Just as the First Amendment protects an independent press so that it may perform a "checking function" against the government, the right of the people to bear arms serves as the ultimate check.

353. Firearms Act 1968, §§ 46–50.

354. Ibid.

355. Lord Gifford, "Debate on the Police and Criminal Evidence Bill," House of Lords, June 26, 1984, reprinted in DuQuesne and Goodman, p. 111. The original prohibition against

carrying "offensive weapons" was the Prevention of Crimes Act 1953, 1 and 2 Elizabeth II, ch. 14.

356. Ewing and Gearty, p. 23.

357. Emsley, pp. 155–56.

358. Lorton, pp. 73–74.

359. "Unmodified Pumps and Autos," *Guns Review,* November 1989, p. 825.

360. George Wallace, "Shotguns and the Law," *Shooting Magazine,* October 1989, p. 28; Mid Glamorgan, "Police Policies," in "Letters to the Editor," *Guns Review,* January 1991, p. 56.

361. *Guidance to Police* (London: Her Majesty's Stationery Office), para. 6(8)(f). See generally Cadmus, "Magazine Mischief," *Guns Review,* September 1990, p. 645.

362. "Colin Greenwood Reviews Police Policy," *Shooting Times and Country Magazine,* December 27, 1979; Cadmus, "A Question of Numbers," *Guns Review,* November 1978, p. 665 (police statement in letters to gun owners who were attempting to renew certificates).

363. Greenwood, "A Waste of Police Time." The proposal (never enacted into law) to ban new gun collections or additions to old collections was made in the Green Paper, p. 17. For a prospective collector's difficulty with the police, see *Hutchison* v. *Chief Constable of Grampian,* 1977 S.L.T. (Sh. Ct.) 98 (Sheriff Court of Grampian, Highland and Islands at Elgin, June 3, 1977).

Sometimes police zeal to enforce gun laws turns silly. The Essex County police have prosecuted a sailing club for not having a license for the fifty-pound blackpowder cannon used to start their races. Mark Edward Crane, "Brickbats," *Reason,* June 1988, p. 14.

364. "Fees," *Guns Review,* January 1991, p. 9. According to a study by the accounting firm Cooper and Lybrand Deloitte, a reasonably efficient firearm certificate licensing system should cost no more than £35 pounds to administer. Ibid.

365. The NCCL turned away a racist transsexual who was pursuing a legal claim to state medical care. The NCCL also rejected a rank-and-file member of the racist National Front who was roughed up while the police conducted a warrantless search of her home and destroyed her property. Larry Gostin, "Editor's Notes," in Larry Gostin, ed., *Civil Liberties in Conflict* (London: Routledge, 1988), pp. 118–19.

366. Ken West, of the National Pistol Association: "We certainly do not believe that one should be able to obtain firearms by buying them from a supermarket." Transcript, "Gun Control Special," *European Journal* #20/89 (Oregon Public Television).

367. Jan A. Stevenson, "Sit Perpetuum? 100 Years at Bisley," *Handgunner,* November 1990, p. 21. The Clay Pigeon Association endorsed the new controls as well.

368. The Right Honorable The Lord Scarman OBE, House of Lords, "Foreword," in *Civil Liberties in Conflict,* p. xiii. When the Law Lords upheld a temporary injunction against the publication of *Spycatcher,* one of the dissenting Lords complained: "Having no written constitution, we have no equivalent in our law to the First Amendment to the Constitution of the United States of America." *Attorney-General* v. *Guardian Newspaper Ltd.* [1987], 3 All E.R. 316 (Lord Bridge of Harwich, dissenting).

369. Lorton, p. 104.

370. John Dunn, "Rights and Political Conflict," in *Civil Liberties in Conflict,* p. 23.

371. Ibid.

372. James Atlas, "Censorship in Britain," *Rocky Mountain News,* March 5, 1989, p. 57.

373. L. S. Amery, *Thoughts on the Constitution* (London: Oxford University Press, 1964), pp. 12–13, 21, 33.

374. *Documentary History of the United States,* vol. II (Mfm. Supp. 1976), pp. 1778–80.

375. Amery, p. 21.

4

Canada: Love of Government

Gun control in Japan and Great Britain ranges from near-prohibition to merely severe. It is not plausible to expect America to adopt controls even close to the British or Japanese models. A far more plausible model for American gun control is provided by Canada, which has a uniform federal system that, while stricter than the United States, generally is more lenient than some American jurisdictions. While Japan and Great Britain have been relatively unarmed for centuries, Canada has one of the highest rates of gun ownership in the world. There are almost as many rifles per capita in Canada as in the United States.[1] And although there are important cultural differences, Canada and the United States "probably resemble each other more than any two nations on earth," observes sociologist Seymour Martin Lipset.[2]

Nevertheless, American firearms advocates reject the Canadian example. They point to the December 1989 rampage of Marc Lépine, in which fourteen female students at the École Polytechnique in Montreal were murdered and twelve more wounded. Lépine used a Ruger Mini-14 semi-automatic rifle that he had purchased after passing a background check.[3] If Canadian controls have not stopped massacres within Canada, the American gun groups argue, there is no reason to expect that Canadian-style controls in America would work either.

After summarizing the history of guns and gun control in Canada, I will examine the structure of Canadian firearms laws, which shows that it is possible for a nation to legislate strict control of handguns but not

136

slip into undue restrictions on most sporting long guns. (The assumption that strict handgun controls will inevitably lead to strict long-gun controls is the great fear of the American gun lobby, and the great hope of the anti-gun lobby.) After briefly examining what collateral effect, if any, the advance of Canadian gun controls has had on other civil liberties in Canada, I turn to the evidence regarding the efficacy of Canadian controls. Because Canada implemented a much tougher national system in 1977, having previously had almost no controls on long guns, it is possible to examine the effects of particular changes in the law. Armed crime and firearms suicide are examined in detail, and some well-known studies of the Canadian laws are investigated. The social implications of firearms ownership are also studied, with particular emphasis on police and civilian attitudes and practices regarding armed self-defense. Finally, I examine the cultural implications of Canadian firearms controls and whether those controls would be suited for the United States. [In this chapter, and all succeeding chapters, "firearm" is used in its normal sense rather than the British interpretation, that is, shotguns are included along with rifles and handguns.]

HISTORY

Justice Holmes observed that, "[t]he rational study of law is still to a large extent the study of history";[4] certainly Canadian gun control cannot be understood outside the context of that country's history. From the start, the Canadian advance on the frontier was much less violent than America's. French fur traders could cooperate with Indians, and French inhabitants of Canada therefore had little to fear from the indigenous tribes. The Hudson's Bay Company's motto for Indian relations was "Never shoot your customers."[5] Unlike the English settlers to the south, the white inhabitants of New France had rarely crossed the Atlantic with the intent of staying forever. The aim was to make some money through commerce and return to Europe. The British who sailed to America, though, usually came to stay. They planned to farm, and, unlike the French traders, had to fight with the Indians for control of the land.[6] Thus, while America had sixty-nine Indian wars, Canada had none.[7]

The most important trade in France's Canadian colony was muskets for beaver pelts. By the time the French were divested of Canada and the Louisiana Territory, almost all the tribes as far west as the Rockies were armed, thanks to French enterprise and Indian wholesalers.[8]

One of the cultural features left behind in New France (Quebec) was a tradition of authoritarianism, which historian Kenneth McNaught finds has not entirely disappeared from modern French Canada.[9] Under the firm and direct command of Paris, the French in Quebec developed few customs of self-government. There was less religious freedom than in France itself. After Britain took Canada from France, the British governor, Guy Carlton, decided not to exterminate French culture, for in "the authoritarian structure of Quebec society he thought that he discerned a sheet anchor for British power in North America."[10]

Two decades after Britain seized Canada, the United States of America wrenched itself from Britain after an eight-year war for total independence. One hundred and twenty thousand Americans, dismayed at the violent revolt against the king, fled to Ontario, New Brunswick, Nova Scotia, and Quebec and called themselves United Empire Loyalists. Their disgust with American "mob" democracy would powerfully influence Canada.[11] In contrast to the American revolutionaries, the Loyalists were not afraid of what the government would do to them; they were afraid of what would happen if the government collapsed.[12] The settlers who came to Canada in the next century would usually be British subjects who had decided that they would like to continue living under the Crown; conversely, immigrants to the United States were more likely be people who rejected European governments. So, for example, while the Northern Irish Anglicans often migrated to Canada, Irish Catholics came to the United States.[13]

In 1867, almost a century after the United States won its independence, the Dominion of Canada was peacefully granted autonomy for domestic affairs within the British Commonwealth by the British North America Act.[14] While there is a particular moment when the United States became an independent nation—the Continental Congress's ratification of the Declaration of Independence—there is no precise day of Canadian independence. As late as World War II, Canada was still legally a "dominion" rather than an independent nation, and it was not clear how much authority Canada had to carry out a foreign policy separate from the British Commonwealth.[15]

Thus, the American national character has been shaped by the violent, armed assertion of national independence, whereas Canada has been shaped by a reaction against the American tradition of armed violence. The contrasting attitudes, which have shaped America and Canada ever since, were especially visible in the War of 1812.

One of the most important factors aggravating tensions between the United States and Britain in the prewar years was Britain's use of its Canadian colony as a trading post with the American Indians: in particular, Britain's giving the Indians weapons that were ostensibly intended for hunting, but were also used for killing encroaching American frontiersmen. After the battle of Tippecanoe, in what is now the state of Indiana, General William Henry Harrison and his troops plundered the Shawnee village of Prophets

Town. The American soldiers discovered weapons that Britain had supplied to its Indian allies. Definitive proof that the British were trading arms to the Indians enraged the American people.

America was ready for war, and expected its ordinary citizens bringing their own arms to battle would win a speedy victory. Sentimental and not always accurate memories of the War for Independence convinced the American public that the virtuous citizen militia could easily defeat any professional army. Representative Henry Clay, leader of the War Hawks in Congress, boasted: "I verily believe that the militia of Kentucky are alone competent to place Montreal and Upper Canada at your feet."[16]

In Canada, the settlers who awaited the American invasion were very different from their exuberantly bellicose southern neighbors. Writes historian Pierre Berton:

> This is a pioneer society, not a frontier society. No Daniel Boone stalks the Canadian forests, ready to knock off an Injun with a Kentucky rifle or do battle over an imagined slight. The Methodist circuit riders keep the people law abiding and temperate. . . . [C]ard playing and horse racing are considered sinful diversions; the demon rum has yet to become a problem. There is little theft, less violence. . . . The new settlers will not volunteer to fight. But most are prepared, if forced, to bear arms for their new country and to march when ordered.[17]

Kentuckians rushed to militia service, and marched north.[18] Mounted volunteers under the command of Samuel Hopkins, a congressional War Hawk turned major-general, charged off to claim Canada. Two weeks later, lost and hungry, the volunteers were attacked by Indians and retreated in shame. Kentucky Governor Shelby observed, "[T]he flower[s] of Kentucky are now returning home deeply mortified by the disappointment."[19] Some American troops did reach the British colony, but they, too, were disappointed; their commanders could have captured Montreal, and hence Canada, with a coordinated and intelligent attack, but the American officers, chosen by the people, were incompetent. Aristocratic Canadian leaders such as Sir George Prevost and Major-General Isaac Brock pulled off a difficult defense and trounced the Americans.

Berton summarizes:

> [T]he key words in Upper Canada were "loyalty" and "patriotism"—loyalty to the British way of life as opposed to American "radical" democracy and republicanism. Brock—the man who wanted to establish martial law and abandon habeas corpus—represented these virtues . . . [Brock] came to represent Canadian order as opposed to American anarchy. . . . Had not Canada been saved from the invader by appointed leaders who ruled

autocratically? . . . This attitude—that the British way of life is preferable to the American; that certain sensitive positions are better filled by appointment than by election; that order imposed from above has advantages over grassroots democracy (for which read "license" or "anarchy") flourished as a result of an invasion repelled. Out of it, shaped by an emerging nationalism and tempered by rebellion, grew that special form of state paternalism that makes the Canadian way of life significantly different from the more individualistic American way.[20]

Another key difference between the American and Canadian historical experiences was the taming of the Western frontier. Settlers of the American West staked their claims years before a government was around to protect their lives and property. The westerners enforced their own law and order with their personal arms. They lived in a Hobbesian, chaotic world, where government was ineffectual, and individuals had to protect themselves or die. Citizens adapted to the practice of local control. When the time came to form the western state governments, westerners drew on their existing experience of local control, and created particularized laws made for local conditions.

The law came to the Canadian West before the people did. The Laurentian Shield—a giant stretch of brushy, barren soil sitting on hard precambrian rock—blocked Canada's westward expansion. Only when railroads penetrated this barrier in the nineteenth century did settlers reach the rich interior prairie. Those settlers came directly from the "civilized" eastern provinces and brought their established practices with them. In fact, the North-west Mounted Police came to establish law and order (and help guard against Americans) before many settlers arrived. The central government, and the semi-feudal Hudson's Bay Company, established standardized and national laws before Canadian citizens ever set foot on their western farms.[21] Prime Minister Alexander Mackenzie had created the Mounted Police specifically to avoid the American pattern of frontier development.[22] Unlike the United States, therefore, Canada did not go through a "recurring pioneering experience," as the frontier was pushed west one farm at a time.[23] Explains Canadian historian Kenneth McNaught: "Partly because of much slower growth, Canada did not suffer the long and bloody wars that marked the American occupation of the far west. The Mounted Police maintained much tighter control of western settlements and the six-shooter never became the symbol of Canadian freedom. Ottawa negotiated treaties with the plains Indians which secured relatively peaceful opening of the most fertile land. . . ."[24]

In the early days of the Canadian West, the Mounted Police discouraged eastern settlers from carrying handguns.[25] By effectively providing for the security of the settlers, the Mounted Police obviated the need for defensive weaponry. Although many Americans urged the creation of an American federal police force for the frontier, western communities resisted it, as an encroachment by military rule on local autonomy.[26]

By the British North America Act of 1867, which granted Canada autonomous Dominion status within the British Commonwealth, all firearms legislation is within the national government's jurisdiction. Canada's first significant firearms law, in 1892, required a permit to carry a pistol if the carrier lacked "reasonable cause to fear an assault" on his person or property.[27] A 1913 revision eliminated the fear of assault exception to the permit law, and required a permit to carry any handgun.[28]

The next important change came in 1919, following the end of World War I. Nineteen-nineteen had at first seemed a heady year for the Canadian labor movement, in light of the growing strength of the British Labour party and the success (or so it seemed) of the Russian Revolution. Canadian labor went on an unprecedented wave of strikes. The business community, terrified of lost profits and red revolution, convinced the government to continue the wartime censorship laws.

In May of 1919, the Winnipeg Trades and Labour Council called a general strike in that town. Although the strike leaders were British born and the strikers were seeking only a nonviolent improvement in their working conditions, the business community claimed that the strike was led by "alien scum" bent on Communist revolution. Accordingly, the Winnipeg government replaced the local police with the national Royal Northwest Mounted Police, called up the militia (mostly ex-soldiers), and ordered the arrest of strike leaders. Defying the mayor's ban on parades, the strikers held a protest march. The Mounted Police and the militia attacked the crowd; one marcher was killed and thirty were injured.[29]

Shortly thereafter, the Canadian House of Commons, terrified by the Winnipeg strike, took up the issue of gun control. The strike was blamed on alien (non-Commonwealth) anarchists. One member of Parliament asked: "Are we to allow these aliens, to bring their bad habits, notions, and vicious practices into this country?"[30] Parliament enacted legislation requiring aliens to receive a permit to possess any gun, and in 1920 the permit requirement was extended to all persons for all types of guns.[31] The 1920 bill was probably influenced by the 1920 pistol and rifle legislation in Britain, another nation frightened by "foreign-born" anarchists. Aliens in Canada were deported in violation of the law, and loosely defined "seditious" speech was prohibited.[32] By 1921, things had calmed, and Canada repealed the gun controls affecting nonaliens. Citizens needed a permit only to carry or purchase handguns.[33]

Gangsterism and attendant publicity in the 1930s sparked a major round of gun control on both sides of the Atlantic. A universal registration law was enacted for handguns, and the silencer* was sharply restricted.[34]

Another transatlantic round of weapons restrictions occurred in 1968. Handgun carry permits were effectively eliminated.[35] By the mid-1970s, carrying or possessing a weapon, or imitation weapon, for a purpose "dangerous to the public peace" was punishable by up to five years in prison.[36] Simple unlicensed possession, other than in the home or place of business, was punishable by up to two years in prison, or by a summary conviction.[37] But as of 1976, no permit was required to buy a long gun to keep in one's house or business; indeed, long guns were subject to hardly any control.[38]

NEW RESTRICTIONS IN 1977

The push for the modern version of gun control in Canada began in 1974, after two incidents in which boys with rifles ran amok in schools. The public demanded executions, and the government responded, as the British government of 1967 had, by offering gun control to distract public attention from the death penalty.[39] Many ideas were discussed, and in 1977, Prime Minister Pierre Trudeau's government introduced a bill, C-58, that would have required a prospective gun purchaser to receive police approval to buy a weapon and to supply the police with two character references. Although a Gallup Poll reported that 85 percent of the populace supported Bill C-58, it was met with over fifty amendments in the Canadian House of Commons, and a firestorm of protest from gun owners. Accordingly, the Trudeau government withdrew C-58, and introduced a milder measure, Bill C-51, which became the Criminal Law Amendment Act.[40]

Like the 1968 U.S. Omnibus Crime Control Bill, Canada's 1977 Bill C-51 pleased liberals because it tightened gun control and pleased conservatives because it eased restrictions on wire-tapping. The liberal/ conservative "anti-crime" coalition sailed through the House of Commons by a 95-40 vote, although 150 other MPs did not vote at all.[41]

In the 1979 election, thirty-three of the MPs who had voted for C-51 were defeated, and the National Firearms Association gave itself some of the credit. The new Conservative Prime Minister, Joe Clark, had won election as part of a Western Canadian revolt against "big government" in the East, and he promised to modify the gun law. His government foundered, though, and was swept out of office in 1980, with the 1977 law left intact.[42]

---

*A "silencer" is a mechanical device that reduces or eliminates the sound of a gun firing (R. A. Steindler, *The Firearms Dictionary* [Harrisburg, Penn.: Stackpole, 1970], p. 230).

Firearms Acquisition Certificate

Under the system created in 1977, Canadians who wish to purchase any sort of gun must acquire a $10 Firearms Acquisition Certificate from the police. For purchasers of almost all long guns (rifles and shotguns), the FAC is the only legal step needed.[43] People who owned long guns before the bill was enacted were not required to apply retroactively for certificates. The FAC entitles its holder to buy most long guns anywhere in Canada for a period of five years.[44] Police may reject an applicant if they believe "it is desirable in the interests of the safety of the applicant or of any other person that the applicant should not acquire a firearm."[45]

To obtain a Firearms Acquisition Certificate, an applicant must provide identification and background information, including addresses for the past five years.[46] Unlike in some American states, applicants are not required to supply confidential medical information to the police.[47] And unlike in the United States as a whole, mail-order sales of both handguns and long guns are permitted.[48] (Some additional controls on FAC applicants, put into law in late 1991, are discussed below at pages 167–68.)

Although American opponents of gun control often claim that it is impossible to devise any licensing system to constrain police abuse of authority, the Canadian system appears to prevent arbitrary rejections in most cases. Less than 1 percent of FAC applications are denied.[49] In case of denial, the police must produce a written justification, and the applicant may appeal to a provincial court judge.[50] (Provincial court is the trial court of general jurisdiction, similar to district courts in most U.S. states.) The judge is required to set a date for hearing the appeal.[51] At the hearing, hearsay evidence may be used against the applicant.[52] The burden of proof is on the firearms officer to justify the denial.[53] About half of all appeals are successful.[54]

Police must keep records of all gun transactions they approve or are informed about, except that police need not keep a list of FAC holders on file. (The law neither forbids nor requires the police to maintain lists of FAC holders.)[55] The police are specifically barred from asking for the serial numbers or other identification of guns that are not restricted weapons.[56] (Restricted weapons, detailed below, are all handguns and certain "bad" long guns.)

Gun dealers must keep records of their sales, but they need not report long-gun transactions to the police. After five years, the dealer may discard his transaction records.[57] New Zealand also allows dealers to destroy records after five years; America requires that records be retained for at least twenty years and turned over to the Bureau of Alcohol, Tobacco and Firearms when the dealer goes out of business.[58]

Thus, in regard to most long guns, Canada is less restrictive than many American jurisdictions. Retail dealers have less burdensome paperwork requirements. While California and New Jersey mandate police approval for every single firearms transaction, Canada requires no police approval for long guns, beyond the initial issuance of the Firearms Acquisition Certificate. Of course Canada's FAC system is also stricter than that of other American states, such as Vermont or Idaho, which do not require purchasers of long guns (or handguns) to pass through any kind of police screening.

RESTRICTED WEAPONS

While the FAC system creates a relatively lenient legal climate for most long guns, guns that are considered to be more dangerous are subjected to a more intense system of controls under the "restricted weapons" classification. "Restricted weapons" include all handguns, as well as "bad" long guns. That the legal system refers to these guns as "weapons" rather than as "firearms" reflects the legal judgment that the guns are also more likely to be misused by criminals. Still, the fact that the guns are merely restricted rather than prohibited shows a recognition that the guns do have legitimate sporting uses. Centerfire semi-automatic rifles with a short barrel or a folding stock are the most numerous type of long guns that are classified as restricted weapons.[59]

Significantly, the Governor in Council (the federal cabinet) may place any gun it chooses on the restricted list.[60] The Governor in Council's decision to restrict a firearm is not subject to judicial review.[61] In 1983, the council placed the FN-FAL rifle (a large Korean war–era semi-automatic from Belgium) on the restricted list, even though it had been implicated in only one crime, a 1962 bank robbery by "the beetle bandit."[62] The Colt AR15 Sporter rifle was once listed, but gun-owner protests forced a recision.[63] The placing of formerly unrestricted long guns on the restricted weapons list has aroused considerable resentment among some Canadian gun owners. Since restricted weapons must be individually registered, some gun owners fear that registration of the FN-FAL or other weapons may be a prelude to confiscation.[64] Compliance with registration requirements for the M1 carbine (a short-barreled, lightweight semi-automatic rifle) is estimated at only 5 to 20 percent; compliance for the FN-FAL is at 3 percent, and compliance for the AR15 (during the time when registration was required) was 5 percent.[65]

Following the March 1989 U.S. ban on the import of many semi-automatic firearms, the Canadian Association of Chiefs of Police imposed a similar import ban. Toronto police reported a 50 percent increase in illegal guns seized in 1988 compared to 1987, which the police said were mostly a result of the drug trade.[66] Canadian gun owners charged that most seizures were of legal, registered firearms that had been retroactively classified as illegal.[67] (Proposals for further legal restrictions on semi-automatics are discusssed below.)

While there is sometimes heated debate about which long guns should be restricted weapons, there is no such debate about handguns. All handguns are restricted.[68]

To receive a Restricted Weapon Registration Certificate, an applicant has the burden of proving that the gun will be used for one of four purposes: "to protect life where other protection is inadequate," or "in connection with a lawful profession or occupation," or for use in target practice under the auspices of a shooting club, or as part of a gun collection by a "bona fide gun collector."[69]

The first step for a prospective handgun purchaser will typically be to join a shooting club and to shoot with club members' guns at the range. Some clubs may observe the applicant for a while before writing a letter of recommendation to the police to attest that the applicant may be entrusted with a handgun.[70] Other prospective handgun owners may simply state that they are buying their first handgun as the beginning of a collection.

After paying for a handgun or other restricted weapon at a gun dealer, the applicant takes a detailed bill of sale to the Registrar of Firearms at the local police station. The registrar completes an application to register a restricted weapon for the applicant, and at this time the applicant may show his shooting club recommendation. The police run a background check, which varies considerably in intensity from area to area. Some police conduct personal interviews in the applicant's home. The police may visit the place (usually the home) where the applicant intends to store the handgun and ensure that the gun will be locked up. While talks with neighbors and employers are not uncommon, the most typical background check simply involves a look at computer records. London, Ontario, used to require a thirteen-question psychological test.[71] In some areas, a handgun permit may be issued in an afternoon, with the only background check being a search of computer records to ensure that the applicant does not have a criminal record.[72] Some jurisdictions allow the handgun purchaser to register his gun and take it home the day he buys it; other jurisdictions (mostly in larger cities) delay final approval until, after three months or so, the Royal Canadian Mounted Police (RCMP) headquarters in Ottawa completes its paperwork for registering the gun.[73] (Some additional controls regarding restricted weapons, enacted in late 1991, are discussed at pages 167–68 below.)

In any case, once the police are satisfied, they will register the gun.[74]

The police fill out a registration form, give two copies to the purchaser, and keep other copies for themselves. The purchaser must return one copy to the gun vendor and then return directly to the police station with the gun. A Permit to Convey allows the citizen to pick up his gun from the gun dealer, bring it to the police station for verification of registration information, and then take the gun to his residence or place of business.[75] The police stamp the purchaser's copy of the registration form. The police send their copy of the form to the RCMP in Ottawa, who in a few months will send the purchaser an official certification that he legally owns the gun.

A registration application contains space for the registration of two restricted weapons. Even after a person has passed the screening process and been granted a Registration Certificate, he must begin the whole process anew for purchases of additional restricted weapons.[76] Even inoperable guns must be registered in some provinces.[77]

The federal government and many U.S. states prohibit anyone with a felony conviction from legally obtaining any kind of gun for the rest of his or her life. The Canadian police, though, will issue even Restricted Weapon Certificates to people whose last felony occurred more than ten years prior to the application.[78]

Any person may appeal the police refusal of a restricted weapons certificate by petitioning a provincial court judge. Unlike the Firearms Acquisition Certificate (for ordinary long guns), the applicant for a restricted weapon certificate bears the burden of proving that the police erred in rejecting the application.[79]

In practical terms, handguns are still obtainable; an applicant merely has to be a gun collector or belong to a target-shooting club. Although collecting firearms is a statutorily valid reason for purchasing a handgun, applicants who wish to start (rather than add to) a handgun collection are sometimes denied registration. Occasionally a firearms registrar may claim that a particular handgun is not suitable for collecting, even though there is no legal authority for the police to make such a determination.[80]

Permits to transport restricted weapons to target ranges must be renewed at periodic intervals, usually once a year.[81] They must be carried with the gun when the gun is transported. Separate one-time "carriage permits" are required to take a handgun or other restricted weapon to a gunsmith for repairs, to a gun show, or to a new home.[82]

As in many American cities, it is virtually impossible for an ordinary citizen to obtain a permit to carry a loaded handgun for self-defense. Handgun carry permits for self-protection are issued "only in exceptional cases" where the issuing officer is "satisfied" of the applicant's need.[83] If the applicant lives in an area that has a police force, no matter how remote the location might be, a carry permit for self-defense will be denied.[84] Even people who live in the far North are denied permits, unless they must carry all their equipment on their person, as geologists or prospectors do.[85] In the rare case where a permit to carry for protection of life is granted, the permit may include a condition forbidding use of the gun in anything less than a life-threatening situation. By the terms of the permit, a permit holder would be forbidden to draw or fire the gun to prevent serious bodily injury, rape, or someone else's murder.[86] Even on a person's own property, carrying a loaded handgun is not permitted, although it is doubtful that prosecution would result.[87]

As with ordinary long guns, the Canadian laws for handguns (and for restricted long guns) are more moderate than in some U.S. jurisdictions. Following an example first set in the Chicago suburb of Morton Grove, several other Chicago suburbs, Chicago itself, and Washington, D.C., totally bar handgun purchases. New York City police for several years simply refused to issue handgun applications, until thrice ordered to do so by the state court. New Jersey allows handgun purchases, but (despite a requirement for thirty-day application processing) the police often take half a year or more to issue a license. In some Canadian jurisdictions the police run a background check and authorize a handgun purchase in an afternoon, whereas states such as California require fifteen-day waiting periods for every single handgun, rifle, or shotgun purchase (and in practice California authorities take much longer than fifteen days to issue their approval).

The majority of U.S. states, though, are more lenient than Canada, requiring only that a retail handgun purchaser fill out a federal form at the point of sale, or obtain a one-time-only license. Only a few states impose any restrictions on private handgun transfers among adults. Some Canadian firearm activists prefer the Canadian system to the American one, since a uniform national system prevents local prohibitions.

PROHIBITED WEAPONS

Short shotguns, sawed-off rifles, and silencers are completely illegal in Canada.[88] Fully automatic weapons are legal only if they were registered to their current owner before January 1, 1978.[89] To comply with the new law, many gun owners had their full automatics permanently converted to semi-automatic.* As semi-automatics, the guns were subject to the same relaxed controls as other standard rifles. But in 1988, the government began confiscating many of the converted semi-automatics, and charging the owners with felony possession of a prohibited weapon. The government reasoned

---

*A full automatic fires continuously as long as the trigger remains depressed. A semi-automatic fires only one bullet for each trigger squeeze.

that if the guns had been converted from full to semi-automatic, they could be reconverted back to fully automatic. Of course the guns could be; most semi-automatics (whatever their prior history) can be converted to full automatic by a skilled gunsmith who has a long afternoon or more to spare and is willing to commit a serious felony. Canadian gun owners were incensed by the confiscations; the gun owners felt that they had made the original full automatic to semi-automatic conversion a decade ago to comply with the law. Over a decade later, their efforts to comply were being twisted into a rationalization for gun confiscation.[90] As a result, many owners of converted semi-automatics, who complied with the 1978 law have begun concealing their guns, in fear of anticipated confiscation.[91] (New controls on converted semi-automatics are discussed below at pages 167–68.)

The government from time to time issues new "Prohibited Weapons Orders"; these orders completely prohibit the possession of particular classes of weapons, even if the weapon was legally owned and registered before the order was enacted. Some of the weapons retroactively prohibited by the orders are small tear-gas canisters, Mace, and electric stun guns.[92] In contrast, these same weapons are legal and totally uncontrolled in almost all American states; the reasoning is that these self-defense items are less dangerous than firearms. But Canadian legal authorities reject the idea of armed self-defense in all its forms.

CIVIL LIBERTIES

American opponents of gun control claim that infringements on the right to bear arms are inevitably accompanied by infringements on other rights. Canadian gun control does involve police activity that would be questionable from the viewpoint of an American strongly committed to civil liberties. But overall, most of the civil liberties issues directly raised by the Canadian law are no more troublesome than those raised by the existing American controls.

The Canadian practices that would most offend American sensibilities all involve Fourth Amendment issues: e.g., encouraging the police who process gun-license applications to drop in on people's homes and to ask neighbors about a person's activities seems troublesome. As we have seen, the Japanese have extensive police "home visits" for everyone. While Britons and Canadians seem to accept home visits in the gun-control context, it is unlikely that Americans would. Indeed, the NRA gets great political mileage out of raising fears that American gun-control proposals would permit police home visits.

When a Canadian peace officer has reasonable grounds to believe that a person, vehicle, or premises (other than a home) has an illegal firearm, he or she may search for it without a warrant. Warrants for home searches and gun confiscation may be issued whenever a magistrate "believes that it is not in the interest of the person or not in the public interest that a person should have in his possession a firearm."[93] In such situations, the authorities may use restricted weapon registration lists to determine whether the home has a gun to confiscate.[94]

New controls imposed by the Parliament in 1991 require all "gun collectors" (that is, the owners of most of the handguns and selected long guns that have been registered as restricted weapons) to consent to warrantless government searches of their homes.[95] Government witnesses promised a legislative committee that the "inspections" would only be carried out during reasonable daylight hours.[96]

Warrantless home searches are also allowed when the peace officer reasonably believes that possession of the firearm "is not desirable in the safety of that person, or of any other person" and that obtaining a warrant would be "impracticable."[97] One rationale for warrantless searches is that a gun should be removed as soon as possible from a volatile domestic situation; moreover, in the North, magistrates are scarce. After a home search, the prosecutors must report the results to the magistrate so that the courts can monitor the implementation of the gun law.[98] In practice, search results are only reported to magistrates when guns are found that the police want to have forfeited.[99] Some gun owners have alleged that informants have tricked the police into confiscating neighbors' weapons by filing false reports of violent threats.[100]

Like the U.S. Bureau of Alcohol, Tobacco, and Firearms, the Canadian police perform roughly one warrantless inspection of every gun dealer every year. Dealers complain that the inspections are sometimes used for harassment,[101] and the limit of one per year was added in a 1986 American reform statute bitterly resisted by the gun-control lobby. Unlike the BATF, the RCMP does not seize dealer records of firearms sales, except to investigate particular crimes. In contrast, the BATF in its operation "Forward Trace" has engaged in mass seizures of U.S. dealer firearms records with no link to any crime, and despite the fact that such seizures are specifically forbidden by federal law.[102]

Both Canadian and American gun laws have helped undermine the traditional principle of Anglo-American criminal law that persons may only be convicted of a criminal offense if they have a *mens rea* (guilty mind). That principle has been eroded as courts have upheld laws making a person guilty of a criminal offense even if there is no proof that the person had a culpable mental state.[103] The Supreme Court's decision in *United States v. Freed* declared that criminal intent was not necessary for a conviction under the Gun Control Act of 1968.[104]

Canadians who possess an unregistered handgun are guilty of a felony under principles of strict liability. The individual's mental state is irrelevant. One person was convicted of failing to obtain a registration certificate, despite the defense's claim that he had relied on an official's statement that his particular rifle was not a restricted weapon.[105] Possession of a firearm by persons under an order not to possess firearms is also a strict liability offense.[106]

Similarly, in *United States* v. *Thomas,* the defendant found a sixteen-inch-long gun while horseback riding. Taking it to be an antique pistol, he pawned it. But it turned out to be short-barreled rifle, which should have been registered before being sold. Although the prosecutor conceded that Thomas lacked criminal intent, he was convicted of a felony anyway.[107]

Guilt by association is usually not an acceptable legal concept in the Anglo-American legal tradition, but it has been upheld in the case of gun laws. In *Ulster* v. *Allen,* the U.S. Supreme Court validated a law stating that if one person in an automobile possessed an illegal gun, all other passengers in the car would be presumed to be in unlawful possession as well, unless they could prove they did not know about the gun. Canada does not go quite so far; the Crown must prove that people in the car with the illegal possessor knew about the presence of the gun. Still, convictions for unlawful possession are allowed even if the occupants had no control over the gun.[108]

Under traditional common law principles, ordinary carelessness is not a criminal mental state. To be prosecuted for an offense involving criminal negligence (such as killing someone with a car), the defendant must have been in "gross disregard" of appropriate standards of care. Simply being careless might make a person vulnerable to a civil lawsuit for money damages, but is not the basis for a criminal conviction. That traditional common law principle was changed in Canada by the 1977 gun law. A person who carelessly uses or stores a gun that injures someone else is guilty of a criminal offense; courts have upheld convictions based on ordinary negligence, rather than the traditional standard of "gross disregard."[109]

American civil libertarians are right to point out that gun controls can lead to the infringement of other civil liberties. Nevertheless, the infringements under the existing U.S. federal controls seem to be approximately equal to the infringements under the Canadian model. Accordingly, the fear that U.S. adoption of federal controls along the Canadian model would lead to significantly greater infringements of other civil liberties might not be valid. On the other hand, as will be discussed below, the Canadian police enjoy a less adversarial relationship with the Canadian people than the American police do with U.S. citizens. Accordingly, some American police might be inclined to enforce a particular law more severely than Canadian police would be.

HAS CANADIAN GUN CONTROL REDUCED GUN MISUSE?

While American newspapers and commentators have touted the 1977 Canadian law, it is not clear that the law has had any measurable positive effect on levels of crime or suicide in Canada. To begin with, there seem to be plenty of illegal guns still available. In the mid-1970s, RCMP estimated there to be an estimated 50,000 unregistered restricted weapons, mostly handguns, in private hands; other government analysts found the 50,000 figure far too low.[110] Today, criminals have an easy time purchasing illegal handguns, many of which are smuggled in from the United States. The head of Toronto's detective unit opined that he would not have to walk more than two kilometers "to pick up a hot piece."[111] Even without U.S. imports, the Canadian pool of more than 45,000 stolen and missing weapons is more than sufficient for criminal purposes.[112]

Crime

In 1983, a study commissioned by the Canadian government did conclude that the 1977 act had positive results.[113] Indeed, the well-publicized results of the study closed the door to consideration about modifying the act. Yet while the study's strong conclusions supported gun control, its data were not so clear-cut.

For example, the study announced that the new gun law had cut the murder rate. In fact, the murder rate had declined immediately following the gun law's implementation. But as the study's data showed, murder had been increasing from 1961 to 1975, and had declined slowly from 1975 to 1981. Since the gun-control law only went into effect in 1978, it should not have been given credit for a trend begun in 1975.

In four major Canadian cities—but not the country as a whole—the percentage of firearms used in attempted murders dropped significantly after 1978. The most dramatic fall was in Vancouver, where firearms had been used in 51 percent of attempted murders in 1975–1977, but only 27 percent in 1978–1981.[114] Knives displaced guns in homicides and attempted homicides.[115] Nationally, the percentage of homicides perpetrated with guns remained stable.[116]

The use of firearms in "rape and indecent assault, assault, and woundings," was already low, and showed no change.[117] Most rapists do not use any weapon, let alone a gun, even in gun-ridden America, since male strength is usually enough to overpower a female victim.[118] As the Canadian experience affirmed, rape is not likely to decline as a result of gun control.

The Canadian robbery rate increased, and the use of guns in robberies increased at a slightly slower rate. In 1977, guns were used in 38.5 percent of robberies, and in 1981 they were used in 34.4 percent.[119] It might be that the (relative) decline in armed robbery, if it is statistically significant, resulted mostly from the mandatory sentencing provisions for use of a gun in a felony.[120] On the other hand, the mandatory sentence is not *really* mandatory, since it is usually plea-bargained away to assure conviction on lesser charges.[121] The Canadian government study did find that the legislation had led to longer jail terms for robbers armed with guns, and shorter terms for robbers who used other weapons.[122] To the small extent that robbery with firearms decreased, it was replaced by robbery with other weapons, particularly knives.[123] The study's confident proclamations that the new gun laws markedly reduced the armed robbery rate were somewhat overstated. To the extent that the Canadian government study found evidence for a general decline in the use of guns in crime (as in attempted murder), the decline was mostly in long-gun crimes; handgun misuse proved more resistant to legal controls.[124] The fact that the data from the study showed very little, if any, benefits from the new gun law should not be considered conclusive proof of the law's failure. After all, the study only had data available for years up through 1981. A relatively moderate law like Canada's, which did not take full legal effect until 1979, should not be expected to produce immediate dramatic results.

The more important question is how the Canadian law has performed over the long term. During the first decade of the law's life, the Canadian trends in firearm misuse generally followed the American pattern. Firearm homicides became a smaller percentage of total homicides, and the overall homicide rate declined from 2.7 to 2.6 per 100,000 population. In the United States the percentage of firearms used in homicides decreased, and the homicide rate fell from 9.2 to 8.9.[125] Domestic homicide fell in Canada, and dropped even more sharply in America.[126]

The most significant change in the years following the new Canadian controls was in armed robbery as a percentage of total robberies. In 1988, only 25 percent of Canadian robberies involved a firearm, whereas in 1977, 38 percent had. Again, knives generally displaced firearms as robbery weapons. In the United States, where gun laws were becoming less restrictive, the number of robberies involving firearms as a percentage of total robberies declined by almost exactly the same amount.[127] Robbery as a whole rose rather sharply, while robbery in America rose somewhat less quickly.[128]

That the United States and Canada might have generally similar crime trends, even though one country was tightening controls while the other loosened, seems intuitively unreasonable. Several criminologists have attempted to refine the analysis of Canadian and American gun control by comparing particular groups of Canadians or Americans.

For example, criminologist Paul Blackman observes that in the late

1970s and early 1980s, northern-tier U.S. states (which would seem to be the most comparable to Canada) saw a much slower rise in the robbery rate than did Canada. Blackman infers that the Canadian law had little effect on robbery, and therefore gun controls in general do not reduce crime.[129]

Direct U.S.-Canadian comparisons, such as Blackman's, must be reviewed carefully to control for the many cultural and social differences that might be far more important than differences in statutory firearms law. One of the most important U.S.-Canada comparative studies (in terms of influence on public consciousness) is of rather limited utility because the study failed to consider social variables.

On the morning of a hotly contested handgun-control referendum in Maryland in November 1988, the *Washington Post* broke an embargo against early release to run a story comparing American and Canadian gun laws.[130] The *Post* article summarized the findings in a forthcoming article in the *New England Journal of Medicine,* which analyzed handgun homicide rates in Vancouver and Seattle.[131] The *NEJM* article and *Washington Post* summary contrasted Seattle's higher homicide rate with Vancouver's lower rate. The article observed that Vancouver had stricter handgun laws than Seattle, and a lower handgun-homicide rate. Virtually all of the excess deaths in Seattle were due to handguns. Moreover, the Seattle-Vancouver difference could not be the result of economic effects on crime, the authors said, because the two cities had comparable average incomes.

Unfortunately, there were serious gaps in the *NEJM*'s reasoning. While Seattle and Vancouver do have the same *average* income, they have very different *below average* income groups. The low-income groups in Seattle have a high proportion of racial minorities that have been brutalized by a history of racial discrimination and destruction of basic family structures. If one limits the Seattle-Vancouver comparison to non-Hispanic whites, the homicide rates and gun victimization rates in the two cities are equal—despite Canada's stricter laws.[132]

The *New England Journal of Medicine* article by John Sloan et al., had other flaws as well. It attributed Vancouver's lower handgun-homicide rate to the 1977 Canadian law, which in practice barred acquisition of a handgun for self-defense, and almost totally outlawed carrying handguns for defense. Yet Vancouver's handgun (and overall) homicide rate after the law went into effect remained the same as in the years *before* the law. As noted above, the homicide rate from long guns had fallen substantially in Vancouver, but the drop in long-gun homicides was entirely matched by an increase in knife homicides. Thus, it was specious to conclude that the strict handgun law was the main cause of the low homicide rate.

Evidence from other sources indicates that the problem of crime involving arms in Vancouver has worsened since 1977. In 1982 the Vancouver

Police Union demanded a shotgun in every patrol car, more powerful handguns, and increased weapons training to cope with a huge surge in armed robberies.[133] Yet even as the police were arming themselves, the Vancouver police chief said he would press for a complete ban on all handguns. "The only reason for a handgun is protection, but we don't have a community that needs that kind of protection."[134]

The *New England Journal of Medicine* article professed to draw on support from other researchers, when the researchers in fact offered no support. The article cited *Under the Gun: Weapons and Crime and Violence in America,* by James Wright, Peter Rossi, and Kathleen Daly, to support the proposition that stricter gun control would reduce homicide. In fact, the book concludes that there is no persuasive evidence that any form of gun control has reduced or would reduce homicide.[135] The authors of the journal article also cited surveys by Decision Making Information (a conservative polling company) and by Cambridge Reports, Inc. (a liberal polling company), for the proposition that gun control would reduce accidents in the home, although the DMI study had not asked about accidents at all, and Cambridge had not asked where the accidents occurred.

While Sloan et al.'s research received widespread favorable coverage in general circulation print media, the study was sharply criticized in a number of letters to the *New England Journal of Medicine.* In self-defense, the article's authors asserted that they had not been evaluating the 1977 Canadian gun laws, but rather the general and long-standing Canadian policy of stricter control. The authors did not respond to the charges that they had attributed to Wright, Patrick Caddell, and DMI conclusions that those researchers had never made, and in some cases had pointedly rejected.[136]

The Seattle-Vancouver study was paid for by U.S. government funding from the Centers for Disease Control. The CDC had allocated a budget of over twenty million dollars for the express purpose of proving that the United States suffers from an "epidemic" of firearms. It does not seem likely, however, that understanding of the gun issue will be advanced by polemics from medical doctors and masters of public health who have been selected for research grants by a federal agency that already knows what results it wants to see.

Some Canadian criminologists, like American physicians, are not always persuasive in their insistence that Canadian gun control saves lives. For example, a 1989 article in the *Canadian Journal of Criminology* (a leading professional research publication) offered research data showing that the Canadian homicide rate had remained essentially stable in the decade following the enactment of the 1977 law. Any homicide decline resulting from the law was so small as to be virtually imperceptible. Nevertheless, the authors, Professors Catherine F. Sproule and Deborah J. Kennett, titled their article, "Killing with Guns in the U.S.A. and Canada 1977–1983: Further Evidence for the Effectiveness of Gun Control."[137] Their argument for the effectiveness of the Canadian law was essentially this:

1. Canada has strict gun controls and the United States does not.

2. The U.S.-Canada ratio of handgun murders is higher than the ratio of other types of murders.

3. Therefore, handgun control does not lead to the substitution of other equally effective murder weapons.

4. Therefore, Canada's low murder rate is "to a large measure the result" of gun control.

Sproule and Kennett's reasoning did not offer an explanation for why the Canadian gun law should be given the credit for Canada's relatively lower handgun-homicide rate. Indeed, Sproule and Kennett conspicuously ignored the Canadian government study that showed handgun crime to be particularly unaffected by the gun law. The only academic studies they cited to support their view that the Canadian law had any benefits were their own work, and the Seattle-Vancouver study discussed above.[138]

The evidence that Canadian gun policy causes crime is at least as convincing as arguments that the controls reduce crime. Even before the 1977 bill, Canadian civilians were more lightly armed than Americans; perhaps as a result, five times as many burglaries were committed against occupied Canadian residences than their counterparts in America. A Toronto study found that 48 percent of burglaries were against occupied homes, and 21 percent involved a confrontation with the victim; only 13 percent of U.S. residential burglaries are attempted against occupied homes. Similarly, most Canadian residential burglaries occur in the nighttime, while American burglars are known to prefer daytime entry to reduce the risk of a confrontation.[139] When an American burglar strikes at an occupied residence, his chance of being shot is at least equal to his chance of being sent to jail.[140] Since the 1977 gun law took effect, the Canadian breaking and entering rate rose 25 percent, and has surpassed the American rate, which has been declining.[141]

The post-1977 burglary increase was part of a general crime escalation. Hence, it might be that the 1977 gun restrictions had nothing to do with the burglary surge. The pattern of burglary against occupied residences in Canada had been established long before the 1977 gun law went into effect. The high burglary rate (if it has any relation at all to gun issues) may be blamed less on the particulars of Canadian law than on the country's gun culture, which has never emphasized the ownership of guns for armed home defense. By choice, Canadian homes have always been protected by loaded guns much less often than have American homes.

Although there are no studies indicating what percentage of Canadians keep a loaded gun at home for self-defense, it seems reasonable to infer that the percentage is markedly lower than in the United States because of the Canadian legal culture's greater hostility to armed defense. This hostility is expressed not only in the near-prohibition of gun acquisition for self-defense, but also in the legal treatment of people who use a gun for self-defense.

Even gun owners who obtain a gun for sport, but use it in an emergency for defense of self or property may be prosecuted, although they are usually acquitted.[142] Likewise, the carrying of a lawful, unregulated weapon (such as a knife) for self-defense has resulted in criminal prosecution for intent to possess a weapon for a dangerous purpose (although again, judges and juries have usually refused to convict).[143]

In the United States, the most common use of a firearm in a home for self-defense is not against a stranger perpetrating a burglary, but against a relative perpetrating an assault. The American judicial system seems to tolerate such results. In Detroit, for example, 75 percent of wives who shot and killed their husbands were not prosecuted, because the wives were determined to be defending themselves or their children against felonious attacks. In Miami the self-defense/nonprosecution figure was 60 percent, and in Houston it was 85.7 percent. But in Canada, the percentage of wives whose homicide cases were deemed not appropriate for prosecution was only 31.7 percent.[144]

Accidents and Suicide

The Canadian evidence regarding guns and crime does not show a profound anti-crime effect. Criminals, though, are not the only targets of gun control. Most gun laws embody the intuition that, in some circumstances at least, ordinary citizens should not be trusted with deadly weapons. Laws that cannot affect criminals—who, after all, have ready access to the black market—may be more effective among law-abiding citizens. The results of the Canadian experience support this intuition.

Seventy-one percent of Canada's firearms deaths in the years preceding Bill C-51 were suicides. Of all Canadian suicides, 35 percent were by gun.[145] The Canadian gun controllers, by making the purchase of an individual's first gun more time-consuming, likely hoped that impulsive gun suicides would decrease. Keeping a potential suicide who already owns one gun from buying another does little good. Nor does reducing the overall gun density of a region. Philip Stenning and Sharon Moyer found no correlation between the number of guns in an area and the number of firearms suicides.[146]

Delaying those who are purchasing their first gun might give some potential suicides time to reconsider. Therefore, it made sense for a Parliament concerned about suicide to concentrate enforcement resources at the point of initial gun purchase, with the Firearms Acquisition Certificate. Acquisition of additional long guns by FAC holders was left mostly unregulated, with no police decision point or even notification.

The Parliament's decision to concentrate on first-time gun purchasers worked. Suicides involving firearms dropped noticeably after 1978, reversing the previous trend.[147] Unfortunately, the overall Canadian suicide rate increased slightly. America's suicide rate declined slightly during the same period (and firearms suicides remained much higher as a percentage of total American suicides).[148]

The explanation may be that people who only wanted to make a gesture did not use a deadly weapon in the first place. People who really wanted to kill themselves and maintained that desire for a period of at least several hours apparently found time to employ other methods. The only potential suicides whom gun control could affect were people who had a serious but brief determination to kill themselves; theoretically, making suicide instruments not readily accessible might stop these potential suicides. Yet the Canadian experience seems to indicate that this third group of potential suicides is quite small and that almost all of them, deprived of guns, quickly found an alternative suicide instrument.

Even the physicians who had performed the Seattle-Vancouver handgun crime-death study found that gun control in Vancouver was not associated with lower suicide rates. Although Seattle's handgun-suicide rate was five times higher than Vancouver's, the latter's overall suicide was greater. Interestingly, the data showed that the suicide rate in Vancouver (where handgun controls were stricter, and individual freedom perhaps slightly more limited) was higher than Seattle's for all age groups except one. That one group was age fifteen to twenty-four, and the physicians chose to emphasize this fact in their presentation, arguing that gun control might reduce young people's suicide, even if it had no overall effect. The assertion seemed questionable in light of the fact that gun controls in Canada are actually less formally restrictive toward teenagers than are American laws.[149]

Another investigation of city pairs looked at Toronto and San Diego. The study found that the Canadian gun laws had decreased firearm suicides by men. The San Diego portion of the study looked only at mental patients, who are forbidden by California law to possess guns, and also found that the law reduces firearm suicides by men. (The firearm suicide rate for women was already low.) Unfortunately, while suicides in Toronto and San Diego involving firearms declined, the overall suicide rate did not. "[T]he difference was apparently offset by an increase in suicide by leaping."[150]

A policy that could save even one life was deemed worth considering. In weighing the costs and benefits of American gun control, however, one should expect that even a stringent gun prohibition would save very few if any of the Americans who take their lives with firearms.

As for fatal accidents involving firearms, Canada in the years after 1977 continued to enjoy a long-term decline in such accidents. This decline had actually begun in the 1950s.[151] The accident rate had been falling sharply for two years, but then hit a plateau in 1976–1977. After the enactment of the law, the accident rate dropped sharply again in 1978, plateauing again in 1979. Compared to crimes or suicides in which firearms played a key role, accidents had always been a minor problem. Evaluating gun use in Canada in the early 1970s, before the new law was enacted, Stenning and Moyer found that "contrary to popular belief, accidental firearms deaths are quite rare in Canada." Teenage males fifteen to nineteen constituted the largest group of victims.[152]

In sum, to the extent that analysis of the effects of the 1977 Canadian law demonstrates anything about the efficacy of gun control, it shows a lack of relation between gun control and crime control. The gun law appears to have had little or no effect on the overall levels of murder, suicide, gun accidents, or robbery. True, the percentage of guns used in murders and suicides has declined, but the result merely reinforces the anti-controllers' argument that if guns are less available, other, equally deadly weapons will be substituted.

One possible explanation for why the Canadian controls appear not to have had much effect is that gun control is not effective. Another explanation, which is also consistent with the data, is that the Canadian controls were not severe enough. While the laws regulated gun possession, they did not seek aggressively to reduce guns to an absolute minimum (as the British laws have). Because the Canadian controls were relatively lenient, the absolute number of firearms in Canada, and the number per capita, actually rose in the decade after controls were imposed.[153] Arguably, stricter Canadian controls would have succeeded where looser controls failed.

On the other hand, the analysis of Britain has shown that strict laws, while successful in reducing gun ownership by law-abiding citizens, appeared to have little impact on criminals. In any case, Canada, having a much more socioeconomically diverse tradition of recreational firearms use than does Britain, would be unlikely to ever adopt controls as severe as Britain's.

Regardless of whether the 1977 gun reforms had any effect, it could be that Canada's lower overall gun density has contributed to the lower Canadian homicide and robbery rates. Before reaching conclusions about the effect of Canada's gun density, it is necessary to consider other factors that may impact crime rates in the United States and Canada.

Sociological Variables

The American crime and violence rate is not uniformly high for all groups. If one looks only at the American states that border Canada, the homicide rate in these states is generally no higher (and often lower) than in adjacent Canadian provinces.[154] Similarly, if one excludes Americans born in southern states (of all races) from American crime statistics, America's crime rate is comparable to Canada's.[155]

The North-South contrast in crime rates in the United States may not be due to gun laws. American southerners have no more access to handguns than northerners do, and yet they commit far more crime.[156] The high southern crime rate cannot be due mainly to guns, since most of the southern guns are in rural areas, and most of the southern crime is in urban areas. Southerners also have an abnormally high nongun assault rate.[157]

Other studies have also found the difference in Canadian and American crime rates to be associated with the different sociological mix of the two nations. The overall death rate for non-Hispanic white Americans from all types of shootings (murder, suicide, accident, etc.) is the same as the rate for Canadians.[158] One study, by Robert J. Mundt, compared twenty-five Canadian cities with twenty-five comparably sized American cities. When the covariables of "percent black" and "city size" where considered, the difference between American and Canadian samples diminished to the point of insignificance.[159] In other words, the higher American homicide rate in relation to Canada was attributable to the fact that America is much more densely urban than Canada, and that America has a much higher percentage of blacks in its population.

Further research by Mundt, however, called into question the adequacy of city size and race as explanatory factors in the differing Canadian and American homicide rates. Mundt conducted in-depth comparisons of Winnipeg and Minneapolis/St. Paul, and of Duluth and Thunder Bay, each city pair having many similarities. Mundt found that the American cities had far higher violent crime rates than their Canadian counterparts, and that much, although not all, of the increased crime was due to increased gun crime. (The major exception was that Thunder Bay had a higher robbery and armed robbery rate than Duluth.) After factoring out the variables of race and city size, Mundt found that there was still a substantial gap in the American and Canadian gun crime rates. Accordingly, stricter Canadian gun laws could not be ruled out as an explanation for Canada's relatively crime-free status.[160]

In all of the U.S./Canada comparisons, except for Mundt's four-city study, sociological differences, including race, urbanization, and the presence of southerners, can statistically account for all the homicide differences between the United States and Canada. If Americans, to the extent that they are as rural, Caucasian (and nonsouthern) as Canadians, have the same homicide rate, even though Americans have much looser gun laws, the Canadian gun laws are not a satisfactory explanation of Canada's low homicide rate. On the other hand, Mundt's four-city study suggests that sociological variables may not always explain the U.S./Canada differences, and it is therefore not possible to say with certainty that the Canadian gun laws do not work.

Even to the extent that the sum of all the research undermines the claims of the Canadian gun controllers, the research does not undermine the claims of the American gun controllers. Precisely because America is more urbanized, suffers from more racial tension, and is (arguably) afflicted by a southern subculture of violence, America might be all the more in need of gun controls. Perhaps some parts of America are so mired in a culture of violence that they must be disarmed.

On the other hand, it might be argued that since gun laws per se are not associated with crime reduction (the Canadian experience and the evidence from most comparisons among Canadian and U.S. cities and regions seems to so indicate), it might be that other strategies would better address America's urban and ethnic violence. Perhaps the effort should be to deal directly with the social conditions that make southerners, blacks, Hispanics, and urbanites so much more likely to be victims and perpetrators of crime.

WOULD CANADIAN-STYLE LAWS WORK IN AMERICA?

Even if it could be demonstrated that the Canadian gun laws have an enormously beneficial impact in Canada, the conclusion that America should adopt a similar system of controls does not necessarily follow. Before concluding that a Canadian-style system would fit well in America, the characteristics of American gun owners and their guns—to the extent they differ from or resemble their Canadian counterparts—should be examined.

Gun Density and Gun Owners

In regard to long guns, the differences between the United States and Canada are not large. The percentage of Canadian households with a rifle is nearly equal to that found in the United States.[161] As for the percentage of overall gun possession, the divergence is greater, but not tremendous. About half of all American households contain a firearm, whereas a quarter to a third of Canadian households do.[162] There is substantial variation among the Canadian provinces. Approximately 67 percent of Yukon/Northwest Territory households contain firearms. The rate of ownership is lowest in the central part of the nation, where, for example, 15 percent of Ontario residents own a gun. The rate is higher on the great plains (35 percent in Saskatchewan and 39 percent in Alberta) and along the Atlantic coast (32 percent in Atlantic provinces).[163]

Regarding handguns, the contrast between America and Canada is profound. The RCMP estimated the pre-1978 pool of illegal handguns in Canada to be about 50,000; even if this figure is too low by a factor of ten, it is minuscule compared with America's illegal gun stock. In New York City alone, conservative estimates put the number of illegal handguns at over 700,000.[164]

There are also many more legal handguns in the United States. About one-third of American firearms are handguns; only 6 percent of Canada's are.[165] As of 1989, there were 847,072 registered "restricted weapons" (mostly handguns), with an annual growth in registrations of 30,000 to 35,000;[166] in the United States handguns comprise about one-third of the roughly 200 million guns. Only 1 to 3 percent of Canadian adults will admit to a pollster that they own a handgun.[167] Pollster Gary Mauser found that about 10 to 30 percent more Canadians supported particular forms of gun control than Americans did. As a general rule, both nations favored "moderate" controls on firearms, such as a police permit and registration. The sharpest difference was on handgun prohibition, with 66 percent of Canadians in favor, but only 36 percent of Americans.[168]

Perhaps more important than the numbers of guns is the characteristics of the gun owners. American opponents of gun control, when challenged with arguments about the gun-control system in Britain, typically reply that British gun owners are simply different; the British shooters are mostly an aristocratic gentry who do not mind controls on their bird-hunting shotguns. The common folk of Britain, not owning guns, do not mind strict controls. While the image of the gun in Britain as a toy of the landed gentry is not entirely accurate, it is widely shared.

The similarities between Canadian and American gun owners are more numerous than the differences. Gun ownership is three times as common for rural men as for those living in metropolitan areas, a ratio similar to the American figures.[169] Although guns in general are less common in urban areas, as in America, a relatively high percentage of legal urban guns are handguns.[170] Much like in America, self-employed men and employers in Canada are more likely to own guns, compared to employees.[171] University graduates are more likely to own guns than people with only a high school education.[172] The most important difference between America and Canada is that no more than 1 percent of Canadian women own guns, while female gun ownership in America is at least fifteen times that rate.[173]

The Police Model

The British police are mostly unarmed, and the Japanese police hardly ever draw their guns. Few people in either nation own guns. The Canadian police are well-armed, and much more likely to use their guns than their British or Japanese counterparts. When Canadian police use their guns they legitimize gun use in general; police gun use is an important explanation for why Canada is so much more heavily armed than Japan or Great Britain.

While some of Canada's local peace officers are unarmed, the federal RCMP (some of whom act as provincial or municipal police under contract from the provincial attorney general) all carry guns.[174] In general, the police are quite well supplied. Most police cruisers carry a shotgun with buckshot loads in the trunk. The emergency response team (like an American SWAT team) may carry tear gas, rifles, shotguns, or submachine guns.[175]

The RCMP and the municipal police formerly used standard round-nosed bullets, but have switched to hollow-point bullets. The RCMP force in British Columbia explains the reasons for the change to hollow-points as follows:

> Round-nosed bullets do not deform upon impact. The lack of deformation increases the chance that the bullet will exit the target's body and strike an innocent bystander.
>
> Hollow-point bullets deform inside the target's body, expending all their energy there. A hit from a round-nosed bullet might kill the victim in a few hours, but would likely not immediately incapacitate the victim. The hollow-point hit, by increasing the likelihood that the target assailant can be stopped with one shot, reduces the need to continue shooting the target. In the long term, this reduces the chance that the suspect will have to be killed.[176]

While the police have adopted hollow points, such handgun cartridges are illegal for civilians, even though they are safer for self-defense, whether the person be a potential victim, an innocent bystander, or a criminal.[177] Since the police have determined self-defense to almost never be a justification for civilian gun ownership, cartridges made especially for self-defense have no place in civilian hands.

Although the Canadian police are well-armed, they do not use their firearms as frequently as their southern counterparts. In America, about one person a day is killed by the police, almost always with legal justification. In Canada the per capita rate of homicide by police is less than a third of that for the Americans.[178] The high rate of gun use by the police in the United States sets an example that encourages the already high rate of civilian gun ownership to become even higher; the police example of gun use is more important than the anti-gun pronouncements of some urban police chiefs.

Self-Defense

Canadian police culture is apparently more restrictive of police rights to use firearms against criminals, and Canadian legal culture is similarly restrictive for civilians. Ordinary citizens may only use deadly force to protect themselves "or any one under their protection," from "death or grievous bodily harm."[179] American citizens in most states may use deadly force to protect anyone, including a complete stranger, from violent felonies, regardless of whether "grievous bodily harm" is feared.

Yet while the Canadian police and legal system send strong messages against civilian self-defense, Canadians seem nearly as supportive of the concept of armed self-defense as are Americans. About 70 percent of citizens in both countries believe that retail store owners are at least sometimes justified in using a firearm in self-defense.[180] Fifty-eight percent of Canadians would even allow store owners to have licensed handguns. The Canadian-American agreement about self-defense for store owners breaks down, though, on the issue of home defense. Only 40 percent of Canadians believe that homeowners should be allowed to have defensive handguns, even with a police license.[181]

Whatever the theoretical support for self-defense in some circumstances, Canadian citizens do not feel a personal need for self-defense guns. A mere 5 percent of Canadians, mostly in prairies remote from any police station, tell pollsters that self-defense is their main reason for owning guns. In contrast, about a quarter of America's gun owners claim self-defense as their reason, and most of them live in cities.[182]

In theory and in practice, American citizens, both police and civilians, need and use guns for self-defense much more than do their Canadian counterparts.[183] It seems likely that people who own guns for self-defense will be especially likely to disobey prohibitive gun control statutes. Thus, even though Canadian and American gun owners have many similarities, efforts to impose a Canadian-type system on the United States would need to consider a particular class of American citizens who would be especially likely to disobey a restrictive gun law: the citizen—predominantly urban and often female—who believes that ownership of a firearm—usually a handgun—is essential for personal safety.

Attitudes toward Gun Control

Neither Canada's culture nor its constitution have inculcated in its citizens a determination to own or carry handguns. For example, when the 1978 law went into effect in Ontario, with an amnesty period for illegal guns, thousands were surrendered,[184] a number far higher than in most American gun amnesties (which are usually lucky to break the three-digit barrier).[185] One Canadian police officer observed, "We don't have the tradition here of people believing it's an inherent right to carry a gun. I've had people come in to a police station after a relative had died, and they'll bring in a box carrying his collection. I tell that to American policemen, and they think I'm lying."[186] But while few Canadians do believe they have a right to carry a handgun, a majority of Canadians believe they have a right to own a gun. The important point is that they do not believe that the right extends to handguns, and they do not seem to believe that the current system of controls violates their right to a gun.[187]

Because the Canadian law matches the intuitions of the Canadian people, there is no need for draconian penalties. Judges usually give only suspended sentences or probation to defendants convicted of illegally possessing a gun (even a machine gun), unless the person was carrying the gun for use in a crime.[188] The typical penalty for possession of an unregistered handgun is a $50 fine.[189] In the United States, gun laws sometimes come along with mandatory minimum sentences. New York and Massachusetts have mandatory one-year prison terms for carrying a loaded handgun without a license, and have imposed prison terms even though the defendant was conceded to have been carrying the gun only for self-protection.[190] The American use of severe mandatory sentences reflects the expectation that many ordinary citizens will resist gun controls, unless terrified into compliance by rigid penalties.

The willing obedience to gun control is one aspect of Canadians' greater acceptance of government power. The *Los Angeles Times'* Toronto correspondent described Canadians as "a conservative people who accept authority more readily than do most Americans."[191] When asked about whether people would comply with a number of hypothetical laws, such as a public ban on smoking, a prohibition on alcoholic beverages, firearms registration, or a handgun surrender law, Canadians anticipated a much higher degree of voluntary compliance than did Americans.[192] In other polls, Canadians were more tolerant than Americans of civil rights restrictions during a crisis and placed a relatively higher value on order over unrestricted free speech.[193]

The deference to authority is reflected in the politics of gun control. Because, says the *Times* writer, Canadians "do not feel that they can have a real role in ironing [government policies] out," most Canadian firearms owners have never involved themselves in politics to become a dominant force in the gun-control debate the way American firearms owners so often have.[194] Although the Canadian gun lobby, the National Firearms Association, has succeeded in rousing more Canadians in recent years, the NFA is not renowned and feared in Ottawa the way the NRA is in Washington, D.C. Canada's NFA has only seven thousand members, and a strong membership base only in the western province of Alberta.[195] The American NRA has 2.5 million members, and a substantial base in every state. The NRA's power is rooted in the political activism of American citizens in general. Americans, and gun owners in particular, write to their elected officials, donate to political campaigns, and become angry when government ignores their wishes.

The quietitude of Canadian gun owners, however, is not without limits. It is true that Canadian gun owners, unlike their more ideological American counterparts, apparently do not believe in the right of revolution as the basis for civilian gun ownership. Nor are even the political activists among Canadian gun owners generally willing to articulate self-defense against crime as a legitimate reason for gun ownership. (The fear of raising the self-defense issue may be an overly timid approach on the part of the gun owners, given the general public's fairly broad support for use of licensed handguns in self-defense.) But there is one gun-control issue for which Canadian gun owners *will* fight. That issue is responsible use of sporting arms.

In the mid-1970s, the Trudeau government announced gun controls that would have made possession of all guns, including hunting rifles and shotguns, subject to strict controls and bureaucratic obstacles. (The particular proposals have been discussed above.) An unorganized but large reaction from Canadian gun owners scuttled those controls. The controls that did emerge in 1977 had virtually no adverse impact on traditional Canadian sporting use of arms. Possession of handguns for self-defense was almost completely outlawed, and automatic firearms placed on the road to extinction, but very few Canadians show any interest in possessing guns for self-defense or in collecting machine guns anyway. What a large number do care about is use of long guns for sporting purposes (and for animal control in rural areas). The 1977 controls placed almost no restrictions on these latter uses, requiring only that a person seeking to buy a rifle or shotgun apply for a Firearms Acquisition Certificate, which would allow unlimited long-gun purchases during the next five years.

The political clout of the Canadian gun owners—on the single issue of sporting use of long guns—was manifested again after the Marc Lépine massacre of the fourteen female students at the École Polytechnique de Montréal in December 1989. Lépine's massacre was perpetrated with a semi-automatic rifle, the Ruger mini-14, which Lépine had acquired lawfully under the Firearms Acquisition Certificate system. (A report by coroner Teresa Sourer stated that Lépine's use of the mini-14 was not an important factor in the shootings, since a standard hunting rifle "probably would have had similar results.") After invading the university classroom, Lépine had excused the male students, and told the female students "You're all a bunch of feminists" before murdering them. The nation was understandably horrified.[196] Minister of Justice Doug Lewis, voicing skepticism about more gun controls, stated "You cannot legislate against insanity."

Leaders of feminist organizations voiced support for the complete abolition of civilian gun ownership, which they saw as a manifestation of patriarchal values.[197] At the same time, the Progressive-Conservative ruling party was finding itself in political trouble with urban females due to the party's tightening of abortion laws. Whether motivated by political expediency, or genuine concerns for public safety, or both, the government proposed a broad range of severe new gun laws.

The ruling party's new minister of justice, Kim Campbell, introduced Bill C-80, which was speedily endorsed by the other two major parties. The bill banned rifle magazines of more than five rounds, and handgun magazines holding more than ten rounds; required applicants for Firearm Acquisition Certificates (FAC) to be vouched for by two persons engaged in professions that the government would designate; subjected the persons offering the voucher to potential civil liability for any misuse of the gun; imposed a twenty-eight-day waiting period on issuing the certificate; authorized the government to administratively ban as many semi-automatic rifles and handguns as it chose; and made a large number of technical modifications that expanded police authority to seize firearms and revoke gun licenses without prior or subsequent judicial review.[198]

Despite the support of all three major parties, Bill C-80 raised a blizzard of opposition from gun owners. Target shooters argued that the magazine ban would have a substantial adverse impact on their sport; and gun owners of all types feared that the government was out to place gun ownership on the road to extinction.[199] Although the Canadian gun owners lacked a strong organizational leader comparable to the American NRA, individual gun clubs, wildlife federations, and gun owners mustered in large numbers. The volume of mail that Parliament received in opposition to Bill C-80 was rivaled only by mail on the abortion issue. Although the Progressive-Conservatives had the votes to pass the bill, the party apparently decided not to alienate its prairie members and their constituents. (The Progressive-Conservatives face a strong challenge in Western Canada from the new Reform party, which has some libertarian inclinations.)

Bill C-80 was sent to a special parliamentary committee, which recommended modifying its most severe features.[200] When Parliament was prorogued, the bill died. Justice Minister Campbell brought a new gun bill back for the 1991–1992 legislative session. Rejecting the position of the Advisory Committee, the new bill, C-17, retained many of the severe features of the original Bill C-80.[201]

As finally enacted by Parliament, Bill C-17 accomplished the following:

- Imposed a twenty-eight-day waiting period on FAC issuance.[202]

- Reenacted government authority (which already existed under the 1977 law) to restrict or ban by administrative regulation any gun that the government does not consider to be commonly used for hunting or other sporting purposes.[203] The guns that are expected to be banned by regulation are centerfire semi-automatic rifles having "military" accessories such as a pistol grip or folding stock. Based on a point system, guns with several accessories would become prohibited weapons, while guns with fewer accessories would become restricted weapons. Current owners of the newly prohibited guns would be "grandfathered," allowed to retain the guns, and allowed to sell them to other persons who own prohibited semi-automatic weapons when the C-17 regulations go into effect.[204]

- "Large capacity cartridge magazines" would be outlawed.[205] The government will likely specify by regulation that "large capacity" means five cartridges for centerfire semi-automatic rifles and ten for centerfire handguns, with no new limit for rimfire or non-semi-automatic firearms.[206] Competition target shooters could receive permits to possess oversize magazines.[207] Current owners of large magazines could retain them by retrofitting the magazine to reduce permanently its cartridge capacity.[208]

- The government would be given authority to ban by administrative decree any firearms accessory not "of a kind commonly used for hunting or sporting purposes in Canada."[209]

- The requirement for a safety training class before obtaining an FAC—which had been enacted in 1977 but never implemented—will begin to be enforced.[210]

- FAC applicants must obtain recommendations from "two persons who belong to a class of persons prescribed by regulation who have known the applicant for at least three years."[211] The persons giving the recommendation are immune from civil liability.[212]

- Officers considering an FAC application may interview the applicant's neighbors, co-workers, and family[213] (as was already the practice for restricted weapon applicants.).

- Safe-storage regulations would be promulgated for all firearms.[214] The regulations are expected to require that guns be stored with a trigger lock, and the ammunition be locked away separately.[215]

Between the first gun-control proposal and final approval of the new law by Parliament, pro-gun activists won numerous concessions on technical issues (such as immunizing persons signing an FAC recommendation from civil lawsuit). Although final regulations have yet to be developed, the number of guns to be prohibited may be substantially less than was originally hoped by the anti-gun activists. At the same time, the FAC application process will become significantly more cumbersome, and the many target shooters who use semi-automatic rifles with a military appearance face a much higher level of regulation.

But unless the police abuse their new powers from the 1991 gun controls, persons who wish to use long guns other than centerfire semi-automatics for hunting or target shooting will likely not find the Canadian controls unbearably onerous.

While the widespread sporting use of long guns in Canada remains reasonably intact, supporters of gun prohibition also express satisfaction with the new laws. The prohibitionists view Canadian gun control as a one-way street, and consider any movement down that street as progress toward the inevitable goal.

Thus, in both the mid-1970s and the early 1990s, Canadian gun owners have shown the political strength to turn back some gun controls despite strong central government support. Canadian gun owners have demonstrated their limited clout only on the issue of sporting or farm use of long guns, and not on self-defense uses of handguns.

Trust the State

Strong as the Canadian right-to-bear-arms movement may sometimes be, the Canadian movement is not even remotely as powerful as its sister in America, in terms of popular support or political success. The relative weakness of the right in Canada comports with the relative weakness in Canada of most other liberties guaranteed in the American Bill of Rights.

The sweeping search and seizure laws that are used to enforce the gun controls in Canada reflect a greater acceptance of government intrusions. Canadian courts still sometimes issue "writs of assistance," which allow the Royal Canadian Mounted Police to conduct broad searches, without specifying what they are searching for. Until recently, the courts simply gave the RCMP fill-in-the-blank search warrants. In the United States, writs of assistance were abolished over two centuries ago, after the American Revolution.

Other rules of criminal procedure also favor the state. The Crown can appeal a "not guilty" verdict in a criminal trial, whereas the American Constitution mandates "nor shall any person be subject for the same offence to be twice put in jeopardy of life or limb."[216] There is no requirement that Canada provide a defense attorney when it prosecutes an indigent for a felony. The right to jury trial exists only in cases involving at least a five-year prison term.[217] There is no guarantee against coerced self-incrimination and the police have no obligation to inform a suspect of his right to silence. If a suspect asks to see his lawyer and the police refuse, voluntary statements made by the suspect may be used in court.[218]

Not until 1987 did the Canadian Security and Intelligence Service disband its "countersubversion branch," which kept files on certain popular labor and anti-war groups. Government internal security has files on 600,000 people, one out every forty Canadians.[219]

Like Britain, Canada has an Official Secrets Act, which lets the government prohibit publication of government secrets, even if the "secret" has nothing to do with national security.[220] Whereas free speech in America is nearly absolute, Canada bans the import of "hate literature," has seized some offending items from a university library, and has even jailed a pamphleteer who denied that the Holocaust took place. There have been a number of convictions and prosecutions of racist or anti-Semitic hate-mongers.[221] The legal boundaries of free speech are narrower in Canada, and Canadians are less inclined to exercise the rights they do have. Even after adjusting for population differences, Canada sees far fewer protest demonstrations than does the United States.[222]

When advertising, persons in the gun business are specifically forbidden to "depict or extol violence against another person."[223] Thus, while self-defense theoretically (although not in practice) remains a lawful reason for gun ownership, police regulations have forbidden even advertising that extols self-defense.

Canada has no separation of powers between the executive and legislative branches of government, nor is the power of the national government confined to specified subjects. The majority party in Parliament enjoys nearly unlimited power for its five-year term.[224] The United States was created out of rebellion against a strong central government; Canada was created by rebels against rebellion, for whom, in the words of former Canadian Minister of Justice Mark MacGuigan, "the state was perceived as a benign presence" to help the struggle against a harsh climate and challenging terrain.[225]

Canada did not have a Bill of Rights until 1960, and today its status is merely that of a statute, subject to easy repeal at any time.[226] In 1984, Canada implemented a Charter of Rights and Freedoms, derived from its Commonwealth British heritage.[227] The Charter of Rights is much harder to change, and provides a solid foundation for the rights contained in America's First Amendment (freedom of speech, religion, and assembly).[228] But the Charter of Rights, in contrast to the earlier Bill of Rights, does not forbid the taking of property without due process. Therefore, ruled Canada's highest court, the government may take personal property—including guns— without due process of law.[229]

And while the American Bill of Rights is framed in absolute terms (e.g., "Congress shall make no law . . . no soldier shall . . . no Warrants shall issue . . . no person shall be held to answer . . . nor shall any person be. . . . In all criminal prosecutions . . . no fact tried by a jury. . . ."), the Charter of Rights and Freedoms is a self-constricting document, its guarantees of freedom being subject to "reasonable limits."[230] Moreover, many of the charter's "guarantees" can be overridden by a federal or provincial law that says it will operate "notwithstanding" the charter.[231] It is no wonder that some Canadian nationalists believe American television is subversive because it makes youth believe they have constitutional rights.[232]

Unlike in the United States, Canadian government regulatory agencies face little judicial scrutiny and are trusted to exercise substantial discretion. At the same time, agencies rely less on harsh sanctions than do their American counterparts, because Canadians are expected to obey government regulations of their own volition.[233]

More trusting of their government, Canadians expect more from it. Canada's government plays a much larger role in the economy than the American government does. The welfare state is far larger, and the populace more supportive of high rates of government spending and taxation. All three major parties are several steps to the left of American Democrats on economic policy.[234] As in Great Britain, the two dominant political ideologies are Tory and Socialist—each one a European-derived philosophy that emphasizes the community and the state over the individual.[235] Historian David Bell calls the Canadian attitude "cratophilia" (love of government).[236]

The Canadian government fits with the people. Cross-national surveys find Canadians more tolerant of ruling elites and less oriented toward individual achievement than are Americans.[237] Three religions—Roman Catholic, Anglican, and the United Church (an amalgam of Protestant denominations)—each have a tradition of state support, and together they account for 87 percent of all Canadians. Belonging to a Canadian church has traditionally meant membership in a large structure that is allied with the government. In contrast, the majority of Americans have traditionally belonged to dissident Protestant sects who feared oppression, and sought safety in the separation of church and state.[238]

Canadian poet Margaret Atwood considers "the frontier" the best symbol of America, because the frontier "is a place for the new, where the old order can be discarded." She contrasts the treatment of the family in American and Canadian literature: "if in America it's a skin you shed, then in Canada it's a trap in which you're caught."[239] Virtually all comparative analysts of Canadian and American literature find Canadian fiction to extol more passive and conservative values. One critic notes that in father-son conflicts in literature, American sons succeed in their rebellion, and Canadian sons usually fail.[240] Other scholars describe Canada's literature as emphasizing the feminine and the accommodating, in contrast to the more domineering, masculine model of American fiction. Female writers, it is suggested, occupy more central positions in Canadian literature because the personal female experience is the political Canadian experience (accommodation and submission in playing the helpmate to Britain and the United States).[241] Other scholars note that Canadian art rarely celebrates populism,[242] and has contributed little to the avant-garde.[243]

Canadian historians neglect violence in Canadian history. Contemporary witnesses to violence (such as the 1919 Winnipeg strike) blame the violence on foreigners. Violence is condemned not merely as immoral in itself, but as an affront to a nation whose very identity is based on a rejection of Americanism and violence.[244]

One Canadian author summarizes the different Canadian attitudes toward liberty and authority as follows:

> Canadians do not lack entrenched civil liberties because their form of government makes it difficult to provide them; they accept a governmental structure under which liberty cannot be guaranteed because they are highly ambivalent about personal freedom and because they genuinely believe that government is designed to be an instrument for advancing the general welfare, and is not, in principle, anything to fear. . . . Canada doesn't want the American political system, doesn't need it, and couldn't make it work. But life in Canada could be made much freer, and political institutions more stable, if Canadians could get the message that is already grasped at some level by most Americans: that authority is, in every sense, inherently questionable.[245]

A man on a saddle with rifle and revolver symbolized the West in both nations. America's character was the independent cowboy, and Canada's the Royal North-West Mounted Policeman.[246] In fact, the "Lone Ranger" would have been an outlaw in Canada, since Canadian law forbade carrying a firearm while "masked or disguised."[247] A typical scene in American frontier fiction is the hero confronting the bad guys in a shoot-out; in the typical Canadian scene, the American desperado surrenders his revolver when so commanded by the mounted policeman.[248] Americans made a national symbol out of their frontier West. Even today, the West is thought to be the most American of all regions. Canadians pay much less historical attention to their own West, and honor the nineteenth-century West only rarely with monuments.[249]

While American history's heroes were often strong individualists, Canadians admired more the organization man, or the organization itself: the loyal servant of New France, the Hudson's Bay Company fur trader, the Mounted Police, or the Saskatchewan grain-growers' associations.[250] As Atwood observes, rebels and revolutionaries, to the extent that they appear at all in Canadian literature, are rarely heroes.[251] Writes Gaile McGregor: "the culture hero is not the gunslinger, triumphing over opposition by a demonstration of natural powers and anarchistic individual will, but rather the Law itself: impersonal, all embracing, pre-eminently social."[252] Canadian criminologist John Hagan contrasts the mounted policeman with another American symbol, the eagle, "a fiercely independent animal prone to outbursts of violence."[253] (The National Rifle Association's symbol is an eagle with crossed rifles in its talons. The symbol of the Canada's National Firearm Association is a Royal Crown with a heraldic shield underneath.)

Symbols such as mounted policemen, cowboys, and eagles reflect and create social reality. So do constitutions. Professor Friedland contrasts the American Constitution with its right to keep and bear arms, and the Canadian Constitution, which simply provides for "peace, order and good government," and signifies obedience to authority.[254] The very names of the founding documents express the divergence between America and Canada. America achieved full independence through its unilateral Declaration of Independence; America's system of government is based on a Constitution deriving its authority from "We the people." Canada's attainment of dominion status within the Commonwealth, as well as its basic structure of government, were not won in revolution by the people, but granted by the British North America Act of 1867.

CONCLUSION

To an American civil libertarian, the Canadian exaltation of the police and of orderliness may seem unpleasant. But the policy has its benefits. As Hagan explains, "the police role has become preeminently symbolic, a reminder that social order precedes individual liberties."[255] The streets are cleaner, teenagers get along better with their parents, and teenage pregnancy is rarer.[256]

Canadian gun control works in Canada. True, the comprehensive system of controls enacted in 1977 has yielded little provable direct benefit. The studies purporting to show good results from the 1977 law are generally of dubious competence. But for most Canadians, that is not the point. Gun control, the exaltation of the police, deference to authority, and rejection of violence are all threads in the unified tapestry of Canadian culture. Canada has a much stronger tradition of sporting long-gun use than Britain or Japan, and Canadian gun laws are correspondingly milder.

The Canadian system works for most Canadians because it symbolically affirms deeply held values of orderliness and nonviolence. Before deciding to transplant the Canadian system to America, it must be asked whether the Canadian system would mesh as well with American values as it does with Canadian ones. There being little evidence that the Canadian gun controls actually reduce crime, the main benefit of the laws is symbolic, and it should be considered how much of a symbolic benefit that Canadian-style gun control would yield in the American culture.

Discussion of the symbolic role of guns and gun control in American culture is taken up in chapters 9 and 10. The previous three chapters have offered detailed examination of the three countries which are most commonly suggested as gun-control models for the United States. The next two chapters look at Australia and New Zealand. The focus is less on the criminological details of gun control in those nations than on the social and political aspects. Besides the United States, Australia is the only nation with a large, aggressive, and powerful gun lobby that is often in open conflict with the police. Nowhere is the war between gun control and gun rights fiercer than Australia. Australia is also the only English-speaking nation, besides the United States, to devolve gun control to the state level.

New Zealand is as different from Australia as Canada is from America. Police and gun owners live together contentedly under a set of reasonable controls that all sides accept. The relation between the government and the governed, as brought out by the firearms debate, is the topic of the next two chapters.

NOTES

1. In the province of British Columbia, 29 percent of all households own a rifle. Gary Mauser, *Ownership of Firearms in British Columbia: Self-Defense or Sportsmanship?* (manuscript in progress, Faculty of Business Administration, Simon Fraser University, Burnaby, British Columbia), p. 4.

2. Seymour Martin Lipset, "Canada and the United States: The Cultural Dimension," in American Assembly, *Canada and the United States: Enduring Friendship, Persistent Stress* (Englewood Cliffs, N.J.: Prentice-Hall, 1985), p. 109. [Hereinafter, Lipset, *Canada and the United States.*]

3. "Killer Fraternized with Men in Army Fatigues," *The Globe and Mail,* December 9, 1989; "Killer's Letter Blames Feminists," *The Globe and Mail,* December 8, 1989.

4. O. W. Holmes, "The Place of History in Understanding Law," in John Honnold, ed., *The Life of the Law* (New York: Free Press, 1964), p. 3.

5. Holger Jensen, "Canada on Brink of War with Indians," *Rocky Mountain News,* September 21, 1990, p. 4.

6. Robin W. Winks, *The Relevance of Canadian History: U.S. and Imperial Perspectives* (Lanham, Md.: University Press of America, 1988), pp. 12–16; Paul Blackman, "The Canadian Gun Law, Bill C-51 Its Effectiveness and Lessons for Research on the 'Gun Control' Issue," paper presented at American Society of Criminology, Cincinnati, Ohio, November 7–11, 1984, p. 1.

As of 1642, the colony of New France included only 300 ethnic French, a group far too small to need to wrest large tracts of land from the Indians. Francis Jennings, *The Ambiguous Iroquois Empire: The Covenant Chain Confederation of Indian Tribes with English Colonies* (New York: W. W. Norton, 1984), p. 91.

7. "Canada on Brink of War with Indians," *Rocky Mountain News,* September 21, 1990, p. 4.

Modern Canada has not been so pacific in its Indian relations. During the spring and summer of 1990, Mohawk Indians led by the Mohawk Warrior Society armed with semi-automatic Kalashnikov rifles and other weapons seized and held part of the town of Oka, near Montreal, to prevent the expansion of a golf course and housing project onto a pine forest which was Mohawk ancestral land and onto the Mohawk's Pine Tree Cemetery. Besides Kalashnikovs, the Mohawks had Fabrique Nationale semi-automatics, high-powered hunting rifles, shotguns, a variety of handguns, RPK machine guns, Molotov cocktails and other homemade explosives, and a large number of booby traps. After the Mohawks repulsed a raid by the tactical squad of the Sûreté de Québec (the provincial police), Québec Premier Robert Bourassa eventually asked the Canadian army to intervene because his provincial force was outgunned by the warriors. The Mohawks saw themselves as the legitimate armed forces of a sovereign nation, defending their territory from attack. After some skirmishing, the federal government agreed to buy the golf course and give it to the Mohawks, and the Mohawks surrendered, ending the seventy-seven-day siege. A similar siege had taken place in upstate New York, where Mohawks seized and held an abandoned girls' camp near Moss Lake from 1974 to 1977, eventually forcing the state government to lease them two tracts of land near Plattsburgh, New York. "Rough Justice," *Maclean's* (August 6, 1990): 17–20; "A Ravaged Town," *Maclean's* (August 6, 1990): 21; "An Ancient Warrior Code," *Maclean's* (August 6, 1990): 22–23; "Fury in the Ranks," *Maclean's* (August 6, 1990): 24–25; John Coleman, "Canada's Civil War," *Soldier of Fortune* (December 1990): 38–47; "Mohawk Refugees Pelted," (New York) *Daily News,* August 29, 1990, p. 15; "Canadian Troops Move on Mohawk Settlement," *Washington Post,* September 2, 1990, p. A38

(Associated Press); "Canada on Brink of War with Indians," *Rocky Mountain News,* September 21, 1990, p. 4; "Mohawk Surrender Turns into One Last Brawl," *Toronto Globe and Mail,* reprinted in *Rocky Mountain News,* September 27, 1990, p. 33.

8. The French trade with the North American Indians is discussed in chapter 9.

9. Kenneth McNaught, *The Penguin History of Canada* (Ontario: Penguin, 1988), p. 27.

10. McNaught, p. 48; Link, p. 12.

11. Seymour Martin Lipset, *Continental Divide: The Values and Institutions of the United States and Canada* (New York: Routledge, 1990), p. 13 [hereinafter, Lipset, *Continental Divide*]; Nicholas N. Kittrie and Eldon D. Wedlock, Jr., *The Tree of Liberty: A Documentary History of Rebellion and Political Crime in America* (Baltimore: Johns Hopkins, 1986), p. 71; McNaught, p. 57.

12. Judy M. Torrance, *Public Violence in Canada* (Kingston: McGill-Queen's University Press, 1986), p. 101, citing David V. J. Bell and Lorne Tepperman, *The Roots of Disunity: A Look at Canadian Political Culture* (Toronto: McClelland and Stewart, 1979).

13. Lipset, *Continental Divide,* p. 183.

14. Canada did revolt briefly in the 1830s. But when revolutionary leader William Lyon Mackenzie began to embrace radical American democracy, the country pulled back. McNaught, pp. 84–86. While the American revolution was the product of a "sensitive" and "aggressive" nationalism, the demands of the Canadians who rebelled were simply for greater control of their local affairs. L. S. Amery, *Thoughts on the Constitution* (London: Oxford University Press, 1964), p. 108.

15. Formal control by the British Parliament was not surrendered until 1982.

16. Speech to Senate, February 22, 1810, quoted in Pierre Berton, *The Invasion of Canada, 1812–1813* (Ontario: Penguin Books Canada, 1980), p. ii.

17. Berton, p. 163.

18. Some state militias, though, refused to move outside their borders. McNaught, p. 70. In doing so, they vindicated the expectations of the authors of the Constitution: basing American power on militias made up of all able-bodied males, rather than a professional standing army, was the best way to keep America out of foreign conflict.

19. Berton, p. 374.

20. Ibid., p. 426. "Has the U.S. a Rabble under Arms?" asked G. Donaldson in *Maclean's,* September 3, 1966, p. 3.

21. Seymour Martin Lipset, "The 'Newness' of the New Nations," in C. Vann Woodward, ed., *The Comparative Approach to American History* (New York: Basic Books, 1968), p. 70; Link, pp. 15–16; Lipset, *Continental Divide,* p. 51, citing Edgar W. McInnis, *The Unguarded Frontier* (Garden City, N.Y.: Doubleday, 1942), pp. 306–307; Douglas Fetherling, *The Gold Crusades: A Social History of the Gold Rushes 1849–1869* (Toronto: Macmillan of Canada, 1989). The major exceptions to the rule were British Columbia and Vancouver, where locals made their own government and laws until the 1870s.

A force of 300 men comprising the North-West Mounted Police was organized in 1873. Their primary mission was to shut down the trading of alcohol to the Indians in exchange for buffalo hides. The force was renamed the Royal North-West Mounted Police in 1904, and the Royal Canadian Mounted Police in 1920. Royal Canadian Mounted Police, *The RCMP: Its History, Its People, Its Function* (Ottawa: Royal Canadian Mounted Police Public Relations Branch, 1987), p. 2.

Except in Hollywood, the term "Mounties" is not used; RCMP or RCM Police is preferred.

22. McNaught, p. 146.

23. Ray Billington, "Frontiers," in *The Comparative Approach to American History,* p. 76.

24. McNaught, p. 176.

25. William Tonso, *Gun and Society: The Social and Existential Roots of American Attachment to Firearms* (Lanham, Md.: University Press of America, 1982), p. 263.

26. Ibid., p. 179.

27. Firearms Law of 1892, ch. 29, 1892 S.C. § 105 (Can.), cited in Donna Lea Hawley, *Canadian Firearms Law* (Toronto: Butterworths, 1988), p. 2.

28. Act of 1913, c. 13, S.C. § 4 (Can.), cited in Hawley, p. 2.

29. The Canadian militia, composed mostly of the "best" citizens in an area, or of ex-soldiers, intervened a number of times to break strikes in the late nineteenth and early twentieth century. The militia was also hostile to Irish Catholic immigrants and to Acadians. There were a number of instances, though, where the militia behaved impartially, protecting strikers and scabs from each other. Torrance, pp. 27–32, citing Morton Desmond, "Aid to the Civil Power: The Canadian Militia in Support of Social Order, 1867–1914," *Canadian Historical Review* 51 (1970): 407–25; David J. Bercuson, "The Winnipeg General Strike," in I. Abella, ed., *On Strike: Six Key Labour Struggles in Canada, 1919–1949* (Toronto: James Lewis and Samuel, 1974): 1–32; McNaught, p. 232.

The militia is mostly forgotten in both Canada and America, but Canada still does formally provide for one militia: far north Eskimos who are armed and trained to act as guides for the regular army, and to warn the regular military of unusual events. Drawn from the Inuit and other indigenous peoples, the "Canadian Rangers" are issued .303 bolt action rifles. "Far North Has Militia of Eskimos," *New York Times,* April 1, 1986, p. A14; R. A. Watt, letter to author, March 26, 1990, p. 3.

30. M. L. Friedland, "Gun Control: The Options," 18 *Criminal Law Quarterly* (1975–76), p. 42.

31. Friedland, pp. 41–43; McNaught, pp. 224–26. Perhaps another reason for the Canadian gun law was a reaction, similar to the one in Britain, against all forms of violence, in response to the carnage of World War I. Total Canadian casualties for that war were 60,000, far higher on a per capita basis than America's 48,000 deaths. America's disgust with World War I was based mostly on a feeling of having been manipulated and cheated by the British and French; there was no American reaction against violence in general.

32. McNaught, p. 228.

33. Friedland, pp. 41–43.

34. Blackman, "The Canadian Gun Law," p. 3; Friedland, pp. 43–45.

35. Blackman, "The Canadian Gun Law," p. 3.,

36. Library of Congress, *Gun Control Laws in Foreign Countries,* rev. ed. (Washington, D.C.: Library of Congress, 1976), p. 41. [Hereinafter, "Library of Congress (1976)."]

37. Library of Congress (1976), p. 43.

38. Ibid., p. 44; Friedland, p. 56.

39. Friedland, p. 33. B. Bruce-Briggs, "The Great American Gun War," *The Public Interest* 45 (Fall 1976), p. 61.

40. Library of Congress, *Gun Control Laws in Foreign Countries* (Washington, D.C.: Library of Congress, 1981), p. 19. [Hereinafter "Library of Congress (1981)."]

41. Canadian House of Commons, *Bill C-51: An Act to Amend the Criminal Code, the Customs Tariff, the Parole Act, the Penitentiary Act and the Prisons and Reformatories Act.* Thirtieth Parliament, second session. First reading April 20, 1977, passed in the House of Commons July 18, 1977 (Ottawa: Supply and Services Canada, 1977). The bill extended the length of time allowed for a tap, and the delay in notifying the subject about the tap. "Canada's Lower House Backs Gun Control Law," *New York Times,* July 21, 1977, p. A2; Library of Congress (1981), p. 20; Blackman, "The Canadian Gun Law," p. 5.

42. Library of Congress (1981), p. 6.

43. Canadian Criminal Code, §§ 82(1), 104.

44. Criminal Code, § 104(10) and (12).

45. Criminal Code, § 104(4).

46. Royal Canadian Mounted Police, *Application for Firearms Certificate (FAC)*, PIB No. CMP/P-PU-035, March 1986. For a time the Social Insurance Number was used to identify applicants, but civil libertarian protests ended the practice. The social insurance number had been introduced in the 1960s with the explicit guarantee that it would only be used to track social welfare payments. Carruthers, "Canada's Identity Number Debate," *Washington Post*, April 15, 1979. As in America, government agencies, banks, and other institutions have essentially adopted the social insurance number as a universal identification number, over the protests of civil libertarians.

47. Royal Canadian Mounted Police, *National Firearms Manual*, chapter 3, § K.2.a.4, note (September 30, 1988). New Jersey, for example, requires gun applicants to waive the confidentiality of all mental health records, and to disclose any instance of consultation of a psychiatrist or other mental health treatment, however brief. State of New Jersey "Application for a Firearms Purchase Identification Card, form STS-3 (rev. 9-1-79).

48. The purchaser must send the vendor an original of his FAC. Gun collectors often apply several times for an FAC, in order to have several originals, so that there is always a spare copy for mail-order sales. If the gun is a restricted weapon, the purchaser must also obtain a permit to convey the gun from the gun store to the purchaser's home, and must send the permit to convey to the vendor. In some cases, the police will require the mail-order handgun to be sent directly to the local police station, for registration before the individual takes possession. *National Firearms Manual*, chapter 3, § O (September 30, 1988); Watt, March 26, 1990, p. 1.

49. Royal Canadian Mounted Police, *Annual Firearms Report to the Solicitor General of Canada by the Commissioner of the R.C.M.P.* § *106.9 Criminal Code 1986*, p. 6. In 1986, there were 171,609 Firearms Acquisition Certificates issued, and 1,364 rejections. The low refusal rate may stem from police prescreening and discouraging of applicants who are likely to be refused. Elisabeth Scarff, Decision Dynamics Corporation, *Evaluation of the Canadian Gun Control Legislation* (Ottawa: Canadian Government Publishing Centre, 1983), p. 39.

People with a felony conviction are only barred from gun possession for ten years. Criminal Code, § 106(4). In the United States, the prohibition is for a lifetime. 18 U.S.C. § 922.

Denials for plainly illegal reasons do sometimes occur. One man, who lawfully held an FAC, punched another man in the nose during an argument, and as a result paid a fifty-dollar fine. Three years later, the man was denied a renewal of the FAC, based on the single punch. David Tomlinson, *Canadian Gun Control—As It Really Works!* (Calgary: National Firearms Association, 1990), pp. 3–4. (Tomlinson is president of the NFA.) In another case, one Vancouverite who was an outspoken opponent of gun controls was rejected for a dealer license, allegedly because of the high incidence of gun crime and frequency of gun thefts in the area. (The two factors are not legal considerations for dealer licenses.) *A.G.B.C.* v. *Martinoff,* [1977] 6 W.W.R. 764, 768 (B.C.C.A.).

50. Hawley, p. 18.

51. Criminal Code, § 100(5).

52. *Unterreiner* v. *Regina,* [1980] 51 C.C.C. (2d) 373, 377–78 (Ont. Co. Ct.) (Killeen, J.). Courts have split on whether they are limited to the administrative record, or may conduct a trial de novo. Contrast *Unterreiner* v. *The Queen* (1979–80), 4 W.C.B. 216 (Ont. Co.

Ct.) (administrative record) with *Regina* v. *Dhillon* (1982), 7 W.C.B. 131 (B.C. Co. Ct.) (*de novo*); *Regina* v. *Kokoshki* (1980), 4 W.C.B. 472 (Ont. Prov. Ct.) (*de novo*).

53. Hawley, p. 20.

54. Scarff, p. 35.

55. Criminal Code, § 106(1) and (2).

56. Criminal Code, § 106(10); *National Firearms Manual,* chapter 3, K.3.d (September 30, 1988).

57. Ibid., chapter 6, F.1.h. (April 29, 1988).

58. 27 Code of Federal Regulations § 178.129. While American ammunition dealers need not obtain a license, Canadian dealers must possess a permit, although they are not subject to inspection. *National Firearms Manual.* ch. 6, § F.1.g. (April 29, 1988); 18 United States Code Annotated 923(a)(3) (1990 pocket part). Neither Canada nor America require records to be made of ammunition transactions. New Zealand recently abandoned control of ammunition sales, while Britain has added new controls.

59. Criminal Code, § 82(1)(b).

60. Criminal Code, § 82(1).

61. *Lawrence* v. *Regina,* (1978) F.C. 782, 42 C.C.C. (2d) 230 (Fed. Ct.).

62. Restricted Weapons Order, amendment, S.O.R./83-550, June 24, 1983 (*Canada Gazette* July 13, 1983, p. 2674), cited in Hawley, p. 10. The FN-FAL ban may have been motivated by the government's dislike of the particular firearms dealer who was the sole importer of the rifle. The official justification for the restriction of the FN-FAL was that because many nations were replacing their FN-FALs with more modern guns, Canada would be flooded with imports. The Canadian army adopted the fully automatic cousin of the FN-FAL (the FNC1 and FNC1A1) in the late 1950s, and has only recently started replacing it with the M16. R. A. Watt (Alberta firearms dealer), letter to author, March 26, 1990, pp. 1–2.

63. Balfour Q.H. Der and Ian F. Kirkpatrick, *The Law of Firearms and Weapons* (Toronto: Carswell, 1989), p. 128. The AR15 Sporter is the civilian version of the U.S. Army M16 assault rifle. The major difference between the two guns is that the M16 can fire automatically (as long as the trigger is squeezed, bullets will be fired), whereas the AR15 can only be fired semi-automatically (one trigger squeeze fires one bullet).

One version of the M1, the M1 carbine, is on the restricted list because it has a short barrel. Shorter rifles are disfavored by the police, but favored by some gun owners, because shorter guns are more maneuverable, a virtue that is especially important in a home-defense situation. An owner of an M1 carbine did *not* have to register if he changed the gun by making the barrel more than twenty inches long (by changing to a longer barrel, or by permanently affixing a flash suppressor or muzzle brake). With the extra two inches of barrel length, the new, "long-barreled" M1 carbine became a normal long gun, rather than a restricted weapon. Because the barrel was long enough, the gun owner could then replace his M1's wooden stock with a folding stock. The folding stock could make the gun as much as twelve inches shorter. Thus, the government got what it wanted (fewer short rifles, as defined by barrel length), and the M1 owners got what they wanted (an even shorter rifle than they had before the law was introduced). Other gun owners, seeing the example set by owners of the M1 carbine and the folding stock, began adding folding stocks to their own guns. The net effect of the law against short rifles, then, was to greatly increase the number of short rifles. Tomlinson, p. 7.

The Heckler and Koch 91, another short rifle with a military appearance, is also classified as restricted. Id.

64. National Firearms Association, *Point Blank,* February 1989, p. 2.

65. Tomlinson, pp. 7–8.

66. Ajit Jain, "Canada's Police Chiefs Seek Similar Ban on Guns as U.S. to Curb Drug, Gang Wars," *New York Tribune*, March 20, 1989.

67. Tomlinson, 1990, pp. 1–2.

68. The only exception is "antique" handguns, that is, guns manufactured before 1898 for which there are no commercially available cartridges.

69. Criminal Code, § 109(3); *National Firearms Manual*, chapter 4, § E.4.c (April 5, 1988).

70. In some provinces, an applicant need only present a club membership card, since the police will know a club, and be familiar with its training procedures. A. D. Olmstead, professor of sociology, University of Calgary, letter to author, March 19, 1990, p. 1.

71. Blackman, "The Canadian Gun Law," pp. 6–7; Tomlinson, 1990, p. 2.

72. F. W. Noftall, National Firearms Association, letter to author, February 24, 1988.

73. Noftall letter; Watt, September 1990.

74. *National Firearms Manual*, chapter 4, § E.4.a.1 (April 5, 1988). They will also issue a Firearms Acquisition Certificate (required for all gun purchasers) if the purchaser does not already have one.

75. Criminal Code, § 110(3); Hawley p. 23; *National Firearms Manual*, chapter 4, § F.3 (April 5, 1988).

76. *National Firearms Manual*, chapter 4, § E.4.b (April 5, 1988); Watt, March 26, 1990, p. 1–2.

77. *National Firearms Manual*, chapter 4, § E.2 (April 5, 1988).

78. The time bar used to be five years, until changed by the 1991 law discussed below. *National Firearms Manual*, chapter 4, § H.2.a.4.6 (April 5, 1988).

79. Criminal Code, § 112(12).

80. Watt, March 26, 1990, p. 1.

81. Hawley, p. 27. In some provinces, the permit to convey may be issued by the local registrar of firearms. Olmstead letter, March 19, 1990, p. 1.

82. Criminal Code, § 110(3); *National Firearms Manual*, chapter 5, § L.1.a (April 4, 1988); Hawley, pp. 31–32; Tomlinson, p. 6.

83. Scarff, pp. 4–5; *National Firearms Manual*, chapter 5, §§ E and F (April 4, 1988).

84. Hawley, p. 28.

85. *Re Purdy*, (1974) 20 D.L.R. 2d 247 (N.W.T. Sup. Ct.); Hawley, pp. 29, 54.

86. *National Firearms Manual*, chapter 5, § H.2.e.1; chapter 5 (April 4, 1988), Appendix 5–3 contains a model restriction: "At no time will the permit holder draw his restricted weapon except where he believes it is absolutely necessary to protect his life."

87. Permits may be issued for carrying a handgun to a part of one's own property for target shooting, if no commercial or public target range is nearby. *National Firearms Manual*, chapter 5, appendix 5–6, p. 1 (April 18, 1988); Watt, March 26, 1990, p. 2.

88. Criminal Code, § 84(1).

89. *National Firearms Manual*, chapter 4, E.4.f (April 5, 1988); Solicitor General, *Gun Control in Canada: Working Together to Save Lives* (Ottawa: Solicitor General of Canada, 1978), p. 3. [Hereinafter, "Solicitor General, *Gun Control.*"]

Owners of registered automatics may sell to each other, but no person who was not a collector of automatics may ever acquire one. The aim is to eliminate ownership of automatics within a generation, even though there had never been a case of a crime or suicide committed with a registered automatic. Tomlinson, p. 3.

It is even against the law to invent an automatic in Canada, since building the prototype would be illegal. Ibid., p. 9.

One firearms collector found registering a gun more than a little difficult. He owned a deactivated WWII machine gun, a war trophy. Thinking that he might someday want to reactivate his trophy, the man went to the Firearms Unit of the Toronto Police, to register it before the January 1, 1978, deadline. The firearms clerk informed the collector that because the machine gun was not operable, it could not be registered. The only way to register the gun would be to activate it, which would be difficult to do in the few remaining days before the January 1 deadline. The collector took his gun home, worked on it all day, and brought his reactivated machine gun to the police for registration. They confiscated it, citing import restrictions promulgated by the province's attorney general. "Dangerous Bureaucratic Red Tape," *Canada GunSport,* February 1978, p. 4.

90. Kim Pemberton, "Mayor, Police Target City Guns," *Vancouver Sun,* March 23, 1989; National Firearms Association, *Point Blank,* September 1988, p. 1; National Firearms Association, "The Doctrine of Utter Contempt for the Public," *Point Blank,* July 1989, p. 2; National Firearms Association, "Gun Owners Declare Enough is Enough," *Point Blank,* October 1989, p. 2.

91. Tomlinson, p. 2.

92. *National Firearms Manual,* appendix 9–1, p. 1, "Order Declaring Certain Devices to be Prohibited Weapons," (April 4, 1988); C.R.C. (Consolidated Regulations of Canada) 1978, chapter 433 (tear gas); S.O.R. /78-278 (Canada Gazette) (April 12, 1978), p. 1272 (stun guns); cited in Hawley, pp. 6–7. *Re Repa and The Queen,* (1982) 68 D.L.R. (2d) 231 (Man. Ct. Q.B.), (weapon that had been lawfully registered earlier).

93. *National Firearms Manual,* chapter 1, § F. (April 5, 1988); Solicitor General, p. 8; Criminal Code, § 101(1).

94. One practical impediment to use of restricted weapon registration lists is that the information is available onlyŕfr o the Firearms Records Section of the RCMP in Ottawa, which is only open during business hours. Watt, March 26, 1990, p. 4.

95. Criminal Code, § 84(1), as amended by Canada House of Commons, *Bill C-17: An Act to Amend the Criminal Code and the Customs Tariff in Consequence Thereof,* 34th Parliament, 3d. sess., 40 Eliz. II, passed by House of Commons November 7, 1991, "'genuine gun collector' means an individual who . . . has consented to the periodic inspections, conducted in a reasonable manner and in accordance with the regulations, of the premises in which the restricted weapons are to be kept . . ."

96. Canada Senate. Standing Committee on External Affairs, *Proceedings,* November 28, 1991, p. 2: 29 (Mr. Richard Mosley, Senior General Counsel, Department of Justice: "Reasonable inspection is limited to daylight hours, from 9 to 5 or when convenient for the householder.")

97. *National Firearms Manual,* chapter 1, § F.2 (April 5, 1988); Blackman, "The Canadian Gun Law," p. 12; Criminal Code, § 103(2).

98. Criminal Code, § 103(3); *National Firearms Manual,* chapter 1, § F.2.c (April 5, 1988).

99. Solicitor General, p. 12.

100. Blackman, "Civil Liberties and Gun-Law Enforcement," paper presented at annual meeting of the American Society of Criminology, November 7, 1984, p. 6.

101. Tomlinson, 1990, p. 2. In the United States, the author participated in a radio talk show in March 1989 regarding the semi-automatic issue; the radio program was broadcast live from Colorado's largest gun store, the Firing Line. The day after the show was broadcast, the Bureau of Alcohol, Tobacco, and Firearms conducted an unannounced search of the Firing Line.

102. The search and record-keeping provisions are both contained in 18 United States Code § 923(g).

103. E.g., *Armour Packing Co.* v. *United States,* 209 U.S. 56 (1908); *Morissette* v. *United States,* 342 U.S. 246 (1952).

104. *United States* v. *Freed,* 401 U.S. 601 (1974).

105. *Regina* v. *Maginnis,* (1981) 64 C.C.C. (2d) 430, 440–41 (Ont. Co. Ct.) (Vannini, D.C.J.). Other courts have split on the issue. New Brunswick courts take a firm line with strict liability; Alberta and Ontario still require mens rea. Discussed in *Regina* v. *Somers,* [1985] 2 W.W.R. 468, 16 C.C.C. (3d) 357, 32 Man. R. (2d) 167 (Q.B.) (mere possession allowed inference of guilty intent; burden of proof on defendant to disprove guilty intent). See also, *Regina* v. *Simonovic,* [1973] 3 W.W.R. 189 (Y.T. Mag. Ct.); *Regina* v. *Hutchison,* (1978) 8 B.C.L.R. 328 (Prov. Ct.); Der and Kirkpatrick, pp. 118–21.

106. Criminal Code, § 103(10).

107. Robert Batey, "Strict Construction of Firearms Offenses," *Journal of Law and Contemporary Problems* 49 (Winter 1986), pp. 184–85.

In Florida, as everywhere else, it is illegal for a felon to possess a gun. One Florida ex-felon discovered this when he wrested a pistol away from someone who was attacking him only to be convicted of illegal possession of a weapon. *Thorpe* v. *State,* 377 So.2d 221 (Fla. App., 1979).

108. Der and Kirkpatrick, pp. 132–33.

109. *Regina* v. *Wright,* [1980] 4 W.W.R. 92 (Sask. Prov. Ct.); Hawley, pp. 45–46.

110. Philip C. Stenning and Sharon Moyer, *Firearms Ownership and Use in Canada: A Report of Survey Findings* (Toronto: Working Paper of the Centre for Criminology, 1981), p. 52.

111. Kashmeri, "Illegal Firearms Easily Bought," *The Globe and Mail,* September 26, 1984, p. 1.

112. *Annual Firearms Report 1986,* p. 5, reporting 45,585 firearms lost/stolen since 1974 and not yet recovered.

113. See Elisabeth Scarff in note 49 above.

114. For completed homicides in Vancouver, firearms had accounted for 21.4 percent before the law, and 14.3 percent after. Scarff, pp. 2, 6.

115. Scarff, pp. 4, 15. Research commissioned by the Canadian government a few years before had found no relationship between firearms availability and firearms homicides. Stenning and Moyer, p. 168.

As in Britain, life imprisonment is mandatory upon conviction of murder. Duncan Chappell and Linda P. Graham, *Police Use of Deadly Force: A Canadian Perspective* (Toronto: Centre for Criminology, 1985), p. v.

116. Catherine F. Sproule and Deborah J. Kennett, "The Use of Firearms in Canadian Homicides 1972–1982: The Need for Gun Control," *Canadian Journal of Criminology* 30, no. 1 (1988): 31–37.

117. Scarff, p. 3.

118. Only 7 percent of rapists use guns. A gun-armed rapist succeeds 67 percent of the time, a knife-armed rapist 51 percent. Philip J. Cook, "Gun Availability and Violent Crime," *Crime and Justice* 4 (1982), p. 61, n.8, analyzing data in Joan McDermott, *Rape Victimization in Twenty-Six American Cities* (Washington, D.C.: Government Printing Office, 1979), pp. 20–21. Rate of firearms use in rape is from Department of Justice, *Report to the Nation on Crime and Justice,* p. 14.

119. Scarff, p. 3.

120. Solicitor General, *Gun Control,* p. 10.

121. Watt, September 1990.

122. Scarff, pp. 7–10.

123. Ibid., p. 72.

124. Ibid., p. 4.

125. Robert J. Mundt, "Gun Control and Rates of Firearms Violence in Canada and the United States," *Canadian Journal of Criminology* 32, no. 1 (January 1990), p. 140. The quoted homicide rates are the means for the periods 1974–78 and 1979–88.

126. Blackman, "The Canadian Gun Law," p. 18, citing data through 1982.

127. Statistics Canada, "Memorandum," February 17, 1989, quoted in Mundt, "Gun Control," pp. 139, 144–45.

128. Blackman, "The Canadian Gun Law," p. 18, citing data through 1982.

129. Blackman, "The Canadian Gun Law." According to the theory of the gun-control lobby, one major reason for the apparent inefficacy of American controls is that guns from states with weak laws are brought into states with strong laws. Thus, Florida's weak laws undermine New York's strong ones. Accordingly, relaxation of gun laws in any state would be expected to increase gun crime in the northern tier states. The most significant change in gun laws during the 1970s was that many states, including several northern tier states, enacted preemption laws to erase existing city and county gun controls, and to bar the enactment of more such controls. Thus, the 1970s changes in American law, even though they were enacted at the state and local level, would be expected to have national impact, including in the northern tier states.

130. The NRA spent nearly seven million dollars on the referendum, and suffered one of its worst losses ever, by a 58–42 percent margin. Because the NRA referendum failed, Maryland now has a commission that must specifically approve the sale of all models of handguns. In practice, the panel has not been as anti-gun as had been feared, and has approved the sale of nearly 99 percent of handguns examined.

131. J. H. Sloan, A. L. Kellerman, D. I. Reay, J. A. Fenis, T. Koepsell, F. P. Rivara, C. Rice, L. Gray, and J. Logerfo, "Handgun Regulations, Crime, Assaults, and Homicide: A Tale of Two Cities," *New England Journal of Medicine* no. 319 (November 10, 1988): 1256–62.

132. Seattle whites had a homicide rate of 6.2 per 100,000; Vancouver whites 6.4. Seattle blacks were 36.6, and Seattle Hispanics 26.9. Ibid., p. 1260.

133. Chappell and Graham, p. 193, citing *The Province,* January 3, 1983, p. 2.

134. Pemberton.

135. In the late 1970s, the National Institute of Justice offered a grant to the former president of the American Sociological Association to survey the field of research on gun control. Peter Rossi began his work convinced of the need for strict national gun control. After looking at the data, however, Rossi and his University of Massachusetts colleagues James Wright and Kathleen Daly concluded that there was no convincing proof that gun control curbs crime. James Wright, Peter Rossi, and Kathleen Daly, *Under the Gun: Weapons, Crime and Violence in America* (Hawthorne, N.Y.: Aldine, 1983).

136. "The intent of our article was not to evaluate the effect of the 1978 Canadian gun law, which has been done by others . . ." *New England Journal of Medicine* 320 (May 4, 1989), p. 1216. The *NEJM* authors' assertion that they were not evaluating the 1978 Canadian law (enacted in 1977) called the original article into rather serious question since: 1. The article has discussed only the present laws in Canada, and made no mention of the historical development of the laws; 2. The first and foremost difference between American and Canadian laws mentioned in the article (Canadians cannot own handguns for self-defense) was a change adopted in 1978; 3. Aside from "carry" laws, the only Canadian statutes specifically cited were those that took effect in 1978 and 1979; 4. The only data presented were from after the 1977 law took effect; 5. Before 1978, Seattle and Vancouver had generally similar

controls on handguns—police permission was needed for a purchase, but permission was freely granted, and self-defense and other lawful reasons were all acceptable.

137. Catherine F. Sproule and Deborah J. Kennett, "Killing with Guns in the U.S.A. and Canada 1977–1983: Further Evidence for the Effectiveness of Gun Control," *Canadian Journal of Criminology* 31 (July 1989): 245–51.

138. Catherine F. Sproule & Deborah J. Kennett, "The Use of Firearms in Canadian Homicides 1972–1982: The Need for Gun Control," *Canadian Journal of Criminology* 30 (1988): 31–37.

139. U.S. Bureau of Justice Statistics, "Household Burglary," January 1985, p. 4; Gary Kleck, "Crime Control Through the Private Use of Armed Force," *Social Problems* 35 (February 1988), p. 16; Norman Okihiro, *Burglary: The Victim and the Police* (Toronto: University of Toronto Press, 1978), p. 31 (Toronto study). A study of an unnamed "northern city" in Ontario for the years 1965–70 also appears to show a relatively high level of burglary against occupied residences. The study reported that 12.2 percent of burglaries were daytime, 69.5 percent were nighttime, and 18.3 percent were unknown. It is certain that no person was home for the "unknown" burglaries since if someone had been home, the time of entry would be known. A large percentage of the nighttime burglaries may have involved a person at home, since most people are at home at night. Peter Chimbros, "A Study of Breaking and Entering Offenses in 'Northern City' Ontario," in Robert A. Silverman and James J. Teevan Jr., eds., *Crime in Canadian Society* (Toronto: Butterworths, 1975), pp. 325–26.

140. The risk of either outcome for a burglar is about 1–2 percent. James Wright, Peter Rossi, and Kathleen Daly, *Under the Gun: Weapons, Crime and Violence in America* (New York: Aldine, 1983), pp. 139–40 (study for National Institute of Justice). A number of criminologists attribute the preference of American burglars for daytime over nighttime entry (even though, in general, night provides better cover) to burglars' fears of confronting an armed homeowner. George Rengert and John Wasilchick, *Suburban Burglary: A Time and a Place for Everything* (Springfield, Ill.: Charles C. Thomas, 1985), p. 30; J. Conklin, *Robbery and the Criminal Justice System* (Philadelphia: Lippincott, 1972), p. 85.

141. Blackman, "The Canadian Gun Law," p. 19.

142. *Regina* v. *Haverstock*, (1979) 32 N.S.R. (2d) 595 (Co. Ct.) (homeowner pointed rifle at trespasser to make him leave); *Regina* v. *Anderson*, (1981) 13 Man. R. (2d) 441 (C.A.) (man pointed unloaded rifle at person who was chasing a girl). Compare *Regina* v. *Weare*, (1983) 56 N.S.R. (2d); *Regina* v. *Ernst*, (1982) 1 C.C.C. (3d) 454 (B.C.C.A.) (shooting into ground to frighten away trespassers in isolated area).

143. *Regina* v. *Thornton*, (1970) 2 C.C.C. (2d) 225 (Ont. C.A.); *Regina* v. *Calder*, (1984) 111 C.C.C. (3d) 546 (Alta C.A.); *Regina* v. *Proverbs*, (1983) 9 C.C.C. (3d) 249 (Ont. C.A.). Some police officials have begun lobbying to outlaw the carrying of knives. Mario Toneguzzi, "Feds Consider Limits on Knives," *Calgary Herald*, March 17, 1990, p. B4.

144. Martine Daly and Margo Wilson, *Homicide* (New York: Hawthorne, 1988), pp. 15, 200 (table). The Miami figures are for 1980, Houston for 1969, and Canada for 1974–83. Data regarding the circumstances of the domestic homicides are not sufficiently detailed to allow a determination of whether the American women were more likely than the Canadian women to be in circumstances where self-defense was better justified.

145. Stenning and Moyer, p. 174–75.

146. Ibid., p. 177.

147. Scarff, pp. 5, 29.

148. Mundt, "Gun Control," pp. 144–46; Blackman, "The Canadian Gun Law," p. 17. The total Canadian suicide rate rose from 12.8 in 1970–77 to 14.1 in 1978–85.

149. John Henry Sloan, Frederick P. Rivara, Donald T. Reay, James A. J. Ferris, Arthur L. Kellerman, "Firearms Regulations and the Rate of Suicide: A Comparison of Two Metropolitan Areas," *New England Journal of Medicine* 322 (February 8, 1990): 369–73. Canadian law until late 1991 allowed long-gun purchases at age sixteen, and handgun purchases at age eighteen. Canadian Criminal Code, §§ 106(2)(a), 109 (3)(a). (The long-gun age was raised to eighteen by a bill enacted November 18, 1991. The bill is discussed in detail below.) In the United States, the corresponding legal ages are 18 and 21. See 18 United States Code, § 922(b)(1). Further, the authors never suggested a reason that Canada's generally more restrictive gun laws would produce a lower suicide rate in one and only one age group, and a higher suicide rate for all other age groups. Nor did the authors compare the current Canadian suicide rates with the rate before the 1977 control system went into effect.

The physicians responded to the above criticisms by again stating that they were not trying to prove anything about the 1977 law. They were looking at Canada's general overall gun density and the resulting lesser accessibility of guns to teenagers.

One critic who wrote to *NEJM* to criticize the suicide study as biased and unprofessional was James D. Wright, a sociologist at Tulane. The *NEJM* authors did not respond to his particular criticisms, and dismissed them with the observation that "Wright's long-held views on the issue of gun control" are "well known," and hence his criticism "was predictable." John Henry Sloan, Frederick P. Rivara, Arthur Kellerman, "Firearms Regulations and Rates of Suicide" (reply to letter to the editor), *New England Journal of Medicine* 323, no. 2 (July 12, 1990): 136–37. Of course Wright's views are well-known (in the sociology and criminology worlds). He authored the National Institute of Justice's studies of firearms under first the Carter administration, and then the Reagan administration. He began his research strongly in favor of gun control, and changed his mind because of the research. The fact that Wright's views on guns (like his views on many other subjects) are well-known among academic sociologists is not in itself proof that his views are invalid. In any case, since Wright's views are well-known, it is difficult to understand why the *NEJM* authors, in their first Seattle/Vancouver study, asserted that Wright's research had found that handgun control would reduce homicide, when Wright had said just the opposite.

150. Charles L. Rich, James G. Young, Richard C. Fowler, John Wagner, Nancy A. Black, "Guns and Suicide: Possible Effects of Some Specific Legislation," *American Journal of Psychiatry* 147, no. 3 (March 1990): 342–46.

151. Scarff, pp. 5, 27; Gary Mauser, letter to author, May 28, 1990.

152. Stenning and Moyer, p. 174.

153. In 1977, there were about 44,500 firearms per 100,000 people in Canada; in 1988, there were about 46,000 per 100,000. As for handguns per 100,000 population, there were 2,970 in 1976 and 3,560 in 1988. Estimates from Mundt, "Gun Control," pp. 150–51.

154. Brandon S. Centerwall, "Homicide and the Prevalence of Handguns: Canada and the United States, 1976–1980," *American Journal of Epidemiology* 134 (December 1991), pp. 1247–51. The homicide rates for New Brunswick (2.9 per 100,000 population per year) and Quebec (3.0) were higher than Maine (2.7), New Hampshire (2.6), and Vermont (2.8). Ontario (2.1) was much lower than New York (11.3) and Michigan (10.1). [Excluding the large metropolitan centers of New York City, Detroit, and Toronto, the rates were Ontario (2.0), New York State (3.4), and Michigan (5.0).] The rate in Manitoba (3.7) was higher than in Minnesota (2.4) and North Dakota (1.2). Saskatchewan (3.8), Alberta (3.4), and British Columbia (3.6) were lower than Montana (4.7), Idaho (4.9), and Washington (4.7). Yukon (16.9) was higher than Alaska (11.6).

155. Bruce-Briggs, p. 57. For more on the South, see Sheldon Hackney, "Southern

Violence," in *Violence in America: Historical and Comparative Perspectives* (Washington, D.C.: Government Printing Office, 1969), p. 387, report to National Commission on Causes and Prevention of Violence. The "southern" variable may simply be a proxy for poverty. Wright, Rossi, and Daly, p. 110.

156. The urban South, being especially crime prone and especially desirous of disarming blacks, was the first American region to implement handgun control. Among southerners, "gun ownership is unrelated to violent values indicative of subcultures of violence." Alan J. Lizotte and Jo Dixon, "Gun Ownership and the 'Southern Subculture of Violence,'" *American Journal of Sociology* 93 (1987), p. 383.

157. Hackney, p. 518. Gun control in the South is discussed in chapter 9.

158. Paul Blackman, *Firearms and Violence, 1983/84* (Washington, D.C.: NRA/ILA, July 1985), pp. 20–21.

159. Robert J. Mundt, "The Effect of National Differences in Political Structure and Culture on Urban Violent Crime in Canada and the United States," paper presented at the 1990 meeting of the Urban Affairs Commission, Charlotte, North Carolina, April 20, 1990.

160. Robert J. Mundt, "A Tale of Four Cities: Firearms and Violence in the U.S. and Canada," paper presented at the 1991 meeting of the American Political Science Association, Washington, D.C., August 19, 1991.

161. Mauser, "Ownership of Firearms in British Columbia," p. 4.

162. Ibid., (one-third, applying figures for British Columbia to nation as a whole); Angus Reid Group, *Firearms Ownership in Canada,* discussed in Kirk LaPointe, "Gun Owners' Reasons Play Down Protection," *Vancouver Sun,* August 6, 1991 (23 percent) [hereinafter Angus Reid Group]. The Angus Reid estimates may have been low, since it was taken at a time when many gun owners were afraid of confiscation, and consequently might have been reluctant to divulge themselves to a stranger on the telephone.

163. Angus Reid Group.

164. The high-end estimate of illegal handguns in New York City is about 1,900,000, based on the police estimate of 2,000,000 handguns in the city, and 50,000 handgun permits (assuming that permit-holders legally own an average of two handguns apiece). "Guns Offer New York Teenagers a Commonplace, Deadly Allure," *New York Times,* November 5, 1990, p. A1.

165. For Canada, the Stenning and Moyer estimate is for 1976. Stenning and Moyer, p. 31. For America, Gary Kleck, *Point Blank: Weapons and Violence in America* (New York: Aldine de Gruyter, 1991), p. 18.

166. Royal Canadian Mounted Police, *1989 Annual Firearms Report.* The story is the same for fully automatic weapons such as assault rifles. The United States has about 170,000 legally registered full automatics; as of 1974, 2,500 Canadians owned 4,000 automatics. Stenning and Moyer, p. 29, citing Solicitor General, 1976.

167. Stenning and Moyer, p. 27. *Maclean's*-Decima Poll, "A North-South Dialogue," *Maclean's,* July 3, 1989, p. 48, cited in Lipset, *Continental Divide,* p. 98; Gary A. Mauser and Michael Margolis, "The Politics of Gun Control: Comparing Canadian and American Patterns," paper presented at the meeting of the American Political Science Association, August 30, 1990, San Francisco, p. 4 [hereinafter "Mauser & Margolis"] (6 percent of households); Angus Reid Group (12 percent of the 23 percent gun-owning households have a handgun, or approximately 3 percent of all households).

Interestingly, the Stenning-Moyer survey, in the mid-1970s, found that 1 percent of adults admitted owning a handgun. The *Maclean's* survey, in March 1989, found 3 percent so admitting. Sampling error is the most likely explanation for the different results. If the results are reliable, though, they indicate an important trend—Canadian ownership of handguns is increasing rapidly, or Canadian handgun owners are becoming less ashamed or fearful about revealing themselves.

168. Gary A. Mauser, "A Comparison of Canadian and American Attitudes Toward Firearms," *Canadian Journal of Criminology* 32 (1990): 573-89; Mauser and Margolis, pp. 17-18.

169. Thirty-one percent of rural Canadian male over the age of fifteen own guns. Eleven percent of Canadians in large urban areas do. Stenning and Moyer, p. 67.

170. Stenning and Moyer, p. 50.

171. Ibid., p. 23.

172. Ibid., pp. 52-53.

173. Self-employed Canadian females, even though part of a gun-owning economic group, owned guns at only a 2 percent rate. Stenning and Moyer, p. 73. Even that rate was above the rate for almost all other groups of women.

174. "Newfoundland Police Want to Carry Guns," *Gun Week,* January 3, 1975. The Ontario Provincial Police and the Quebec Provincial Police (Sûreté du Québec) are independent forces not part of the RCMP.

175. Dr. R. J. McCaldon, "Readers Write," *The American Rifleman* (November 1988), p. 28.

176. Chappell and Graham, pp. 121-22, 176-77, citing Royal Canadian Mounted Police, *Discussion Paper: .38 Calibre Service Revolver Ammunition* (Fall 1981); and quoting British Columbia Police Commission. Not all local police forces have made the switch. The Calgary police adopted and then abandoned Glaser Safety Slugs (a brand of self-defense cartridges with high stopping power, which has the advantage of *not* penetrating walls and putting nearby innocents at risk) and other local forces have adopted and abandoned .357 magnum cartridges (another powerful variety). Public relations concerns made it untenable for some police forces to employ cartridges considered highly lethal. Olmstead letter, March 19, 1990, p. 3.

177. Massad Ayoob, "Self Defense and The Law: Your Gun Can Be A Liability," *Peterson's Handguns* (March 1989), pp. 33-34. As a technical matter, it is hollow-point handgun cartridges that have been outlawed. Hollow-point rifle cartridges are still legal. "New Regulations," *Canadian Handgun,* Winter 1990, p. 12. Moreover, while hollow-point ammunition is illegal, hollow-point bullets are not. A Canadian handloader could legally purchase hollow-point bullets, and load them into his own cartridges. Watt, September 1990.

178. Chappell and Graham, pp. 5-6, citing Sulton and Cooper, "Summary of Research on the Police Use of Deadly Force," in U.S. Department of Justice, *A Community Concern: Police Use of Deadly Force* (Washington, D.C.: N.I.L.E. and C.J., 1979), p. 69; U.S. Department of Justice, *Uniform Crime Reports: Crime in the United States 1980* (Washington, D.C.: Government Printing Office, 1981); Statistics Canada, *Crime and Traffic Enforcement Statistics (1974-76)* (1981), catalogue #85-205.

179. Chappell and Graham, p. 35; Criminal Code, § 34(2) (1988) defense against assault.

180. Mauser, "A Comparison of Canadian and American Attitudes," pp. 578-79; Mauser and Margolick, p. 18. When a Calgary drugstore owner was prosecuted (and acquitted by a jury) for shooting two robbers, he received overwhelming public support. "Arms Against Crime: A Citizen's Right?" *Chatelaine,* December 1987: 42-44.

181. Mauser, "A Comparison of Canadian and American Attitudes," pp. 582-83. Mauser's results are summarized in "Gunplay," *Vancouver Sun,* August 28, 1989. The 58 percent result is inconsistent with the poll reported at note 168, which suggests that either or both polls may be inaccurate.

182. Stenning and Moyer, pp. 129-31; Blackman, "The Canadian Gun Law," (for U.S.), p. 3; Mauser and Margolick (4 percent said protection was the "most important reason" for their owning a gun).

183. American police uses are discussed above. For civilians, one study indicates that handguns are used in roughly 645,000 self-defense actions each year—a rate of once every forty-eight seconds. (Most defensive uses simply involving brandishing the gun, rather than firing it.) Gary Kleck, "Crime Control and the Private Use of Armed Force," 35 *Social Problems* (February 1988): 1–21. Kleck was analyzing survey data collected by pollster Peter Hart for the no longer active National Alliance Against. Hart's question had asked if the person or someone in their household had used a handgun for self-defense at least once in the last five years. The frequency of armed self-defense in America is discussed in more detail in chapter 11.

184. Rich, Young, Fowler, et al., p. 345.

185. See, for example, Curtis L. Taylor, "27 Weapons Turned In To Police: Gun Amnesty a Dud, Critics Say," *New York Newsday,* August 27, 1990, p. 7; "Massachusetts: The Shot Heard 'Round the States," *State Government News,* May 1975, p. 2 ("In New York City, a recent 'amnesty' program resulted in the return of about 500 guns. . . . A similar 'forgiveness' program had very little effect in Washington, D.C."). One *New York Times* article explains:

"Nobody will turn in their guns," said Russell Miller, who runs a hardware store near the 34th Precinct station house in Washington Heights in Manhattan. "This is a jungle, and in a jungle you don't lay down your weapons. Everyone around here has considered buying a gun."

James Barron, "Amnesty Starts and One Owner Turns in 3 Guns: He Is Only One to Take Offer From Dinkins," *New York Times,* August 2, 1990, p. B3. Gun buybacks (in which the police pay a moderate sum, such as $50, for each gun surrendered) are often more successful. The buybacks often attract hundreds, or even thousands of citizens who take an opportunity to remove an unwanted gun from their home. Buybacks also attract large numbers of gun enthusiasts exchanging broken or low-quality firearms for a bounty greater than the firearms' market value.

186. "Gun Controls," *San Francisco Sunday Examiner and Chronicle,* September 6, 1981, p. A18.

187. Mauser, "A Comparison of Canadian and American Attitudes," pp. 577–80; Mauser and Margolick, p. 19. While the United States Constitution and forty-three state constitutions contain an explicit right to bear arms, in Canada the right is only a common law tradition, derivative of the 1689 British Bill of Rights. See also note 232.

Mauser's survey on Canadian attitudes covered only the Pacific coast province of British Columbia. Mauser, "A Comparison of Canadian and American Attitudes," p. 575. Mauser found that 63 percent of British Columbia citizens thought they had a right to own a gun. The percentage might be lower in Canada as a whole, taking into account the statist sentiments of populous Ontario.

188. Richard M. Weintraub, "Guns Abroad," *Washington Post,* December 21, 1980. In some areas, the typical fine for a prohibited weapon (usually a fully automatic rifle) is $300. Watt, September 1990.

189. Michael J. Martinoff, " 'A Tale of Two Cities' A Vancouverite's Perspective," *Point Blank,* April 1989, p. 2.

190. One of the early test cases under the Massachusetts Bartley-Fox law was the successful prosecution of a young man who had inadvertently allowed his gun license to expire. To raise money to buy his high school class ring, he was driving to a pawn shop to sell his gun. Stopping the man for a traffic violation, a policeman noticed the gun. The teenager spent the mandatory year in jail with no parole. Another Massachusetts case involved a

man who had started carrying a gun after a co-worker began threatening to murder him. The Civil Liberties Union of Massachusetts had opposed Bartley-Fox precisely because of the risk that innocent people would be sent to jail. David Hardy, "Legal Restrictions on Firearms Ownership as an Answer to Violent Crime: What Was the Question?" *Hamline Law Review* 6 (July 1983), p. 407; Brief for Civil Liberties Union of Massachusetts as *amicus curiae, Commonwealth* v. *Jackson,* pp. 22–26, cited in James Beha, "And *Nobody* Can Get You Out," *Boston University Law Review* 57 (1977), p. 110, n.55.

The New York law includes an escape provision that is sometimes invoked for first offenders. New York Penal Law, § 70.15.

191. Meisler, "Canada: Mired in a Nice Quiet Identity Crisis," *Los Angeles Times,* December 4, 1983, p. IV:2.

192. Mauser, "A Comparison of Canadian and American Attitudes," p. 8.

193. *Maclean's*-Decima Poll, Paul M. Sniderman et al., "Liberty, Authority, and Community: Civil Liberties and the Canadian Political Culture" (Centre of Criminology, University of Toronto, and Survey Research Center, University of California, Berkeley, 1988), both discussed in Lipset, *Continental Divide,* pp. 94, 111.

194. "A Nice Quiet Identity Crisis."

195. The NFA considers itself strong all over, and points out that its membership surged in 1990, in response to government proposals for new controls. Tomlinson, 1990, p. 2.

196. Victor Malarek, "Killer's Letter Blames Feminists," *The* (Toronto) *Globe and Mail,* December 8, 1989, p. 1. During the shooting, police and emergency telephone operators argued over whether the call should be transmitted to the police directly; police dispatchers provided police officers only with the school's address, and not the building where the crime was taking place, and the police did not enter the building until eight minutes after Lépine had taken his own life, still having 60 unused rounds of ammunition.

197. One manifestation of the campaign against guns per se came at the University of Toronto, where a committee of students and faculty has urged the closing of a target range, under the theory that use of firearms is "inappropriate" and that "Many people are revolted that there are individuals who take delight in firearms." "Taking Aim at University Marksmen," *The* (Toronto) *Globe and Mail,* May 18, 1991, p. 10.

198. *Bill C-80: An Act to Amend the Criminal Code and the Customs Tariff in consequence Thereof,* Second Session, Thirty-fourth Parliament, 38–39 Elizabeth II, 1989–90; Department of Justice, Canada, *Safer and Better Firearms Control: Proposals for Change* (Ottawa: Department of Justice, Canada, 1990).

199. For example, R. A. Watt, *Bill C-80—A Layman's Critique* (privately published, 1990); *The Outdoorsman,* October 1990; British Columbia Wildlife Federation, *Response to Bill C-80* (Langley, B.C.: B.C. Wildlife Federation, October 1990); *The Barnet Marksman* 24, no. 1 (March 1991).

200. *Report of the Special Committee on The Subject-Matter of Bill C-80 (Firearms),* House of Commons, Issue no. 12, Second Session of the Thirty-Fourth Parliament, February 1991.

201. Among the features in the original C-17 found objectionable by Canadian firearms owners are a section which would allow the government to ban ammunition that can be fired in prohibited firearms (such ammunition includes the common .303 British, .30 '06, .308, 12 gauge shotgun, 9mm pistol, and .45 ACP pistol calibres, all of which are commonly used for target shooting or hunting); a magazine capacity limit of five for rifles and ten for handguns (rather than the Advisory Committee's suggested 10/15 limit); an undetailed requirement for "safe storage" (which Canadians fear could be interpreted like the British safe-storage requirement, forcing gun owners to spend thousands of dollars on safes and

electronic alarms, thereby making gun ownership unaffordable to many citizens); and a $50 per FAC fee (which is said to exceed actual administrative costs, and which could be arbitrarily increased by the central government to discourage gun ownership).

202. Criminal Code, § 106(1), as modified by Bill C-17, p. 24.

203. Criminal Code, § 84(1), as modified by Bill C-17, p. 2.

204. Author's personal communication with Gary Mauser, professor of business, Simon Fraser University, February 14, 1992.

205. Criminal Code, § 84(1), as modified by Bill C-17, pp. 3–4.

206. Ministry of Justice, "Review of Major Legislative and Regulatory Firearms Proposals," November 18, 1991, FA2-TBL.08E, p. 5. [Hereinafter "Review of Major Firearms Proposals."]

207. Criminal Code, § 90(3.2), added by Bill C-17, p. 5.

208. "Review of Major Firearms Proposals," p. 5.

209. Criminal Code, § 84(1), as modified by Bill C-17, p. 2.

210. Criminal Code, § 106(2)(c), as modified by Bill C-17, p. 25; Mauser communication.

211. Criminal Code, § 106(8), as modified by Bill C-17, p. 27.

212. Criminal Code, § 106(8.1), as modified by Bill C-17, p. 27.

213. Criminal Code, § 106(9.1), as modified by Bill C-17, p. 27.

214. Criminal Code, § 116, as modified by Bill C-17, p. 36.

215. Mauser communication.

216. Can. Const. (Constitution Act of 1982) pt. I (Canadian Charter of Rights and Freedoms), § 10(h); Lipset, p. 102; United States Constitution, Amendment V.

217. Lipset, pp. 102–103.

218. John Hagan, *The Disreputable Pleasures* (Toronto: McGraw Hill Ryerson, 1984), p. 179.

219. John F. Burns, "Canada to End Countersubversion Unit," *New York Times,* December 2, 1987, p. A2.

220. Edgar Z. Friedenberg, *Deference to Authority: The Case of Canada* (White Plains, N.Y.: M. E. Sharpe, 1980), p. 33.

221. John F. Burns, "Canada Puts Neo-Nazi's Ideas on Trial, Again," *New York Times,* March 30, 1988, p. A12, col. 1; *Chronicle of Higher Education,* September 19, 1984, p. 34, cited in Blackman, "The Canadian Gun Law," p. 23; David Bercuson and Douglas Wertheimer, *A Trust Betrayed: The Keegstra Affair* (Toronto: Doubleday Canada, 1985) (criminal prosecution of high school teacher for teaching anti-semitic propaganda); Lipset, pp. 105–106, citing B. P. Elman, "The Promotion of Hatred and the Canadian Charter of Rights and Freedoms: A Review of *Keegstra* v. *The Queen,*" *Canadian Public Policy* 15 (March 1989), pp. 74–75.

222. Lipset, p. 95, analyzing data for 1948–82 from the *World Handbook of Political and Social Indicators.*

223. Regulations Respecting the Control of Restricted Weapons and Firearms, § 6. The advertising ban might be argued to be in violation of the Charter of Rights.

224. The British North America Act of 1867, creating Canada's basic structures of government, took account of the American Civil War, which the British and Canadians thought to be caused by the weakness of the United States federal government and by the emphasis on states' rights.

While the United States had fractured government power, to prevent any faction, or any majority, from oppressing minorities, Canada took the opposite approach—hoping that a strong national government would best guard minority rights.

225. Michael T. Kaufman, "Canada: An American Discovers Its Difference," *New York Times Magazine,* May 15, 1983, pp. 60–61, 80–85, 88.

226. The Bill of Rights does not apply to matters within provincial jurisdiction.

227. Constitution Act, 1982, R.S.C. 1985, Appendix II, No. 44, Part I, Canadian Charter of Rights and Freedoms. Enacted by the Canada Act, 1982 (U.K.), chapter 11.

228. Charter of Rights, § 2; U.S. Const. Amend. I.

229. Lipset, p. 103.

230. Charter of Rights, § 1.

231. Parliament or the legislature of a province may declare that a provision will operate for five years notwithstanding sections 2 (free speech, religion, and assembly) or sections 7 through 15 (due process, equal protection of the law, and criminal procedure protections). Charter of Rights, § 33. See also Anne F. Bayefsky, "The Judicial Function under the Canadian Charter of Rights and Freedoms," *McGill Law Journal* 32 (1987), p. 818.

232. Friedenberg, p. 12. Interestingly, the Charter of Rights claims to guarantee the "security of the person," a provision which might one day be used as a legal basis for protecting a Canadian right to bear arms.

233. Lipset, p. 132, citing Peter N. Nemetz, W. T. Stanbury, and Fred Thompson, "Social Regulation in Canada: An Overview and Comparison of the American Model," *Policy Studies Journal* 14 (June 1986): 594. Charter of Rights, § 7.

234. Robert T. Kudrle and Theodore R. Marmor, "The Development of Welfare States in North America," in Peter Flora and Arnold J. Heidenheimer, eds., *The Development of Welfare States in Europe and America* (New Brunswick, N.J.: Transaction Books, 1981), pp. 110–12 (ideology is the key reason that most welfare state innovations appear first in Canada rather than America, despite similar economic conditions in the two countries); Lipset, pp. 139, 141–42, citing Vicki L. Templin, "Predicting Policy Choices of Individual Legislators: A Comparative Study of Canada and the United States," *Population Research and Policy Review* 6 (1987): 254–56; "Bleeding Heart Conservatives," *Economist,* October 8, 1988, p. 4.

It should be noted that there is a new party, the Reform party, which espoused conservative economic ideology and does not embrace gun control. In 1990, the party rapidly gained strength in western Canada, and may achieve significant electoral success there, especially in Alberta.

235. Gad Horowitz, "Red Tory," in William Kilbourn, ed., *Canada: A Guide to the Peaceable Kingdom* (New York: St. Martin's Press, 1970), p. 256.

Socialism, in the form of social democracy, has enjoyed better times in Canada than in America, in part due to the differences in the two nations' history. Socialism came to Canada from immigrant Britons (fellow subjects of a common monarch) and from repatriated students who had studied at British universities. Accordingly, socialism did not seem an alien idea. Canada's greater emphasis on community duties over individual rights made Canadians receptive to the socialist message. But the United States, with its revolution, had rejected Europe and all it stood for. U.S. socialists could never overcome the presumption that socialism was "un-American." McNaught, p. 399.

Canada's less individualist, more collectivist mentality is also illustrated by the greater success of Canadian trade unions. Union density is 40 percent in Canada, nearly twice the U.S. rate. Canadian unions began as international extensions of American unions, and Canada's National Labor Relations Act is patterned after the American one. Seymour Martin Lipset explains the continued durability of Canadian unionism: "As compared to her more populous neighbor, Canada is a more elitist, communitarian, statist and particularist (group-oriented) society." Seymour Martin Lipset, "North American Labor Movements," in Seymour Martin Lipset, ed., *Unions in Transition: Entering the Second Century* (San Francisco: 1986), pp. 442–43; David Brody, "Barriers of Individualism: In the Path of American Unions," *Dissent* (Winter 1989), pp. 75–76.

236. David V. J. Bell, "The Loyalist Tradition in Canada," *Journal of Canadian Studies* 5 (1970), pp. 27–29, discussed in Torrance, p. 101 n.6.

237. Michael A. Goldberg and John Mercer, *The Myth of the North American City: Continentalism Challenged* (Vancouver: University of British Columbia Press, 1986), p. 247. See also Craig Crawford and James Curtis, "English-Canadian Differences in Value Orientations: Survey Comparisons Bearing on Lipset's Thesis," *Studies in Comparative International Development* 14 (Fall-Winter 1979), pp. 23, 40; Peter C. Pineo and John Porter, "Occupational Prestige in Canada" in James E. Curtis and William G. Scott, eds., *Social Stratification: Canada* (Scarborough, Ont.: Prentice-Hall Canada, 1973); L. Neil Guppy, "Dissensus or Consensus: A Cross-National Comparison of International Prestige Scales," *Canadian Journal of Sociology* 9 (Winter 1983–1984).

238. Lipset, pp. 49, 74–75, 80, 83, 88.

239. Margaret Atwood, *Survival: A Thematic Guide to Canadian Literature* (Boston: Beacon Press, 1972), pp. 55, 131, quoted in Lipset, p. 60.

240. Russell M. Brown, "Telemachus and Oedipus: Images and Authority in Canadian and American Fiction" (unpublished dissertation, Department of English, University of Toronto, 1979), discussed in Lipset, p. 62.

241. Gaile McGregor, *The Wacousta Syndrome: Explorations in the Canadian Langscape* (Toronto: University of Toronto Press, 1985). Canadian literature emphasizes dangers of ambition, impossibility of escape, and the vulnerability of man alone. While Americans fear the loss of self in society, Canadians define the self through society. See Lipset, pp. 63–65, 71, citing Mary Jean Green, "Writing in a Motherland" (French Department, Dartmouth College, Hanover, N.H., 1984). See also Hugh MacLennan, "The Psychology of Canadian Nationalism," *Foreign Affairs* 27 (April 1949), pp. 414–15 (Canada's feminine characteristics are based in part on proximity to the larger and dominant United States); Robert Fothergill, "Coward, Bully, or Clown: The Dream Life of a Younger Brother," in Seth Feldman and Joyce Nelson, eds., *Canadian Film Reader* (Toronto: Peter Martin Associates, 1977), pp. 235–41; Robert Kroetch, *The Lovely Treachery of Words: Essays Selected and New* (Toronto: Oxford University Press, 1989); R. Bruce Elder, *Image and Identity: Reflections on Canadian Film and Culture* (Waterloo, Ont.: Wilfrid Laurier University Press, 1989); Russell M. Brown, "A Search for America: Some Canadian Literary Responses," *Journal of American Culture* 2 (1980): 676; Susan Swan, *The Biggest Modern Woman of the World* (Toronto: Lester and Orpem Dennys, 1983), pp. 273–74.

242. Northrop Frye, "Preface to an Uncollected Anthology," in Eli Mandel, ed., *Contexts of Canadian Criticism* (Chicago: University of Chicago Press, 1971), p. 184; Claude A. Bissell, "The Place of Learning and the Artist in Canadian Life," in Richard A. Preston, ed., *Perspectives on Revolution and Evolution* (Durham, N.C.: Duke University Press, 1979); Claude A. Bissell, "A Common Ancestry: Literature in Australia and Canada," *University of Toronto Quarterly* 25 (January 1956): 133–34, all discussed in Lipset, p. 65.

243. Ross Skoggard, "Old Master," *Saturday Night* 103 (May 1988), pp. 68–69; George Bowering, "Modernism Could Not Last Forever," *Canadian Fiction Magazine,* nos. 32–33 (1979–80): 4; Stanley Fogel, *A Tale of Two Countries: Contemporary Fiction in English Canada and the United States* (Toronto: ECW Press, 1984), all discussed in Lipset, pp. 65–66.

244. Torrance, pp. 100–106.

245. Friedenberg, p. 130.

246. Robert Thacker, "Canada's Mounted: The Evolution of a Legend," *Journal of Popular Culture* 14 (Fall 1980), pp. 303–11.
Wrote Washington Irving, "With his horse and his rifle, he is independent of the World,

and spurns all its restraints." Washington Irving, *The Adventures of Captain Bonneville USA in the Rocky Mountains and the Far West, digested from his journal by Washington Irving* (first published in New York, 1843; reprinted, Norman: University of Oklahoma Press, 1961), p. 11.

Or as a Canadian artist, with a bleaker view of the U.S. frontier put it: "The U.S. frontier is the West and its hero is an outlaw; the Canadian frontier is the North, and its hero is a policeman." Robertson Davies, "Signing Away Canada's Soul: Culture, Identity, and the Free Trade Agreement," *Harper's,* January 1989, p. 43.

247. Friedland, p. 41; Blackman, "The Canadian Gun Law," p. 2. The present law only forbids being masked while possessing a firearm and intending to commit a felony. Canadian Criminal Code, § 351(2).

The Enforcement Acts of the Reconstruction period in the United States also forbade wearing a mask, but only if the actor intended to deprive a person of his/her civil rights.

248. Lipset, p. 90, quoting Susan Wood, "Ralph Connor and the Tamed West," in L. L. Lee et al., eds., *The Western Experience in American Literature: Bicentennial Essays* (1977), p. 199.

249. Robert Athearn, *The Mythic West in Twentieth-Century America* (Lawrence: University Press of Kansas, 1986); Link, pp. 18–21; Lipset, p. 91, citing Dick Harrison, "Popular Fiction of the Canadian Prairies: Autopsy on a Small Corpse," *Journal of Popular Culture* 14 (Fall 1980): 329; Dick Harrison, "The Insignificance of the Frontier in Western Canadian Fiction," in Wolfgang Kloos and Hartmut Lutz, eds., *Kanada Geschichte: Politic Kultur,* German-English Yearbook Band 19 (Berlin: Argument-Verlag, 1987), pp. 49–57.

250. Link, p. 18.

251. Atwood, *Survival,* p. 171.

252. McGregor, p. 61, quoted in Lipset, p. 90.

253. Bellows, "Attitude Canada's Key to a Lower Crime Rate," *Niagara Gazette,* August 4, 1985, p. 5A, quoting Hagan's book *The Disreputable Pleasures,* 2d ed. (Toronto: McGraw Hill Ryerson, 1984).

254. "Gun Controls," *San Francisco Sunday Examiner and Chronicle,* September 6, 1981, p. A18. The same point is made by William A. Stahl, *"May He Have Dominion . . ."* *Civil Religion and the Legitimation of Canadian Confederation* (Luther College, University of Regina, 1986), p. 4, quoted in Lipset, pp. 43-44.

255. Hagan, p. 233.

256. Lipset, p. 115, discussing Elise F. Jones et al., *Teenage Pregnancy in Industrialized Countries* (New Haven, Conn.: Yale University Press, 1986), pp. 89, 92.

5

Australia: No One Is Happy

In "America as a Gun Culture," historian Richard Hofstadter dismissed the idea that America's frontier heritage could explain its present attachment to guns: "This is, after all, not the only nation with a frontier history. Canada and Australia had theirs, and yet their gun control measures are far more satisfactory than ours."[1] Essayist Tom Wicker and historian Arthur Schlesinger both make the same point. Australia and Canada had a frontier heritage, but now each has rational gun controls. Why cannot America do the same?[2]

Surely Australia started with enough potential for bloodshed. Like Georgia, much of Australia was a penal colony, filled with debtors, convicts, emancipists, and various victims who chose "transportation" over incarceration or execution. Gun registration was imposed in 1802, fourteen years after the first penal colony had been established.[3] There were occasional uprisings: in March 1804, an Irish convict named William Johnston led his fellow Irish prisoners—armed with sticks, staves, hoes, and a few rifles—on a march to conquer Sydney, in the Castle Hill uprising. British troops speedily shot them down.[4]

Once Australia's eastern seaboard was settled and controlled, the frontier experience was no longer a significant part of national consciousness. Americans pushed into Alabama, Tennessee, Ohio, and beyond, while Australia's "frontier experience" stopped short when settlers, having passed through the gaps in the Great Dividing Range, were halted by the vast interior deserts.[5] The states not on the eastern seaboard—South Australia,

193

Western Australia, and the Northern Territory—were not settled by movement across a continental frontier.

Although the Aborigines would sometimes launch mass attacks on isolated settlers, the natives, fighting with stone-age weapons, were militarily ineffectual against the whites. Indeed, roving bands of escaped Irish prisoners were sometimes a more serious threat than the Aborigines.[6] The Murngin or Aranda tribes were not warriors like the Cherokee, the Apache, or the Sioux. Compared to the American Indian wars, the conflict in Australia "seems a mere parody of war."[7] Still, laws were enacted preventing the transfer of firearms to Aborigines.[8]

And like Canada, Australia brought a centrally controlled police force into new areas as soon as settlers arrived—although this force lacked the popularity and the effectiveness of the Canadian Mounted Police.[9] The original government was designed to secure the submission of men in servitude, rather than the assent of free citizens.[10] Indeed, some states of Australia still retain one of the strongest anti-police traditions in the world,[11] an adversarial relationship that continues today in the gun debate.

Australia did experience something of a "wild west" phase in the "back-blocks" (back country) where pistols became common.[12] But in the more settled and urban areas, handgun density never approached the level of the United States. Rifles and carbines were much more numerous than pistols and revolvers.[13] During the 1850s, British observers contrasted the orderly behavior of Australian gold miners with that of the lynch law in California. Only rarely did Australians resort to vigilante justice.[14] In contrast to the British observers, the Australian miners often compared their situation—oppressed by the police and exploited by the aristocracy—unfavorably to California's.[15]

Just as the Australian frontier was more peaceful, so were the cities. Once order had been established in older, coastal cities and regions, there was neither civil war nor destabilizing ethnic immigration. In Australia and Canada, urbanization and industrialization never approached the frenzied and helter-skelter intensity of the United States.[16]

Australia had little need for a militia to combat indigenous tribes or foreign invaders. Only once did the weakness of the militia threaten the national interest. During the period after Pearl Harbor, when the Japanese were contemplating invasion, home militia defenses were undermanned and feeble, and the regular army (and navy) was in the Mediterranean, Africa, or Southeast Asia defending the British Empire.[17]

In sum, Australia's experience falls somewhere between America's and Canada's. The central police never had the respect or power that they did in Canada, but Australians still found themselves with a safer, more stable nation—both frontier and city—far sooner than America did. Because both the cities and the frontier were so much more secure, guns were not so necessary as a means of self-defense against humans. Accordingly, handguns did not proliferate in Australian society. Shooting nonhuman animals was and is the main social justification for gun ownership in Australia. Today, all groups except gun abolitionists and animal rights activists acknowledge that many rural landholders need long guns to control wild ducks, dingoes, wild dogs, rabbits, and other animals.

THE BATTLE OVER CONFLICTING STATE LAWS

Japan's National Police Agency enforces a national firearms law. Canada's Royal Canadian Mounted Police supervise the gun laws for the national government. Britain's uniform law is enforced with some variations in all of the national police districts. Only Australia and the United States, among the English-speaking countries, leave gun-control laws at the state level, to be enforced by state police.

In earlier times, leaving gun control to the states seemed to work because most states adopted similar policies. Modern gun controls were introduced in Australia in the 1920s and early 1930s, when all eight states enacted pistol and revolver registration.[18] Australia, like Canada, Britain, and New Zealand, panicked at the thought of red revolution, and imposed restrictions on speech, labor unions, and immigrants, as well as on guns.[19] New South Wales, the most populous state, added long-gun registration but repealed it in 1927.

By the New South Wales Pistol License Act of 1927, handgun licenses were only to be issued "for good reason," which the police commissioner interpreted to mean "never."[20] Elsewhere, "registration" eventually became so severe that persons were forbidden to own handguns for target shooting in a licensed club. Only in 1956, the year of the Melbourne Olympics, did target shooting again become a legal reason to own a handgun.[21]

Conflict over Long Guns

While all states have maintained a consensus about handgun control, there is a fierce battle over conflicting state regulations of rifles and shotguns. In recent years several states have imposed stringent long-gun controls, and have insisted that their sister states fall in line.

The southeast island state of Tasmania and the northeast agricultural state of Queensland maintain the least restrictive gun-control systems. Except for Tasmania, all Australian states have long outlawed possession of fully automatic firearms.[22] When Tasmania refused to submit to federal pressure for a ban, the federal government threatened to bar the import of firearms into that state.[23]

For long guns, the general practice is to require a prospective long-gun owner to obtain a one-time "shooter's license," which (like a Canadian Firearms Acquisition Certificate) allows unlimited long-gun purchases. The conflicts over long-gun controls center on three topics: whether there should be a waiting period to buy guns after the waiting period required to obtain a shooter's license; whether long guns should be registered; and whether some or all semi-automatic long guns should be subject to special controls.

In approximate order of decreasing liberality of gun controls, the Australian states have the following systems: Queensland (Weapons Act of 1990) requires a shooter's license for long guns but no additional waiting period beyond the twenty-eight-day period for issuance of a license. Long guns are registered by the dealer at the point of sale but registration forms are not sent to the government. There are no special restrictions on semi-automatics. New South Wales (Firearms Act of 1989) requires a shooter's license with a twenty-eight-day waiting period for issuance of the licensee, but has and no registration. Temporary restrictions are placed on centerfire semi-automatic transfers, in effect pending further review of the issue. (The lengthy conflict over semi-automatic restrictions in New South Wales is discussed below.) Tasmania (Firearms Act of 1932) also requires a shooter's license but no registration. When Tasmania imposed a seven-day "cooling-off period," the disappointed anti-gun lobby stated that it would have preferred a "three- to four-month cooling-off period."[24] Permits for centerfire semi-automatics were issued only on the basis of demonstrated need. In South Australia (Firearms [Amendment] Act of 1988) all guns are registered.[25] A lengthy waiting period is required for the first-time buyers, and a graded shooter's license is enforced. Licenses to own centerfire semi-automatics are far more difficult to obtain than licenses for other long guns. Persons living in Victoria (Firearms Act of 1958) and the Northern Territories (Firearms Act of 1977) also have a lengthy waiting period before they can buy their first gun. Registration is required for all long guns. Permits for centerfire semi-automatics are issued only for demonstrated need. (Victoria laws are discussed below). Western Australia (Firearms Act of 1973) registers all guns, and centerfire semi-automatics are prohibited.

The federal government's action on gun control is limited mainly to customs controls. It has barred the import of selected semi-automatic rifles.[26]

One long-gun issue on which there is national consensus is that, as in other Commonwealth countries, the police have broad powers to search for and seize firearms.

In New South Wales, the police were granted power to confiscate on the spot any firearm that they deem "unsafe."[27] The South Australia police may seize any weapon they reasonably suspect to be unregistered.[28] In 1975, one state's premier drafted legislation to allow home searches for weapons "on reasonable grounds," without a warrant.[29]

Consensus on Handguns

Queensland and Tasmania both follow the strict handgun policies of the rest of Australia. Pistol licenses are available only to members of target-shooting clubs, and to those who are found to need the gun professionally, such as government employees or bank security guards.[30] There are no licenses for handgun hunting, a sport that is rapidly growing in popularity in the United States, but is illegal in Australia.[31] Handgun licenses are issuable and revocable at the "absolute discretion" of the police.[32] In many states, a separate license is required each time a person wishes to purchase an additional handgun.[33]

Throughout Australia, club shooters who use handguns are careful guardians of their privilege and screen out potential members who might be undesirable.[34] Accidental misuse of target shooters' handguns is virtually nonexistent.[35] Some ordinary citizens do obtain target licenses so that they can surreptitiously keep a handgun at home for protection.[36] And it is not unheard of for politically connected individuals to receive handgun permits without meeting the standard criteria.[37]

Safety

All states agree about the need for some kind of legislation for safe gun storage. Some states simply require "reasonable" precautions, while others mandate that the guns be locked. Gun owners are criminally liable for damage resulting from negligent storage.[38]

A written safety test for gun licensees is required in most states. Even Western Australia, with strict controls on all guns, has a simple test, and almost all applicants who pass are granted a long-gun license.[39] The test excludes only applicants who believe that one may toss a loaded gun over a fence or shoot drunk.[40] Interestingly, the fatal shooting accident rate per capita in Western Australia is twice as high as in Queensland, which has more guns, and no safety test.[41]

Police-Made Laws

Most Australian gun laws are enacted by elected legislatures. But like the police in Britain and America, the police in Australia sometimes create their own gun controls. The New South Wales police, without legal authority, add a special condition to the usual "safe storage" requirement for guns: owners of two or more handguns must keep them in an approved steel safe that is bolted to the structure of the house. The police inspect handgun license applicants' homes to ensure that the safe is properly installed.[42] Police in two states conduct interviews with the neighbors of those who apply for handgun licenses.[43]

In one major city, the senior police officer took the view that no one except the police should possess firearms. Contrary to the state's licensing rules, he instructed subordinates to reject gun licensees at every possible opportunity. In many parts of Australia, shooters complain that the interpretation of the laws by the police varies radically from year to year.[44]

The Need for National Uniformity

States sometimes attempt to apply their local gun laws to interstate commerce. Section 92 of the Australian Constitution guarantees the right to engage in "commerce" freely across state borders, and guns have been held to be "legitimate articles of commerce." In *Chapman* v. *Suttie,* the State of Victoria prosecuted a Victoria firearms dealer who had sold guns by mail to buyers in another state who did not hold a Victoria firearms license. The High Court held that Victoria could not compel buyers beyond its borders to obtain Victoria licenses.[45]

States with strict gun control, such as Victoria, do not want to export guns; they want to export gun control. The situation in Western Australia illustrates why. Western Australia was the first state to implement severe gun control, starting in 1931.[46] (The law forbade gun ownership by non-whites, unless they were "of the Jewish or Lebanese races."[47]) Today, a person in Western Australia may only buy ammunition for the particular weapon for which he holds a license.[48] Along with several other states, Western Australia requires urbanites who claim they want a long gun for hunting to produce written permission from rural landholders stating that the urbanite may hunt on their land.[49] Western Australia police interview the landholders to make sure that the hunting sites are safe.[50]

Fourteen percent of households in Western Australia's capital of Perth own a gun; 43 percent of rural households in the state own one.[51] Yet Perth is one of Australia's most dangerous cities.[52] Western Australia suffers the highest per capita rate of gun crime, and the fastest rate of increase in violent crime. "Right to bear arms" supporters blame the Western Australian gun laws, which are said to encourage criminals to attack a defenseless population.[53]

Gun-control advocates, however, agree with Minister of Police W. R. B. Hassell's 1980 complaint that Western Australia's gun crime problem was due to weapons imported from other states.[54] Likewise, the general secretary of the Police Association of New South Wales protested: "Australia's gun laws are farcical and chaotic. They can be broken by anyone who wants to cross a state boundary. In New South Wales, Queensland, and Tasmania, there is no adequate register of firearms nor of people buying them. All private sales go unrecorded."[55]

"REDNECKS, REACTIONARIES, AND RAMBOS"

Many leading police officials insist that gun control in Australia cannot work until all states adopt uniform, strict controls, including registration of every gun. As in Britain and America, highly publicized incidents of gun crime give the police an opportunity to push hard for more control. One day in June 1984, two gangs of road warriors opened fire on each other in the "Milperra bikie massacre" (also known as "The Father's Day Shoot-out"). A few years passed without another famous massacre. Then, in August 1987, in Melbourne, seven people were killed and nineteen injured by a deranged gunman. A week later, the Hungerford Massacre in England splashed onto the newspapers. Four months after that, on Queen Street in Melbourne, a despondent ex-law student shot to death eight people and wounded five with an M1 carbine, and then hurled himself through a window.[56] Following the second mass murder, one state government took action almost immediately, and all of Australia wondered if something had gone seriously wrong with society.

Since 1973, New South Wales had required long-gun owners to be licensed.[57] The New South Wales government announced a new set of laws to tighten the licensing system:

- all licensees would have to wait for a fourteen-day "cooling off" period;
- the commissioner of police would apply stricter requirements in issuing licenses;
- each purchase of a long gun would (like a handgun under present law) require specific police permission;
- people who wished to purchase a gun would have to show they had good cause for ownership;
- good cause would include gun-club membership or rural property ownership, but not self-defense;
- ammunition would be sold only to a person with a proper license;
- mail-order firearms purchases would be outlawed;[58]
- airguns would brought under the same controls as other guns.[59]

Two additional proposals aroused the most anger from gun owners: the government would strictly enforce a confiscation and ban on self-loading (the Australian term for "semi-automatic") rifles, after a two-month period during which people would be ordered to surrender these arms.[60] All remaining rifles and shotguns, and even airguns, still left in private hands would be registered. The Labor government had determined to deal with the fact that of the estimated one million illegal guns in the New South Wales, all but six hundred remained unaccounted for.[61] Press reaction to the new controls was "universally favorable" according to law professor Richard Harding, Australia's leading academic gun-control advocate.[62] The Police Association of New South Wales protested that the new controls did not go far enough.[63]

Many gun owners felt betrayed. In the 1984 election in New South Wales, the minister for police for the incumbent Labor party had promised to "fully consult" with the gun lobby in any gun-control laws. The opposition Liberal and National parties had also fished for gun-owner support, announcing that "stricter gun control will do little to achieve" lower crime.[64]

The Labor government was re-elected in 1984, and in 1985 the Labor-controlled Parliament passed the gun controls described above, without consulting the gun lobby.[65] Premier Barrie Unsworth did not proclaim (put into effect) the gun laws immediately. He waited until the start of the next election cycle in 1988, and proclaimed the law shortly after the Queen Street massacre.

In response, the two major pro-gun organizations, the Firearms Advisory Council and the Sporting Shooters Association of Australia, formed a joint task force.[66] The gun lobby did not scare anyone. True, the Australian edition of *Reader's Digest* had blamed the Sporting Shooters (SSAA) and the Field and Game Federation of Australia for blocking tighter gun controls.[67] But in a 1982 Victoria election, three candidates targeted by the gun lobby suffered no discernible damage.[68] Harding warned the gun owners: "[I]f you think you can bring down a government on the basis of this, you are fooling yourselves."[69]

The gun lobby went ahead and tried to topple the Labor government. Membership in one gun lobby, which had stood at four hundred in 1985, soared to ten thousand.[70] In the cities, the lobby approached the election with moderate advertisements that raised concerns about crime and put the gun issue in terms of other civil liberties violations by Unsworth's government. Alleged violations included the illegal sacking of the Sydney City Council, and the confiscation of land for national parks and for mining.[71]

The gun-lobby effort was designed to lower the emotional pitch of the gun debate. The task force rejected calls for mass rallies of gun owners, or for marching on Parliament.[72] The task force ads seemed to neutralize the gun laws as an advantage for Premier Unsworth.[73] Nick Greiner's opposition Liberal party agreed with the firearms groups: "Labor's new guns laws are nothing more than a red herring" designed to deflect attention from other Labor failures.[74]

In rural areas, aggressive ads by the gun task force aimed to "maintain the rage." Ads reminded voters that 1988 was the two hundredth anniversary of the year that British prisoners first arrived in Australia. "Free Men Own Guns—Convicts Don't" announced one ad for the "Bicentennial of the New Convict." Print advertising in ethnic areas—translated into nine different languages—showed Premier Unsworth accompanied by a pair of storm troopers coming to confiscate guns. Ethnic voters were reminded that they had fled their homelands because of government tyranny.[75] The task force's quarter-million-dollar advertising budget, almost all of it in print media, was the highest spending by any group besides the two major parties.[76]

The gun lobby itself became an issue. Australia's largest newspaper, the *Sun-Herald,* ran a front-page headline that read "Slush Fund to Defeat Unsworth." The paper described the campaign funds as lawfully raised from gun retailers and manufacturers. Another *Sun-Herald* banner headline screamed "Foreign Arms Cash," although the story itself found only one foreign donor, a safari club.[77]

Labor welcomed the gun controversy. The government ran extensive public service advertisements, explaining the new law to gun owners in moderate terms.[78] Labor played up the gun issue as a centerpiece of the campaign theme that, despite twelve years in power, the Labor government was launching important new initiatives. Attempting to raise the emotional stakes and polarize the issue, Unsworth denounced opponents of the gun law as "Rednecks, Reactionaries, and Rambos."[79] One Labor MP's ad implored "Stop the slaughter," and mocked a Liberal's statement that "to restrict access to guns is an infringement of basic liberties."[80] "A vote for McClelland is a stand against guns," declared another Labor candidate.[81] The Labor party itself took out full-page ads, riddled with bullet holes, reproducing pro-gun quotes by the opposition party. "The Unsworth Labor Government will not compromise on gun control," the ad affirmed.[82]

When pre-election polling indicated that the gun issue was hurting Labor, its MPs from rural areas asked Unsworth to ease off. He refused: "I will not back down. The stakes are too high." He warned, "If we don't act now, Sydney will become an armed camp like many American cities."[83] All in all, Labor spent over one million dollars of advertising solely on the firearms debate.[84]

In the March 19, 1988, New South Wales general state election, the Labor party suffered its worst defeat in fifty years. Labor received only 39 percent of the vote.[85] According to the *Sun-Herald,* "in the country, the controversial new gun laws cost the government seats." Other news-papers agreed.[86] Resigning as party head, Barrie Unsworth confessed, "Clearly as leader I must accept the major proportion of the blame for the defeat, particularly in terms of my decision on the gun issue. . . ."[87] One retiring Labor veteran complained: "I told [Unsworth] he was running a one-man band, especially regarding the gun laws . . . in this case he was pig-headed and arrogant. He was prepared to go down into the Valley of Death like the Charge of the Light Brigade, taking all his mates with him. Now he's done that. Bloody mates that have worked their guts out and mates of quality." In the steel and coal heartlands of Newcastle, Cess-nock, and Swansea, solid Labor districts suffered a swing of over 25 percent of the vote.[88]

Unsworth had expected a favorable pro-control response from urban women to far outweigh any loss of rural males. In marginal urban districts, polling the year before the election showed that two-thirds of undecided voters were women.[89] By waiting to proclaim the 1985 gun laws until just before the 1988 election, Unsworth thought he was giving Labor a large boost in close urban races. Polling indicated, however, that 60 percent of the voters who considered the gun issue important were male, and that *all* of the voters who were going to switch their vote because of the gun issue were males voting against Labor.[90]

Australian Labor party post-election polling indicated that the gun issue was one of the party's three major liabilities in the campaign. Unsworth's successor as party leader, Bob Carr, promised that guns would not be an issue in the next election. "It's no good having a morally appropriate policy if you are never going to have a chance to adopt it."[91]

The new Liberal government ordered the return of the self-loading rifles that had been surrendered.[92] Police officials declared that the 10,300 semi-automatics turned in represented "just the tip of the iceberg."[93] The new premier, Nick Greiner, stated that the ban "was clearly unenforceable and made criminals of decent, law-abiding citizens. Our action means that these people will no longer be branded as criminals simply because they own a self-loading rifle. Less than one percent of these guns were surrendered, making an absolute mockery of an ill-conceived law."[94] Premier Greiner rescinded plans for a gun registry. As substitute reforms, Greiner suggested that firearms license applicants be scrutinized for "good character" and required to pass a safety test.

Worried newspapers looked closer at the powerful new gun lobby. One tabloid compared it to Oliver North and to American backers of the Vietnam War. A spokesman for America's National Rifle Association admitted that the NRA had provided the Australian lobby with encouragement, moral support, and some research assistance, but no financial help.[95]

In 1991, as new elections approached, the Australia Labor party announced its new position on firearms. The announcement was made at the sports stadium in the mining town of Cessnock, north of Sydney. On that spot in February 1988, two thousand miners had rallied against the incumbent Labor government's anti-gun laws, and in the elections that followed Cessnock had turned against Labor for the first time in eighty-seven years.

The Labor announcement was made by Peter Anderson, presently serving as Labor spokesman on law-and-order matters. Anderson had lost his seat in the 1988 elections, and had tried to persuade Premier Unsworth to abandon the gun-control issue. Anderson announced that in response to the community: "The ALP now acknowledges that the people of NSW, both in metropolitan and nonmetropolitan areas, delivered a clear message at the last election regarding gun laws. . . . We will not remove the right of law-abiding citizens in NSW to possess and use firearms, nor will we impose further restrictions on the ownership of firearms." The NSW Labor party also began pressing the federal Labor government to loosen its stand on firearms imports.[96] In place of registration and confiscation, the new government instituted a twenty-eight-day "cooling-off" period for license applicants, and a requirement that applicants take a safety class administered by a gun club.[97]

Despite the fears of the press and the hopes of the Australian shooters, gun owners have not become an invincible political force. A few months after the New South Wales elections of 1988, gun activists failed to score a decisive win in the next electoral contest, in the southeastern state of Victoria. Premier John Cain had proposed a ban on semi-automatics similar to the one in New South Wales. Gun-owner reaction had been fierce. A rally in Melbourne attracted a crowd between 30,000 and 50,000, the majority waving Australian flags and denouncing gun control as "un-Australian."[98] After the election in New South Wales, Premier Cain completely rescinded the ban on low-powered rimfire semi-automatics (about 200,000 owners in Victoria). As for the relatively high-powered centerfire semi-automatics (about 12,000 owners), Cain decided to allow the possession of some such guns under a carefully controlled permit. Having defused much of the firearms community's opposition, Cain won re-election by a small margin.[99] Cain's close call, coming on the heels of Unsworth's defeat, did defuse pressures for federal gun control.

The Victoria government proceeded with plans to confiscate all semi-automatic centerfire rifles that it considered not to be appropriate for sports.[100] Some of the semi-automatics surrendered to the police might be returned at some point, the government said, if the police thought it wise to do so. And Premier Cain did at least promise to pay "market value" for the confiscated guns, as determined by two independent licensed gun dealers.[101] Semi-automatics remained available to rifle-club members, hunters, and farmers under special licensing procedures.

Victoria's severe restrictions on semi-automatics were the first such restrictions in the Commonwealth or the United States. An internal police report later described the controls as "very difficult and impractical."[102]

Registration enforcement in Victoria became a serious matter. One government "public service" advertisement pictured five naked men from the rear, lined up against a wall in a prison shower. The uniformed police looked on. "Think About It Now . . . Or You Could Get 12 Months to Think About Nothing Else." The final gun surrender amnesty was coming to a close, and the ad concluded: "This is your last chance. . . . After Saturday December 17, you've got no excuse."[103] When firearms are registered, the registrant is forced to make a "statutory declaration" that all firearms in his possession are registered.[104] At the time the program began in 1985, an estimated 250,000 unregistered firearms were in private hands in Victoria. Three years later, before the start of the final amnesty period, compliance with Victorian registration was estimated by the police to be only 59 percent.[105] (Registration in Victoria is discussed in more detail below.)

There was much more to the new Victorian law. Private gun transactions were outlawed. Advertising for firearms was barred everywhere except gun-club journals. First-time gun buyers were required to pass a four-week waiting period to obtain a shooter's license, renewable every three or six years.[106] S. H. Crabb, the police minister for the Labor government, said the police were satisfied with the new laws, the toughest in Australia.

Tough as the new Victorian gun laws are, they are only partially as strong as the laws Labor Premier John Cain first proposed. Police Minister Crabb said the government "had been surprised" by gun owners' opinion "that gun ownership was their right." Even more surprising, said Crabb, was how quickly public opinion, "which the government believed was overwhelmingly in favor of greater gun restrictions, turned lukewarm after other unrelated issues received publicity."[107]

Robin Cooper, the police spokesman for the Opposition thought "too much rhetoric . . . had been focused on the wrong issue." He added: "Concentrating on law-abiding citizens is absolute nonsense. You have got to have some controls on firearms, and law-abiding shooters are prepared for that. But all those other ratbags who are buying their guns in pubs and whatnot are still able to continue uncheckered. The key is to get firearms out of criminal hands."[108]

John Crook, president of Gun Control Australia, praised the government for instituting new controls, but added, "I think there still is a lot to do." More intense restrictions on multi-shot shotguns (i.e., almost all shotguns) and handguns were Crook's agenda for more action.

"The gun law debate was a knee-jerk reaction to the shootings," said Julian Knight, the Hoddle Street mass murderer, who thought there should be a psychological test for gun buyers because there were too many guns around: "I could just go home, pick them [firearms] up and go out." In the Queen Street massacre, "it was that [the killer] was able to get his hands on [guns] so easily."[109]

Victoria's government, in its manual for gun owners, proclaimed that the new laws "strike a careful balance between the rights of nonshooters, and the genuine sporting shooters in our community."[110] Some of the new rules actually were moderate. Indeed, one page of the ad showed a wholesome teenager with a gun, supervised by his father. People between the age of twelve and eighteen could still shoot, after receiving a "junior permit" allowing them to carry a gun in the company of an adult with a shooter's license.[111] Importantly, some rejected license applicants could appeal to the Firearms Consultative Committee, made up of lawyers, the police, and shooters. Further appeal was available to the Magistrate's Court.[112]

Some parts of the Victorian law turned out more severe in practice than on paper. The Gun Law Handbook circulated by the police promised that firearms licenses could be issued for up to a six-year term. But Police Minister Crabb only issued licenses for a three-year term.[113]

On August 17, 1991, a taxi driver wielding a semi-automatic SKK Chinese-made rifle and a machete killed seven people in a shopping mall in Strathfield, New South Wales.[114] Rupert Murdoch's tabloid the *Telegraph Mirror* collected one million anti-gun signatures on petitions from its readers. Both the Liberal and the Labor parties of New South Wales abandoned their policies, and jointly declared that more gun control on the Victorian model was desirable. Firearms activists staged a 25,000-person rally at Parliament House in Sydney, and Sporting Shooters Association of Australia president Ted Drane told the crowd, "We admit there be some need for restrictions on military-style weapons . . . but they'd better leave everything else alone or there will be trouble."[115]

Following a meeting of the Police Ministers Council in October 1991, the heads of all the state governments agreed to introduce legislation in 1992 that would:

- require a twenty-eight-day waiting period for issuance of a firearms license;
- ban the possession of detachable centerfire rifle or shotgun magazines holding more than five rounds;
- require that firearms and ammunition be stored separately; and
- require owners of "military" centerfire semi-automatics to possess a special license.[116]

Queensland, New South Wales, and Tasmania all rejected the suggestion that the states register all guns, and require a separate permit for each gun purchase.[117]

How the political conflict over guns in Australia will end, if it ever does end, is difficult to predict. Many governmental leaders seem determined to take Australia a long distance down the road that Great Britain has traveled, to make civilian gun ownership an exceptional occurrence. It is doubtful that even the enactment of the full panoply of restrictions presently under debate will make massacres impossible, and hence it is unlikely that the push for still more gun control will lose momentum. At the same time, Australia's traditional distrust of government, combined with a state rather than a national system of gun control, has produced a powerful gun-rights movement, rivaled in the English-speaking world only by the American gun movement. The Australian gun lobby has found the volunteer force, the grassroots commitment, and the money necessary to allow a head-on confrontation with ruling governments and their police administrators. Sometimes the gun movement wins, as in New South Wales, and sometimes it loses, as in Victoria. Whatever the results of the future struggle for stricter gun control in Australia, a large and active citizens' movement will be fighting back and making a difference.

THE ANTI-GUN LOBBY

Two states are always criticized for their lax gun laws: Queensland and Tasmania.[118] Is the gun problem worse in these states? Queensland's per capita homicide rate, per gun homicide rate, and per capita gun accident rate are all at or below the national averages.[119] In Tasmania in 1986, there were two fatal gun accidents and one murder with a gun. In 1987, there were no murders.[120] Disappointed that Tasmania is not stricter, the anti-gun lobby complains that the Tasmanian shooters' organizations "have a path straight to the Minister's door."[121] In New South Wales, the most populous state, and one also criticized for laxity, there were only sixty-one murder *attempts* with guns in 1983.[122]

Is it possible that the anti-gun lobby is not primarily concerned with crime reduction? The former attorney general of New South Wales summarized the parliamentary debate on gun control: "The debate was not about guns or crime or legal control or research or the eradication of vermin by the 'man-on-the-land.' It was about 'society' and what goes to make up the 'good life' within that 'society.' "[123] The attorney general compared gun control to the environmental movement, in placing a greater emphasis on quality of life and less reliance on unconstrained individualism.[124]

The moralistic strain of the anti-gun sentiment is illustrated by comments at a meeting of the leaders of the anti-gun coalition. "We reject the right for people to answer violence with violence," says university lecturer Martha McIntyre.[125] She expresses the view of many in the anti-gun movement that the person who violently resists crime has sunk to the level of the criminal.

Gun control is only one aspect of a full-scale rejection of violence. The Reverend Wes Campbell, of the Uniting Church, agrees with Harding that the anti-gun issue should be integrated into the nuclear disarmament issue,[126] although thus far, an anti-bomb, anti-gun alliance has only barely begun to materialize.

American opponents of guns have campaigned against toy guns. Campbell goes a step further and suggests elimination "of bad toys, like inhuman monsters, robots, etc."[127] He also urges a ban on shooting on Sundays.[128]

The campaign against violence includes not only symbolic controls of "violent" objects, but also an attempt to abolish violence against animals. The animal-rights lobby has signed on with the anti-gun lobby. During the 1988 New South Wales election, they linked opposition to duck hunting to support for the Labor government's strict new gun laws.[129]

Animal Liberation (the leading animal rights group) and the rest of the anti-gun coalition have won the support of a smaller party, the Australian Democrats. Far from political power, the party can speak its mind freely on the gun issue. The Democratic party helps publicize Animal Liberation's efforts to eliminate duck hunting.[130] A draft Democratic party platform calls for the abolition of sport hunting, a complete gun ban in urban and other "gun-free areas," a ban on all long guns that can hold more than two rounds of ammunition, and a six-month waiting period for any firearms transaction. Neighborhood residents could prohibit a neighbor from possessing a gun if they felt uncomfortable with firearms in their neighborhood.[131] The Australian Democrats get their draft policy from Gun Control Australia, states GCA president John Crook.[132]

The more powerful national Australian Labour party accepts a step-by-step campaign against hunting as one element in the campaign against private gun ownership. As a delegate at one ALP conference put it, the hunters and firearms owners are too powerful to be tackled en masse. The way to extend control is to "chip away" at the edges, with selective bans on hunting.[133]

In Britain the animals-rights movement (The League Against Cruel Sports) is the main anti-gun lobby. In the United States, connections between animal rights and restrictions on gun rights are more tenuous. *The Animals' Agenda,* a leading American animal-rights magazine, does take frequent potshots at the National Rifle Association. Other United States animal-rights supporters, though, are also gun-rights advocates.[134] Unlike Australia and Britain, socially legitimate gun ownership in America is not confined to "sporting use." Many American guns are owned for defense of innocent human life against criminals, not for killing innocent animals for sport. Thus, animal-rights crusaders in America can stand up in defense of the right to bear arms, as long as the right is placed in a context that legitimizes self-defense, and delegitimizes or ignores hunting.

Professor Harding, Australia's leading gun-control advocate, suggested for years "without notable success" that gun control become a feminist issue since most gun homicide victims are female and most gun criminals are male.[135] (In fact, most gun victims are male.) Nevertheless, in response to the increased activity of the NSW gun lobby in the late 1980s, Ms. Lee O'Gorman founded New South Wales Women Against Guns. The organization has a thousand (mostly inactive) members. Women Against Guns can bring out several thousand people for a rally, in contrast to the gun lobby, which can bring out tens of thousands.[136]

Although not a part of the organized anti-gun lobby, the Council for Civil Liberties does favor gun control. The council argues that fear of crime makes people "hostages in their own homes" and hence less free; moreover, fear of crime leads to undesirable and repressive criminal laws.[137] (The council's position is somewhat at odds with the fact that the gun laws themselves are sometimes enforced quite harshly, and in violation of other civil liberties, such as freedom from warrantless search and seizure.[138])

The money for the anti-gun lobby comes chiefly from the Australian Bankers' Association and Australian Bank Employees Union.[139]

The Australian anti-gun lobby's cultural disdain for shooters is clear. One strategist complains that "shooters, being simple, write simplistic letters" that get printed in the newspapers.[140] Mr. Laurie Levy, head of Animal Liberation, believes that firearms are phallic symbols for the sexually maladjusted.[141]

Foreign countries figure prominently in the Australian gun debate. Harding warns Australians about America. The United States, he writes, has passed the point of no return. Gun density has made American gun use "destructive, volatile, self-perpetuating, and intractable." Unless Australia acts quickly, it, too, will find gun control a lost possibility.[142] (Professor M. L. Friedland of the University of Toronto convinced his fellow Canadians of the same point in the mid-1970s.)

On all counts, from the Australian viewpoint, America seems a bad example. Even Australian proponents of stricter control are leery of the way gun control has been administered in America. For example, law reformer J. David Fine insists on assurance that Australian gun law enforcement would not be politicized as it had been in the United States, especially in New York City, where carry permits are only available for the rich and famous.[143] (Fine's confidential interviews with police departments uncovered evidence that some Australian police may already be as politicized as some American ones.)

The anti-gun lobby also contrasts Australia and America, in that America has an explicit right to bear arms, and Australia does not. Australian gun advocates reply that the Australian firearms right descends from Australia's common-law heritage with Britain, and Parliament's 1689 recognition of a right to bear arms.

When Australian shooters urge their countrymen to look at foreign examples, they point not to America, but to New Zealand, where the police abandoned gun registration in 1983. The most that shooters say about the United States is to point out—albeit defensively—that the American areas with the most restrictive gun laws are generally the areas with the most crime.

A crucial element of the Australian anti-gun coalition is the mainstream press. America's most influential academic voice for gun control is University of California Professor of Law Franklin Zimring. In a 1981 visit to Australia, Zimring opined that Australia had no gun problem, but that Australian shooters had a media problem.[144] Zimring is right, for as long as any guns exist in civilian hands, there will always be Queen Street or Milperra massacres that arouse the press and inflame public fears. Agreeing with Zimring, Fine criticized press coverage of the massacres for creating "a sense of urgency and hysteria which is not conducive to sound policy formulation." He complained that "this unfortunate style of media reporting" has given "a highly exaggerated sense of the magnitude and frequency of firearms-related death and injury in Australian society."[145]

From what we have seen in other English-speaking countries, though, gun-control laws are enacted predominantly in times of public hysteria over an exaggerated and often nonexistent threat. Laurie Levy, of Animal Liberation, offers the following rationalization: "The public responds to emotion, not intellect. We have to make our appeal emotional."[146]

In Britain and Canada and Australia no amount of gun control has satisfied the anti-gun lobby. If, as the attorney general for New South Wales, explained, gun control is more an issue of morality than one of criminology, Australian (and American?) gun control can never be satisfied until firearms, those potent symbols of violence, are eradicated.

MORE AND MORE GUNS

The urgency of the anti-gun lobby to turn the first massacre that comes along into the next step of gun control is a sensible tactic. Firearms ownership is up all over Australia.[147] In South Australia from 1980 to 1984, the number of licensed shooters and the number of legally registered firearms increased four times faster than the rate of population increase. And the increase in South Australia was lower than that for the nation as a whole.[148] In 1979, there was one gun for every five or six Australians; by 1988, the figure was one gun for every four Australians. Roughly 30 percent of households own one of Australia's three to four million guns and the figure is rising rapidly.[149] Put another way, about 10 percent of Australia's fifteen million people personally own a gun.[150]

Most guns are purchased for sport or as part of a collection, but about 20 percent are acquired primarily for self-defense. The only states that deviate significantly from this percentage are the two with the least restrictive controls: Queensland, where about a third of all gun ownership is for self-protection, and Tasmania, where only 7 percent of gun owners are concerned with self-defense.[151] The Queensland police list of legitimate reasons for owning a gun includes sport and collecting, but not self-defense.[152]

Although gun ownership is increasing, handguns remain rare. In Western Australia, for example, there are twenty-five times as many long guns as handguns.[153] About 60 percent of Australian guns are rifles, 30 percent shotguns, 6.5 percent airguns, and 3.5 percent handguns.[154]

Gun ownership is three times higher in rural than in urban areas.[155] Western Australia, with almost all of its population concentrated in metropolitan Perth, has the lowest household rate of gun ownership, 20 percent; Tasmania, with a highly dispersed population, has the highest gun-owning rate, 32 percent.[156] Gun owners are most likely to be younger men working in middle-class or primary-industry jobs.[157] In terms of marital status and social stability, firearms owners are identical to the rest of the population.[158] That gun owners are so much like nonowners is one of the reasons Australia has so much less gun control than Britain, where gun owners are seen as a special class.[159] (Immigrants from Britain, incidentally, are considerably less likely to own guns than are native Australians.[160])

CRIME CONTROL

According to Fine, senior police officials have unanimously asserted that—despite the strict handgun laws—"handguns were still readily available to criminals who wanted them."[161] One officer stated that a criminal need only walk into a certain pub in the state's capital city, "indicate that he wanted a pistol and wasn't fussy about make or calibre, and then wait about an hour."[162]

Homicide

Variations in gun laws among the Australian states seem to have little relation to crime. The homicide rate in New South Wales, with relatively weaker laws, is 2 victims per 100,000 people per year.[163] The rate in other states is similar, except for the Northern Territory (with stricter laws), where homicide is six times as common, 11.8 people per 100,000.[164] The Northern Territory's rate is even higher than that of the United States. The national homicide rate has stayed fairly constant for the last fifteen years, and is far lower than a century ago.[165]

Just as the interstate gun law variations do not seem to make a difference, the rural/urban differences in gun density do not seem to have an impact. Although there are many more guns in rural Australia, urban and rural areas have almost identical homicide rates—1.9 and 2.0, respectively.[166]

United States gun-control advocates note that handguns are the most common firearm used in murders, including murders by family members and acquaintances. Because handguns are so easy to pick up, in contrast to bulky long guns, it is argued that handguns pose a special threat in volatile domestic disturbances. Yet in Australia, where handguns are much more difficult to obtain than long guns, most murders are still domestic or acquaintance.[167] The Australian anti-handgun policy does work, in that, unlike in the United States, most gun homicides are not by handgun. This is evidence that many killers in Australia are not determined criminals who can procure a handgun if they wish, but instead simply reach for the handiest weapon, which, if it is a gun, is more likely to be a long gun rather than a handgun.

In general, domestic homicide follows patterns similar to those in the United States. A quarter of all homicides are by spouses, with men doing the killing three-quarters of the time.[168] Guns are more common in spousal homicides (40.9 percent) than in other homicides.[169] Husbands who killed their wives were much less likely to use a gun or other weapon than were wives who killed their husbands. All women suspected of killing their husbands used a gun or some other weapon; 22.6 percent of males who killed their wives used no weapon at all. "This is not an unexpected result given the difference in physical strength between men and women," observes a criminal justice report.[170] Wife-to-husband violence is often committed in defense of self or a child, says the National Committee on Violence. "Murders committed by wives are usually desperate, last-ditch responses after receiving years of brutal violence."[171]

Gun control might not reduce the number of killings of wives by husbands, because husbands retain the advantage of physical strength. An effective gun prohibition might well reduce the killings of husbands by wives, but this result might not be a step forward for social justice. In 35 percent of killings by wives, the women had been previously assaulted, and claimed they killed their husbands in response to an imminent threat of attack.[172] Few women killed men from whom they were separated. But almost half of the women who were killed had already separated from their spouse. Notes the New South Wales attorney general, "Victims of domestic violence are commonly blamed for not leaving a violent relationship. . . . [L]eaving the relationship did not necessarily end the violence, and for some women [it] had lethal consequences."[173] Guns being more common in rural areas, 54 percent of spousal killings there involved a gun; the figure is only 35 percent for urban areas.[174]

Robbery

The conclusions about gun control that can be drawn from Australian efforts to control armed robbery are ambiguous. In the last fifteen years, the robbery rate has more than doubled, following a fairly steady upward slope. The robbery rate has still remained significantly below the American and Canadian levels.[175] In New South Wales, about a third of all reported robberies involve a gun, and about 18 percent involve some other kind of weapon, usually a knife.[176] Residents of Sydney suffer an armed robbery rate that is thirty times as high as the rest of New South Wales.[177]

In South Australia, 32 percent of robberies involve the use of some weapon. Reported Australian armed robberies involved firearms at about the same rate (60 percent) as American one.[178] Of the robberies in South Australia in which a firearm was used, handguns were present 26 percent of the time; in Victoria and New South Wales, the percentages were 44 percent and 36 percent, respectively.[179]

Although handguns are much more difficult to obtain than long guns, and are only a small percentage of the Australian gun stock, handguns still had a high percentage of use in robberies. This suggests that even stringent gun-control policies may not be able to reduce handgun robbery below a certain minimum. Any illegal item can always be obtained at the right price. For a professional robber, a handgun costing as much as several thousand dollars may be a worthwhile investment.

Of course determined, professional criminals are not the only people who use guns unlawfully. The Queensland Police Department, while rejecting the idea that gun control could prevent homicide or suicide, favors handgun control to keep guns out of the hands of casual criminals.[180] Richard Harding agrees that while "amateurish" gun misuse may be deterred by reducing the availability of guns, professional gun use by criminals (such as robbers of commercial premises) is unlikely to be affected by any gun-control system. A study Harding conducted involving felony prisoners in Western Australia found that the criminals had little difficulty obtaining guns, although Western Australia's gun laws are the sternest in the nation.[181] Harding suggests that disarming of marginal, inexperienced criminals is enough reason for gun control; professional criminals are less likely to shoot their victims than are drug-crazed tyros who may fire the gun in a panic.[182]

In any case, robberies involving handguns compose a significantly smaller percentage of gun robberies in Australia where guns of any kind are involved than they do in the United States. This suggests that a strict gun policy aimed primarily at handguns may force some robbers to switch from handguns to long guns as a robbery tool. Whether or not forcing the change is desirable is unclear. Sawed-off rifles and sawed-off shotguns are concealable, as are handguns, but they are much more deadly.[183]

Suicide

Firearms account for approximately a quarter of Australian suicides, compared to two-fifths in the United States and Canada. Not surprisingly, the local availability of guns affects their use in suicide. In New South Wales, for example, rural areas of the state have a gun suicide rate forty-four times higher than urban Sydney. Yet for total suicides, Sydney's rate is nearly twice as much as that of the rural areas.[184] Harding finds no connection between the availability of firearms and their use in suicide, and no connection between the rate of suicides involving guns and the overall rate of suicides.[185] The Australian suicide rate is approximately the same as America's.[186] Thus, Australia's experience with gun control and suicide is consistent with other nations: the availability of particular weapons does not seem to have an impact on the overall suicide rate.

One clear effect of the Australian controls is that when a gun is used in a robbery or an attempted murder, the gun is less likely to be a handgun than in a comparable situation in the United States. Likewise, handguns are used relatively infrequently for suicides in Australia, compared to the use of long guns. If the strict handgun laws have resulted in some suicides substituting long guns for handguns, the laws will have caused an increase in mortality, since suicide by handgun is more survivable than suicide by rifle or shotgun.

Analysis of Australian statistics regarding homicide, robbery, and suicide may be interesting for non-Australian observers, but the statistical inquiry is of virtually no importance to the Australian gun debate itself. While the American pro-gun and anti-gun lobbies hurl (sometimes dubious) statistics and studies at each other, such numerical argument is noticeably absent in the Australian gun debate. The irrelevance of academic research to the Australian debate is particularly apparent in report titled *Violence: Directions for Australia,* produced by the National Committee on Violence. Created in response to two mass shootings in Melbourne in 1987, the national committee conducted lengthy hearings on all aspects of violence in Australia, from boxing matches to spousal abuse to gun crime. The committee operated under the direction of Dr. Duncan Chappell, director of the Australian Institute of Criminology. A respected international criminologist, Chappell has produced the kinds of carefully reasoned, analytic studies typical of a highly competent social scientist.[187]

Violence: Directions for Australia, however, bears little resemblance to standard criminological arguments (except that it does contain several thorough bibliographies). On the whole, its policies and sensibility closely resemble those of a 1970 American progressive. Violence in virtually any form is bad. Bad environments and bad influences impel people to violence and it is the government's duty to alter those environments and influences. There is little suggestion that some violence may result from the perpetrator's decision to choose evil conduct, or that the decline of traditional moral training bears any relation to some criminals' refusal to control their evil impulses. (Indeed the word "evil" would perhaps seem quaint and silly to the book's authors).[188]

The book's five-page discussion on firearms reflects the view that firearms should be cleansed from the environment. The national committee encourages a reduction in the number of firearms as a worthwhile goal in itself. Canadian gun control is touted for reducing the percentage of homicides committed with firearms, but not the number of overall homicides, as if a society where people are killed with knives is better than a society where an equal number of people are killed with guns. In addition to a panoply of restrictions on the sale and possession of firearms, the national committee even recommends national firearms registration; yet there is no credible academic study finding firearms registration to have any relation to reducing firearms violence, and no such study is cited by the committee. The committee simply declines to discuss the fact, brought to its attention by witnesses, that the New Zealand police scrapped their nation's gun registration system after finding it to be nothing more than a drain on police resources.[189]

If a national commission chaired by the director of the Australian Institute of Criminology can call for sweeping firearms controls, while the weight of criminological research provides no support for or actually demonstrates the inefficacy of such controls, can other Australians be blamed for not caring about studies or statistics? As the former attorney general of New South Wales observed, while his government enacted gun-confiscation legislation, the gun control debate is not about crime control, or the needs of farmers, but rather about what makes a good society. To the Australian gun-control movement, to much of the Australian media, and to the Australian Institute of Criminology, it is self-evident that a good society should not have guns. Of what use are statistics in a debate about decency?

SOCIAL CONTROLS

Previous chapters have explained the low crime rates, including the low crime rates involving guns, in Japan, Britain, and Canada primarily in terms of social control, rather than gun control. It would not be plausible to contend that Australia's system of social controls is as pervasive or as powerful as those in Japan or Great Britain or, perhaps, even in Canada. Nevertheless, Australia does have one system of control that is lacking in America: the likelihood that violent criminals will go to prison. About 20 to 30 percent of robberies in Australia result in an arrest,[190] a rate not much different from that in the United States. Once a person is arrested, however, he or she is very likely to go to jail. For defendants charged with serious robbery offenses (e.g., those involving use of any weapon, those in which two or more people participate, or offenses in which personal violence results), 63 percent pleaded guilty as charged; 22 percent were convicted as charged; and 9 percent were convicted of a lesser charge. Thus, 94 percent of charged defendants were convicted, a rate far higher than in the United States.[191]

In South Australia, a robber's first offense could find him or her in prison for up to fourteen years. If the victim is seriously injured, or if the robber uses a weapon (including a club), the maximum sentence is life imprisonment.[192] While courts do not seem to readily use the lengthiest terms available, jail is the normal result of a conviction. Of the defendants convicted of robbery in South Australia, 74 percent went to jail, and 38 percent went to jail for more than five years.[193] The state of Victoria followed a comparable sentencing policy. New South Wales sentenced 90 percent of its convicted defendants to jail, and 60 percent for longer than five years.[194] As chapter 10 will detail, the comparable rates of imprisonment are much less in the United States.

Other aspects of Australian social control (or lack thereof) are similar to those in the United States. Alcohol is involved in 70 percent of all homicides, about the same as in the United States.[195] The criminalization of heroin and other opiates, by driving up the price, leads many addicts to pursue robbery careers, which account for most of Australia's robberies.[196]

A survey of felony prisoners in Western Australia seems to validate the hypothesis that use of a firearms in crime depends less on the availability of guns than on the social conditioning toward them. For example, rural Aborigines in the northwest grow up in a culture where they are surrounded by guns, yet those who become criminals are far less likely to use guns to perpetrate their crimes than their white counterparts. As one Aborigine prisoner put it, "Guns are for shooting tucker (food), not people."[197] Likewise, criminals who had been introduced to firearms by authority figures, such as their father or grandfather, were less likely to commit armed offenses than were criminals who had been introduced to guns by peers, such as brothers or friends.[198]

REGISTRATION: "AN ELABORATE CONCEPT OF ARITHMETIC WITH NO TANGIBLE AIM"

Analysis of gun control in Britain and Canada suggested that national systems of control, if they had any relation to national crime levels, had an inverse relation: crime worsened after gun control was imposed. While Australia offers important lessons about the political dynamics of gun control, the criminological lessons are less clear.

Variations in state laws, the possibility of interstate arms transfers, and the absence of detailed national criminal justice statistics make assessment of the laws difficult. Australia does have a uniform system of strict handgun control. Although no one asserts that handguns are unavailable to determined criminals, controls may have placed handguns beyond the reach of inexperienced criminals, or the mentally unstable. To the extent, if any, that the special policy for handguns has encouraged sociopaths like the failed law student on Queen Street, or potential suicides, or spouses, to substitute long guns for handguns, the policy has increased the death rate. But to the extent that long guns were not substituted for handguns, the policy has likely reduced that rate. Australia's homicide rate is less than one-quarter of America's and has remained stable, even as overall crime has soared. Of course, even without American homicides involving guns, America would still have a higher homicide rate. America's problem with homicides stems almost entirely from racial minorities subject to discrimination, who compose over 20 percent of the United States's population. Australia's most victimized minority, the Aborigines, compose only 1 percent of the population.

Whatever conclusions academics might draw would matter little to either side in the Australian gun debate. The pro-control forces, which include the National Committee on Violence, have supported controls primarily as a moral issue, without requiring evidence that controls would really reduce crime. The pro-gun forces likewise take a moral approach. While their public advertising (like their adversaries') may discuss the crime issue, the central question is whether a free citizen has the right to own a gun.

There is one lesson, however, that can very clearly be drawn from the Australian experience: gun registration does not work. That lesson comes not from the Sporting Shooters Association, but from the police. Fine, after comprehensive interviews with police officials around the nation, was unable to find a single instance where firearms registration had helped solve a crime.[199] In earlier interviews, Fine asked whether registration prevented some criminals from obtaining guns. "The author was not sufficiently brave to continue to raise this possibility with police across the country, as he found himself thought to be extraordinarily naive, or a typically muddle-headed academic, merely for raising the suggestion."[200] Fine's police officers also concluded that ammunition controls were ineffective and a waste of police time.[201]

Fine reports that police administration of the licensing and registration system has been less than efficient. He was present when two police officers arrived unannounced at a licensee's door to take away "your unlicensed pistols." The licensee produced his current, valid license, which—despite what the police computer said—had been properly renewed.[202] He also reports a number of incidents where police improperly recorded firearm serial markings—for example, confusing the scope manufacturer with the firearm manufacturer, or incorrectly recording the cyrillic alphabet characters on some guns.[203] Registration is more than just a useless diversion for police officers who do not know foreign alphabets. The strain on limited police resources seems severe. The police in Victoria take up to a year to issue firearms licenses.[204] As of January 1989, the Victoria Firearms Registry for that state had a staff of forty-three, urgent requests for more staff overtime, and a backlog of 46,000 firearms to register.[205]

The most severe problem with registration and similar "paperwork" controls is not how many police officers and financial resources the programs pull off of anti-crime patrol. The worst problem is how many criminals the registration laws create. The late Stanford law professor John Kaplan argued that when a law criminalizes behavior that its practitioners do not believe improper, the new outlaws lose respect for society and the law. Kaplan found the problem especially severe in situations where the numbers of outlaws was very high, as in the case of alcohol, marijuana, or gun possession.[206] Citizens who would otherwise consider themselves law-abiding members of the community, but who fear that a registered firearm today will be a confiscated firearm in a few years, violate the registration laws. Australia's David Fine worries that widespread disobedience with respect to registration breeds disrespect for firearms laws and alienation from society.

He recommends that registration be abolished to better promote other gun controls, such as a uniform system for licensing first-time purchasers.[207]

The rate at which gun registration laws are disobeyed is high. The lowest estimate of noncompliance comes from Harding, who figures that perhaps 10 to 15 percent of all guns are unregistered.[208] Harding derives his figure by noting that about 10 percent of guns involved in accidents were unregistered. Yet unregistered guns may be less likely to be used on a day-to-day basis, and hence less likely to be involved in an accident. Indeed, unregistered guns may be most likely to meet the strict safe-storage requirements: hidden and protected so that only one person even knows about them. Fine puts the noncompliance rate for gun owners at around 50 percent.[209] (The American rate at which registration is disobeyed is even higher.)[210] Fine's estimate comports with other evidence about widespread disobedience to the gun laws. While carbines with revolving cylinders were formerly legal in Queensland, they were banned in the early 1980s. In the subsequent amnesty in Queensland, only six such guns were surrendered, even though a single dealer in Queensland had imported two thousand of just one brand of such guns. (The guns were relegalized in the Weapons Act of 1990.)

The low compliance rate makes the Queensland police skeptical of any new registration system.[211] Even John Marsden, director of research for the Australian Bankers Association (one of the main backers of gun control), warns, "Registration will bring massive noncompliance."[212]

Victoria is the latest state to push hard on gun registration. In 1979, the Australian Police Federation had suggested that the law forbid persons (other than police officers) from personally owning more than three guns, unless the person could "show cause." To implement the three-gun rule, gun registration would be required. Although the gun limit was never enacted, registration went into effect. In late 1987, the police estimated that only 59 percent of guns have been registered.[213] For the guns that are registered, approximately 60 percent of the registration records are thought to be incorrect.[214] A registration amnesty during the first six months of 1987 was labeled "a dismal failure" by the police.[215] A final amnesty for late registrants expired on December 31, 1988, resulting in a compliance rate of approximately 82 percent.[216]

An internal police report, obtained under the freedom of information law and released to the press in April 1988, branded Victoria's gun registration "an elaborate concept of arithmetic with no tangible aim. Probably, and with the best of intentions, it may have been thought, that if it were known what firearms each individual in Victoria owned, some form of control may be exercised, and those who were guilty of criminal misuse could be readily identified. This is a fallacy, and has proven not to be the case."

The police report concluded: "Previous experience in New Zealand and South Australia, and now indeed in the State of Victoria, indicates that firearms registration in the way in which it is implemented is costly, ineffective, and achieves little." The police officer who authored that report was transferred to another job.[217] The Victoria registration system continues in force, with an annual cost of over two million Australian dollars.

The Victorian Labor government listened not to the police officer, but to Police Minister Crabb (who had been selected for his post because his anti-gun views differed from those of his predecessor). Police administrators such as Crabb could not produce evidence that registration would reduce crime. Against the common sense of police experience, the Victorian government insisted on a gun-control program that seemed designed to do little more than intimidate ordinary gun owners. And intimidation may not be citizens' only worry; Professor Harding, an advocate of strict gun controls on civilians, argues that police misuse of deadly force is routine, and usually covered up.[218] In some ways, the attitude of police officials toward the people has changed little since the first prisoners arrived two centuries ago. The determination of at least some people to resist also remains.

CONCLUSION

The story of police/community relations told in these chapters has been an unhappy one. In Britain and Japan, and to some extent in Canada, police officials have pressed harsher gun laws on legitimate firearms owners. Often, the gun laws spring from an attitude that controlling the populace and eliminating gun ownership is good in itself. In response, an increasingly alienated body of gun owners is drawn into a bitter conflict with the government. Where traditions of individualism and distrust of government are strongest, as in Australia, the gun owners may achieve some political success, but they can never lose their sense of being embattled. Disobeying ever-stricter laws, many Britons, Canadians, and Australians have refused to register their firearms.

Is there no room for a spirit of cooperation; and for the police to abandon particular gun controls that are patently irrelevant to crime control; and for the gun lobby to accept reasonable regulation of sporting arms, while the police enforce regulations reasonably? There is a place where police administrators and sport shooters live together cooperatively. That place is New Zealand.

NOTES

1. Richard Hofstadter, "America as a Gun Culture," *American Heritage,* October 1970, p. 82.

2. Tom Wicker, "Violence and Hypocrisy," *The New York Times,* July 9, 1990, p. A17. Arthur M. Schlesinger, Jr., *The Crisis of Confidence: Ideas, Power, and Violence in American Life* (New York: Bantam, 1968), p. 15.

3. Malcolm Brown, "A Nation Won by Guns," *Sydney Morning Herald,* February 27, 1988, p. 68. The registration was enacted in New South Wales.

4. Manning Clark, *A Short History of Australia* (New York: Mentor, 1963), pp. 35–36.

5. Ray Allen Billington, "Frontiers," in C. Vann Woodward, ed., *The Comparative Approach to American History* (New York: Basic Books, 1968), p. 78.

6. Clark, pp. 38, 68–69.

7. William Tonso, *Gun and Society: The Social and Existential Roots of the American Attachment to Firearms* (Lanham, Md.: University Press of America, 1982), p. 169.

8. A New South Wales law to this effect was enacted in the 1850s. Brown, p. 68.

9. Tonso, pp. 179–80.

10. Clark, p. 22.

11. C. McGregor, *Profile of Australia* (1966), pp. 81–85, cited in Tonso, p. 182.

12. Brown, p. 68.

13. The number of antique pistols currently available in Australia does suggest that pistols were not uncommon. Colin Greenwood, letter to author, November 24, 1989; Tonso, p. 263.

A carbine is a short, light rifle with a barrel less than twenty-two inches long. Like most rifles, the carbine was originally invented for the military, but is now commonly used by hunters.

14. Clark, pp. 116–17.

15. In October 1854, the miners went on strike. At the Eureka Stockade in Victoria, the strike was ultimately crushed and the armed miners massacred. The government did, however, begin to recognize that reform was necessary. Clark, pp. 121–24; Brown, p. 68.

16. Tonso, p. 199.

17. Objecting to a standing army, the Australian people had only a small pre-war regular army of a few thousand regular forces; unfortunately, the militia was not an effective substitute for a standing army, consisting only of 80,000 men who spent twelve days a year in training. Once the Axis attack began in 1939, Australia spent most of its military resources defending the British Empire in the Mediterranean, rather than in expanding the militia and bringing it up to strength. The Chief of the General Staff, Sir Brudenall White, informed the government that in the event of invasion, there were only enough guns and ammunition to supply the militia for a month. "That is what you cannot tell the public," replied Sir Keith Murdoch, director general of information.

On February 19, 1942, one hundred Japanese planes attacked the coastal town of Darwin, capital of the Northern Territory. Uniformed defenders and townspeople alike panicked, with desertions and widespread looting as the result. Darwin knew that it lacked the aircraft and guns necessary to resist the expected Japanese follow-up invasion. David Day, *The Great Betrayal: Britain, Australia and the Onset of the Pacific War 1939–42* (New York: W. W. Norton, 1988), pp. 14–15, 57, 76, 186, 267.

18. Firearms Act 1921 (Victoria); Gun Licence Ordinance 1925 (Australian Capital Territory); Gun Licence Act 1920 (New South Wales); Firearms Licence Act 1927 (Queensland); Pistol Licence Act 1929 (South Australia); Firearms Act 1931 (Western Australia); Firearms

Act 1932 (Tasmania); Firearms Registration Ordinance 1932 (Northern Territory), all cited in Richard Harding, *Firearms and Violence in Australian Life: An Examination of Gun Ownership and Use in Australia* (Nedlands, Western Australia: University of Western Australia Press, 1981), p. 167 n.2. [hereinafter "Harding, *Firearms*"].

A little Australian geography: The western third of Australia is the state of Western Australia, whose largest city is Perth. The middle third comprises the Northern Territory and South Australia. In the eastern third, Queensland sits atop New South Wales, which sits atop Victoria. The capital of New South Wales is Sydney, and the capital of Victoria is Melbourne. The island state of Tasmania lies off the southeast coast.

Australia's national capital of Canberra, in the Australian Capital Territory (A.C.T.), is a separate jurisdiction (like Washington, D.C.) which lies in New South Wales. A few small islands, such as Norfolk Island, are separate jurisdictions.

19. Clark, pp. 202–205.

20. Pistol License Act 1927; Tunney, "Commentary on Professor Harding's Paper," in University of Sydney Faculty of Law, *Proceedings of the Institute of Criminology: No. 64 Gun Control* (Sydney: University of Sydney, 1985), p. 75. In the act's earliest years (the late 1920s), persons who already owned handguns were usually granted licenses to keep them.

21. Tonso, p. 264.

22. J. David Fine, *An Agenda for the Reform of Firearms Laws* (Recommendations to the Criminology Research Council for Practical Reforms to and the Harmonization of Australia's State and Territorial Firearms Laws) (Edgewater: University of Western Australia, 1988), pp. 21–22; Queensland Police Department, *A Police Perspective on Gun Control,* (Melbourne, reprinted by Australian Firearms Law Institute: 1982), p. 4; *Seminar on Gun Misuse* (Report of meeting held June 5, 1988, at Australian Bank Employees Union, North Melbourne), pp. 2–3.

Technically, most Australian states allow ownership of automatics with a special permit. Usually the permit is given only to theater and film producers. Rod Marvell, "Editor's Notebook," *Australian Shooters Journal,* January 1989, p. 3. It is debatable whether a film company making a *Rambo*-type movie glorifying violence poses less of a threat to society than does a gun collector.

23. Ross Dunn, "Tasmania Faces Guns Blockade," *Sydney Morning Herald,* March 19, 1988, p. 3. Although the federal government retreated from its threat to cut off firearms commerce, it did announce a "Positive Generic Arms Statement" to prohibit import of most semi-automatic firearms and all magazine clips holding more than five centerfire semi-automatic rifle cartridges. The gun lobby's most intense objection to the Positive Generic Statement has been its potential retroactivity, meaning that legally owned semi-automatic firearms would become illegal. Before the regulations were even approved by the Senate, the Federal Police already began seizing lawfully owned semi-automatics from some citizens. Australian Senate, *Senate,* May 29, 1991, pp. 3813–31 (debate on proposed import regulation); John Horgan, "The Positive Generic Arms Statement, Part 3," *Australian Shooters Journal,* March 1991, p. 2.

24. *Seminar on Gun Misuse,* p. 3.

25. Amendment to Firearms Act 1958, § 22AA(2A); "Confusion Greets New Gun Laws in Victoria." Firearms Act 1977.

26. See note 23.

27. Fine, *Firearms Laws,* p. 6; 1985 Amendment Act, § 45(1) and (3).

28. South Australia Firearms Act, § 32(1)(a).

29. Mitton, "An Historical Insight into the Background of Firearms Legislation in Australia," pp. 7–8. Such searches might well have declared to be in violation of the Australian Constitution.

30. Queensland Police Department, pp. 6–7.

31. Fine, *An Agenda for Reform,* p. 13.

32. South Australia has a similar system. Licenses may denied to anyone not "fit and proper" or "for any other reason." South Australia, Firearms Act 1977, § 12(3). Nevertheless, the expectation in all states except Western Australia seems to be that if there are no particular grounds to disqualify an applicant, he is entitled to a license. Harding, *Firearms,* p. 21.

33. § 21(1). J. David Fine, *Firearms Laws in Australia* (North Ryde, New South Wales: CCH Australia, 1985), pp. 33, 48–49. In South Australia and Victoria, license rejections are appealable to a police committee and then to a magistrate. According to Fine, the South Australia police committee has a reputation for impartiality. The appeals committee, the Firearms Consultative Committee, was the first of its kind in Australia. Victoria later established a similar one. P. T. Anderson (Minister for Police and Emergency Services, Labour Government of N.S.W.), "Gun Laws—Reform of Restriction," in *Proceedings of the Institute,* p. 22. The South Australian committee is an important step away from the general Australian model that, while refusals to grant a handgun license may formally be appealed, police discretion to refuse is essentially unreviewable. Harding, *Firearms,* pp. 8–11.

34. Fine, *An Agenda for Reform,* pp. 12–13.

35. Ibid., p. 13.

36. Ibid., pp. 14–15.

37. Ibid.

38. See, for example, Firearms Regulations 1979 (South Australia), §§ 12(1), 12(2); Firearms Act 1973 (Western Australia; citizens must affirmatively take "all reasonable precautions to ensure the safe-keeping" of the gun). About thirteen people a year are prosecuted in Western Australia. Harding, *Firearms Ownership,* p. 136.

39. Harding, *Firearms Ownership,* pp. 134–35; Richard Harding, "Gun Law Reform in New South Wales: Better Late Than Never," in *Proceedings of the Institute,* p. 43. South Australia's testing provisions are codified in Reg. 24: Regulations: Sch. 1. Prospective licensees in Victoria must correctly answer nine of thirteen multiple-choice questions. Re-takes (with different questions) are allowed after two days. Firearms Regulations 1979 (South Australia), § 25(4).

40. Fine, *An Agenda for Reform,* p. 27. Western Australia test reprinted in Harding, *Firearms,* p. 95.

41. Carl Vandal, *Firearms Control* (Melbourne: reprinted by Australian Firearm Law Institute, 1984), p. 14.

42. Fine, *An Agenda for Reform,* p. 37.

43. Ibid., p. 23. Fine's work included confidential interviews with police administrators. He did not name the two states.

44. Ibid., p. 56. After a party allied to pro-gun activists was elected, New South Wales created an ombudsman within the police department to supervise uniform and nonarbitrary enforcement of the gun laws.

45. 110 C.L.R. 321, 36 A.L.J.R. 342 (1963). The case essentially overruled *Coghlan* v. *Fleetwood,* which had upheld the conviction of a South Australian dealer for selling by mail to a New South Wales resident. [1951] S.A.S.R. 163.

Mail-order sales do not seem to pose a risk of circumventing the gun licensing laws. One gun owner reports that when he received a mail-order handgun, the police arrived soon after to inquire why he had not notified them. Rod Marvell, "Editor's Notebook," *Australian Shooters Journal,* January 1989, p. 3.

Several jurisdictions still have statutes that contradict the rule of *Chapman* v. *Suttie.* Firearms Act 1958 (Victoria), § 33(c). Also, Firearms Act 1932 (Tasmania), § 11(c); Gun Licence Ordinance (A.C.T.), § 8(5), both cited in Harding, *Firearms,* p. 18.

Similar issues of state control over interstate commerce arise in the United States. Until Congress intervened in 1986, New York State required Pennsylvania hunters on their way to Maine to obtain a New York State pistol license, even if the pistol was locked in a case in a trunk for the entire trip through New York. The statute regarding interstate transport is 18 United States Code § 926(a).

46. Firearms Act 1931 (Western Australia). See also Richard Harding, *Firearms Ownership and Accidental Misuse in Western Australia* (Nedlands: University of Western Australia, n.d.), reprinted from *University of Western Australia Law Review* 12 (1975), p. 124.

47. Firearms Act 1931 (Western Australia), § 8(3). The administrators of the 1931 Act did repeal existing laws that had forbidden Aborigines to own guns. Firearms Act 1905, § 47, superseded by Regulation 29, *Government Gazette*, March 24, 1932, p. 391. The same year, the Northern Territory banned gun ownership by Aborigines. The anti-Aborigine law was repealed in 1964. Firearms Ordinance, 8 (No. 40 of 1964). All of above cited in Harding, *Firearms*, p. 2.

48. Firearms Act, § 10(1).

49. Fine, *An Agenda for Reform*, p. 20–21.

50. Vandal, pp. 12–13.

51. Harding, *Firearms Ownership*, p. 125.

52. "Perth is the Most Violent City in Aust," *Sunday Times*, January 7, 1979, citing Australian Institute of Criminology data.

53. Tunney, "Commentary on Professor Harding's Paper," in *Proceedings of the Institute*, p. 74.

54. W. R. B. Hassell, minister for police and traffic, letter to Hon. A. A. Lewis, M.L.C., July 7, 1980; Fine, *An Agenda for Reform*, p. 22.

55. Armstrong, "Needed: Stricter Control of Firearms—Now," *Reader's Digest* (Australian ed.), March 1982, pp. 31, 33.

56. Duncan Chappell, "Violence, Crime, and Australian Society," no. 1 in series *Violence Today* for National Committee on Violence (Woden, ACT, Australia: Australian Institute of Criminology, 1989); National Committee on Violence, Violence in Australia (Canberra, Australia: Australian Institute of Criminology, 1989), pp. 1, 15. The two massacres led to the creation of the National Committee on Violence, to study the causes and prevention of all types of violence.

The semi-automatic M1 rifle was originally used by American soldiers during World War II. Versions of the M1 are in common use today as high-quality target match guns and as hunting arms. In the United States debate over bans on semi-automatics, the M1 is usually included in initial lists of guns to be banned, since it is a military model. By the time legislation is enacted, the M1 is usually off the list. Since several million M1s are in private hands, law-makers often conclude that stringent controls would be unrealistic.

57. Firearms and Dangerous Weapons Act (1973).

58. Mail-order gun sales in the United States have been illegal since 1968, unless the sale takes place between dealers certified as Federal Firearms Licensees.

59. New South Wales gun owners charged that the sole motive for registering airguns was to collect the registration fees, since no crimes had been committed with airguns. Norman Blake, "Discussion Paper 1," in *Proceedings of the Institute*, p. 61.

60. New South Wales Firearms and Dangerous Weapons (Amendment) Bill, 1985, summary in *Proceedings of the Institute*, pp. 25–27; New South Wales Government, "Changes to Firearms Laws," *Sunday Telegraph*, December 27, 1987 (government advertisement); same in *St. George and Sutherland Shire Leader*, March 10, 1988, p. 16; Harding, "Gun Law Reform," p. 43.

61. *The Times,* January 9, 1988 (Associated Press report).

62. Harding, "Gun Law Reform," p. 45.

63. Ibid., p. 46.

64. Minister Peter Anderson, letter to Mr. Mitton, president SSAA, March 9, 1984; Nick Greiner, leader of the Opposition, letter to Mr. Mitton, March 10, 1984.

65. "Shooters Gaze Down the Government's Barrel," *Sydney Morning Herald,* March 12, 1985. For a good overview of the amendments, see J. David Fine, "Issues in Firearms Control," *Australia and New Zealand Journal of Criminology* 18 (December 1985): 257–71.

66. Skip Gordon, "Aussie Shooters Help Mug Labor Party," *Gun Week,* April 15, 1988, pp. 1, 15.

67. "Needed: Stricter Control of Firearms—Now," pp. 34–35.

68. Harding, "Gun Law Reform," p. 46.

69. Richard Harding, in "Discussion," in *Proceedings of the Institute,* p. 103.

70. The lobby was the New South Wales arm of the Firearms Sports Association, Ltd. Matthew Condon, "The Waking Tiger Snarls," *Sun Herald,* February 7, 1988, p. 8.

71. Civil liberties objections had earlier made the New South Wales government back off from a proposal to tighten the "consorting" laws. Harding, "Gun Law Reform," p. 32.

72. Sporting Shooters Association of Australia and Firearms Advisory Council, *Rednecks, Reactionaries, and Rambos* (Dubbo, New South Wales: Macquarie Publications, n.d.) (unpaginated).

73. "Rednecks, Reactionaries, and Rambos."

74. N.S.W. Liberal party, *News from the Shadow Ministry,* January 14, 1988 (press release).

75. Advertisement, *Sunday Telegraph,* February 21, 1988, p. 39; "Rednecks, Reactionaries, and Rambos."

76. "Rednecks, Reactionaries, and Rambos."

77. Matt Condon, "Slush Fund to Defeat Unsworth," *Sun-Herald,* March 6, 1988, p. 1.

78. "Rednecks, Reactionaries, and Rambos."

79. Ibid.

80. Advertisement of Frank Walker, *St. George and Sutherland Shire Leader,* February 18, 1988, p. 25; similar text in "Ken Gabb on the Gun Laws Argument," *St. George and Sutherland Shire Leader,* March 10, 1988, p. 30 (advertisement).

81. Advertisement, *St. George and Sutherland Shire Leader,* March 10, 1988, p. 37. The ad argued "The United States murder rate doubled between 1960 and 1980—and they're soft on guns! The gun lobby has many U.S. politicians paralysed with fear."

82. Advertisement, *Sun-Herald,* January 17, 1988, p. 4.

83. "Rednecks, Reactionaries, and Rambos"; "Focus on the Gun Debate," *Sun-Herald,* February 7, 1988, p. 46 ("Some MLAs were distinctly jittery about the tightening of gun controls and the impact it may have on their seats—and the government itself. Yet Premier Barrie Unsworth reportedly said there would be no climb-down on the new laws."); "Slush Fund to Defeat Unsworth," p. 1.

84. "Rednecks, Reactionaries, and Rambos."

85. Warren Owens, "It's Premier Greiner! Labor Routed in 'Worst Ever' Loss," *Sunday Telegraph,* March 20, 1988, p. 1.

86. "Libs Win," *Sun-Herald,* March 20, 1988, p. 1; James Morrison, "Coalition Takes 15 ALP Seats," *The Australian,* March 21, 1988, p. 2 ("The swing to the Coalition in the country was a backlash from traditional Labour voters over the tough new guns laws. . . .")

87. Barrie Unsworth, *Labor Leadership* (news release), March 22, 1988.

88. "Why Voters Turned Their Backs on ALP," *Sun-Herald,* March 27, 1988, p. 12; Warren Owens, "Coalition Has to Work to Keep Power," *Sunday Telegraph,* March 27, 1988, p. 50.

89. "Rednecks, Reactionaries, and Rambos."

90. Tim Dodd, "Greiner Sprints Ahead in Poll," *Sun-Herald,* March 6, 1988.

91. Jack Taylor, "Carr-isma," *Sunday Telegraph,* April 3, 1988, p. 13.

92. New South Wales Government, "Return of Self Loading Rifles," *Sun-Herald,* March 27, 1988, p. 136 (government advertisement).

93. Malcolm Brown, "The Surrendered Guns Are Going Home . . . To the City," (newspaper article, publication uncertain).

94. Tracey Ausin, "Coalition to Hand Back 10,500 Guns," *Sydney Morning Herald,* March 26, 1988, p. 5. While the gun-surrender law was in effect, plumbing supply stores had reported large sales of 150mm pipe, apparently used for burying newly illegal guns.

95. "Who Is Behind the Gun Lobby?" *Sun-Herald,* November 20, 1988, p. 4.

96. Matthew Moore, ". . . While Bob Fires a Shot for Shooters," *Sydney Morning Herald,* May 18, 1991, p. 1; Malcolm Farr, "Carr Surrenders to Gun Men," *Daily Telegraph Mirror,* April 27, 1991, p. 27; Peter Grimshaw, "Double-Barrel Poll Win for Shooters," *Daily Telegraph Mirror,* April 27, 1991, p. 11; Bob Carr, leader of the Opposition, letter to secretary, Sporting Shooters Association, May 1, 1991; "The ALP's Firearms Policy," April 1991.

97. Firearms Act of 1989.

98. Alan Tate, "God, Guts, and Guns," *The Good Weekend* (Sydney Morning Herald Magazine), February 20, 1988, p. 29; Matthew Ricketson, "Ducking for Cover over Gun Violence," *The Weekend Australian,* February 6–7, 1988, p. 20.

99. "The Battle to Beat Off the Gun Lobby," *The Sun-Herald,* November 20, 1988, p. 4.

100. "Tougher Gun Laws Urged After Aussie Student Kills 8," (Springfield, Mass.) *Union-News,* December 10, 1987, p. 15 (Associated Press wire story).

101. *Gun Law Handbook* (Victoria government, June 1989), p. 23.

102. D. J. Keogh, Chief Inspector, Registrar of Firearms, "Report of the Operations of the Firearms Registry for 1988/89 Annual Report," July 14, 1989, p. 2.

103. Government public service advertisement, *The Sun,* December 13, 1988, p. 20.

104. *Gun Law Handbook,* p. 14. A statutory declaration is a sworn statement, similar to affidavit under American law.

Permits to own semi-automatic rifles will be granted to members of the Military Rifle Club, International Practical Shooting Clubs, and the Australian Army Rifle Club. The guns may only be used at club ranges, and only by members who attend at least six practice or competition sessions per year. Rifle club member semi-automatics may have pistol grips, folding or telescopic stocks, and large capacity magazines.

Hunters may be issued licenses for semi-automatics that have a magazine capacity of five or less, no telescopic or folding stock, and no pistol grip. Depending on the animal to be hunted, the guns must be of a certain minimum caliber (e.g., persons wishing to hunt sambar must use a gun of at least .270 caliber). M1 carbines are not allowed for hunting.

Farmers ("primary producers") may be licensed for semi-automatics of any calibre that do not have a pistol grip or folding/telescopic stock. The farmer must show a need for the particular type of rifle.

Any person wishing to own more than one semi-automatic must provide a "good reason." Permits for semi-automatics will be issued only to persons who have already had a shooter's license for three years, and have experience with other types of rifles (such as bolt action).

P. J. Keogh, Chief Inspector, Registrar of Firearms, Victoria Police, "Guidelines for the Issue of Authorities for Semi-Automatic Centre Fire Rifles" (no date).

Semi-automatics must be stored in a locked receptacle or a strong room. P. J. Keogh, Chief Inspector, Registrar of Firearms, Victoria Police, "Minimum Security Requirements for Semi-Automatic Rifles," 1989.

105. A. Newgreen, Chief Inspector, Registrar of Firearms, "Firearms Registration System: C.R.B. File: 39–1–1385/84," February 26, 1987, Melbourne.

106. Victoria Government, *The Gun Law Handbook* (n.d.).

107. Innes Wilcox, "Lingering Bitterness in the Gun Debate," *The Age* (Melbourne), August 12, 1988.

108. Ibid.

109. Ibid.

110. *The Gun Law Handbook,* p. 3.

111. *Gun Law Handbook,* p. 10.

112. Victoria, Firearms Act 1958, §§ 53–54; *Gun Law Handbook,* p. 31. The Victoria Consultative Committee has no legislative advisory role, but its N.S.W. counterpart is frequently consulted. Robert Mitton, "Legislation," *Australia Shooters Journal,* April 1989, p. 34.

113. Hon. Roger M. Hallam M.L.C., letter to the Hon. S. M. Crabb, M.P., Minister for Police and Emergency Services, February 28, 1989; exchange in Parliament between Mr. Hallam and Mr. Crabb of March 29, 1989, reprinted in Rod Marvell, "Editor's Notebook," *Australian Shooters Journal,* June 1989, p. 3.

114. "Report of the Joint Select Committee on Law Reform" (October 15, 1991, New South Wales legislature), p. 23.

115. Sue Quinn and Marc McEvoy, "People Power Takes to the Streets," *Sunday Telegraph,* September 22, 1991, p. 2; Stephen Skinner and Alison McClymont, "You Need Semi-automatics, MP Tells Shooters' Rally," *Sunday Telegraph,* September 22, 1991; Ron Scherer, "Australia Moves to Ban Sale of Semiautomatic Weapons," *Christian Science Monitor,* September 5, 1991.

116. Ted Pickering, New South Wales Minister for Police and Emergency Services, letter of November 22, 1991, to A. Sutcliffe, attachment, p. 3. Proposed legislation in New South Wales would implement the November 1991 proposals, require proof of "genuine reason" for owning any gun (including an air rifle), and consider protection not to be a "genuine reason." Firearms Legislation (Amendment) Bill 1992, introduced in the New South Wales Parliament March 4, 1992.

117. Ibid.

118. The population of these two states is not densely concentrated, whereas in New South Wales, Western Australia, South Australia, and Victoria, much of the population lives in a few urban centers.

119. Vandal, p. 10.

120. *Seminar on Gun Misuse,* p. 3; Rod Marvell, "Editor's Notebook," *Australian Shooters Journal,* September 1989, p. 75.

121. *Seminar on Gun Misuse,* pp. 3–4.

122. Harding, "Gun Law Reform," p. 33.

123. T. W. Sheahan, "Gun Laws in New South Wales—A Perspective," in *Proceedings of the Institute,* p. 13.

124. Sheahan, "Gun Laws," p. 14.

125. *Seminar on Gun Misuse,* p. 11.

126. Ibid., p. 12.

127. Ibid.

128. Ibid., p. 13. Shooting on Sundays has been legal in New South Wales since 1973.

129. Ibid., pp. 13–14; Matt Condon, "Duck! Here Come the Guns," *Sun-Herald,* March 13, 1988, p. 6.

130. Rod Marvell, "Editor's Notebook," *Australian Shooters Journal,* May 1989, p. 3.

131. *Australian Democrats National Journal,* November 1988, reprinted in Rod Marvell, "Editor's Notebook," *Australian Shooters Journal,* February 1989, pp. 3, 74.

132. Bill Royson, "On Target," *Australian Shooters Journal,* September 1989, p. 77.

133. Bill Royson, "On Target," *Australian Shooters Journal,* October 1989, p. 12.

134. Donald B. Kates, the leading theoretician of the United States gun-rights movement, is a vegetarian who has never hunted. David Kopel's joint statement with police leaders in opposition to semi-automatic prohibition was reprinted in the Congressional Record, and followed a few weeks later by a Congressional Record reprint of Kopel's call for a ban on intensive factory farming of veal calves. "Insight into Gun Ownership," *Congressional Record,* May 15, 1989, p. E 1676; "Veal Calf Protection Act," *Congressional Record,* July 25, 1989, p. E 2661.

135. Harding, "Gun Law Reform," p. 37.

136. *Seminar on Gun Misuse,* p. 14.

In the U.S., gun control is not an explicitly feminist issue, although the National Organization of Women and it publication *Ms.* magazine do support it. For example, *Ms.* ignored the results of a readers' poll about most admired women and named Handgun Control's Sarah Brady one of its women of the year. As in Australia, American women are relatively more supportive of gun control than men. While American men view the National Rifle Association favorably by a 5–1 ratio, American women support the NRA by a much smaller margin.

137. Beverly Schurr, Secretary, N.S.W. Council for Civil Liberties, "Discussion," in *Proceedings of the Institute,* pp. 93–94.

138. South Australian police may break and enter, without a warrant, into any home or other premises where they reasonably suspect an illegal gun may be. Firearms Act 1977, § 32(3). See also the discussion of Victoria's registration campaign, below.

139. Arms and Militaria Collectors' Association of NSW, "Counter Submission to Appendix A to Mr. Anderson's Paper," in *Proceedings of the Institute,* p. 85.

One study of Australian bank robberies suggested that bank employees not be armed, because they lacked the training to win a shoot-out with a criminal. Peter Lettkemann, *Crime as Work* (Englewood, N.J.: Spectrum Books, 1973), pp. 114–15, cited in Harding, *Firearms,* pp. 78–79. The bank organizations, like the police, are in the somewhat awkward position of possessing guns for defense while being allied with gun-control groups that believe people should not use guns for defense.

For an excellent survey of current data regarding Australian bank robberies, see Geoff Griffiths, "Armed Robbery Reduction: A Strategic Approach from a Major Australian Bank," paper presented at the 42d annual meeting of the American Society of Criminology, Baltimore, Md., November 7–10, 1990.

140. *Seminar on Gun Misuse,* p. 16.

141. Bill Roysson, "On Target," *Australian Shooters Journal,* February 1989, p. 12.

Psychiatrist Bruce Danto notes that if gun owners were searching for phallic symbols, they would want the largest guns possible, such as .40-calibre elephant guns, and would want guns with long-barrels. But hardly anyone besides hunters of African game buys the largest-sized guns, and long barrelled-guns are predominantly owned by the people who would be expected to use long barrels—people who hunt in open country where long-range accuracy is important. Nicole Varzos and Donald B. Kates, Jr., "Aspects of the Priapic Theory of Gun Ownership," in William Tonso, ed., *The Gun Culture and Its Enemies* (Bellevue, Wash.: Merril Press, 1990), pp. 93-107.

142. Harding, *Firearms,* p. 158.

143. David Fine, "Issues in Firearms Control," *Australia-New Zealand Journal of Criminal Law* 18 (1985), p. 265; "Permit 29,000 to Pack Guns," (New York) *Daily News,* June 22, 1981 (most of the permit-holders were ex-police or persons with political or financial clout); Susan Hall, "Nice People Who Carry Guns," *New York,* December 12, 1977; Donald B. Kates, Jr., and Carol Ruth Silver, "Self-Defense, Handgun Ownership, and the Independence of Women in a Violent, Sexist Society," in Donald B. Kates, Jr., ed., *Restricting Handguns: The Liberal Skeptics Speak Out* (Croton-on-Hudson: North River Press, 1979), p. 153; William Bastone, "Born to Gun: 65 Big Shots with Licenses to Carry," *Village Voice,* September 29, 1987, p. 11.

144. W. Woolmore, "Why Gun Registration?" in *Proceedings of the Institute,* p. 69.

145. J. David Fine, "Impediments to the Purposeful Reform of Firearms Laws," in *Gun Control Examined,* collection of papers from the conference on Gun Control, Melbourne University, August 27-28, 1988, p. 44.

146. *Seminar on Gun Misuse,* p. 17.

147. In 1981, Harding had analyzed late 1970s data and warned that firearms ownership was rising faster than the population. Harding, *Firearms,* pp. 51-52.

148. Harding, "Gun Law Reform," p. 41. As Harding points out, some of the numerical increase in South Australia may be attributed to gun owners who belatedly decided to comply with the long-gun registration and licensing law that was promulgated in 1977 and went into effect in 1980. The "new" gun owners who registered, for example, in 1982, were not really new gun owners. On the other hand, the South Australia total excludes the guns and gun owners who have chosen not to register; the total therefore may be too low.

149. Australian Bankers' Association, p. 11; "Guns: A Matter of Responsibility," *Sydney Morning Herald,* April 4, 1988, p. 6. A telephone survey in early 1989, conducted as part of an international crime study, reported that 20.1 percent of Australian households admitted that they contained a firearm. Martin Killias, "Gun Ownership and Violent Crime: The Swiss Experience in International Perspective," *Security Journal* 1, no. 3 (1990), p. 171 table 1. Given the tense relations between gun owners and the police administration, and given the very high noncompliance rate with gun registration laws, it may well be that a significant percentage of gun owners decided not to reveal themselves to a stranger on the telephone.

Richard Harding's estimate of gun ownership in 1975 was that there were 2,197,000 guns in Australia, distributed among 26.3 percent of the households. Harding, *Firearms,* pp. 37-52. Harding's data were based on extrapolations from household surveys in Western Australia. Harding's analysis for Western Australia starts with the assumption that "the community more or less operates within the parameters set by law." Therefore, says Harding, one can infer that Western Australians' response to pollsters' question "Do you own a gun?" was truthful. Harding, *Firearms Ownership,* p. 124.

That assumption of truthful responses to the pollsters might not be accurate. If a remnant of Western Australians held illegal guns, guns that might have been illegal and kept hidden since the gun laws of half a century ago, that remnant might be cautious about confessing to a crime. As detailed below, the evidence is fairly clear that a significant percentage of Australian gun owners do not comply with registration laws.

Accordingly, Harding's 1975 estimate of 26 percent of households with guns may be too low, and Killias's 1989 estimate of 20 percent of households with guns is almost certainly too low; hardly any Australians would not agree that gun ownership has been rising faster than population in recent decades.

150. Harding, "An Ounce of Prevention . . . Gun Control and Public Health in Australia," *Australia and New Zealand Journal of Criminology* 16 (1983), p. 3. Harding approvingly noted that America's "National Institute of Justice has recently granted funding for seven projects which, in toto, will constitute the most well-focussed gun research programme that has ever been attempted." Ibid. p. 5. The researcher of one those projects (a past president of the American Sociological Association) began the research as a proponent of national handgun control. He and his colleagues ended up convinced of the efficacy of guns in deterring crime, the near impossibility of keeping them out of the hands of criminals, and the futility of gun control as a way to reduce crime or suicide. James D. Wright, Peter H. Rossi, and Kathleen Daly, *Under the Gun: Weapons, Crime, and Violence in America* (New York: Aldine, 1983).

151. Harding, *An Ounce of Prevention,* p. 7; Harding, "Gun Law Reform," pp. 34-35; Australian Bankers' Association, p. 11.

152. Queensland Police Department, p. 5.

153. Harding, *Firearms Ownership,* p. 126.

154. Harding, *Firearms,* p. 54.

155. Australian Bankers' Association, p. 11.

156. Ibid.

157. Harding, *Firearms,* pp. 61-65; Australian Bankers' Association, p. 11; Firearms Dealers Association, Queensland, "Analysis of Firearms Sold by Occupation of Purchaser," December 1989 (study of Queensland retail gun purchasers, based on dealer records).

158. Richard Harding, *Firearms and Violence in Australian Life* (Nedland, Western Australia: University of Western Australia Press, 1981), p. 69.

159. See chapter 3, notes 143-54, and accompanying text.

160. British immigrants to Australia own guns at twice the domestic British rate, still much lower than the Australian rate. Harding, *Firearms Ownership,* p. 129. Harding, *Firearms,* p. 67.

161. Fine, *An Agenda for Reform,* p. 78.

162. Ibid.

163. N.S.W. Bureau of Crime Statistics and Research, "Homicide," *Crime and Justice Bulletin,* no. 5 (Sydney: Government Printing Office, April 1988), p. 1 (1985 data). In the Northern Territory, semi-automatic rifles are licensed strictly as handguns. See discussion of state laws, above.

164. "Homicide," p. 1.

165. *Violence in Australia,* pp. 9-10; Chappell, p. 2, citing Peter N. Grabosky, *Sydney in Ferment: Crime, Dissent, and Official Reaction 1788-1973* (Canberra, Australia: Australian National University Press, 1977).

166. "Homicide," p. 3.

167. "Trends in Serious Crimes in N.S.W.," *Crime and Justice Bulletin,* June 1987, p. 2; "Homicide," p. 3; National Committee, p. 21.

168. "Homicide," p. 4. All statistics are for 1968-86.

169. About 35 percent of overall Australian homicides are by gun, compared with 60 percent in the United States. "Homicide," p. 4.

170. "Homicide," p. 4.

171. Jane Mugford, "Domestic Violence," no. 2 in series *Violence Today* for National Committee on Violence (Woden, ACT, Australia: Australian Institute of Criminology, 1989), p. 2. The author was applying to Australian conditions the United States study by Murray A. Straus and Richard J. Gelles, "Societal Change and Change in Family Violence from 1975 to 1985 as Revealed by Two National Surveys," *Journal of Marriage and the Family* 48, no. 3 (August 1986): 465-79.

172. "Homicide," p. 4.

173. Ibid.

174. Ibid.

175. *Violence in Australia,* p. 11 Figure 4; *Robbery in South Australia,* p. 5.

176. Statistics record 27 percent "gun" and 9 percent "assumed gun." Bureau of Crime Statistics and Research, *Robbery Study,* First Interim Report Police Reports of Robberies in N.S.W. (New South Wales: Attorney General's Department, February 1986), p. 25.

177. Department of the Attorney General and of Justice N.S.W., "Intentional Shootings," Statistical Report 2, series 2 (May 1975), p. 9.

178. The South Australia rate was 65 percent. *Robbery in South Australia,* p. 37. The rates were 65 percent in Victoria, and 54 percent in New South Wales. Bureau of Crime Statistics and Research, Armed Robbery, Research Report 2 (Department of the Attorney General and of Justice N.S.W. Bureau of Crime Statistics & Research, December 1977), p. 14 [hereinafter *"Armed Robbery* (Dec. 1977)"].

179. *Robbery in South Australia,* p. 39. See also *An Historical Insight into the Background of Firearms Legislation in Australia,* p. 4, citing Report to the Standing Committee of Attorneys General, Armed Robbery, May 1977 (N.S.W. Bureau of Crime Statistics and Research); *Armed Robbery* (Dec. 1977), p. 8.

180. Queensland Police Department, p. 8.

181. Richard W. Harding and Ann Blake, *Weapons Choice by Violent Officers in Western Australia: A Pilot Study,* Research Report, no. 1. (Nedlands, Western Australia: Crime Research Centre, Univeristy of Western Australia, n.d.), pp. 16–17.

182. Harding, *Firearms and Violence,* p. 119; Harding, "Gun Law Reform," p. 37.

183. Gary Kleck, *Point Blank: Guns and Violence in America* (New York: Aldine de Gruyter, 1991), pp. 91–94. During the New South Wales gun debate, Harding pointed to the huge increase in armed robbery in that state in late 1970s and early 1980s. R. B. Tunney, a gun advocate, noted such an increase was forecast in 1972, when New South Wales introduced new restrictions. Tunney, "Commentary on Professor Harding's Paper," p. 74.

184. "Intentional Shootings," p. 5. In gun suicides, police sometimes find newly opened packets of fifty bullets, with just one used. Ballistics experts speak of "The 49 club." Ibid. p. 4. It is not known how many of the newly opened packets were also newly bought.

185. Harding, *Firearms,* pp. 115–19.

186. The Australian rate for 1984 was 11.5 per 100,000. For males the rate was 16.9, and for females the rate was 5.2. The American rate for 1983 was 12.5, with 19.2 for males, and 5.4 for females. Bureau of the Census, *Statistical Abstract of the United States, 1988* (Washington, D.C.: Government Printing Office, 1987), pp. 802–803.

187. See, for example, Duncan Chappell and Linda P. Graham, *Police Use of Deadly Force: A Canadian Perspective* (Toronto: Centre for Criminology, 1985), whose findings are discussed in chapter 4.

188. The authors' sensibilities are sometimes revealed in small details. For example, the national committee notes that assault on Australians at work is, fortunately, "minimal, compared to the People's Republic of China, where, according to *People's Daily,* 13 tax collectors have been murdered and over 6,000 beaten up since 1985." National Committee, p. liv. Are assaults on tax collectors from a Communist dictatorship really a compelling example of "intimidation" in the workplace, or are such assaults legitimate resistance to a kleptocracy? Are attacks on Communist tax collectors really the most serious examples of mass intimidation in the workplace that the committee could find? Would a China where tax collectors had no fear for their physical safety imply a China where ordinary citizens were even less safe from governmental violence?

189. National Committee, pp. 173–77.

190. Armed Robberies, p. 17 (Victoria and New South Wales); Bureau of Crime Statistics and Research, "Robbery Study: First Interim Report of Robberies in N.S.W." (Attorney General's Department N.S.W., 1986), p. 40.

191. Office of Crime Statistics, "Robbery in South Australia," series II, no. 3 (n.p., February 1980), p. 55.

192. Criminal Law Consolidation Act §§ 155, 156, 158, quoted in "Robbery in South Australia," p. 3.

193. "Robbery in South Australia," p. 56.

194. Ibid., p. 59.

195. Richard Harding, "Extract from Firearms and Violence in Australian Life," in *Proceedings of the Institute,* p. 55; Harding, *Firearms,* p. 127, citing New South Wales Bureau of Crime Statistics and Research, "Gun and Knife Attacks," Statistical Report, no. 9 (1974).

196. New South Wales Bureau of Crime Statistics and Research and N.S.W. Criminal Law Division, "Heroin Use and Crime," *Crime and Justice Bulletin,* no. 3 (June 1987) (Sydney: Government Printing Office), and same, "Trends in Serious Crime in N.S.W." no. 1 (June 1987).

197. Richard W. Harding and Ann Blake, *Weapons Choice by Violent Officers in Western Australia: A Pilot Study,* Research Report no. 1. (Nedlands, Western Australia: Crime Research Centre, University of Western Australia, n.d.), pp. 16–17.

198. Harding and Blake, pp. 20–21.

199. Fine, *An Agenda for Reform,* p. 73.

200. Ibid.

201. Ibid., pp. 84–85.

202. Ibid., pp. 79–80.

203. Ibid., p. 80.

204. Tunney, "Commentary on Professor Harding's Paper," p. 75.

205. A. D. J. Ryan, Acting Chief Inspector, Acting Registrar of Firearms, memorandum to A. O'Hea, Executive Officer, Operations Department, Firearms Registry, January 17, 1989, "Request for funding for overtime to reduce backlog of work due to Amnesty."

206. John Kaplan, "Controlling Firearms," *Cleveland State Law Review* 28 (1979), p. 8.

207. Fine, *An Agenda for Reform,* p. 76.

208. Harding, *Firearms Ownership,* p. 127.

209. Fine, *An Agenda for Reform,* pp. 75–76.

210. In Illinois, for example, a 1977 study showed that compliance with handgun registration was only about twenty-five percent. Donald B. Kates, "Handgun Control: Prohibition Revisited," *Inquiry,* December 5, 1977, p. 20, n.1. The rate of compliance for Denver's registration of semi-automatics is only one percent. David B. Kopel, "Denver Gun Law Violates Constitutional Rights," (Colorado Springs) *Gazette Telegraph,* January 11, 1990, p. B7. The one percent estimate was based on the about 130 gun registrations during the lawful registration period, and the estimate of 10,000 guns covered by the ordinance being privately possessed in Denver. The 10,000 figure assumes that Denverites own the covered firearms at a rate no higher than the average United States rate. In general, Colorado has one of the highest per capita rates of gun ownership. Of the 300,000 "assault weapon" owners in California, approximately 10 percent have registered themselves as required by law. The rate of compliance with semi-automatic bans in Boston, Cleveland, and other American cities has been about one percent. In New Jersey, between 100,000 and 3,000,000 firearms are covered by the state's "assault weapons" law (depending on how broadly the law's inexact definitions are read). At the end of a year-long transitional period, the Firearms Section of the New Jersey State police reported that 947 guns had been registered, 888 had been rendered inoperable, and 4 surrendered to the police. All the rest had apparently

been moved out of state, or were possessed by owners who decided to ignore the law. Wayne King, "New Jersey Law to Limit Guns Being Ignored," *New York Times,* October 26, 1991; Howard Rabb, "New Jersey Politicians' Nightmare Comes True: Gun-owners Stage Successful Mass Rebellion," *GSSA Sentinel,* Fall 1991, p. 4.

In New York City, at least 250,000 to 300,000 persons possess long guns which they purchased lawfully, but which they have not registered as required by City law. Gerald Preiser, testimony before Committee on Public Safety, New York City Council, July 24, 1991, pp. 48–50 (estimate based on discrepancy between number of hunting licenses and number of gun registrants).

211. Queensland Police Department, p. 10.

212. *Seminar on Gun Misuse,* p. 9.

213. Report on the (Firearms) Amendment Bill, p. 30; A. Newgreen, Chief Inspector, Registrar of Firearms, memorandum to G. Brown, Chief Inspector, Operations Department, Victoria Police, "Annual Report—1986/87 Firearms Registry," July 14, 1987, p. 3. Newgreen took the number of licensed shooters, multiplied the number by 2.8 (the estimated number of guns owned per shooter), and arrived at an estimate of 739,303 guns in the community. The 435,337 registered guns amounted to 58.9% of total estimated guns. The estimate of total guns would be too low (and hence the registration percentage would be smaller) if there were a significant number of persons owning long guns who had never obtained a shooter's license, or who had let their license expire without disposing of their gun.

214. Tony O'Brien, "Canada and Firearm Registration," *Australian Shooters Journal,* September 1990, p. 58.

215. A. Newgreen, Chief Inspector, Registrar of Firearms, "Firearms Registration System: C.R.B. File: 39-1-1385/84," February 26, 1987, Melbourne; "Record Owners, not Guns: Report," (Melbourne) *Herald Sun,* November 2, 1990, p. 7; Greg Roberts, "Vic Gun Register Branded a Failure," *Sydney Morning Herald,* April 7, 1988. Earlier government reports had advised against introducing registration for shotguns, and successfully urged abolition of registration for rifles. Statute Law Revision Committee, "Report from the Statute Law Revision Committee upon the Desirability of Restricting the Use of Shotguns" (Melbourne: Government Printer, September 9, 1964), p. 5; Statute Law Revision Committee, "Report from the Statute Law Revision Committee upon Proposed Amendments to the Firearms Act 1958 together with Minutes and Evidence" (Melbourne: Government Printer, April 27, 1966), p. 4; Victoria Legislative Assembly, Hansard, Debate on Firearms (Amendment) Bill, March 17, 1972, p. 3963. (Government finds gun registration "cumbersome, costly, and generally ineffective.")

216. The police estimated that the gun pool consisted of 2.8 guns for each person holding a shooter's license. There were 308,508 licensed holders with (an estimated) 866,822 guns. A total of 704,145 guns ended up being registered. Victoria Police, "Firearms Registry Annual Report for 1989/90" reporting data for 1990/91 and 1989/90). The compliance rate is only a rough estimate. If the 2.8 guns per shooter estimate is too high, then the noncompliance rate would be lower. If a large number of guns are illegally possessed by persons without a shooter's license, the compliance rate would be lower.

217. Antony O'Brien, "State Bank Gunned Down," *Australian Shooters Journal,* November 1990, p. 22.

218. Harding, *Firearms,* p. 147; Richard Harding, *Police Killings in Australia* (Melbourne: Penguin Books, 1970); Richard Harding, "Changing Patterns of the Use of Lethal Force by Police in Australia," *Australia and New Zealand Journal of Criminology* 8 (1975), p. 128. Harding opposes civilian gun ownership for self-defense because even if it could be proven to make the individual safer, it contributes to the "fear-violence spiral." For the same reason, Harding opposes police officers carrying guns on routine duty. Harding, *Firearms,* p. 157.

6

New Zealand: Everyone Is Happy

In Japan, Canada, Great Britain, and Australia, the general trend set by legislation enacted in the 1980s has been toward more and more gun control. Governments have listened to what the police hierarchy has told them to do. The government in New Zealand also listens to its police. That is why the government substantially loosened controls in the 1980s.

At first thought, a person might expect New Zealand's gun-control culture to be something like Australia's. Yet the two are quite different. As Canada rejects the firearms control model of its more powerful and populated (and only) neighbor, New Zealand has veered sharply from the Australian example.

SUBDUING THE MAORI AND CONTROLLING THE WORKERS

In the United States, the fierce resistance of American Indians made the white invaders fight their way across the frontier one bloody step at a time. The indigenous resistance in Canada and Australia was weaker. Consequently, conquest of the Canadian and Australian frontiers was not so protracted, and frontier gun ownership was less of a necessity. In New Zealand, on the other hand, the native peoples fought long and hard against the white attack.

When Captain Cook sailed into Mercury Bay, the Maori mistook the whites for goblins, and their ship for a god. Captain Cook, the chief goblin, astonished the Maori by using what appeared to be a stick to kill a bird in mid-air.[1]

European settlement began in earnest in the early nineteenth century with the arrival of whaling and sealing gangs from Australia, over 1,200 miles to the northwest. The Maori eagerly traded flax for European goods, especially muskets. Once the gun demand was saturated, Maori interest in trade waned.[2]

To the Maori, "the great god of the white man" was the *pu,* the gun. According to historian Keith Sinclair, the Maori economy became "a musket economy."[3] The various Maori tribes of the North Island turned the guns on each other in the Musket Wars 1818–1833. Armed tribes attacked unarmed ones, and forty thousand Maori were killed in intertribal warfare. Finally, when all the Maori were armed, the balance of power was restored, and the killing ended.[4]

In Africa, the British traded cheap "sham dam iron" guns made especially for the export to the indigenous tribes. The Maori, though, were able to insist on higher-quality guns: first, top-quality flintlocks and then percussion locks and double-barreled shotguns. Like the American Indians, the Maori never learned gun repair or ammunition manufacture; but the Maori did maintain rough arms parity with the white invaders.[5]

The few hundred white settlers had not only the Maori to worry about, but sometimes each other. Like the settlers of the American West, the whites turned to vigilantism as a response to the lack of an effective government criminal justice system. In 1838, a vigilance committee called the Kororareka Association was formed to protect persons and property, especially property of the middle and upper classes. While the tarring and feathering of criminals did reduce the crime level, the vigilance committee was also turned against personal enemies of the leadership.[6]

The Maori were disciplined fighters who fought a long, often successful struggle against white encroachment. Unlike the American Indian chiefs, for whom warfare meant sporadic surprise attacks, the Maori kings were excellent military strategists who led disciplined armies that could fire in volleys.[7]

While the Maori at first outnumbered the white settlers, the British usually had numerical superiority during a particular battle. Although the British and the Maori both used one- or two-shot weapons, the British effectively had a higher rate of firepower because of their greater numbers. (In the American West, the whites' five- or six-shot revolvers also gave them an advantage in rate of fire.) The Maori adapted successfully to the British advantage by inventing trench warfare, with timber and earthworks structures called *pa.* Just as trenches protected European soldiers from rapid-fire of machine guns in World War I, the *pa* shielded the Maori from the numerically superior British fire.[8]

When the Maori and the Europeans fought, the Maori won at least as often as they lost. Nowhere else in the nineteenth-century world did indigenous peoples handicapped by smaller fighting forces resist so long and so successfully.[9] It was neither superior tactics by the Europeans nor cultural collapse of the Maori that finally extinguished the resistance to invasion. As historian James Belich puts it, the whites "won for the same reason the Goths beat the Romans: overwhelming numbers."[10] Like the Japanese of the sixteenth century, the nineteenth-century Maori knew nothing about guns when Europeans arrived by sail; both groups of islanders learned firearms quickly and well.

New Zealand and the United States are the only nations in this book to face a prolonged and often successful indigenous resistance to European conquest. Like the United States, New Zealand had to rely on citizen militias bringing their own arms to battle for a good deal of the fighting.

And just when the Maori wars entered their most intense phase, British imperial forces were withdrawn from the New Zealand wars.[11] The lack of British support made the New Zealanders more reluctant to prosecute the wars, but also more confident of their own prowess. Indeed, the New Zealand militias, like their New England counterparts, thought themselves superior fighters to the British regulars.[12]

Peace seemed to be at hand in 1840 with the Treaty of Waitangi; Queen Victoria's government guaranteed the Maori full possession of their lands, and the Maori in return ceded sovereignty to the Crown. Unfortunately, the English and Maori versions of the treaty differed as to whether the queen was given merely titular sovereignty, or the actual authority to rule. War promptly resumed.[13] The "Wairau massacre" of 1843 and the sacking of Kororareka in 1844 convinced the government to do something about guns.

By the Arms Importation Ordinance of 1845, the lieutenant-governor of New Zealand gave the governor power to regulate the import and sale of arms and gunpowder. There were substantial fines for violators.[14] The ordinance lamented that "certain tribes of the Native race of New Zealand have taken up arms against the Queen's sovereign authority."[15] The 1845 gun controls did little to disarm the Maoris. The Maori/Caucasian war that lasted from 1845 to 1848 was particularly fierce. One historian argues that the controls were ineffective because they only regulated gun transactions, not gun possession.[16]

Fierce war continued, with irregular periods of peace. In 1860, the New Zealand general assembly, to prevent the further arming of the "Aboriginal natives," enacted licensing and registration laws for all firearms owners. Lesser controls having failed in 1845, the general assembly tried more controls on gun possession by whites, to disarm the Maori. White settlers, particularly residents of the mostly mountainous South Island, where there were few Maori, resented the new law.[17] (New Zealand consists of the North Island, the South Island, and a host of smaller islands. The capital, Wellington, is on the North Island.) In 1862, a Maori named Te Ua saw a vision of the Archangel Gabriel, who revealed the *pai marire* or new "Good and Peaceful Religion." This combination of Christianity with traditional Maori beliefs promised adherents that they would be immune to bullets in combat if they raised their right hand and yelled "Pai marire, hau! hau!" The *hau hau* warriors were bold and fierce in combat.[18] Yet, like the Sioux Ghost Dancers of the 1890s who also chanted "Hau! Hau! Hau!" the Maori *hau hau* looked in vain for divine help to transcend the bullet.

Still, the Maori resistance had gained something. Once subdued, the Maori were given designated seats in New Zealand's parliament, while the Australian Aborigines were denied basic citizenship.[19] With the Maori resistance vanquished, gun control loosened. In the early 1880s, the Arms Act (1860) was suspended for the mountainous South Island and relaxed for the North Island. European settlers were allowed to possess almost any firearm they wished.[20]

The government did add laws requiring "native applicants" to sign receipts for purchase of ammunition and required them to obtain permits. As an English literacy test for gun owners, ammunition receipts were required to be filled out "at length," with words rather than numbers. While many Maori were literate in their native language, English literacy was rare.[21]

Like the natives, the whites in New Zealand were literate (unlike many of the whites and natives in Australia). Immigrants to New Zealand generally came as a matter of choice.[22] The government saw no need to disarm the white population. Many of the British settling in New Zealand, not being aristocrats, had not been allowed to hunt or fish in their native land,[23] but they enjoyed unrestricted big-game hunting in their new homeland. Rifles and big game were scarce in England; both flourished in New Zealand.

In the present century, however, wildlife populations and hunting have both declined, and with them gun ownership.[24] In the 1950s, the sight of people carrying unloaded rifles on their shoulders through mid-city traffic, on their way to the mountains or a range, would not have been uncommon. Today, such a sight would arouse fear in a citizenry concerned about crime.

The first twentieth-century gun controls were enacted in 1908, one year after the nation was granted dominion status in the British Commonwealth. The laws came at the request of the British government, perhaps as a result of the Boer War (a white rebellion in South Africa against British rule).[25] Conditions in South Africa, though, probably mattered less to the New Zealand government than domestic radical labor agitators. During the decade before World War I, the International Workers of the World (the "wobblies") and the Federation of Labour (the "red feds") failed to mobilize the working the class, but did manage to terrify the government.[26]

As in the western United States and Australia (and South Africa) the gold fields were sometimes violent places. A government attempt to force striking gold miners back to work led to a clash with armed strikers in the town of Waihi. In 1910, only three years after New Zealand had been granted dominion status, London's "Siege of Sidney Street" further intensified fear of anarchism. (The siege was an overblown incident in which the police mistook three Lithuanians for a vast terror network.)[27] The fear gave birth to the War Regulations Act of 1914, which required a license for the purchase of any gun except a shotgun, and controlled the carrying of firearms in public places. Laws were simultaneously enacted against publication of seditious material.[28]

As in America, government propaganda campaigns during the Great War whipped the nation into a xenophobia that endured beyond the war. The Irish revolution against the British Crown had begun on Easter Sunday 1916, and continued in earnest from 1919 until independence was granted in 1921. New Zealand's minority Catholic population cheered the Irish, thereby enraging an already hostile Protestant majority, and increasing fears of Catholic sedition. The Labour party, having opposed conscription during the war, was also considered potentially subversive.[29]

The return of servicemen from the Great War, bringing home their service guns (war booty or trophies), greatly augmented the firearms stock and made the authorities apprehensive of large-scale industrial demonstrations or riots. In 1919, the police requested further controls, particularly on handguns, which they said were "freely" sold. Parliamentary debates on gun-control proposals reflected grave concern about the "automatic revolver" (a poorly made and poorly understood gun thought to be capable of rapid fire.)[30]

By the Arms Act 1920, every gun, including shotguns, had to be registered with the police. Carrying a handgun without a license was outlawed. Half a century later, the police explained that in the 1920s, registration was introduced "because of fear a riot could occur."[31]

Ordinary gun owners had little say in the legislation, but did help to bring about some amendment a decade later.[32] The paperwork burden of gun registration had become heavy on the police; about half the police district officers favored relaxing registration. In 1930, the registration requirement for shotguns was abolished at police request.[33] For several decades, the police suspended enforcement of the law requiring shotgun purchasers to have a permit like other gun owners. In 1968—a year when civil turmoil led to new gun controls in Britain and the United States— a permit to procure a shotgun was again put into force.[34] No permit was needed to continue to possess a gun already owned. Once granted a license, shotgun owners still did not need separate permission for each new gun purchase.[35]

The president of the Deerstalkers' Association attributed the looser regulation to the view of the shotgun as "a gentleman's gun."[36] Britain, which looks on shotguns as "the toy of the landed gentry," has also regulated shotguns less stringently than rifles, even though shotguns are potentially more lethal at close range.

THE POLICE RELAX GUN CONTROL

The crime rate in New Zealand, as in most of the Western world, began curving up in the mid-1960s. The percentage of firearms used in crime remained stable.[37] Shootings account for less than 20 percent of all homicides, a percentage that continues to decline even as the number of homicides increases.[38] (Guns are used in about 60 percent of U.S. homicides.)

In the early 1980s, the problem of crime involving guns did not seem out of control, and, again, the police thought that gun registration requirements were taking up too much of their time.[39] Police officials found that the registration system was not a cost-effective way to fight gun-related crime.[40] Senior-Sergeant Jones, a police spokesman, opined, "Whatever law you have, if criminals want to commit a crime with a gun, they will get a gun."[41] The official police report on the subject also concluded: "It is unlikely that firearms registration controls firearms use in domestic violence."[42] In general, the police found no correlation between the number of guns and the number of crimes.[43]

The registration system, so useless in crime control, was falling apart under its own weight. The error rate of registration certificates was about two-thirds, and correcting the certificates would have taken at least five years of intensive police work.[44] The police persuaded the government to recodify New Zealand's gun laws in the Arms Act of 1983.

Persons who wished to purchase rifles or shotguns had to apply for a license and pass a safety test. Once granted the license, these persons could buy unlimited numbers of rifles and shotguns for the rest of their lives; none of the gun purchases needed to be registered.

The Arms Act tightened other controls. The long-gun licensing system was made universal, including even people who owned only old shotguns that were family heirlooms. The nation's gun owners were given eight months to get their licenses.

Under the arms act, which remains in force today, licenses "shall be issued" to any person over sixteen years of age who, at the discretion of the police, is considered "a fit and proper person to be in possession of a firearm or airgun."[45] The police may revoke the license of any person they no longer consider "fit and proper."[46] License applications include the applicant's date and place of birth, address, occupation, the name and address of a near relative, and a reference who is not a near relative.[47]

Private transfers of firearms are legal. It is the seller's responsibility to ensure that the buyer is legally qualified.

Any New Zealander in possession of a firearm may be requested by the police to produce a license, and supply full name, address, and date of birth.[48] If the license-holders do not have the license in their possession, they must furnish it to the police within seven days.[49] If the gun owner moves, the police must be informed within thirty days.[50] If a firearm is lost or stolen, the police must be notified.[51]

Unlike the firearms licenses issued by other nations or by American states, which are simply bureaucratic-looking slips of paper, the New Zealand license is a small booklet with a stiff red fabric cover, of the same stock as New Zealand's diplomatic passports. Australia's J. David Fine praises the high-quality New Zealand gun licenses as a sign of police respect for gun owners.[52] The fee for a firearms license is a reasonable 45 New Zealand dollars (about $16 U.S. currency).[53]

Another change in the police-sponsored Arms Act of 1983 was the reduction of ammunition controls. No longer would an individual permit be legally required every time a person wanted to buy a box of cartridges.[54] In practice, the ammunition-permit rule had only been enforced against people in possession of an unlawful weapon.[55] Further, since the law had been enacted, handloading (creating one's own ammunition from used casings) had become increasingly popular and rendered the law irrelevant.

Airguns are completely free of control for adults over eighteen years of age; anyone over sixteen may own an airgun if the person possesses a firearms license.[56]

The arms' act made one major change in the handgun laws, namely, relegalizing the ownership of semi-automatic handguns. Licenses for handguns of all types remained available for members of an incorporated, police-approved club or for collectors.[57] Most clubs require a person to shoot regularly for six months before they issue the recommendation to the police that the person receive permission to procure a pistol.[58] Pistol ownership is so rare, and so private, that, as the head of a sports safety group explained, "few members of the nonshooting public realize that pistol shooters exist, or that they have guns at home."[59]

Handgun licensees may buy additional guns at retail or informally, after receiving a permit to procure. They must, however, register with the police a description of the firearm and the serial number.[60]

Carrying a pistol outside the property surrounding one's dwelling requires a police permit.[61] These carry-permits allow only the transport of the pistol to an approved club, gunsmith, or licensed dealer.[62] No one may carry a loaded firearm, or even a loaded magazine, in a vehicle.[63] If an act is committed with a firearm and would be illegal without a permit, the burden of proof is on the accused to prove that he or she possessed a permit.[64]

Automatics (including genuine assault rifles) and mortars (small cannons) are "restricted weapons." An arms collector may add one to his collection, but may not fire it.[65] The governor-general, by Order in Council, may declare any firearm, or even an airgun, to be a restricted weapon.[66]

Like American gun dealers, New Zealand dealers are required to keep gun sale records, but need not report the sale to the government.[67] New Zealand dealers may destroy their sales records after five years, while United States dealers must keep their records for twenty years, turning them over to the government when they go out of business.[68]

The final significant change New Zealand's 1983 law was to greatly increase penalties for criminal misuse of a weapon.

One pro-gun leader rejoiced about "a significant advance" and stated that, despite certain restrictions, New Zealanders had "greater freedom now than many U.S. states."[69] It is considerably easier to buy a long gun in New Zealand than in New Jersey, New York City, or Washington, D.C. While California examines every firearms transaction, New Zealand examines gun owners once, and then lets them buy as they wish. On the other hand, no state treats handguns as strictly as does New Zealand, which allows handgun ownership only by gun club members or collectors. (Washington, D.C., and Chicago, though, have outlawed handgun acquisition.)

One factor in the general contentment with arms laws may be police behavior. Police officers do not routinely carry handguns, and thereby help set the tone for a society where people do not believe that self-defense handguns are necessary.[70]

Perhaps the most important difference from the United States is that both New Zealand's gun organizations and its high-ranking police officials were content with the existing laws. Much of the credit for the harmonious situation goes to the New Zealand police, who had the common sense to abolish gun controls that manifestly were not working. Another share of the credit goes to New Zealand's gun organizations, which have done an outstanding job of promoting responsible gun ownership.

THE NEW ZEALAND MOUNTAIN SAFETY COUNCIL

No pro-gun citizen organizations in the world enjoy so much official recognition and respect as those in New Zealand. In formulating the Arms Act of 1983, the government consulted with New Zealand's outdoor life association—the New Zealand Mountain Safety Council (NZMSC)—as well as with gun organizations such as the New Zealand Deerstalkers' Association.[71] The Mountain Safety Council, organized in 1966 to promote safe enjoyment of the backcountry, has six hundred certified volunteers who teach firearms safety and administer the safety test for gun-license applicants. New Zealand Police Arms Officers—the official licensing officers—are required to be familiar with these safety procedures.[72]

Over the last half-century, there has been a significant decline in firearms deaths and injuries in New Zealand, even as the number of guns has soared.[73] There has been a similar trend in the United States, which writers such as Don Kates and I have attributed to the substitution of (less powerful) handguns for long guns as home-defense weapons. Yet the hypothesis is contradicted by the New Zealand experience: handguns there are much more difficult to obtain than long guns, yet the accident rate has still dropped sharply.

One explanation for the mortality decline in both the United States and New Zealand is improvements in medical care. The Mountain Safety Council tentatively suggests the increased use of low-cost, low-power .22 rimfire rifle and pistol ammunition as another explanation for declining accident deaths.[74]

Safe-storage requirements might also help reduce accidents. New Zealand licensees are required to take "reasonable steps" to keep their guns from being obtained by a young child or a thief, and must store guns so that a person who obtains access to them does not obtain access to the ammunition.[75] The Mountain Safety Council advises that loaded firearms should never be kept in a home.[76] Police-NZMSC brochures suggest that firearm, bolt, and ammunition be stored and locked separately.[77] Handguns, mortars, and automatics *must* be stored with a vital part removed.[78]

The downside of safe-storage requirements is that they usually make it difficult to access a loaded firearm in an emergency, such as a nighttime burglary. No American jurisdiction has handgun safe-storage rules as strict at New Zealand's. But the requirement apparently works little hardship on New Zealand gun owners, since only .6 of 1 percent of them own a gun for personal protection.[79] Even the gun-rights lobby considers the legitimate uses of firearms to be "hunting, target shooting, vermin control, antiques or collecting," rather than self-defense or resistance to tyranny.[80]

One other factor in the low New Zealand gun accident rate may be the safety campaigns conducted by the Mountain Safety Council since 1965.[81] The council engages in a variety of public education efforts to promote firearms safety. Firearms license applicants must take a safety course and pass a written test.[82] The volunteer instructors develop an effective rapport with their students, impressing the importance of responsible exercise of the privilege of sport shooting. Test-takers must correctly answer twenty-eight of the thirty questions, including all seven of the "compulsory" safety questions. The pass rate is 90 percent, and ten thousand new applicants become firearms licensees every year.[83]

As in other nations, people between the ages of sixteen and thirty are disproportionately involved in firearms accidents. A fifth of New Zealand gun accidents involve people under the age of sixteen, the minimum age for possession of a gun without adult supervision.[84] In America also, a fifth of fatal gun accidents involve children under sixteen.[85] New Zealand's official approach to gun safety for youngsters differs markedly from the official American approach. The Mountain Safety Council, in a pamphlet co-produced with the police, promotes gun use by children, promising that "airgun ownership can contribute in a positive way to growing up."[86] The council also publishes, in conjunction with the police, a gun-safety comic series called "Billy Hook," which teaches children gun-safety rules. The comic endorses supervised gun use by children.[87] The official police instruction book for gun owners, the *Arms Code,* advises parents: "While children should not handle a firearm except under the supervision of a firearms license holder, it can ease their curiosity to show them your firearm and explain that it must never be touched except when you are there."[88]

New Zealand promotes gun safety by promoting responsible gun use, but other nations take the opposite approach. A government researcher in Western Australia concluded that firearms safety classes in high schools might reduce injuries.[89] Nevertheless, the researcher opposed the idea because classes might encourage an interest in firearms and because instructors might suggest it was legitimate to own firearms.[90]

Unlike the New Zealand Mountain Safety Council, America's National Rifle Association is not subsidized by the government. The NRA does follow the New Zealand lead, though, by publishing a gun safety comic book. The NRA's "Eddie Eagle" comic might be considered less contro-versial than New Zealand's "Billy Hook," since Billy Hook endorses child-hood gun use, while Eddie Eagle does not even endorse adult gun ownership. The message of the NRA's comic is simply "No. Go. Tell." Don't touch an unattended gun, leave the area, and tell an adult. The comic's only statement that could be construed as pro-gun is, "You should be around guns only if an adult is present."

Although Eddie Eagle could not have a blander message, and although the comic is recommended by the National Association of Chiefs of Police, and the Police Athletic League, the NRA comic has aroused intense opposition. Many school districts have refused to accept free copies. Some districts have substituted alternate "gun safety" programs in which gun control advocates tell children to urge their parents to dispose of all guns, and to report to the police illegal guns owned by their parents.

While New Zealand and Billy Hook have reached a state of equilibrium— moderate gun controls and promotion of sporting-gun use by children— America enjoys no such tranquility. The American debate is polarized between opponents of all regulation, and people who vehemently object to the slightest implication in a comic book that some adults legitimately own guns.

NEW ZEALAND BY THE NUMBERS

As of December 1991, 352,232 New Zealanders held firearms licenses (for long guns); 2,332 held handgun target permits; and 2,661 held handgun collector permits. If airguns are included, about 435,000 people lawfully own a gun. The number of licensed gun owners is increasing at a 2.8 percent annual rate.[91] Gun ownership being almost exclusively male, about one in four adult New Zealand males has a firearms license.[92] There are about 1,010,000 legal guns in the nation. By type, there are approximately 500,000 rifles; 250,000 shotguns; 250,000 airguns; and 10,000 handguns.[93] The average gun owner owns 2 to 3 guns. Gun owners who had never hunted (only 7 percent of gun owners) possessed an average of 1.5 firearms.[94]

Firearms amnesties, to surrender illegal guns without fear of prosecution, are held periodically, especially when concern about gang violence is high. A typical amnesty will bring in one thousand to two thousand long guns, and approximately three hundred handguns. These numbers have stayed fairly constant since the early 1970s. New Zealand amnesties collect illegal guns at about the same rate as amnesties in Canada or Britain. Amnesties in Australia and America are far less successful.

Interestingly, the number of surrendered handguns in a given New Zealand amnesty equals about 3 percent of the lawful handgun stock. This may indicate that there is a substantial pool of illegal handguns, and that the pool has not diminished in recent decades.[95] The police report that at least twenty thousand lost or stolen firearms have never been recovered.[96]

Crime involving firearms in New Zealand is relatively rare. There are fewer than one hundred firearms-related robberies, homicides, and attempted homicides per year.[97] Yet newspapers accord 81 percent more space to violent offenses with firearms than to all other violent offenses combined.[98]

All types of violent crime, including robbery and homicide, have increased sharply since the early 1960s. Firearms use in most crimes has increased at the same rate (except for robbery, where the rate of gun use has fallen from 13 percent to 7 percent).[99] Although handguns are only 1 percent of the total gun stock, they are used in approximately 25 percent of those crimes in which a gun is involved.[100]

The suicide rate per 100,000 population aged fifteen and over is 12.5, about the same as the Australian and American rates.[101] Twenty-two percent of New Zealand suicides are by firearms, a percentage that has showed little change over the last two decades.[102] As in Japan, the United Kingdom, Australia, and the United States, the male suicide rate is far above the female rate.[103] New Zealand males are ten times as likely to use firearms in suicide, while females are twice as likely to use "analgesic and soporific" poisons.[104]

POLICE POWERS

Although the New Zealand police leaders have behaved more reasonably than most of the highest-ranking police leaders in the countries discussed above, or in America, New Zealand is not without civil liberties violations in enforcement of the gun laws. Freedom from search and seizure, is, as in other countries, the civil liberty most immediately impacted by tough gun laws. The New Zealand police may, without a warrant, enter and search the home of any person they believe to possess a firearm and to be "by reason of physical or mental condition, however arising, incapable of having proper control of the firearm." The firearm may also be seized.[105]

By the Police Offenses Amendment Act the police are allowed to stop and search a person or vehicle or enter a building on "reasonable grounds" without a warrant if they believe an illegal weapon is being carried.[106] After a search pursuant to the above provision, the officer is required to inform the police commissioner in writing.[107] Canada has a similar notification provision for reporting of warrantless searches, which seems to be honored mostly in the breach.

The definition of "offensive weapons" is broad enough to include a tire iron. The person searched for an "offensive weapon" can be detained "as long as is reasonably necessary." A skeptical law review note worries that the "identity of the person, or occupants of the vehicle," might be the determining factor in police discretion to search.[108]

In regard to searches for "offensive weapons," New Zealand appears to have slid down the same slippery slope as has Britain. Few New Zealanders objected when the police were given power to search for weapons and drugs without a warrant. Then, technical redefinition of the term "offensive weapon" expanded the class of people subject to the possibility of discretionary searches including many people who do not own guns, but who do own tire irons and the like.

If an illegal gun is found in a dwelling place, all occupants of the dwelling place are deemed in illegal possession of the gun, and bear the burden of proving that they had no knowledge of the gun. This is true even if the gun is hidden in a secret wall compartment.[109]

While police search-and-seizure powers are broader than an American civil libertarian might prefer, the friendly relationship between police and gun owners in New Zealand is a refreshing change from the tense relations in other parts of the world. The New Zealand police, unlike their British counterparts, are not out to abolish civilian gun ownership.

In the early 1980s, the New Zealand police proposed a tightening of gun controls. The gun lobby held an international conference to discuss gun laws, and the conference raised doubts in the minds of the police leadership. The police began their own research and study of gun control and concluded that New Zealand's gun laws should be loosened.[110]

Remember Colin Greenwood, the British police officer whose research on Britain has been ignored by British governments, because he contends that British gun control is a failure? The New Zealand police used Greenwood as a consultant for revision of New Zealand's firearms laws. They abolished a gun registration system that did nothing to reduce crime. In promoting the new law, the police did not claim that it (or any other gun law) would reduce the use of firearms in crime. Instead, they emphasized that the new law would free the police from bureaucratic work, simplify their record-keeping jobs, and help them determine "who is in unlawful possession of firearms."[111]

Seventy-one percent of the general population opposed the less-restrictive law. Key objections were the absence of limit on the number of guns that could be accumulated and lack of ongoing checks on suitability of firearms licensees.[112] Yet the police pushed for the looser gun controls despite public opposition. They praised the system of a one-time licensing of firearms owners, rather than a continual gun-by-gun licensing and registration system, as "enlightened legislation and superior to that in other Western countries."[113]

The Canadian government has outlawed hollow-point handgun cartridges, claiming that they are only useful for homicide. The government-funded New Zealand Mountain Safety Council, on the other hand, touts hollow-point bullets for small-game hunting.[114] The police/NZMSC *Arms Code* not only explains New Zealand gun laws, but also offers an introduction to firearms mechanics and gives hunting tips.[115]

THE ARAMOANA MASSACRE AND THE BREAKDOWN OF CONSENSUS

During the 1980s, New Zealand enjoyed a set of gun laws that sports persons and police alike found reasonable. The mutual antagonism typical of Britain, Canada, and Australia was absent. It is not clear, however, whether New Zealand will be able to carry its consensus into the 1990s and beyond, for the 1990s have begun with the first outbreak of political warfare between gun owners and the police, caused by concern over semi-automatic rifles.

New Zealand police discretion to limit firearms imports is broad but not unlimited.[116] In February 1989, the United States banned the import of certain self-loading firearms; a few months earlier, Britain had ordered owners of almost all semi-automatics to sell their guns outside the country, or to surrender them to the government for half-price. The New Zealand police, fearing that their nation might become a dumping ground for British and American guns, banned the import of some semi-automatics and limited the import of some others to five-unit lots.[117] Police Inspector John Meads, national firearms coordinator at police headquarters in Wellington, had initially defended the availability of semi-automatics: "Semi-automatic weapons have been on sale in New Zealand for many years. Their owners are generally responsible people whose fitness to purchase firearms has been established by the police."[118] Although the press aroused public concern about "military-style" guns, Police Commissioner John Jamieson reassured the public that no "assault-style rifles" had almost never been used in homicides or robberies in New Zealand in 1990.[119] The media, meanwhile, editorialized against rapid-fire automatic rifles, although the guns in question were not automatics.[120]

The import policy was studied during the following months. A Firearms Selection Committee recommended that imports be permanently limited to ten per dealer, and ownership be restricted to one per licensee.[121] An internal police report concluded that semi-automatic firearms in the hands of licensed owners were not a threat to anyone in New Zealand.[122] Jamieson rejected the committee's advice, and instead banned imports completely, while proposing no restrictions on semi-automatics currently in New Zealand.[123] The import ban marked the first time in over a decade that the police had come into conflict with the firearms community. As in the United States, the prospect of a ban prompted record sales of the guns in question. The ban was voided by the High Court in 1991 because an absolute prohibition was not in the police's statutory power.[124]

A few months after the 1989 ban on semi-automatic imports, a thirty-three-year-old man named David Gray, unemployed and nearly illiterate, ran amok in the small South Island oceanside retirement town of Aramoana. Gray first burned down his neighbor's house, killing two eleven-year-old girls inside. When the neighbor returned, Gray shot him dead, and wounded the neighbor's nine-year-old daughter. A six-year-old who happened upon the scene, as well as a man and his wife and their six-year-old daughter who came upon the burning house, were shot and killed. The couple's four-year-old daughter was wounded in the abdomen. A police sergeant arrived, and he, too, was murdered; Gray took the dead sergeant's .38 calibre revolver. As more people came to help put out the fire, they were killed. All together, thirteen people died.

Gray was eventually surrounded in his home by a special police anti-terrorist squad. The wounded four-year-old girl lay in the back of a pick-up truck for over two hours, until a detective risked his life to come to her rescue. "Please don't shoot me," she asked him. Twenty-three hours after Gray's rampage had begun, he bolted from his home. Carrying a Norinco 84(s) 5.56mm semi-automatic rifle, he screamed "Kill me, kill me." The anti-terrorist squad obliged.

Gray had no criminal record, and while he was known in the small community as a mentally disturbed, angry, and reclusive person, he had no official record of mental illness. A licensed firearms owner, he legally owned seven different guns. Although it is not clear what guns he used to murder his victims, in his final siege with the police he relied on the Norinco semi-automatic with a thirty-round magazine and a rimfire Remington semi-automatic with a seven-round magazine.[125]

The rampage shocked New Zealand, and many voices in the media wondered whether more gun control was appropriate. The police promised to review the entire Arms Act.[126] Less than two weeks after the Aramoana massacre, Police Commissioner Jamieson visited with the New Zealand Shooters Rights Association, and suggested that the import ban was required because as few as six people in the nation were the type who had to be prevented from having such weapons. The commissioner also left the door open for reevaluation of the ban regarding particular high-quality models used in match competition.[127]

In the early summer of 1991, the police unveiled a sweeping set of new gun-control proposals. The restrictive standards currently applicable to handguns would also apply to all semi-automatic long guns, including .22 rimfires. Secure-storage standards would make the cost of possessing a semi-automatic over one thousand New Zealand dollars. In addition, police permission would be needed for each individual purchase of a semi-automatic. Persons possessing semi-automatics would be forbidden to possess magazines holding more than ten rounds.[128]

At the time of the import ban, concerned firearms owners founded a New Zealand Shooters Rights Association, the first gun organization in the country concerned with policy rather than sports.[129] A number of other gun-rights groups have also arisen. Although the firearms activists have yet to be tested in an election, advocates of gun prohibition are already complaining about "strong gun lobbies," and Police Commissioner Jamieson noted with displeasure: "We have people absolutely obsessed with rights."[130]

After an extensive public comment period, a modified government proposal was introduced in November 1991. Ownership of a semi-automatic long gun maintained in a "military configuration" would require a special license, similar to a handgun license. "Military configuration" would mean the presence of features such as a folding stock, a pistol grip, or a magazine of over five rounds (fifteen for low-power rimfire guns). The bill also would allow the government to ban imports of gun accessories, as well as guns.[131] Asked why the bill did not provide for confiscation of New Zealand's sixty thousand to seventy thousand "military" semi-automatics, the minister of police said, "I take my advice from the police."[132]

CONCLUSION

The current battle over semi-automatics may signal a widespread deterioration in relations between police and gun owners. New Zealand may be starting to take the path of Australia, where gun owners feel besieged by a push for severe controls, and politicians alternate between disdain and fear of a powerful gun lobby.

Still, it should be remembered that Commissioner Jamieson's proposed controls for New Zealand, even if adopted in full, would leave that nation's gun laws less severe than most Australian states. Given the harmonious record of police and gun owners up until 1990, it may be that the two groups will confine their disagreement to the single issue, and retain their otherwise amicable relations. Whatever the future holds, New Zealand in the 1980s did achieve a consensus over gun control that no other English-speaking nation was able to attain.

Why during the last decade was there such a pacific state of affairs and a moderate attitude on the part of all parties? Perhaps New Zealanders, with no penal colonies in their past, lack the mistrust of authority held by Australians. Unlike Canada and Britain, New Zealand remains a small, homogenous nation, where the people and the government may still know each other well enough to share a degree of mutual respect. For whatever reason, the New Zealand police, unlike most of their Commonwealth counterparts, have not adopted the view that reducing the number of guns in their nation is a good in itself.

Another factor helping New Zealand was that the police and gun owners shared mutual objectives. Unlike some American police chiefs, the New

Zealand police hierarchy rejected gun prohibition. Indeed, the sporting use of long guns was something that the police positively encouraged, particularly for children under parental supervision. Because almost no one in New Zealand wished to possess a gun for self-defense, gun owners could accept a system of controls that was designed to protect and promote sporting-gun use.

Further, New Zealand gun owners accepted the system because they trusted the police to administer it fairly. And the experience of reasonable enforcement of the laws validates the New Zealanders' trust. Even in the dispute over semi-automatics, police enforcement has generally stayed within the bounds of statutory authority—quite a contrast to the police approach in Britain.

Where should American gun owners turn if they wish to trust police administrators? To New York City, where the police department has refused to issue legally required licenses, even when commanded by courts to do so? The department refused even to hand out blank application forms.[133] To Gary, Indiana, where the police also followed orders never to give anyone license application forms?[134] To New Jersey, where the law requires that the authorities act on gun-license applications within thirty days, but delays of several months are common, and some applications are delayed for years, for no valid reason?[135] To St. Louis, where gun permits have routinely been denied to homosexuals, nonvoters, and wives who lack their husbands' permission?[136] New Zealand gun owners have good reason to trust their nation's police to administer laws fairly; United States gun owners have every reason not to.

The experience of Britain, Canada, Australia and, to a lesser degree, New Zealand should perhaps caution Americans who favor stricter legal controls of guns. In general, there does not seem to be a strong factual association in these countries between gun control and crime control. In addition, a simple handgun-permit system seems to develop a momentum of its own, until handguns are nearly banned and long guns become subject to ever-more severe controls.

Of course the banning of handguns and the careful regulation of long guns might be a good idea. Still, it is easy to see why people who own only rifles or shotguns may see handgun-only control as the starting point in a process that might one day deprive them of their long guns.

In Japan and the British Commonwealth, gun control is often accompanied with searches and seizures that are unacceptable under American constitutional norms—and there are other civil liberties violations as well. The association of gun control with government heavy-handedness, present in the most stable English-speaking democracies, becomes especially clear when one examines a less stable Commonwealth democracy, Jamaica.

NOTES

1. Keith Sinclair, *A History of New Zealand,* rev. ed. (Auckland: Penguin, 1988), pp. 32–33. The word "Maori" is used to describe all of the different tribes in New Zealand. The tribes only used the word "maori," meaning "normal," to contrast themselves to the whites. Ibid., p. 117.

2. Ibid., p. 39.

3. Ibid., p. 41.

4. James Belich, *The New Zealand Wars and the Victorian Interpretation of Racial Conflict* (Auckland: Penguin, 1988), pp. 19–20; Sinclair, pp. 41–42.

5. Belich, pp. 21–22.

6. Sinclair, p. 54.

7. Belich, p. 24.

8. Ibid., pp. 293–97.

9. Ibid., p. 291.

10. Ibid., p. 298.

11. Robin W. Winks, *The Relevance of Canadian History: U.S. and Imperial Perspectives* (Lanham, Md.: University Press of America, 1988), p. 31.

12. Belich, pp. 84–85, 126.

13. The New Zealand government in later years has refused to consider the treaty binding law. Hilary Charlesworth, "Book Review: A Standard of Justice," *Australian Journal of International* Law 81: 796.

14. Charles I. H. Forsyth, *Firearms in New Zealand* (Thorndon, Wellington: New Zealand Mountain Safety Council, 1985), pp. 85–86 [hereinafter "Forsyth (1985)"].

15. Robert Badland, "New Zealand Firearms Control," in *Gun Control Examined,* a collection of papers from the "Conference on Gun Control," Melbourne University, August 27–28, 1988, p. 46.

16. P. S. O'Connor, *Arms Control in New Zealand 1845–1930* (Auckland: University of Auckland, 1981), cited in Forsyth (1985), p. 86.

17. Arms Act 1860, 24 Victoria no. 38; Forsyth (1985), p. 86, citing O'Connor.

18. Sinclair, pp. 140–41.

19. Winks, p. 31.

20. Forsyth (1985), p. 87, citing O'Connor.

21. Forsyth (1985), p. 87; Charles I. H. Forsyth, letter to author, March 8, 1990 [hereinafter "Forsyth, March 8, 1990"]. Sinclair, p. 219.

22. Winks, p. 25.

23. Forsyth (1985), pp. 123–24.

24. Hong Tse, "What Does the Future Hold for Firearms Owners in New Zealand?" in *Proceedings of the International Shooting Sports Symposium* (Wellington, New Zealand: New Zealand Mountain Safety Council, 1981) (symposium held October 25, 1980); New Zealand Police, *Arms Code: Firearms Safety Manual Issued by the New Zealand Police* (Upper Hutt, New Zealand: Wright and Carman, n.d.), p. 40.

The New Zealand Deerstalkers' Association reports that deer recently have been found in new areas. Charles I. H. Forsyth, letter to author, March 1, 1988. Small game is increasing in rural areas of the South Island, and becoming something of a menace. Bob Badland, letter to author, December 7, 1989. Goats, varieties of wallaby, deer, chamois, thar, wapiti, and feral pigs remain available for hunters who want to make the trek into less accessible areas. New Zealand Mountain Safety Council, *Selecting a Firearm,* bulletin 32 (Wellington: N.Z.M.S.C., n.d.), p. 4.

25. Forsyth (1985), p. 88.

26. Sinclair, pp. 202–203.

27. Sinclair, pp. 209–11; George Dangerfield, *The Strange Death of Liberal England, 1900–1914* (New York: Perigree; published in the United States by G. P. Putnam's Sons, 1935), pp. 89–91. See chapter 3, note 98 and accompanying text.

28. Forsyth (1985), p. 89. Regulations promulgated on September 20, 1915, extended the gun controls. Ibid.

29. Sinclair, pp. 241–44.

30. New Zealand Police, *Background to the Introduction of Firearms User Licensing Instead of Rifle and Shotgun Registration Under the Arms Act 1983* (n.d.), p. 2 [hereinafter "New Zealand Police, *Background*"]; New Zealand Police Department, *Project Foresight* (Melbourne, Australia: reprinted by Australian Firearms Law Institute, 1984), p. 4; Forsyth (1985), pp. 89–91. The automatic revolver's mechanical features and criminal (dis)utility are discussed in chapter 3 at notes 95–97 and accompanying text.

31. Forsyth (1985), p. 90.

32. Ibid., p. 91.

33. New Zealand Police, "Background," pp. 2–3; Charles I. H. Forsyth, "Education Favoured for Firearms Safety," *Otago Daily Times,* February 28, 1991, p. 8; Charles I. H. Forsyth, March 1, letter to the author, 1988; Forsyth, March 8, 1990; Forsyth (1985), citing New Zealand Police, *Firearms Registration in New Zealand* (unpublished, Support Services Directorate, 1982).

34. New Zealand Police, "Background," p. 3; Forsyth, March 8, 1990.

35. New Zealand Police, "Background"; Forsyth (1985), p. 93.

36. "Gun Law No Barrier to Criminals," *New Zealand Herald,* April 28, 1983, p. 17.

37. Forsyth, *Firearms in New Zealand* (Wellington, New Zealand: New Zealand Deerstalkers' Association, 1977), pp. 14–15 [hereinafter "Forsyth, (1977)"].

38. Forsyth (1977), pp. 18–19.

39. New Zealand Police, *Background,* p. 3.

40. Ibid., pp. 3–4.

41. "Gun Law No Barrier to Criminals," p. 17.

42. *Firearms Registration,* cited in Forsyth (1985), p. 122.

43. Remarks of Inspector Neville Cook, in *Proceedings of the International Shooting Sports Symposium,* pp. 14–15.

44. New Zealand Police, *Background,* pp. 4–7.

45. "An Act to consolidate and amend the law relating to firearms and to promote both the safe use and the control of firearms and other weapons," enacted by the General Assembly of New Zealand November 29, 1983, § 24 [hereinafter: "Arms Act"]; New Zealand Police, Arms Code (Upper Hutt: Wright and Carman, n.d.), p. 13.

Despite the "shall be issued" statutory language, the applicant bears the burden of satisfying the issuing officer that he is entitled to a license, and bears the burden of proving to the appeals court that the officer's initial denial was incorrect. The police and the court may both consider hearsay evidence against the applicant. *Police* v. *Cottle,* 1 N.Z.L.R. 268 (High Court, Dunedin, 1986). The New Zealand system contrasts with the Canadian one, where the police bear the burden of proving that a long-gun license denial was correct. See chapter 4, note 53 and accompanying text.

46. Arms Act, § 27.

47. The Arms Regulations 1984, Order in Council, May 14, 1984, § 13 [hereinafter "Arms Regulations"].

48. Arms Act, § 40.

49. Arms Act, § 26.

50. Arms Act, § 34. Owners of pistols or restricted weapons must also notify an Arms Officer of provisions made for safe custody of the gun during the move. Ibid.

51. Arms Act, § 39.

52. J. David Fine, *An Agenda for Reform of the Firearms Laws* (Nedlands, Western Australia: University of Western Australia Faculty of Law, 1988), pp. 30–31.

53. Arms Regulations, First Schedule, p. 11; Bob Badland, letter to author, December 7, 1989.

54. "New Zealand Eases Firearms Restrictions," *Gun Week,* September 7, 1984, p. 1; A. G. McCallum, Inspector, Arms Co-ordinator, Official Letter, March 6, 1984.

55. Forsyth, March 8, 1990.

56. Arms Act, § 21.

57. Arms Act, § 29.

58. Arms Code, p. 43.

59. Alan Trist, Executive Director New Zealand Mountain Safety Council, letter to Hon. Peter Tapsell, Minister of Police, April 6, 1989, appendix B.

60. Arms Regulations 1984, enacted May 14, 1984 (1984/121), §§ 19–22 [hereinafter "Arms Regulations"].

61. Arms Act, § 36.

62. Arms Code, p. 43.

63. Traffic Regulations, 1976.

64. Arms Act, § 17.

65. Arms Code, p. 43; Forsyth (1985), p. 97; Forsyth, March 8, 1990. A mortar is a small, short cannon that loads from the muzzle and fires projectiles a short distance at very steep angles.

66. Arms Act, § 4.

67. Arms Regulations, § 5. While the United States government does not require reporting, some states and cities do.

68. Arms Regulations, § 5(c)(5) (New Zealand); 27 Code of Federal Regulations § 178–179 (U.S.).

69. "New Zealand Eases," *Gun Week,* September 7, 1984, p. 1.

70. John Osborne, *Handguns and Police in New Zealand 1840–1990* (Te Awanga, New Zealand: South Pacific Armoury, 1990), p. 2.

71. "New Zealand Eases," p. 1; Proceedings of the International Shooting Sports Symposium, Wellington, N.Z., October 25, 1980 (New Zealand Mountain Safety Council, 1981).

72. Badland, "Firearms Safety Education in New Zealand," in *Proceedings of the International Shooting Sports Symposium.*

The N.Z.M.S.C. is funded in part by the government's Lotteries Commission, and in part by the state-owned Accident Compensation Corporation. New Zealand Mountain Safety Council, *Firearms Safety Training Scheme* (October 1987); Bob Badland, letter to author, December 7, 1989.

73. Forsyth (1985), pp. 2, 121.

74. Ibid., p. 21.

75. Arms Regulations, § 16.

76. New Zealand Police, *Do's and Don'ts for Firearms Users* (4-page brochure, n.d.); New Zealand Mountain Safety Council, *Lock Away Firearm, Bolt, Ammunition, SEPARATELY!* (one-page flyer, n.d.).

77. Ibid.

78. Arms Regulations, § 23.

79. Graham Nugent, "Hunting in New Zealand: Survey Results" (Christchurch, New Zealand: Forest Research Institute, November 1989), p. 8.

80. New Zealand Shooters Rights Association, undated one-page flyer.

The courts seem to be hostile to self-defense. In one case, a man and his son shot an enraged neighbor who was charging at them with a metal bar on their own property. The son was convicted of manslaughter, and the appeals court chastised the family for arming itself in response to the neighbor's repeated violent threats. *Regina* v. *Dwight,* 1 N.Z.L.R. 160 (Court of Appeal, Wellington, 1989).

81. Forsyth (1985), p. 26.

82. Arms Regulations, § 12. In-person New Zealand Mountain Safety Council lectures are the most common type, of course, although an applicant may instead complete the correspondence course offered by the Technical Correspondence Institute. Federation of Mountain Clubs of N.Z., *Bulletin* (no. 99, September 1989), p. 14.

83. Forsyth (1985), p. 157.

84. Ibid., p. 15.

85. National Safety Council, *Accident Facts 1988 Edition* (Chicago: National Safety Council, 1988), pp. 13, 24. In 1985, there were 1,649 fatal gun accidents in the United States, out of a total of 93,457 fatal accidents. The number of children killed was ages 0–4: 43; ages 5–9: 58; ages 10–14: 177; ages 15–16: 109.

86. New Zealand Police and New Zealand Mountain Safety Council, *Beginning with Airguns* (Wellington, Government Printer, 1986), p. 2.

87. In *Billy Hook Goes to Manuka Lodge,* young Billy learns essential gun-safety rules. Home from the lodge, he goes target shooting with his father. See also, New Zealand Police and New Zealand Mountain Safety Council, *Gun Safety with Billy Hook* (n.d.).

88. Arms Code, p. 33.

89. O. F. Dixon, *Review of Firearms Legislation: Report to the Minister for Police and Traffic* (Perth, Australia: Government Printer, 1981), cited in Forsyth (1985) p. 121.

90. Ibid.

91. Charles I. H. Forsyth, "The Reduction of Firearms-Related Injuries in New Zealand," speech delivered at *Firearms Control: How do We Reduce Firearm-Related Injuries in N.Z.?* symposium sponsored by Public Health Association of New Zealand, Dunedin, August 15, 1991; Charles I. H. Forsyth, "Firearms Statistics," *New Zealand Guns,* January/ February 1992, p. 6.

92. Peter Maxwell, "The New Arms Bill," *New Zealand Guns,* January/February 1992, p. 2.

93. Tim Murphy, "Big NZ Arsenal," *Otago Daily Times,* May 16, 1989, p. 3; Forsyth (1985), p. 116, citing Heylen Research Center, *Firearm Consumer Research* (Wellington, 1983), and *New Zealand Official Yearbook* (Wellington: Department of Statistics, 1984); Nugent, p. 6; Bob Badland, letter to author, December 7, 1989; Forsyth (1985), pp. 116–17, citing P. Stirling, "The Right to Shoot," in *New Zealand Listener* (Broadcasting Corporation of New Zealand, May 28, 1983), and J. Leigh, "Why More Women Should Know What to Do with a Gun," *New Zealand Women's Weekly,* July 4, 1983, pp. 34–35.

Before rifle registration was abolished, 280,000 people owned 460,000 registered rifles. The number of shotguns is impossible to estimate with precision, since they were not usually individually registered. When a permit to procure a shotgun was still necessary, about 100,000 were extant. Forsyth (1985), p. 116.

Approximately 42,500 people belong to one of New Zealand's sporting shooting organizations. Forsyth (1985), p. 103; Forsyth, "Membership of Sport Shooting Clubs in New Zealand (1989)," *Otago Firearms Coalition Newsletter,* n.d.

94. Graham Nugent, "Hunting Firearms in New Zealand—A Survey" (unpublished paper), pp. 1–2.

95. Forsyth (1985), pp. 135–36.

96. New Zealand Police Department, *Project Foresight,* p. 5.

97. Forsyth (1985), p. 67. In 1988, there were 28 gun homicides. Police Commissioner John Jamieson, Report to Police Minister Richard Prebble, discussed in Hugh Barlow, "Rifle Concern Not Supported Say Police," *Dominion Sunday Times,* March 18, 1990, p. 3.

98. Forsyth (1985), p. 31.

99. Ibid., p. 68.

As in the U.S., blunt instruments (such as bottles) are likely to be used against a victim, while deadlier weapons (such as firearms and knives) are less likely to be used, since their intimidation value suffices to make a victim submit. Forsyth (1985), pp. 40–41, citing M. J. Kun, *Criminal Violence* (unpublished, 1977).

Also as in the United States, the majority of homicide offenders know their victim. Forsyth (1985), p. 52, citing Department of Justice, *Crime in New Zealand* (Wellington: Government Printer, 1968).

100. Based on a report of the 48 firearms crimes in 1981 where the offender was caught. New Zealand Police, *Firearms Registration in New Zealand* (1982).

101. Bureau of the Census, *Statistical Abstract of the United States, 1988* (Washington, D.C.: Government Printing Office, 1987), pp. 802–803. The Australian rate was 11.5, and the American rate 12.2.

102. Forsyth (1985), p. 83.

103. Erwin Stengel, *Suicide and Attempted Suicide* (England: Pelican, 1970); *Statistical Abstract of the United States, 1989.* See chapter 2, note 211.

104. Forsyth (1985), p. 81.

105. Arms Act, § 60.

106. Arms Act, §§ 60, 61. The current provisions re-codified existing standards.

107. Arms Act, § 61(3).

108. Comment, "Legislation," *New Zealand University Law Review* 9 (1980): 194.

109. Arms Act, § 66; *Bright* v. *Police,* [1971] N.Z.L.R. 1016 (Supreme Court, Hamilton).

110. Colin Greenwood, letter to author, November 24, 1989.

111. New Zealand Police Department, *Project Foresight,* p. 8.

112. Forsyth (1985), p. 151, citing Heylen Research Centre.

113. Inspector John Meads, national firearms co-ordinator, quoted in Dominic Andrae, "New Zealand Criminals' Armoury Alarms Local Police," *Police Review,* March 17, 1989. (Despite the headline, only one administrator was "alarmed." The rest of the police hierarchy saw no threat.)

114. New Zealand Mountain Safety Council, *Bulletin No. 32: Selecting a Firearm,* p. 2.

115. Arms Code.

116. Arms Act, § 18.

117. "Review of Rifle Imports," *Otago Daily Times,* March 28, 1989.

118. Dominic Andrae, "New Zealand Criminals' Armoury Alarms Local Police," p. 24; "Review of Rifle Imports," *Otago Daily Times,* March 28, 1989, p. 24.

119. Hugh Barlow, "Rifle Concern Not Supported Say Police," *Dominion Sunday Times,* March 18, 1990, p. 3.

120. "Weapons Ban Justified," *The Southland Times,* June 27, 1990.

121. Police National Headquarters, "Police Ban Semiautomatics," news release, June 25, 1990.

122. "Self Loading Rifle Hysteria," *Guns Review,* September 1990, p. 639.

123. Police National Headquarters, "Police Ban Semiautomatics," news release, June 25, 1990. The import ban only applied to semi-automatic rifles with a military-style look, and to a few shotguns. Semi-automatic handguns, which were re-legalized by the reforms of the previous decade, were not affected.

124. Dene Mackenzie, "Rush to Buy Last Semi-automatic Rifles," *Otago Daily Times,* June 29, 1990; *Woods and the Practical Shooting Institute* v. *Police,* [1991] N.Z.L.R. (High Court) (Tipping, J.) ("The absolute ban was beyond the commissioner's powers and therefore invalid.").

125. Police Complaints Authority, "Aramoana—The Police Complaints Authority Report," *Otago Daily Times,* December 21, 1991, p. 10; Michael Holland, "Survivors to Bury Dead as Memories Stalk Streets," *New Zealand Herald,* November 17, 1990, section 1, p.1; "Mental Maze of a Mass Murderer," *New Zealand Herald,* November 17, 1990, section 2, p. 1; "Gunman on Rampage," *Otago Daily Times,* November 14, 1990, p. 1; "Hours of Terror End," *Otago Daily Times,* November 15, 1990, p. 1; "Gunman Called 'Kill Me' as He Rushed Police," *Otago Daily Times,* November 16, 1990, p. 1; " 'Don't Shoot Me' Wounded 4-Year-Old's Plea," *Otago Daily Times,* November 16, 1990, p. 2; Cadmus, "Aramoana Horror," *Guns Review,* February 1991, p. 110. Gray's other guns included a single-shot .22 Winchester rifle with a silencer, a single-shot .22 Vickers rifle, a semi-automatic .22 Squires Bingham rifle, a semi-automatic SKS 7.62 x 39mm rifle, and an air rifle. Police Complaints Authority.

New Zealanders call massacres such as Aramoana "amok" killings. "Amok" is a Malay word referring to a person who tears through a village using a machete to kill anyone he can find. The last "amok" killing before Aramoana occurred during World War II, when a man refused to surrender his rifle in order that it to be given to New Zealand's army.

126. Richard Boock, "Room for Improvement to Gun Laws, Says Expert," *Otago Daily Times,* November 17, 1990, p. 3.

127. *Newsletter* (New Zealand Shooters Rights Association), p. 5 (November 28, 1990, meeting with N.Z. Shooters Rights Assoc.). It is estimated that there are about 10,000 semi-automatic rifles privately owned in New Zealand. Ibid., p. 6. Semi-automatics constituted about 20 percent of all firearms sold in New Zealand in the 1980s. Charles I. H. Forsyth, letter to Commissioner of Police, June 27, 1991, p. 1.

128. Office of the Minister of Police, Arms Amendment Act 1991 (draft proposal). Other proposed controls included a ban on the mail-order sale of firearms; a ban on ammunition sales to persons who do not possess a firearms license; and a requirement that firearms licenses include a picture of the licensee. Some gun-rights advocates objected to the last measure because it could create incentives to make licenses renewable periodically, rather than valid for life, as they are presently.

The proposed restrictions on semi-automatics, which the gun groups opposed, included a special exemption for the TV and movie industry. The Otago/Southland Firearms Coalition suggested eliminating the special film exemption, because "the emergence of *Rambo*-type films" is seen as "providing consistently poor role models." Otago/Southland Firearms Coalition, letter to Commissioner of Police, May 15, 1991.

129. The founder was the late Mervyn Stanley, a recent immigrant from Britain. New Zealand Shooters Rights Association, *Newsletter* (December 1990), p. 2.

130. Kay Sinclair, "Judge Urges Firearms Ban," *Otago Daily Times,* May 17, 1991, p. 1 ("strong gun lobbies"); "The Situation Now," *Newsletter* (New Zealand Shooters Rights Association), April 1991, p. 3 (Jamieson quote, from March 8, 1991, article in *Auckland Star*).

131. Arms Amendment Act 1991, Hon. John Banks.

132. John Banks, Minister of Police, "Holmes Programme," November 29, 1991, television transcript reprinted in "Television," *New Zealand Shooters Rights Association* (newsletter), January 1992, p. 13.

133. For some examples of the New York City Police Department's flagrant abuse of the statutory licensing procedure, see *Shapiro* v. *Cawley,* 46 A.D.2d 633, 634, 360 N.Y.S.2d 7, 8 (1st Dept. 1974) (ordering N.Y.C. Police Department to abandon illegal policy of requiring applicants for on-premises pistol license to demonstrate unique "need"); *Turner* v. *Codd,* 85 Misc. 2d 483, 484, 378 N.Y.S.2d 888, 889 (Special Term Part 1, N.Y. County, 1975) (ordering N.Y.C. Police Department to obey *Shapiro* decision); *Echtman* v. *Codd,* no. 4062-76 (N.Y. County) (class action lawsuit that finally forced Police Department to obey *Shapiro* decision).

Also: *Bomer* v. *Murphy,* no. 14606-71 (N.Y. County) (to compel department to issue blank application forms for target-shooting licenses); *Klapper* v. *Codd,* 78 Misc.2d 377, 356 N.Y.S.2d 431 (Supreme Court, Special Term, New York County) (overturning refusal to issue license because applicant had changed jobs several times); *Castelli* v. *Cawley, New York Law Journal,* March 19, 1974, p. 2, col. 2. (Applicant suffered from post-nasal drip, and repeatedly cleared his throat during interview. His interviewer "diagnosed" a "nervous condition" and rejected the application. An appeals court overturned the decision, noting that the applicant's employment as a diamond cutter indicated "steady nerves.")

134. *Motley* v. *Kellogg,* 409 N.E.2d 1207 (Ind. App. 1980).

135. Statement of Robert F. Mackinnon, on behalf of the Coalition of New Jersey Sportsmen, before the House Committee on the Judiciary, on *Legislation to Modify the 1968 Gun Control Act,* part 2, serial no. 131, 99th Congress, 1st and 2d sess., February 27, 1986 (Washington, D.C.: Government Printing Office, 1987), p. 1418.

136. Donald B. Kates, "On Reducing Violence or Liberty," *Civil Liberties Review* (August/September, 1976), p. 56.

7

Jamaica: War on Guns

"I shot the sheriff, but I swear it was in self-defense."

—Bob Marley, "I Shot the Sheriff"

When Jamaica gained sovereign status in the British Commonwealth in 1962, the nation enjoyed one of the better economies and one of the strongest traditions of democracy in the Third World. Yet for the lower classes of Jamaican society, the necessities of life—including social justice—were in short supply, and the people themselves in a condition of servitude.

Even in the early 1970s the Jamaica Tourist Board still promised foreign visitors beach cottages "equipped with gentle people named Ivy or Maud or Malcolm who will cook, tend, mend, diaper, and launder for you. Who will 'Mister Peter, please' you all day long . . . admire you when you look 'soft' (handsome), giggle at your jokes and weep when you leave."[1] Advertisements in the *New York Times* suggested: "Rent a Villa, Rent a Car, Rent a Nanny."[2] In the years that Jamaica struggled to establish social justice for people named Ivy or Maud or Malcolm—people who dubbed themselves "the sufferers"—Jamaica would also implement the most severe effort at gun control ever attempted by a democratic nation. The structure of democracy was much more fragile in Jamaica than in the other nations discussed in this book. The relative weakness of the democracy would make the strict gun-control experiment possible, and would impact how the control was carried out.

THE VIOLENCE BEGINS

From the first years of Jamaican independence, the nation was troubled by violence. The machete had a long and brutal history as the favorite murder instrument. Yet, all in all, the crime level seemed tolerable.

Around 1964, Jamaica started to export large quantities of "ganja" (marijuana) to the United States. Because the export business was illegal, the merchants could not rely on the government to guard the ganja fields and protect shipments from hijackers. Accordingly, the exporters imported guns from the United States, in exchange for ganja. Groups of unemployed youths were hired as enforcers. Gangs such as Skull, Zulu, Vikings, Dirty Dozen, and others terrified the citizenry and the police.[3]

At the same time, politicians were finding that alliances with armed gangs could be useful. Michael Manley, a future prime minister, conducted his trade union activities while surrounded by formerly unemployed "bad men."[4] Leading gangsters called "top-rankings" and their gangs of impoverished youths took up the offers of political bosses, and allied with political parties. Top-rankings helped a party control the streets, and thereby prevent opposition political activity, such as voter registration. By frightening away poll-watchers, top-rankings and their gangs facilitated vote fraud.[5]

In December 1965, electoral warfare broke out with Molotov cocktails and revolvers. The lower-class Central and West Kingston neighborhoods of Denham Town, Trenchtown, Back O'Wall, and Moonlight City suffered the first gun battles.[6] The next May, armed gangs of unemployed West Kingston youth violently raided opposition political strongholds. That summer, the government bulldozed West Kingston shanties to make way for a public housing project called Tivoli Gardens. Pro- and anti-government gangs turned West Kingston into a battleground.[7] The project was eventually built, and filled with supporters of the Jamaica Labour party (JLP) loyal to Michael Manley's arch-enemy, Representative Edward Seaga, himself a future prime minister.[8]

The *Daily Gleaner*—the leading newspaper and an ally of the JLP—engineered peace talks in August, but negotiations broke down. Thus far, most of the violence was confined to willing combatants; nevertheless, upper-class fears intensified with rumors that the director of public prosecutions had told the police to eschew "interference" in political violence.[9]

The JLP government declared a state of emergency in October 1966 and raided the headquarters of the JLP and the opposition People's National party (PNP). Violence abated until the state of emergency was lifted in November.[10] The next year, just before the national elections, the Farquharson Institute, a public policy organization, reminded voters: "This is your country. Jamaica doesn't belong to a couple hundred half-wits with revolvers."[11]

The arming of top-rankings and their followers was not the official policy of either the JLP or PNP. Still, some functionaries within each party continued to equip their gang supporters. By the late 1960s, firearms were the primary weapon of the top-rankings. By the early 1970s, the lower-class gangs, armed by the political establishment, had learned nonpolitical uses for the gun and were beyond the establishment's control.[12] Explains one observer: "After this short introduction to politics within the system, some of these gangs reverted to ordinary criminal activities, others turned to more revolutionary politics and some used their newly acquired guns to terrorize the rest of society, particularly, the national bourgeoisie."[13]

Having begun to climb in the mid-1960s, the murder and robbery rates soared. Criminal use of weapons rose even faster, and the gun replaced the machete as the most popular instrument for committing murder.[14] By 1973 Jamaicans were comparing their country to Vietnam. Not only were people afraid to go out, they were afraid to stay in. In many sections of Kingston, family members would take turns keeping watch on the home during the night. Robbers and rapists shot their victims, perhaps to eliminate them as witnesses. Crime witnesses were killed, or intimidated into not testifying for the Crown.[15] The homicide rate, while extremely high, was below the rate in the most violent American cities in the same period.[16]

SOCIAL CONTROLS COLLAPSE

In 1972 a rising popular mood demanding social justice swept Michael Manley and his People's National party into office. The lower-class Rastafarian community strongly supported Manley.[17] Manley's campaign used a 45 rpm record by reggae star and Rastafarian Bob Marley promising "Power for the people, if they need it; Power for the people, let them have it." The song segued into Michael Manley's voice: "I warn this country we are heading for an explosion because the faith of the people is running out. . . . Only a just society can be viable because it is only justice that endures in human affairs."[18]

Prime Minister Manley's first years in office consisted of moderate reformism; then the government took a hard turn toward state socialism in 1974. One element of the change was a strict approach to gun control, prompted by shocking new levels of violence.

In March 1974, Leo Henry, a businessman prominent in sports and charitable organizations, was shot. The business community was outraged, and the *Daily News* headline demanded: "Get the Guns."[19] Two days later, Montego Bay attorney Robert Stennet was shot in his home. Shortly thereafter, gunmen murdered Montego Bay attorney Paul Ritz-Ritson, the chairman of National Sports.[20] The Jamaican Council of Churches, the Council of Human Rights, and the Young Lawyers Association called for surprise roadblocks to search cars for illegal guns.[21]

A large segment of public opinion attributed the murders to the breakdown in respect for social institutions and for the upper classes.[22] The nation was ready to sacrifice liberty to obtain safety, and so was Michael Manley.

"RADICAL SURGERY FOR A GRAVE DISEASE"

Prime Minister Manley told the Jamaican people that the nation needed "radical surgery for a grave disease." He insisted, "There is no place in this society for the gun, now or ever."[23] The House of Representatives rapidly approved a set of strict new laws:

The Dangerous Drugs Act increased penalties for trade and possession of ganja. Under the supervision of Security Minister Eli Matalon, the government gave the United States Drug Enforcement Agency broad powers to conduct an anti-marijuana offensive—Operation Buccaneer—in Jamaican territory. Eventually, the United States was carrying out full-scale military maneuvers in rural areas.[24]

The Juveniles Act authorized use of firearms in reform schools by Correctional Officers. Children over the age of fourteen who were accused of gun offenses were made subject to the same justice process as adults.

The Suppression of Crime Act allowed warrantless searches of homes, persons, and motor vehicles in designated areas. The act, which periodically expires, was repeatedly renewed by the House of Representatives and remains in force today.

The Gun Court Act and the Firearms Act essentially outlawed private ownership of guns and ammunition.[25] The upper and middle class had long controlled the gun-permitting process, and therefore had a virtual monopoly on legal gun ownership. Licensed gun owners were allowed to retain their guns, but not to accquire new ones.[26]

According to the Gun Court Act and the Firearms Act, once defendants were arrested for a gun offense—even possession of a single bullet—they were to be detained, tried, and sentenced within a seven-day period, all in the same compound in Kingston. The special stockade, the "Rehabilitation Centre," was like a concentration camp, with barbed wire, watchtowers, and machine guns. Painted blood red, it was meant to be a prominent and harsh reminder of the fate of gun criminals. Kingston residents called it "Stalag 17."[27]

Gun possession trials were closed to the public, and the court had the power to keep the names of witnesses confidential and to bar publication of any news of the trial, except for the name of the accused, the charge, the verdict, and the sentence.[28] There was no bail and no jury, except in capital cases.

Persons caught in the presence of another with a gun were themselves considered guilty.[29] Many American states have similar rules; those persons found in the passenger compartment of a car that contains an illegal gun are presumed to have illegally possessed the gun. It is up to the defendants to prove their innocence by demonstrating that they were not aware of the gun.[30]

Despite some severe restrictions on due process, the Gun Court did not have an excessive conviction rate. To the contrary, over one-third of all people tried by the court were acquitted—a very high percentage for serious crime prosecutions. The number of people held without trial, however, was always large. Defendants were usually imprisoned for two years before being tried.[31] The Manley government used emergency powers to detain some people even after they had been formally acquitted. Moreover, convictions based on uncorroborated, malicious accusations were common.[32]

Once convicted, a Gun Court prisoner faced indefinite detention.[33] In 1976, the Judicial Committee of the Privy Council (the highest legal body of Commonwealth nations) ruled that the indefinite detention provision was unlawful. Prime Minister Manley and the House of Representatives revived the Gun Court by making any conviction of a gun offense—including possession of a single bullet—mandatory life imprisonment.[34] One American tourist who accidentally brought a .22 calibre bullet to Jamaica—in a suitcase borrowed from his uncle—was speedily imprisoned, and escaped a life sentence only because of the intervention of the U.S. ambassador.[35]

The same day that the Jamaican House of Representatives revived the Gun Court, Manley banned all protest marches and demonstrations.[36]

From the first day of the Firearms Act, gun scenes in movies and on Jamaican Broadcasting Corporation television were censored. Movie attendance declined; karate film imports surged.[37] The objective of censorship and of the harsh gun "rehabilitation" prison was to delegitimize firearms criminals as popular heroes, and to crush the notion that gun violence was exciting.[38]

With the warrant requirement abolished, the police raided and searched from house to house, shanty to shanty in West Kingston. Police corruption and political loyalties prevented the searches from rooting out gunmen.[39] Curfews were enforced in selected areas, starting with the upper-class section of downtown Kingston, with no one allowed in or out after dark.[40]

All of these measures involved crime control from above—crime control carried out by the government. The People's National party also created neighborhood watch groups called the "Home Guard," whose members had the authority to make arrests. They were accompanied on patrols by police officers, and were often given handguns to carry while on patrol. (Many of the police by this point were patrolling with automatic weapons.[41]) In the long term, the Home Guard became not an independent base of popular power, but an appendage of the police, "with members becoming fixtures at the local police station, drinking rum or playing dominoes with the boys."[42]

While black power publications did not support civil disarmament, the middle- and upper-class press had called for strict gun legislation long before the government finally acted. Newspapers urged citizens to surrender their guns, but only 150 people did so.[43] Clerics told their parishioners that God commanded them to turn in persons who owned guns.[44] Some sportspersons had been allowed to retain their guns with a license; the *Daily Gleaner* complained that there were 24,000 licensed guns still in the possession of citizens, and those citizens refused to give up their firearms.[45] Despite the calls to take guns away from current license holders, the minister of national justice and security stated that he would allow one gun per household.[46]

In the early months of the Gun Court Act of 1974, the Jamaican Bar Association, as well as some newspaper columnists, began to object that the act had been passed hastily and that fair trials would not be possible.[47] The bar association president complained that the gun court would "humiliate" the principles of law.[48]

The main designer of the Gun Court Act and rehabilitation center had been the president of the World Federation for Mental Health, Dr. Michael Beaubrun. He insisted that the gun court was a scientifically designed approach to behavioral change. He warned that amendments suggested by lawyers—who did not understand psychology—would undermine the act. The *Daily Gleaner* praised the "fire brigade red" painting of the gun stockade as "a psychological weapon" emphasizing the seriousness with which the government viewed firearms crimes.[49]

A citizens' group from Montego Bay asked the government to supply all citizens with guns and to teach them how to use the firearms. The Jamaica Rifle Association warned that the disarming of law-abiding citizens would eventually create a crime wave that would make the current one pale to insignificance. The newspapers scoffed at the claim.[50] The people agreed with the newspapers. As of June 1974, public opinion supported the Gun Court Act by a margin of 86 percent to 9 percent.[51]

The firearms ban, the Gun Court, and other severe measures were an immediate and spectacular success. In the year before the gun court there were 124 murders involving guns. In the year following the act there were 55. In the first six months of the act murders in which guns played a part were 78 percent below the previous year's rate; in the second six months the figure was 22 percent below. Nongun-related murders (i.e., with machetes) rose from 99 to 144. Overall, murder of all types declined 14 percent.[52]

Shooting with criminal intent fell by 52 percent in the first six months, and 20 percent in the second six months,[53] but then returned to its old level and stabilized there. Robbery with a gun declined 28 percent over the law's first year. Nongun-related robbery fell 58 percent in the first six months, then rose 30 percent in the second six months.[54] Larceny increased slightly, while breaking and entering and assaults showed no significant change.[55] Overall, the gun court benefits were strongest in urban areas.[56]

By the fall of 1974, only a few months after the act took effect, the Farquharson Institute was calling for its repeal. The institute argued that act had only a short-term effect on criminals and that its continuation would weaken government credibility.[57]

Gun-control supporters complained that the due process criticisms of the gun court were undermining its effectiveness. One *Daily Gleaner* columnist mocked "the criminals, wooly-minded do-gooders, and petty fogging attorneys" who opposed the law. The Jamaica Union of the Travellers Association called for the death penalty for gun crimes, and so did Education Secretary Robotham.[58]

By early 1975, violence was up and the murders of important businessmen again became sensational stories. The government blamed criticism of the Gun Court and a breakdown in public confidence in the police. Malcolm Short, a columnist for the *Daily Gleaner,* retorted that greater police action, and not the gun law, had produced the drop in gun crime. He sneered at curfews and helicopter patrols as "tranquilizers for the middle class." The government's attempt to blame crime on people who criticize the Gun Court, wrote Short, had made society "want to arrest six-year-olds without ID cards, establish vigilante groups, bring the Army into the Police, and substitute Gun Court justice for our traditional justice."[59] By the end of 1975, crime was as bad as ever, and most of the public wanted the Gun Court eliminated. Stories of police brutality circulated in Kingston.[60]

POLITICAL VIOLENCE WORSENS

The political parties continued to use guns. One factory worker explained, "Political parties gave guns to people in certain neighborhoods, strongholds of the opposition party, to stir up trouble; in order to create unhappiness and perhaps gain a political foothold."[61] Lamented another Jamaican: "During elections one side declares war on the other. If they thought you were on the other side, they would kill you; not so much in the rich areas, but in the poor areas. You see we can't afford to pay off the police for protection."[62]

Again, while politically connected gunmen were given weapons for political purposes, they also used the weapons for nonpolitical criminal offenses.[63] Some of the poor chose "to live by the gun," as the only way to survive economically, to get "free money."[64] One teenager explained:

> Well, it was called free money because most of the time you would do nothing and you would still collect it. . . . Sure I knew what I was doing was illegal and I knew there was a chance that I would be caught and sent to Gun Court for the rest of my life. But I needed money and I was told that I needed to do what they were telling me to do so that the government would change and things would get better.[65]

(Apparently this youth was working for Seaga's opposition JLP party.) One disgruntled executive of the Jamaica Labour party resigned to protest the party's giving firearms to "half starved and maltreated youngsters and encouraging them to take up a life of crime and violence in an effort to win the election."[66]

Socialist historian Michael Kaufman attributes almost all of the initiation of gun violence to Seaga and the JLP; during the years of Manley's PNP rule, Seaga and the JLP used violence to destabilize the government.[67] Kaufman adds that for uneducated youths, there were only three ways out of the ghetto: the first, to become a reggae star as Bob Marley had; the second, to become a gunman—a "ranking" and eventually a "top-ranking" (rankings still lived in the ghetto, but enjoyed material wealth); the final way out of the ghetto was in a coffin.[68]

As the 1976 election approached, firearms crime continued to escalate, worsened by the intense crowding of Kingston, where three-quarters of the population lived in a fifteen-block area, and many of the apartment buildings were public housing projects controlled by one of the two parties.[69] In this election, individuals not in the political gang system were also victims.[70] Automatic weapons became common, and the CIA, under then-director George Bush, was reported to be attempting to destabilize Manley's pro-Castro government.[71] Violent crime in the Corporate Area (Kingston and environs) was rampant by 1976. The combination of crime, economic problems, and worries about Manley's commitment to democracy led to large-scale emigration by skilled workers and professionals.[72] Almost every household contained a machete for self-defense.[73] As the violence intensified, the Manley government declared a state of emergency and arrested Jamaica Labour party members, who were said to be plotting a coup.[74] A leading radio station was declared a "social institution" and expropriated by the government.[75]

Prime Minister Michael Manley proudly campaigned for re-election on his program of "heavy manners" (discipline) to promote social justice.[76] "We Know Where We're Going," promised his PNP campaign slogan.[77] The Jamaican people gave Manley and the PNP 57 percent of the vote, the biggest landslide in Jamaican history.[78] For the most part, the urban poor stuck with the PNP. Those poor people who had jobs had seen their real incomes rise. PNP patronage had benefitted some, and all the poor, thanks to Manley, had enjoyed a rush of self-confidence and self-worth.[79]

THE PEOPLE BETRAYED

Crime grew worse and worse. A November 1978 poll of the Kingston area showed that one of three adults had been robbed that year. Low- and high-income areas were equally likely to be victimized. In rural areas, the robbery rate was one person in five each year.[80]

People organized spontaneous vigilance organizations. Youth groups would set up roadblocks. Older men would spend the night playing dominoes to pass the time during the watch.[81]

In 1978, gang leaders Claudie Massop and Bucky Marshall negotiated a truce, defying their patrons Seaga and Manley.[82] Bob Marley played a peace concert in April at the National Stadium. He brought Michael Manley and Edward Seaga onto the stage and lifted their hands together in the air to the tune of "One Love" in a triumphant gesture of peace before 85,000 people. But by the summer the truce was unraveling.[83]

The economy, in part because of CIA destabilization, teetered near collapse.[84] The urban poor turned against Manley. Graffiti told the story:

- "IMF = Is Manley's Fault" (Jamaica was in a serious debt conflict with the International Monetary Fund.)

- "The Poor Can't Take No More"

- "Joshua = Judah" (During the 1972 campaign, Manley had adopted the name "Joshua," and brandished the "rod of correction," a cane given to him by Rastafarian deity Haile Selassie, emperor of Ethiopia.[85])

- "Deliverance Is Near," promised Edward Seaga's Jamaica Labour party.[86]

The problem with firearms violence was the problem with the economy: the slogan "power to the people" had been twisted into "power to the government." Historian Michael Kaufman, while critical of the JLP for arming the political gangs, blames the ruling PNP for its loss of public support. He rebukes Manley's party for believing that "state management could do the job for the people . . . rather than initiating and leading a process within which the sufferers would become the actual producers of their own political destiny."[87] Kaufman explains that Manley never intended to change the power relationship between the people and the government. What Manley intended was a more responsive government, more concerned with the needs of the people.[88] But the Rastafarians and the rest of the lower class thought they were getting "power for the people," in the words of Manley's 1972 campaign song. As Manley later put it, the poor voted "for a change which we symbolized more than specifically promised."[89]

For example, the land reform program, Project Land Lease, was carried out not by peasants with government support, but by the government for the good of the peasants. Writes Carl Stone: "Project Land Lease has preserved the traditional pattern of small peasant political impotence and total subjugation to the hegemony of the Civil Service technocracy. . . . [T]here is a total lack of belief [of the technocracy] in democratic decision making whereby persons affected should have a say in policies that affect them."[90] Frustrated with the government, tens of thousands of peasants turned to "land capturing"—moving onto and farming land that was not being used by large landowners.[91] Kaufman calls the government "rigidly hierarchical and paternalistic."[92]

Likewise, the Manley government's effort to stem violence was carried out through repressive, top-down criminal laws, or through drawing citizens into government service as auxiliary police. There was no effort to help citizens operating outside of the direct chain of command of the government to resist or prevent crime.

Violence in the 1980 election reached the worst levels ever. Nine hundred and thirty-three Jamaicans were killed that year, 556 by gunmen, and 234 by security forces. (In other words, about a quarter of that year's homicides were perpetrated by the police or the army.) By 1980, a majority of the armed forces and police, along with the rest of the country, opposed Manley. Junior Minister of Security Roy McGann was surrounded in his car by a JLP mob and shot.[93]

THE GUN COURT'S BANKRUPTCY

Some Rastafarians had protested against Manley soon after he implemented Operation Buccaneer (the American drive to eradicate ganja) and the rest of the campaign against guns and marijuana. Max Romeo's song "No Joshua No" pleaded with Manley to change his course.[94]

Likewise, Peter Tosh and Bob Marley had told the Rastas to resist Manley's anti-ganja drive and other anti-democratic measures: "Get up, stand up, stand up for your rights."[95] While many Rastas stuck with Manley during the 1976 election, as they—and other members of the lower class— saw innocent youths hauled off to Gun Court, saw the promises of "power to the people" cynically inverted, and watched the socialist economy collapse, they turned against the Gun Court, and eventually Manley.[96]

At Manley's request, a United Nations team evaluated the Gun Court system. The study "found people in cages. We also tasted the food there. It was not fit for human consumption. . . . Moreover, the Gun Court placed tremendous pressures on other aspects of the criminal justice system."[97]

Criminologist William Calathes states that the Gun Court Act targeted only middle- and lower-level political players, plus apolitical street criminals. The connections of the top-ranking gunmen with one party or the other kept them safe. Politicians would often go to a police station to secure a gunman's release. Calathes concludes that the act was "aimed at the population which contributed the least to the high level of firearm crime."[98]

The act made it easy for lower-class people to be accused and convicted, since they could not afford private counsel, and public counsel was scarce. A defense attorney reported: "When you come into the Gun Court as an accused man, the judge makes you know that you are the lowest form of human life in the whole world. I think them call you boy. They call you this and that and push you around in court. You are guilty in the minds of all the judges."[99]

Hardly any Gun Court defendants were middle or upper class.[100] However, the conviction (and prohibition of press reports thereof) of two real estate developers following a police raid on their homes and offices helped turn the more prosperous elements of society against the act.[101]

NEW GOVERNMENT, OLD REPRESSION

Edward Seaga's Jamaica Labour party had initially supported the Gun Court Act, including the mandatory life sentences. Eventually, though, the JLP came to the public conclusion that the act should be repealed. In the violent 1980 election, a landslide brought Seaga and the JLP to power.[102] But instead of repealing the Gun Court Act, party officials used the Manley laws to carry out political vendettas in retribution for those that had been inflicted on them.[103] The cynicism that Rastas felt about Babylon's "politricks" and its "shitstem" was reinforced.

As of December 1982, life sentences had been meted out to 460 persons. That month, 400 of them went on an internationally publicized hunger strike to demand a review of the Gun Court.[104] Another 1,782 people were detained while awaiting trial.[105]

The Gun Court neared administrative collapse due to the length of trials, the limited resources of the government ballistics expert, non-attendance by civilian and police witnesses, inefficient process servicing of witnesses, frequent adjournments, lack of police transport vehicles, and shortage of defense attorneys.[106]

In 1979, a government advisory committee had recommended that the Gun Court be phased out.[107] A few years later, during Seaga's tenure, a select committee of the House of Representatives proposed revision of the court. A minority of the committee, along with Jamaican legal groups, called for more extensive reforms or outright repeal.[108] The House of Representatives repealed the mandatory life sentence and allowed judges in most parishes to exercise discretion whether or not to send a case to the Gun Court.[109] During the reign of the Gun Court, from 1974 to 1983, approximately 1,200 individuals had been convicted.[110]

Political violence continued as before. Rival groups of JLP supporters, some attempting to leave the party, fought a days-long battle with M16s and other automatic weapons in West Kingston in 1984. Some of the gunmen were caught, tried, and acquitted in 1987 when one witness recanted her testimony and other witnesses failed to appear. JLP supporters greeted the acquittal by marching through downtown Kingston, firing shots, and sending other people fleeing in panic.[111]

As the 1987 election neared, one wire service reported: "[W]hile both major parties continue to make pious appeals for an end to gun violence, politicians are arming gangs to prepare for the bitter tribal wars that usually accompany elections. . . . Police Commissioner Herman Rickets yesterday confirmed that many illegal guns were coming into the island through a big guns-for-marijuana trade."[112] The rate of homicides per 100,000 population had risen from 4.6 per in 1954 to 13.6 in 1974, and up to 22.6 in 1987.[113] The Privy Council interpreted the amendments to the Gun Court Act still to allow prosecutors virtually unlimited discretion to bring a case in Gun Court.[114]

Some of the gang leaders, no longer needed by their political patrons, headed north to Miami or Brooklyn to found drug-dealing posses. According to Delroy "Uzi" Edwards, a convicted murderer and posse boss, "It was the politicians who first brought guns" into his Kingston neighborhood. "Seaga," he says, "is the biggest gangster of them all."[115]

To the extent that Edward Seaga (denounced as "CIAga" by his political opponents) and his American patrons introduced armed warfare into Jamaican political life, the invasion of America by the Jamaican posses is poetic justice, as the Frankenstein gun monster has turned on its creator.

Yet the story of Jamaican guns and gun control is more than the story of the perfidy of Edward Seaga and the CIA. It is the sad story of a nation whose political elite chose a seemingly expedient form of repression as an alternative to empowering the sufferers.

At the worst, the gun laws were not simply a political distraction; they were an invitation to murder. The human-rights group Americas Watch analyzed Jamaican homicides in the early 1980s. About a third of homicides in those years were committed by the police. Indeed, in some years the rate of Jamaicans killed by police officers was higher than the rate of Americans killed by anyone. Although the police usually reported that the killings took place in a shoot-out with the victims, Americas Watch contends that the police were lying. Many of those killings, the human-rights group said, were deliberate killings of personal enemies of particular policemen. Bob Marley's song "I Shot the Sheriff" told the story of a young man on the run after shooting a sheriff in self-defense.

Even the slayings of genuine criminal suspects were often not really in a shoot-out, but rather deliberate police executions; innocent bystanders or people mistaken for the criminal suspect were frequently murdered.[116] The public fervor over guns—initiated by the middle-class press and augmented by the government—provided a handy excuse for homicidal police officers. The statement that a victim of police homicide had been killed in a shoot-out was readily accepted without investigation, even when no gun was recovered from the victim.[117] The excesses of police violence, claimed Americas Watch, drove Jamaica to new heights of violence, because the police example legitimated violence in the eyes of both criminals and ordinary citizens.[118] The Jamaican gun laws have deprived Jamaicans of the most effective means of self-defense against ordinary street criminals, and of self-defense against a far more dangerous group of criminals—those who wear police uniforms and employ the authority and resources of the government in furtherance of their crimes. The failure of gun control in Jamaica—where police kept their guns and used them against the populace—contrasts with the much greater levels of obedience to gun control in Britain, where the police were unarmed when gun control was instituted.

CONCLUSION

Studies of the Firearms Act and the Gun Court have been nearly unanimous in their condemnation. Criminologist William Calathes writes that while the Gun Court Act did not lower the rate of firearm-related crime, the people were expected to believe in the act's deterrent value, even as both political parties used firearm violence, and the Gun Court Act itself, for their own political objectives.[119] Calathes continues: "Although the Act professed to deter firearm crime, it eliminated fundamental constitutional rights and sharply refocused the attention of the people from the social and economic reasons for crime to the more modest hope of deterring firearm crime."[120]

"The social control functions of the Gun Court Act cannot be over-emphasized," he says. "The Act always had the potential for social control due to its oppressive legislative form since its immediate cause was the legislators, the agents of political crime, and its true purpose was not the resolution of firearm crime but, more immediately, the balance of class forces, economic necessity, and ideological pressures."[121] Calathes argues that Jamaica faced "contradictions between relatively developed political tendencies and relatively backwards economic forces." The government reconciled the contradiction "by highly developed skills of political management," in propagating myths of the deterrent value of oppressive legislation.[122]

C. Thomas Surridge, a former commissioner of corrections in Jamaica, and Paul Gendreau, a consultant psychologist for the Corrections Department, complain that "the Gun Court drama diverted Jamaican society from the more difficult tasks of revising the judiciary and constitutional processes to deal with some of the social problems that contribute to crime in the country."[123]

Although a long-term failure, Gun Court did cut gun crime for about a year. A Jamaican government minister opines that the reason the Gun Court had shown at least some success was that on an island, a concentrated effort and psychological climate to fight a particular type of crime could be created.[124]

Another study argues that while the overall package of repressive legislation had a limited but positive short-term impact on crime, the gun law had been relatively ineffectual even regarding the initial drop in crime, except in changing firearms homicides into homicides with other weapons. The authors suggest that most illegal guns had remained in circulation, and that more important than the laws to reduce the absolute number of guns had been the laws providing enhanced sentences for crimes committed with firearms, as opposed to other weapons.[125]

A United Nations criminologist asserts that the Gun Court aggravated crime, because it alienated the people from the government. The severe criminal sentencing in Jamaica, especially the life sentencing for guns, "through its punitiveness contributed more than anything to the deterioration of the crime situation."[126]

Dudley Allen, also a commissioner of corrections for Jamaica, notes that the crime wave had taken place during a period of rising national prosperity. He blames the epidemic on the "breakdown of traditional social roles and institutional controls over the behavior of young and old alike." (Canada, Great Britain, and America also experienced crime increases in that period, under similar social conditions.) Commissioner Allen argues that all the criminal laws of 1974 were selectively enforced. He accuses the police of beating and torturing confessions out of defendants, and condemns police conduct for perpetuating the nation's cycle of violence. Many of the Gun Court prisoners vehemently asserted their innocence, and many of them came "from the underprivileged or disadvantaged classes or followers of the Rastafarian subculture." Allen pleads for "warm compassion and a preparedness to tolerate diversity" as the key to dealing with Jamaica's criminal offenders.[127]

Jamaica's crime wave came with the breakdown of controls over behavior, and gun control could not cure it. Having examined five Commonwealth democracies, we have seen that social and cultural controls, rather than gun ownership or gun controls, best explains variations in crime rates. Gun control in Commonwealth nations is accompanied by violations of American standards of civil liberties—particularly searches and seizures without probable cause. In Jamaica, where traditions of civil liberties and democracy were less strong, the new gun laws were enforced with horrible violations of human rights.

Data from the other Commonwealth countries have in general failed to show a correlation between the severity of gun control and the year-to-year crime rate. Jamaica, on the other hand, enacted its gun laws in conjunction with a number of other repressive criminal measures. These combined measures led to a spectacular drop in crime for several months; but within two years the crime situation was as bad as ever and growing worse.

The enforcement of the Firearms Act long after it had outlived its usefulness did more than waste limited police resources. The continuing focus on the act distracted the government into a "top-down" response to criminal violence, rather than a "power to the people" approach to the root causes of injustice and crime. Those root causes—including colonialism, poverty, and debt—are difficult for any nation to solve. The temptation to tackle what seemed to be a simpler problem—firearms possession—was understandable. Yet the focus on the "simple" problem had the effect, in the long run, of making the real problems of violence and social alienation all the worse.

Gun violence in Jamaica's capital is political, while gun violence in America's capital is drug related. In each case, the epidemic of violence at the center of power prompted an urgent determination to "do something." The "War on Drugs" has already prompted legislation that would confiscate millions of self-loading firearms and make possession of one such gun a ten-year felony offense.[128] Other proposed legislation bars the production of all rifles not specifically designed for hunting, under the theory that self-defense is not a legitimate reason for gun ownership. Legislation has been proposed to use registration lists to round up guns that would be retroactively banned.[129] A significant minority of Americans wants to ban all handguns, and a third of that group wants the ban enforced with house-to-house searches.[130]

The Jamaican experience should be a caution to those who back draconian gun laws. Severe gun control in Jamaica enjoyed near-unanimous initial support and was buttressed by a host of other strict criminal laws. But unlike Japan, the Jamaican government did not, and could not, ensure the success of gun control by taking control of society. That the great Jamaican experiment in gun prohibition ended in such abject failure should at least make other nations think twice before embarking on a similar path.

The political use of gun laws to distract attention from other issues is not unique to Jamaica. It will be recalled from our earlier discussions that the British instituted shotgun controls in the 1960s to divert the public from the death penalty, and in the 1970s, the Canadian government used gun control to forestall public clamor for the death penalty.[131]

Gun control costs no money yet it offers legislatures a quick and easy way to "do something." But as Jamaica illustrates, a government and nation that decide to "do something" about gun control may be distracted from the real work of social control. Indeed, the diversion of society from the real fight against crime by the offering of a gun-control panacea may be one of the most destructive, criminogenic effects of efforts to control guns.

Study of Japanese and Commonwealth gun control has produced little evidence that gun laws reduce gun crime. The political and social culture in which Japanese and Commonwealth gun controls thrive is a climate relatively hostile to American-style civil liberties and individualism. Only in New Zealand have police and gun owners learned how to live together and respect one another.

Of course, the fact that strict firearms laws have not accomplished much in other nations does not mean that the United States must reject the idea of gun control. The United States indisputably has a more serious crime problem, and hence a more serious gun problem, than almost all other democracies. Even if Japan and the Commonwealth do not provide us with handy gun-control roadmaps there is no reason America cannot work toward gun-control policies appropriate for its own unique culture.

To some partisans in the American gun debate, though, no form of gun control is acceptable. Gun advocates point to Switzerland as a peaceful nation where every household is armed with weapons of war. Yet in pointing to Switzerland, American gun advocates unknowingly make the case for gun control in America.

NOTES

1. Frank Taylor, *Jamaica—the Welcoming Society* (Kingston: ISER, UWI, 1975), working paper no. 8, quoted in Michael Kaufman, *Jamaica Under Manley: Dilemmas of Socialism and Democracy* (Westport, Conn.: Lawrence Hill and Co., 1985), p. 36.
2. Horace Campbell, *Rasta and Resistance* (Trenton: Africa World Press, 1987), p. 88.
3. Ibid., p. 111.
4. Ibid.
5. William Calathes, "Gun Control in a Developing Nation: The Gun Court Act," *International Journal of Comparative and Applied Criminal Justice* 14, no. 1 (Winter 1991), p. 324. [Hereinafter Calathes, "Gun Control."]
Calathes, a criminology professor at the Jersey City State College, is the leading American expert on Jamaica's firearms control experiment.
6. Kaufman, p. 114.
7. Calathes, "Gun Control," p. 324.
8. Kaufman, p. 113.
9. Calathes, "Gun Control," pp. 324–25.
10. Ibid., p. 325.
11. *Daily Gleaner,* October 15, 1967, quoted in Calathes, "Gun Control," p. 325.
12. Calathes, "Gun Control," p. 326.
13. Terry Lacey, *Violence and Politics in Jamaica 1960–70: Internal Security in a Developing Country* (Totowa, N.J.: Frank Cass, 1977), pp. 32–33.
14. Dudley Allen, "Urban Crime and Violence in Jamaica," in Rosemary Brana-Shute and Gary Brana-Shute, eds., *Crime and Punishment in the Caribbean* (Gainesville, Fla.: Center for Latin American Studies, 1980), p. 31.
15. Calathes, "Gun Control," pp. 327–28. The cases involving constitutional challenges to the draconian Gun Court (discussed below) took judicial notice of the crime problem. *Regina* v. *Moses Hind, R.M.C.A. no. 41–44 (1974); Regina* v. *Trevor Jackson, R.M.C.A. no. 53 (1974).
16. E. B. Mann, "Jamaica's Anti-gun Fiasco," *Field and Stream,* September 1975, p. 20. In 1973, the homicide rate in Kingston was 27. The rates in some of the worst American cities for the year were New York City, 21.4; Los Angeles, 17.7; Cleveland, 41.3; Detroit, 40.1; and Washington, D.C., 32.8.
17. Rastafari is a biblically derived religion popular with the Jamaican lower class. Its tenets include the divinity of former Ethiopian Emperor Haile Selassie, the wearing of hair in "dreadlocks" to help communicate with God, the sacramental use of "ganja" (marijuana), and the corruption of the nonreligious world ("Babylon"). See generally, Ras-j-Tesfa, "The Living Testament of Rasta-for-i," (no city or publisher, 1980).
18. Kaufman, pp. 71–72.
19. *The Daily News,* March 15, 1974, quoted in Calathes, "Gun Control."
20. Calathes, "Gun Control," p. 328.
21. Paul Gendreau and C. Thomas Surridge, "Controlling Gun Crimes: The Jamaican Experience," *International Journal of Criminology and Penology* 6 (1978), p. 45.
22. Calathes, "Gun Control," p. 328.
23. "Stalag in Kingston," *Time,* September 23, 1974, p. 55.
24. Campbell, p. 109. Prime Minister Manley's decision to allow the United States to intervene apparently backfired, as Jamaicans later downplayed his (probably accurate) claims that the CIA was trying to remove him from office.
25. Gun Court Act 1974, enacted April 1, 1974.

26. Author's conversation with William Calathes, February 20, 1992.

27. Edward Diener and Rick Crandall, "An Evaluation of the Jamaican Anticrime Program," *Journal of Applied Social Psychology* no. 1 (March 1979), pp. 135–46; "Stalag in Kingston," *Time,* September 23, 1974, p. 55; Colin Greenwood, quoted in Donald B. Kates, Jr., ed., *Why Handgun Bans Can't Work* (Bellevue, Wash.: Second Amendment Foundation, 1982), p. 16; Hanley, "Gun Control Laws Vary," *Poughkeepsie Journal,* April 19, 1981, p. 9A; William Calathes, "Criminal Justice and Underdevelopment: A Case Study of the Jamaican Gun Court Act," *Journal of Caribbean Studies* 6 (Autumn 1988), p. 328.

28. Gun Court Act § 13(1); Allen, p. 31.

29. Calathes, "Gun Control," p. 335; Calathes, "Criminal Justice and Underdevelopment," p. 327.

30. *Ulster County Court of New York* v. *Allen,* 442 U.S. 140 (1979).

31. *Bell* v. *Director of Public Prosecutions,* [1985] 1 A.C. 937, [1985] 2 All E.R. 585, [1985] 3 W.L.R. 73, [1985] Criminal Law R. 738 (Privy Council) ("a delay of two years in the Gun Court is a current average period of delay in cases in which there are no problems for witnesses.")

32. Calathes, "Criminal Justice and Underdevelopment," pp. 329, 349.

33. Gun Court Act, §§ 8(2), 22(1) and (2).

34. The case history: *Henry Martin,* in which Jamaica's Appeals Court declared the act constitutional by a 2-1 vote (R.C.M.A. no. 41–44 [1974]); *Trevor Jackson,* in which Jamaica's Appeals Court then declared the act unconstitutional by 2-1 vote. The Attorney General appealed to the Privy Council of England, and announced that the act would remain in effect pending appeal—even though the most recent court ruling had declared the act unconstitutional. *Hinds & Others* v. *The Queen* [1976] 1 All E.R. 353, [1976] 2 W.L.R. 366 (Privy Council). The Judicial Committee of the Privy Council declared the indefinite sentence aspect of the law unconstitutional because it vested authority to terminate the sentence in nonjudicial officers, rather than committing sentencing decisions to the judiciary. The committee also objected to the Resident Magistrates being seated in the Full Court Division. Jamaica repaired this problem by reassigning gun cases to Supreme Court judges. The constitutional cases are discussed in L. G. Barnett, *The Constitutional Law of Jamaica* (New York: Oxford University Press, 1977), p. 313, cited in Calathes, "Gun Control," p. 330. *See also* Gendreau and Surridge, pp. 56, 59, n.22.

35. "American Tourist Freed in Jamaica," *Gun Week,* October 8, 1976.

36. Michael Manley, *Jamaica: Struggle in the Periphery* (London: Writers and Readers, 1982), p. 149. Manley's advisors believed that the violence was perpetrated by well-paid opposition gunmen.

37. Gendreau and Surridge, p. 58, n. 9.

38. Calathes, "Criminal Justice and Underdevelopment," p. 328.

39. Kaufman, pp. 113–15.

40. Gendreau and Surridge, pp. 45–46.

41. Kaufman, p. 116.

42. Ibid. Kaufman blames the pro-JLP police for excluding Manley's PNP supporters.

43. Gendreau and Surridge, pp. 45–46; William Calathes, letter to author, November 1989.

44. Mann, p. 22.

45. Gendreau and Surridge, p. 47, citing *Daily Gleaner,* April 8, 1974.

46. Gendreau and Surridge, p. 47; William Calathes, letter to author, November 1989.

47. Gendreau and Surridge, p. 46.

48. Ibid., p. 47.

49. Ibid., p. 48; the *Daily Gleaner,* June 13, 1974; William Calathes, letter to author, November 1989.

50. John Maxwell, a leading political columnist, noted that guns in civilian hands were stolen at the rate of one per day. Guns crimes with stolen rich people's guns were then perpetrated against poor people who could not afford their own gun, and whom the police did not effectively protect. Gendreau and Surridge, pp. 46–47.

51. Gendreau and Surridge, p. 48,

52. Ibid., p. 50. Gendreau and Surridge argue that the increase in nongun-related murders, which partially offsets the decline in gun-related murders, was not statistically significant.

53. Ibid., pp. 50–51.

54. Ibid., p. 51.

55. Ibid., p. 55.

56. Ibid.

57. Farquharson Institute, quoted in the *Daily Gleaner,* October 15, 1974, cited in Calathes, "Criminal Justice and Underdevelopment," p. 330.

58. Gendreau and Surridge, pp. 48–49.

59. Ibid., p. 49, citing the *Daily Gleaner,* various issues in February and March 1975. Malcolm Short's proposed alternative to the Gun Court was an improved criminal justice and police system, which he admitted would probably never be enacted because it might "smack of going soft on criminals, of idealism . . . liberalism."

60. Calathes, "Criminal Justice and Underdevelopment," p. 331.

61. Calathes, "Gun Control," p. 333.

62. Ibid., pp. 333–34.

63. Ibid., p. 335.

64. Ibid., p. 334.

65. Ibid.

66. Kaufman, p. 117, citing *Daily Gleaner,* June 19, 1976.

67. Kaufman makes it clear that he is a partisan of Manley, and wished Manley's socialist experiment success. In analyzing the fall of the Manley government Kaufman suggests that next time, the press be more closely regulated. "Whatever problems existed in Jamaica, press freedom was not one." Kaufman, p. 190.

68. Ibid., pp. 114–15. One 18-year-old told this story to a magistrate: "De money I go for. I son [my son], I son sick." The man burglarized a house to look for money and for food for the baby. Confronted by the homeowner, the man panicked, and hacked him to death with a machete. In tears the man continued his story: "I beat down. De world beat I down. I not want to steal. De jobs, they have none for I. I dant [don't have] de clothes to look nice and de good food for I son, but it not I to have? Why not for I? Kill? I not try to. I not." *Washington Post,* September 6, 1976, quoted in Kaufman, p. 19, n.20.

69. Courtland Milloy, "Political Gang Warfare in Jamaica Kills 100 in 6½ Months This Year," *Philadelphia Inquirer,* July 18, 1976 (*Washington Post* service).

70. Calathes, "Criminal Justice and Underdevelopment," p. 331.

71. Laurie Gunst, "Johnny-Too-Bad and the Sufferers," *The Nation,* November 13, 1989, p. 567.

72. Kaufman, p. 95.

73. Ibid., p. 112.

74. Ibid., p. 117, citing *Daily Gleaner,* June 30, 1976.

75. Ibid., p. 227.

76. Ibid., p. 125, citing *Daily Gleaner,* December 14, 1976.

77. Ibid., p. 127.

78. Ibid., p. 125.

79. Ibid., p. 127.

80. Carl Stone, *The Political Opinions of the Jamaican People (1976–1981)* (Kingston: Blackett Publishers, 1982) (pamphlet), p. 68, cited in Kaufman, p. 178.

81. Kaufman states that most of the attacks were against PNP communities, and chastises the PNP for being so slow to respond. He quotes a PNP Youth Organization leader who complained that while the JLP would attack with automatic weapons, the PNP victims would have only a .38 snub-nose revolver with which to fire back. Kaufman, pp. 178–79.

82. Gunst, p. 568.

83. Kaufman, p. 149.

84. Ibid., p. 183.

85. Ibid., p. 71.

86. Ibid., p. 187.

87. Ibid., p. 183.

88. Ibid., p. 72.

89. Ibid.

90. Carl Stone, "Tenant Farming Under Capitalism," in C. Stone and A. Brown, eds., *Essays on Power and Change in Jamaica* (Kingston: Jamaica Publishing, 1976), p. 133, quoted in Kaufman, p. 99.

91. Kaufman, p. 100.

92. Ibid., p. 173. Kaufman notes that Jamaicans refer to the state in a singular, personified, paternal form, as in "Government announced a new programme yesterday."

93. The previous three years, annual killings were between 334 and 383. Kaufman, pp. 188–89.

94. Quoted in Campbell, p. 137.

95. Campbell, p. 137.

96. Calathes, "Gun Control," p. 333; Campbell, p. 114.

97. The study was reported in Gerhard Mueller, Crime Prevention and Criminal Justice Branch/Center for Social Development and Humanitarian Affairs, *Crime and Justice in Jamaica* (unpublished report, 1977). The quote is from Prof. Calathes's interview with Mueller, November 11, 1984, quoted in Calathes, "Criminal Justice and Underdevelopment," p. 345.

98. Calathes, "Gun Control," p. 334.

99. Calathes, "Criminal Justice and Underdevelopment," p. 339.

100. Ibid., p. 333.

101. Ibid..

102. Seaga's party won 51 of 60 seats in Parliament, in an election in which 80 percent of the electorate voted. Jo Thomas, "After Bullets and Ballots, Jamaican Hopes Rise," *New York Times,* November 2, 1980, p. 2.

103. Mark Kurlansky, "Countdown in Jamaica," *New York Times Magazine,* November 27, 1988, p. 93; Calathes, "Criminal Justice and Underdevelopment," pp. 348–49.

104. "Jamaican Inmates Fast to Urge Gun Law's Repeal," *Daily Breeze* (Torrance, Calif.), September 11, 1982, p. A5 (Associated Press); Calathes, "Criminal Justice and Underdevelopment," p. 350.

105. Advisory Committee of the Ministry of Justice, *Report of the Advisory Committee of the Ministry of Justice in Relation to the Gun Court Legislation* (Kingston: 1983), cited in Calathes, "Gun Control," p. 332.

106. Calathes, "Gun Control," p. 332.

107. Calathes, "Crime and Underdevelopment," p. 16 (the report was published in 1983).

108. Calathes, "Criminal Justice and Underdevelopment," p. 350.

109. Ibid., p. 352.

110. Calathes, "Gun Control," p. 330. Criminal justice statistics do not explain what happened to the approximately 750 persons who were convicted during the course of the act, but were not in prison in 1983. The most reasonable deduction is that some were released early, and some completed their life sentence by dying in prison.

111. "Jamaica: Warning Issued on 'Incipient Anarchy,' " *Inter Press Service,* July 8, 1987. The *Daily Gleaner* reported that in 1985, 1986, and the first half of 1987 combined, the police seized 600 guns from criminals, most of them illegally imported. Desmond Allen, "Jamaica: Armed Gangs, Drug Dealers, and Angry Citizens," *Inter Press Service,* August 13, 1987.

112. "Jamaica: Armed Gangs, Drug Dealers, and Angry Citizens." See also Kaufman, p. 148.

113. Numbers from "Jamaica: Tributes to Peter Tosh, Concern Over Violence," *Inter Press Service,* September 14, 1987.

114. *Da Costa* v. *Regina,* [1990] 2 W.L.R. 1182 (Privy Council).

115. Gunst, pp. 567–68.

116. Americas Watch Committee, *Human Rights in Jamaica* (New York: Americas Watch Committee, September 1986).

117. Ibid.

118. Ibid.

119. Calathes, "Gun Control," pp. 331–39.

120. Ibid., p. 338.

121. Ibid.

122. Calathes, "Criminal Justice and Underdevelopment," p. 354.

123. Gendreau and Surridge, p. 55.

124. Ibid., p. 60, n.43.

125. Diener and Crandall, pp. 141–42.

126. Mueller interview, quoted in Calathes, "Criminal Justice and Underdevelopment," p. 344.

127. Dudley Allen, pp. 56–57.

128. One such bill was introduced by Represenative Howard Berman (D-California) in early 1989, H.R. 669.

129. Proposed in Illinois, during the summer of 1989.

130. Paul Blackman, "Civil Liberties and Gun Law Enforcement," paper presented at the American Society of Criminology, Cincinnati, 1984, p. 2. Blackman was reporting the results of private polls conducted for the National Rifle Association by Decision-Making Information, a polling firm headed by conservative pollster Richard Wirthlin.

131. The British and Canadian chapters contain more details, chapter 3, text at note 117; and chapter 4, text at note 39.

8

Switzerland: The Armed Society

Was bruucht e rëchte Schwyzerma
nes subers Gwehrli a der Wand,
nes heiters Lied fürs Vaterland?

(*What does a true Swiss man need?*
A clean little gun on the wall
And a cheerful song for the Fatherland)[1]

Ever since American gun banners began touting the advantages of gun control in Britain and Japan, American gun owners have been pointing to Switzerland. Like Israel, Switzerland distributes weapons of war to its civilians, has a high rate of gun ownership—especially of assault weapons—and yet suffers virtually no gun crime. Professor Richard Harding of Australia outlines what he calls the "Swissraeli Syllogism":

1. Switzerland and Israel are heavily armed;
2. Switzerland and Israel have very low crime rates;
3. Therefore guns do not cause crime.[2]

The American anti-gun lobby, though, rejects the "Swissraeli syllogism." Indeed, according to Handgun Control, Inc.'s analysis, Switzerland is one of the more advanced gun-controlling societies. Gun registration is universal, and permits and background checks are required for handgun ownership.[3] In the eyes of Handgun Control, Switzerland is merely one more nation with sensibly strict gun laws and a low crime rate. Is Switzerland a model

278

for widespread gun ownership, as the American gun lobby asserts? Or for strict gun control, as the American anti-gun lobby asserts? Before deciding which side of the American debate Switzerland supports—if it supports any side at all—let us look at what the gun laws in Switzerland really require, and at what role guns play in Swiss culture.

ARMS FOR INDEPENDENCE

Like America, Switzerland won independence in a revolutionary war fought by an armed citizenry. In 1291, three cantons (states) began a war of national liberation against Austria's Hapsburg Empire. In legend, the revolution was precipitated by William Tell, although there is no definitive proof of his existence.[4] While America's war for independence took eight years, Switzerland's took two centuries. In the battles of Morgarten (1315), Sempach (1386), and Näfels (1388), the three original cantons, joined by five others, won effective autonomy. Over the next century, the Swiss militia liberated most of Switzerland from Austrians and other foreigners. In 1499, Hapsburg Emperor Maximilian I granted the Swiss almost total independence.

The ordinary citizens who composed the Swiss militia used the assault weapons of the time: pikes, halberds (lengthy pole-axes), swords, and cross-bows.[5] Known as fervent warriors in close combat, the Swiss were reluctant to adopt firearms.[6] They did eventually adopt a new gun, the harquebus, a short smoothbore matchlock that rested on two sticks, which absorbed some of the recoil. Military historian Robert O'Connell ties the successful fighting tactics of the Swiss with their democratic values:

> Poor but independent, not serfs but free peasants and burghers, the Swiss naturally gravitated towards each other fighting in close formation. . . . [T]he spirit of equal participation, more than obedience, drove the Swiss formations into battle.[7]

Swiss officers fought in the front lines with everyone else. The Swiss peasants paid no attention to courtly traditions of noble combat and surrender. One historian notes that they "fought with a fierceness that appalled con-temporaries."[8] The German scholar Trithemius complained that the Swiss were presumptuous and hostile to princely authority.[9] "They want to become Swiss" was the German expression for persons who desired independence.[10]

In Machiavelli's analysis of the state, the control of force was the central issue. His books *The Prince, The Art of War,* and *The Discourses on the First Ten Books of Titus Livius* theorized that when the central gov-ernment controlled the power of the sword, the government would tend toward absolutism. The best security of a free state, wrote Machiavelli, was a well-organized and well-armed citizenry, protecting freedom from dangers both domestic and foreign.[11] Machiavelli drew on the Swiss as an example of an armed and free people, crediting Switzerland's universal armament with protecting it from invasion. The Swiss were, he wrote, "*armatissimi e liberissimi*"—most armed and most free.[12] He noted that harquebus was used effectively by the Swiss "who, being poor and wishing to live in freedom, were and are obliged to resist the princes of Germany, who, being rich, are able to keep horses."[13] Swiss tactical innovations with firearms and pikes demonstrated that citizen infantry armies could defeat aristocratic cavalry and armor.[14] The evolution of fighting technologies had been important in the Swiss victories, but the most important factor was motivation of the free Swiss militia.[15]

The independent Swiss kept on fighting, both against neighboring nations and against other cantons. At the battle of Marignano in 1518, the Swiss infantry, which had gained a reputation for invincibility, was destroyed by adroit use of French artillery and cavalry.[16] The Swiss abandoned their efforts to control Milan and other parts of Italy, signed a "perpetual alliance" with France, and adopted a policy of armed neutrality.

For the next four centuries, the great empires of Europe rose and fell, swallowing many weaker countries. Russia and France both invaded Switzerland, and the Austro-Hungarian Empire remained a special threat. The empire's most skillful diplomat, Prince Metternich, contemplated invading Switzerland during the 1830s because it served as a refuge for liberals seeking to overturn the European empires.[17] But Switzerland almost always retained its independence. The Swiss policy was "*Prévention de la guerre par la volonté de se défendre.*" (Prevention of war by willingness to defend ourselves.) The whole able-bodied male population was enrolled in the militia; and, until 1874, they were required to provide their own weapons.[18]

During World War I, both France and Germany thought about invading the northern Swiss lowlands to attack each other's southern flank.[19] In World War II, Hitler wanted the Swiss gold reserve, and needed free communications and transport through Switzerland to supply Axis forces in the Mediterranean. Official German maps pictured Switzerland as part of the Reich.[20] But when military planners looked at Switzerland's well-armed citizenry, mountainous terrain, and civil defense fortifications, Switzerland lost its appeal as an invasion target.[21] While two world wars raged on all sides, Switzerland enjoyed a secure peace.

Armed neutrality did not mean that Switzerland withdrew from world affairs. Having defeated Austria's mercenaries, the Swiss became mercenaries themselves. The well-armed Swiss were often hired for fighting by European monarchies which did not trust their own citizens with guns. The mercenaries provided Switzerland with one of its main sources of revenue, and an outlet for overpopulation.[22] *Pas d'argent, pas de Suisses* (no money, no Swiss) was the saying.[23] From the fifteenth to the nineteenth century, two million Swiss soldiers fought in foreign armies.[24]

The Swiss developed only a weak central government, leaving most authority in the hands of the cantons or lower levels of government. Since power was, quite literally, in the hands of the people themselves, it made sense for government authority to be concentrated at a level close to the people. The tradition of local autonomy helped keep Switzerland from the bitter civil wars between Catholics and Protestants that devastated Germany, France, and England. That Switzerland escaped the religious wars is all the more remarkable considering that John Calvin's Geneva and Huldrych Zwingli's Zürich were the hotbeds of the Protestant Reformation. Zwingli and Protestant Zürich came into conflict with the "Forest Cantons" (the original three that led the Swiss revolution, plus Lucerne), which preferred to keep their Catholicism. Zwingli imposed a trade embargo on the Catholic Forest Cantons; war broke out in 1531; Zwingli was killed at the battle of Kappel; and the Reformation's advance in Switzerland was halted.

For the next century, climaxing with the Thirty Years War of 1618–1648, most of the rest of Europe tore itself apart in religious war. Germany in particular was devastated. Yet the Swiss stayed neutral; unable to agree on religion, the Swiss cantons simply governed themselves, and stayed relatively free of religious warfare.[25]

Although a Swiss aristocracy eventually came to dominate the country, Switzerland remained a comparatively democratic nation, surrounded by monarchies or other dictatorships. In *The Prince,* Machiavelli explained that a "republic armed with its own citizens is less likely to come under the rule of one of its citizens than a city armed with foreign soldiers. . . . The Swiss are extremely well armed and are completely free."[26]

The revolution that had begun in France in 1789 spread throughout Europe in the next half century. Every major industrial city in Europe witnessed at least one attempt at popular revolution. In 1847 and 1848 the European revolution climaxed, and liberals throughout Europe rose up against aristocratic rule. Only in Switzerland did they succeed, taking control of the whole nation following a brief conflict called the Sonderbund War. (Total casualties were ninety-eight.)[27] Civil rights were firmly guaranteed, and all vestiges of feudalism abolished.[28]

During the worldwide industrial upheaval in 1918, Switzerland had a general strike; but even then, the well-armed Swiss remained pacific. Not one striker employed the military rifle that he kept at home.

Despite the hopes of German reformers, the Swiss did not send their people's army into Germany in 1848 to assist popular revolution there,

or anywhere else, ever.[29] The next decade, after the German revolution
had failed, autocratic Prussia considered invading Switzerland, but decided
the task was impossible.[30]

MODERN MILITARY SERVICE

Today, military service for males is universal. At about age twenty, every
Swiss male goes through 118 days of recruit training in the *Rekrutenschule.*
Because units are organized by canton, they are usually linguistically homogeneous.[31] (Switzerland has four official languages: German, French, Italian,
and Romansch; German is the native tongue of about 70 percent of the
population, French of about 20 percent, and Italian of about 4 percent.
Romansch, a name for several Romance dialects, is the native language
for less than 1 percent of the Swiss.[32]) Nevertheless, the army experience
plays an important role in building national unity. Carol Schmid, an American scholar analyzing Switzerland's successful creation of a multilingual
society, observes:

> The recruit school brings the young men of the country together at a
> very impressionable age. Besides informal civic instruction which stresses
> the Swiss national position and attitude, it introduces Swiss, from whatever
> linguistic group, to the varied landscape of their country, and gives them
> something in common to talk about for the rest of their lives.[33]

Even before required training begins, young men (and women, too) may
take optional courses with the Swiss Army's military rifle. They keep that
gun at home for three months, and receive six half-day training sessions.

From age twenty-one to thirty-two, a Swiss man serves as a "frontline"
troop in the *Auszug,* and devotes three weeks a year (in eight of the twelve
years) to continued training. By the Federal Constitution of 1874, military
servicemen are given their first equipment, clothing, and arms. After the
first training period, conscripts must keep rifle, seventy-two rounds of sealed
ammunition, gas masks, and other equipment in their homes until the end
of their term of service.[34] Enlisted men are issued fully automatic rifles,
and officers are given pistols.[35] Once a year, the man must demonstrate
his weapons proficiency on a rifle range, or spend three days in remedial
marksmanship instruction.[36]

From age thirty-three to forty-two, Swiss men serve in the *Landwehr*
(like America's National Guard, except that everyone belongs); every few
years, they report for two-week training periods. Finally, from ages forty-
three to fifty (fifty-five for officers), they serve on reserve status in the

Landsturm; in this period, they only spend thirteen days total in "home guard courses." Over a soldier's career he also spends scattered days on mandatory equipment inspections, and on required target practice. Thus, in a thirty-year military career, he spends a total of about one year in direct military service.[37] After discharge from service, the man is given a rifle, free from registration.[38] Starting in the 1994, the government will give ex-reservists full automatic rifles (although there is some discussion of down-converting them into semi-automatics). Officers are given their pistols at the end of their service.[39]

The Swiss government makes it easy for any adult, whether or not in the military, to learn how to use military weapons. When the government adopts a new infantry rifle, it sells the old ones to the public.[40] Three thousand shooting ranges give every Swiss an easy opportunity for target practice.[41] The army sells to arms "collectors" (usually former soldiers) a variety of machine guns, as well as anti-tank weapons, howitzers, anti-aircraft guns, and cannons. Purchasers of these weapons require a cantonal license, and the weapons are registered.[42] Thus, in a nation of six million people, there are at least two million guns, including 600,000 fully automatic assault rifles (more than in the whole United States) and half a million pistols.[43]

The government also subsidizes ammunition purchases. The Swiss are encouraged to buy military ammunition (7.62 and 5.56 mm for rifles, 9 and 7.65 mm Luger for pistols), which is sold at cost by the government, for target practice. About eighty million rounds of service ammunition are fired outside of military duty each year.[44] Nonmilitary ammunition for long-gun hunting, and .22LR ammo are not subsidized, but are subject to no sales controls. Nonmilitary, nonhunting ammunition more powerful than .22LR (such as .38 special) is registered at the time of sale by recording the buyer's name in a book.

Swiss military ammunition must also be registered if bought at a private store, but need not be registered if bought at a range. The nation's shooting ranges sell the overwhelming majority of ammunition. Technically, ammunition bought at the range must be used at the range, but the rule is barely known, and almost never obeyed. Switzerland allows the purchase of any type of ammunition, including hollow-point bullets.[45] The government maintains gunpowder production as a state monopoly.[46]

Besides subsidized military surplus, the Swiss can buy other firearms easily, too. While long guns require no special purchase procedures, handguns of military size (caliber larger than 6 mm) are sold at retail only to those with a purchase certificate issued by a cantonal authority.[47] A "firearms purchase certificate" is issued to every adult applicant who is not a criminal, mentally infirm, or otherwise unfit.[48] The gun is not registered. Thus, the assertion by the U.S. lobby Handgun Control, Inc., that "Switzerland and

Israel strictly control handgun availability," is more than a little inaccurate.[49] There is no real impediment to the Swiss buying any type of gun.

There are no restrictions on the carrying of long guns. Fifteen of Switzerland's twenty-six cantons, representing about 57 percent of the population, have permit procedures for carrying handguns, and the other half has no rules at all. There is no discernible difference in the crime rate between the cantons as a result of the different policies.

Thanks to a lawsuit brought by the Swiss gun lobby, ProTell, semi-automatic rifles require no purchase permit and are only registered by the dealer. Thus, the only long guns registered by the government are full automatics. (Three cantons do require collectors of more than five or ten guns to register them.) Gun sales from one individual to another are regulated in five cantons, and completely uncontrolled in all the rest.

Retail gun dealers must keep records of some over-the-counter gun transactions; transaction records are not reported to or routinely collected by the government. In Switzerland, purchases of hunting long guns and of small-bore rifles from dealers are not even recorded by the dealer. In other words, the dealer would not record the sale of .30-06 hunting rifle, but would record the sale of a .30-06 Garand, since the Garand was directly based on a military design. As in other countries, a gun's history or look rather than its function may determine the way it is regulated.[50]

"SWITZERLAND DOES NOT HAVE AN ARMY; IT IS AN ARMY."

The nation defended by responsible, trained civilians has been a political ideal in diverse locations: James Harrington's seventeenth-century England, Thomas Jefferson's eighteenth-century America, and Aristotle's Greece. The nation that has best maintained "a well-regulated militia" is Switzerland. Even in the early eighteenth century, when the British right to bear arms was flourishing, Whig political philosophers looked enviously at Switzerland's citizen militia.[51] Later, Adam Smith pronounced Switzerland the only place where the whole body of the people has successfully been drilled in militia skills.[52] Indeed, the militia is virtually synonymous with the nation.[53] As the Austro-Hungarian diplomat Metternich was once said to have remarked, "Switzerland does not have an army; it is an army."[54]

Fully deployed, the Swiss army has 15.2 men per square kilometer; in contrast, the United States has only .2 soldiers per square kilometer. Indeed, only Israel is denser with soldiers.[55] The Swiss citizen-army can start mobilization in the morning, and be ready for combat by the afternoon.[56] With only 1,500 full-time soldiers, the Swiss can mobilize 650,000 soldiers within twenty-four hours.[57] The mobilized Swiss citizen-army is twice as large as the entire United States army stationed in Europe.[58]

Militarized as Switzerland is, the army has no general during peacetime. The existence of an officer of such a rank except during a state of war would be considered a contradiction of democratic values.[59]

The military doctrine calls for making the aggressor's gains as costly and bloody as possible. Swiss fighters would retreat from the borders, and fight instead in the more defensible interior terrain. In the event the army and air force were destroyed, the doctrine calls for obstinate and bitter guerilla resistance.[60]

Since 1291, when the people's assemblies formed circles in the village squares, and only men carrying a sword could vote, weapons have been synonymous with citizenship. As a Federal Military Department spokesman said, "It is an old Swiss tradition that only an armed man can have political rights."[61] This tradition helps explain why the political and social emancipation of women has taken so much longer in Switzerland than in the rest of the Western world. (Women today have the same right to purchase firearms as men do.)[62]

To be sure, there are voices of opposition to the idea that the Swiss national identity should be primarily defined by militia service. In 1977, the Münchenstein Initiative proposed allowing citizens to choose social or hospital work over military duty, but was rejected at the polls, and in both houses of the legislature.[63]

As foreign threats recede, Switzerland, like other democratic nations, is beginning to question the importance of military strength. The generations that kept Switzerland armed, ready, and free during World War II and the most dangerous phases of the cold war were proud of their intensive, demanding national service. Such service was one part of "spiritual national defense." Today, one writer observes that young Swiss "are free of the porcupine mentality which was justified back then, but is a handicap now."[64] A 1989 referendum to abolish the army, sponsored by the six thousand-member "Group for Switzerland without an Army," lost by a wide margin, but did attract a substantial minority vote (although one commentator suggests that many of the anti-army votes came from people who expected the referendum to fail, but wanted to warn the army against excessive spending).[65]

The Federal Military Department has already begun a partial demilitarization of Swiss society. The service age will be reduced from fifty to forty-two, and eventually to forty. The department is considering shortening basic training.[66]

For now at least, Switzerland remains the nation of the well-regulated militia. There are provisions for conscientious objectors, but this group only numbers 0.2 of 1.0 percent of conscripts.[67] A current dictum explains the political rationale of an armed citizenry: "If weapons are a token of power, then in a democracy they belong in the hands of the people."[68] Or as another Swiss saying puts it: "If the government cannot trust the people, the people cannot trust the government."[69]

GUN CONTROL AND GUN-RELATED CRIME

Switzerland is not immune to pressures for gun control, although in Switzerland's case, much of the pressure comes from abroad. In 1978, Switzerland refused to ratify a Council of Europe Convention on Control of Firearms. Since then, Switzerland has been pressured by other European nations, which charge that it is a source for terrorist weapons.[70] Thus, in 1982, the federal government proposed barring foreigners in Switzerland from buying guns they could not buy in their own country (foreigners legally resident in Switzerland have the same rights to buy guns as Swiss citizens); and also extending the coverage of the licensing law to other weapons besides handguns, automatics, and artillery. Outraged Swiss gun owners formed a group called ProTell, named after national hero William Tell.[71] The next year, the Federal Council abandoned the gun-control proposal because "the opposition was too heavy," and suggested that the cantons regulate the matter.[72] A few months earlier, the Cantonal Council of Freiburg had already enacted such a law, by a one-vote margin. A popular referendum overturned the law the next year, by a 3 to 2 margin.[73]

Whatever the effect of Swiss guns abroad, they are a very small problem domestically. Despite all the guns, murder is only 15 percent of the American rate. Although equal to or slightly higher than the Japanese and English homicide rates, the Swiss rate is far below the Canadian, Australian, New Zealand, and Jamaican homicide rates, even though Switzerland has more guns per capita than all of them.[74] In 1987, there were fifty murders involving any type of gun.[75] To the extent that Swiss guns are used in crime, the weapon is usually a stolen pistol or revolver.[76]

In recent years, the overall gun-crime problem has not gotten worse. In 1991, for example, the number of homicides with guns declined to forty, out of ninety-nine total murders that year. Switzerland has, however, suffered several sensational mass murders with guns: in March 1992 (when a man killed six people in their homes), in May 1991 (when a businessman killed five family members and himself), and August 1990 (when a jeweler murdered five people and then shot himself).

Accordingly, there is some momentum for granting the federal government the power to regulate guns. Such a grant of authority to the federal government would have to be passed by both houses of the legislature, and then enacted by the people in a referendum.

Possible items in a new federal gun law could include: federalizing the handgun permit system created by the intercantonal agreement, putting semi-automatic rifles under a similar permit system, requiring a permit to carry a loaded handgun (ProTell is working to make issuance of the permit mandatory to all qualified persons, without proof of "necessity"), and placing some restrictions on purchases of guns by foreigners.

While the sensational killings in Switzerland, like those in Britain, do attract international media attention, it should be remembered that gun crime in both Switzerland and Britain is much rarer than in the United States.

Perhaps one of the reasons for the low Swiss crime rate is that potential violent criminals know that their potential victims are trained in armed and unarmed combat defense, may be carrying a gun, and may well have a gun in their home. Few burglars want to confront an American shotgun or a Swiss military rifle. Then again, the deterrent effect of firearms may be superfluous. Crime is so low that purse-snatchings are newsworthy even in Geneva.[77]

The suicide rate is high, though, over double the American rate. Guns are used in 23 percent of Swiss suicides.[78]

Again, not all Swiss agree that guns in the home are not a problem. A significant percentage of women object to the policy of militiamen keeping guns at home. And criminologist Martin Killias, of the University of Lausanne, contends that, contrary to the popular myth, Switzerland does suffer serious gun problems. Killias, along with Pat Mayhew of the British Home Office and Jan van Dijk of the Netherlands, surveyed victimization rates, attitudes toward crime, and gun-ownership rates in fourteen Western democracies.[79] What they found was enough to convince Killias that widespread gun ownership harms both Switzerland and the United States.

The authors found no relationship between handgun density and armed robbery. That a country was relatively high in handgun density did not mean that it would be relatively high in armed robbery. The one country that did have a high armed robbery rate combined with plentiful handguns was the United States. Killias suggests that as long as handgun density stays at a relatively low threshold, armed robbery will be rare, regardless of whether handgun ownership is almost nil, or just fairly low. Having exceeded the handgun density threshold, the United States suffers from frequent armed robbery.[80]

But evidence presented in earlier chapters indicates that even in countries with stringent handgun laws, such as Japan and Britain, criminals can easily purchase a black-market handgun. An alternative explanation for the relatively high American armed robbery rate would be that America has a relatively higher percentage of criminals. (This issue is discussed in more detail in the concluding chapter.)

Killias states that he has found "a substantial impact of gun ownership on homicides committed with firearms," and hence overall higher homicide rates. His argument is simply to point out that Switzerland and the United States both have much higher firearms homicide rates than Britain.[81]

The data do not support his strongly stated conclusion. Killias presents homicide statistics for Switzerland and eight other countries. Switzerland has more guns per capita than any country but the United States. Yet Switzerland has fewer firearms homicides per capita than six of the eight countries.[82]

Killias also finds "a rather strong impact of gun ownership on suicides committed with firearms." Here, presenting data for only six countries, Killias does show that the countries with the most guns have the most suicides involving guns. The countries for which Killias provides data are England and Wales, the former Federal Republic of Germany, Belgium, Australia, Canada, Switzerland. The foregoing list is in order of increasing gun density, and increasing gun-related suicide rates, the order being the exact same for both.[83]

Here, Killias's conclusions are better attuned to his evidence. The more serious problem is that his observation, while likely correct, borders on the trivial. Countries with many guns may have relatively more gun-related suicides for the same reason that countries on the ocean have relatively more drowning-related suicides—the availability of a suicide instrument (firearms or water) to which some cultural importance is attached.

The more crucial question is whether gun density correlates with overall suicide rates. If fewer guns lead only to more suicides of other types, anti-gun laws would not be helpful. When the displacement effect is considered, the anti-gun argument is not as strong. On the one hand, Switzerland (a country which is three-quarters German-speaking), has a nongun-related suicide rate almost identical to the former West Germany's (suggesting a similar cultural attitude toward suicide), but has a gun-related suicide rate that is over four times as high as West Germany's.[84] The data imply that Switzerland's higher gun density could increase suicide.

On the other hand, Belgium, possessing guns at only 52 percent of the Swiss rate, has 94 percent as many suicides. Australia and Canada have only half as many suicides as West Germany and Belgium, even though they have twice as many guns per capita.[85]

More fundamentally, the sample of six countries is somewhat arbitrary. Killias and his coauthors were not able to obtain gun-related suicide data for the other countries in their study. If Killias had had the United States data, he would have seen that gun density does accompany a very high gun-related suicide rate. But he would also have seen that the overall United States suicide rate is slightly less than Canada's, even though Canada possesses far fewer guns per capita. And America's suicide rate is much lower than Switzerland's, even though Killias's survey found 32.6 percent of Swiss households have guns, and 48.9 percent of American ones do. In addition, it should be remembered that many countries with very high suicide rates—such as Japan, Hungary, or Rumania—have virtually no guns at all. More guns do mean more gun-related suicide. Whether more gun suicide necessarily means more overall suicide is not so clear. The evidence from previous chapters regarding Great Britain and Canada suggests that the enactment of firearms control laws to screen and delay gun purchasers does lower firearms-related suicide but does not reduce overall suicide.

The case of Switzerland does not prove that every society should give everyone a gun. But Switzerland's experience does demolish the notion "more guns, more gun crime."[86] A society with a great deal of guns is not necessarily a society with a great deal of gun problems. More important than the number of guns is their cultural context. The next section examines the cohesive social structure that keeps crime low in Switzerland.

SOBER ATTITUDES TOWARD FIREARMS

Some psychologists in the United States have argued that the mere presence of guns causes a "weapons effect" and makes people anti-social and aggressive. Although the "weapons effect" theory has been widely publicized, the actual experimental data are far from conclusive about the existence of any such effect.[87] Switzerland disproves the most extreme versions of the "weapons effect" theory—that the mere sight or presence of a firearm will make otherwise placid individuals aggressive and murderous—"Guns Make People Crazy," in the words of one newspaper.[88] If the "weapons effect" were universally true, the Swiss would long since be dead from machine-gun massacres.[89] Notably, in Sweden and Belgium, where gun control is more prohibitive, tentative studies do show a "weapons effect." Accordingly, it may be that the "weapons effect" is inverse to an individual's or culture's day-to-day familiarity with guns.[90] Many of the people who think guns make people crazy have their own irrational and extreme thoughts about guns.

The sober Swiss attitude makes it understandable that while the Swiss own "Rambo" guns, they have banned Sylvester Stallone's "Rambo" movies. International airlines note the Swiss taste in film: "They hate violence."[91]

Switzerland has more automatic firearms in homes than does the entire United States but there are no massacres with these guns. The Swiss have easy access to everything from revolvers to anti-aircraft guns, but violent crime is as rare as it is in Japan, where guns are almost totally prohibited. In sum, Switzerland illustrates, in the words of two historians of the gun in America: "More important than the number of weapons is their perceived role, which determines how they will be used."[92]

EVERYONE IS HIS OWN POLICEMAN

When the case of Switzerland is raised in the American gun debate, the first reply of American prohibitionists is that Switzerland is a homogeneous, rural society. But that is simply untrue. German, Italian, and French speakers all live in Switzerland. The three groups share no common language nor religion nor culture. Switzerland includes large, ethnically diverse cities, as well as isolated mountain communities.[93]

Does the explanation for the low crime rate lie in a severe criminal justice system? To the contrary. The Commonwealth nations discussed in previous chapters impose long prison terms for violent crimes more often than does America; but Switzerland does not. For all crimes except murder, the Swiss rarely inflict a prison term of more than a year; most of the serious offenders receive suspended sentences.[94] As in Japan, the focus of the criminal justice system is on the reintegration of the offender into the community.[95]

While widespread civilian gun ownership may have some influence on the low crime rate in Switzerland, guns are not the important reason why crime is low. Switzerland's low crime rate does not stem per se from the ownership of guns. Rather, it is the emphasis on community duty, of which gun ownership is one important part, that best explains the low crime rate. Criminologist Marshall Clinard contrasts the low crime rate in Switzerland with the higher rate in Sweden, where gun control is more extensive. The higher Swedish rate is all the more surprising in view of Sweden's much lower population density and its ethnic homogeneity.[96] One of the reasons for the low Swiss crime rate, says Clinard, is that Swiss cities grew relatively slowly.[97] Most families live for generations in the same area. Therefore, slum cultures in large cities never developed.[98]

Moreover, the political structure is organized to promote citizen involvement and responsibility. With the weakest central government of any world democracy, Switzerland is governed mainly by its 3,095 communes (substates of a canton).[99] Upon the presentation of 100,000 signatures or upon the request of eight cantons, federal laws and international treaties must be submitted to popular referendum.[100] Unlike in the rest of Europe, the police force is decentralized.[101] Judges are popularly elected.[102] With less mobility, and more deeply developed community ties, there is less crime.

The saying is that everyone is his own policeman. Foreign visitors are surprised to see Swiss pedestrians always waiting at traffic lights, even when there is no traffic; the mass transit systems successfully depend on voluntary payment.[103] Clinard infers that Sweden's strong central government weakens citizen initiative, whereas Switzerland is decentralized, and relies more on individual responsibility. Thus, while crime shot up everywhere in Western Europe in the 1960s, as social control weakened, crime in Switzerland remained stable. He concludes, "Communities or cities that wish to prevent crime should encourage greater political decentralization by developing small government units and encouraging citizen responsibility for obedience to the law and crime control."[104]

In *Nations Not Obsessed with Crime,* Freda Adler comes to many of the same conclusions as Clinard. She, too, emphasizes the communal system of government—in which all laws are enacted by popular vote— and the stability of residential patterns. Moreover, schools are strict, and teenagers have less freedom than in most of the rest of Europe. Communications between the generations are open. According to some studies Swiss teenagers—in contrast to most adolescents—do not prefer their peers to their parents.[105] Most Swiss still live in traditional patriarchal families. In fact, Switzerland has the lowest percentage of working mothers of any European country.[106]

Among the factors contributing to the intergenerational and intercultural harmony is military service, which provides an opportunity for all groups to interact.[107] Adults and youth share many sports, such as skiing and swimming. Sunday target shooting is another important shared pastime, with community awards and team trophies often displayed in restaurants and taverns. The Swiss Rifle Association has 500,000 members (many of whom are militiamen required by law to belong to shooting clubs).[108] At the annual *Feldschießen* weekend, over 200,000 Swiss attend national marksmanship competitions.[109] The yearly shooting festivals have long been a civic celebration and instruction, a "school of morals for the young" in the words of one nineteenth-century author.[110] The Federal Military Department strongly encourages and assists recreational target shooting.[111]

The civic virtues are not taught only once a year. In the words of American author John McPhee, "While a father cleans his rifle at the kitchen table his son is watching, and 'the boy gets close to the weapon.' "[112] Because weapons of war must be kept in the home, writes Clinard:

> much activity associated with the proper care of weapons, target practice, or conversations about military activities become common in the family. All of this, together with the other varied activities carried out in Switzerland across age lines, has served to inhibit the age separation, alienation, and

growth of a separate youth culture that has increasingly become char-
acteristic of the United States, Sweden, and many other highly developed
countries. Although these factors represent only one aspect of a total Swiss
way of life, they play no small part in the low crime rate and the crime
trend.[113]

WHY THE SWISS SYSTEM CANNOT WORK IN AMERICA

Both the anti-gun and the pro-gun lobbies in the United States try to turn
the Swiss example to their advantage. In neither case does the effort succeed.
The leading anti-gun lobby, Handgun Control, Inc., offers literature called
"Handgun Facts," which is wrong about every single "fact" it mentions
concerning Switzerland. If Handgun Control really approves of the Swiss
system, the organization ought to reverse a number of its current policies.

First of all, Handgun Control should oppose the handgun prohibition
laws in Washington, D.C., Chicago, and other cities—since the Switzerland
experience "proves" that lenient licensing is all that is needed to stop gun
crime. Second, Handgun Control should work to repeal laws that prohibit
Americans from owning howitzers, anti-aircraft guns, and other military
weapons. Switzerland allows ownership of these weapons by anyone who
can meet the simple requirements for a license. And thanks to the "howitzer
licensing" system, there is no howitzer crime in Switzerland. Since Swiss-
style handgun licensing is the main reason Switzerland has no handgun
crime (claims Handgun Control), a Swiss-style system of howitzer licensing
would also be a good idea for America. Lastly, Handgun Control should
reverse its policy and work for repeal of America's ban on the possession
of fully automatic firearms manufactured after 1986. Handgun Control
should push America to adopt the Swiss policy: having the government
sell automatics at discount prices to anyone with an easily obtained permit.

It is not likely, though, that Handgun Control will follow the logic
of its advertising and work to let Americans own licensed machine guns
and howitzers. But until Handgun Control does so, it should stop talking
about what a good handgun licensing system Switzerland has.

While Handgun Control does not convincingly offer Switzerland as
a reason for American gun control, Marshall Clinard does propound a
highly plausible argument in favor of American gun control. Reasons
Clinard: "In a country like the United States, where there has been a long
history of both personal and collective violence, it is essential that rigid
regulations for both registration and control be adopted."[114]

Clinard's argument regarding American gun control cannot be dismissed
out of hand. After all, few Americans would want the United States to

adopt the lenient criminal sentencing practices of Switzerland. Opponents of lenient sentencing would argue, correctly, that America does not have the stable, integrated community structures of Switzerland. Thus, the American government must take a more coercive, authoritarian role in controlling prisoners, to make up for the lack of community controls.

The same point might be made about guns. Although guns are more available in Switzerland, Swiss gun culture is more authoritarian than America's. Gun ownership is a mandatory community duty, not a matter of individual free choice.[115] In Switzerland, defense of the nation is not relegated to professional soldiers or to people who join the army to learn technical skills for civilian jobs. Defense of the nation is the responsibility of every male citizen. Unlike the guns in America, many of the weapons that the Swiss possess in their homes are government issue, with concomitant government-imposed responsibilities.

That an "assault-rifles-for-everyone" policy works in Switzerland does not mean it would work in America. American gun advocates should consider whether an unmanned American mass transit system could count on payment by the honor code. Further, America obviously has a large criminal class of gun abusers, and Switzerland does not.

Pro-gun Americans cannot realistically embrace Switzerland as a model. Although a Western democracy with a decentralized government, Switzerland is generally more authoritarian than the United States. The Swiss impose restrictions on free speech, including the banning of violent movies, that would never be legal in America.[116] In early 1990, the Swiss found out that security officials had compiled files on 50,000 people, sometimes for legal political activity, or even for working at a day-care center. Until 1973, the Swiss Constitution banned the Jesuits from the nation and forbade the establishment of new monasteries.[117] While America was debating the Equal Rights Amendment, Switzerland was wondering whether women should be allowed to vote.[118] America has integrated women into almost all noncombat roles in the armed forces; Swiss women volunteers serve in a relatively unimportant auxiliary corps.[119] The little song quoted at the beginning of this chapter highlights the difficulty of moving Swiss gun-control techniques to America: "What does a good Swissman need, except a clean gun on the wall, and a cheerful song for the fatherland?" In Switzerland, fathers still rule the family and the nation. The Swiss may think of their nation as a real "fatherland" since their father—and every other ancestor as far back as anyone knows—was born in Switzerland.[120] No one in the United States can make that claim, except for American Indians, whose distant ancestors crossed what is now the Bering Strait.

CONCLUSION

Switzerland is a special combination of opposites: a local democracy like Athens and a premier military state like Sparta. Highly armed, yet peaceful; democratic, yet authoritarian. In the patriarchal Swiss "fatherland," social gun controls more than make up for the scarcity of legal gun controls. These strong Swiss social controls would be nearly impossible to duplicate in individualistic America.

Cultural conditions, not gun laws, are the most important factors in a nation's crime rate. Young adults in Washington, D.C., are subject to strict gun control, but no social control, and they commit a staggering amount of armed crime. Young adults in Zürich are subject to minimal gun control, but strict social control, and they commit almost no violent crime. As a Swiss politician explains, "This [low crime] rate doesn't depend whether you have a weapon at home or not. It depends on a state of society, or a morality of criminality in society."[121]

America—with its traditions of individual liberty—cannot import Switzerland's culture of social control. Teenagers, women, and almost everyone else has more freedom in America than in Switzerland.

Therefore, the American gun advocates' reference to Switzerland proves little. True, the Swiss are powerfully armed, with everything from handguns to anti-aircraft missiles, and legal controls range from nonexistent to mild. Yet the Swiss learn to use their guns through mandatory militia training. The United States has no such mandatory training. While Switzerland may prove that easy access to handguns and anti-aircraft missiles is acceptable in a patriarchal nation with universal male militia service, America's patriarchy is weaker and militia training is close to nil.

True, gun control in America might be even more difficult to implement than in the Commonwealth countries (and they have not been wholly successful); and it might involve privacy problems. Being aware of the practical difficulties, however, does not mean one has to abandon completely the idea of American gun control. Our examination of the Commonwealth and Japan has led to the conclusion that gun control has not been a significant cause of low crime rate; self-control has mattered more. Yet it is the United States that has such a large fraction of its population without self-control. It might be that because America is different—because there is less self-control—there is all the greater need for gun control. To evaluate the hypothesis, we must now turn to America, to examine guns and gun control in American culture.

NOTES

1. Jonathan Steinberg, *Why Switzerland?* (Cambridge: Cambridge University Press, 1978), p. 164.

2. Richard Harding, "An Ounce of Prevention . . . : Gun Control and Public Health in Australia," *Australia and New Zealand Journal of Criminology* 16 (March 1983), pp. 3, 5. Technically speaking, the statement is not in the form of a syllogism.

3. Handgun Control, Inc., *Handgun Facts* (Washington, D.C.: Handgun Control, Inc., n.d.), unpaginated (Question and Answer number 8).

4. On August 1, 1291, the three cantons of Schwyz, Uri, and Nidwalden formed an alliance called "The Everlasting League," which ousted the Austrian bailiffs who ruled Switzerland. Carol L. Schmid, *Conflict and Consensus in Switzerland* (Berkeley: University of California Press, 1981), p. 77.

In legend, the revolution did not begin until 1307, when Werner Stauffacher of Schwyz, Walter Fürst of Uri, and Arnold von Melchtal of Nidwalden met in the town of Rütli and swore the Rütli Oath on the shore of Lake Lucerne. William Tell, supposedly a follower of Stauffacher, refused to pay obeisance to one of the Austrian bailiffs, Gessler. As punishment, Tell was forced to shoot an apple off his son's head. After completing that feat, Tell fled, and later shot Gessler in an ambush at Küssnacht, precipitating the revolution that gained Switzerland its freedom on January 1, 1308.

August 1 in Switzerland, like July 4 in the United States, is a national celebration in honor of men who voluntarily formed an association to carry out a violent revolution for their rights and liberties. Gérard Pflug, *Histoire de la Suisse* (Fribourg: Départements du Instruction Publique, Fribourg et Valais, 1960), p. 83, quoted in Schmid, pp. 77–78.

One of the factors casting doubt on the Tell legend's authenticity is the existence of similar legends in Norway, Denmark, Sweden, the Faeroe Islands, and Iceland. J. Murray Luck, *History of Switzerland* (Palo Alto, Calif.: SPOSS Inc., 1985), pp. 123–24.

Today Switzerland contains 20 cantons and 6 half cantons. Luck, p. 738.

5. Luck, p. 222.

6. Ibid., p. 91.

7. Robert O'Connell, *Of Arms and Men: A History of Wars, Weapons, and Aggression* (Oxford: Oxford University Press, 1989), p. 102, citing Charles Oman, *Art of War in the Middle Ages: A.D. 378–1278,* vol. 2 (Ithaca, N.Y.: 1953), pp. 254, 280.

8. O'Connell, p. 102, citing Oman, pp. 75–76, 280. "There is no one quality so universally recognized among the *Switzers,* as that of valour." A. Stanyan, *An Account of Switzerland* (London: 1714), p. 128, quoted in Luck, p. 134. Luck summarizes: "[I]n every engagement from Morgarten (November 1315) onwards, the Swiss displayed a tactical skill and a primitive disdain for death in combat that knew no equal in the warfare of the middle ages." Luck, p. 134.

9. Johannes Trithemius (1460–1516) was Abbott of Spanheim by Kreuznach in the Rheinland. Luck, pp. 134, 170.

10. W. Oechsli, *History of Switzerland 1499–1914* (Cambridge, England: 1922), p. 7, quoted in Luck, p. 134. The Glasgow theology professor Gilbert Burnet, after visiting Bern, reported "The men are robust and strong, and have generally an extream sense of liberty." He noted that the Bern was "always ready for war," and could raise 80,000 men, while Zurich could muster 50,000 in twenty-four hours. Gilbert Burnet, *Some Letters containing an Account of what seemed most remarkable in Switzerland, Italy, etc.* (Rotterdam: Abraham Rocher, 1686), pp. 21, 47, quoted in Luck, pp. 178, 180.

11. Niccolò Machiavelli, *The Prince* (1532), chapters 12, 13; *Discourses on the First*

Ten Books of Titus Livius (1531), Book I: chapters 21, 43; Book II, chapter 20; *The Art of War* (1521) Book I, pp. 491–506, all in Peter Bondanella and Mark Musa, ed. and trans., *The Portable Machiavelli,* (New York: Penguin Books, 1979). [Unless otherwise noted, all subsequent references to Machiavelli are to the Penguin edition.]

12. Machiavelli, *Il Principe* (Venice: 1537), chap. 12, p. 24.

13. Niccolò Machiavelli, *The Art of War,* book II (Florence: 1521), reprinted in Allan Gilbert, trans., *Machiavelli: The Chief Works and Others* (Durham, N.C.: Duke University Press, 1965), p. 597.

14. G. A. Hayes-McCoy, *Irish Battles: A Military History of Ireland* (Belfast: Appletree, 1989), p. 94, citing H. Seitz, "Some Traits of the International Expansion of Edged Weapons During the XVI Century," in *Armi Antiche* (Turin: 1956). At the battles of Morgarten and Sempach, Swiss pikemen in articulated columns (*Gewalthaufen*) devastated the Austrian array of feudal knights. Gordon A. Craig, *The Triumph of Liberalism: Zürich in the Golden Age* (New York: Collier Books, 1988), p. 4.

15. Steinberg, *Why Switzerland?* p. 164; Foco Bank, "The Defense of Switzerland," *Swiss Economic Viewpoint* 15, no. 4 (October 1983).

16. Craig, p. 12.

17. Ibid., p. 68. Metternich was deterred not only by the Swiss militia, but also by concerns about how Britian, France, or Russia might react.

18. Luck, pp. 221–22, 276. Also, "[T]he whole body of the People, from 16 to 60, is enrolled in the Militia." Stanyan, p. 193, quoted in Luck, p. 181.

19. Later in the nineteenth century, Swiss military drills held during the visits of German Prince Wilhelm Hohenzollern were informally called the "Crown Prince's Maneuvers." According to one (perhaps apocryphal) story that was recounted on a widely circulated postcard in the early twentieth century, Hohenzollern (who would rule as Germany's Kaiser during World War I) asked the Swiss commander, "How many men have you under arms?" When the commander replied "one million," Hohenzollern asked, "What would you do if five million of my men came across the frontier tomorrow?" Replied the Swiss commander, "Each of my men would fire five shots and go home."

20. Luck, p. 803.

21. George S. Patton and Lewis Walt, "The Swiss Report," in Morgan Norval, ed., *The Military in 20th-Century America,* 1st ed. (Falls Church, Va.: Gun Owners Foundation, 1985), p. 161.

22. Luck, pp. 98, 264, 407–12.

23. O'Connell, p. 102. Alternatively, "point d'argent, point de Suisses." Luck, p. 207.

24. Marshall Clinard, *Cities with Little Crime: The Case of Switzerland* (Cambridge: Cambridge University Press, 1978), p. 8.

The Bourbon Kings of France made particularly heavy use of the Swiss Guards. The Guards valiantly defended Louis XVI and the Tuileries Palace against a revolutionary mob in 1792. After the French Revolution, many citizens named their children after William Tell—even though Switzerland served as a counter-revolutionary base of operations for the Royalists.

After overthrowing the first republic, Napoleon used the Swiss Guards in his Russian campaign. And when the Bourbon Kings were restored after Napoleon's defeat, the Swiss Guard were rehired. Finally, the French people overturned the monarchy for good in 1830, and Switzerland stopped leasing mercenary soldiers. Today, the only remnant of the Swiss Guards are the volunteers in the "army" of Vatican City.

25. Since the Reformation, Switzerland has been about 55 percent Protestant and 43 percent Catholic. The religion percentages are based on 1970 census data from the *Annuaire*

Statistique de la Suisse (Basel: Birkhäuser, 1976), pp. 28, 30, quoted in Schmid, p. 16. Prior to the 1848 Constitution, the Catholic and Protestant cantons had separate federal legislatures.

26. Machiavelli, *The Prince,* chap. 12, p. 117.

27. In addition, 493 were wounded. Some commentators suggest that the low casualties showed the Swiss not to be as militarily expert as they claimed; other commentators contend that the Swiss simply tried to avoid killing each other, preferring instead to concentrate on pillage and rapine. Craig, p. 75.

28. The Swiss Constitution of 1848 was modeled after the American Constitution. P. I. V. Troxler, *Die Verfassung der Vereinigten Staaten Nord Amerikas als Musterbild der Schweizerischen Bundesreform* (Schaffhausen: 1849), cited in Luck, p. 365.

29. Craig, pp. 82–83.

30. Ibid., p. 90.

31. Schmid, p. 28.

32. Ibid., p. 16. Romansch is actually a "national language," rather than an "official language" as are German, French, and Italian. Federal government administrative functions are never conducted in Romansch, but the government subsidizes the perpetuation of Romansch and its associated culture.

33. Schmid, p. 28. One of the reasons that Switzerland, like America and unlike Canada, has successfully built a positive national identity shared by its diverse cultures is that the national identity is primarily defined in terms of a shared political culture. Ibid., pp. 112–24.

34. Federal Constitution of May 29, 1874; Ordinance of November 15, 1974, cited in Library of Congress, *Gun Control Laws in Foreign Countries* (Washington, D.C.: 1981), p. 166 (home storage) [hereinafter "Library of Congress, (1981)"]; John McPhee, *La Place de la Concorde Suisse* (New York: Farrar, Straus, and Giroux, 1983), p. 40. The Swiss practice of requiring soldiers to store all military gear at home is unique to that nation. "Swiss Coalition Presents Petition on Referendum to End Army," *New York Times,* September 14, 1986, p. 6.

35. The rifles are Sturmgewehr 541 (.223); SG 510-0 (7.5 mm); or SG 550 (5.56 × 45 mm). The pistols are SIG-Sauer 9 mm. The current pistol was adopted in 1975, replacing the Sig P210, which had been adopted in 1949, and is still available for civilian sales. "News About 5.56MM Small Arms," *News From The Institute for Research on Small Arms in International Security* 1, no. 2 (February 1990), p. 6; Donald B. Kates, Jr., "Gun Rights," *Peterson's Handguns,* October 1989, p. 8; Duncan Long, *Automatics: Fast Firepower, Tactical Superiority* (Boulder, Colo.: Paladin Press, 1989), p. 74. ("SIG" is an acronym for Schweizerische Industrie Gesselschaft.)

36. Patton and Walt, p. 163.

37. Foco Bank, "The Defense of Switzerland," p. 1; Clinard, p. 134; Trimborn, *Los Angeles Times,* October 1, 1980, pp. 1, 14. Officers serve for much longer periods, but are still civilians on leave from their jobs. There being no military academy, officers first serve as enlisted men and N.C.O.s. Since officers come mostly from the educated middle and upper class, their service in non-officer positions early in their career helps reduce social stratification in the army. Clinard, p. 134.

38. In recent years, shortage of the Stgw. 57 has resulted in the government giving retirees the Karabiner 31.

39. Library of Congress, *Gun Control Laws in Foreign Countries* (Washington, D.C.: Library of Congress, 1976), p. 179 [hereinafter "Library of Congress (1976)]; Hanspeter Baumann, President ProTell, letter to author, February 23, 1988.

40. William Tonso, *Gun and Society: The Social and Existential Roots of the American Attachment to Firearms* (Lanham, Md.: University Press of America, 1982), p. 6.

41. Hanns Neuerbourg, "Guns Abound at Shootin' Time in Switzerland," *Philadelphia Inquirer,* August 7, 1979 (Associated Press).

42. Hanspeter Baumann, letter to author, February 24, 1988. Silencers are legal in some cantons, but not in others. Luck, p. 272.

43. McPhee, p. 41.

44. R. A. I. Munday, "Switzerland Without an Army," *News From The Institute for Research on Small Arms and Security* 1, no. 2 (February 1990), p. 1.

45. The hollow point makes the bullet expand more fully in its target. Hollow points in America are commonly used for varmint and small-game hunting and for self-defense.

46. Library of Congress (1981), p. 163.

47. "Intercantonal Agreement Re Commerce in Weapons and Munitions," March 27, 1969, ratified by the *Bundesrat* on January 13, 1970, articles 2-3, para. 1 (English translation by National Firearms Association of Canada, Edmonton) [hereinafter "Intercantonal Agreement"]; Library of Congress (1976), pp. 175-76. The handgun purchase certificate is valid for three months. Intercantonal Agreement, article 4.

48. The following groups are forbidden to buy handguns: 1. people under eighteen; 2. the insane or the mentally weak; 3. persons under judicial disability; 4. alcoholics placed under supervision; 5. persons forbidden to make purchases in liquor stores; 6. criminals who have been required to post a bond that they will not commit further crimes; 7. those convicted of violent crimes or misdemeanors; 8. those sent to prisons more than one time; 9. persons who might use the guns dangerously against themselves or others. Intercantonal Agreement, article 5, para. 1; Library of Congress (1981), p. 169.

49. *Handgun Facts.*

50. For handguns, dealers must retain a copy of the firearms purchase certificate, and also record the date of sale, personal identification of the purchaser, and serial number and model of the handgun. Intercantonal Agreement, article 6.

51. "Were our militia well regulated . . . we'd need not fear a hundred thousand enemies. . . . That this is not only practicable but easy, the modern example of the Swissers and Swedes is an undeniable indication." Roger Molesworth, "Introduction," in *Franco-Gallia* (London: 1721), p. xxviii. "The Swiss at this day are the freest, happiest, and the people of all Europe who can best defend themselves, because they have the best militia. . . ." Andrew Fletcher, *A Discourse of Government with Relation to Militias* (1737). Both Molesworth and Fletcher were widely read in the American colonies. David Hardy, *The Origins and Development of the Second Amendment* (Chino Valley, Ariz.: Blacksmith, 1986), pp. 46-48, citing (for Molesworth) H. Trevor Colbourn, *The Lamp of Experience: Whig History and the Intellectual Origins of the American Revolution* (New York: W. W. Norton, 1965).

52. Adam Smith, *The Wealth of Nations* (New York: Random House, 1937) (1st pub. 1776), Book V, chap. I, part III, article II, p. 739.

53. Steinberg, p. 165.

54. Munday, p. 1.

55. "The Defense of Switzerland," p. 2. Switzerland is also the only Western nation to provide shelters, fully stocked with food and enough supplies to last a year, for *all* its citizens in case of war. The banks and supermarkets subsidize much of the stockpiling. The banks also have plans to move their gold into the mountainous center of Switzerland in case of invasion. Ibid. Around 4,000 permanent obstacles and more than 2,000 demolition devices lie in wait for an aggressor. Patton and Walt, p. 154.

Swiss defenses include preparation for nuclear attack. The idea of evacuating population centers was rejected because the country is too small to make evacuation possible, and because evacuees would interfere with military use of the roads. Private homes and all new construction of any type are required to have shelters built to federal specifications. Unlike most American shelters, the Swiss shelters are meant not only to provide a refuge from radiation, but to protect from nearby nuclear blasts. Public shelters must be built to withstand three atmospheres of overpressure—enough to shield people from a one-megaton explosion nine-tenths of a mile away. Males aged fifty to sixty must spend several days a year in mandatory training as civil defense workers. Every private home is required by law to contain two weeks worth of food. Richard F. Jansen, "An Alternate World Underground: Swiss Civil Defense Setup," *Wall Street Journal,* October 17, 1977, pp. 1, 33; Luck, pp. 773-75; Patton and Walt, pp. 169-70.

56. McPhee, p. 41.

57. "Meet the Swiss Weekend Warrior," *Christian Science Monitor,* May 4, 1988, p. 16, col. 1.

58. Munday, p. 1.

59. The highest peacetime rank is corps commander. Luck, p. 774.

60. H. R. Kurz, "Swiss National Defense,' in J. Murray Luck, ed., *Modern Switzerland* (Palo Alto, Calif.: SPOSS, 1978), pp. 415-16; Patton and Walt, p. 166.

61. "Most Swiss Own Guns But Crimes Are Rare," *New York Times,* May 31, 1977 (United Press International story quoting Ernest Moegeli).

62. Women volunteers in the army do not receive weapons training, and are not permitted in combat roles. The government may soon allow them to carry pistols. Claire Nullis, "Swiss Army Tough Stint for Women," *Rocky Mountain News,* October 21, 1990, p. 41 (Associated Press).

63. John A. Callcott, " 'Left' Seeks to Disband Swiss Way of Life—Its Army," *Los Angeles Times,* August 31, 1986, p. 18 (United Press International).

64. Roger Bernheim, "Jubilee Time," *Swiss Review of World Affairs,* August 1991, p. 11.

65. Munday, pp. 1, 3. Opponents of the army recognized that it was the most important socializing institution in Switzerland, and blamed it for "maintaining patriarchal, sexist power structures, the bodyguard of the bourgeoisie, the brake on progress." Abolitionist flyer distributed in Biel, November 1989, and quoted in Munday, p. 3.

66. "FA-18s for the Swiss Army," *Swiss Review of World Affairs,* August 1991, p. 31.

67. *The Defense of Switzerland,* p. 3. Persons who object for ethical or religious reasons and are found to pass the "test of conscience" are required to serve in environmental protection, health care, mountain rescue, or a similar service for a period of one and one-half times as long as the military service refused. In 1990, 199 persons requested conscientious objector status. "Work Service for Conscientious Objectors," *Swiss Review of World Affairs,* July 1991, p. 32.

68. Eugen Heer, Director, Swiss Institute of Arms and Armour, letter to Prime Minister Margaret Thatcher, reprinted in Rod Marvell, "Editor's Notebook," *Australian Shooters Journal,* August 1989, p. 3.

69. Quoted in Munday, p. 4.

70. In 1977, a German official was assassinated with a Heckler and Koch 43 rifle that had been legally bought in Malters, in Lucern canton. Luck, p. 772.

During the Algerian war for independence from France, both the Algerians and the French living in Algeria procured guns from Switzerland.

71. Reuters, September 29, 1982. As of 1991, ProTell had 6,000 members. Philip B. Bürgel, "Report on Martin Killias Gun Ownership and Violent Crime," September 22, 1991 (ProTell), p. 5.

72. The federal council (the executive) is made up of seven members chosen from

the assembly, and includes the president of the Confederation, who is elected annually by the assembly.

73. Hanspeter Baumann, letter to author, February 24, 1988.

74. Comparative homicide and suicide statistics are set forth in chapter 11, at note 5 and accompanying text. See also Martin Killias, "Gun Ownership and Violent Crime: The Swiss Experience in International Perspective," *Security Journal* 1, no. 3 (1990), p. 171, table 2.

75. Felix Auer, member of Parliament, "European Journal: Gun Control Special," *Oregon Public TV* episode #20/89, Story-Nr. P 16 765.

76. Luck, p. 772, citing *Neue Zürcher Zeitung,* March 8-9, 1980.

77. "Staying on the Safe Side: A Traveler's Guide to Scams, Ripoffs and Other Concerns in 22 Cities Around the World," *New York Times,* June 24, 1990, p. 19.

78. United States Census Bureau, *Statistical Abstract of the United States, 1989* (Washington, D.C.: Government Printing Office); Clinard, p. 2; Hanspeter Baumann, letter to author, February 24, 1988; Killias, p. 171 table 2.

79. The countries were the United States, England and Wales, Scotland, Northern Ireland, Canada, Australia, Switzerland, France, West Germany, Norway, Finland, and Spain. Jan van Dijk, Pat Mayhew, Martin Killias, *Experiences of Crime Across the World: Key Findings of the 1989 International Crime Survey* (Deventer, Netherlands: Kluwer, 1990). Only some of the data has been released and interpreted. More books discussing the data are in progress.

80. Killias, p. 173.

81. Ibid.

82. The firearms homicide rates, are, in ascending order: Netherlands, England and Wales, Switzerland, Finland, Australia, Canada, Belgium, France, United States. Ibid., p. 171, table 2.

The correlation of gun homicides wtih gun density appears valid only at the extremes. The Netherlands and England and Wales are the lowest by far in gun density, and the United states the highest. For the other six countries, there is no correlation at all.

83. Killias, pp. 171, table 2; 173.

84. Ibid., p. 171, table 2.

Killias's description of Swiss firearms laws is sometimes misleading. For example, he writes that "The ammunition for the automatic army rifle is not on sale in any arms shop." The statement is true, and the reader is left with the impression that Swiss militiamen have no access to ammunition for their assault rifles except through government channels. But while Swiss ordnance cartridges are not on sale in commercial gun stores, foreign ammunition that fits the Swiss assault rifles is readily available for over-the-counter purchase.

85. Killias, p. 171, table 2.

86. Quote from former New York Senate candidate Mark Green, *Winning Back America* (New York: Bantam, 1982), p. 222.

87. The theory was popularly introduced in Leonard Berkowitz, "Impulse, Aggression and the Gun," *Psychology Today* 2 (September 1968): 19-22. Notably, Berkowitz and other academics whose research Berkowitz promotes did not test whether people who actually used or owned guns were more aggressive. The research showed only that people were more likely to respond more aggressively when someone else, such as a scientist conducting an experiment was associated with a weapon. For example, motorists reacted more aggressively to other vehicles slow to accelerate when a red light turned green if the slow car had a rude bumper sticker and a rifle in a gun rack. Leonard Berkowitz, "How Guns Control Us," *Psychology Today* 15 (June 1981): 11-12. See generally, Donald G. Fischer, Harold

Keim, and Ann Rose, "Knives as Aggression-Eliciting Stimuli," *Psychological Reports* 24 (1969): 755–60; Desmond P. Ellis, Paul Weiner, and Louis Miller III, "Does the Trigger Pull the Finger? An Experimental Test of Weapons as Aggression Eliciting Stimuli," *Sociometry* 34 (1971): 453–65; Adam Fraczek and Jacqueline R. Macauley, "Some Personality Factors in Reaction to Aggressive Stimuli," *Journal of Personality* 39 (1971): 163–77; Charles W. Turner, John F. Layton, and Lynn Stanley Simons, "Naturalistic Studies of Aggressive Behavior," *Journal of Personality and Social Psychology* 31 (1975): 1098–1107.

Tests of people actually firing or owning guns found "no evidence that the presence, firing, or long-term use of guns enhances subsequent aggression." A. Buss, A. Brooker, and E. Buss, "Firing a Weapon and Aggression," *Journal of Personality and Social Psychology* 22 (June 1972): 296–302, quoted in Donald B. Kates, Jr., "Firearms and Violence: Old Premises and Current Evidence," in Ted Robert Gurr, ed., *Violence in America* (Vol. 1, *The History of Crime*) (Newbury Park, Calif.: Sage, 1989), p. 202.

88. Luedens, "Guns Make People Crazy," *Milwaukee Journal,* April 7, 1986.

89. Donald B. Kates, Jr., and Mark Benenson, "Handgun Prohibition and Homicide," in Donald B. Kates, Jr., ed., *Restricting Handguns: The Liberal Skeptics Speak Out,* (Croton-on-Hudson, N.Y.: North River Press, 1979), p. 115.

90. Gary Kleck, "Assumptions of Gun Control," in Donald B. Kates, Jr., ed., *Firearms and Violence* (Cambridge, Mass.: Ballinger, 1984), p. 29.

Like Switzerland, Israel has universal military training, and distributes government weapons such as full automatic Uzis and Galils to law-abiding adults. Writes one reporter: "Although Israel is pervaded by guns, it is not excited by them. They are a common appliance, familiar to most 18-year-olds, inspiring neither aversion nor awe. . . . [T]here is a sober approach to weapons." Shipler, "Jerusalem Talks of Guns," *San Francisco Chronicle,* April 16, 1981.

The hypothesis that "weapons effect" varies inversely with weapons familiarity is also consistent with the work of sociologist Barbara Stenross, whose study of hunters, target shooters, and gun collectors finds them contemptuous of people who get an emotional charge from the idea of firearms violence. Barbara Stenross, "The Meaning of Guns," paper presented at the Popular Culture Association, Montreal, March 28, 1987.

91. Ken Perkins, "Airlines Very Choosy About In-flight Movies," *Denver Post,* April 11, 1989 (reprinted from the *Dallas Morning News*).

92. Lee Kennett and James L. Anderson, *The Gun in America: The Origins of a National Dilemma* (New York: Westport Press, 1975), p. 249.

93. Significantly, the one-million foreign guest workers are approximately a sixth of the total population. These workers have an even lower crime rate than native-born Swiss. Hanspeter Baumann, letter to author; Clinard, pp. 5, 151.

94. Clinard, pp. 116–17.

95. Freda Adler, *Nations Not Obsessed with Crime* (Littleton, Colo.: Fred B. Rothman, 1983), pp. 15–23, 118. The recidivism rate for ex-prisoners (50 percent-70 percent) is about the same as in the rest of Europe. Clinard, p. 120.

96. Clinard, p. 10. There is some suggestion that Clinard misses Swiss underreporting of crime. Flemming Balvig, trans. Karen Leander, *The Snow-White Image: The Hidden Reality of Crime in Switzerland* (Oslo: Norwegian University Press, 1988).

97. Clinard, p. 152.

98. Ibid., p. 105.

99. Ibid., pp. 106–107. The federal government is granted only limited powers by the Constitution of 1874, and the cantons retain their sovereignty.

100. Luck, pp. 367, 415, discussing Article 89 of Swiss Constitution. As of 1985, there were 1,141 federal laws, of which 67 had been submitted to referenda by citizen or canton

petition. Of these, the voters rejected outright 49. Eleven others were rejected but replaced with government counterproposals. Luck, p. 719.

101. Ibid., p. 108

102. Adler, p. 18.

103. Ibid., pp. 112–13.

104. Clinard, p. 156.

105. Ibid., p. 130.

106. Adler, p. 17; Clinard, p. 130: "Most Swiss marry young, and few women work after marriage. . . . For the most part the Swiss woman is a homemaker who supervises her children and the household yet remains subservient to her husband in questions of educational and disciplinary matters."

107. Clinard, p. 133.

108. Luck, pp. 751, 754. The Association was founded in 1824, and is Switzerland's largest and oldest sports federation. Ibid.

109. Michael Yardley and Jan A. Stevenson, eds., *Report on the Firearms (Amendment) Bill* (London: Piedmont, 2d ed. 1988), p. 73.

110. Craig, p. 158, quoting Gottfried Keller's Story "The Little Banner of the Seven Upright Ones."

111. Luck, p. 754. For the once-intimate relationship of America's National Rifle Association to the United States Army, see Edward F. Leddy, *Magnum Force Lobby: The National Rifle Association Fights Gun Control* (Lanham, Md.: University Press of America, 1987), pp. 55–71.

112. McPhee, p. 41.

113. Clinard, pp. 134–35. During World War I, the General Secretary of the International Peace Bureau, who hoped to do away with war entirely, suggested that in that eventuality, "Switzerland ought merely to do away with the ammunition," the militia "being otherwise the best school of civic virtues." Julian Grande, *A Citizen's Army: The Swiss System* (London: Chatto and Windus, 1916), p. 106.

114. Clinard, p. 157.

115. Australia's Harding notes "in Swissrael gun ownership is an aspect of a citizen's obligation to the community, whereas in the United States and Australia it is a means of self-expression." Harding, "An Ounce of Prevention," p. 5.

116. E.g., "Swiss Doubter of Nazi Camps Is Forbidden to Teach History," *New York Times,* February 22, 1987.

117. Schmid, p. 27.

118. The franchise was extended in federal elections in 1971. Clinard, p. 8. It now includes all local elections as well, with a very few exceptions. Luck, p. 821.

119. Trimborn, *Los Angeles Times,* p. 14.

120. To be precise, the Swiss are unlikely to think of Switzerland as their fatherland. The citizen's commune or canton is more likely to receive this type of loyalty. A citizen of the canton of Appenzell feels his primary loyalty to that canton, and feels derivative loyalty to Switzerland, in that the Swiss confederation is what has preserved Appenzell's freedom. Denis de Rougemont, *La Suisse ou l'histoire d'un peuple Heureux* (Lausanne: Libraire Hachette, 1965), p. 199; Herbert Lüthy, "Has Switzerland a Future? The Dilemma of the Small Nation," *Encounter* 19 (1962), p. 18; both discussed in Schmid, p. 92.

121. Felix Auer, member of Parliament, "European Journal: Gun Control Special," *Oregon Public TV* episode #20/89, Story-Nr. P 16 765.

9

Civilization and Savagery: America's Half-Remembered Violent Past

"We call them savages because their manners differ from ours, which we think the perfection of civility. They think the same of theirs."

—Benjamin Franklin, on American Indians[1]

As the case of Switzerland illustrated, guns do not cause trouble on their own; if the people are willing to control their own behavior, they will use guns only in a responsible manner. Conversely, when social cohesion collapses, as in Jamaica in the 1970s, guns cause tremendous problems, and so does gun prohibition. Before coming to conclusions about the right gun policy for America, or importing foreign controls on the New Zealand/ Canada or other models, it is necessary to examine the gun in American culture.

The full story of the gun in America is a topic beyond the scope of a single chapter, or even a single book. My focus will be on six themes of America's historical experience with firearms. Each of the themes is often thought to be unique to the American experience, and to be important in creating the special American attitude toward the gun: armed conflict with Indians; the role of the armed citizen, through the militia, in creating the early republic; the "Wild West" and vigilantism; "hillbilly" feuds; racial conflict; and urban crime and ethnic violence. Each topic could easily fill a book in itself; my aim here is only to illuminate the most salient features of each topic, and to see how Americans perceive their own relation to firearms and violence.

Each of the topics involves a conflict between civilization and savagery, and raises the question of the degree to which America can consider itself a civilized nation, in light of its record of violence. Before tackling the conflict of civilization and savagery, I will set forth the ideal of civilization, as seen by American advocates of gun control.

GUNS AND THEIR OWNERS—ENEMIES OF CIVILIZATION

To some, it is incomprehensible that America has not followed the lead of other democracies and sharply restricted civilian gun ownership. Writes the founding chair of Handgun Control, Inc., "The rest of the civilized world looks with horror at the lack of gun controls in the United States."[2] To essayist Garry Wills, gun control is the very essence of civilization: "Until we are willing to outlaw the very existence of civilian handguns, we have no right to call ourselves citizens or consider our behavior minimally civil."[3] He writes that "Every civilized society must disarm its citizens against each other."[4] Maryland's former Senator Joseph Tydings (a leading sponsor of gun control until his 1970 defeat, widely attributed to an NRA ad campaign) found it "tragic that in all of Western civilization the United States is the one country with an insane gun policy."[5] President Johnson decried "the insane traffic in guns" and called for national gun registration.[6] As his attorney general Ramsey Clark put it: "Every civilized nation but one has acted to control guns. . . . In Britain, France, the Soviet Union, Italy, and West Germany, the ownership of a firearm is a strictly regulated privilege."[7] Former Massachusetts Congressman Robert Drinan calls for an "international commission against violence," which would criticize nations with the worst handgun records. "This international agency has to civilize barbarous countries like the United States."[8] "In our kind of civilization, I can't tolerate any kind of weapon," writes a Harvard law professor.[9] Former Screen Actors Guild President Edward Asner demands a handgun ban because "it is time to set the house of civilization in order."[10] *Time* magazine asks "How can America think of itself as a civilized society when day after day the bodies pile up amid the primitive crackle of gunfire across the land?"[11]

Firearms advocates are sometimes seen as so far outside the paradigm of civilization that their very adherence to humane or sane standards is questionable. A scientist calls America's gun habits "simply beastly behavior."[12] "Gun Lunatics Silence the Sounds of Civilization," writes the *Miami Herald;* the paper's columnist finds NRA reasoning "difficult to understand from a civilized view." The reason for the NRA's failure to understand civilization? "Handgun Nuts Are Just That—Really Nuts."[13] To Atlanta newspaper columnist Lewis Grizzard, gun owners are simply "bulletbrains."[14] Another columnist considers gun-control opponents "dolts" and "bumpersticker cretins."[15] The Coalition to Stop Gun Violence diagnoses gun ownership as a "national paranoia."[16] A little more tactfully, Senator Edward Kennedy decries the "mindless proliferation of handguns."[17]

The typical American firearms owner is a rural or smalltown Protestant male[18]—no surprise to many prohibitionists. Science fiction author Harlan Ellison, in an editorial urging his readers to send donations to Handgun Control, recalled his first thought when he heard that Mark Chapman had murdered John Lennon: "You watch: he'll turn out to be a Christer."[19] "Why should a civilized society tolerate 30 gun deaths every single day?" wondered New York City newspaper columnist Harriet Van Horne in a column where she sneered at "Backwater, Tenn." and "the Gospel-tent tradition of poor, backward, rural America," and castigated Jimmy Carter for "attributing all his talk of love and humility to the teachings of Jesus."[20] Manhattan's satire magazine *Spy* headlines its article about the rest of America, "Big Dumb White Guys with Guns."[21]

If gun owners may not comprehend a civilized society, in the view of control advocates, then certainly the National Rifle Association does not. Handgun Control, Inc.'s Jeanne Shields calls NRA members "macho men who don't understand the definition of a civilized society."[22] Fundraising letters for Handgun Control carry a large-type message on the outside envelope: "Your first real chance to tell the National Rifle Association to go to hell! . . ."[23] New York Governor Mario Cuomo denounces opponents of his mandatory seat belt law as "NRA hunters who drink beer, don't vote and lie to their wives about where they were all weekend."[24]

The intuition of Cuomo and others that gun values are not the values of cosmopolitan society are correct. As a National Institute of Justice report explained, gun values:

> are best typed as rural rather than urban: they emphasize independence, self-sufficiency, mastery over nature, closeness to the land, and so on. . . . [T]raining in the operation and use of small arms is very much a part of what fathers are expected to provide to their sons.[25]

But the anti-gun lobby's concerns for civilization extend to more than just the rural/urban conflict; firearms themselves are considered a public health problem of the first magnitude. The American Academy of Pediatrics calls for a complete ban on all handguns and even many airguns.[26] Anti-gun physicians advise the public that gun-ownership by law-abiding citizens is a public health disaster.[27] Gun owners are portrayed as "unstable, violent, and dangerous."[28] Garry Wills calls them "gun fetishists" and "traitors, enemies of their own *patriae*."[29] They are an alien, infectious presence; in the words of a *Miami Herald* columnist:

> Thus we find ourselves surrounded by gun-toting psychopaths, druggies, urban trash from the North, dangerous yokels from the South, van gypsies, half wits, and other losers of every stripe imaginable.[30]

The anti-gun position articulates a fear that our cities are besieged by "an enemy within."[31] An enemy whom Garry Wills terms "the sordid race of gunsels."[32]

Advocates of gun control do not, of course, always engage in vituperation in the style of the *Miami Herald* or Handgun Control, Inc. Even so, guns still represent something deeply wrong with America: its violent and independent national character. D. H. Lawrence wrote that "the essential American soul is hard, isolate, stoic, and a killer." American historian Richard Hofstadter traces the problem to American gun owners.[33] "We were once again proven a savage, uncontrollable, unpredictable, gun-ridden, and murderous people," lamented psychologist Robert Coles when Charles Whitman launched his sniper barrage from a tower at the University of Texas.[34] Violence is "as American as cherry pie," claimed H. Rap Brown.[35] Writes Robert Sherrill: "Could any response be more American than that of the two New York youths who shot and killed a storekeeper because they asked for apple pie and he had offered them Danish pastry instead? Or the husband who shot and killed his wife for being thoughtless enough to run out of gas on the way home?"[36] Or the "McDonald's massacre" (a 1984 mass killing of patrons in a San Ysidro, California, fast-food restaurant)?[37]

Observed the president of the American Sociological Association and his two coauthors:

> In the minds of many, the gun symbolizes all that is wrong with American culture: it symbolizes male dominance, sexual frustration, aggression, violence, and a host of other pathologies that are offensive to a civilized society. In this view, the gun is blood lust incarnate. But in the minds of many others, the same gun symbolizes all that is right in this culture: it symbolizes manliness, independence, self-sufficiency, outdoorsmanship, and a willingness to die for one's beliefs. In this view, the gun is a virtual embodiment of traditional American values.[38]

For good or ill, guns are central to American culture. To devise gun laws that can work in American culture, it is necessary to understand the role of the gun in America's past and its present. What exactly is it about the gun and America that binds them?

CONQUERING THE CONTINENT

As different waves of Europeans arrived in North America, each took distinct approaches to relating to the Indians, including whether to trade guns with them. The Dutch who came to New Netherlands (now lower New York state), came from one of history's greatest trading empires. The Dutch settlers of the Hudson River Valley bartered guns to the Mohawk tribes. In 1643, some of the Mohawk launched a two-year war against Dutch settlements, but took care to spare the Hudson communities that continued to sell them guns.

The Dutch attempted to license gun traders in 1650, with a view to shutting off the Indians' supply. The West India Company, a giant mercantile trading concern, protested, arguing that Indians would pay a black market price so high that controls were impossible. In 1656, the government decreed that settlers could possess only matchlock rifles; modern flintlock rifles, which were more reliable, and easier and faster to fire, were banned. A death penalty for selling guns to the Indians was enacted, but the laws failed to stop the trade.[39] The Dutch story in North America ended when the Dutch lost New Netherlands to the British in 1664.

No matter what the Dutch did, the natives had a ready supply of guns from the French. Based in Canada, the French penetrated deep into the interior of the continent and traded firearms as they went. One firearm, usually a musket, was worth twenty beaver pelts. The main partners of the French were the Ottawa (whose name means "to trade"), who brought guns even deeper into America, and shared the French prosperity—much to the annoyance of their rivals the Iroquois.

In the early seventeenth century, the Iroquois nation allied with the Dutch settlers in the Hudson Valley or with the nearby British, and bought guns. By mid-century, the Iroquois were heavily armed. They began a decades-long campaign, called the Beaver Wars, to destroy the trade of France and her Indian allies, especially the Ottawa. The Iroquois's main objective was to replace the Ottawa as middle-men trading western beaver pelts for European guns. The French and Ottawa prevailed, however, and their trade continued to expand.[40]

The victory in war with the Iroquois confirmed to the governor of New France, the Comte de Frontenac, that friendship with Ottawa traders was the best policy. Building an empire of commerce that stretched deep into what would become the Louisiana Territory, Frontenac did everything possible to supply the Indians with guns. Because the gun made big-game hunting so much more profitable, and because many Indian tribes were involved in wars with each other, firearms were the most valuable commodity a European could offer. The French explorer La Salle observed: "The savages take better care of us French than of their own children. From us only can they get guns and goods."[41]

Frontenac's policy was the right one for France. Unlike the English (and later the Americans), the French were not settling the land with waves of immigrant farmers. Trade was what the French wanted, and the sparse French population needed to trade throughout the Louisiana Territory. Canada did not threaten the Indians. Thanks to the success of commerce with the Indians, the French, coming down from Canada, reached western Pennsylvania and Ohio before English settlers from the Atlantic coast found their way through the gaps in the Appalachian mountains.

But with the victory of Britain and its colonies in the French and Indian War of 1754–1763, the French were expelled from North America; the French trading posts vanished and the French gun trade with the Indians ceased. In a hundred years, the French had sold the Indians 200,000 guns.[42]

Exploring the southern part of North America, the Spaniards adopted the opposite policy from the French, and enslaved the Indians to expand the Spanish empire. In 1501, only nine years after the discovery of the New World by Spain's navigator Columbus, King Ferdinand and Queen Isabella banned the sale of guns to Indians.[43] Many Florida and Southwest Indians, though, stole guns from the Spanish, or bought them from the trading network linked to the French. The enslaved Pueblo Indians of New Mexico acquired and hoarded guns one at a time. They revolted in 1680. Pueblo attacks in the next sixteen years killed hundreds of whites, and pushed white settlement out of Santa Fe, all the way back to El Paso. In the 1750s, Comanche raiders, using guns supplied by the French, forced Spain to abandon north Texas.[44]

At first, the English colonizers followed a policy similar to the Spanish. Officially, arms trading with the Indians was prohibited. In 1641, the Crown ordered that no person should give the Indians "any weapons of war, either guns or gunpowder, nor sword, nor any other Munition, which might come to be used against ourselves." But despite the Crown's orders, many merchants in the diverse North American colonies found trade with the Indians advantageous.

Soon enough, though, the British were trading guns with tribes in Illinois and the rest of what would become the Northwest Territory. As trouble with the American colonists worsened, the British saw the advantage of arming the Indians to attack the encroaching American farmers and backwoodsmen.[45]

Without firearms, life itself would have been impossible for the new people who would be called "Americans." Mastery of a gun was essential to survival. Historian Daniel Boorstin notes, "Shooting small game with a bow or a gun and throwing a tomahawk became lifesaving skills when Indians attacked."[46] Because frontiersmen had to hunt their food and defend themselves against Indians, "civil and military uses of firearms dovetailed as they had not generally done in Europe."[47]

In Canada and Australia, native resistance to white invasion did not amount to long-term, continual war. New Zealand's Maori did fight back, hard, for half a century. Significant armed aboriginal resistance to the white invasion of the United States spanned over two centuries. The western frontier was pushed ahead one farm at a time, a recurring pioneering experience. Step-by-step expansion across the continent meant that America was usually in some kind of armed conflict from the seventeenth century until nearly the turn of the twentieth.

Canadians or Australians or Europeans confronted by a highway robber could probably surrender their property and escape harm. Americans confronted by criminals could often do the same. An American attacked by an Indian could defeat the Indian, escape, or die. Red and white Americans were both determined to possess the same territory; one would live, and one would die.

Survival meant not only fighting Indians, but also hunting for food. The European emigrants who settled America abandoned aristocratic anti-poaching rules. Game animals in the American wilderness were a public bounty, not a private possession.[48]

The special demands of the American gun market led to major innovations in firearms production. Civilian rifle output and design had been stunted in Britain ever since the seventeenth century, owing to lack of big game; America soon took the world lead in making rifles for its people. The .45 calibre Kentucky rifle was introduced for hunting game and for killing Indians, and also served well in the wars with Britain.

Pistols gained popularity as back-up sidearms, in case a rifle jammed, or more rapid fire was needed.[49] The introduction of the revolver into combat in the 1840s changed the face of warfare. Almost all predecessors to the revolver needed to be reloaded after one or two shots; the few guns that could hold three or more rounds (such as the "pepperbox") were eccentric and unreliable. With the mass production of Colonel Samuel Colt's revolving handguns, the whites gained massive firepower superiority over the Indians.

The first major application of Colt technology was in Texas; there, Indians on horseback could launch arrows at a higher rate than settlers could fire and reload single-shot rifles. Moreover, a rifle was heavy and difficult to discharge from horseback. With Colt revolvers, Texans could exceed the Indians' rate of fire, and could shoot while mounted. The leap in technology from single-shot guns to the revolver was of far greater significance than subsequent refinements of multi-shot weapons. According to historian Carl Russell, the "Colt is strongly in evidence as the arm which marked the turning point in Indian warfare in the Far West by giving the white man superiority."[50] The gun had been what the Indians had wanted in trade from the whites. But the gun, so potent at first for the Indians, had become their undoing.

"The gun had a greater influence in changing the primitive ways of the Indians than any other object brought to America by the white man," Russell says.[51] The spread of French guns into the Louisiana Territory changed relations among the many tribes. Warfare was already endemic. The French trade shifted the balance of power to tribes that could get guns, and set all tribes on a feverish arms-trading race.[52] Moreover, tribes that lived near the encroaching whites faced "the choice of buying guns to defend themselves, or else being killed or enslaved."[53]

Guns were used for more than war. Especially for the Plains Indians, the combination of guns and horses (brought to the New World by the Spanish) engendered a new era of material prosperity. Hunting and survival became much easier, and the standard of living skyrocketed.

Nevertheless, the firearm remained a symbol of white superiority. Most tribes did not know how to make gunpowder.[54] No tribes knew how to manufacture or repair guns. A malfunctioning rifle was apt to be coerced with ancient tactics of fire, water, and brute force. Indian weapons were also destroyed through neglect and lack of maintenance.[55] While the natives mastered the breeding and care of horses, the manufacture and repair of firearms were beyond the grasp of a people who had been using stone-age technology. Moreover, the gun trade itself drew the Indians into an economically dependent relationship with the whites.[56]

As Indian cultures one at a time faced extermination, prophets would arise. By returning to the old ways, the prophets said, to the ways before the gun and whites and the technology that could never be mastered, the tribes could restore harmony with the spirits. An essential teaching of these prophets was that Indians should not use firearms. The spiritual rejection of firearms and other white technologies was first preached by a Delaware in 1764, and taken up by Pontiac in his efforts to unite all eastern tribes to push the whites into the sea. Half a century later, as the whites were conquering the upper midwest, the mystic Tenskwatawa implored the tribes of the Northwest Territory to reject firearms, alcohol, and other evils introduced by the Europeans. The mystic's half-brother, Tecumseh, accepted Tenskwatawa's preaching and organized tribes from Alabama to North Carolina to Canada in a grand alliance to stop white expansion. Tecumseh disdained firearms because the explosions frightened the deer. Practicality intervened, though, and the prophecy was elaborated to allow guns for fighting the whites, but not for hunting, and eventually the taboo against firearms was fully lifted. In any case, Tecumseh, like Pontiac before him, could not drive the whites away, with or without firearms.

As the white campaign for domination neared completion at the end of the nineteenth century, the great warriors of the plains, the Lakota Sioux, danced the Ghost Dance. Wearing their muslin "ghost shirts" and praying for a revival of the "old buffalo days," they believed they could become immune from bullets. The medicine men in the dance would chant "Hau! Hau! Hau!" But like the New Zealand Maori with their "Hau" cry, the Sioux and the rest of the tribes of the United States could neither defeat nor transcend the white man and his guns. The Ghost Dance—and the last hope that Indians could resist the whites—died with the massacre at Wounded Knee.[57]

The frontier war against the Indians meant that for over two centuries, many Americans were armed and ready to kill at a moment's notice. The Indian conflict helped build traditions of individual self-reliance, of violence, and of racism, that remain today. America's brutal war of racial genocide, savagely fought by both sides, does explain how our nation's development diverged from that of Australia or Canada. While the savage war between whites and Indians laid a foundation for America's attachment to the gun, it does not provide a convincing explanation of why America still cherishes the gun, long after the danger of an Indian raid has passed.

THE MILITIA

America won its independence by an armed revolt, the first colony of its epoch to do so. While George Washington's Continental Army garnered most of the American victories, irregular formations of citizens—the militia— were an essential component in the triumph of the Revolution. Of the approximately 400,000 men in active service against Great Britain, the militia amounted to about 165,000.[58]

Militias comprised the able-bodied males in the township or county.[59] They elected their own officers, who usually reported to commanding officers controlled by the state governor. Militiamen were responsible for supplying their own weapons and short-term equipment. If the militia went on a longer expedition, the state governments would supply what they could.[60] Whereas the firearms for the English militias were sometimes centrally stored by the government, American militias were armed by the militiamen. Instead of taxing the populace to buy common guns, the American states required citizens to own and carry private guns, bringing these guns to militia duty when necessary.[61] While many towns kept central armories that contained gunpowder, lead, and artillery, the militiaman's firearm was expected to be his contribution to community defense.

The militias wore no uniform. They were the deliberate opposite of uniformed professional forces. "[T]he gun offered the sole emblem of an individual militiaman's commitment," writes historian Marie Ahearn.[62] The militias existed virtually from the first days of white settlement, for many colonies were intermittently at war with the Indians. Frontier settlements were sometimes in a permanent state of war. In theory the British were supposed to protect the colonists, but in practice the colonists usually protected themselves.[63]

The independent characteristics of the American militiaman sometimes produced unexpected victories. At the port of Louisbourg, in French Canada in 1745, New England militias were ordered to make a frontal attack on the French fortress. The militiamen, seeing a speedy and futile death ahead, refused. Forced to abandon the frontal assault that would likely have failed, the commanders continued with a siege that eventually captured Louisbourg. The victory at Louisbourg reinforced for the people of New England the religious message preached at special militia assemblies: New Englanders were chosen by God to claim land in his name, as Israel had in the Old Testament. Aggressive war against the French or Indians was the modern version of the war against the Amalekites.[64]

The Americans believed they were both morally and tactically superior to professional European armies. The militias were composed of the solid middle class, people who were citizens first, and soldiers second. It was not uncommon for a troop of militiamen to debate whether to follow a commander's order.[65]

Life in a professional European army was brutal. Soldiers were drilled and disciplined until they could no longer think. They were expected to obey unquestioningly, and to move in precise lock-step formations. Only people who had no other choice joined the army, and the army was, in the words of the middle class, composed of "the dregs of society" rounded up from gin mills and jails.[66]

While the Americans thought themselves the citizen army of God, the English had a less inflated view of the Americans. The militias had generally performed badly in the French and Indian War. Being less afraid of their own officers than of the enemy, and being inclined to break out of formation and take cover when attacked, the American militias did not measure up to European standards.[67]

The colonial victory at Louisbourg had been the exception. The militias were not good for fighting far away from home. Most declined to go on long campaigns. Indeed, for most campaigns more than a short distance from home, the militia ideal of universal mandatory service was replaced by volunteers who enlisted for financial incentives. Even when under direct British command, American men at arms were not once able to defeat the French regular army in battle during the French and Indian War. The British concluded that the Americans were poor fighters compared to regular troops from Britain—troops who were drilled and drilled until they could perform coolly and automatically in the heat of combat, troops who did not question whether orders made sense.[68]

In 1775, the American Revolution came. The British thought they could quickly crush the slovenly, self-important Americans. The Americans expected that their skill in backwoods warfare with the Indians would enable numerically inferior citizen militias to smash the Redcoat puppets and the aristocratic snobs who commanded them.[69] The contest would prove to be more difficult and protracted than either side expected.

It was a British attempt to seize the colonists' armory that began the war. In April 1775, the British army, responding to a rumor that the Americans had come into possession of a cannon, marched on Concord, Massachusetts, to confiscate the weapons of war in the armory there. On the way to Concord, the British were met by a militia on the Lexington Green. About seventy men, half the town's adult male population, were there. "Disperse ye Rebels— Damn you, throw down your arms and disperse!" ordered British Major John Pitcairn.[70] One volley from the British regulars, followed by a bayonet charge, sent the American militia scurrying in disarray. The rout at Lexington confirmed what the French and Indian War had already shown the British. Americans could hold their own against the savage Indians; but the undisciplined American militia could never defeat civilized European regulars. The Redcoats marched on to Concord and destroyed the armory there.

At the North Bridge in Concord, the Redcoats met another militia. As the militia advanced, the British fired a volley, but the militia did not break. The militia "fired the shot heard 'round the world," and a battle raged for two or three minutes. The Redcoats panicked and ran.

The militia was unable to carry out a coordinated pursuit. "Every man was his own commander," remembered one participant.[71] Individually the Americans pursued the Redcoats as they left town on the Bay Road. Rather than fight in open fields, as professional European soldiers did, the Americans hid behind natural barriers, ambushed the British in indefensible natural traps, and harried the Redcoats all along the road back to Lexington. One British officer complained that the American had acted like "rascals" and fought as "concealed villans" with "the cowardly disposition . . . to murder us all." An American remembered "a grait many [British] lay dead, and the Road was bloddy."[72]

Back in London, William Pitt urged the House of Lords to conciliate with the Americans, instead of attempting to subjugate them by force, and warned that the armed American people were a formidable opponent: "My Lords, there are three millions of whigs. Three millions of whigs, my Lords, with arms in their hands, are a very formidable body. 'Twas the whigs my Lords, that set his Majesty's royal ancestors upon the throne of England."[73]

A few months after Lexington and Concord, the British and Americans fought again, at Breed's Hill north of Boston. The British army commander and the American militia commanders both made drastic errors. The battle was a draw. To the Americans, a draw was the same as victory. And in fact, they had inflicted twice as many casualties as they suffered. What the British called the "rabble in arms" had held their own against the mighty British army. In American memory, the draw at Breed's Hill became the glorious Battle of Bunker Hill. The official American national myth that the citizen militiaman was always superior to the professional soldier grew stronger than ever, regardless of the facts.[74]

As in the French and Indian War, the Americans declined to go far from home for very long. Even Americans who formally enlisted in the national Continental Army resisted signing up for more than a year. At the end of their year, they would leave for home and farm, sometimes in mid-campaign.[75]

In the winter of 1775, an American force headed north to seize Canada. The expedition was a disaster. In January 1776, half the American enlistments were set to expire, and in late December of 1775 the American generals launched a desperate—and unsuccessful—attack on Montreal, during a blizzard no less, before their "army" melted away.[76]

Because Americans insisted on returning to their farms at least once a year, or never wanted to stray far in the first place, George Washington and the Continental Congress never had a Continental Army as large as they wanted. This was to the better, as it turned out. Local militia service enabled men to fight the British sometimes, and keep the economy going the rest of the time. Further, since the British controlled the waters and could travel by sea, they could move faster than the Continental Army. Because the militia was widely dispersed, it could arise wherever the British deployed. Thus, the American side developed a tactical mobility to match the British mobility at sea. As Daniel Boorstin put it, "The American center was everywhere and nowhere—in each man himself."[77] Ironically, the insistence of the people on staying rooted to their land gave the American war effort a quick reaction time that it otherwise would have lacked.

When British regulars met American militias on open fields, the British training usually prevailed. At the battle of Kip's Bay in Manhattan, the

Connecticut militia broke and fled in terror, despite General Washington's attempts to restore order. The ranks of the militia collapsed again at the battle of Camden in 1780.

The Americans could afford some losses in battle; a large fraction of the adult white male population was available to fight British who ventured nearby. British soldiers, though, were more difficult to replace, since they had to be imported from across the Atlantic. The British held major coastal cities such as Boston and New York City, but control of the vast interior proved impossible. The militiamen had learned warfare from the Indians; in the mountains and swamps and forests they denied use of the country to the British. For example, after the 1780 capture of Charleston, the British quickly seized more towns in the interior, along the Savannah River. In the country around the river, chaotic civil war broke out between Tories loyal to the king and patriots seeking independence. As a result, the Redcoats could control nothing beyond the cities on the banks of the Savannah.[78]

The militia had good days to match the bad ones. At the battle of Cowpens, in South Carolina, the militia, under the command of Brigadier General Daniel Morgan, pretended to break and flee after firing a few shots. The British rushed ahead to rout the fleeing militia. With the British committed, American cavalry swept in on the left and right of the attacking Redcoats. In front of the Redcoats, the militia stopped "fleeing" and took up pre-arranged positions in the line with the Continental Army. General Morgan's double envelopment destroyed almost all the British contingent. Only a small force of cavalry reserves escaped.[79]

In the campaign of 1777, the British attempted to move down from Canada and up from New York City to meet in between on the Hudson River to isolate New England from the rest of the colonies. The militia of upstate New York and Vermont rose in large numbers wherever the British appeared. Ready to fight, the American populace had been outraged at the murder of a beautiful white woman by Indians who had been armed by the British. British General John Burgoyne complained "Wherever the King's forces point, militia in the amount of three or four thousand people assemble in 24 hours; they bring with them their subsistence, etc., and the alarm over, they return to their farms. . . ."[80] At the battle of Freeman's Farm, near Saratoga, riflemen hiding in the woods killed many Redcoats. Weeks later, when Burgoyne was in full retreat from New York, the militia sliced his supply lines. His six thousand men and all their military provisions fell into the hands of the Americans.[81] Fear of the "countryside in arms" led the British War Office to ban expeditions to the interior in 1778.

In 1778–1779, the Kentucky militia, led by George Rogers Clark, captured key British posts on the Wabash River in the future states of Indiana and Illinois. The victories helped legitimize the United States's claim to all British territory east of the Mississippi, which Britain later recognized in the Treaty of Paris.[82]

The militiamen brought their privately owned guns to battle. For the most part, they fought with the Kentucky rifle, which had a "shattering" effect against British Redcoats. The British muskets could fire three times as fast as the Kentucky rifle, and were well-suited for use by disciplined linear formations in open terrain. Redcoats were not expected to aim, depending instead on the cumulative effect of rapid fire. American guerrillas, though, did not fight formal pitched battles, but instead hid behind rocks and trees and sniped at the enemy.[83] The Kentucky rifle was effective only in the hands of a skilled marksman, who could hit a target the size of a man's head from two hundred yards away. A lucky shot could travel four hundred yards. The rifling of the gun's bore, which gave the bullet a spin, vastly extended the effective combat range for gunmen.[84] The American riflemen specialized in sniping at the British officers, causing them considerable apprehension, and distracting them from command.[85]

As George Washington often noted, the militia could rarely hold its own against regular troops. Echoing the criticisms of British commanders during the French and Indian War, Washington complained that the militia's "want of discipline and refusal, of almost every kind of restraint and Government, have produced . . . an entire disregard of that order and subordination necessary to the well doing of an army."[86] But the militia did not have to fight by European standards and win battles against disciplined linear formations. Because almost every free male was armed, the American resistance existed wherever the American people lived. The British occupied every major port. When they fought, they usually won. But defeating America was not simply a matter of capturing its major cities or crushing its uniformed army.[87] With every American male a militiaman, the British could triumph only by occupying the entire United States, and that task was far beyond their human resources. The Americans never really defeated the British; the war could have continued long past Yorktown. After eight years of winning most of the battles but getting no closer to winning the war, the British simply gave up.

Because of the war with the Indians, American whites were already proficient gun users, comfortable with using violence to get what they wanted. In most households, the gun was the most advanced piece of technology. Firearms fascinated many Americans, including their first president, who had a personal collection of over fifty guns, a third of them handguns. The War for Independence reinforced the existing American admiration of firearms and violence. The war vindicated the democratic ideal of the armed husbandman as the embodiment of republican virtue. As a twentieth-century presidential commission on American violence explicated, the War for Independence sanctified the philosophy that noble ends justify violent means.[88]

The experience of the Revolution helps explain why America's rulers did not even consider disarming the country in future years, although leaders of many other nations would have done so. In 1786, three counties in western Massachusetts erupted in "Shays's Rebellion" against oppressive state taxes and heavy-handed sheriffs.[89] While the rebellion was crushed quickly, the national government was weak, with the thirteen states in conflict (sometimes armed conflict) with each other. New York and Vermont, for example, had a long-running, intermittent border war, in which Vermont fought for and won independence. Chaos that would lead to reconquest by Europe seemed possible. George Washington feared that the nation was "faster verging to anarchy and confusion!"[90] Congress called for a national convention in Philadelphia to find ways to strengthen the federal government and to prevent another Shays's Rebellion that might blaze out of control.

With revolution in the air, countries such as Britain or Japan would have tried to disarm the people and build up a strong standing army around an executive. The Constitution adopted by the Philadelphia Convention took the opposite approach.

In regard to both the army and the militia, Congress was given the primary powers, with the executive to act only as commander in chief.[91] Limited to a two-year appropriation, the standing army was put under the congressional thumb.[92]

The grant of congressional militia powers immediately followed the grant of congressional power over the army. Congress was authorized "To provide for calling forth the Militia to execute the Laws of the Union, suppress Insurrections and repel Invasions," and "To provide for organizing, arming, and disciplining, the Militia, and for governing such Part of them as may be employed in the Service of the United States, reserving to the States respectively, the Appointment of Officers, and the Authority of training the Militia according to the discipline prescribed by Congress." In other words, Congress, not the president, had the power to set standards by which the states would train state militias, while states would appoint the militia officers. Congress could call the militia into national service, but unlike the army, the militia could not be sent overseas; the only purposes allowed were domestic: to execute the law, suppress insurrection, and repel invasion.

The grant of legislative and executive powers presumed the existence of both a standing military and a militia that was usually under state control, but subject to a federal call in an emergency. In the late nineteenth century the Supreme Court stated in dicta that even if there were no Second Amendment, state laws which disarmed citizens would be unconstitutional because they would deprive the federal government of its militia.[93]

During a time of internal rebellion, the framers of the Constitution chose to build stability and national security on the presumption that most adult white males would be personally armed. In retrospect, the decision made sense; although the War for Independence was over, a European invasion of at least some parts of the vast nation was not out of the question. The militia remained necessary for national defense. Of course in the long run, there was a risk that an armed people might revolt against the Constitution itself, and if successful, overthrow it.

Yet that risk was not seen as a defect in the structure of government. The potential for armed revolution was seen then (and later) as a safeguard.[94] When anti-federalists argued that the proposed Constitution could turn the central government into a dictatorship, Alexander Hamilton and James Madison replied in the newspaper essays later collected as *The Federalist Papers* that as long as a militia existed, no national dictator could long endure. Madison rejoiced in "the advantage of being armed, which the Americans possess over the people of almost every other nation." A national standing army could not, as a practical matter, amount to more than thirty thousand men, Madison said. "To these would be opposed a militia amounting to near half a million of citizens with arms in their hands. . . . It may well be doubted whether a militia thus circumscribed could ever be conquered by such a proportion of regular troops." He predicted that the European governments, who were "afraid to trust the people with arms," would be "speedily overturned" if ever opposed by a popular militia directed by locally controlled governments and officers.[95] James Madison's friend Tench Coxe explained:

> The powers of the sword are in the hands of the yeomanry of America from sixteen to sixty. The militia of these free commonwealths, entitled and accustomed to their arms, when compared with any possible army, must be tremendous and irresistible. Who are the militia? Are they not ourselves. . . . Congress have no power to disarm the militia. Their swords, and every other terrible implement of the soldier, are the birth-right of an American. . . . [T]he unlimited power of the sword is not in the hands of either the federal or state governments, but, where I trust in God it will ever remain, in the hands of the people.[96]

The armed people were the ultimate check in the system of checks and balances.

Nevertheless, anti-federalists feared that the new central government might become oppressive. Richard Henry Lee warned that Congress might create a "select militia" of "one-fifth or one-eighth part of the men capable of bearing arms." Lee insisted that the militia always include "all men capable of bearing arms."[97] Afraid of congressional control of the militia, at the Virginia ratifying convention, George Mason warned that the government might gradually increase its power "by totally disusing and neglecting the militia." Fellow anti-federalist Patrick Henry agreed, repeatedly stressing that a Congress that controlled the militia could prevent popular rebellion against federal tyranny. "The militia, sir, is our ultimate safety. . . . The great object is that every man be armed . . . . everyone who is able may have a gun."[98]

Because of anti-federalist protests, a Bill of Rights was added, including: "A well-regulated Militia, being necessary to the security of a free state, the right of the people to keep and bear arms shall not be infringed." As the Supreme Court has stated repeatedly, the amendment guarantees the right of individual citizens to own firearms.[99] The Supreme Court interpretation accords with evidence of contemporaneous intent from the period of the Second Amendment's ratification.[100]

In a 1939 decision, the Supreme Court noted the historical understanding of the militia: that most able-bodied citizens would be personally armed, would train together sometimes, and would serve together in an emergency. The unanimous Court wrote: "The Militia comprised all males physically capable of acting in concert for the common defense. . . . Ordinarily when called for service these men were expected to appear bearing arms supplied by themselves and of the kind in common use at the time."[101]

The modern definition of militia comports with the Supreme Court and historical definition. The United States Code states: "The militia of the United States consists of all able-bodied males at least 17 years of age and . . . under 45 years of age." The next section of the code distinguishes the organized militia (the National Guard) from the "unorganized militia."[102]

The Second's Amendment's phrase "a well-regulated militia" is sometimes said to mean "a militia subject to nearly unlimited bureaucratic regulation." Hence, gun controls not amounting to prohibition would be permissible restrictions on the "well-regulated militia."

Another, perhaps more plausible interpretation, looks at the phrase "well-regulated" as it refers to firearms. In firearms parlance, "regulating" a gun means adjusting it so that successive shots hit as close together as possible. If the objective is achieved, the gun is "well-regulated." For example, the 1989 *Gun Digest,* in an article about double-barrelled rifles, notes, "The well-regulated double [rifle] shoots closely enough with both barrels to hit an animal at normal ranges."[103] The *Rifle Guide* notes that "All of these [older, larger, black-powder, British] double rifles are regulated for a given bullet weight and a specific powder charge. Regulating, in this instance, means that both barrels will shoot very close together."[104] *The Firearms Dictionary* does not define "regulated," but does define "regulating barrels," which is "a tedious job needed to make both barrels of a side-by-side or O/U [over and under] gun shoot to the same point."[105] A magazine article about a Smith & Wesson pistol notes, "The sights are perfectly regulated to center for standard weight bullets."[106]

The colonial political usage of the phrase "well-regulated militia" also suggests that the word "regulated" was an exhortation to competence, not an invitation to bureaucracy. Before independence was even declared, Josiah Quincy had argued for the necessity of "a well-regulated militia composed of the freeholder, citizen and husbandman, who take up their arms to preserve their property as individuals, and their rights as freemen."[107]

Thus, "a well-regulated militia" would be an effective citizen militia whose members hit their targets. Government regulations to make the militia "well-regulated" would seem permissible, whereas regulations that did not promote militia quality would be suspect. Requiring all militia members to achieve minimum target-range competence or else take supplementary shooting classes, as Switzerland requires of its militia, would seem legitimate under the Second Amendment. Particular firearms policies, some of which would promote "a well-regulated militia," are discussed in more detail in chapter 11.

The Second Amendment was meant to prevent oppression by a standing army; such oppression was to be prevented by ensuring that the people would be universally armed and trained in the use of arms. As Madison put it, no tyranny could endure "without a standing army, an enslaved press, and a disarmed populace."[108] But could a government based on Madison's theory remain stable?

Early in President Washington's first term, in 1794, parts of Virginia (today, West Virginia) and western Pennsylvania revolted against high federal taxes on whiskey.[109] The president exercised his power (which had been delegated to him by Congress) to call forth the militia to suppress the Whiskey Rebellion; he warned that if local militias could not or would not do the job, he would call forth militia from other states.[110] The local militia responded, and the insurrection was crushed.[111]

The decisions of the framers of the Constitution and of President Washington today seem predictable, but they ran against the dominant course of world history. A weak federal government, faced with armed rebellion against its authority, responded by creating a government structure that presumed the whole citizen population would individually own weapons of war, and would be trained in their use.

The War of 1812 is sometimes called the Second War for Independence. Filled with glorious, not wholly accurate, memories of militia valor in the first War for Independence, the United States eagerly took on Britain a second time.[112] As discussed in chapter 4, the militia of Kentucky and other states marched off to what was expected to be the rapid conquest of Canada.

The invasion of Canada turned into a humiliating defeat for the American militia, and an affirmation (for Canada) of the superiority of a disciplined nation led by an aristocracy.

The war ended in 1815 in a draw, with the Treaty of Ghent, signed in Belgium. News traveled slowly, and a few weeks after the war had officially ended, General Andrew Jackson and the men of Kentucky destroyed the British at the Battle of New Orleans. As usual, Americans forgot the humiliation of 1812, glorified the victory of 1815, and congratulated their citizen-soldier selves on their extraordinary fighting ability.

Jackson's troops had brought their own rifles to war, most being superbly crafted weapons made by the Pennsylvania Dutch. These Pennsylvania rifles were the same "Kentucky rifles" discussed above.[113]

Even if the militia was not always as "well regulated" as the Constitution had hoped, and even if the American militiaman was not so invincible in fact as he was in memory, the citizen militia had changed the course of American and world history. That Americans had guns was a necessary condition for winning independence from the world's strongest colonial power. The military historians Coakley and Conn explain that the revolution helped democratize war, turning it from a contest between professional soldiers into a struggle between the people of two nations.[114]

The militia in England had withered from lack of use once William and Mary ascended to the throne in 1688. England's fighting was no longer done in England by citizens, but overseas by soldiers.[115] As the American frontier closed, the militias began to fade from disuse. The annual militia muster began to amount to little more than a get-together for veterans of the old fighting militia, and a day of drinking for everyone. Citizens drilled when times were dangerous, but, fortunately for America, things seemed to grow more peaceful at home.[116] After the Civil War, few Americans fought on American soil. The new American wars were overseas, a theater where the militia had no value (except perhaps as an introduction to military training for future soldiers).

In the decades between the Civil War and World War II, the militia was most frequently seen in the often-violent clash between working people and capital. At times the militia was on the populist side, as when North Dakota Governor William Langer threatened in 1933 to call out the militia to shoot any sheriff who attempted a farm foreclosure.[117]

More often, the militia sided with capital.[118] The presence of armed citizens, including militias, on both sides of the economic conflicts helped give the United States "the bloodiest and most violent labor history of any industrial nation in the world."[119] The problem was not only that the people (both strikers and militia) had guns. American businessmen, who usually controlled the police and private armies (e.g., the Pinkertons and the Baldwin-

Felts "detectives") were less accustomed to accommodation than their British counterparts, and more inclined to take the law into their own hands to break a strike.[120] Historian Michael Wallace suggests that American "labor violence" would be better labeled "capitalist violence."[121]

The coal miners who took up arms in places like Matewan, West Virginia, or Huerfano County, Colorado, were continuing an American tradition of using violence as a last resort to protect their homes and freedom from destruction by outside forces.[122] Yet the citizen militias that crushed so many labor rebellions were also part of the American tradition. They thought they were defending their way of life against assault by alien or immigrant influences.

The aristocracies of Europe had been afraid that an armed population would perpetrate revolutionary class warfare. The United States, on the other hand, began with the radical precept that most citizens should be armed. And in the United States, perhaps because of the opportunities offered by American freedom (including all the free land from exterminating the Indians), the armed populace turned out to be the ally of conservative respect for private property and inequality of wealth.[123] The intuitive trust of the authors of the Constitution (many of them conservative and wealthy) in the stability of an armed society was vindicated.[124]

Over time, economic conflicts grew less violent as the New Deal took hold, collective bargaining rights were protected, and the farm crisis ameliorated.[125] With little fear of enemies, foreign or domestic, state governments and the people continued to let the militia decay from neglect.

Within days after the attack on Pearl Harbor, when for the first time in over a century America faced a serious risk of invasion, the militia reactivated en masse. The first months of war seemed especially dangerous. German submarines were seen patrolling off the East Coast. Japanese bombs occasionally exploded on the Oregon coast; the Japanese army seized several Alaskan islands. A Japanese landing on the West Coast was feared, predicted as a tactic to divert Americans from the main front in the Pacific. The National Guard had already been sent into overseas combat. Governors and other officials in Hawaii, Maryland, Virginia, and Oregon called on the long-dormant unorganized militia of individual citizens to bring their own guns to guard beaches and patrol landing areas. Tens of thousands responded.[126] All over the country people took up arms.[127] After the National Guard was federalized for overseas duty, "the unorganized militia proved a successful substitute for the National Guard," according to a Defense Department study. Militiamen, providing their own guns, were trained in patrolling, roadblock techniques, and guerilla warfare.[128]

Following World War II, America became virtually immune from invasion. The citizen militia has vanished even from the memory of the people.

All that remain are drawings in the history books of places called "Lexington" and "Bunker Hill."[129]

Important as the militia has been to America's past, it is no longer a significant part of America's national culture. Having helped to democratize gun ownership and validate the just use of force, the militia makes no significant continuing contribution today to America's gun culture. The militia will remain mostly forgotten until, perhaps, as in World War II, an unexpected crisis requires armed American citizens to restore order or defeat an invader.

The Soviet empire having collapsed, America faces a choice. America could demobilize much of its worldwide standing army, under the theory that large standing armies are made for war, and the cold war is over. Or America could conclude that the drug war is the next mission for the standing army. Deployment of the army in border interdiction may lead to the use of the army in purely domestic law enforcement. To James Harrington or James Madison, the sight of uniformed national army troops, armed with rapid-fire guns, and conducting commodity raids (most likely without probable cause) would be quite alarming.

As an alternative, America might demobilize much of the standing army, and consider whether American nuclear, naval, and air power, backed up by armed citizens and a smaller army, would be more than sufficient for realistic security needs.

PRIVATE LAW ENFORCEMENT:
THE "WILD WEST" AND THE VIGILANTE TRADITION

Having secured independence from Europe in 1783, Americans turned their attention to the North American continent for the next century. There were no impassable barriers of gigantic deserts or uninhabitable scrubland in the path of westward settlement. Pioneers moved west faster than government-provided law and order could catch up. Settlers had to enforce the law themselves. While the militia tradition developed by the colonies and the early republic would eventually fade from the American psyche, the popular enforcement of law and order on the frontier West would become an American myth, one that remains vivid to this day. I will examine two aspects of the frontier myth: vigilantism (crowds taking action to punish perceived lawbreakers) and the "Wild West" (where a gun on every hip is usually thought to have produced chaos and crime).

On the frontier and in the more easterly towns, there were not enough resources to support a professional law enforcement infrastructure, particularly one that could pursue criminals beyond the town border.[130] Accordingly, as many as five hundred different vigilante movements arose in the United States in the years before 1900. No other nation developed such a powerful vigilante tradition.[131] In practice (although not in modern memory) vigilantism was a rational and mostly constructive response to the weakness of the formal law enforcement system.

One of the first groups described by historians as vigilantes was organized in Revolutionary War Virginia by Colonel Edward Lynch. There being no established courts in rural Virginia, Lynch set up criminal courts to try suspected Tories. His "Lynch mobs" whipped people and drove them from the community, but did not hang them.[132]

A decade before the Revolutionary War, in 1766–1767, South Carolina's back country was ravaged by outlaw gangs. They abducted girls to be their mates in outlaw villages, and robbed, raped, and tortured plantation masters and their wives. With no local courts or sheriffs, middle- and upper-class citizens banded together as "Regulators." They broke up the outlaw gangs, flogged the idle, and drove the worst criminals out of the area. Although the two-year Regulator campaign succeeded in breaking the outlaw crime wave, the Regulators became increasingly sadistic and arbitrary. An opposition group called the "Moderators" arose, and fought the Regulators to a standstill until 1769, when the colonial government finally provided local courts and sheriffs.[133]

The name "regulator" had at times been adopted by armed groups who protected their territory against oppressive nonlocal governments. The Boston Tea Party, many other local reactions against the British, and Shays's Rebellion were all acts of regulators. So were many uprisings against economic oppression and undemocratic government in the 1830s and 1840s, such as the Dorr War in Rhode Island.[134]

The South Carolina regulators, however, were less concerned with oppressive government than with the absence of any effective government. Their concern was crime, not despotism. In coming years, similar anti-crime groups would be called vigilantes.

Over the nineteenth century, vigilantes would kill at least seven hundred people, perhaps many more. Thousands and thousands would be driven out of town or whipped. Vigilante groups, though, were not the raucous and disorganized mobs portrayed on modern television. Vigilantes formed temporarily into organized hierarchies of command. At the top were usually the wealthiest and most powerful men in the community. Vigilantes never wore masks or disguises, because they saw themselves as upholding the law. Sometimes they even held trials, which produced acquittals.[135] The sheer mass of an assembly of most the adult males in a community was what gave the vigilantes their coercive force, although for good measure many brought along their personal firearms.

One of the first vigilante organizations was the anti-horse-thief move-ment, which originated soon after the Revolutionary War and spread nation-wide. In many states the Anti-Horse-Thief Association was officially recog-nized as an adjunct to the regular law enforcement structure. By 1900, the association included hundreds of thousands of members; only with the advent of the automobile did the Anti–Horse-Thief Association disappear.[136]

In the 1830s, Mississippi River towns were overrun by faro gamblers who branched into murder and robbery. Vigilantes drove out and killed gamblers in Vicksburg. The "antigambling crusade" spread up and down the Mississippi River and beyond, reaching New Orleans, Natchez, Louisville, Cincinnati, and Chicago.[137]

Most vigilantes followed what historian Richard Maxwell Brown called the "socially constructive model," as exemplified by the Illinois Regulators of 1841. Outlaw gangs ruled several northern counties. Local government was weak, and in some counties controlled by the outlaws. Led by a bank president and a wealthy settler, middle-class farmers banded together, and with whippings, hangings, and firing squads, the vigilantes destroyed the outlaws and made their counties safer.[138] Most vigilante committees were short-lived, having been formed to deal with a discrete problem, and dis-banding after their success.

In Bannack, Montana, in the early 1860s, the sheriff himself secretly headed a network of highwaymen, horse thieves, and murderers. Eventually, the townspeople realized that the sheriff and his appointed deputies were assisting the reign of terror in Bannack and nearby Virginia City. Several vigilante organizations formed openly, held elections for officers, conducted trials, and carried on their activities in daylight with no masks. During the winter of 1863–1864, thirty criminals were hung, including Sheriff Plummer.[139] The vigilante leader, Wilbur Fiske Sanders, went on to found the Montana Bar Association and was elected one of Montana's first two United States senators in 1889.[140]

Vigilante organizations "often drew their leaders from the top levels of local society," and "their following came largely from the solid middle class," writes Richard Hofstadter.[141] Richard Maxwell Brown, the foremost historian of vigilantism, explains that vigilantism protected conservative values of property and order, "represented a genuine community consensus," was not usually directed against minorities, and was often socially con-structive.[142] Most vigilance committees comprised several hundred mem-bers, who amounted to a large fraction of the able-bodied men in their communities.[143] Vigilantes were by definition violent, but not always lethal. Hanging one or two offenders and expelling the rest from the community usually sufficed to restore order.[144]

In 1813–1814 John Marshall—while serving as Chief Justice of the

United States Supreme Court—joined other Virginia leaders to found a "Committee of Vigilance" to provide local defense against a possible British attack.[145] While serving as president, Andrew Jackson applauded Iowa farmers' vigilante tactics.[146] The enshrinement of popular sovereignty as an American value during the Jackson administration coincided with a tremendous upsurge in vigilantism.[147]

Vigilantes were exalted when the nineteenth century began and when it ended. Young Theodore Roosevelt begged to join a North Dakota group that was tracking down rustlers and horse thieves.[148] (Seeing him as a "skim milk cowboy," the group refused to let him join.) In 1890, there were four ex-vigilantes in the U.S. Senate. Statesmen and governors pointed with pride to their own experiences as vigilantes.[149] Vigilantes justified themselves on the grounds that "self-preservation is the first law of nature," and advocated popular sovereignty, the need for efficient and inexpensive justice, and, when the government became unbearably corrupt, "the sacred right of revolution."[150] As one newspaper of the time put it, "Deplore, as we may, that condition of a society that requires the gathering of a mob to execute the decrees of justice, it is an improvement over that other high state of civilization which allows murder to run riot in a community and allows assassins to walk the streets unharmed."[151]

Vigilantism was an appropriate response to the social conditions of nineteenth-century America. Because jails were nonexistent or inadequate, the only way the frontier—or sometimes a city—could deal with a criminal was to drive him out (the most common result), execute him, or surrender to him.[152] In part vigilantism was spurred by the lack of economic resources for a professional criminal justice system on the frontier and the corrupt nature of the forces that did exist.[153]

There might have been other solutions. But tax increases for a bigger criminal justice system (or for any other purpose) were never popular, least of all with the wealthy men who led the vigilantes. In most of the frontier communities, the sparse population simply could not afford an extensive government law enforcement apparatus.[154] Although some Americans urged the creation of strong American federal police force for the frontier, similar to Canada's Mounted Police, western communities resisted it as a military encroachment on local autonomy.[155]

Given the resistance to taxation and to federal control, vigilantism was a necessary antidote to what would have been anarchy. Far from being a symbol of lawlessness, "Vigilantism was a violent sanctification of the deeply cherished values of life and property," writes Brown.[156] Accordingly,

The vigilante credo was accepted by legal scholars, judges, and lawyers, as well as by men of action, during the late 1800s and early 1900s. On the whole, the legal illuminati granted qualified approval to vigilantism as a rational response to the inadequacies of the criminal justice system.[157]

Today, "vigilante" is an epithet. People who are afraid of citizens bearing arms for self-defense warn that "vigilantism" is unacceptable in modern America. But what modern gun prohibitionists usually mean by "vigilantism" is random, uncontrolled, self-directed, and racist violence. For example, in a national poll, *Newsweek* magazine asked if Bernhard Goetz's shooting of four men who allegedly tried to rob him—an act which *Newsweek* called "vigilantism"—was acceptable. But the real historical meaning of vigilantism had nothing to do with individual self-defense against crime. Vigilantism meant organized, community effort to rid a locality of lawbreakers.

America's less-than-accurate historical recollection of vigilantism is matched by a wildly inaccurate "memory" of the so-called Wild West. Modern America remembers the "gun-totin' " Wild West as an intensely violent place, overrun with crime, where citizens were nearly always in fear for their lives. The assumption is that no matter how bad crime may be today, permitting citizens to carry guns is unacceptable, because that would bring a return to the Wild West. Brooklyn District Attorney Charles Hynes— who has made his office's top priority the prosecution of unlicensed firearms possession—rejects the idea that ordinary citizens ought to be allowed to carry guns. He decries the notion of licensed, trained citizens carrying guns as "leading to a Dodge City atmosphere."[158]

But while the assumption that the American West was extremely violent has been commonly shared, it has never been rigorously proven. Historian Roger McGrath's book *Gunfighters Highwaymen & Vigilantes* put the "Wild West" under a microscope.[159] Studying the nineteenth-century Sierra Nevada mining towns of Aurora and Bodie, McGrath found far less violence than the Wild West myth remembers.

Aurora and Bodie certainly had as much potential for violence as any places in the West. The population was mainly young transient males subject to few social controls. There was one saloon for every twenty-five men; brothels and gambling houses were also common. Governmental law enforcement was ineffectual, and sometimes the sheriff was himself the head of a criminal gang. Nearly everyone carried a gun. (Aurorans usually carried a Colt Navy .36 six-shot revolver, while Bodeites sported the Colt Double Action Model known as the "Lightning.")[160]

Was the homicide rate in those towns high? Yes. The "bad men" who hung out in saloons shot each other at a fearsome rate, although Aurora's rate was less than the rate in modern Washington, D.C.[161] The presence of guns turned many petty drunken quarrels into fatalities.

But other crime was virtually nil. The per capita annual robbery rate was 7 percent of modern New York's. The burglary rate 1 percent. Rape was unknown.[162] "The old, the weak, the female, the innocent, and those unwilling to fight were rarely the targets of attacks," McGrath found. One resident of Bodie did "not recall ever hearing of a respectable women or girl in any manner insulted or even accosted by the hundreds of dissolute characters that were everywhere. In part this was due to the respect depravity pays to decency; in part to the knowledge that sudden death would follow any other course."[163] Everyone carried a gun and, except for young men who liked to drink and fight with each other, everyone was far more secure than today's residents of cities with gun prohibitions.[164] If innocent people not living in fear of criminal attack is one index of civilization, Aurora and Bodie were more tranquil, civilized places than most modern American cities.

The experience of Aurora and Bodie was repeated throughout the West. One study and five major cattle towns with a reputation for violence— Abilene, Ellsworth, Wichita, Dodge City, and Caldwell—found that all together the towns had less than two criminal homicides per year.[165] During the 1870s, Lincoln County, New Mexico, was in a state of anarchy and civil war. Homicide was astronomical, but (as in Bodie and Aurora) confined almost exclusively to drunken males upholding their "honor." Modern big-city crimes such as rape, burglary, and mugging were virtually unknown.[166] A study of the Texas frontier from 1875 to 1890 found that burglaries and robberies (except for bank, train, and stagecoach robberies) were essentially nonexistent. People did not bother locking doors, and murder was rare, except of course for young men shooting each other in "fair fights" that they voluntarily engaged in.[167] (The "Urbanization, Immigration, and Ethnic Relations" section of this chapter details how precarious personal security was in the urbanized East.)

In sum, historian W. Eugene Hollon found "the Western frontier was a far more civilized, more peaceful, and safer place than American society is today."[168] Another historian concludes "this last frontier left no significant heritage of offenses against the person, relative to other sections of the country."[169] Frank Prassel suggests that "in the American West, crime may have been more closely related to the developing urban environment than the former existence of a frontier."[170]

Yet the "mild" West is not what America "remembers" from the frontier. California and Nevada newspapers carried hyperbolic stories of the gunmen of Bodie, full of fictitious quotes and events. The papers never told their readers that for people who did not enjoy drunken fights, there was no place in the United States safer than Bodie.[171] Popular consciousness of the American "Wild West" resembles more closely the memories of the city audiences who attended the enormously popular "Buffalo Bill

Wild West Show." The show opened in 1883, and featured a stagecoach robbery, shooting contests, numerous gunfights, and terrifying Indians.[172] Historian Robert Athearn's *The Mythic West* explains how the "Wild West," exemplified (or invented) by the Buffalo Bill show, became a symbol of the purest, most rugged form of Americanism.[173]

Guns had been important in the preservation of law and order on the nineteenth-century frontier. Criminal violence would likely have made settlement nearly impossible, if citizens had not been armed. But they were armed, and things were, for a frontier, relatively well ordered, especially when compared to the cities of the East (although Indians were of course a threat, as detailed above). Yet America's historical "memory," with its mythic fascination with violence, tells of crazed, bloodthirsty masked vigilante mobs, and the frightening, crime-ridden "Wild West."

FEUDS

The historical memory of the crime-filled frontier West and its vigilantes and gunfighters is out of alignment with the true historical West. Other aspects of historical memory are also skewed. One of the most widely shared American images of gun ownership in the nineteenth century is the feud: hillbilly families shooting each other in the Appalachian Mountains. Indeed, the most famous feudists of all, the Hatfields and McCoys, are more widely recognized than many American presidents. The Hatfield-McCoy feud symbolizes to modern America an episode of psychotic blood lust, of man's basest instincts turned into genocide by firearms.[174] The reality of the Hatfield-McCoy feud was more complex, as Altina L. Waller details in *Feud: Hatfields, McCoys, and Social Change in Appalachia, 1860–1900*.[175] In the Tug Valley that straddled West Virginia and Kentucky lived the descendants of poor people who had migrated from the British Isles. Since the best eastern seaboard land had been taken, they moved inland to less fertile land in the Appalachian Mountain valleys.

The Hatfields lived on the West Virginia side of the Tug River. Operating a logging business, they were among the first families of the valley to earn a living from the emerging world of commerce, rather than from the local world of farming. The McCoys lived across the river in Kentucky; they also lived in near poverty on their farms as they practiced traditional slash-and-burn agriculture, and complained bitterly and jealously about the more prosperous Hatfields. The conflict between the Hatfield and McCoy families simmered for years, with the different sides conducting lawsuits and urging law enforcement authorities to prosecute the other.[176]

On election day 1882 (a traditional day for drunkenness), a gang of three McCoys got into a fight with a Hatfield and killed him. The Hatfields formed an unofficial posse, captured the three McCoys, and executed them.

That ended the killing. Most people in the Tug Valley, except for clan leader Ranel McCoy, accepted the results of that election day. Life returned to normal.

Five years later, though, Ranel McCoy prevailed upon a distant relative, a lawyer named Perry Cline, to help the McCoys get even. Cline convinced the governor of Kentucky to offer a reward for the Hatfields who had executed the McCoys.

The outside power of the state of Kentucky upset the resolution that the valley had achieved. Kentucky posses and gangs of Pinkerton detectives raided Hatfield territory, killing one Hatfield and capturing nine others.[177] In retaliation, on New Year's Day 1888, the Hatfields burned the McCoys' home, killing two children in the process. The national press reported that the counties were in a state of war and that nearby towns might be incinerated. The governors of Kentucky and West Virginia prepared to send in the militia to restore order. As the governors found out, however, the valley was tranquil, except for the two extended families involved in the conflict.

West Virginia Governor Wilson, outraged at the unlawful raid into West Virginia territory, tried to free the Hatfields imprisoned in Kentucky. He asked the federal courts to issue a writ of habeas corpus to return the Hatfields from the Kentucky jail because they had been feloniously kidnapped. The case was eventually heard before the United States Supreme Court. The Court agreed that the Hatfields had been abducted in violation of extradition laws, but said that there was no federal remedy for West Virginia to retrieve its citizens unlawfully held in Kentucky jails.[178]

Of the nine Hatfields held in Kentucky, eight were imprisoned for life, and one was executed. The Kentucky government's execution was the last act of violence. Violence had flared for a couple days in 1882, and for several weeks in 1887-1888, when Kentucky government agents invaded West Virginia.[179] The feuding families had comprised only 3 percent of the population of the Tug Valley; murder was rare enough so that the entire valley was shocked by the killings.

Waller argues that the bloodshed was no proof of "white savagery." Rather, the deaths were caused by the efforts of outside industrialists, through the governor of Kentucky, to assert control over the Tug Valley; indeed, two of the killings were perpetrated by the state of Kentucky and its agents, and it was the murders by Kentucky that incited the brief episode of violence that turned the local conflict into a grossly exaggerated national sensation.

For Kentucky's governor, the issue was state government control over the Tug Valley—control to assist the railroads and mining companies that were moving in to "develop" the valley. For the national press, the issue was what the *New York Times* called "the purely savage character of the population." The *Times* repeated as fact the tall tale that Hatfield family leader Devil Anse had five wives. "A long course of common schools, churches, soap and water is required," the *Times* proclaimed, "before these simple children of nature will forbear to kill a man whenever they take a dislike to him."[180]

For the developers and the newspapers, the feud was justification for the imposition of a new way of life, to reform the mountain "savages." The outsiders regarded the residents as lazy and stupid, and considered them "irrational" for not adjusting the rhythms of their lives to the demands of work in the coal mines. A popular contemporary book about the feud, *An American Vendetta: A Story of Barbarism in the United States,* condemned the mountain folk for their "excessive independence of thought," loose sexual standards, and affinity for whiskey, all of which supposedly created a culture of violence in the community.[181] Ironically, it was the efforts of the outsiders and modernizers to assert control—through the Kentucky government's capture of the West Virginia Hatfields—that created the second, sensationalized phase of the feud, a phase used as justification to civilize the savages.

Industrial development brought violence rather than civilized peace. In 1921, the coalminers of nearby Matewan attempted to form a United Mine Workers local and go on strike. The coal companies imported "detectives" from the Baldwin-Felts agency to force the miners back to work at gunpoint. Matewan's chief of police, Sid Hatfield, an orphan who had been adopted by the Hatfields, confronted the detectives as they tried to evict families from their company-owned homes. In the resulting "Matewan Massacre," the agents killed several townspeople, and Sid Hatfield shot seven agents. Hatfield was tried for murder, and acquitted on grounds of self-defense. A year later, as Sid Hatfield and his wife were walking up the steps of a courthouse to testify, he was gunned down by Baldwin-Felts detectives. The detectives were tried and acquitted by a jury composed of nonunion coal company employees; many witnesses did not testify because of fear of retribution from the company.[182] Observes Waller: "Once feuding, whiskey, and guns were eliminated, [outside developers and reformers] argued, an impartial judicial system would readily bring about order. Now, coal companies enforced their wishes with guns, reinforced by a county government and judicial system they had bought and paid for."[183]

The image of the feuding Hatfields and McCoys is unlikely to be changed by books such as Waller's from university presses. The myth of the gun-totin' feuding hillbillies, like the myth of the gun-totin' crime-ridden Wild West, is a near inversion of reality. The images today reinforce the beliefs of Americans who believe that guns cause violence; that gun ownership is a primitive urge which must be controlled for the good of rationality and peace. Ironically, as the Hatfield-McCoy episode illustrates, it was the determination of cosmopolitan America to control and "civilize" the "savages" of rural America that was the most important cause of violence.

RACE RELATIONS

In the decade preceding the Civil War, the ubiquitous belief of American citizens that violent enforcement of their moral principles was more important than adherence to the law helped destroy the Union. Part of the Compromise of 1850 was the Fugitive Slave Act, which ordered federal marshals in northern states to return escaped slaves to the South.[184] The Fugitive Slave Act authorized the marshals to call out the *posse comitatus*. While the militia was under the control of state governors or their appointees, and was (ideally) a well-regulated and trained body with officers, the posse comitatus was more informal. It was (and in many states still is) simply the adult males in a locality, all of whom must assemble at the command of the sheriff to apprehend local lawbreakers.[185]

But when the federal government called for help with slave-catching, the northern people balked. Armed vigilance committees resisted enforcement of the Fugitive Slave Act and liberated slaves at gunpoint from the federal authorities.[186] Massachusetts Judge Lemuel Shaw reasoned that the Constitution was the highest law, and ordered runaway slaves returned to their masters. Crowds of anti-slavery activists, though, enforced their version of natural law, invaded the courthouse, and freed captive slaves.[187]

The South already had its vigilance committees devoted to dealing with "servile insurrection" or potential abolitionist trouble.[188] The southern patrols also searched for slaves who were off the plantation after dark or who held illegal meetings, and summarily punished all offenders. These patrols were the social ancestor of the postwar Ku Klux Klan.[189]

A nation in arms was racing toward confrontation. In "bleeding Kansas," free-soil "Jayhawks" fought a guerrilla war with pro-slavery settlers.[190] John Brown's raid, panic over slave rebellion in the South, northern mobs freeing slaves from the custody of the courts—all symbolized the collapse of the social order.[191]

After the Civil War, the defeated southern states aimed to preserve slavery in fact if not in law. Keeping blacks disarmed had always been an issue; the first mention of Negroes in Virginia's laws had been a 1644 provision barring free Negroes from owning firearms, but with emancipation, the civil status of ex-slaves assumed a paramount importance. The states enacted Black Codes, which barred the black freedmen from exercising basic civil rights, including the right to bear arms. Mississippi's provision was typical: No freedman "shall keep or carry fire-arms of any kind, or any ammunition. . . ."[192] *The Special Report of the Anti-Slavery Conference of 1867* complained that freedmen were "forbidden to own or bear firearms and thus . . . rendered defenseless against assaults" by whites.[193]

Despite the statutes, and at the suggestion of Reconstruction governors and other leaders, blacks often formed militias to resist white terrorism.[194] For example, in June 1867 in Greensboro, Alabama, the police let the murderer of a black voting registrar escape; in response, a freedman who would later serve in the Alabama state legislature urged his fellow freedmen to create a permanent militia. "Union League" militias were formed all over central Alabama. The freedmen slipped from white control. One planter protested that his workers were "turbulent and disorderly," coming and going when they wished, as if they had a choice whether or not to work. The Union League, protested another ex-master, was advising freedmen "to ignore the Southern white man as much as possible. . . . [T]o set up for themselves."

The next spring, the Ku Klux Klan came to central Alabama. The Klansmen, unlike the freedmen, had horses, and thus the tactical advantages of mobility. In a few months, the Klan triumph was complete. One freedman recalled that the night riders, after reasserting white control, "took the weapons from mighty near all the colored people in the neighborhood."[195]

The same dynamic existed throughout the South. Sometimes militias consisting of freedmen or Unionists were able to resist the Klan or other white forces.[196] In places like the South Carolina back-country, where the blacks were a numerical majority, the black militias kept white terrorists at bay for long periods.[197]

While many blacks participated in informal, local militias, most of the Reconstruction governors set up official state militias that were racially integrated. Like many other facets of the Reconstruction governments (and the racist governments that followed them), the integrated "black" state militias were corrupt. The state militias, which sought to protect the state governments and the election process, were frequently in conflict with informal white militias. Arms shipments from the federal government to arm the militias were often intercepted and seized by white militias.[198]

Official or unofficial, the black militias were the primary target of the white racist resistance.[199] In areas where the black militias lost and the Klan or other white groups took control, "almost universally the first thing done was to disarm the negroes and leave them defenseless," wrote Albion Tourgée. (An attorney and civil rights worker from the North, Tourgée would later represent the civil rights plaintiff in *Plessy* v. *Ferguson*.)[200] Afraid of race war and retribution, whites were terrified at the mere sight of a black person with a gun.[201] As one historian notes, "From the southern white's point of view, a well-armed Negro militia was precisely what John Brown had sought to achieve at Harper's Ferry in 1859."[202]

The Vicksburg white riot of 1874 typified the problem. According to a congressional investigation, the whites conducted "unauthorized searches by self-constituted authority into private homes[;] searches for arms converted, as is unusual, into robbery and thieving. . . ."[203]

The Radical Republican Congress observed the South with dismay. The Republicans intended to use federal power to force freedom on the South. One of the Radical Republicans' most important tools was the Fourteenth Amendment to the Constitution, which required states to respect basic human rights.[204] While the vague language of the amendment has produced disagreement about exactly what is covered, the congressional backers of the amendment seem to have intended, at the least, protecting some of the core freedoms listed in the national Bill of Rights. Announced Representative Clarke of Kansas: "I find in the Constitution an article which declared 'the right of the people to keep and bear arms shall not be infringed.' For myself, I shall insist that the reconstructed rebels of Mississippi respect the Constitution in their local laws."[205]

The amendment was quickly emasculated by the United States Supreme Court. Following the 1872 elections in Louisiana, two separate governments—one Unionist and one racist—had declared themselves the winner and the official government of the state. In the town of Colfax, armed blacks occupied the courthouse and the surrounding district to assert the legitimacy of their side's control of the local government. A rioting band of white farmers attacked the courthouse, burned it to the ground, and murdered blacks who tried to escape the flames. William Cruikshank and other leaders of the riot were tried in federal district court for violating federal civil rights ordinances. By the terms of what were called the Enforcement Acts,[206] Cruikshank was found guilty of conspiring to deprive the blacks of the rights they had been granted by the Constitution, including the right peaceably to assemble and the right to bear arms.[207]

The *Cruikshank* case forced the United States Supreme Court to squarely address the issue of whether the enumerated provisions of the Bill of Rights, particularly the Second and Fourth Amendments, were made enforceable against the states by the Fourteenth Amendment and the congressional laws enacted pursuant to the amendment. The issue had arisen a few years before, in a federal prosecution of South Carolina Klansmen for conspiring to deprive blacks of their arms and to destroy the black militias. There, the lower federal courts had held the Fourteenth Amendment did not incorporate the Bill of Rights. The Supreme Court evaded review on procedural grounds.[208]

In *United States* v. *Cruikshank,* a divided Supreme Court held the

Enforcement Acts unconstitutional. The Fourteenth Amendment, the Court acknowledged, did give Congress the power to prevent interference with rights granted by the Constitution. The right to assemble and the right to bear arms, however, were not rights conferred by the Constitution, the Court said. Those rights predated the Constitution; the Constitution merely recognized the validity of those already existing rights. The right of the people peaceably to assemble and the right of the people to keep and bear arms were natural human rights that were "found wherever civilization exists."[209] Hence, the Fourteenth Amendment gave Congress no authority to prevent infringements of the right to assemble and the right to bear arms. The Court also ruled that the Fourteenth Amendment only allowed Congress to legislate against state interference with civil rights, and not against private conspiracies against those rights.[210]

As a matter of interpreting the First and Second Amendments, the Court was plainly correct in recognizing that the authors of those amendments did believe the right peaceably to assemble and the right to bear arms to be preexisting fundamental human rights. The Court's analysis of the Fourteenth Amendment, however, was a (perhaps deliberate) misinterpretation of what the authors of that amendment had intended. The amendment was enacted to protect a core set of fundamental human rights (such as the right to bear arms, the right to assemble, the right to contract), most of which predated the Constitution. Rights that were actually created by the Constitution (such as the right to interstate travel) were not the focus of the Fourteenth Amendment. The *Cruikshank* decision essentially ruined the Fourteenth Amendment as a check on state abuses of human rights, until the amendment was revived in the 1920s.[211]

The Supreme Court understood the social realities of the South. The *Cruikshank* decision gave the green light to the Klan, unofficial white militias, and other racist groups to forcibly disarm the freedmen and impose white supremacy.[212] One state at a time, white racists took control of government by using armed violence and the threat of violence to control balloting on election day. Freedmen and their white allies also resorted to arms. But white Republican governors were usually afraid that employing the black militias fully would set off an even broader race war.[213] The white South, while defeated on the battlefield in 1865, had continued armed resistance to northern control for over a decade. When the North, a hostile occupying power, grew weary of the struggle and abandoned its black and Republican allies in the South, the white South was again the master of its destiny.[214] As the British army had failed to control the armed United States, the federal army was unable to impose its will on the armed white South. The white South, acutely aware of the balance of power, made every effort to insure its own dominance by disarming the black South.

Even in the states where white supremacy was back in control for good, laws to disarm Negroes now had to be cloaked in neutral, nonracial terms. Tennessee took the lead in 1870 with creative draftsmanship. The legislature barred the sale of any handguns except the "Army and Navy model." The ex-confederate soldiers already had their high-quality "Army and Navy" guns. But cash-poor freedmen could barely afford lower-cost, simpler firearms not of the "Army and Navy" quality. Arkansas enacted a nearly identical law in 1881, and other southern states followed suit.[215] Other southern states enacted gun registration and handgun permit laws.[216] By the early twentieth century, most of the South had racially neutral laws covering gun ownership. As one Florida judge explained, the laws were "passed for the purpose of disarming the negro laborers . . . [and] never intended to be applied to the white population."[217]

The "Army and Navy Law" is the ancestor of today's "Saturday Night Special" laws. Inexpensive guns unsuited for sports are disproportionately owned by low-income blacks for self-defense. As the federal district court in Washington, D.C., noted, "Saturday Night Special" laws selectively disarm minorities, who, because of their poverty, must live in crime-ridden areas.[218] One National Institute of Justice study concluded:

> The people most likely to be deterred from acquiring a handgun by exceptionally high prices or by the nonavailability of certain kinds of handguns are not felons intent on arming themselves for criminal purposes (who can, if all else fails, steal the handgun they want), but rather poor people who have decided they need a gun to protect themselves against the felons but who find that the cheapest gun in the market costs more than they can afford to pay.[219]

The very phrase "Saturday Night Special" may derive from a combination of "suicide special" and "niggertown Saturday night."[220]

Vigilantes, regulators, the militia, the mob—all are manifestations of the same phenomenon, the people taking collective violent action. Frontier vigilantism was a benign form of the phenomenon. Vigilance committees rarely executed their targets, preferring instead to run them out of town. Vigilantes almost always focused on genuine criminals—horse thieves, robbers, and other felons. After the Civil War, frontier vigilantism continued to exist in much of the West.

An uglier form of collective action took hold in the South, and sometimes elsewhere. The abolition of slavery brought blacks a measure of potential independence, and white violence was generally used to keep them from achieving it. Southern white lynch mobs, like their counterparts in almost all such movements, were generally led or encouraged or assisted by the "better men" of the community. Before abolition, vigilante groups or un-organized mobs had hardly ever lynched blacks (except for revolution), since slaves were too valuable to kill. But between 1882 and 1927, about five thousand persons were lynched, around 70 percent of them black.[221]

Whereas vigilantism had primarily occurred on the western frontier, mob lynching of blacks took place mainly in the South.[222] Although about three-quarters of southerners who were lynched were black, non-southern lynch-ings mostly involved whites. In all regions, by far the most common reason for lynching a person was the accusation that he had allegedly committed murder. The second most common reason was alleged rape, and together these two crimes accounted for about 80 percent of all lynchings.[223] Like most vigilante actions, most racist lynchings did not need firearms to succeed. The capability of a mob of several dozen or several hundred people to overpower one or two individuals made firearms nonessential.

At the turn of the century, one of the most important black spokesmen was Booker T. Washington, who believed that America would ease racial oppression only when white America learned that "colored" people were not dangerous. Washington's theory of accommodation to white supremacy reflected a general sense of powerlessness in some black communities. Blacks offered only minimal resistance to white rioters in Wilmington, New Orleans, Akron, and New York.[224]

Neither did the blacks fight back in the East St. Louis riot of 1917.[225] Still, the Missouri legislature thought blacks a threat, and enacted a law requiring a permit to obtain a handgun. The St. Louis police, over half a century later, continued to enforce the law unequally against blacks.[226]

Yet if blacks would not protect themselves, no one would protect them. The government (in the form of the police or the military) and the white upper- and middle-class majority (in the form of the militia or vigilance committees) were generally indifferent to protecting blacks from anyone. Often enough, the government forces themselves actively attacked the blacks.[227]

While Booker T. Washington called for pacifism, many blacks began to listen instead to radicals such as W. E. B. Du Bois, who wrote, "[L]ynching of Negroes is going to stop in the South when the cowardly mob is faced by effective guns in the hands of people determined to sell their souls dearly."[228] Sometimes, as in Memphis, the mere presence of armed blacks constrained white police or mob behavior.[229] Other times, resistance produced heavy bloodshed on both sides.[230]

Black resistance, like black nonresistance, led to more repression and gun control by whites. In the Atlanta suburb of Brownsville in 1906, the press incited the city over a nonexistent epidemic of black rape; a wave of beatings and shooting of blacks followed. The police arrested Negroes who armed themselves against further attack.[231] In Michigan, handgun permit laws were enacted after Dr. Ossian Sweet, a black, shot and killed a person in a mob that was attacking his house because he had just moved into an all-white neighborhood. The Detroit police stood nearby, refusing to restrain the angry crowd.[232] In the 1921 Tulsa riots, armed blacks protected an alleged black rapist from a lynch mob. A small white army, led by the American Legion and approved by the police and city government, burned a one-mile square black district to the ground. As many as two hundred blacks died, but about fifty whites also lost their lives in the riot. The act of resistance greatly raised the self-esteem of the black community.[233]

White attacks continued during World War II. Placed in segregated army units, blacks would often find themselves in training camps in the deep South, where race hatred was most severe and blacks were beaten or killed for no reason at all.[234] Black civilians who left the South to work in military factories in Los Angeles were crowded into ghettos. In the "Zoot suit riots," mobs of white soldiers and sailors attacked blacks and Hispanics wearing flamboyant Zoot suits.[235]

In the 1950s and 1960s, a new civil rights movement began in the South. White supremacist tactics were just as violent as they had been during Reconstruction. Over a hundred civil rights workers were murdered during that era, and the Department of Justice refused to prosecute the Klan or to protect civil rights workers adequately. Help from the local police was out of the question in areas where Klan dues were sometimes collected at the local station.[236]

Blacks and civil rights workers armed themselves for self-defense.[237] John Salter, a professor at Tougaloo College and chief organizer of the NAACP's Jackson Movement during the early 1960s, wrote, "No one knows what kind of massive racist retaliation would have been directed against grassroots black people had the black community not had a healthy measure of firearms within it." Salter personally had to defend his home and family several times against attacks by night riders. After Salter fired back, the night riders fled.

State or federal assistance sometimes came not when disorder began, but when blacks reacted by arming themselves. In North Carolina, Governor Terry Sanford refused to command state police to protect a civil rights march from Klan attacks. When Salter warned Governor Sanford that if there were no police, the marchers would be armed for self-defense, the governor provided police protection.[238]

Civil rights workers and the black community generally viewed nonviolence as a useful tactic for certain situations, not as a moral injunction to let oneself be murdered on a deserted road in the middle of the night. Based in local churches, the Deacons for Defense and Justice set up armed patrol car systems in cities such as Bogalusa and Jonesboro, Louisiana, and completely succeeded in deterring Klan and other attacks on civil rights workers and black residents. (Unlike in the 1860s, these modern black militias had the mobility to arrive quickly at the scene of Klan threats, thanks to automobiles and telephones.) Sixty chapters of the Deacons were formed throughout the South.[239] Of civil rights workers killed, almost none were armed.[240]

In Monroe, North Carolina, Robert Williams, the president of the local NAACP, chartered an official National Rifle Association gun club, where blacks were encouraged to learn armed self-defense. At the same time, Williams was leading demonstrations against the whites-only policy at the city swimming pool. Ku Klux Klan death threats came by telephone. Thousands of people gathered at Klan rallies to denounce both Williams and Dr. Albert Perry, another Monroe civil rights advocate.

Civil rights volunteers, in groups of fifty a night, took turns standing guard at Perry's house. They dug foxholes, piled up sandbags, and kept steel helmets and gas masks handy. They also stockpiled over six hundred firearms, including automatic carbines and machine guns.[241] On the night of October 5, 1957, a Klan motorcade approached the Perry house. The civil rights workers opened fire, having been told not to shoot unless necessary:

> The fire was blistering, disciplined and frightening. The motorcade of about eighty cars, which had begun in a spirit of good fellowship, disintegrated into chaos, with panicky, robed men fleeing in every direction. Some had to abandon their automobiles and continue on foot.[242]

Two years later, Williams began to advocate more than mere resistance to white attacks. On the steps of a courthouse, following a trial in which a white man was acquitted of allegedly raping a pregnant black woman, Williams called for black lynching of white criminals: "[I]f it's necessary to stop lynching with lynching, then we must be willing to resort to that method."[243]

Williams was suspended from the NAACP. When he appealed, the national convention upheld the suspension, and also resolved, "We do not deny but reaffirm the right of individual and collective self-defense against unlawful assaults."[244] Dr. Martin Luther King, Jr., took the same position. King predicted that mass nonviolent actions—boycotts, marches, sit-ins, and the like—would liberate blacks, and armed struggle would not. At the same time, King distinguished Williams's call for lynchings from violence "exercised in self-defense." King described the latter type of violence "as moral and legal" in all societies, and noted that not even Gandhi condemned it.[245]

The spirit of resistance, kindled by the civil rights movement, ignited into uncontrollable rage within a few years. In the summers of 1966–1968, blacks rioted in almost every major U.S. city. With the cities in flames, anti-Vietnam protest out of control, exaggerated reports of sniper attacks during the riots, and assassins gunning down Martin Luther King and Robert Kennedy, Congress responded with the Gun Control Act of 1968, which banned imports of the inexpensive foreign handguns and low-cost foreign military surplus (mostly bolt-action rifles) that were thought to be the favorite guns of rioters.[246]

For over three centuries, the racial impact of gun control has been a central issue in the American gun debate. Are blacks safer with the means to defend themselves, or are they better protected by forgoing self-defense, and placing their trust in the police and government to protect their rights?

The absence of guns in American society would not have made white violence against blacks less vicious. Lynch mobs do not need guns. Two hundred unarmed people can have their way with two unarmed people. If only the government has guns, only the people the government cares to protect are safe. In America, black communities have often been denied effective protection.

Whether to threaten to use force, or to actually use force, in self-defense is not a question for which one answer is always correct. When civil rights workers in the South in the 1960s let themselves be arrested and manhandled by brutal police officers, their actions were effective and morally correct. Civil rights workers also stood guard at their friends' homes all night ready to lay their lives on the line to protect innocent lives from the Ku Klux Klan. Who will call their actions immoral?

While the large majority of black political leaders have opted to trust the authorities, a sizeable fraction, and sometimes a majority, of blacks in different states have voted against gun control, apparently opting to retain the choice to defend themselves.[247] Are the civil rights struggles over? Is it time to conclude that from this point forward in American history minorities will no longer be attacked by mobs, and that the government will always protect the oppressed, and not assist the oppressor?

The story of gun control as race control concludes with an irony. The British aristocracy applied gun control to the subordinate classes of Britain. Now the disarmed lower and middle classes are pushing, successfully, to disarm the aristocracy. In the United States, white southerners disarmed southern blacks. Today, the "rednecks" thought to compose the rural South are themselves the targets of gun control. To many sophisticates of the northeast corridor, the "rednecks" in the South are just as frightening and dangerous as the blacks and Hispanics in nearby slums.

URBANIZATION, IMMIGRATION, AND ETHNIC RELATIONS

Although the frontier closed in the large cities of the East, public safety did not improve. Ethnic and class division led citizens to arm themselves against each other.[248] The ethnic diversity that would become one of America's greatest strengths also emerged as an important cause of violence.

Some immigrants brought their habits of violence with them. For example, the Irish often rioted in New York City, continuing an Irish tradition that was incited by hostility from Americans of English descent.[249] Some of the newer immigrants, such as Poles and Italians, came from countries where civilians were unfamiliar with guns, and moved into large American cities with no access to hunting.[250] Nevertheless, those burgeoning cities, growing two or three times as fast as comparable British cities, experienced predictable tensions, and many residents reacted by arming themselves.[251]

The first urban police forces were not even established until the 1840s and they focussed mainly on containing riots and on liquor controls. Professional police forces even got involved in combat, as in the 1857 conflict in which the Metropolitan Police took control of New York City from the Municipal Police. In 1858, disgruntled New York City senior police and fire officers assaulted and burned down the yellow fever hospital on Ward's Island.[252]

Roger Lane's *Violent Death in the City: Suicide, Accident & Murder in 19th Century Philadelphia* explains the deadly role guns played in one big city. Some evidence seems to show a link between increased gun density and death. Pistols were not widely available until two-dollar self-defense handguns—with names like "Protector" or "Tramps Terror" or "Little All Right"—came on the market from the 1870s through the 1890s. In that period, the suicide rate almost doubled.[253] Handguns were used in an increasing percentage of suicides, and poisons (most predominant before 1840) declined.

On the other hand, the suicide rate did not increase steadily, and sometimes declined, even as handguns grew more available. Germans, Bohemians, and Hungarians were becoming an increasing fraction of the population, and these groups had high suicide rates, as did the unarmed countrymen they had left behind in Europe.[254]

Another, earlier trend in gun ownership that might have increased urban deaths was the carrying of guns. In the 1850s, frightened gentlemen in New York City and Philadelphia began to carry pocket pistols.[255] With handguns more widespread, drunken brawls in the 1850s became deadlier. For the rest of the century, though, the homicide rate declined, despite the ever-increasing popularity of guns.[256] Indeed, "the habit of going armed" became so common in the East that in the late nineteenth century, men's trouser's had a "revolver pocket" on the right hip.[257] Well-armed, many urbanites did use their guns for lawful self-defense. Even in the first third of the twentieth century, statistics from major American cities indicated a high level of justifiable homicide.[258] (The modern American rate of justifiable homicide remains high, and is discussed in chapter 11.)

Ethnicity, of course, had much to do with gun and other weapon misuse. Germans were unlikely to be involved in homicide; the Irish very likely.[259] And the people most likely to shoot or get shot were Philadelphia's blacks.

In Philadelphia, blacks were usually well-armed, first with knives, and then—to catch up with whites—with guns. Forced to the margins of the urban economy, blacks had to live near centers of criminal activity. Outside their own ghettos they were subject to harassment, and inside the ghettos there was always the risk of mob invasion.[260] Consequently, "many blacks found eternal battle-readiness an essential survival mechanism."[261] Like the southern or western blacks who sometimes took up arms to resist white assaults, Philadelphia blacks were forced to arms as a defense against white racism.

Guns were equally available to all groups; but only the black homicide rate soared.[262] The 1839 white homicide rate of 2.8 per 100,000 per year has remained mostly stable to this day. The black homicide rate mushroomed from 7.5 (1839–1901) to 24.6 (1948–1952) to 64.2 (1972–1974).[263]

For other societies, urbanization was not so unsettling. Unlike the United States, Europe and Japan did not experience the destabilizing trends of urbanization and industrialization at the same time. Urbanization and industrialization in Canada and Australia were never so frenzied as in the United States.[264] In heterogeneous American cities, Old World social controls lost their exclusivity and power—often before New World social controls had taken hold. Crime by some immigrant groups became a serious problem.

Gun control had come to the South as a way to disarm black "immigrants" and their descendants, who had been kidnapped and brought to America by force. Gun control came to the Northeast out of fear of another kind of immigrant: the central, southern, or eastern European.

A major nineteenth-century Supreme Court interpretation of the Second Amendment involved a German group Lehr und Wehr Verein marching in military exercise in public. The case grew out of an Illinois arms-control measure enacted in response to the labor uprisings of the late 1870s. Militias and the federal army had brutally suppressed peaceful strikes. When workers began forming self-defense organizations such as Lehr und Wehr Verein, the state government outlawed private militias, and the Supreme Court upheld the action.[265]

New York State passed the 1911 Sullivan Law to license handguns while the *New York Tribune* complained about pistols found "chiefly in the pockets of ignorant and quarrelsome immigrants of law-breaking propensities" and condemned "the practice of going armed . . . among citizens of foreign birth."[266] The *New York Times* noted the affinity of "low-browed foreigners" for handguns.[267] Even before the Sullivan Law, the New York City police had been canceling pistol permits in the Italian sections of the city. A 1905 law had forbidden aliens to possess firearms "in any public place."[268] The first man sentenced under the Sullivan Law, an Italian immigrant who lived in New Jersey and was passing through New York City on his way to work in Connecticut, was lectured by the judge: "It is unfortunate that this is the custom with you and your kind, and that fact, combined with your irascible nature, furnishes much of the criminal business in this country."[269] In the first three years of the Sullivan Law, 70 percent of those arrested had Italian surnames.[270]

The West Coast had its own worries about immigrants. Oregon (1913) and Hawaii (1934) passed handgun controls after strikes led by "foreign-born radicals." California enacted a waiting period for handgun purchases during the hysteria over the San Francisco "Red Raids" of 1934.[271] Taking a more traditional approach, Colorado banned the sale of guns to Indians, long after the frontier wars were over.[272] While statutory gun control was the product of late nineteenth- and early twentieth-century fears of blacks and immigrants, the practice of disarming dissenters dated back to Puritan Massachusetts.[273]

The gun controls placed on immigrants were not simply a matter of irrational prejudice. Italian and Jewish immigrants did have a high crime rate. Mainstream America, which was still overwhelmingly of northwest European stock, considered the immigrant Italians beyond the pale. Crime statistics separated Italians from "non-Italian white," just as modern statistics distinguish Hispanics from "non-Hispanic white."

Over time, of course, the Italians and Jews, like the "Wild Irish" before them, were socialized and brought into the American mainstream. Their crime rates dropped to near the levels of other white Americans. Blacks, though, remained excluded from the expanding economy and forced to live in high-crime neighborhoods. Black crime remained high, and many law-abiding blacks continued to feel a need to carry weapons every day for self-defense.[274]

In the rest of the English-speaking world, gun controls were also partly motivated by anti-alien sentiment. British gun control had always had a history of being applied to suspect citizens (Protestant, Catholic, Jew, or the poor depending on the monarch).[275] The 1919 gun-control debate in the Canadian House of Commons followed the Winnipeg General Strike, which (like most labor agitation) was falsely blamed on alien anarchists.[276]

Today, the same view is manifest in legislation such as America's Gun Control Act of 1968. Although the initiative that year came from the assassinations of Robert Kennedy and Martin Luther King, Jr., the actual act did not affect the weapons used in those murders. It was somehow easier to achieve a consensus that cheap imported guns were evil and should be banned.

The point of banning "cheap" guns is that people who can only afford cheap guns should not have guns. The prohibitively high price that some firearms licenses carry ($500 in Miami until recently) suggests a contemporary intent to keep guns away from lower socioeconomic groups.[277] California and many other states impose stricter firearms regulations on aliens than on citizens.[278] While the different treatment of aliens might partly be ascribed to the fact that noncitizens by definition do not belong to the militia and have no obligation to defend the state, it seems likely that the anti-alien restrictions are at least somewhat motivated by prejudice.[279]

It might be argued that selectively disarming the poor, including blacks and immigrants who are poor, might be a prudent gun policy. After all, it is the poor who commit a disproportionate number of gun-related crimes, both premeditated and spontaneous. The problem with the argument is that it assumes the poor are all criminal. In truth, the huge majority of poor people are law-abiding; only a small fraction perpetrate gun-related crime. The rest are potential victims, who deserve the option of self-defense.

Moreover, a gun-control strategy of selectively disarming the poor and the outcast (that is, the strategy of most gun control for most of American and British history) must fail. People on the margins, including those victimized by the dominant groups, are the least likely to be affected by a commodity ban, especially in urban capitalist societies.[280] To the extent that the poor and outcast obey gun controls, only the lawful are disarmed.

CONCLUSION

Guns may not cause America's problems, but they sometimes make the problems worse. While the United States was ready to tear itself apart over slavery in the 1850s, violent slave-rescuing by northern abolitionists seriously aggravated tensions. There were plenty of reasons for blacks in Philadelphia to commit crimes; but the growing availability of cheap handguns probably made those crimes deadlier. Eric Monkkonen estimates that without the Civil War's infusion of firearms into civilian society, the homicide rate in the postwar decade might have been 10 to 20 percent lower.[281]

Widespread gun ownership also made America possible. Without the militia, the American Revolution would have failed. The continent could not have been seized from the Indians without a constantly advancing frontier of armed settlers. The practice of vigilantism and of individual armed self-defense provided most of the defense against crime in most of America for most of its history. If the 1950s and 1960s civil rights workers had not been armed, the movement would have been exterminated, as it was during Reconstruction.

The American experience offers little reason to trust that government will reduce violence against victimized groups. Too often, the government and its police and army ally with and help to arm an already dominant and oppressive group, such as company bosses or the Ku Klux Klan. The Canadian people trust a strong government to mediate conflicts between different interests. In America, the people have been unwilling to surrender their own right to use force, and skeptical that the government would use a monopoly on force to ensure justice. Too often, American governments have turned disarmament into racial or ethnic oppression.

It is sometimes thought that the types of people who own guns are more likely to be racists who would perpetrate violence against dissidents or minorities. But research regarding people who have intolerant attitudes approving of violence against social deviants and dissenters shows that such people are no more likely to own guns than are Americans as a whole. Moreover, people who approve of violence against dissidents are less likely as a group than are gun owners to approve of the use of defensive force.[282] Perhaps the intolerant persons' disapproval of defensive force is based on the accurate assessment that defensive force might be used against violent aggressors such as themselves.

Reducing violence depends less on eliminating particular instruments of violence than on eliminating its cause. Says a popular bumper sticker: "If you want peace, work for justice." The end to American labor violence came not with gun control or with repressing workers or with deporting foreign labor leaders or with outlawing strikes or even with militia assistance. Labor violence ended because America finally chose a national policy of labor justice; President Roosevelt's National Labor Relations Act gave legal protection to union organization and to strikes. Labor violence vanished as quickly as capital began to accept the new system. Likewise, debtor-farmer uprisings were common in the 1930s. Crowds of farmers seized property that had been legally foreclosed by banks; the farmers held "shotgun sales" and sold the farms back to their original owners for pennies. The New Deal quelled farm violence not with gun bans but by redressing farmers' grievances.

The American experience suggests that a United States where everyone can choose to be armed is less likely to be oppressive than a society, like the Jim Crow South, where the government can choose who is armed.

While the militia is a forgotten relic to most Americans, the "Wild West," the crazy vigilantes, and the bloodthirsty feuding Hatfields and McCoys remain an important part of American national consciousness.

In all three cases, myth and reality are sharply out of kilter. Except for badmen shooting each other in saloons, the West was mostly free of violent crime. The vigilantes were usually controlled and constructive. The Hatfield-McCoy troubles were primarily the fault of cosmopolitan outsiders, not the so-called white savages in the Tug Valley.

America remembers a violent past that is in part a fiction. What does it say about a nation that mythologizes its past by exaggerating and misunderstanding its actual historical record of violence? Perhaps there is something about random, uncontrolled violence that is so appealing to the American character that Americans are driven to "remember" a past of pathological violence, regardless of whether that past really existed. A more realistic view of America's violent history might better focus on the East and South, rather than the West, and consider how much of America's violence might be caused by racial and ethnic prejudice, rather than the presence of firearms.

The historical reality and the lurid mythology of the gun in America continue their struggle today. Extremists on each side are drawn to the same myth. The mythology attracts some "pro-gun" types into a swaggering world of combat fatigues and hypermasculinity. The mythology convinces other Americans that the gun is horrible and evil and even demonic. While the historical reality is more complex than either extreme will admit, America's view of the history of the gun is shaped as much by the myth as by the reality.

NOTES

1. Quoted in Reginald and Gladys Laubin, *Indian Dances of North America: Their Importance to Indian Life* (Norman: University of Oklahoma Press, 1977), p. xvi.

2. Pete Shields, *Guns Don't Die—People Do* (New York: Arbor House, 1981), p. 62.

3. Garry Wills, "John Lennon's War," *Chicago Sun-Times,* December 12, 1980.

4. Garry Wills, "Gun Rules . . . or Worldwide Gun Control?" *Philadelphia Inquirer,* May 17, 1981, p. 8-E.

The list of all the nations that have done as Wills requires, and totally banned civilian handguns would not qualify as the world's most civilized: Albania, Cyprus, Greece, Guinea, Ireland, Morocco, Tanzania, and the former USSR. List from George Newton and Franklin Zimring, *Firearms and Violence in American Life* (Washington, D.C.: Govermment Printing Office, 1970), pp. 119-120.

Wills's response to assertion of the Constitutional right to arms is that "The founding American document did not intend to undo the role of all social compacts and return us to a war of everyone against everyone. . . ." Wills is certainly correct; the framers and people did not intend a reversion to Hobbesian world of all against all. But neither did they intend to revert to the other Hobbesian world that Wills prefers, in which citizens surrender their right to self-defense by surrendering their autonomy to the Leviathan of government.

At least some Americans have defined civilization differently from Wills. According to the United States Supreme Court in *United States* v. *Cruikshank,* 92 U.S. 542, 551–53 (1875), the right to bear arms, like the right peaceably to assemble, derives " 'from those laws whose authority is acknowledged by civilized man throughout the world.' It is found wherever civilization exists."

5. Quoted in Richard Hofstadter, "America as a Gun Culture," *American Heritage,* October 1970, p. 4.

See also, Henry Fairlie, quoted in Richard Strout, "Gun Control and the Death of Bobby Kennedy," in *TRB: Views and Perspectives on the Presidency* (New York: Macmillan, 1979), p. 329: "There is an element of violence in American society which the outsider has to learn to comprehend. . . . However much I may love and admire America, its gun laws come near to ruling it out of civilized society"; Albert L. Wyman, "Sale of Firearms," letter to the editor, *New York Times,* August 9, 1910, p. 8, col. 5 (praising strict foreign gun laws "As a commentary on the relative civilization of our country and China and Japan.").

6. President Johnson's address to the nation reprinted in *Congressional Record,* June 24, 1968: H5371–72. When voting for a law to prohibit possession of "assault rifles," in New York City, including rifles which had been lawfully purchased and registered under the city's gun laws for many years, council member Stanley Michels explained:

We have to, once again, bring this City back to sanity and to civilization. We must get rid of these weapons, and, unfortunately, innocent people, who probably would never use these weapons in an illegal manner will have to bear the brunt of the sacrifice, because the most important thing we must do is to civilize this City and to let people know that we will no longer tolerate the murder that goes on in our street from weapons such as this. I vote aye.

Committee on Public Safety, City Council of New York City, July 24, 1991, p. 65. Is making innocent people suffer in order to express displeasure with the criminal acts of third parties a civilized act? Is such infliction of harm rational, and if not, does it meet the definition of "civilize"—"to bring to a technically advanced and rationally ordered stage of cultural development"? *Webster's Ninth New Collegiate Dictionary* (Springfield, Mass.: Merriam-Webster, 1984), p. 244.

7. Ramsey Clark, *Crime in America: Observations on Its Nature, Causes, and Control* (New York: Simon and Schuster, 1970), p. 86. Clark noted approvingly: "Throughout most of Russia, private ownership of rifles and firearms is punishable by up to two years in prison." Clark neglected to note that ownership of photocopy machines and Bibles was subject to similar sanctions. It is astonishing to see the former Soviet Union cited as a good example of crime control, or of civilization.

8. "Drinan Proposes International Gun Control," *The Sun* (Lowell, Mass.), May 22, 1981.

9. Arthur E. Sutherland, quoted in Carl Bakal, *No Right to Bear Arms* (New York: Paperback Library, 1968), p. 329. A contrary view was expressed by British historian Thomas Carlyle, who considered "gunpowder, printing, and the Protestant religion" to be the "three great elements of modern civilization."

10. *Newark Star-Ledger,* quoted in "Anti-Gun Crusaders Pin Hopes on Dukakis," *Gun Week,* September 23, 1988, p. 1.

11. "Death by Gun," *Time,* July 17, 1989, p. 31.

12. Dr. Humphrey Osmond, Director of Bureau of Research in Neurology and Psychiatry at New Jersey Neuropsychiatric Institute, quoted in "Gun Toting: A Fashion Needing Change," *Science News* 93 (June 29, 1968), p. 614. See also Cincinnati psychologist Dr. Karl Heiser's opinion that his city contains "about 10,000 psycho gun addicts" who "use

guns as sex symbols." *Los Angeles Times*, August 22, 1968. The *Washington Post* condemns "the need that some homeowners and shopkeepers believe they have for weapons to defend themselves" as representing "the worst instincts in the human character." Editorial, "Guns and the Civilizing Process," *Washington Post*, September 26, 1972.

13. Braucher, "Handgun Nuts Are Just That—Really Nuts," *Miami Herald*, January 29, 1981; Braucher, *Miami Herald*, July 19, 1982. See also Luedens, "Wretchedness Is a Warm Gun," *Progressive* 48 (1984), p. 50.

14. Lewis Grizzard, "Bulletbrains and the Guns that Don't Kill," *Atlanta Constitution*, December 18, 1980 ("You simply can't argue with bulletbrains about gun control. . ."). For a columnist trying to combat the American gun culture, Grizzard chooses odd titles for his books, such as *My Daddy Was a Pistol and I'm a Son of a Gun*.

15. George Rice, "Constitution and Handgun Control: No Kinship," *St. Paul Sunday Pioneer Press*, April 13, 1975, Focus section, p. 2.

16. National Coalition to Ban Handguns [former name of the CSGV], "A Shooting Gallery Called America" (undated, unpaginated pamphlet).

17. Fund-raising letter for Handgun Control, Inc., quoted in Alan Gottlieb, *The Gun Grabbers* (Bellevue, Wash.: Merril Press, 1986), p. 13.

18. James Wright, Peter Rossi, and Kathleen Daly, *Under the Gun: Weapons, Crime and Violence in America* (Hawthorne, N.Y.: Aldine, 1983), p. 109. One explanation is that Protestants and rural folk are more likely to be descended from older American stock and to retain cultural values of the "individualistic orientation that emanated from the American frontier. . . ." Young, "The Protestant Heritage and the Sport of Gun Ownership," *Journal of Scientific Study of Religion* 28 (1989), p. 307.

19. Harlan Ellison, "Fear Not Your Enemies," *Heavy Metal*, March 1981, p. 34.

20. Harriet Van Horne, *New York Post*, June 2, 1978.

21. *Spy*, June 1988, p. 71.

22. Jeanne Shields, "Why Nick?" *Newsweek*, May 8, 1978, p. 23.

23. Envelope in author's files. Ellipses in original.

24. "Rifle Group Criticizes Statement by Mario Cuomo," *New York Times*, May 3, 1985, p. B5, col. 5. Cuomo later apologized that it was "unintelligent and unfair" to "disparage any large group." "Hunting for Trouble," *Time*, May 27, 1985, p. 33.

25. Wright, Rossi, and Daly, p. 113.

26. "Firearms and Adolescents, *AAP News*, January 1992, pp. 21-22.

27. See chapter 10, not 97 and accompanying text.

28. Wright, Rossi, and Daly, p. 122.

29. Wills; "John Lennon's War."

30. "Handgun Nuts."

31. "Armed and Dangerous: The Enemy in Our Cities," *Detroit Free Press*, January 26, 1977.

32. Wills, "Gun Rules . . . or Worldwide Gun Control?"

33. Hofstadter, "America as a Gun Culture," p. 82.

34. Whitman's 1966 shooting a rifle from a tower at the University of Texas bore a sad resemblance to Lee Harvey Oswald's assassination of President Kennedy with a rifle from the sixth floor of the Dallas Schoolbook Depository. Perhaps sick minds view highly publicized murders, and imitate the "successful" psychopaths who make the television news. Would it be impossible for intense media coverage of isolated shootings with Kalashnikov rifles to spur more such shootings? Compare "Copycat Suicides," *Rocky Mountain News*, September 12, 1990, p. 3 (Italian media voluntarily limits coverage of suicides to cope with spate of copycat suicides).

35. William C. Culberson, *Vigilantism: Political History of Private Power in America* (New York: Praeger, 1990), p. 168.

36. Robert Sherrill, *The Saturday Night Special* (New York: Charterhouse, 1975), p. 5. Also, Max Lerner, "Myth America," *The New Republic,* September 7, 1987, p. 12. Lerner calls America's "obsession with guns" a symptom of "internal decline." If he is right, America has been in decline virtually since its settlement by whites.

37. In 1984, a man named James Huberty announced that he was going out to "hunt humans," and went out to kill twenty-one at a McDonald's in San Ysidro, California. Richard Price, "Senseless Death of 21 Shocks Us All," *USA Today,* July 20, 1984, p. 1A.

38. Wright, Rossi, and Daly, p. 8. An explicit link of gun ownership with male dominance was made in a 1977 newspaper advertisement by the National Abortion Rights Action League, calling opponents of abortion, "The same kind of people who oppose the ERA, gun-control, aid to dependent children. . . ." *New York Times,* October 23, 1977, p. IV-5, col. 1. The author of the ad might be surprised that Senator George McGovern, the sponsor of the food stamp legislation, generally opposed gun control, as have pro-choice liberals such as the late Frank Church and Tom Foley.

39. Carl P. Russell, *Guns on the Early Frontiers* (Lincoln: University of Nebraska Press, 1957), pp. 10–13.

In 1648, the directors of the Dutch East India Company had observed that the Indians were so determined to obtain firearms that they would start a war if the trade were cut off. The directors suggested that private firearms trade with the Indians be outlawed, and the Dutch East Indian Company be allowed to sell small quantities to the Indians. Francis Jennings, *The Ambiguous Iroquois Empire: The Covenant Chain Confederation of Indian Tribes with English Colonies* (New York: W. W. Norton, 1984), p. 84. [Hereinafter, "Jennings, *Iroquois Empire.*"]

40. See generally, Jennings, *Iroquois Empire.*

41. Bil Gilbert, *God Gave Us This Country: Tekamthi and the First American Civil War* (New York: Atheneum, 1989), p. 40; Russell, p. 19; Frederick Jackson Turner, *The Character and Influence of the Indian Trade in Wisconsin: A Study of the Trading Post as an Instititon,* (Ph.D. dissertation Johns Hopkins University, 1891; reprinted Norman: University of Oklahoma Press, 1977), p. 37 (La Salle quote).

42. Russell, pp. 16–23. Although there were no more imports, French merchants within formerly French territory (midwestern North America) kept on trading their existing stocks of guns to the Indians. The French regained the Louisiana territory in 1800 through the treaty of San Ildefonso, and sold it to the United States in 1803.

43. *Recoplicon de Leyas de las Reynes de las Indias,* Tomo II, Libro VI, Titulo I (Madrid: 1943), p. 196. Cited in John C. Ewers, "The Indian Trade of the Upper Missouri before Louis and Clark: An Interpretation," *Bulletin of the Missouri Historical Society* 10 (July 1954), p. 436.

44. Russell, pp. 26–34; J. Manual Espinosa, ed., *The Pueblo Indian Revolt of 1696* (Norman: University of Oklahoma Press, 1988). When the guns were not going into Spanish territory, the Spanish realized that gun trade with Indians could be in Spain's interest. For example, Spanish Florida supplied firearms to the Indians of the Gulf Plains, to be used to harass American settlers in Georgia and Alabama. Russell, pp. 38–39.

45. Russell, pp. 41–50. With Indians who did not pose an immediate threat to Britain's interests, the arms trade thrived. When the British did cut off the arms trade, as they did in the Great Lakes region in 1763, the Indians were outraged. Chief Pontiac—acting on the advice of a prophet who preached that guns should be rejected as evil instruments of the whites—organized the Ottawa and nine other tribes into a confederacy that annihi-

lated numerous English frontier posts in the West. But the American Indians were incapable of carrying out sustained warfare, and when English reinforcements arrived, the Indians retreated to Illinois.

46. Daniel Boorstin, *The Americans: The Colonial Experience* (New York: Random House, 1965), p. 365.

47. Lee Kennett and James LaVerne Anderson, *The Gun in America: The Origins of National Dilemma* (New York: Westport Press, 1975), p. 41.

48. Ibid., p. 41.

49. William Tonso, *Gun and Society: The Social and Existential Roots of the American Attachment to Firearms* (Lanham, Md.: University Press of America, 1982), pp. 244–46. The practice of carrying two guns persisted even after flintlocks were replaced with more reliable guns; most western gunfighters sported a pair of revolvers. Joseph G. Rosa, *The Gunfighter: Man or Myth?* (Norman: University of Oklahoma Press, 1969), p. 193.

50. Russell, pp. 95–96, 194; Walter Prescott Webb, "The American Revolver and the West," *Scribner's,* February 1927, pp. 171–178; Walter Prescott Webb, *The Great Plains* (Boston: Ginn, 1931), pp. 167–79.

51. Russell, p. vii.

52. Turner, pp. 77–78; Ewers, p. 437; Russell, pp. 36–37; Jennings, *Iroquois Empire,* p. 81. Even after the French were gone, the dynamic continued. For example, British traders from the Hudson's Bay Company in Canada exchanged guns for beaver (twenty beaver for one gun) with the Kutchin, who in turn used the guns for defense against the Eskimos. Shepard Krech III, " 'Throwing Bad Medicine': Sorcery, Disease, and the Fur Trade Among the Kutchin and Other Northern Athapaskans," in Shepard Krech III, ed., *Indians, Animals, and the Fur Trade: A Critique of Keepers of the Game* (Athens: University of Georgia Press, 1981), pp. 78–79.

53. Charles M. Hudson, Jr., "Why the Southeastern Indians Slaughtered Deer," in *Indians, Animals, and the Fur Trade,* pp. 166–67.

54. Allan R. Millett and Peter Maslowski, *For the Common Defense: A Military History of the United States of America* (New York: n.p., 1984), pp., 2, 9–18, quoted in Walter LaFeber, *The American Age: United States Foreign Policy at Home and Abroad Since 1750* (New York: W. W. Norton, 1989), p. 7.

55. Turner, p. 136; Russell, p. 141.

56. Turner, p. 36; Jennings, *Iroquois Empire,* p. 81.

57. For the Sioux, "Hau, Hau," was a declaration of belief in the Ghost Dance prophecies. The Ghost Dance was created in Nevada by a Paiute named Wovoka. It spread faster than any religion in history, reaching as far as the upper midwest and south central region. It incorporated visions of an Indian messiah probably derived from Mormon missionaries. The concept of a ghost shirt that would make the wearer immune from bullets was confined almost entirely to the Sioux and other midwest tribes.

Faith in the Ghost Dance's vision of the imminent destruction of the whites led many Sioux to abandon the reservations and head for the Badlands of South Dakota. They lived outside of federal authority for several months, until starvation forced them to return to reservation life and meager rations from the whites. At Wounded Knee, the Seventh Cavalry disarmed one group as cavalry Colonel Forsyth ordered, "Now you tell Big Foot [a chief] he need have no fear in giving up the weapons I know his people have, as I wish to treat them with nothing but kindness." As the Sioux were surrendering their guns, the Seventh Cavalry opened fire, massacring men, women, and children. The patent failure of the ghost shirts to provide protection destroyed faith in the Ghost Dance. Several thousand other Sioux, seeing the massacre, kept up an armed resistance for several weeks longer, but eventually surrendered from starvation. David Humphreys Miller, *Ghost Dance* (Lincoln: University of Nebraska Press, 1959). See also Pierre Berton, *The Invasion of Canada: 1812–1813* (Ontario: Penguin, 1988), pp. 654–69; Laubin, pp. 52, 58–66; Gilbert, p. 219.

58. Robert Sprecher, "The Lost Amendment," *American Bar Association Journal* 51 (June 1965), p. 556 n.27. The militia was often the only force opposing the British. In the twenty-eight battles in the South Carolina Back Country in 1780, the militia fought eighteen unassisted by the Continental Army. In 1781, of the thirty-nine Back Country battles, the militia fought alone in twenty-two, the Continental Army fought alone in one, and the two forces fought side by side in sixteen. Richard Maxwell Brown, *Strain of Violence: Historical Studies in American Violence and Vigilantism* (New York: Oxford University Press, 1975), pp. 76–77.

59. Between 1620 and 1775, "almost the entire male population of New England actively participated in the militia." Marie Ahearn, *The Rhetoric of War: Training Day, the Militia, and the Military Sermon* (Westport, Conn.: Greenwood Press, 1989), p. 2. The Concord militia "included nearly everyone between the ages of sixteen and sixty." Robert A. Gross, *The Minutemen and Their World* (New York: Farrar, Straus, and Giroux, 1976), p. 70.

60. Robert W. Coakley and Stetson Conn, *The War of the American Revolution* (Washington: Center of Military History United States Army, 1975), p. 11.

61. "[I]t is further ordered that every freeman or other inhabitant of this colony provide for himself and each under him a sufficient musket and serviceable peece for war and bandeleros [ammunition bandolier] and . . . two pounds of powder and ten pounds of bullets." The 1632 law of New Plymouth in William Brigham, *The Compact with the Charter and Laws of the Colony of New Plymouth* (Boston: 1836), p. 31. "That men shall not go to work in the ground without their arms and a centinell upon them . . . that the commander of every plantation take care there be sufficient powder and ammunition within the plantation. . . ." The 1623 Virginia law in William Hening, ed., *The Statutes at Large, being a Collection of all the Laws of Virginia,* Vol. I (1823), p. 127, both quoted in David Hardy, *Origins and Development of the Second Amendment* (Chino Valley, Ariz.: Blacksmith, 1986), pp. 42–43.

62. Ahearn, pp. 33–34.

63. LaFeber, p. 11. While the militia was a hastily assembled volunteer body of most adult males in the area, the Minutemen were a more intensively trained citizen force. Although created to deal with sudden British raids, the minuteman concept traced back to forces that had first been formed to protect New England towns against Indian attacks. As the name stated, they were ready for combat at a minute's notice. John R. Galvin, *The Minute Men: The First Fight: Myths and Realities of the American Revolution* (Washington, D.C.: Pergamon-Brassey's, 1989, published in conjunction with the Institute of Land Warfare Association of the U.S. Army); Gross, p. 59.

64. Ahearn, pp. 89–101.

65. Ray Allen Billington, *Land of Savagery, Land of Promise: The European Image of the American Frontier in the Nineteenth Century* (Norman: University of Oklahoma Press, 1981), p. 248. The English commander at Louisburg complained that the American militiamen "have the highest notions of the Rights, and Libertys, of Englishmen, and indeed are almost Levellers, they must know when, how, and what service they are going upon, and be Treated in a manner that few Military Bred Gentlemen would condescend to. . . ." Douglas Edward Leach, *Roots of Conflict: British Armed Forces and Colonial Americans, 1677–1763* (Chapel Hill: University of North Carolina Press, 1986), p. 69.

For an analysis of the ancient Israelite militia, see James B. Jordan, "The Israelite Militia in the Old Testament," in Morgan Norval, ed., *The Militia in 20th Century America* (Falls Church, Va.: Gun Owners Foundation, 1985), pp. 23–39. The Philistines, when occupying Israel, outlawed blacksmithing, "Lest the Hebrews make swords or spears" (1 Samuel 13:19).

66. Gross, p. 71.

67. Leach, p. 109. One British commander during the war called the American citizen-soldiers "Naturely an Obstinate and Ungovernable People, and Uterly Unaquainted with the Nature of Subordination in General." Lieutenant Alexander Johnson, letter of December 20, 1756, in Leach, pp. 131–132.

68. Robert O'Connell, *Of Arms and Men: A History of War, Weapons, and Aggression* (Oxford: Oxford University Press, 1989), pp. 154–57; Coakley and Conn, pp. 17–21, Harold E. Selesky, *War and Society in Colonial Connecticut* (New Haven, Conn.: Yale University Press, 1990) (distant expeditions).

69. Leach, p. 165.

70. *Essex Gazette,* April 25, 1775, p. 3, col. 3. British seizure of Virginia gunpowder led to the first confrontation with rebel militia in that state. Thomas M. Moncure, Jr., "Who Is the Militia—The Virginia Ratification and the Right to Bear Arms," *Lincoln Law Review* 19 (1990), p. 6.

71. Gross, pp. 125–27.

72. Ibid., pp. 60, 117–29; Coakley and Conn, pp. 25–26. Total deaths were 273 British and 95 Americans. Culberson, p. 70.

73. William Gordon, *The History of the Rise, Progress and Establishment of the Independence of the United States,* Vol. I, p. 443, quoted in Hardy, p. 60. Later, during the war, Pitt told the House of Lords, "If I were an American, as I am an Englishman, while a foreign troop was landed in my country, I would never lay down my arms—never—never—NEVER! You cannot conquer America." William Pitt, Earl of Chatham, Speech in the House of Lords, November 18, 1777.

Shortly before the outbreak of war, one of Britain's leading political philosophers had blamed the royal governors' oppressions of the American colonists upon the fact that the governors were emboldened by the presence of a standing army. James Burgh, *Political Disquisitions,* Vol. II (London: 1775), pp. 473, 476, quoted in Hardy, p. 49. Burgh's book was enormously influential in America. Bernard Bailyn, *Ideological Origins of the American Revolution* (Cambridge, Mass.: Harvard University Press, 1967), p. 41.

74. Coakley and Conn, pp. 25–29.

75. Ibid., pp. 29–33.

76. Ibid., pp. 33–35.

77. Boorstin, p. 370. See also William Marina and Diane Cuervo, "The Dutch-American Guerrillas of the American Revolution," in Gary North, ed., *The Theology of Christian Resistance: A Symposium,* Vol. 2 of *Christianity and Civilization* (Tyler, Tex.: Geneva Divinity School Press, 1982), pp. 242–65.

78. Coakley and Conn, pp. 39–42, 48, 70, 73.

79. Ibid., pp. 74–76. The militia comprised about 75 percent of the American combatants at Cowpens.

80. Ibid., pp. 60–61.

81. Edward Countryman, *A People in Revolution: The American Revolution and Political Society in New York, 1760–1790* (New York: W. W. Norton, 1989), p. 76; Coakley and Conn, pp. 60–62.

When British victory appeared in sight in 1777, Colonial Undersecretary William Knox authored a plan "What is Fit to Be Done in America?" Knox suggested establishment of a state church, unlimited tax power, a governing aristocracy, a standing army, repeal of the militia laws, a ban on arms manufacture, a ban on arms imports without a license, and "the Arms of all the People should be taken away." Howard W. Peckhom, ed., *Sources of American Independence*, Vol. 1 (Chicago: University of Chicago Press, 1978), p. 1786.

82. LaFeber, p. 20.

83. Contrary to popular memory, though, the Americans did not win the war by hiding behind trees while inflexibly managed British army formations stupidly marched in lockstep, to be picked off by American riflemen. Most of the fighting was still done by the British Redcoats engaging the Continental Army or the militia in conventional battle in open fields.

84. Tony Jackson, *Legitimate Pursuit: The Case for the Sporting Gun* (Southampton, England: Ashford Press, 1988), p. 19; Coakley and Conn, pp. 21–22.

85. The British officers, in turn, denied the American riflemen quarter, considering them executioners rather than honorable soldiers.

86. George Washington, letter to the President of Congress, New York, September 2, 1776, in John C. Fitzpatrick, ed., *The Writings of George Washington*, Vol. VI (Washington, D.C.: 1931–1944), p. 5, quoted in Steven Rosswurm, *Arms, Country and Class: The Philadelphia Militia and the "Lower Sort" during the American Revolution* (New Brunswick, N.J.: Rutgers University Press, 1989), p. 72.

87. Coakley and Conn, p. 82.

88. Brown, "Historical Patterns of Violence," in Hugh Graham and Ted Robert Gurr, eds., *Violence in America: Vol. I*, Report to the National Commission on the Causes and Prevention of Violence (Washington, D.C.: Government Printing Office, 1969), pp. 62–64.

89. Shays's list of grievances for which the people, "now at arms," demanded reforms dealt mostly with taxes and other financial issues. There were also complaints about the suspension of habeas corpus and the "unlimited power" granted to law enforcement officers by a Riot Act. The last of eight reforms the Shaysites demanded was "Deputy sheriffs be totally set aside as a useless set of officers in the community. . . ." Thomas Grover, letter "To the Printer of the Hampshire Herald," December 7, 1786, in Henry Steele Commager, *Documents of American History*, Vol. II (New York: Appleton-Century-Crofts, 1948), pp. 127–28. Styling themselves as "regulators," the Shaysites were insisting that law enforcement be returned to local, community control. Alden T. Vaughan, "The 'Horrid and Unnatural' Rebellion of Daniel Shays," *American Heritage*, June 1966, pp. 50–53, 77–81.

90. Vaughan, p. 50.

91. "The President shall be Commander in Chief of the Army and Navy of the United States, and of the Militia of the several States, when called into actual service." U.S. Constitution, Article II, § 2, cl. 1.

Consolidating the victory against one-man executive power that had been won by the Glorious Revolution, the Constitution listed Congressional powers first. The ultimate power "To declare War" was placed in the hands of Congress. U.S. Constitution, Article I, § 8.

In regards to federal relations with state government, the Constitiution again recognized that the power to call for military action should be primarily in the legislature, rather than a single leader. The United States as a whole is obliged to protect "every State" against "Invasion," upon the "Application of the Legislature, or of the Executive (when the Legislature cannot be convened) against domestic violence." U.S. Constitution, Article IV, § 4.

92. Congress was granted the authority "to raise and support armies, but no Appropriation of Money to that Use shall be for a longer Term than two years; To provide and maintain a Navy." U.S. Constitution, Article I, § 8, cl. 12, 13.

93. *Presser v. Illinois*, 116 U.S. 252, 265 (1886): "It is undoubtedly true that all citizens capable of bearing arms constitute the reserved military force or reserve militia of the

United States, and, in view of this prerogative of the general government . . . the States cannot, even laying the Constitutional provision in question [the Second Amendment] out of view, prohibit the people from keeping and bearing arms, so as to deprive the United States of their rightful resources maintaining the public security, and disable the people from performing their duty to the general government."

94. Mr. Lenoir, quoted in Jonathan Elliot, ed., *Debates on the Several State Conventions,* Vol. IV (Philadelphia: Lippincott, 1937, 1st ed., 1836), p. 203 (North Carolina); Joseph Story, *Commentaries on the Constitution* (Durham, N.C.: Carolina Academic Press, 1987, 1st ed., 1835), § 1001.

95. James Madison, *The Federalist Papers,* no. 46, Clinton Rossiter, ed. (New York: Mentor, 1961; 1st ed., 1788). Madison's predicted half-million militiamen amounted to most of the adult white male population under fifty. In Federalist 28, Hamilton scoped out one scenario of resistance to:

the enterprises of ambitious rulers in the national councils. If the federal army should be able to quell the resistance of one State, the distant States would have it in their power to make head with fresh forces. The advantages obtained in one place must be abandoned to subdue the opposition in others; and the moment the part which had been reduced to submission was left to itself, its efforts would be renewed, and its resistance revive.

Noah Webster echoed the idea: "Before a standing army can rule, the people must be disarmed; as they are in almost every kingdom of Europe. The supreme power in America cannot enforce unjust laws by the sword; because the whole body of the people are armed . . ." A Citizen of America (Noah Webster), "An Examination Into the Leading Principles of The Federal Constitution Proposed by the Late Convention" (Philadelphia: Prichard and Hall, 1787), p. 43, reprinted in Paul Ford, ed., *Pamphlets on the Constitution of the United States* (Brooklyn: n.p., 1888), p. 56.

Henry Knox, the first secretary of war, proposed a militia plan that would periodically train all citizens. He forecast that "A Republic constructed on the principles herein stated would be uninjured by events, sufficient to overturn a Government supported solely by the uncertain power of a standing army." Henry Knox, *A Plan for the General Arrangement of the Militia of the United States,* January 21, 1790, reprinted in Charlene Bangs Buckford and Helen E. Veit, eds., *Documentary History of the First Federal Congress 1778–1791,* Vol. V (Baltimore: Johns Hopkins University Press, 1986), p. 1439.

96. Tench Coxe, *Pennsylvania Gazette,* February 20, 1788, quoted in Stephen Halbrook, "To Keep and Bear Their Private Arms: The Adoption of the Second Amendment, 1787–1791," *Northern Kentucky Law Review* 10 (1982), p. 17.

97. Richard Henry Lee, *Letters from the Federal Farmers to the Republican,* November 8, 1787, quoted in Hardy, pp. 66–67.

98. David Robertson, *Debates and Other Proceedings of the Convention of Virginia,* (2d ed., 1805), George Mason remarks at Virginia Convention, June 14, 1788; Patrick Henry, remarks at Virginia Convention, June 5, June 9, June 14.

99. The Supreme Court's most recent statement on the Second Amendment was that the "right of the people to keep and bear arms" and "the right of the people peaceably to assemble," protect the same class of people as "the right of the people to be secure in their persons, houses, papers and effects against unreasonable searches and seizures." In all cases, the Court said, the "right of the people" refers to individual American citizens. (And therefore, a Mexican citizen in Mexico City could not complain he was unreasonably searched by American drug agents.) *United States* v. *Verdugo-Urquidez,* 494 U.S. 259, 265 (1990).

For discussion for the original meaning of the Second Amendment, see Sanford Levinson, "The Embarrassing Second Amendment," *Yale Law Journal* 99 (1989): 637–59; Donald B. Kates, "Handgun Prohibition and the Original Understanding of the Second Amendment," *Michigan Law Review* 82 (1983): 203; Shalhope, "The Ideological Origins of the Second Amendment," *Journal of American History* 69 (1982): 599–614; Joyce Malcolm, *Arms for Their Defense: Origins of an Anglo-American Right* (forthcoming); Senate Subcommittee on the Judiciary, Subcommittee on the Constitution, *The Right to Keep and Bear Arms*, 97th Congress, 2d sess., Senate Doc. 2807 (Washington, D.C.: Government Printing Office, February 1982). [This document is out of print. Reprints are available from the Second Amendment Foundation, in Bellevue, Wash.]

Among the Court decisions recognizing the right to bear arms as an individual one are *Presser* v. *Illinois* (discussed at notes 93 and 265); *United States* v. *Cruikshank* (notes 4 and 209–11); and *United States* v. *Miller* (note 101).

100. The only commentary available to Congress when it ratified the Second Amendment was written by Tench Coxe, one of James Madison's friends. Explained Coxe: "The people are confirmed by the next article of their right to keep and bear their private arms." A Pennsylvanian (Coxe's pen name), "Remarks on the First Part of the Amendments to the Federal Constitution," *The Federal Gazette and Pennsylvania Evening Post*, June 18, 1789, p. 2, quoted in Stephen Halbrook, *That Every Man Be Armed* (Albuquerque: University of New Mexico Press, 1984), p. 76. After Coxe sent Madison a copy of his article, Madison wrote back that the move for a Bill of Rights would "be greatly favored by explanatory strictures of a healing tendency, and is therefore already indebted to the cooperation of your pen." James Madison, letter to Tench Coxe, June 24, 1789, in Robert A. Rutland and Charles F. Hobson, eds., *The Papers of James Madison*, Vol. 12 (Charlottesville: University Press of Virginia, 1979), p. 257.

Madison's original structure of the Bill of Rights did not place the amendments together at the end of the text of the Constitution (the way they were ultimately organized); rather, he proposed interpolating each amendment into the main text of the Constitution, following the provision to which it pertained. If he had intended the Second Amendment to be mainly a limit on the power of the federal government to interfere with state government militias, he would have put it after Article 1, section 8, which granted Congress the power to call forth the militia to repel invasion, suppress insurrection, and enforce the laws; and to provide for organizing, arming, and disciplining the militia. Instead, Madison put the right to bear arms amendment (along with the freedom of speech amendment) in Article I, section 9—the section that guaranteed individual rights such as habeas corpus. Donald B. Kates, Jr., "Second Amendment," in Leonard Levy, ed., *Encyclopedia of the American Constitution* (New York: Macmillan, 1986), p. 1639. See also Robert Shalhope, "The Ideological Origins of the Second Amendment," *Journal of American History* 69 (December 1982): 599–614; Joyce Malcolm, "The Right of the People to Keep and Bear Arms: The Common Law Tradition," *Hastings Constitutional Law Quarterly* 10 (Winter 1983): 285–34.

101. *United States* v. *Miller*, 307 U.S. 174, 179 (1939).

102. 10 United States Code § 311(a). When a person enlists in the National Guard, he takes one oath of allegiance to the state government, as a member of the National Guard of that state. He takes another oath of allegiance to the United States government, as a member of the National Guard of the United States. Members of a National Guard unit are considered to be part of the state guard, unless they are called into federal service, at which point their status as state guard members disappears, and they function solely as members of the National Guard of the United States. The U.S. National Guard was specifically raised under Congress's power to "raise and support armies," not its power to

"Provide for organizing, arming and disciplining the Militia." When a national guardsman is serving as a member of a state's organized militia, he cannot be sent overseas. When a guardsman is federalized into national service, he can be sent overseas, as the Guard was during World War II, and more recently in the Persian Gulf War. Senate Committee on the Judiciary, Subcommittee on the Constitution, *The Right to Keep and Bear Arms,* 97th Congress, 2d sess., Senate Doc. 2807 (February 1982): 20–23; House Report No. 141, 73d Cong., 1st sess. (1933), pp. 2–5.

Although it is sometimes asserted that the Second Amendment guarantee protects only the right of states to have a National Guard unit, the National Guard's weapons plainly cannot be the arms protected by the Second Amendment, since guard weapons are owned by the federal government. 32 United States Code § 105(a)[1].

In a passage cited approvingly by the Supreme Court, nineteenth-century commentator Thomas Cooley wrote: "The alternative to a standing army is 'a well-regulated militia'; but this cannot exist unless the people are trained to bearing arms." Thomas Cooley, *Constitutional Limitations* (Boston: Little, Brown, 8th ed., 1927; 1st ed., 1868), p. 729, cited in *United States* v. *Miller,* 307 U.S. at 183 n.3. Cooley further stated:

The right is general—It may be supposed from the phraseology of this provision that the right to keep and bear arms was only guaranteed to the militia; but this would be an interpretation not warranted by the intent . . . [I]f the right were limited to those enrolled [by the government in the militia], the purpose of this guaranty might be defeated altogether by the action or neglect to act of the government it was meant to hold in check. The meaning of the provision undoubtedly is that the people from whom the militia must be taken shall have the right to keep and bear arms, and they need no permission or regulation of law for the purpose.

Thomas Cooley, *General Principles of Constitutional Law* (Boston: Little, Brown, 3d ed., 1898), p. 298.

103. Howard E. French, "Double Rifles Had Glamour," in *Gun Digest 1989,* 43rd Annual Edition (Northbrook, Ill.: DBI Books, 1988), p. 73. Other phrases from the article:

these 8-bore bullets regulated perfectly . . . When people speak of how double rifles group they always mention "regulating." The barrels of double rifles are not parallel, the bores are angled from rear to front. If the barrels were aligned side-by-side, the right barrel would shoot to the right and the left barrel to the left. To align the barrels of a double rifle they are fastened at the breech while the muzzles are held in a device that allows the barrels to be moved by wedges or by re-soldering until the bullets from both barrels shoot properly. Only then are the muzzle perfectly affixed. The regulating of a double is simple in theory but difficult in practice. Probably most double rifles were regulated to shoot in the tropics, using Cordite, where temperatures could run as high as 120 degrees.

Ibid.

104. R. A. Steindler, *Rifle Guide* (South Hackensack, N.J.: Stoeger, 1978), p. 96. Some other uses: "Guns like the now obsolete 'Paradox,' 'Jungle Gun,' 'Explora,' 'Fauneta,' and other similar 'ball and shot guns' were regulated for heavy bullets." Jack Lott, "Double Gun Actions," in Hans Tanner, ed., *Basic Gun Repair,* (Los Angeles: Peterson Printing, 1973), p. 57; "Due to the difficulty in regulating side-by-sides, this gun should probably be an over and under." Jack Lott, "The Cape Gun," *1975 Guns and Ammo Annual,* p. 140; "A moderate load should be selected for regulating the barrels, something in the neighborhood of 2¾ drams. . . . Luckily, most old pairs of barrels will have been regulated during manufacture so no additional adjustments will be necessary." William R. Brockway,

Recreating the Double Barrel Muzzle-Loading Shotgun (York, Penn.: George Shumway, 1985), p. 180.

105. R. A. Steindler, *Firearms Dictionary* (Harrisburg, Penn.: Stackpole, 1970), p. 193.

106. Terry Murbach, "Sixgun or Auto Pistol . . . Smith has a fine new .45 for You!" *Peterson's Handguns,* September 1989, p. 52.

107. Quoted in Clinton Rossiter, *The Political Thought of the American Revolution* (New York: Harcourt, Brace and World, 1953), pp. 126–27.

108. Madison autobiography, manuscript collection, Library of Congress, quoted in Hardy, pp. 50–51. That the Second Amendment was intended most directly as a safeguard against tyranny does not mean that individual defense against crime was foreign to its purpose. Defense against criminal governments was seen as a large-scale application of the natural right and duty of self-defense against individual criminals. Donald B. Kates, Jr., "The Second Amendment and the Ideology of Self-Preservation," *Constitutional Commentary* 9 (1992): 87–104.

109. Far western farmers needed to distill their corn into whiskey in order to shrink it for transportation for sale. The Virginians and Pennsylvanians were angry that the tax bore so one-sidedly on them, and that it was enforced so rigorously by the federal government.

110. Proclamation of August 7, 1794, reprinted in Commager, pp. 163–64.

111. Gerald Carson, "Watermelon Armies and Whiskey Boys," in Roger Lane and John J. Turner, Jr., eds., *Riot, Rout, and Tumult: Readings in American Social and Political Violence* (Lanham, Md.: University Press of America, 1978), pp. 70–79, originally printed in Gerald Carson, *The Social History of Bourbon: An Unhurried Account of Our Star-Spangled American Drink* (New York: Dodd, Mead, 1963). Washington pardoned the rebels.

112. Robert E. Shalhope, "The Armed Citizen in the Early Republic," *Law and Contemporary Society* 49 (Winter 1986), p. 140.

113. Ian V. Hogg, *The Illustrated Encyclopedia of Firearms* (Secaucus, N.J.: Chartwell, 1978), p. 46.

114. Coakley and Conn, p. 83.

115. David T. Hardy, "The Second Amendment and the Historiography of the Bill of Rights," *Journal of Law and Politics* 4 (1987), pp. 13–15.

116. In the 1840s and 1850s, many men joined "volunteer companies," which emphasized target shooting and other training. German and Irish immigrants often organized into such groups. Volunteer companies were generally seen as admirable organizations promoting civic virtue. It is not known how effective the companies actually were in combat, since the Union and Confederate military commands did not integrate the volunteer companies into the armies as whole units. Marcus Cunliffe, *Soldier and Civilians: The Martial Spirit in America 1775–1865* (Boston: Little Brown, 1968).

117. William Langer, Speech to National Farmers Union 1933 Convention, *Minutes* (N.F.U., 1934), in National Farmers Union Historical Archives, Western Historical Collection, University of Colorado, Boulder, Colo., discussed in Roy T. Wortman, "Populism's Stepchildren: The National Farmers Union and Agriculture's Welfare in Twentieth-Century," in Frank Annunziata, Patrick D. Reagan, and Roy T. Wortman, eds., *For the General Welfare: Essays in Honor of Robert H. Bremner* (New York: Peter Lang, 1989), p. 173.

118. Philip Taft and Philip Ross, "American Labor Violence: Its Causes, Character, and Outcome," in *Violence in America: Historical Perspectives,* pp. 281–395. In many cases, as in the Colorado coal wars at the turn of the century, the citizen militia had been replaced by a uniformed National Guard, precisely the kind of select, standing army that the framers had feared would be used to suppress internal dissent.

119. Taft and Ross, p. 281.

120. Ben C. Roberts, "On the Origins and Resolution of English Working-Class Protest," in *Violence in America*, pp. 245, 278.

121. Michael Wallace, "The Uses of Violence in American History," in *Riot, Rout, and Tumult*, pp. 18–19. Another historian writes: "One of the major themes in American urban history since the 1850s has been the struggle of the municipal authorities and their business-class allies to gain a monopoly on the use of violence. The problem was not that the elected official lacked a monopoly on the use of legally authorized violence; rather they struggled to convince turbulent portions of the populace that all other violence was illegitimate." Michael Feldberg, "The Crowd in Philadelphia History: A Comparative Perspective," in *Riot, Rout, and Tumult*, p. 142.

122. For an excellent history of the coal wars of Pennsylvania and Colorado, see Priscilla Long, *Where the Sun Never Shines: A History of America's Bloody Coal Industry* (New York: Paragon House, 1989).

123. The Northerners who violently prevented escaped slaves from being returned to the South might be said to be undermining private property. The Northerners, though, did not consider the slaves to be property; the semi-feudal Southern slave system was considered a threat to the North's "free labor" capitalist policies.

124. The American people were not necessarily more conservative than other peoples. The Canadian militia helped break the Winnipeg strike of 1919, and the British militia participated in the routing of the demonstrators at Peterloo in 1819. See chapter 3, note 79 and chapter 4, note 29.

125. During the last year of the Hoover presidency, in 1932, direct farmer action halted 140 farm foreclosures. John Shover, "The Farmer's Holiday Association Strike, August 1932," in *Riot, Rout, and Tumult*, pp. 281, 288. Originally published in *Agricultural History* 39 (1965): 196–203.

126. Governor O'Conor of Maryland delivered a radio address on March 10, 1942, in which he called for volunteers to defend the state: "[T]he volunteers, for the most part, will be expected to furnish their own weapons. For this reason, gunners (of whom there are sixty thousand licensed in Maryland), members of Rod and Gun Clubs, of Trap Shooting and similar organizations will be expected to constitute a part of this new military organization." *State Papers and Addresses of Governor O'Conor*, Vol. III, p. 618, quoted in Bob Dowlut, "The Right to Bear Arms: Does the Constitution or the Predilection of Judges Reign?" *Oklahoma Law Review* 36 (1985): 76–77. See also Donald B. Kates, *Why Handgun Bans Can't Work* (Bellevue, Wash.: Second Amendment Foundation, 1982), p. 74, citing Baker, "I Remember 'The Army' with Men from 16 to 79," *Baltimore Sun Magazine*, November 16, 1975, p. 46; M. Schlegel, *Virginia On Guard—Civilian Defense and the State Militia in the Second World War* (Richmond: Virginia State Library, 1949), pp. 45, 129, 131. According to Schlegel, the Virginia militia "leaned heavily on sportsmen," because they could provide their own weapons. Ibid., p. 129, quoted in Bob Dowlut, "State Constitutions and the Right to Keep and Bear Arms," *Oklahoma City University Law Review* 2 (1982), p. 198; Don McLean, "Tillamook Guerrillas: Defenders of the Oregon Coast," *Soldier of Fortune*, January 1990, pp. 72–77, 102–103, 107.

127. "To Arms," *Time*, March 30, 1942, p. 1. According to a New York appellate case, "Six hundred thousand of our citizens in cities have sat in shelters at the top of tall buildings and in the country on lonely hillsides every hour day and night for more than eighteen months." The opinion noted that under the present circumstances in which citizens were on guard against paratroop attack from the air, a man "who could shoot with accuracy, would be a more useful citizen than one who, if attacked, could only throw a bootjack

at his assailant." *Moore* v. *Gallup,* 45 N.Y.S. 2d 63, 69; 267 App. Div. 64; *affirmed* 59 N.E. 2d 847, 294 N.Y. 699 (1943) (Hill, Presiding Judge, dissenting).

128. Office of the Assistant Secretary of Defense, *U.S. Home Defense Forces Study* (March 1981), pp. 32, 34, 58–63, quoted in Dowlut, "State Constitutions," p. 197.

129. During the 1960s, when the idea that many people could survive the first round of a limited nuclear attack was still a legitimate thought, government advice to civilians about the aftermath of an attack included details about how to form militias and vigilance committees and administer justice. Office of Civil Defense, Department of Defense, *Shelter Management Textbook* (Washington: 1967).

130. Richard Maxwell Brown, "The American Vigilante Tradition," in Hugh Davis Graham and Ted Robert Gurr, eds., *Violence in America: Historical and Comparative Perspectives* (New York: Praeger, 1969), p. 178. The *Violence in America* series is republished every decade, with some old articles and some new ones. To distinguish the 1969 edition from other ones, the 1969 edition is hereinafter cited as *"Violence in America: Historical and Comparative Perspectives."*

131. Brown, "The American Vigilante Tradition," p. 154. As discussed in the New Zealand chapter, New Zealand did resort to vigilantism for several years. See chapter 6, note 6 and accompanying text. Rural Russia also had episodes of vigilantism, in which peasants executed horse thieves. James Elbert Cutler, *Lynch-Law: An Investigation into the History of Lynching in the United States* (New York: Longmans, Green, 1905), p. 3, citing *Washington Times,* December 14, 1902.

132. Names for the same process in Great Britain were "Cowper law," "Jeddart justice" (named for a Scotch border town), and Lydford law. William C. Culberson, *Vigilantism: Political History of Private Power in America* (New York: Praeger, 1990), p. 37.

133. Brown, "The American Vigilante Tradition," p. 159; Richard Maxwell Brown, *The South Carolina Regulators* (Cambridge, Mass.: Belknap, 1963).

134. Altina L. Waller, *Feud: Hatfields, McCoys, and Social Change in Appalachia, 1860–1900* (Chapel Hill: University of North Carolina Press, 1988), p. 169. Not all reactions against nonlocal control were denominated as the acts of regulators. For example, during the years of British rule, rioting colonists in Maine and New Jersey had resorted to "swamp law" or "club law" to drive away colonial authorities who had attempted to keep Americans from harvesting timber that legally belonged to the King. John Perlin, *A Forest Journey: The Role of Wood in the Development of Civilization* (New York: W. W. Norton and Co., 1989), pp. 300–307.

135. For example, Article 8 of the "Constitution of the Committee of Vigilantes of San Francisco" (May 16, 1856) required "that no persons, accused before this body, shall be punished until after fair and impartial trial and conviction," reprinted in *Documents of American History,* Vol. I, p. 339.

The criminal act that had spurred the formation of the San Francisco vigilante movement of 1851, the robbery and beating of a clothing store owner, led to the trial before a vigilante court of two suspects, with the vigilantes' leader acting as prosecutor. The jury voted nine for guilty, and three for acquittal. The suspects were returned to the legal authorities. Alan Valentine, *Vigilante Justice* (New York: Reynal and Co., 1956), pp. 28–29; Bruce Benson, *The Enterprise of Law: Justice Without the State* (San Francisco: Pacific Research Institute, 1990), pp. 316–17.

For a carefully ordered description of a vigilante trial see Kenneth Jessen, *Colorado Gunsmoke* (Boulder, Colo.: Pruett Publishing, 1986), p. 22, describing a Denver case that was presided by a professional judge in a trial that lasted several days and was heard before a twelve-man jury. Jessen's book contains a number of well-told histories of vigilante actions in Colorado.

136. Richard Maxwell Brown, "Historical Patterns of Violence," in Ted Robert Gurr, ed., *Violence in America: Protest, Rebellion, Reform* (Vol. II in *Violence in America* series) (Newbury Park: Sage, 1989), pp. 37–38. [The volume is hereinafter cited as *Violence in America: Protest.*] Joseph G. Rosa, *The Gunfighter: Man or Myth?* (Norman: University of Oklahoma Press, 1969), p. 19.

137. Clement Eaton, "Mob Violence in the Old South," in *Riot, Rout, and Tumult,* p. 147, citing *Southern Argus* (Columbus, Miss.), July 25, 1835, and *Niles' Weekly Register,* 48, p. 401. Originally published in *Mississippi Valley Historical Review* (now *Journal of American History*) 24 (December 1942): 351–70; Richard Hofstadter and Michael Wallace, eds., *American Violence: A Documentary History* (New York: Knopf, 1971), p. 450. [Hereinafter, "Hofstadter and Wallace, *American Violence.*"]

138. Brown, "The American Vigilante Tradition," pp. 184–85. The one instance of excess occurred when the Regulators burned down a local newspaper after it published a hostile editorial.

139. Thomas J. Dimsdale, *The Vigilantes of Montana: Being a Correct and Impartial Narrative of the Chase, Trial, Capture, and Execution of Henry Plummer's Notorious Road Agent Band* (Norman: University of Oklahoma Press, new ed., 1953); Hofstadter and Wallace, pp. 462–63. The standard survey of vigilantism in Montana and the Northwest is N. P. Langford, *Vigilante Days and Ways* (Missoula: Montana State University Press, 1957; 1st ed., 1893, D. D. Merrill).

140. Brown, "The American Vigilante Tradition," p. 177.

141. Hofstadter, "Reflections on Violence in the United States," in Hofstadter and Wallace, *American Violence,* p. 22.

142. Richard Maxwell Brown, "Historical Patterns of Violence," in *Violence in America: Historical Perspectives,* p. 68; Richard Maxwell Brown, "The American Vigilante Tradition," pp. 121–80.

143. Brown, "The American Vigilante Tradition," p. 172.

144. Ibid., p. 176. One of the exceptional committees was the Montana group described above, which killed 30 people in a two-year span. Ibid.

145. Brown, "The American Vigilante Tradition," p. 179.

146. "As law emanates from the people, written or not, [and is] nothing [but] certain rules of action by which a people agree to be governed, the unanimous decision among that people to put a man to death for the crime of murder, rendered the act legal." Jackson quoted in *Niles' Register,* quoted in Cutler, p. 98. Also, Rosa, p. 55. Jackson's letter is frequently said to be related to vigilantism in Missouri rather than Iowa; the confusion results from Iowa's status as part of the original Missouri territory.

147. Brown, "The American Vigilante Tradition," p. 182.

148. Brown, "Historical Patterns of Violence," p. 69.

149. Brown, *Strain of Violence,* pp. 162–67. Among them: Leland Stanford, Sr., California governor (1861–63), U.S. senator (1885–93), founder of Stanford University; Francis Cockrell, senator from Missouri (1875–1905); Alexander Mouton, sugar planter, U.S. senator from Louisiana (1837–42), governor (1843–46); Augustus French, governor of Illinois (1846–53); John Osborne, governor of Wyoming (1893–95); Fennimore Chatterton, governor of Wyoming (1903–1905); Miguel Otero, governor of New Mexico (1897–1906); George Curry, governor of New Mexico (1907–11), U.S. representative (1912–13); Granville Stuart, American ambassador to Paraguay and Uruguay (1894–98); William J. McConnell, Idaho's first U.S. senator (1890–91), governor (1893–96). McConnell's autobiography of his youth and vigilante career, *Frontier Law: A Story of Vigilante Days* (1924), was written as a primer on good citizenship for American boys. Senator William Borah, one of the era's greatest progressives,

wrote a laudatory introduction. For an adult book by McConnell on vigilantism, see W. J. McConnell, *Early History of Idaho* (Caldwell, Idaho: Caxton, 1913).

150. Dimsdale, p. 16; Hofstadter, "Reflections on Violence in the United States," p. 22. The regulators of LaGrange and Noble counties in Indiana in 1858 echoed the Declaration of Independence in their explanation: "that the people of this country are the real sovereigns, and that whenever the laws, made by those to whom they have delegated their authority, are found inadequate to their protection," it is "the right of the people" to enforce the laws themselves. Brown, *Strain of Violence,* p. 62, citing M. H. Mott, *History of the Regulators of Northern Indiana* (Indianapolis, 1859).

As legal philosopher Lon Fuller put it, when government grossly deviates from its obligation to obey the law, the government's misconduct "must—if we are to judge the matter with any rationality at all—release men from those duties that had as their only reason for being, maintaining a pattern of social interaction that has now been destroyed." Lon L. Fuller, *The Morality of Law* (New Haven, Conn.: Yale University, 1964), p. 22.

151. Virginia City *Territorial Enterprise,* January 20, 1882, quoted in Roger D. McGrath, *Gunfighters, Highwaymen & Vigilantes: Violence on the Frontier* (Berkeley: University of California Press, 1984), p. 243.

152. Frantz, "The Frontier Tradition," p. 130.

153. Brown, p. 185–91; "Special Project: Self-Help," *Vanderbilt Law Review* 37 (1984), p. 845 n.280.

154. Brown, *Strain of Violence,* pp. 155–56.

155. Tonso, p. 179.

156. Brown, "The American Vigilante Tradition," p. 156.

157. A. Karmen, "Vigilantism," in Sanford Kadish, ed., *Encyclopedia of Crime and Justice* (New York: Free Press, 1983), pp. 1616–17.

158. "Enforcing New York City's Gun Law," *Newsline New York,* Show no. 8, January 31, 1990 (television show transcript), p. 2. The Brooklyn prosecutions do not excuse people whose illegal possession was solely for self-defense.

159. Roger D. McGrath, *Gunfighters, Highwaymen & Vigilantes: Violence on the Frontier* (Berkeley: University of California Press, 1984).

160. The Lightning was a double-action version of the famous Peacemaker or Frontier revolver. Ian V. Hogg, *The Illustrated Encyclopedia of Firearms* (Secaucus, N.J.: Chartwell, 1978), p. 121.

161. The homicide rate in Washington, D.C., is 71.8 per year per 100,000 people. FBI Uniform Crime Reports, *Crime in the United States 1990* (Washington, D.C.: U.S. Department of Justice, Government Printing Office, 1991), p. 61. The homicide rate in Aurora and Bodie was approximately 64 per 100,000 and 116 in Bodie. McGrath, p. 116.

162. Bodie had a robbery rate of 84 per 100,000 persons per year. The rate in New York City in 1980 was 1,140; in San Francisco–Oakland, 521, and the United States as a whole, 243.

The Bodie burglary rate was 6.4 per 100,000 population per year. The 1980 New York City rate was 2,661; the San Francisco–Oakland rate was 2,267. The overall American rate was 1,668.

The Bodie theft rate was 180, in contrast to New York's 3,369 and San Francisco–Oakland's 4,571. The American rate was 3,156.

All figures from McGrath, pp. 247–54.

163. Grant Smith, "Bodie, Last of the Old Time Mining Camps," *California Historical Society Quarterly* 4 (March 1925), p. 78, quoted in McGrath, p. 157. As McGrath points out in his bibliographical essay, most of the historical works about the "violent"

West have assumed that the West was violent, without offering proof beyond a detailed history of some anecdotal violent events.

Another reason that women were generally well-treated was that they were scarce. Billington, *Land of Savagery*, pp. 260–61.

164. In other parts of the American West, citizens successfully used a variety of mechanisms to protect property rights in the absence of effective government. Terry L. Anderson and P. J. Hill, "An American Experiment in Anarcho-Capitalism: The *Not* So Wild, Wild West," *Journal of Libertarian Studies* 3, no. 1 (1979): 9–29.

165. Robert A. Dykstra, *The Cattle Towns: A Social History of the Kansas Cattle Trading Centers* (New York: Alfred A. Knopf, 1968), pp. 144–47. During the sixteen years studied by Dykstra, the five towns had a total of forty-five homicides. Of those, sixteen were justifiable homicides by law enforcement officers or civilians. Two others were lynchings.

Dodge City and the other Kansas cattle towns attempted a variety of gun controls, such as requiring visitors (particularly Texas cowboys) to check their guns with the sheriff for the duration of their stay. The town's gun laws, like their laws against gambling and prostitution, were nearly impossible to enforce. Their main function was to raise revenue through nominal fines. Rosa, pp. 62–63, 74–75, 84. One of the few marshals who had any success enforcing the gun laws was Thomas J. "Bear River Tom" Smith, Marshal of Abilene in 1870. Smith "exercised a brand of law enforcement completely alien to the Texans— he used fists instead of pistols to make an arrest. Baffled by this approach, everyone in town allowed himself to be completely ruled by Smith." Rosa, p. 85. Smith's success provides an interesting parallel to the experience of Great Britain (and to a lesser degree some of the other Commonwealth nations), where unilateral police disarmament was a necessary precondition to civilian disarmament.

166. Robert M. Utley, *High Noon in Lincoln: Violence on the Western Frontier* (Albuquerque: University of New Mexico Press, 1987), pp. 173–79. Again, as in Aurora and Bodie, the ubiquity of firearms turned many drunken quarrels into homicides.

167. William C. Holden, "Law and Lawlessness on the Texas Frontier 1875–1890," *Southwestern Historical Quarterly* 44 (October 1940): 188–203.

168. W. Eugene Hollon, *Frontier Violence: Another Look* (New York: Oxford University Press, 1974), p. x.

169. Frank Richard Prassel, *The Western Peace Officer: A Legacy of Law and Order* (Norman: University of Oklahoma Press, 1972), p. 17.

170. Prassel, pp. 22–23. See also Lynn I. Perrigo, "Law and Order in Early Colorado Mining Camps," *Mississippi Valley Historical Review* 28 (1941): 41–62.

171. McGrath, pp. 221–23.

172. Ray Allen Billington, *Land of Savagery, Land of Promise: The European Image of the American Frontier in the Nineteenth Century* (Norman: University of Oklahoma Press, 1981), p. 48; Rosa, p. 7.

173. Robert G. Athearn, *The Mythic West* (Lawrence: University of Kansas, 1986).

174. The Hatfield-McCoy feud (1873–88) is the most famous feud. Others included the Martin-Tolliver (1884–87) and Hargis-Cockrell (1902–1903). Southwestern feuds include Sutton-Taylor (1869–99); Horrell-Higgins (1867–77); Jaybird-Woodpecker (1888–90); and Stafford-Townsend-Reese-Hope (1890–1906). The ultimate feud took place in New Mexico between the cattle-raising Grahams and the sheep-raising Tewksburys. In the words of the Zane Grey novel that details the feud, the battle continued "to the last man." Brown, "Historical Patterns of Violence," pp. 48–50; Zane Grey, *To the Last Man* (New York: Harper, 1922).

175. Altina L. Waller, *Feud: Hatfields, McCoys, and Social Change in Appalachia, 1860–1990*.

176. Actually, many people who were McCoys by blood sided with the Hatfields, and vice versa. Contrary to the standard view of the mountain folk, the economic and social networks of the valley were more important than familial relations.

177. "Devil Anse," the leader of the Hatfields, had learned of the possibility of interference by Frankfort several weeks before the governor's proclamation. Forty-nine Hatfields and kin took the name "Logan County Regulators" (the traditional name for a group fighting external interference in local affairs) and warned against action by Kentucky. In the minds of the Regulators, they were upholding the law as they knew it, the tradition of leaving local justice to local communities.

178. *Mahon v. Justice,* 127 U.S. 90 (1887).

179. Two other deaths related to the feud: In 1880, two McCoys got into an argument with a witness who had testified in court in favor of a Hatfield who had been accused of stealing Ranel McCoy's hogs. The McCoys killed the witness, were tried, and acquitted on grounds of self-defense. An infant born to a Hatfield-McCoy union died of natural causes in 1880. Waller, pp.3-4.

180. *New York Times,* February 18, 1888, p. 4, col. 2 (untitled).

181. Waller, pp. 225-28.

182. The composition of the jury has only been recently uncovered. Michael Hinds, "Labor Wars Recalled as the Past is Dug Up," *New York Times,* June 18, 1990, p. A8. Hinds's article ascribes the acquittals of both Sid Hatfield and the Baldwin-Felts detectives to fear of retaliation.

183. Waller, pp. 244-47.

184. Fugitive Slave Act, *U.S. Statutes at Large,* Vol. IX, p. 462 ff., reprinted in Henry Steele Commager, ed., *Documents of American History,* 5th ed. (New York: Appleton Century Crofts, 1949), pp. 319, 321-22.

185. Joseph Story, *Commentaries on the Constitution of the United States* (abridged version) (Durham, N.C.: Carolina Academic Press, 1987), § 587; Pauline Maier, "Popular Uprisings and Authorities in Eighteenth Century America," in *Riot, Rout, and Tumult,* p. 39, originally printed in *William and Mary Quarterly,* 3d series, 27 (1970): 3-35. "Posse comitatus" literally means "power of the country." Use of the posse comitatus continued long past the Civil War. Even in the early twentieth century, Colorado law provided for punishment of anyone failing to join the posse comitatus. Revised Statutes of Colorado, § 229 (1908). In June 1977, the Aspen, Colorado, sheriff called out the posse comitatus (ordinary citizens with their own guns) to hunt for escaped mass murderer Theodore Bundy. A typical modern posse comitatus statute is Kentucky's: "Any sheriff, deputy sheriff or other like officer may command and take with him the power of the county, or a part thereof, to aid him in the execution of the duties of his office, and may summon as many persons as he deems necessary to aid him in the performance thereof." Kentucky Revised Statutes Annotated, § 70.070 (Baldwin, 1991).

186. Brown, *Strain of Violence,* p. 7; Hofstadter and Wallace, *American Violence,* p. 85.

187. In one incident, two free blacks rescued a captured slave from government custody while a crowd of whites cheered. Charles Adams, *Richard Henry Dana: A Biography,* Vol. 1 (Boston: Houghton, Mifflin, 1890), pp. 182-83.

188. Brown, *Strain of Violence,* p. 7. Newspapers or speakers who supported abolitionism were often suppressed by militias or mobs. Clement Eaton, "Mob Violence in the Old South," in *Riot, Rout, and Tumult,* pp. 155-56 (first published in *Mississippi Valley Historical Review* 29 [December 1942]: 351-70), pp. 146-81; Brown, "The American Vigilante Tradition," p. 180. Nat Turner's rebellion was put down by militias and vigilantes. Michael Wallace,

"The Uses of Violence," in *Riot, Rout and Tumult*, p. 12. (Originally printed in *The American Scholar* 41, no. 1 [Winter 1970-71]: 81-102.)

189. Albion Winegar Tourgée, *The Invisible Empire* (Baton Rouge: Louisiana State University Press, 1989; 1st ed., 1880), pp. 137-328; George C. Rable, *But There Was No Peace: The Role of Violence in the Politics of Reconstruction* (Athens: University of Georgia Press, 1984), p. 28.

190. Jay Monaghan, *Civil War on the Western Border, 1854-1865* (Lincoln: University of Nebraska Press, 1955).

191. John Brown, having participated in the civil war in Kansas during the 1850s, led a takeover of the United States arsenal at Harper's Ferry, Virginia (now West Virginia), in a plan to set off a slave rebellion throughout the South. The militia and a U.S. marine force led by Robert E. Lee defeated Brown and his men. Brown was executed a few weeks later. Brown had believed he was acting under God's command to ignite a race war that would destroy the evil of slavery. He was eulogized as a martyr in the North. In the South, his raid set off a flurry of panic about servile insurrection, and a severe round of repression against abolitionist speech and suspected abolitionists.

During the election years of 1856 and 1860, there were (false and hysterical) reports of slave rebellions all over the South. Eaton, p. 156.

192. 1865 Mississippi Laws 82, 4, § 1. A person informing the government about illegal arms possession by a freedman was entitled to receive the forfeited firearm. Ibid. White men were forbidden to give or lend freedmen firearms or knives. Section 3, reprinted in Nicholas N. Kittie and Eldon D. Wedlock, Jr., eds., *The Tree of Liberty: A Documentary: History of Rebellion and Political Crime in America* (Baltimore: Johns Hopkins University Press, 1986), pp. 208-209.

193. Quoted in Harold Hyman, ed., *The Radical Republicans and Reconstruction* (New York: Bobbs-Merrill, 1967), p. 217. As one observer detailed:

The militia of this county have seized every gun found in the hands of so-called freedmen in this section of the county. They claim that the Statute Laws of Mississippi do not recognize the Negro as having any right to carry arms.

Letter, December 2, 1865, in *Harper's Weekly*, January 13, 1866, quoted in Otis P. Singletary, *Negro Militia and Reconstruction* (Westport, Conn.: Greenwood Press, 1984; reprint of Austin: University of Texas Press, 1957), p. 5.

Congress's "Report of the Joint Committee on Reconstruction" set forth the factual need for a Fourteenth Amendment to protect the liberties enumerated in the federal Bill of Rights. At the committee's hearings, General Rufus Saxon testified that throughout the South, whites were "seizing all fire-arms found in the hands of the freedmen. Such conduct is in clear and direct violation of their personal rights as guaranteed by the Constitution of the United States, which declares that 'the right of the people to keep and bear arms shall not be infringed.' " *Report of the Joint Committee on Reconstruction*, House of Representatives Report No. 30, 39th Cong., 1st sess., part 2, pp. 118-19, quoted in Stephen Halbrook, "The Right to Bear Arms in Texas: The Intent of the Framers of the Bill of Rights," *Baylor Law Review* 41 (1989), p. 642.

194. Rable, pp. 25-26; Hofstadter and Wallace, *American Violence*, p. 224.

195. Michael W. Fitzgerald, " 'To Give Our Votes to the Party': Black Political Agitation and Agricultural Change in Alabama, 1865-1870," *Journal of American History* 76, no. 2 (September 1989): 489-505; Rable, pp. 25-28. Tourgeé observed that the Klansmen's having horses indicated that the wealthier men in the community were either participating or lending material assistance. Tourgée, p. 37.

196. Rable, pp. 70–71, 105.

197. Herbert Shapiro, *White Violence and Black Response: From Reconstruction to Montgomery* (Amherst: University of Massachusetts Press, 1988), pp. 21–22.

198. The best history of the black state militias is Otis P. Singletary, *Negro Militia and Reconstruction,* cited in full in note 193.

199. For white assassination of militia leaders, barring militia members from employment, and stealing militiamen's firearms, see Singletary, pp. 120–28.

"Pitchfork" Ben Tillman, the foremost U.S. Senate advocate of racism for many decades, joined a "Sweetwater Sabre Club," whose members seized control of South Carolina's Edgefield Country from a black militia in 1874–75, and attacked a black militia at Hamburg, South Carolina, in 1876. Brown, *Strain of Violence,* pp. 88–89.

200. Tourgée, pp. 54–55. The Klan's objective in disarming the blacks was to leave them unable to defend their rights. *Ku Klux Klan Conspiracy,* Vol. 5 (Washington, D.C: Government Printing Office, 1872), p. 1672, reprint of *Testimony Taken by the Joint Select Committee into the Condition of Affairs in the Late Insurrectionary States* (South Carolina, Vol. 3), 42d Cong., 2d sess., cited in Kermit L. Hall, "Political Power and Constitutional Legitimacy: The South Carolina Ku Klux Klan Trials, 1871–72," *Emory Law Journal* 33 (1984), p. 925; Williamson, p. 262.

201. George C. Rable, *But There Was No Peace: The Role of Violence in the Politics of Reconstruction* (Athens: University of Georgia Press, 1984), pp. 25–27.

202. Hall, p. 927.

203. The Congressional Report detailed one arms roundup:

One poor old man, half crazed, but harmless, sitting quietly in a neighbor's house, is brutally shot to death in the presence of terrified women and shrieking children. He gained his wretched living by hunting and fishing, and had a shot-gun. No one pretended that Tom Bidderman had anything to do with the fight, but he was black, and had a gun in his house, and so they murdered him for amusement as they were going from the city to restore order in the country.

Vicksburg Troubles, House of Representatives Report No. 265, 43rd Cong., 2d sess., in Hofstadter and Wallace, *American Violence,* p. 228.

In modern Chicago, the police conducted a similar "Operation Clean Sweep," sealing off public housing projects, and conducting apartment-to-apartment warrantless, suspicionless searches for guns and drugs. "Complaint of Rose Summeries, Jane Does 1–3, and John Doe," United States District Court for the Northern District of Illinois, case no. 88C10566, December 16, 1988. The police desisted under the threat of an American Civil Liberties Union lawsuit.

204. "All persons born or naturalized in the United States, and subject to the jurisdiction thereof, are citizens of the United States and of the States wherein they reside. No State shall make or enforce any law which shall abridge the privileges or immunities of citizens of the United States; nor shall any State deprive any person of life, liberty, or property without due process of law; nor deny to any person within its jursidiction the equal protection of the laws. . . . The Congress shall have power to enforce, by appropriate legislation, the provisions of this article." Amendment XIV, §§ 1, 5.

205. Cong. Globe, 39th Cong., 1st sess., p. 1838 (1866). The earlier Freedman's Bureau Bill had also been squarely aimed at protecting the right to bear arms. The bill guaranteed federal protection of "the full and equal benefit of all laws and proceedings for the security of person and estate, including the constitutional right of bearing arms." *Congressional Globe,* 39th Cong., 1st sess. (1866), p. 743, quoted in Michael Kent Curtis, "Still Further

Adventures of the Nine-Lived Cat: A Rebuttal to Raoul Berger's Reply on Application of the Bill of Rights to the States," *North Carolina Law Review* 62 (March 1984), p. 526.

The best discussion of the right to bear arms in the context of the Fourteenth Amendment is found in Stephen Halbrook, *That Every Man Be Armed: The Evolution of a Constitutional Right* (Albuquerque: University of New Mexico Press, 1984), chap. 5.

206. 16 Stat. 140 § 6 (1870): "That if two or more persons shall band or conspire together, or go in disguise upon the public highway, or upon the premises of another . . . or intimidate any citizen with intent to prevent or hinder his free exercise and enjoyment of any right or privilege secured or granted him by the Constitution or laws of the United States. . . ."

207. Rable, pp. 125–29. Enforcement Acts, 16 Stat. 140; 18 United States Code §§ 241, 242.

208. *United States* v. *Crosby*, 25 F. Cas. 701 (Dist. South Car. 1871); *United States* v. *Arvey*, 80 U.S. (13 Wall.) 251 (1871). The cases are discussed in Hall, "Political Power and Constitutional Legitimacy: The South Carolina Ku Klux Klan Trials, 1871–72," *Emory Law Journal* 33 (Fall 1984): 921–51.

209. 343 U.S. at 551–53.

210. *United States* v. *Cruikshank*, 92 U.S. 542 (1876).

211. Robert Palmer argues that "*United States* v. *Cruikshank* accomplished the nullification of the fourteenth amendment that scholars traditionally attribute to *Slaughter-House.*" Palmer argues that Justice Waite's opinion in *Cruikshank* misread *Slaughter-House,* and wrongly assumed that state and federal privileges and immunities were absolutely distinct. Robert C. Palmer, "The Parameters of Constitutional Reconstruction: Slaughter-House, Cruikshank, and the Fourteenth Amendment," *University of Illinois Law Review* 1984 (1984): 739–70.

Cruikshank was overruled by implication by *DeJonge* v. *Oregon,* which held, directly contrary to *Cruikshank,* that the right peaceably to assemble was guaranteed by the Fourteenth Amendment. Because *Cruikshank* had applied identical reasoning to find that the First Amendment (assembly) and Second Amendment (arms) were not protected by the Fourteenth Amendment, there is no reason for *Cruikshank* to be considered good law today in regard to the Fourteenth Amendment's protection of the right to bear arms.

212. Rable, p. 129.

213. Singletary, pp. 145–46; Wallace, p. 14; Shapiro, p. 11; W. E. B. Du Bois, *Black Reconstruction* (New York: Harcourt, Brace, 1935), p. 690 ("the Reconstruction governors were afraid to use these militia forces lest they start a race war. . . .").

214. The election control tactics were particularly successful in Mississippi and Louisiana in the early 1870s, although they were duplicated all over the South. Rable, pp. 122–86; Allen W. Trelease, *Reconstruction: The Great Experiment* (New York: Harper & Row, 1971), pp. 147–92.

215. Alabama (1893), Texas (1907), and Virginia (1925). Donald B. Kates, Jr., "History of Handgun Prohibition in the United States," in Donald B. Kates, Jr., ed., *Restricting Handguns: The Liberal Skeptics Speak Out* (Croton-on-Hudson, N.Y.: North River Press, 1979), p. 14; Donald B. Kates, Jr., *Guns, Murders, and the Constitution: A Realistic Assessment of Gun Control* (San Francisco: Pacific Institute, 1990), p. 38 n.141.

216. Registration: Mississippi (1906), Georgia (1913), North Carolina (1917). Handgun permits: North Carolina (1917), Missouri (1919), Arkansas (1923). Kates, *Guns, Murders, and the Constitution,* p. 38 n.141.

217. *Watson* v. *Stone,* 148 Fla. 516, 450 So.2d 700, 703 (1941) (Buford, J., concurring specially).

218. *Delahanty* v. *Hinckley* (D.D.C. July 1986) (Penn, J.).

219. Wright and Rossi, p. 238. Likewise, arbitrary increases in licensing fees for firearms ownership also impact unequally on blacks. The Congress on Racial Equality, filing an amicus curiae brief in suit to stop New York State's Westchester County from collecting illegal handgun license surcharges, explained: ". . . the obvious effect of the higher fees is to deny the law-abiding poor, including the law-abiding black poor, access to weapons for the defense of their families. That effect is doubly discriminatory because the poor, and especially the black poor, are the primary victims of crime. . . ." Quoted in *The Bullet*, September, 1987, p. 3. (*The Bullet* is the magazine of the New York State Rifle and Pistol Association.)

220. Bruce-Briggs traces the phrase to "niggertown Saturday night." B. Bruce-Briggs, "The Great American Gun War," *The Public Interest* 45 (Fall 1976), p. 50. So-called suicide specials were small, low-priced, single-action revolvers. They were manufactured until 1890, when they were made obsolete by the double-action revolver. Donald B. Webster, *Suicide Specials* (Harrisburg, Penn.: Stackpole, 1958).

221. Wallace, p. 15. In 1882, about one-half of all people lynched nationally were white. After 1902, virtually all lynching victims were black. *To Secure These Rights, The Report of the President's Committee on Civil Rights* (New York: Simon & Schuster, 1947), p. 21.

222. Brown, *Strain of Violence*, p. 150.

223. Cutler, pp. 155–92. Alleged assaults, robberies, and burglaries comprised almost all of the rest. Lynchings for social offenses were particuarly horrible, but were the exception rather than the rule. As Ida B. Wells and other black activists noted, however, many of the alleged rapes were not real rapes, but instead the post-hoc accusations of white women who had been discovered having sex with black men.

224. August Meier and Elliot Rudwick, "Black Violence in the 20th Century: A Study in Rhetoric and Retaliation," in *Violence in America: Historical and Comparative Perspectives*, p. 408.

225. Meier and Rudwick, pp. 311, 314; Wallace, p. 16. The white rioters "burned houses and, with a deliberation which shocked reporters, shot black residents as they fled the flames. They killed them as they begged for mercy and even refused to allow them to brush away flies as they lay dying. The blacks, disarmed by the police and the militia after an earlier riot and defenseless in their wooden shanties, offered little resistance." Robert Fogelson, "Violence as Protest," in *Riot, Rout, and Tumult*, p. 332. Originally published as Robert Fogelson, *Violence as Protest: A Study of Riots and Ghettos* (New York: Doubleday, 1971).

226. According to the American Civil Liberties Union, the St. Louis police have conducted over 25,000 illegal searches under the theory that any black driving a late-model car must have a handgun. The ACLU estimate is cited in Donald B. Kates, Jr., "Handgun Control: Prohibition Revisited," *Inquiry*, December 5, 1977, p. 23. Blacks are not the only victims. Permits in St. Louis have routinely been denied to homosexuals, nonvoters, and wives who lack their husbands' permission. Donald B. Kates, Jr., "On Reducing Violence or Liberty," *Civil Liberties Review* (August/September, 1976), p. 56.

227. Shapiro, p. 31 (officers of the law often joined lynch mobs). Some examples of the hostility of law enforcement to blacks:

In the Wilmington, North Carolina, riot of 1898, a mob destroyed a black newspaper after taking offense at a newspaper opinion. Armed whites gunned down blacks, killing 12. Blacks did not resist. The leader of the mob was elected mayor. Shapiro, p. 73.

In August 1900 in New York City, police joined an anti-black riot, often behaving more brutally than other rioters. The mayor, the police commissioner, and the courts covered up the officers' crimes. Shapiro, pp. 94–95.

The rioters in the extremely destructive East St. Louis riot of 1917 were assisted by the police and by the Illinois state militia. Shapiro, pp. 115–17.

In the Washington, D.C., riots of 1919, policemen refused to protect blacks from rampaging soldiers and sailors. Fogelson, p. 332.

In Tulsa during and after World War I, the police worked closely with the "Knights of Liberty," a group whose members wore masks and attacked blacks and union organizers. Shapiro, p. 181.

When whites and blacks rioted against each other in Detroit in 1943, the police tried to "reason" with the white rioters (to little effect) and killed 17 black rioters. A report by NAACP special counsel Thurgood Marshall blamed the riot on the Detroit police's overescalation of violence. Shapiro, pp. 318–19, discussing Thurgood Marshall, "Activities of Police During Riots June 21 and 22, 1943," in Walter White and Thurgood Marshall, *What Caused the Detroit Riot?* (New York: National Association for the Advancement of Colored People, 1943), pp. 29–37.

In Columbia, Missouri, in 1946, a white radio repairman slapped a black woman. The woman's son attacked the repairman. The woman and son escaped a lynch mob, and fled the state. Five hundred National Guardsmen opened machine gun fire on blacks who had barricaded themselves in their homes, expecting attack. The Guard arrested 101 blacks, 2 of whom were killed in police custody. Shapiro, pp. 362–63.

A report by the President's Committee on Civil Rights, assessing the contemporary problem of lynching, found that "Frequently state officials participate in the crime, actively or passively." *To Secure These Rights: The Report of the President's Committee on Civil Rights,* p. 23.

228. W. E. B. Du Bois, *Crisis,* October 1916, pp. 270–71. Du Bois's editorial was prompted by a Gainesville, Florida, lynching in which a group of blacks with a numerical advantage had handed over a black to a lynch mob. Others advocating self-defense against white attacks included the NAACP. Meier and Rudwick, p. 402.

Some additional voices:

• Ida B. Wells, editor of the Memphis black newspaper *Free Speech and Headlight:* "[S]o long as we permit ourselves to be trampled upon, so long will we have to endure it. Not until the Negro rises in his might and takes a hand in resisting such cold-blooded murders, if he has to burn up whole towns, will a halt be called to wholesale lynching." Brown, *Strain of Violence,* pp. 215–16.

• A. Philip Randolph: "Always regard your own life as more important than the life of the person about to take yours, and if a choice has to be made . . . choose to preserve your own and destroy that of the lynching mob." A. Philip Randolph, "How to Stop Lynching," *Messenger,* August 1919, pp. 8–10, reprinted in Shapiro, p. 170. Randolph's details for action were implausible: When the possibility of a lynching arose, blacks should ask authorities for arms with which to defend themselves, and form voluntary companies built around army veterans. Ibid., p. 172.

• "I advise you to be ready to defend yourselves. I notice the State government has removed some of its restrictions upon owning firearms, and one form of live [sic] insurance for our wives and children might be the possession of some of these handy implements." Hubert H. Harrison, *Baltimore Afro-American,* June 10, 1921, reprinted in Shapiro, p. 159.

• Reverend C. O. Benjamin Davis, editor of a Lexington, Kentucky, black newspaper: "If the whites resort to the gun and the torch, let the Negro do the same, and if blood must flow like water and bonfires be made of valuable property, so be it all around . . ." reported in *Cleveland Gazette,* November 19, 1898, quoted in Shapiro, p. 78.

• Miss M. R. Lyons of Brooklyn, Speech to Calvary Baptist Church, after a riot by white police and a mob in New York City: "Let every negro get a permit to carry a revolver. You are not supposed to be a walking arsenal, but don't you get caught again. Have your houses made ready to afford protection from the fury of the mobs, and remembering that your home is your castle and that no police officer has a right to enter it, unless he complies with the usage of the law, see that he does not." "Negroes' Public Protest," in *New York Times,* September 13, 1900, p. 2, col. 6.

229. Meier and Rudwick, "Black Violence," p. 403. During the Atlanta riots, while blacks "were unable to offer effective resistance when trapped downtown or caught in white sections of the city, they did fight back successfully when the mobs invaded their neighborhoods." John Dittmer, *Black Georgia in the Progressive Era: 1900-1920* (Urbana: University of Illinois Press, 1970), pp. 129-30.

230. In July 1919, a black who had floated into "white" water near a Lake Michigan beach in Chicago was killed. Whites rioted, blacks fought back with rifles, and the police stood aside. Twenty-three blacks and fifteen whites were killed in a week of rioting. Shapiro, pp. 150-51.

231. *Atlanta Constitution,* September 23, 1906, reprinted in Hofstadter and Wallace, *American Violence,* p. 237; Brown, *Strain of Violence,* pp. 210-11. One police officer was shot dead, and sixty blacks were arrested and the black populace disarmed. Happily, the jury acquitted the blacks, with the foreman stating: "We think the Negroes were gathered just as white people were in other parts of the town, for the purpose of defending their homes. We were shocked by the conduct some of the county police had been guilty of." Shapiro, pp. 100-101.

During a 1939 strike by Mississippi sharecroppers, the state police and local sheriffs broke up demonstrations and confiscated their hunting guns. According to an FBI investigation, the only violence at the demonstrations had been perpetrated by law enforcement officers. Shapiro, p. 250.

232. Kates, "A History of Handgun Prohibition," p. 19. Indicted for first-degree murder, Sweet was acquitted after a lengthy trial at which Clarence Darrow served as his attorney. Black newspapers such as the *Amsterdam News* and the *Baltimore Herald* vigorously defended blacks' right to use deadly force in self-defense against a mob. Walter White, "The Sweet Trial," *Crisis* 31 (January 1926): 125-29; Irving Stone, *Clarence Darrow for the Defense* (New York: Doubleday, 1941), pp. 529-47; Shapiro, pp. 188-96, citing *Amsterdam News,* November 18, 1925, and *Baltimore Herald,* November 2, 1925.

Darrow summed up for the jury: "[T]hey may have been gunmen. They may have tried to murder. But they were not cowards. . . . [E]leven of them go into a house, gentlemen, with no police protection, in the face of a mob, and the hatred of a community, and take guns and ammunition and fight for their rights, and for your rights and for mine, and for the rights of every other human being that lives." Clarence Darrow, in Arthur Weinberg, ed., *Attorney for the Damned* (New York: Simon & Schuster, 1957), pp. 241-42.

233. Wallace, p. 16; Shapiro, pp. 181-83. Writes one historian: "The self-confidence of Tulsa's Negroes soared, their businesses prospered, their institutions flourished, and they simply had no fear of whites. . . . After 1921, an altercation between a white person and a black person was not a *racial* incident. It was just an incident." John Hope Franklin, "Foreword to Ellsworth," in Scott Ellsworth, *Death in a Promised Land: The Tulsa Race Riot of 1921* (Baton Rouge: Louisiana State University Press, 1982), p. xvi, quoted in Shapiro, p. 183.

In 1936 in Gordonsville, Virginia, a black man and his sister, William and Cora Wales, shot a sheriff who had come to arrest the man on false charges of threatening a white woman. The arrest was a pretext to force the two blacks to sell their property to the town, for cemetery expansion. An enraged crowd of 5,000 whites assembled outside the home, although the crowd was afraid to attack the two armed blacks. After night fell, the crowd threw a torch on the house, and shot the Waleses as they were silhouetted against the fire. After the fire had cooled, souvenir hunters hacked the Waleses' bodies into tiny pieces. Roy Wilkins, a future head of the NAACP, blamed the racist system for all the deaths. While emphasizing that legal action was the appropriate strategy for blacks, Wilkins wrote, "*The Crisis* defends William and Cora Wales." Shapiro, pp. 288–89, discussing Roy Wilkins, "Two Against 5,000," *Crisis,* June 1936, pp. 169–70.

Resistance was not entirely new to blacks. In the 1841 Cincinnati race riot they had fought back with firearms. Hofstadter and Wallace, *American Violence,* p. 208; August Meier and Elliot Rudwick, "Black Violence in the 20th Century: A Study in Rhetoric and Retaliation," in *Violence in America: Historical and Comparative Perspectives,* pp. 408–409.

234. Shapiro, pp. 305–309.

235. Harvard Sitkoff, "Racial Militancy and Interracial Violence in the Second World War," in *Riot, Rout, and Tumult,* p. 314. Originally published in *Journal of American History* 58 (December 1971): 661–81. The flashy and extreme Zoot suit had a thigh-length jacket with very wide padded shoulders and leg pants with narrow cuffs.

236. John R. Salter, Jr., "Social Justice, Community Organizing and the Necessity for Protective Firearms," in William R. Tonso, ed., *The Gun Culture and Its Enemies* (Bellevue, Wash.: Merril, 1989), pp. 19–23. Originally published in *Against the Current* July/August 1988.

237. Daisy Bates, the leader of the Arkansas NAACP and publisher of a pro-rights newspaper during the Little Rock High School desegregation case, recalls that three crosses were burned on her lawn and gunshots fired into her home. Her husband, L. C. Bates, stayed up to guard their house with a .45 semi-automatic pistol. Some of their friends organized a volunteer patrol. After the Bates's front lawn was bombed, Mrs. Bates telegrammed Attorney General Herbert Brownell in Washington. He replied that there was no federal jurisdiction, and told them to go to the local police. "Of course *that* wasn't going to protect us," Mrs. Bates remembers. Peter Irons, *The Courage of Their Convictions: Sixteen Americans Who Fought Their Way to the Supreme Court* (New York: Free Press, 1988), pp. 124–25.

In 1947, "freedom riders" from the Congress On Racial Equality rode by bus from town to town in the South, defying the segregated transportation laws. At a freedom rider meeting in Chapel Hill, North Carolina, "virtually suicidal young Communists" carried rifles and stood guard on top of a minister's home, and protected it from racist attack. Conrad Lynn, *There Is a Fountain: The Autobiography of a Civil Rights Lawyer* (Westport, N.Y.: Lawrence Hill and Co., 1979), discussed in Shapiro, p. 409 n.82.

238. Salter, "Social Justice." The unburned Ku Klux Klan cross in the Smithsonian Institution was donated by a civil rights worker whose shotgun blast drove Klansmen away from her driveway. Ibid., p. 20.

239. Brown, "The American Vigilante Tradition," pp. 203, 217 n.150.

240. Donald B. Kates, Jr., "Why a Civil Libertarian Opposes Gun Control," *The Great Gun Control Debate* (Bellevue, Wash.: Second Amendment Foundation, 1976), p. 4. For more, see J. Weiss, "A Reply to Advocates of Gun Control Laws," *Journal of Urban Law* 53 (1974): 577. At the time, Weiss was director of the Office of Economic Opportunity's national legal services office for the elderly poor.

241. Shapiro, pp. 457, 522 n.8, citing Robert Carl Cohen, *Black Crusader: A Biography of Robert Franklin Williams* (Secaucus, N.J.: Stuart, 1972), p. 99, and Robert F. Williams, *Negroes with Guns* (New York: Marzani & Munsell, 1962).

242. Julian Mayfield, quoted in James Forman, *The Making of Black Revolutionaries* (New York: Macmillan, 1972), p. 167, quoted in Shapiro, p. 457.

243. Shapiro, pp. 458–59.

244. The NAACP unanimously adopted a preamble to a resolution stating: "In rejecting violence we do not deny but reaffirm the right of individual and collective self-defense against unlawful assault. The NAACP has consistently over the years supported this right as by defending those who have exercised the right of self-defense, particularly in the Arkansas Riot Case, the Sweet Case in Detroit, the Columbia, Tenn., riot cases, and the Ingram Case in Georgia." The resolution observed that Williams was not suggesting self-defense, but rather "violence as a means of redress of wrongs." Daisy Bates, the Little Rock civil rights leader whose family was armed for self-defense with a Colt .45, spoke in favor of the suspension of Williams. Gloster B. Current, "Fiftieth Annual Convention," *Crisis,* August-September 1959, pp. 408–10.

245. Shapiro, p. 461.

Said Malcolm X:

Concerning nonviolence: it is criminal to teach a man not to defend himself when he is the constant victim of brutal attacks. It is legal and lawful to own a shotgun or a rifle. We believe in obeying the law.

In areas where our people are the constant victims of brutality, and the government seems unable or unwilling to protect them, we should form rifle clubs that can be used to defend our lives and our property in times of emergency such as happened last year in Birmingham; Plaquemine, Louisiana; Cambridge, Maryland; and Danville, Virginia. When our people are being bitten by dogs, they are within their rights to kill those dogs.

We should be peaceful and law-abiding—but the time has come for the American Negro to fight back in self-defense whenever and wherever he is being unjustly and unlawfully attacked.

If the government thinks I am wrong for saying this, let the government start doing its job.

Malcolm X, March 12, 1964, in G. Breitman, ed., *Malcolm X Speaks* (New York: Grove Weidenfeld Press, 1965), pp. 20–22.

246. Public Law 90-618, 90th Cong., H.R. 17735, October 22, 1968; codified at 18 U.S.C. § 921 et seq. The House Un-American Activities Committee noted with disapproval the suggestions of Bobby Seale (Black Panther chairman) and H. Rap Brown (a national leader of the misnamed Student Non-Violent Coordinating Committee) that blacks arm for self-defense. "Subversive Influences in Riots, Looting, and Burning: Part 3-A (Los Angeles—Watts)," Hearings before the Committee on Un-American Activities, 90th Cong., 2d sess., June 28, 1968 (Washington, D.C.: Government Printing Office, 1968).

247. In Massachusetts, blacks supported a handgun ban referendum by a 3-to-2 margin. J. V. Holmbert and M. Clancy, *People vs. Handguns: The Campaign to Ban Handguns in Massachusetts* (no city: U.S. Conference of Mayors, 1979), pp. 83–84. In California, 62 percent of blacks opposed a handgun freeze, compared to 63 percent of the total population. Decision-Making Information, *A California Statewide Post-Election Panel Survey for the NRA* (Santa Ana: 1982). Information about black voting on the 1988 Maryland referendum to outlaw "Saturday Night Specials" is less precise. Pre-election polling showed blacks supporting the law in about the same proportion as the general population. The gun ban was upheld by a 58 percent majority.

248. "Self-Help," pp. 892–93.

249. Paul A. Gilje, *The Road to Mobocracy: Popular Disorder in New York City 1763–1834* (Chapel Hill: University of North Carolina Press, 1987), p. 129.

250. Tonso, p. 235.

251. Ibid., pp. 185–86.

252. Ibid., pp. 190–91; Richard Wade, "Violence in the Cities: A Historical View," in *Riot, Rout, and Tumult,* p. 352. Originally published in Charles U. Daly, ed., *Urban Violence* (Chicago: University of Chicago Press, 1969), pp. 7–26.

253. Roger Lane, *Violent Death in the City: Suicide, Accident & Murder in 19th Century Philadelphia* (Cambridge, Mass.: Harvard University Press, 1979), p. 61; Eric Mottram, *Blood on the Nash Ambassador* (London: Hutchinson Radius, 1989), p. 14.

254. Lane, *Violent Death in the City,* p. 27.

255. Kennett and Anderson, pp. 149–51. Apparently pistols were not the primary self-defense weapon of the era's urbanites. An English visitor to New York in the 1850s wrote: "The practice of carrying concealed arms, in the shape of stilletos for attack, and swordsticks for defense, if illegal, is perfectly common." Charles Lockwood, "Gangs, Crime, Smut, Violence," *New York Times,* September 20, 1990.

256. Lane, *Violent Death in the City,* pp. 62–63, 76.

257. Kennett and Anderson, pp. 156–57.

258. Robin, "Justifiable Homicide by Police Officers," in Marvin Wolfgang, ed., *Studies in Homicide* (New York: Harper & Row, 1967), p. 295 n.3 (in 1920, justifiable civilian homicides comprised 26.6 percent of all homicides in Detroit, and 31.4 percent in Chicago; in 1914–18, such homicides were 32 percent of all homicides in Washington, D.C.); James Boudouris, "Trends in Homicide, Detroit 1926–1968," unpublished Ph.D. dissertation, Wayne State University (1970); James Boudouris, "A Classification of Homicides," *Criminology* 11 (1974): 525–40; Arthur V. Lashley, "Homicide (In Cook County)," chap. 13 in *The Illinois Crime Survey* (Illinois Association for Criminal Justice: Chicago, 1929). Boudouris and Lashley are both discussed in Margaret A. Zahn, "Homicide in the Twentieth Century: Trends, Types, and Causes," in *Violence in America: The History of Crime,* Vol. 1 (Newbury Park, Calif.: Sage, 1989), pp. 221–22.

259. Lane, *Violent Death in the City,* p. 103.

260. Elizabeth M. Geffen, "Violence in Philadelphia in the 1840s and 1850s," in *Riot, Rout, and Tumult,* pp. 115–18. Originally printed in *Pennsylvania History* (October 1969): 381–410.

261. Lane, *Violent Death in the City,* p. 112.

262. Ibid., p. 133.

263. Ibid., p. 113.

264. Tonso, p. 199.

265. Levinson, p. 652 n.78; Kennett and Anderson, p. 167; Halbrook, p. 159. Kennett and Anderson, in favor of gun control, call the group "a radical paramilitary organization." Halbrook, opposed to control, describes the group as "a corporation of German immigrants whose stated objectives included education and military exercise to promote good citizenship."

For an excellent history of government use of the militia and the army to crush labor protest, see Robert V. Bruce, *1877: Year of Violence* (Chicago: Ivan R. Dee, 1989; 1st published by Bobbs-Merrill, 1959).

The case involving *Lehr und Wehr Verein* was *Presser* v. *Illinois,* 116 U.S. 252 (1886). The Court held that the Second Amendment did not protect independent militia organizations from state regulation. Further, the Second Amendment did not limit the state governments, because none of the Bill of Rights did. Today, the holding about nonapplication of the Bill of Rights to the states has long since lost any force. The Subcommittee on the Constitution of the Senate Judiciary Committee has concluded from historical analysis that the authors of the Fourteenth Amendment meant the Second Amendment to apply to the states, like the other items in the Bill of Rights. U.S. Senate Subcommittee on the Constitution, *The Right to Keep and Bear Arms*, 97th Cong., 2d sess. (1982). See notes 204–11 above, and accompanying text.

266. *New York Tribune*, November 19, 1903, p. 6. See generally, Kates, "History of Handgun Prohibition," pp. 15–22.

267. "Bargains in the Pawnshops," *New York Times*, August 30, 1911.

268. Kennett and Anderson, p. 178.

269. "First Conviction Under Weapon Law," *New York Times*, September 28, 1911, p. 5, col. 5. The defendant, Marino Rossi, was sentenced to a year in Sing Sing prison. A Newark resident, Rossi said he was passing through Manhattan on his way to New Haven, and was not aware of the new law. He said he carried a revolver—which a policeman saw sticking out of his pocket—because he was afraid of the Black Hand.

270. Brendan Furnish, "The New Class and the California Handgun Initiative: Elitist Developed Law as Gun Control," in Tonso, ed., *The Gun Culture*, p. 133. (Survey of *New York Times* articles from 1911 to 1913 concerning Sullivan Law arrests.)

271. David F. Selvin, "An Exercise in Hysteria: San Francisco's Red Raids of 1934," *Pacific Historical Review* 58 (August 1989): 361–74; Kates, "History of Handgun Prohibition," pp. 18–19.

272. The law was enacted in 1891, and repealed in 1959. Session Laws of Colorado, 1891, and 1959 (making transfer of firearms to Indians for any reason, under any circumstances, a felony).

273. In the 1630s in the Massachusetts Bay Colony, Anne Hutchinson criticized the Puritan government for its legalistic, mechanical interpretation of the Bible, and asserted that the Old Testament was no longer binding law. Hutchinson and others were tried for the seditious offense of spreading antinomian ideas, banished, and their supporters disarmed. Bradley Chapin, *Criminal Justice in Colonial America, 1606–1660* (Athens: University of Georgia Press, 1983), pp. 103–104.

274. Roger Lane, "Social Meaning of Homicide Trends," in Ted Robert Gurr, ed., *Violence in America: The History of Crime*, Vol. 1 (Newbury Park, Calif.: Sage, 1989), pp. 72–73.

275. See chapter 3.

276. See chapter 4, notes 29–32 and accompanying text.

277. Wright, Rossi, and Daly, p. 268. Nearby Monroe County, Florida charged $2,000. Both laws were preempted by statewide legislation that took effect in November 1987. Atlanta requires a $1,000 bond. Paul Blackman, "Carrying Handguns for Personal Protection," paper presented at annual meeting of American Society of Criminology, San Diego, November 13–16, 1986, p. 8.

278. California Penal Code § 12021.

279. Kates, "History of Handgun Prohibition," pp. 15–20.

280. John Kaplan, "The Wisdom of Controlling Handguns," *Annals of the American Academy of Political and Social Science* 455 (May 1981): 11–23.

281. Eric A. Monkkonen, "Diverging Homicide Rates: England and the United States, 1850–1875," in *Violence in America: Crime*, p. 93.

282. Alan Lizotte and Jo Dixon, "Gun Ownership and the 'Southern Subculture of Violence,'" *American Journal of Sociology* 93 (1987): 383–405.

10

Taking the Law into One's Hands: Firearms in Modern America

"The right of the people to take care of themselves if the law does not is an indisputable right."

—Professor Bigger, addressing Johnson County, Missouri, vigilantes in 1867.[1]

THE MODERN FRONTIER

In Japan, Britain, Canada, New Zealand, and Switzerland, citizens have little fear of crime or the government, and most people seem to voluntarily comply with the gun laws. Hardly anyone feels a need to own a gun for self-defense. In Australia and Jamaica, many people are afraid of criminals, or of the government. Civilian resistance to gun controls has been fiercer in those two nations.

Americans did not trust the government for protection in the nineteenth century, and they do not trust it today. If Americans are ever to abandon the practice of arming for defense, they will probably do so after crime has been controlled, not before. The failure or inability of the modern American state to control crime makes it particularly unlikely that Americans could be persuaded by statute to give up their guns.

In the harsher parts of the modern American city, the high crime rate stretches police resources thin, and citizens must protect themselves. The frontier is here. As the late Senator Frank Church wrote, most people

> would not go into ghetto areas at all except in broad daylight under the most optimum conditions—surely not at night, alone or on foot. But some people have no choice. To live or work or have some need to be on this "frontier" imposes a fear which is tempered by possession of a gun.[2]

Chief Justice William Rehnquist agrees that the inner city is out of control: "we are rapidly approaching the state of savagery. . . . In the Nation's Capital, law enforcement authorities cannot protect the lives of employees of this very Court who live four blocks from the building in which we sit."[3]

Former Washington, D.C., mayor Marion Barry enforced a ban on gun ownership for self-defense and insisted "Washington is not Dodge City." Yet modern Washington's per capita homicide rate exceeds Dodge City's.[4] In 1985, a *Washington Post* reporter found women more comfortable on the streets of Beirut than Washington.[5] Some American cities are worse than war zones. During the week that United States forces invaded Panama, twenty-three Americans were killed in that country; during the same week, thirty-six residents of New York City were killed.[6] The chance that an American child now aged twelve years will be the victim of a violent felony during his or her lifetime is 83 percent. The chances of two or more victimizations is 52 percent.[7]

Professor George Fletcher writes: "[I]n contemporary urban America, the government has failed its elementary function of securing the peace."[8] Police administrators in cities such as New York or San Jose insist that citizens do not need guns; all a person requires for protection is access to emergency services by dialing 911.[9] But when citizens are injured because the police negligently fail to protect them, the police departments retreat behind the doctrine of sovereign immunity, and insist that they have no legal obligation to protect the public.[10]

Does the modern big-city criminal-justice system perform much better than the inadequate frontier system? Not in New York City, where a mere 1 percent of felony arrests lead to a term in state prison.[11] Only 9 percent of felony *convictions* lead to more than a year in jail.[12] In the nation as a whole, the figures are better, but not comforting: out of every one hundred felony arrests, thirteen lead to a sentence of a year or more of incarceration.[13] Of juvenile offenders convicted for murder, rape, or assault with a deadly weapon, only 59 percent serve even a day in jail.[14] When the police sometimes take forty-six minutes to arrive at the scene of burglary in progress, it is little wonder that many people choose to be armed.[15] Forty-seven percent of the professional women in New York City have been mugged, robbed, or raped.[16] The crime that modern urban dwellers face is several degrees of magnitude worse than the crime in the roughest towns of the frontier west.

The failure of the government has led the people to protect themselves. Even in suburban villages on Long Island, "We have people getting guns that three to five years ago were members of handgun control groups," reports one firearms instructor.[17] In the gun-prohibition capital of the United States, New York City, firearms license applications have risen sharply; armed self-defense was at one time freakish and unusual, as in the Bernhard Goetz subway shooting, but has now become routine, with one publicized self-defense shooting following another every few weeks.[18]

Twenty years ago, when the crime rate was lower, one Harlem leader condemned vigilantism, but argued that conditions in Harlem were no better than in Dodge City or Abilene, and warned that if the police did not provide more protection, the people would inevitably protect themselves.[19] The conditions have not improved, and Americans are increasingly determined to defend themselves. From 1981 to 1985, the percentage of Americans keeping a gun or other weapon for self-defense jumped from 31 percent to 45 percent.[20] Twenty-five percent of New York City subway riders carry a weapon for protection (mostly knives). Three percent carry a gun.[21]

The cities are not the only places where crime is worse than on the frontier. Many boat owners in Florida have taken to keeping high-tech automatic and semi-automatic weapons on board, to defend themselves against drug smugglers who hijack a boat, kill all the passengers, and then use the boat for a single drug run before discarding it.[22]

A survey of Florida police chiefs and sheriffs reported that 84 percent believed the police's inability to protect citizens at all times justified the possession of guns by civilians.[23] Said Gerald Arenberg, executive director of the National Association of Chiefs of Police: "You are more likely to find a policeman when you run a red light than when you need him in a violent situation."[24]

Criminal violence is common in modern America and so is armed self-defense. According to the FBI's "Crime Clock," there is a violent crime every 17 seconds, an aggravated assault every 30 seconds, and a robbery every 49 seconds.[25] Every 48 seconds, a person uses a handgun to defend him- or herself against another person. (Brandishing a gun, rather than firing it, usually suffices to frighten away the attacker.)[26]

Just as individual self-defense has become increasingly important to a growing fraction of the population, the nation is experiencing a new variation in its long-playing theme of vigilantism.[27] Historian Richard Maxwell Brown observes:

American vigilantism has experienced a revival in recent years. Significant have been the avowedly self-protective and community patrol organizations that have proliferated by the hundreds among urban and suburban white and black Americas since 1964. Arising chiefly in response to the turmoil in race relations exemplified by the black ghetto riots of the 1960s and to the steeply rising crime rate, these organizations—among them such well-known associations as the "Maccabees" of Crown Heights in Brooklyn and the North Ward Citizens Committee (headed by Anthony Imperiale) of Newark—have been viewed as vigilante groups by the police, the press, the public, and themselves. Although they have seldom taken the law into their own hands, they have clearly emerged from the vigilante tradition and identify with it.[28]

This time vigilantes are often unarmed, almost never concern themselves with retrospective punishment of criminals, and never stage formal trials of apprehended targets. (And therefore, the new vigilantes do not fit within the traditional nineteenth-century definition of "vigilante.")

In Detroit, citizens have burned down crack houses and have been acquitted of arson by juries.[29] And while modern Detroit vigilantism includes setting fires, it also includes prevention: on "Devil's Night" in 1985, unarmed citizen volunteers numbering twenty thousand patrolled the city on the night before Halloween to prevent arson. In 1984, before the patrols started, 810 fires were set on Devil's Night.[30] The patrols dramatically reduced the number of arsons in subsequent years. In Oakland, novelist Ishmael Reed writes that a new wave of black vigilantism will take the offensive against "Black terrorists . . . the brutal crack fascists."[31]

Americans watched in horror when television showed the Cambodian-American school children killed by a deranged criminal with a Kalashnikov rifle, in a Stockton, California, schoolyard in January 1989. America's "Drug Czar" William Bennett informed the American people that Kalashnikovs were guns made only for drug traffickers like the Crips and Bloods gangs in Los Angeles. Through Bennett and the television networks, America heard one story about semi-automatic rifles. Another, equally dramatic story, was never heard outside Los Angeles. In May 1988, the Bloods attacked a Los Angeles housing project containing Cambodians. The Cambodians fought back with M1s and Kalashnikovs and drove away the Bloods.[32]

To defend a neighborhood from Bloods on Piru Street, Los Angeles, "some block clubs had to resort to armed guerilla warfare," reports the *Washington Times.* One block club leader met with Mayor Bradley, with Police Chief Daryl Gates, and with the city attorney (all vociferous gun prohibitionists) and achieved nothing. Drug dealers continued to shoot at block club members, but now the block club fired back. After club leader Norris Turner shot and wounded two gang members who had tried to ambush and kill him on the street, Turner threatened to call the media. Police presence increased, and the neighborhood was cleaned up.[33]

The "War on Drugs" took on a new meaning in September 1989 in Tacoma, Washington, where angry citizens gathered for an anti-crime rally. Spurred by the rally, an off-duty sergeant organized a dozen off-duty Army Rangers and went into freefire combat with neighborhood crack dealers. Up to three hundred rounds of handgun, shotgun, and semi-automatic rifle fire were exchanged. No fatalities resulted, and Washington Governor Booth Gardner praised the gunmen: "They were very good shots. They weren't shooting to harm. They were shooting to make a point, I think." The police mediated a truce, whereby the drug dealers agreed to stop dealing in the streets, and the neighborhood agreed to put away its guns.[34]

In most situations, fortunately, actual combat has not broken out. Risk reduction and deterrence have instead been the main objectives, as in Houston, where sales of firearms and burglar alarms increased sharply after a court-ordered release of prisoners due to jail overcrowding.[35]

In Washington, D.C., and Brooklyn, New York, Black Muslims have organized community patrols to drive drug dealers out of neighborhoods. The first day that the Fruit of Islam organization arrived at Washington's Mayfair Mansions housing project, the crack dealers departed, and parents no longer had to keep their children inside to shield them from the cross-fire of gun battles between drug dealers.[36] Elite media outlets such as the New Republic lamented the patrols as "a serious breakdown in civic order"—without understanding that civic order broke down years before and that the patrols were restoring order.[37]

Frustrated by the lack of police protection from gaybashing and from crime in general, many homosexuals in New York City are now carrying guns. A group called the "pink panthers" patrols Greenwich Village to deter anti-gay crime.[38] New York City pedestrians of all sexual orientations have even chased and killed muggers.[39] In addition, there are "a growing number of Brooklyn clergymen arming themselves to defend their families and churches."[40] Even the New York Republican party, once the home of gun prohibitionists such as Nelson Rockefeller and John Lindsay, now calls for armed, licensed "vigilantes" to patrol New York City streets.[41]

Brooklyn's 79th police precinct is one of the city's most drug-infested, and one of its most corrupt. A Sunni Muslim street patrol from the At-Taqwa Mosque helped crush the crack trade on Fulton Street. The citizen patrols spurred the police to greater efforts.[42] Guardian Angels, called in by community groups, patrol the streets to control crackheads in Restaurant Row in Hell's Kitchen.[43] Former New York City Police Commissioner Benjamin Ward decried the Guardian Angels as vigilantes. But police in Minneapolis and Houston have welcomed them.[44] A Department of Justice study concluded that the Guardian Angels enhanced citizens' feelings of security and did not engage in abusive tactics.[45]

In the coastal towns of Louisiana, oyster and crab poachers have driven many fisherman to the brink of bankruptcy. The crab fishermen of Des Allemands Parish have joined mutual protection associations and have begun carrying guns. The sheriff of St. Bernard Parish has deputized members of an oystermen's association.[46]

Vigilantism did not just drop in on the decades of the 1980s and 1990s like a ghost from the distant nineteenth century. During the previous period of crime and civil disorder, the late 1960s, citizens formed community patrols all over New York City.[47] Anti-crime patrols were active in Houston to protect small businesses against robbery; in West Hollywood, Florida, where shotgun-armed patrol cars stemmed business burglaries; in Warren, Michigan, and in Pittsburgh, Oakland, and Detroit. In Bogalusa and Jonesboro, Louisiana, the Deacons for Defense and Justice went armed in patrol cars to protect civil rights workers and black residents.[48] The most common type of vigilante organization was black neighborhood groups concerned with crime. The second most common was white suburbanites concerned about incursions by rioters.[49]

The new round of citizen law enforcement is not without its troubles. To some people, "vigilantism" is feared as a code word for racism. Indeed, some patrols have aroused tensions. Blacks in the Crown Heights neighborhood of Brooklyn complained about unfair treatment by Jewish patrols. Former mayor Edward Koch intervened and helped put together joint Hasidim-black patrols that reduced crime and increased understanding.[50] Understanding is not always guaranteed; in Cleveland, white neighborhood patrols during the 1960s were involved in racist incidents. Some citizen groups do espouse racist or other anti-American ideology.[51]

Officials can help mediate between ordinary citizens. But what about racial purity organizations like the Nation of Islam (Rev. Louis Farrakhan's group) which now patrols housing projects in Washington, D.C.? Farrakhan's organization has had the opportunity to restore order to a grateful neighborhood because the corrupt and inept Washington city government has utterly failed to control crime and has forbidden ordinary citizens to protect themselves by owning guns. Politicians who do not wish to see Nation of Islam patrols in their own cities would do well to increase police protection in poor neighborhoods, and to foster nonracist, anti-crime civic groups who could preempt outside organizations.

The overwhelming majority of citizens involved in modern anti-crime patrols are not racist. But they are human, and humans commit errors. In the rundown east side of New York City, neighborhood groups chase drug dealers and junkies away from their doorsteps. Jerry Vaughn, former head of the International Association of Chiefs of Police, worries that the citizens will one day make a violent mistake.[52]

Over the long run, a mistake, perhaps even a fatal one, is a statistical likelihood. The risks of citizen law enforcement must be considered, but so must the risks of citizen abdication. If the residents of 13th Street followed Vaughn's advice, retreated to their apartments, and put all their faith in dialing 911, would the neighborhood be more safe, or less safe? How many people would be killed or injured by the drug criminals perpetrating violence in the neighborhood?

It should also be noted that while there are 600,000 police officers in the United States (dedicated to protecting the whole population), there are 1,400,000 private security guards dedicated to protecting those who can pay them. "Private security guards are simply vigilantes for the rich," writes West Virginia Supreme Court Chief Justice Richard Neely.[53] If society allows rich people to hire vigilante security guards (most of whom are very poorly trained), is it just for society to forbid less wealthy citizens to protect themselves?[54]

Critics who assume that police training somehow makes policemen perfect are incorrect. The rate of *substantiated* crimes perpetrated by New York City police officers is approximately 7.5 crimes per year per thousand officers. The number of crimes alleged but not definitively verified is 112.7.[55]

True, police officers are trained in the police academy, but the safety and marksmanship training rarely exceeds what a civilian could learn at a good firearms instruction school. A deplorably large number of officers have not practiced marksmanship since they passed their firearms certification test as police recruits. The police also work difficult, stressful jobs day in and day out for many years. Ordinary citizens, if they find themselves under stress, can simply retreat to their apartments. When an off-duty New York City policeman fires a gun, one time out of four the firing will be an accident, a suicide, or an act of frustration.[56] Every time an on-duty New York City police officer fires a gun (outside of a target range), police officials review the incident. About 20 percent of discharges have been determined to be accidental, and another 10 percent to be intentional discharges in violation of force policy. In other words, only 70 percent of firearms discharges by police are intentional and in compliance with force policy.[57] Likewise, when police shoot at criminals, they are 5.5 times more likely to hit an innocent person than are civilian shooters.[58]

Society takes risks by having an armed police force, and society takes risks by allowing violent crime to flourish; the risks of citizens protecting their neighborhoods from crime are comparatively small. With the advent of inexpensive indoor laser target systems and high-technology video trainers for "shoot-don't shoot" programs, and the proliferation of civilian firearms schools, there is no reason citizens willing to devote a dozen or two hours a year to training cannot be effectively schooled in defensive firearms use.

Citizens are sometimes racist, and sometimes kill innocent people, as they did in the racist South; and police officers and sheriffs may do the same. The American tradition has been for citizens to trust themselves more than they trust the government. The history of more than two centuries of American vigilantism has not proven that citizens' faith in themselves was wrong.

GUNS AND VIOLENCE IN AMERICAN CULTURAL LIFE

Only in America and Switzerland have guns become cultural symbols. Britain romanticized the aristocratic knight, Canada saluted the government Mounted Policeman, Japan bowed to the samurai, and America idolized the independent cowboy, and sometimes even the outlaw.[59] Why?

One reason is that violence and disorder have been so common in American life that they are seen as natural. Richard Hofstadter observes:

> Americans, however much they may deplore and fear violence, are not
> so deeply *shocked* by it as the English are. Our entertainment and our
> serious writing are suffused with violence to a notorious degree. . . .
> [Americans endure violence] as part of the nature of things, and as one
> of the evils to be expected from life.[60]

American history is in part a story of idealistic violence. The following conclusion was offered by the National Commission on the Causes and Prevention of Violence:

> [V]iolence has formed a seamless web with some of the noblest and most
> constructive chapters of American history: the birth of the nation (Revo-
> lutionary violence), the freeing of the slaves and the preservation of the
> Union (Civil War violence), the occupation of the land (Indian Wars),
> the stabilization of frontier society (vigilante violence), the elevation of
> the farmer and the laborer (agrarian and labor violence), and the preser-
> vation of law and order (police violence). . . . We must realize that violence
> has not been the action only of the roughnecks and racists among us
> but has been the tactic of the most upright and respected of our people.[61]

Another scholar concludes that Americans share a mystical vision of pur- gation and regeneration through violence.[62]

The attachment to firearms and the idolization of the cowboy also reflect the American traditions of individualism and social equality. Indeed,

Alexis De Tocqueville invented the word "individualism" for his book *Democracy in America*.[63] Individualism pervades American life. Writes Hofstadter:

> [T]he United States has shown an unusual penchant for the isolated, wholly individualistic detective, sheriff, or villain, and its entertainment portrays the solution of melodramatic conflicts much more commonly than, say, the English, as arising not out of a ratiocination or scheme of moral order but out of ready and ingenuous violence.[64]

According to sociologist Philip Slater, Americans put a unique emphasis on self-reliance in every aspect of their lives: "a private house, a private means of transportation, a private garden, a private laundry, self-service stores, and do-it-yourself skills of every kind."[65] Others come up with the same answer for why America has neither a socialist party on the left nor a nationalist/religious party on the right: "the pervasive individualism of American culture."[66]

Equality is an important value in many cultures. The American version is concerned less with equality of wealth than with the fundamental equality of individuals. While income inequalities in America are among the largest of any democracy, social equality remains the rule. The notion of due deference to superior classes has always been seen as un-American. Accordingly, America could never honor a fighting man, like the knight or the samurai, who became a fighting man by virtue of his noble birth.

The cowboy, the archetypal American hero, came from an indifferent family background, and fought—not with an exquisite samurai sword—but with a mass-produced Colt .45 that cost ten dollars. Guns become an article of apparel and a badge of manhood.[67] Firearms, accessible to all citizens, made every man the master of his fate. In a world where everyone has a gun, everyone is equal.

The firearms industry, by emphasizing mass-produced guns for the tight budget, furthered the penetration of guns into American cultural life. Gun manufacture has prospered in America as nowhere else. In the first decades of the nineteenth century, Eli Whitney, Simeon North, and other entrepreneurs created the "American system" of mass production of complex products (firearms) through the use of machine tools capable of fabricating interchangeable parts. The innovation, one of the most important of the Industrial Revolution, was possible in America because the market would accept mass-produced guns, and because craft traditions were weak. In contrast, the British gun market was craft driven, catering to a market insistent on buying a tailor-made gun as a mark of good taste. The mass-produced American firearm became the nation's first significant manufactured export. Later, it was Americans who brought the machine gun onto the world stage. European nations rejected the machine gun because their large standing armies, top-heavy with aristocrats, could not accept the idea of a weapon that would replace individual heroism and mobile warfare with mass firepower in a killing zone. During the nineteenth and early twentieth centuries, America lacked a large standing army with preconceived ideas about how wars should be fought. Instead, America had an endless supply of inventors, and an optimistic, anti-aristocratic faith that technology could overcome all.[68]

Few countries besides America had such a coincidence of causes for armament: open hunting, citizen militias, an armed frontier, violent cities, distrust of authority. Nowhere else in the world did environmental and sociocultural conditions foster use of shotguns *and* rifles *and* handguns.[69]

Finally, the sport popularity of guns in America maintains a link with the frontier heritage. As sociologist George Stone explains, "[A]n important function of play is the recreation and maintenance of obsolete work forms, making history a viable reality for mankind. Thus, canoeing, archery, and horseback riding persist in society today as play."[70]

In most countries guns pervade the media. In America, gun culture pervades ordinary life. American speech is loaded with gun metaphors: shot in the dark; big shot; going off half-cocked; cocksure; misfire; shoot for the moon; primed; a gunner; jump the gun; triggered; flash-in-the-pan; keep your powder dry; top gun; straight shooter; loaded for bear; target date; set your sights on it; square shooter; take another shot at it; a long shot; draw a bead on it; son of a gun; high caliber; stick to your guns; he's a pistol; shoot from the hip; faster than a speeding bullet; bring out the big guns; fire away; bite the bullet; a shotgun approach; lock, stock, and barrel; on target; and on and on.[71]

CITIZENS AND THE LAW: AMERICA AND EUROPE

In the eyes of gun lovers and gun haters, the gun is associated with an individual "taking the law into his own hands." People taking the law into their own hands has always been a principle of the American system—and not just in regard to firearms use.

In a precise legal sense, armed use of force for self-defense is not "taking the law into one's hands." Using deadly force or the threat thereof to defend against a violent felony is legal in all fifty states. There are many circumstances where exercising the choice to use force for self-defense or defense of another is entirely lawful. Using such force, therefore, cannot be "taking the law into one's hands" any more than exercising other lawful choices, such as signing a contract. Similarly, every American state recognizes, at the least, the right of citizens to arrest a person committing a violent felony in his or her presence.

When criminals use force, though, they are violating the law, and thereby taking the law into their own hands. When citizens use or threaten force to stop the law-breaking, they are taking the law back from the criminals, and restoring the law to its rightful owners: themselves.

Regardless of technical definitions, use of force in self-defense is generally approved by the American public. Two 1985 polls asked whether "vigilantism," which was defined as "taking the law into one's hands," is justified by circumstances. Seventy to eighty percent of the population responded "always" or "sometimes."[72]

Although armed self-defense may be legally permissible, some gun control advocates consider it inappropriate. Writes Professor M. Friedland of the University of Toronto, father of Canada's modern gun legislation: "A person who wishes to possess a handgun should have to give a legitimate reason. . . . To protect life or property . . . should not be a valid reason. . . . Citizens should rely on the police, security guards, and alarm systems for protection."[73]

Thus, in the eyes of some gun controllers, the right to life itself must be subjugated to "civilization." David Clarke, former chair of Washington's City Council, claims that his gun-control efforts (outlawing gun ownership for self-defense) "are designed to move this government toward civilization. . . . I don't intend to run the government around the moment of survival."[74] The view that all power to use deadly force or to enforce the law belongs in the hands of the state is in conflict with American legal culture. In most nations, "law" and "violence" are diametrically opposed, philosophically and structurally. Yet in America, writes law professor Robert C. Post: "The law is founded on force and is parasitic on lawlessness, and that has been a major theme of American culture at least since James Fennimore Cooper's *Leatherstocking Tales*."[75]

The fact that the American system of justice supports a citizen role in defense against violent criminals is consistent with the American system's inclusion of a citizen role in other important areas. Most democracies outside the Anglo-American legal tradition see justice as a unitary state function. The inquisitorial continental legal system does not sharply separate the role of the judge and the prosecutor. Finding of fact is by the judge, not a jury.[76]

The British and other Commonwealth systems allow a limited role for citizens. Britain, for example, allows juries to decide serious criminal cases and libel suits.

In America, ordinary citizens retain the rights that were once enjoyed by all citizens in Anglo-American legal systems. American juries determine most civil cases in which the plaintiff wants a jury, and all felony criminal cases (unless the defendant prefers a judge). Significantly, juries are not confined only to finding the facts. Juries possess—and regularly exercise—the power to nullify the law itself.[77] One of the most common situations for nullification is self-defense and defense of property.[78]

Citizens sometimes function not only as triers of facts, but also as prosecutors. Citizen suits to enforce the law began with fraud suits against government contractors in the Civil War, grew at the turn of the century to include antitrust enforcement, and now are a routine tool to compel stringent environmental law enforcement. Under the False Claims Act, citizens may sue fraudulent government contractors and collect a share of the penalty.[79]

The American system of justice, far more than the justice system in other nations, is based on an adversary model with due process as the core objective. The court system in most countries is an inquisitorial one, in which the government attempts to ascertain the truth. The Anglo-American model (which today is far stronger in America than in Britain and the rest of the Commonwealth) places the government merely in the role of one litigant. The ultimate value is not truth, but fair procedure in which all parties can present their arguments.[80]

At the core of the large role of Americans in their judicial system is the unique American concept of popular sovereignty. While most other nations consider law as a vehicle of the state, the American tradition views the law as the servant of the people; as a federal district court put it, "the people, not the government, possess the sovereignty."[81]

In the years leading up the American Revolution, patriots and Tories alike began to use the term "Body of the People" to mean "a majority of the people" and eventually "the united will of the people." Legitimate sovereignty, patriots said, flowed not from "the Crown," but from the "Body of the People."[82] Locating sovereignty in the People, and not in the Crown, meant locating the physical power to preserve the law in the "Body of the People" as well. During the debate over ratification of the Constitution, federalist Noah Webster assured America:

> Before a standing army can rule, the people must be disarmed, as they are in almost every kingdom in Europe. The supreme power in America cannot enforce unjust laws by the sword, because the whole body of the people are armed, and constitute a force superior to any band of regular troops that can be, on any pretense, raised in the United States.[83]

Reserving more power for themselves, Americans grant less power to government. America is one of the few nations without a universal licensing system for all guns and the only nation not to license handguns. But the explanation is not simply that Americans are crazy about guns; Americans resist licensing of all sorts. American licensing programs for drivers are the least stringent of any modern industrial nation.[84] Virtually all nations except Britain, Japan, and America, require citizens to carry a national identification card and to produce it upon police demand.[85]

It is true that America protects the right to bear arms far more vigorously than other nations do. America protects most other rights better as well. The United States is the only nation with a meaningful exclusionary rule to prevent the courtroom use of illegally seized evidence—much to the consternation of former federal Judge Malcolm Wilkey, who maintains that we cannot enforce current or future gun control unless we imitate "other civilized countries," such as Britain, Canada, and Japan, by scrapping the exclusionary rule and the probable cause requirement of the Fourth Amendment.[86] The extensive *Miranda* rules that protect suspects from being coerced to confess would be unimaginable in other nations. Speech is freer in America, and government secrets more discoverable. While other countries have Official Secrets Acts, America has the Freedom of Information Act, which allows the U.S. government to keep far fewer documents secret than can the governments of other democracies.

The American system of adversary courtroom procedure; of checks and balances among the three limited branches of government; and of widespread ownership of firearms reflect the assumption that government is not to be trusted, and that only if the People retain for themselves direct control over the law and law enforcement can the People's liberty be secure.

America chose to be different, consciously to create itself, as the Puritans envisioned, as a shining city on the hill, and, as the Founding Fathers hoped, a beacon to human freedom. From the very first days of colonial settlement, America deliberately rejected British and European precedent. Criminal procedure and criminal law in America were more protective of the rights of suspects, and less brutal in their punishments. The Puritans rejected British practices of mutilation and torture, and reduced the number of capital offenses from 223 to 14.[87] Later, Justice William O. Douglas noted, "one of the objects of the [American] Revolution was to get rid of the English common law on liberty of speech and the press."[88]

The National Rifle Association is sometimes chastised as an obstacle to sane gun laws. But the NRA does not exist in a vacuum. American civil liberties groups of all stripes are more powerful and more militant than elsewhere. The American Civil Liberties Union is the most aggressive rights lobby of its kind in the world. The NRA usually gets its way because the American political system is sensitive to citizens who write their representatives and get involved in politics. (The NRA's clout derives mainly from its ability to mobilize members to contact elected officials; the group's campaign contributions are relatively insignificant in relation to almost all campain budgets.[89]) Are monolithic party voting blocs along the British parliamentary model more representative or wiser?

Simply put, Americans do not trust authority as much as most citizens of the British Commonwealth and Japan do. Unlike the British of 1920, they do not trust the police and government to protect them from crime. They do not trust the discretion and judgment of police officers to search whatever they please.

America places more faith in its citizens than do other nations. The first words of America's national existence, the Declaration of Independence, assert a natural right to overthrow a tyrant by force. In the rest of the world the armed masses symbolize lawlessness; in America, the armed masses are the law.

THE "SYMBOLIC CRUSADE" AGAINST THE DEMON GUN

Thus, while some gun controllers see themselves as defenders of civilization against alien and untrustworthy elements, it is gun control that is out of place in American culture. In rejecting guns and in admiring the "civilized" foreign nations, gun control proposes a less American, more European model for the relation of the individual and the state. Bruce-Briggs summarizes it best:

> [U]nderlying the gun control struggle is a fundamental division in our nation. The intensity of passion on this issue suggests to me that we are experiencing a sort of low-grade war going on between two alternative views of what America is and ought to be. On the one side are those who take bourgeois Europe as a model of a civilized society: a society just, equitable, and democratic; but well ordered, with the lines of authority clearly drawn, and with decisions made rationally and correctly by intelligent men for the entire nation. To such people, hunting is atavistic, personal violence is shameful, and uncontrolled gun ownership is a blot upon civilization.
>
> On the other side is a group of people who do not tend to be especially articulate or literate, and whose world view is rarely expressed in print. Their model is that of the independent frontiersman who takes care of himself and his family with no interference from the state. They are "conservative" in the sense that they cling to America's unique pre-modern tradition—a non-feudal society with a sort of medieval liberty at large for everyman. To these people, "sociological" is an epithet. Life is tough and competitive. Manhood means responsibility and caring for your own.[90]

Sociologist Herman Kahn chastised advocates of gun control: "You had no idea what you were doing. You were hitting America in the teeth, right in the center of the culture."[91]

Gun prohibitionists are not anti-patriots. (Nor are gun owners "anti-citizens," despite Garry Wills's invective.[92]) Some gun prohibitionists are uncomfortable, though, with certain aspects of American culture, including the individualism and violence, and the difficult-to-control minorities, immigrants, and "rednecks." It is certainly possible to love America and hate it at the same time. Part of the way to resolve the cognitive dissonance of loving America but despising certain parts is to rationalize away the parts one despises. If American violence and crime (and the rural values embodied in gun culture) are caused by the very existence of guns, one need only do away with guns. Since, as Ramsey Clark writes, guns "make lions out of lambs," we could all be lambs again if only guns vanished.[93]

By blaming objects, a person can avoid having to blame individuals for their moral choices and lack of self-control. Some gun controllers base their position on their sincere belief that control could reduce crime. Other advocates of gun prohibition seem motivated by a desire to express their disdain for the kind of people who own guns. Other controllers may be reluctant to condemn groups (particularly the black underclass) for their actions, and guns therefore become a substitute scapegoat object.

Indeed, the scapegoat object has long tradition in Anglo-American law. For many centuries, if a criminal killed someone with a sword, the sword would be forfeited. If a boy used a chain to hang himself, the chain would be destroyed.[94] This punishment of physical objects was paralleled in medieval and early-modern European law by the legal punishment of animals. If a pig killed a baby, or if a swarm of locusts ate a crop, the animals would be charged with legal offenses, defended by a court-appointed lawyer, and usually convicted. Animal defendants whom the court could apprehend, like domestic pigs, would be tortured to death, just as were human criminals.[95]

Some scholars suggest that the people who punished swords and executed pigs were not so stupid as to believe that swords or pigs could form criminal intent, or could be deterred by the punishment of their fellows. Rather, suggests one scholar of the phenomena, people were terrified by the seemingly random nature of bad events that befell others, events which implied there was no order to the universe. Thus, the purpose of punishing objects and animals

> was to establish cognitive control . . . the job of the courts was to domesticate chaos, and to impose order on a world of accidents—and specifically to make sense of certain seemingly inexplicable events by *redefining them as crimes* . . . the child's death became explicable. The child had died

as an act of calculated wickedness, and however awful that still was, at least it made some kind of sense.[96]

Perhaps it is easier to trace America's problems to "wicked" objects like guns or drugs, rather than to consider the depressing possibility that America may include a disproportionately large number of wicked people.

Gun control now fashions itself a "public health" concern,[97] and does partly resemble America's greatest public health crusade, the temperance movement. Joseph Gusfield analyzed the temperance crusade as less a battle over alcohol than a "status conflict." Gusfield thought prohibition a "symbolic crusade," in which prohibitionists sought government validation of their lifestyle and condemnation of the perceived lifestyle of drinkers. From the 1900s onward, temperance was a Protestant, rural, nativist movement, increasingly isolated from its liberal reformist allies of the nineteenth century. Once Prohibition was enacted into law, the temperance movement had achieved its goal of status validation of its members. That Prohibition was haphazardly enforced was not a major concern to the prohibitionists; symbolic validation of lifestyle, not actual abstinence, was the true goal, writes Gusfield.[98] The gun-control movement has many similarities to the liquor-control movement. When challenged that gun control will not reduce crime, advocates point to control's important symbolic benefits.[99]

Half a century ago the Reverend Billy Sunday railed against "demon rum." One anti-gun Denver priest claims that "guns are modern-day demons."[100] Demon rum and demon guns are satisfying to denounce, but can they be exorcised by statute? Are they the real causes of America's problems? Would gun prohibition succeed any better than liquor prohibition?

Liquor prohibition has faded as the great public health crusade, replaced by a public health crusade against the gun, led by Dr. Louis Sullivan, secretary of the Department of Health and Human Services. The modern crusade may, however, ultimately be detrimental to public health.

Several centuries ago, physicians treated wounds by caring for the weapon that caused it. According to the 1622 *armarium urguentum* (a metholdology for how to treat wounds from weapons), "If the wound is large, the weapon with which the patient has been wounded should be anointed daily; otherwise, every two or three days. The weapon should be kept in pure linen and a warm place but not too hot, nor squalid, lest the patient suffer harm."[101]

Today, it would seem absurd to deal with gunshot wounds by treating the gun rather than the wound. But prestige organs of the medical establishment such as the *New England Journal of Medicine* and the *Journal of the American Medical Association* claim to have found the solution for the public health problem of woundings—remove guns from society. The better the pathogen of guns is controlled, the safer society will be.

Like the *armarium urguentum* in its time, this view is widely accepted among public health professionals of this time. As in the seventeenth century, a focus on the object that seemed to "cause" the distress—the weapon— was a simplistic solution that missed the real cause of the distress. The distress of a wound, and the distresses of a violent society, have causes more profound than physical objects. Better mental health and criminal justice care are the appropriate direction for public health to take, by directly treating those who are violent, rather than attempting to control a single means of violence. Instead of trying to calm the violence by controlling guns, why not prevent the violence from arising, by incarcerating and treating people who are already displaying, through their arrests and convictions, a propensity for acts of rage?

Patrick Purdy, who murdered five children in Stockton, California, in January 1989 with a semi-automatic Kalashnikov rifle, had a long arrest record for felonies such as robbery, receiving stolen property, and sale of illegal weapons. But instead of being imprisoned for his crimes, he always slipped through the cracks of the system, avoided a felony conviction, and wound up back on the street. In addition, Purdy, a mildly retarded alcoholic, had a record of mental disease for which he should have been committed and treated. He told a state health official that he felt compulsions to commit a mass murder with a gun or a bomb. In April 1987, he was arrested for firing a pistol at trees near Lake Tahoe, and assaulted a police officer. After he smeared his jail cell with blood, was caught reading white supremacist literature and attempted suicide attempt in jail, Purdy was described in a mental health report as "a danger to himself and others." Although he was sentenced to a year in jail, the parole board let him go after forty-five days.

The state's chief law enforcement officer, Attorney General John Van deKamp turned what should have been a humiliating indictment of California's failure into a political victory. Van deKamp convinced the California legislature to ban the guns he termed "assault weapons" (although the final bill did not even ban the type of gun Purdy had used, due to drafting errors). Whatever the independent merits of an "assault weapon" bill, the passage of the legislation satisfied Californians that they had done something about crime, when in fact the state's revolving door criminal and mental health systems were just as overburdened and underfunded as on the day Purdy opened fire.

People on the fringe of society have the least power to assert a claim on social resources. The failure of society to provide decent mental health care to people like Patrick Purdy ends up, often enough, with mentally diseased people doing awful things to themselves. On the rare occasions when mental disease catches the public eye—in a spectacular killing with a gun—there is much ado over controlling guns. The same pathetic individuals who have perpetrated the heinous act of violence, typically ending with their own death, have usually been passed around and passed down by the system. Legislatures content themselves with passing a bill "about guns," as if they have solved something. Sealing up the criminal justice and mental health systems—keeping the Patrick Purdys inside— is more effective than letting the Purdys loose again and again and trying to keep them from getting guns or other dangerous instruments.

In the real public health context, gun control is not simply an irrelevancy. Gun control is an active political obstacle to better public health. Criminologist Gary Kleck summarizes: "Fixating on guns seems to be, for many people, a fetish which allows them to ignore the more intransigent causes of American violence, including its dying cities, inequality, deteriorating family structure, and the all-pervasive economic and social consequences of a history of slavery and racism. . . . All parties to the crime debate would do well to give more concentrated attention to more difficult, but far more relevant, issues like how to generate more good-paying jobs for the underclass, an issue which is at the heart of the violence problem."[102] Gun control distracts the public and the legislature from the more difficult tasks of taking better care of the mentally ill, of confronting the culture of poverty, and of imprisoning violent criminals for lengthy terms.[103]

TRANSPLANTING FOREIGN GUN CONTROLS TO AMERICAN SOIL

In the debate preceding the Sullivan Law, the first major American gun-control law affecting citizens accorded full civil rights, one *New York Times* letter to the editor recommended that New York copy Japan, "where intending purchasers of revolvers must first obtain police permits, and sales must be reported to the police" and therefore revolver possession was "practically nil."[104] In 1987, a letter to the editor of the *New Republic* announced that Japan has so little crime because "citizens forsake their right to own guns in return for safety," and America must do the same.[105] Such sentiments, typical of the pro-control advocates in America, misunderstand foreign gun control, for one cannot simply look at statute books to understand a country's firearms policy without considering its social context.

The statute books of the world are littered with failed attempts to transplant one nation's law into an unreceptive culture.[106] The jury system was tried and rejected in Europe and Africa. Postwar Japan was ordered to follow American antitrust and criminal procedure rules, and to adopt an American-style independent banking system, but soon stopped.[107] The

American-written Japanese Constitution guarantees fair criminal procedure and social equality of the sexes in terms far stronger than the American Constitution. In practice, American freedoms are much broader. The American police cannot hold persons in jail for weeks on end without bringing them before a judge; nor can the police limit a suspect's access to lawyer. America gave Japan a strong human rights constitution, but it could not transplant a tradition of judicial review, and the Japanese Supreme Court has generally been passive.[108]

Automobile and steel factories as well as coal mines are generally similar around the world, yet attempts to impose one nation's labor laws on another's labor force have failed miserably.[109] The British Industrial Relations Act, which was modelled after American statutes, attempted to outlaw the closed shop and to make unions liable for their members' actions, but the law did not work. One commentator concluded that the act's downfall resulted from attempting to change human nature by statute and to alter existing national patterns of labor relations.[110]

It is impossible to transfer political structures to inappropriate cultures. Britain's Prime Minister Clement Attlee was once asked by an enthusiastic American student whether the United States should adopt Britain's style of cabinet and party government. "My dear young man," Attlee replied, "our shoes won't fit your bunions."[111]

CONCLUSION

Guns have a unique role in American culture, one that legislative fiat cannot abolish. America is the only democracy in which a right to bear arms is written into its Constitution.[112] Unlike the British Commonwealth nations of Canada, Australia, New Zealand, and Jamaica, the United States deliberately broke away from Britain and explicitly rejected several British traditions, including infringements on the right to bear arms.[113]

If guns are a public health "epidemic," they are already so widespread that removing or even substantially reducing the pathogen is no longer possible. England had only 1 percent as many handguns per capita when it instituted gun control. Yet the only major study of the British gun laws concludes that there is still a plentiful supply of handguns for criminals who want one. Professors Harding of Australia and Friedland of Canada both urged immediate gun controls for their nations, before an American level of gun density rendered control impossible. Scotland Yard agrees that America is long past the point of no return on gun control.[114] America's per capita handgun ownership rate is at least four times as high as any other nation's. America's most thoughtful gun controllers, George Newton and Franklin Zimring caution, "[N]o other nation in history has ever instituted firearms control with so many firearms already in circulation among persons accustomed to them."[115]

American gun owners—even more so than their counterparts in other countries—will massively resist any form of gun control. In Illinois, for example, a 1977 study showed that compliance with handgun registration was only about 25 percent.[116] A 1979 survey of Illinois gun owners indicated that 73 percent would not comply with a gun prohibition.[117] Registration laws for semi-automatic firearms in Denver and Boston have achieved a 1 percent compliance rate. It is evident that New York City's near-prohibition is not voluntarily obeyed; estimates of the number of illegal guns in the city range from seven hundred thousand to three million. The New York state commissioner of prisons testified to the state legislature that if 1 percent of illegal handgun owners in New York City were caught, tried, and sent to prison for a year, the state prison system would collapse.[118] There is no reason to believe that more restrictive laws would be obeyed more willingly.

The volume of guns alone would make enforcement close to impossible, and the singular difficulty of American enforcement would be compounded by America's distinctive attitude about search and seizure. If the Second Amendment is to be abrogated, the Fourth Amendment must also be. Not only would this be poor constitutional policy, it would be massively resisted. The Japanese accept a policeman looking in a random woman's handbag. Americans would not. Instead of attempting to plant Japanese or British law in American soil, a more realistic gun policy must consider guns in the context of American culture. The next chapter considers what gun controls might work in America's unique civilization.

NOTES

1. Quoted in Hugh D. Graham and Ted R. Gurr, eds., *The History of Violence in America: Historical and Comparative Perspectives* (New York: Knopf, 1969), pp. 181–82.

2. Senator Frank Church, "Foreword," in Donald B. Kates, Jr., ed., *Restricting Handguns: The Liberal Skeptics Speak Out* (Croton-on-Hudson: North River Press, 1979), p. xiii.

3. *Coleman* v. *Balkcom,* 451 U.S. 949, 962 (1981) (Rehnquist, J., dissenting from denial of certiorari).

4. William Safire, "Washington's War," *New York Times,* March 2, 1989, p. A19.

5. S. Evans, "A Crime Victim's Story," *Washington Post,* February 3, 1985.

6. "Life During Wartime," *Spy,* March 1990, p. 25.

7. "83% to be Victims of Crime Violence," *New York Times,* March 9, 1987, p. A13. Nevertheless, the United States Conference of Mayors insists, "The probability of being raped, robbed, or assaulted is low enough to seriously call into question the need for Americans to keep loaded guns . . . ," M. Yeager and the Handgun Control Staff of U.S. Conference

of Mayors, *How Well Does the Handgun Protect You and Your Family?* (Washington: U.S. Conference of Mayors, pamphlet).

8. George Fletcher, *A Crime of Self-Defense: Bernhard Goetz and the Law on Trial* (New York: Free Press, 1988), p. 201.

9. On July 4, 1990, dialers of 911 in Los Angeles reached a recording. While a two-year-old boy lay wounded from a drive-by shooting, it took twenty minutes and the intervention of an operator to reach 911. "The Curse of 911," *Newsweek,* November 5, 1990, p. 31. In Buffalo, 911 calls go unanswered because of understaffing. *Buffalo News,* July 31, 1990. A gun group in Detroit sells t-shirts which play on the disillusionment with 911: "Which will protect you best? 911 or a .38." Motor City Sportsmen's Association t-shirt described in Joseph P. Tartaro, "Urban Numerology: 911 or .38," *Gun Week,* August 24, 1990, p. 11.

10. See, for example, *Bowers* v. *DeVito* 686 F.2d 61 (7th Cir. 1982) (no federal Constitutional requirement that police provide protection); *Calogrides* v. *Mobile,* 475 So. 2d 560 (Ala. 1985); Cal. Govt. Code §§ 821, 845, 846; *Davidson* v. *Westminster,* 32 Cal.3d 197, 185 Cal. Rep. 252; 649 P.2d 894 (1982); *Stone* v. *State* 106 Cal.App.3d 924, 165 Cal. Rep. 339 (1980); *Morgan* v.*District of Columbia,* 468 A.2d 1306 (D.C.App. 1983); *Warren* v. *District of Columbia,* 444 A.2d 1 (D.C. App. 1981); *Sapp* v. *Tallahassee,* 348 So.2d 363 (Fla. App. 1977); Ill. Rev. Stat. 4-102; *Keane* v. *Chicago,* 98 Ill. App.2d 460, 240 N.E.2d 312 (1986); *Jamison* v. *Chicago,* 48 Ill. App. 567 (1977); *Simpson's Food Fair* v. *Evansville,* 272 N.E.2d 871 (Ind. App.); *Silver* v. *Minneapolis* 170 N.W.2d 206 (Minn. 1969); *Weutrich* v. *Delia,* 155 N.J. Super. 324, 326, 382 A.2d 929, 930 (1978); *Chapman* v. *Philadelphia* 434 A.2d 753 (Penn. 1981); *Morris* v. *Musser* 478 A.2d 937 (1984).

The law in New York remains as decided by the Court of Appeals the 1959 case *Riss* v. *New York:* the government is not liable even for a grossly negligent failure to protect a crime victim. In the *Riss* case, a young woman telephoned the police and begged for help because her ex-boyfriend had repeatedly threatened "If I can't have you, no one else will have you, and when I get through with you, no one else will want you." The day after she had pleaded for police protection, the ex-boyfriend threw lye in her face, blinding her in one eye, severely damaging the other, and permanently scarring her features. "What makes the City's position particularly difficult to understand," wrote a dissenting opinion, "is that, in conformity to the dictates of the law, Linda did not carry any weapon for self-defense. Thus, by a rather bitter irony she was required to rely for protection on the City of New York which now denies all responsibility to her." *Riss* v. *New York,* 22 N.Y.2d 579, 293 N.Y.S.2d 897, 240 N.E.2d 806 (1958).

Ruth Brunell called the police on twenty different occasions to beg for protection from her husband. He was arrested only one time. One evening Mr. Brunell telephoned his wife and told her he was coming over to kill her. When she called the police, they refused her request that they come to protect her. They told her to call back when he got there. Mr. Brunell stabbed his wife to death before she could call the police to tell them that he was there. The court held that the San Jose police were not liable for ignoring Mrs. Brunell's pleas for help. *Hartzler* v. *City of San Jose,* 46 Cal. App. 3d 6 (1975).

11. "99% of Felony Arrests in the City Fail to Bring Terms in State Prison," *New York Times,* January 3, 1981, p. A1. Some of the 99 percent do lead to short terms in city jails.

12. Hans Zeisel, "The Disposition of Felony Arrests, *American Bar Foundation Journal* (1981), pp. 450–51.

13. Barbara Boland, Catherine H. Conly, Lynn Warner, Ronald Sones, for United States Department of Justice, Office of Justice Programs, Bureau of Justice Programs, *The Prosecution of Felony Arrests 1987* (Washington: Department of Justice, 1990), p. 3.

14. Susan Jacoby, "Children," *New York Times Book Review,* April 10, 1988.

15. David J. Krajicek and Marcia Kramer, "Police Response Time Hit," (New York) *Daily News,* May 3, 1988 p. 23. In Buffalo, understaffing is so severe police often have three or four serious calls to respond to at once. Juan Forero, "City Police Understaffing Described as Acute," *The Buffalo News,* July 31, 1990, p. C5.

A Staten Island case puts a human face on these statistics. In the Stapleton public housing projects, Bernadette Shabazz heard three people arguing about a drug deal in the hallway. She stepepd outside, and asked them to quiet down, so as not to disturb her baby. One of the men grabbed her from behind and choked her, and another punched her in the mouth and knocked out three teeth. As a result of the choke hold, she suffered brain damage, underwent brain surgery, and will need medication for the rest of her life. None of her attackers was prosecuted. The judge referred the case to a dispute resolution center, which told the attackers they would be in trouble if they bothered Mrs. Shabazz again.

Her husband, Saeed Shabazz, started organizing the community to reduce crime in the housing project. But the promised police co-operation never materialized, and the drug dealers decided to take revenge on Mr. Shabazz and his family. Death threats began coming, and Mrs. Shabazz was surrounded and hit in the eye in an elevator. She immediately informed a policeman, who refused to do anything, since there were no witnesses except the perpetrators. On a Sunday morning, two seventeen-year-olds accosted Mr. Shabazz. One of them had a police record not only for drug sales, but for attempted robbery of an undercover police officer. After a struggle, Shabazz escaped, having shot and wounded the two attackers. Shabazz was arrested and charged with attempted murder. Bob Herbert, "Blind Justice Doesn't See the Horror on S.I.," *Daily News,* September 22, 1988, p. 4.

16. Leah Rozen, "Fear and Living in New York," *New York Woman,* March 1990: 66–69.

17. "Armed and Ready: Suburban Families Fight the Fear," *New York Times,* February 25, 1990, p. 2 (Long Island Section.)

18. For some examples, see Sharon Brussard, "Lady Goetz: I Had to Shoot," (New York) *Daily News,* April 3, 1990, p. 3; Dennis Duggan, "A City Armed to the Teeth," *New York Newsday,* April 3, 1990, pp. 19, 35; David J. Krajicek, "Alarmed and Armed," (New York) *Daily News,* May 8, 1990, pp. 7, 15–16; Eric Pooley, "Frontier Justice: Fed-up New Yorkers Are Taking the Law Into Their Own Hands," *New York,* July 23, 1990: 33–39.

19. Vincent S. Baker, chairman of NAACP anti-crime committee, quoted in Robert E. Maxwell-Brown, "The American Vigilante Tradition," in Hugh Graham and Ted Robert Gurr, eds., *Violence in America,* Vol. I, Report to the National Commission on the Causes and Prevention of Violence (Washington: Government Printing Office, 1969), pp. 207–208.

The New York State Pistol and Rifle Association has given cash awards to "Courageous Citizens," who use guns to resist what it calls "the Barbarians." Critics denounce the awards "as bounties smacking of frontier mayhem." Francis X. Clines, "Smoking Guns in the Big Town," *New York Times,* January 31, 1978, p. 24.

20. "A Goetz Backlash?" *Newsweek,* March 12, 1985, pp. 50–53.

21. D. J. Kenney, *Crime, Fear, and the New York City Subways: The Role of Citizen Action* (New York: Praeger, 1987), pp. 69–71.

22. Patrick Carr and George W. Gardner, *Gun People* (Garden City, N.Y.: Doubleday, 1985), p. 22. Wayne Pacelle, "Animal Rights in Bloom: An Interview with Berke Brethed," *Animals' Agenda,* July/August 1989, p. 11:

There's no more scurrilous a crowd than the NRA. I own guns though. In fact, I own an assault rifle. I keep it to carry on my boats.

A: "In case of shark attack?"
Brethed: "No, in case of piracy."

Boat owners in the Sulu Sea and elsewhere in Southeast Asia are also carrying rifles and pistols for protection from pirates. Melinda Liu, "Terror on the High Seas: Modern-day Pirates Add a New Level of Violence," *Rocky Mountain News,* April 15, 1989 (reprinted from *Newsweek*).

23. "Floridians Preparing for Liberal Gun Laws," Reuters, September 21, 1987 (available in Reuters Library in Nexis).

24. "A Lethal Lucky Charm," *Maclean's,* October 12, 1987, p. 59.

25. U.S. Department of Justice, Federal Bureau of Investigation, *Uniform Crime Reports 1990* (Washington: Goverment Printing Office, 1991), p. 7.

26. Gary Kleck, "Crime Control Through the Private Use of Armed Force," *Social Problems* 35, no. 1 (February, 1990), pp. 2-4. The data regarding armed self-defense are discussed in the next chapter.

27. Kim Remesch, "Vigilance or Vengeance?" *Police,* July 1990, p. 56: "Frustrated by the lack of control they feel, otherwise normal citizens are taking back the streets in their own way."

28. Richard Maxwell Brown, *Strain of Violence: Historical Studies in American Violence and Vigilantism* (New York: Oxford University Press, 1975), p. 58.

29. Isabel Wilkerson, "Crack House Fire: Justice or Vigilantism?" *New York Times,* October 22, 1988, p. 1.

30. "Volunteers Patrol to Combat Arson in Detroit," *Denver Post,* October 31, 1988, p. 3A (Associated Press).

31. Ishmael Reed, "Living at Ground Zero," *Image,* March 13, 1988, p. 15, cited in Mike Davis, "Los Angeles: Civil Liberties between a Hammer and the Rock," *New Left Review* 170 (August 1988), pp. 45-46.

32. *Los Angeles Times,* May 13, 1988, p. II 3, cited in Davis, p. 55 n.52.

33. "Block Clubs Wage the Battle," *Washington Times,* November 25, 1988, p. C6.

34. "Drug Battle Truce," *Rocky Mountain News,* September 29, 1989, p. 4; "Anti-Drug Gun Battle Spurs Demand for Firearms," *Gun Week,* November 3, 1989, p. 9, citing *Spokane Chronicle.*

35. Roberto Suro, "As Inmates Are Freed, Houston Feels Insecure," *New York Times,* October 1, 1990, p. A16, col. 1.

36. William K. Stevens, "Muslim Patrols Fight Capital Drug Trade," *New York Times,* April 24, 1988 p. 20; "In Flatbush, Citizen Patrol Battles Crime," *New York Times,* October 1, 1990.

37. Charles Paul Freund, "The Zeitgeist Checklist," *The New Republic,* May 16, 1988, p. 8.

38. Alisa Solomon, "Fired Up: Should Gays Carry Guns," *Village Voice,* November 27, 1990, pp. 43-44.

39. David Kocieniewski and Mitch Gelman, "Mob Chases Mugging Suspect to His Death on Subway Bed," *New York Newsday,* September 27, 1990, p. 3 (the mugger fled down the subway tracks, accidentally touched the electrified third rail, and was electrocuted); Donatella Lynch, "Robbery Suspect Dies and a Neighborhood is Silent," *New York Times,* August 24, 1990, p. A1 ("A crowd in a crime-ridden Bronx neighborhood took justice into its own hands Wednesday night, surrounding a fleeing robbery suspect and stabbing him to death, the police said. . . . It also relfects what appears to be an increase in vigilante justice in the city in the last several years. . . . Residents yesterday stressed that the stabbing was a positive symbol for those frustrated with crime. 'The neighborhood is so bad that the cops are scared of it.' ")

40. Eddie Borges and Janet Wilson, "Man Found Shot Dead in Church," (New York) *Daily News,* September 30, 1990; Jan Hester and Rocco Parascandola, "Gun-toting Rev Denies Killing Thief," *Daily News,* October 1, 1990, p. 6.

41. The proposal was made by the party's 1990 candidate for Governor, Pierre Rinfert. Frank Lynn, "Rinfert Seeks Volunteer Band of 'Vigilantes'," *New York Times,* September 25, 1990, p. B1; Fredric Dicker, "Rinfert: Arm Vigilantes for Crime War," *New York Post,* September 25, 1990; Joel Benenson and Frank Lombardi, "100,000 More Guns!: Rinfert Says We Need Vigilante System," *Daily News,* September 25, 1990, p. 5.

42. Daniel Kagan, "John Doe Unit to Regain Its Turf," *Washington Times,* November 25, 1988, p. 25; Patrice Gaines-Carter and John Mintz, "Muslims Nurture Legacy of Power," *Washington Post,* April 20, 1988; Mark H. Moore and Mark A. R. Kleiman, "The Police and Drugs," *Perspectives on Policing* no. 11 (National Institute of Justice, September 1989, p. 10.

43. Judge Howard E. Goldfluss, "They Do What Cops Can't," *Newsday,* June 27, 1988 p. 48 (Guardian Angels not bound by restrictions on legal searches); John F. Clarity, "Angels Fight the Addicts on New York's Restaurant Row," *New York Times,* June 12, 1988, p. 8E ("Critics' statements about the danger of vigilantism are only words to residents and businessmen confronted by crack-heads, dealers, and miscellaneous bad actors"); Sarah Lyall, "Anger Grows in West 46th St. Between Police and 'Angels'," *New York Times,* June 14, 1988, p. A1 (police arrest Angels for confronting people when Angels have not observed a crime being committed).

Suffering huge losses because customers were scared away by the crack trade, merchants between 34th and 39th streets, west of 9th Avenue, signed up the Guardian Angels to take back the streets. Guardian Angel President Curtis Sliwa explained: "Our techcnique of physical interdiction was the technique practiced by your parents and grandparents. Then it wasn't the police. It was the men and women coming out of their living rooms and backyards." Frank Sommerfeld, "Crack Up; Local Businesses Under Siege," *Crain's New York Business,* July 11, 1988, p. 1.

44. Kagan, "John Doe."

45. Susan Pennell, Christine Curtis, and Joel Henderson, *Guardian Angels: An Assessment of Citizen Response of Crime* (Washington: U.S. Department of Justice, 1986).

46. Frances Frank Marcus, "Crab-Trap Crime Wave in Louisiana," *New York Times,* April 22, 1988; Chris Cooper, "Oystermen Scooping Up Badges and Guns," *New Orleans Times-Picayune,* March 27, 1988, B1.

47. In Harlem, for example, a Baptist minister started an "armed police militia." *Violence in America: Historical and Comparative Perspectives* (1969): Chap. 5, epilogue.

48. See chapter 9, note 239 and accompanying text.

49. Brown, "The American Vigilante Tradition," pp. 201–207.

50. "Unity Is Key to Fight Against Crime," *Washington Times,* November 25, 1988, p. C6.

51. In Tierra Amarilla, New Mexico, Amador Flores led a real-life version of *The Milagro Beanfield War,* using guns to defend 50 acres against the Vista del Brazos develoment company. Because of Flores' resistance, development was halted and the dispute was sent to court. While many people would be sympathetic to Flores' primary goal of preventing development (even at the expense of property rights), Flores' long-term objective is a return of the southwest United States to Mexico. "Mex It Up," *Westword,* September 14, 1988, p. 9; "Amador Flores Lands in Jail," *Westword,* July 13, 1988, p. 6; Colorado Coalition Against English Only, "Tierra o Muerte!" *Ya Basta!,* August 1988.

52. Joe Davidson, "Some Citizen Patrols Bully Drug Traffickers Until They Flee Away,"

Wall Street Journal, September 26, 1988, p. 16. One example of a violent mistake: "Two Good Samaritan tourists who stopped their car to help an elderly woman cross the street as they were driving through Brooklyn on their way home to Canada yesterday were apparently mistaken for muggers and beaten by a gang of bat-wielding youths in Bensonhurst, police said." Curtis L. Taylor, "Samaritan Tourists Beaten by Teen Gang," *New York Post,* September 25, 1990; Ruth Landa, "2 Tourists Bashed in B'klyn: But Neighbors Offer Aid, Cash," *Daily News,* September 25, 1990, p. 34.

53. Richard Neely, *Take Back Your Neighborhood* (New York: Donald I. Fine, 1990), p. 51.

54. Chief Justice Neely writes:

The same government, academic and media elites who cluck their tongues at even such benign citizen forces as New York's Guardian Angels have nothing unkind to say about bank guards, railroad detectives or the little chap who sits in the guard shack at the entrance to Jonathan's Landing in Palm Beach County, Florida.
Neely, p. 53.

55. Neely, p. 74–75. Other major cities reported similar rates of substantiated allegations.

56. "The Guns of Kennesaw," *New York Times,* March 28, 1982, p. 26, col. 1.

57. Gina Goehl, *1989 Firearms Discharge Assault Report* (New York: Police Academy Firearms and Tactics Section, April 1989) (BM 369). For 1985–89, the cumulative figures are 1,193 total discharges, 824 intentional and not in violation of force policy (69.1%), 112 intentional and in violation (9.4%); 135 accidental but not in violation of policy (11.3%), and 122 accidental and in violation (10.2%). [The percentages and numbers are slightly different from those in the Report itself, due to a Departmental mathematical error in addition; the Department mistakenly totals the number of intentional lawful shootings at 836 (rather than 824), and mistakenly records the total of all incidents at 1,143, rather than 1,193. As a result, Department reports that the sum of all categories of incidents is 105.4%, rather than 100%.]

58. Carol Ruth Silver and Donald B. Kates, Jr., "Self-Defense, Handgun Ownership, and the Independence of Women in a Violent, Sexist Society," in *Restricting Handguns,* pp. 154–55. The problems police encounter do not necessarily imply that the police are poorer shooters, or that they possess worse judgment. Official guidelines may force the police to intervene in situations that ordinary citizens could avoid and may prevent an officer from drawing his weapon at the most opportune time.

59. After Frank and Jesse James and a confederate robbed the gate at a Kansas City fair, the *Kansas City Times* exalted, "It was as though the three bandits had come to us from storied Odenwald, with the halo of medieval chivalry upon their garments and shown us how things were done that poets sing of." Quoted in Joe B. Frantz, "The Frontier Tradition: An Invitation to Violence," in *Violence in America: Historical and Comparative Perspectives,* pp. 127–28. The folk song "Jesse James" eulogized the outlaw as "a friend to the poor." Duncan Emrich, *Folklore on the American Land* (Boston: Little, Brown and Co., 1972), pp. 302–304. For outlaw heroes in general, see Paul Kooistra, *Criminals as Heroes: Structure, Power, and Identity* (Bowling Green, Ohio: Bowling Green State University Popular Press, 1989).

Joseph G. Rosa, a British historian of the American West, begins his book: "The Western gunfighter was the New World's counterpart of the knights in armor and the Robin Hoods of Old. His sword was a Colt .45 and his armor the ability to outdraw and outshoot any rival." Joseph G. Rosa, *The Gunfighter: Man or Myth?* (Norman: University of Oklahoma Press, 1959), p. v.

British Westerns, reflecting British values, made chivalry the basis of the cowboy code of honor. Ray Allen Billington, *Land of Savagery, Land of Promise: The European Image of the American Frontier in the Nineteenth Century* (Norman: University of Oklahoma Press, 1981), p. 173.

In Japan, "the sword replaces the six-shooter and cowboy is a samurai." David E. Kaplan and Alec Dubro, *Yakuza* (Reading, Mass.: Addison-Wesley, 1986), p. 14.

60. Richard Hofstadter, "Reflections on Violence in the United States," in Richard Hofstadter and Michael Wallace, eds., *American Violence: A Documentary History* (New York: Knopf, 1971), p. 6.

61. Robert E. Maxwell-Brown, "Historical Patterns of Violence in America," in Hugh Graham and Ted Robert Gurr, eds., *Violence in America, Vol. I* (report to the National Commission on the Causes and Prevention of Violence) (Washington: Government Printing Office, 1969), 75–76. Some people, this author included, would disagree that the seizure of the continent from the Indians was a "noble" enterprise.

62. J. Cawelti, "Myths of Violence in Popular Culture," *Critical Inquiry* 3 (1975), pp. 537–40.

63. Walter LaFeber, *The American Age; United States Foreign Policy at Home and Abroad since 1750* (New York: W. W. Norton, 1989), p. 86.

64. Richard Hofstadter, "America as a Gun Culture," *American Heritage*, October 1970, p. 82. It is true that Japanese and European movie-goers enjoy American violent entertainment, such as Charles Bronson movies. But their cinema preferences do not reflect the way they structure their society. (Despite the concerns of Andrea Dworkin and Catherine MacKinnon, popular entertainment does not inevitably determine social reality.)

65. Quoted in Patrice Greanville, "Freedom Trails," *The Animals' Agenda*, June 1987, p. 30. Daniel Goleman, "Group and the Individual: New Focus on a Cultural Rift," *New York Times*, December 25, 1990, pp. 37, 41 (discussing worldwide study of 116,000 I.B.M. employees; most individualist countries were, in descending order: United States, Australia, Great Britain, Canada).

66. "The Harumph of the Will," *New Republic*, December 21, 1987, p. 40.

67. William Tonso, *Gun and Society: The Social and Existential Roots of the American Attachment to Firearms* (Lanham, Md.: University Press of America, 1982), p. 281.

68. Joseph Bradley, *Guns for the Tsar: American Technology and the Small Arms Industry in Nineteenth-Century Russia* (Dekalb: Northern Illinois University Press, 1990), pp. 30–31; John Ellis, *The Social History of the Machine Gun* (Baltimore: Johns Hopkins University Press, 1986); Eric Mottram, *Blood on the Nash Ambassador: Investigations into American Culture* (London: Hutchison Radius, 1989), pp. 11–13.

69. Tonso, p. 54.

70. Gregory P. Stone, "Wrestling—The Great American Passion Play," in E. Dunning, ed., *Sport: Readings from a Sociological Perspective* (1972), p. 302, cited in Tonso, p. 30.

71. Indians used to say "My rifle is my mother; it feeds me; it houses me, clothes me, and protects me." Because of this saying, whites called Indians "sons of guns." Bert Levy, *Guerrilla Warfare* (Boulder: Paladin, 1964), p. 48. Another possible origin of the phrase is said to be births induced by the noise of gunshots.

"Riding shotgun," derives from the armament of stagecoach guards. Tony Lesce, *The Shotgun in Combat* (Boulder: Paladin, 1984), p. 4.

72. "A Newsweek Poll: Deadly Force," *Newsweek*, March 11, 1985, p. 53. One Gallup poll in February 1985 and another in March had asked: "Do you feel that taking the law into one's own hands, often called vigilantism, is justified by circumstances?" In the Febru-

ary poll, 8% said "always" and 72% "sometimes." In the March poll, 3% said "always" and 68% said "sometimes."

73. M. L. Friedland, "Gun Control: The Options," *Criminal Law Quarterly* 18 (1975–76), pp. 50–51.

74. Greene, "The Case for Owning a Gun," *The Washingtonian* (March 1985), p. 196. It might be wondered if a government like Washington, D.C.'s, which does not protect its citizens at the moment of survival and will not let citizens protect themselves, ought to call itself civilized. Compare Aleksander Sozlhenitsyn's description of life under Stalinism: "The state, in its Criminal Code, forbids citizens to have firearms or other weapons, but *does not undertake* to defend them!" Aleksander Solzhenitsyn, *The Gulag Archipelago Two* (New York: Harper & Row, 1975), p. 431 (emphasis in original).

75. Robert C. Post, "On the Popular Image of a Lawyer: Reflections in a Dark Glass," *California Law Review* 75 (1987), p. 382. "Judge Colt and his jury of six," was a popular 19th century expression. Rosa, p. 5. (The "six" referred to the Colt revolver having a six-shot capacity.)

76. Attempts to impose the Anglo-American jury system on France, Germany, and Africa failed in the last century. The jury system violated the accustomed distribution of power between bar and bench.

77. Maryland's Constitution explicitly makes the jury "the Judges of Law, as well as of fact." Constitution of Maryland, Declaration of Rights, Article 23. Indiana's Constitution states that "the jury shall have the right to determine the laws and the facts." Indiana Constitution article I, § 19.

Courts today do not inform jurors that they have the power to nullify the law, and the courts have been clear that juries need not be so informed. Even courts which reject instruction about jury nullification, however, are in complete agreement that the jury has the absolute right to nullify the law if it so chooses. "If the jury feels the law under which the defendant is accused is unjust, or that exigent circumstances justified the action of the accused, or for any reason, which appeals to their logic, or passion, the jury has the power to acquit and the courts must abide by that decision." *United States* v. *Moylan,* 417 F.2d 1002, 1006 (4th Cir.1969).

The United States Supreme Court, in its earliest days, sometimes presided over jury trials At one such trial, John Jay, the first Chief Justice, instructed the jury that it had "a right to take upon yourself to judge of both, and to determine the law as well as the fact in controversy." *Georgia* v. *Brailsford* 3 Dallas 1, 4 (1794).

Columbia Law Professor George Fletcher observes that jury nullification might at first seem "to conflict with the rule of law, but careful historical reflection underscores the power of the jury not to defeat the law, but to perfect the law, to realize the law's inherent values." He points to jury acquittal of John Peter Zenger in his 1735 trial for seditious libel. Zenger's lawyer told the jury that they were the ultimate judges of law as well as fact; the jury acquitted Zenger on the grounds that his articles in *The New York Weekly Journal* about a corrupt governor were true—even though the formal law did not yet recognize truth as a defense to seditious libel. Fletcher, pp. 154–55.

78. Valerie P. Hans and Neil Vidmar, *Judging the Jury* (New York: Plenum, 1986), pp. 151–53.

79. False Claims Act, 31 United States Code § 3729 et seq.; Robert L. Vogel, "Citizens' Lawsuits Based on the False Claims Act Have Multiplied," *National Law Journal,* November 26, 1990: 20–23.

80. The American system has long been contrasted unfavorably with the British system

for putting excessive emphasis on due process. See for example, Roscoe Pound, *Criminal Justice in America* (New York: 1930).

81. *Mandel* v. *Mitchell,* 325 F. Supp. 620, 629 (Eastern District of New York, 1971).

82. Brown, *Strain of Violence,* pp. 61–62.

83. Noah Webster, "An Examination into the Leading Principles of the Federal Constitution . . ." in P. Ford, ed., *Pamphlets on the Constitution of the United States* (1888), p. 56.

Anti-federalist Richard Henry Lee insisted that "to preserve liberty, it is essential that the whole body of the people always possess arms and be taught alike, especially when young, how to use them." W. Bennett, ed., *Letters from the Federal Farmer to the Republican* (1975), p. 124.

84. "Freedom Trails," pp. 30–31. The war on drugs, and the mania for urine testing may nullify much of the above analysis of America as a society resistant to random searches.

85. Kent, "ID Card Common Around Globe," *Los Angeles Times,* June 18, 1980.

86. Malcolm Richard Wilkey, "Why Suppress Valid Evidence?" *Wall Street Journal,* October 7, 1977, p. 12. See chapter 3, note 224 for the suggestion by Norval Morris, President Carter's nominee to head the Law Enforcement Assistance Administration, that gun prohibition be enforced by secret walk-through metal detectors in public places.

During the Ford administration, the Justice Department allegedly discussed the possibility of using federal troops to conduct house-to-house searches for handguns, if the government decided to ban them. Morgan Norval, "The Right to Life," in Morgan Norval, ed., *The Militia in 20th Century America* (Falls Church, Va.: Gun Owners Foundation, 1985), p. 6 (Norval's conversation with anonymous "high Justice Dpeartment official").

87. The point is developed at length in Bradley Chapin, *Criminal Justice in Colonial America, 1606–1660* (Athens: University of Georgia Press, 1983). In particular:

• Only 56.5 percent of the colonies' substantive criminal law came from England, the rest being based on colonial reforms or on Biblical precedent. Ibid., p. 5.

• The law was stated positively, in statutes written in straightforward English comprehensible by ordinary people, rather than the confusing "law Latin" and "law French" of England. Ibid., pp. 22–24.

• In England, a defendant's exercise of any right other than the right to a jury was left to the discretion of the trial judge. The colonial codes included specific guarantees of bail, grand juries, a requirement for multiple witnesses in capital cases, no cruel or unusual punishments, no double jeopardy, no corruption of the blood (punishing a defendant's descendants for his crimes) and a right to appeal. Ibid., pp. 22–23, 58–59.

See also E. P. Evans, *The Criminal and Capital Punishment of Animals: The Lost History of Europe's Animal Trials* (London: Faber and Faber, 1987; 1st ed. 1906), p. 29 (number of capital offenses).

88. To "assume that English common law in this field became ours is to deny the generally accepted historical belief that 'one of the objects of the Revolution was to get rid of the English common law on liberty of speech and the press.' " *A Book Named "John Cleland's Memoirs of a Woman of Pleasure"* v. *Attorney General of the Commonwealth of Massachusetts,* 383 U.S. 413 (Douglas, J., concurring), *quoting* Schofield, "Freedom of the Press in the United States" *Publications of the American Sociological Society,* vol. 9, p. 76.

89. Richard L. Benke, "Expensive Lobbying Pays Off for Rifle Association," *New York Times,* September 22, 1988, p. A32 ("The group's real power came from the intensive lobbying drive").

90. B. Bruce-Briggs, "The Great American Gun War," *The Public Interest* 45 (Fall 1976), p. 61.

91. Herman Kahn, *Washington Post,* July 1, 1973, p. C1.

92. See chapter 9, notes 3, 4, and 32 and accompanying text.

93. Ramsey Clark, *Crime in America: Observations on Its Nature, Causes, and Control* (New York: Simon and Schuster, 1970), p. 95.

The gun prohibition lobby apparently believes that firearms turn normal people into criminals, and asserts that each year thousands of gun killings "are done by law-abiding citizens who might have *stayed* law-abiding if they had not possessed firearms . . . most murders are committed by previously law-abiding citizens." Lindsay, National Coalition to Ban Handguns, "A Shooting Gallery called America" (undated, unpaginated pamphlet), cited in Donald B. Kates, Jr., *Guns, Murders, and the Constitution: A Realistic Assessment of Gun Control* (San Francisco: Pacific Institute, 1990), p. 46 n. 159. The assertion that most murders are committed "by previously law-abiding citizens" is patently false. Two-thirds to four-fifths of homicide offenders have prior arrest records, generally for violent felonies. A. Swersey and E. Enloe, *Homicide in Harlem* (New York: Rand Institute, 1975), p. 17 (80%); R. Narloch, *Criminal Homicide in California* (Bureau of Criminal Statistics, 1973), pp. 53-54 (80%); Marvin Wolfgang, *Patterns in Criminal Homicide* (Philadelphia: University of Pennsylvania, 1958), pp. 175-78 (64%); Gary Kleck, "Policy Lessons from Recent Gun Control Research," *Law and Contemporary Problems* 49 (1986), pp. 40-41 (70-75% for domestic homicides).

For the same sentiment, see Mary McGrory, "Plastic Guns: The NRA Gets the Drop," *Washington Post,* October 25, 1987, p. C1. "Pretty soon, all airline passengers might in self-defense slip a plastic pistol into the hand-luggage, and any respectable businessman or housewife could become a potential terrorist." Whether carrying a gun would really turn a "respectable businessman or housewife" into a terrorist seems debatable.

94. Earlier in Britain, objects that "caused" a death were punished. If man fell from a tree, the tree was cut down. If he drowned in a well, the well was filled up. If a criminal killed a victim with a third party's sword, "the sword shall be forfeit as deodand, and yet no default is in the owner." A steam-engine was even forfeited under this doctrine. O. W. Holmes, *The Common Law* (Boston: Little, Brown and Co., Mark DeWolfe Howe, ed., 1963; 1st ed. 1881), pp. 23-24. The "deodand" was a gift to God of the object causing death. In early American law, a tree that fell on someone might be destroyed as deodand. One court ordered destruction of a canoe that had failed "to make way in a storm," causing its owner's death. A Virginia court ordered the chain by which a boy had hanged himself in suicide forfeit as deodand. Chapin, p. 35, citing William H. Browne et al., eds., *Archives of Maryland* 66 vols. (Baltimore, 1983-), vol. IV, *Proceedings of the Provincial Court, 1637-1650* (Baltimore, 1887), pp. 9-10 (tree); Nathaniel B. Shurtleff and David Pulsifer, eds., *Records of the Colony of New Plymouth in New England,* 12 vols. (Boston: 1855-61), Vol. I, p. 88 (canoe); Henry R. McIlwaine, ed., *Minutes of the Council and General Court of Virginia* (Richmond: 1924), pp. 53-54 (chain).

Similarly, in ancient Greece, a sword used by a murderer would be banished beyond the city limits, as would a statue that fell on someone. W. W. Hyde, "The Prosecution of Animals and Lifeless Things in the Middle Ages and Modern Times," *University of Pennsylvania Law Review* 64 (1916): 696-730.

95. E. P. Evans, *The Criminal Prosecution and Punishment of Animals: The Lost History of Europe's Animal Trials* (London: Faber and Faber, 1988; 1st pub. 1906).

96. Emphasis in original. Nicholas Humphrey, foreword in Evans, p. xxvi.

97. One of the most thorough analyses of gun control as public health is contained

in Richard Harding, "An Ounce of Prevention . . .: Gun Control and Public Health in Australia," *Australia & New Zealand Journal of Criminology* 16 (March 1983): 3-19. Harding notes that since Switzerland has the vector (guns) but not the disease (murder), it is not certain that the vector causes the disease. But, argues Harding, since America does have the vector and disease, public health prudence dictates avoiding the vector.

The reasoning, though, fails to consider the possibility that gun control may be an ineffective, quack remedy, like leaching, that may make things worse, and may distract the patient and physician from seeking an efficacious cure.

For more on gun control as public health, see, for example, the not entirely persuasive work of: J. H. Sloan, A. L. Kellermann, D. I. Reay, J. A. Fenis, T. Koepsell, F. P. Rivera, C. Rice, L. Gray, and J. Logerfo, "Handgun Regulations, Crime, Assaults, and Homicide: A Tale of Two Cities," *New England Journal of Medicine* no. 319 (November 10, 1988): 1256-62 (failure to control the effects of ethnicity; discussed in chapter 3, at notes 131-36); Lois A. Fingerhut and Joel C. Kleinman, "International and Interstate Comparisons of Homicide Among Young Males," *Journal of the American Medical Association,* 263 (June 27, 1889): 3292-95 (assertion that firearms availability relates to homicide; no proof offered); Gary J. Ordog, "Socioeconomic Aspects of Gunshot Wounds, in Gary J. Ordog, ed., *Management of Gunshot Wounds* (New York: Elsevier, 1988), pp. 447-48; Norman B. Rushforth et al., "Violent Death in a Metropolitan County," *New England Journal of Medicine* no. 297 (1977): 531-38; Stephen P. Teret and Garen J. Wintemute, "Handgun Injuries: The Epidemoliogic Evidence for Assessing Legal Responsibility," *Hamline Law Review* 6 (1983): 341-50 (assertion that handguns are actually more lethal than long guns—"uniquely lethal"; number of childhood firearms accidents valid only if all persons under twenty-four are considered children); Garen S. Wintemute, "Firearms as a Cause of Death in the United States," *Journal of Trauma* 27 (1987): 532-36; Susan P. Baker, "Without Guns Do People Kill People?";*American Journal of Public Health* 75 (1985): 587-88 (handguns as deadlly as long guns).

One of the ironies of the medical attack on firearms owners is that medical/surgical misadventures kill 62% more people than firearms accidents. National Safety Council, *Accident Facts,* 1991 Edition (Chicago: NSC, 1991), p. 19 (1988 data).

For dangers of turning criminological issues into medical ones, see Peter Conrad & Joseph W. Schneider, *Deviance and Medicalization* (St. Louis: C. V. Mosby, 1980).

98. Joseph Gusfield, *Symbolic Crusade: Status Politics in the Temperance Movement* (Urbana: University of Illinois Press, 1963).

Gusfield's work on symbolic crusades has been deepened and elaborated by a number of researchers. The social reaction of a "moral panic" involves the defining of a group of people or a certain behavior as a threat to social values. The persons/activity are presented in the media in a stereotyped and hysterical fashion in the media. Moral panics are launched by "moral entrepreneurs," who frequently have both theoretical and financial interests in the propagation of the panic. The moral panic is set off in society by an "atrocity tale" which is an event (real or imaginary) that evokes moral outrage, implicitly justifies punitive actions against those considered responsible for the event, and mobilizes society to control the perpetrators. The witch hunts in colonial Massachusetts, the McCarthy persecutions in the 1950s, some aspects of the child abuse concerns today, and the numerous drug wars of the twentieth century have all been studied as moral panics. See Robert L. Chauncey, "New Careers for Moral Entrepreneurs: Teenage Drinking," *Journal of Drug Issues* 10 (1980): 45-70; Howard S. Becker, *Outsiders* (New York: Free Press, 1963); Edwin M. Schur, *The Politics of Deviance* (Englewood Cliffs, N.J.: Prentice-Hall, 1980); Stanley Cohen, *Folk Devils and Moral Panics* (New York: St. Martin's Press, 1980), (British panic over "mods" and "rockers"); Louis A. Zurcher, Jr. and George R. Kirkpatric, *Citizens for Decency: Anti-Pornography Crusades as Status Defense* (Austin: University of Texas Press, 1976); David Downes, "The Drug Addict as Folk Devil," in P. Rock, ed., *Drugs and Politics* (New Brusnwick, N.J.: Transaction, 1977); Thomas S. Szasz, *Ceremonial Chemistry: The Ritual Persecution of Drug Addicts and Pushers* (New York: Doubleday Books, 1975); David G. Bromley, Anson D. Shupe, and J. C. Ventimiglia, "Atrocity Tales: The Unification Church and the Social Construction of Evil," *Journal of Communciation* 29, no. 3 (1979): 42–53; Nachman Ben-Yehuda, "The European Witch Craze of the 14th to 17th Centuries: A Sociologist's Perspective," *American Journal of Sociology* 86, no. 1 (1980): 1–31; Nachman Ben-Yehuda, *Deviance and Moral Boundaries: Witchcraft, the Occult, Science Fiction, Deviant Sciences and Scientists* (Chicago: University of Chicago Press, 1985); Malcolm Spector and John I. Kituse, *Constructing Social Problems* (Menlo Park, Calif.: Cummings, 1977); Erich Goode, *Drugs in American Society* (New York: Knopf, 1989, 3d ed.); Nachman Ben-Yehuda, *The Politics and Morality of Deviance: Moral Panics, Drug Abuse, Deviant Science, and Reversed Stigmatization* (Albany: State University of New York Press, 1990) chapter 5 (May 1982, moral panic in Israel over 50 percent rate of hashish use by high school students. All statistics indicated actual rate of use was 3–5 percent. Panic was promulgated by Israeli drug enforcement officials.)

99. For example, New York City Council Member Walter McCaffery, when voting for an "assault weapon" ban, stated that he would like to say "[T]o those who question the words of symbolism, we live in a world filled with both substance and symbolism. It is my belief that this is an important piece of legislation to send a message, as a piece of symbolism. . . ." Walter McCaffery, City Council of New York, Committee on Public Safety, July 24, 1991, p. 67.

100. Father Marshall Gourley, of Our Lady of Guadalupe Church: "Demons exist in the world today and guns are demons. . . . We look at different possibilities of casting out those demons."

101. Daniel Beckher, *Medicus Microcosmus* (1622), quoted in Christopher Cerf and Victor Navasky, *The Experts Speak* (New York: Pantheon, 1984), p. 33.

102. Gary Kleck, "Guns and Violence: A Summary of the Field," paper presented at the American Political Science Association, August 29, 1991, p. 18.

103. Wrote the *Wall Street Journal* shortly after John Lennon's murder by a mentally ill but not insane young man:

[T]he sudden hue and cry for more gun control at such times is a kind of cop-out, the sort of cop-out that is part of the problem in America.

The country knows that something is wrong. . . . Too many are turning to crimes of violence. The notion that this can be changed by controlling guns, we worry, may be an excuse for avoiding the hard work of making our decrepit criminal justice system start to function, and the even harder work of buttressing what used to be called the nation's moral fiber.

"Guns and Logic," *Wall Street Journal,* December 19, 1980, p. 24, col. 2.

104. Albert L. Wyman, Letter to the Editor, "Sale of Firearms," *New York Times,* August 19, 1910, p. 8, col. 5.

105. "Correspondence," *The New Republic,* March 30, 1987, p. 6.

106. For example, see J. Crump, "T'Ang Penal Law in Early Japan," University of Michigan Center for Japanese Studies, Occasional Papers no. 2 (1953), p. 91: Japan's attempt to import China's penal code failed because Chinese T'ang law could not be understood outside the context of China's social evolution and the Confucian philosophy that underlay the law.

107. "The Japanese explicitly rejected American-style capitalism, with its wide share ownership and independent banks, in favor of a system that allowed the government to control industry directly through the banks. In other words, the cartels that had dominated Japanese business before the war, and had been busted up by the American occupation (on the ground they were the enemies of democracy), were encouraged to come together again." Michael Lewis, "Kamikaze Capitalism," *Manhattan, Inc.* (now "*M. Inc.*"), September 1990, p. 24.

108. W. Howard,"Constitution and Society in Comparative Perspective," *Judicature* 71 (1987), p. 114. In the postwar era, the Japanese Supreme Court has voided only five laws on constitutional grounds. Yasuhiro Okudairo, "40 Years of the Constitution and Its Various Influences," *Law & Contemporary Problems* 53 (Winter 1990), p. 37.

109. O. Kahn-Freud, "Uses and Misuses of Comparative Law," *Modern Law Review* 37 (1974): 1–27.

110. H. Sandison, "A Rejected Transplant: The British Industrial Relations Act," *Industrial Relations Law Journal* 23 (1979): 247–320.

111. Howard, p. 114. It is interesting to note that Lloyd Cutler, who heads the law firm Wilmer, Cutler, and Pickering (a white-shoe firm that is the main legal resource of Handgun Control, Inc.) favors adoption of a British-style parliamentary system in the United States.

112. One other nation, which is not a full democracy, does have a right to bear arms. Article 10 of the Mexican Constitution guarantees the right of Mexicans to have arms of any kind for self-protection or legitimate self-defense, except those which are expressly forbidden by law, or reserved for exclusive use of the military.

Until 1968, small calibre rifles and handguns were freely available. Anti-government student movements, however, scared the government into closing firearms stores, and registering all weapons. Compliance with the registration has been virtually nil. Riding, "Smuggled Guns from U.S. Are Common in Mexico," *New York Times,* January 23, 1977.

113. See chapter 11, notes 51–56 and accompanying text.

114. See chaper 3, note 192; and chapter 5, note 142 and accompanying text.

115. George Newton and Franklin Zimring, *Firearms and Violence in American Life* (Washington: Government Printing Office, 1970), p. 123. Newton and Zimring were not convinced that American gun control would reduce crime much, but they did expect controls to reduce domestic homicide. Their argument is discussed in the next chapter.

116. Donald B. Kates, Jr., "Handgun Control: Prohibition Revisited," *Inquiry,* December 5, 1977, p. 20, n.1.

117. David Bordua, Alan Lizotte, and Gary Kleck, *Patterns of Firearms Ownership, Use, and Registration in Illinois* (Springfield: Illinois Law Enforcement Commission, 1979), p. 253.

118. Kates, *Guns, Murders, and the Constitution,* p. 59.

11

Guns, Crime, and Virtue

"Mistrust the people and they become untrustworthy."

—I Ching

The previous chapters have shown that gun control does not cause the low crime rate in the Commonwealth democracies and Japan, and widespread gun ownership does not cause the low crime rate in Switzerland. Broader cultural forces, of which gun policy is only one element, are more important. This chapter looks at the effects of gun controls in America, and then proposes new controls designed to fit in with existing American culture.

GUN CONTROL AND SELF-CONTROL

Comparative international death statistics are the anti-gun lobbies' stock in trade. The International Association of Chiefs of Police (IACP) publishes a set of graphs (reprinted in Australia by the anti-gun lobby) that show the high homicide rates in American cities compared to the lower rates in comparably sized cities in other democratic countries.[1] The point is meant to be that gun laws reduce homicide. Although the IACP tries to pick low-crime non-American cities and high-crime American cities for the comparison, the graph contradicts its own thesis. Cities with handgun bans and severe long-gun restrictions—such as Chicago and Washington, D.C.—

406

turn out to have far higher homicide rates than cities with more moderate laws, such as Toronto or Calgary.[2]

Writes Handgun Control, Inc.: "In 1980, handguns killed 77 people in Japan, 8 in Great Britain, 24 in Switzerland, 8 in Canada, 18 in Sweden, 23 in Israel, 4 in Australia, and 11,522 in the United States."[3] The Coalition to Stop Gun Violence makes its case for handgun prohibition by contrasting the low handgun-related murder rates in Japan and England with the high rate in the United States.[4]

The obvious point is that as far as gun policy goes, the United States is a barbaric country that must import the gun controls of the civilized world. Yet before enacting controls in America based on the handgun statistics, it makes sense to take a look at the overall death rate. Surely the measure of a nation's level of civilization should not be the violent death rate from one particular object, but the violent death rate as a whole. A compassionate measure of civilization must also take into account suicides as well as homicides. A person caught in the vortex of social circumstances, who takes his or her life out of desperation, is a person at least as valuable to society as a drug dealer who is murdered by a business competitor; premature violent death is always tragic. The anti-gun lobby can have no objection to including suicide in the "civilization" index, since the lobby promises that gun control will reduce suicide. Here then, is a comprehensive index of violent death and other crime in the democracies analyzed (except for Jamaica):

Table 1 (rate per 100,000 persons)

Country	Homicide	Suicide	Total Death	Rape	Robbery	Burglary
Japan	.8	21.1	21.9	1.6	1.8	2351.2
Engl. & Wales	1.1	8.6	9.7	2.7	44.6	1639.7
Scotland	1.7	10.2	11.9	4.4	86.9	2178.6
Canada	2.7	12.8	14.5	10.3	92.8	1420.6
Australia	2.5	11.8	14.3	13.8	83.6	1754.3
New Zealand	1.7	10.8	12.5	14.4	14.9	2243.1
Switzerland	1.1	21.4	22.5	5.8	24.2	976.8
United States	7.9	12.2	20.1	35.7	205.4	1263.7

The above table is based upon U.S. Department of Justice and Interpol figures.[5]

Is the United States an exemplar of civilization by these standards? Certainly not, but neither is it horribly barbaric. In terms of premature violent deaths, the United States is slightly better than civilized, gun-free Japan and gun-laden Switzerland. Japan, Switzerland, and the United States suffer about 50 percent more violent deaths than Australia, Canada, or New Zealand, and twice as much as Britain. Overall, while Japan, the United States, and Switzerland do not do well by the measure of total violent deaths, neither are their death totals so high as to disqualify them from the civilized community.[6]

In discussing how much "extra" crime and death are caused by guns in America, it is always difficult to determine how many gun-related murders or gun-related robberies would have occurred anyway, if guns did not exist. America has many more homicides per capita than England and Wales, and most American homicides are perpetrated with guns. Yet would the absence of guns result in a sharp drop in American homicides?

Only 7 percent of American rapists use guns, so rape might be considered a baseline crime; even if no criminals had guns, the rape rate would be nearly the same. If, compared to a given country, America had five times more rapes per capita, and ten times more homicides, the data would allow the inference that some special American factor, perhaps the ubiquity of firearms, inflates the American violent crime rate beyond what the rate would be absent guns. Conversely, if the homicide ratio were less than the rape ratio, the data would be less supportive of the hypothesis that guns cause excess homicides.

Table 2 (number listed reflects ratio of U.S. crime rate to countries listed)

Country	Rape ratio	Homicide ratio
Japan	22.3	9.9
England & Wales	13.0	7.2
Scotland	8.1	4.6
Canada	3.5	2.9
Australia	2.6	3.2
New Zealand	2.5	4.6
Switzerland	6.2	7.2

The ratios are calculated using the crime statistics from table 1.

In three of the countries (Australia, New Zealand, and Switzerland), the rape ratio was lower than the homicide ratio, suggesting that America might have "extra" homicides caused by the presence of guns. For the other three countries (Japan, England and Wales plus Scotland, Canada), the rape ratio was higher than the homicide ratio, suggesting that America's more relaxed gun laws are not a cause of excess homicide.

It should also be remembered that the official American homicide statistics are artificially high because they include justifiable and excusable homicides (self-defense or defense of others) in the homicide totals. The American homicide statistics are based on arrests rather than convictions, which means that if a person is arrested for homicide, but later acquitted or released without prosecution on grounds of self-defense, his or her act of self-defense winds up in the crime statistics as murder rather than as justifiable self-defense. Criminologist Gary Kleck suggests that 1,500 to 2,800 American homicides each year are committed in self-defense.[7] It is ironic that statistical miscounting of American self-defense is used as an argument in favor of gun control, when in fact a large fraction of American homicides are not crimes, but legitimate defenses against crimes. Were the homicides tabulated according to their ultimate legal disposition, rather than the initial characterization by a police officer who does not want to err on the side of not making an arrest, the arguments of the gun prohibitionists would be less persuasive.

Other nations' homicide statistics are likely not so distorted by miscounting of justifiable self-defense homicides; since such homicides are relatively rarer in Japan and the Commonwealth, the legal culture forbids gun ownership for self-defense, and polls indicate that gun owners have little interest in self-defense (except in Australia).

Interestingly, in the nations with the strongest social controls—Switzerland and Japan—the homicide rate is near zero, and the suicide rate is very high. Martin Gold suggests that suicide and homicide are two alternative methods of dealing with frustration. People socialized to cooperative or group-oriented behavior are more likely to choose suicide over homicide.[8]

Would total violent crime rates, rather than the violent death rate be the better measure of civilization? All the countries studied in this book have stricter legal or social gun controls than the United States. The United States has a higher homicide rate than all but Jamaica, and a lower burglary rate than all but Japan and Switzerland. The overall American violent crime level is much higher than in England, Japan, or Switzerland, and higher but by a smaller margin, than in Canada, Australia, and New Zealand. If burglary is counted as a violent personal crime (and it obviously is when the victims are home) the overall rate of violent crime in Australia, Canada, and New Zealand taken together, is only slightly less than in the United

States.[9] Despite generally more lenient gun laws, the United States would seem as civilized as Australia, Canada, and New Zealand.

Switzerland makes easy availability of assault rifles and anti-aircraft guns an official policy, and has a violent crime rate about the same as England and hence would seem equally "civilized."[10]

There are other measures of civilization to consider also. Wars in "civilized" Europe in this century have killed over fifty million people, a far higher death toll and rate of death from all of America's individual and collective killings in all its three centuries.

Should individual freedom be the measure of civilization? The very terms "civil rights" and "civil liberties" imply that freedom is the mark of civilization. If so, the United States is the most civilized country, and its emphasis on the right to bear arms is just one important thread in a magnificent tapestry of civil liberties.

The point is not that the United States necessarily is the most civilized country in the world, or the best country, although it is among the freest. The point, rather, is that the United States is not less civilized than other democracies, and that it is preposterous to claim that America is less civilized simply on the basis of comparative handgun statistics.

SOCIAL CONTROLS

The United States has a lower level of political assassination by gun or other weapon than many other nations.[11] In the 1920s and 1930s, Japan suffered an assassination spree several times worse than anything experienced by any democracy in the twentieth century. Would it make sense to conclude that America's lenient gun laws prevented assassinations during the 1920s and 1930s, since potential American assassins were worried that nearby armed civilians might shoot them as soon as they drew a gun? Of course not.

Internal social conditions—not gun policy—explain why America has had so much less domestic terrorism than Japan. Internal conditions also explain why America suffers so much more violent crime than Japan or Britain. British gun-related and nongun-related crime was at its lowest level at the turn of the century, when there were no gun controls. As discussed in chapter 3, the low turn-of-the-century crime rate in Britain, and the increase in crime since then, is probably explained by what James Q. Wilson calls "the changing investment in impulse control."[12] Wilson's social control emphasis is consistent with the low crime rate in both Switzerland and Japan, despite their polar differences in gun ownership. In *Nations Not Obsessed with Crime,* Freda Adler compares diverse nations with low crime rates, and finds the common denominator to be some form of strong social control, outside and apart from the criminal justice system. The social systems of which I speak do not aim to control by formal restraint. Rather, they transmit and maintain values by providing for a sharing of norms and by ensuring cohesiveness. Among those social control systems, there is, above all, the family.[13]

The advance and decline of internalized social controls may also explain why crime declined throughout most of the nineteenth century and early twentieth century in Scandinavia, West Germany, France, Austria, Great Britain, and the United States, increased in the mid-1950s, and moved sharply upward in the next two decades.[14] In the 1960s, as social controls collapsed worldwide, crime rates rose in places as diverse as Ireland, Scandinavia, Sri Lanka, and Holland.[15] Jamaica's Commissioner of Corrections Dudley Allen blamed the crime epidemic of the 1960s and 1970s on the "breakdown of traditional social roles and institutional controls over the behavior of young and old alike." Notably, the crime rate did not rise in Japan, Israel, or Switzerland, where the investment in impulse control remained high.[16]

The basic cause of crime is not guns, but the uncontrolled American character. As Charles Silberman writes: "American crime is an outgrowth of the greatest strengths and virtues of American society—its openness, its ethos of equality, its heterogeneity—as well as its greatest vices, such as the long heritage of racial violence and oppression."[17] Indeed, racial and economic inequality, when combined with an ethic that stated that all Americans are created equal, was bound to have explosive results.

America suffers so much crime because it has so little social control. If one social pathology typifies the problems behind America's high crime rate, it is not gun ownership, but the extremely high rate of teenage illegitimate births—even though (or because?) most industrial European nations are more tolerant of teenage sexual activity.[18] America has been out of control for many years, and may always be.

Of course America was not always lacking in social controls. During the first half-century of white colonization, communities had a stable social order and each person knew his or her place. There was no unemployment; everyone had the minimum necessities of life, and disparities of wealth were small. Churches provided a firm structure of social control. As a result, there was very little crime of any type.[19] The low crime rate was all the more remarkable in contrast to England, where the crime rate at the time was much higher, even though the governmental law enforcement system in England was stronger and less constrained by procedural protections for suspects. In general, the only gun controls in colonial America were laws against trading with the Indians, and a requirement that free white males own their own gun.

If America could recreate a strong culture of social control, gun controls would become superfluous. But Americans are not likely to make a long return trip to a more repressed society, even if the trip would result in less crime. The erosion of social control, as Wilson points out, has yielded worthwhile benefits. Female liberation and free thought have greatly expanded the horizons and possibilities of human life and the pursuit of happiness. Notwithstanding the hopes of what was once called the Moral Majority, the United States is unlikely to imitate the localized, patriarchal structure of Switzerland. Nor is America going to become an ethnically homogenous nation that makes its corporations into surrogate families, as Japan does.

Switzerland and Japan have low imprisonment rates because they have strong community ties and a culture of shared responsibility; offenders can be treated with community controls rather than isolation from the community. The alternative to caring for and rehabilitating criminals is long prison sentences, which are what Australia has.

The United States has the worst of all possible worlds. It lacks strong community structures to promote rehabilitation. The first thought most Americans have upon learning that a halfway house might be built in their neighborhood is concern for real estate values. Because community corrections are not a viable alternative, American prisons are jammed beyond capacity, and the drug war ensures that prison space for violent criminals is unlikely to catch up with need.

To the lack of prison capacity there are no solutions in sight except for re-legalizing at least some drugs on a state-by-state experimental basis. If America is not going to re-legalize some drugs in order to increase the prison space that can be devoted to repeat violent offenders, what America needs are better nongovernmental methods to reduce crime, since legal controls have only a limited and inadequate capability. Improving the overall structure of social control, and doing so within the context of a highly individualistic society, is the true long-term solution to the crime problem. The panacea of gun control is a distraction from the difficult task. People who want to "do something" about crime often attempt to "do something" about guns. But in fact, the effort to "do something" about guns is often irrelevant and at worst criminogenic since it distracts attention from more difficult, but more effective, solutions.[20]

American liberals and conservatives share a consensus about crime: it is the Constitution's fault. Liberals blame the high violent crime rate on the "obsolete" Second Amendment and the "insane" gun nuts who obstruct civilized gun control. Conservatives blame the Fourth, Fifth, and Sixth Amendments. They argue that protections against unreasonable searches, rules against coercion of suspects under interrogation, and the guarantee of a right to counsel for felony defendants—all enforced by judges "soft on crime"—riddle the criminal justice system with loopholes through which criminals constantly escape. Data suggest that the availability of guns promoted by the Second Amendment does not increase the crime rate or the death rate.[21] Research on the criminal procedure protections of the Constitution also indicates that strict protections against governmental abuse prevent only a few prosecutions.[22]

If there is one amendment that might be blamed for violent crime, it is not the right to bear arms amendment, or any of the criminal procedure amendments, but rather the First Amendment. Research by the University of Washington's Brandon Centerwall reveals that homicide rates in the United States, Canada, and South Africa all rose steeply after the introduction of television. He noted that after television was introduced in Canada, the rate of homicide nearly doubled, even though the rate of per capita firearms ownership remained stable. In the United States, the rise in firearms-related homicide was paralleled by an equally large rise in unarmed homicide. The data therefore imply that the underlying cause of the homicide increase was not a sudden surge in availability of firearms, since unarmed homicide rose as sharply as firearms-related homicide. Centerwall suggested that one mechanism by which television causes homicide, and perhaps other violent crime as well, is simple imitation. He pointed to a poll of prisoners, which asked "have you ever committed a crime you saw on television?" Over one-quarter of prisoners remembered a specific crime episode they had imitated.[23]

Despite Centerwall's findings, violent television is not always associated with homicide. Japanese television is as violent as any in the world, and the Japanese homicide rate is near zero. It may be that television is associated with violence only when it has a cumulative effect after other social controls, such as family stability, have already been weakened.

Perhaps Centerwall's study is flawed. But hypothesize that it is true. It is consistent with studies showing that people exposed to "slasher" movies are more tolerant of violence against women. If it were proven that violent entertainment causes criminal violence, should censorship be imposed? No. The philosophy of the Constitution is that censorship is itself so dangerous that it is better to suffer certain social harms than to let the government control the content of speech. The conclusion that the First Amendment freedoms of speech and of the press must never be violated comes easily to many cosmopolites.

If infringements on the First Amendment are never acceptable, no matter what the benefits, why should infringements on the Second Amendment be permissible? To treat any provision of the Bill of Rights as less favored than any other provision is to disrespect the rule of law.

WHAT COULD GUN CONTROL ACCOMPLISH IN AMERICA?

The introduction to this book started with the observation that academics often assume that foreign gun controls would work in America. Pro-control academics who have looked at the foreign countries carefully are more circumspect in making these claims. George Newton and Franklin Zimring caution that it is far from certain that "adopting the foreign firearms control systems in this country would reduce our firearms violence to the lower foreign levels. A multitude of other factors—such as traditions and cultural traits —contribute to the level of gun violence in any country."[24]

Newton and Zimring's *Firearms and Violence in American Life* (a report to the National Commission on the Causes and Prevention of Violence) compared Britain and the United States, and observed that America had much higher rates of crimes with guns and crimes without guns. The authors agreed that because cultural determinants were the most important factor in crime, a British-style gun-licensing system might not lower the American crime rate. Nevertheless, Newton and Zimring still favored a restrictive national licensing system for handguns, because comparison with Britain showed that for a given category of crime, a higher percentage of the American crimes were committed with handguns. The authors noted, "When homicide occurs, guns are used three times as often in the United States." The organization Handgun Control, Inc., also applauds Britain for having a lower percentage of its killings take place by gun.[25]

But it is not clear why one mode of death is better than another mode. Dead is dead, and a policy whose only accomplishment is changing one cause of death for another is not compelling.

If changing the type of weapon used in a homicide does not matter, changing the type of weapon used in a lesser crime might. Criminologist Philip J. Cook surmises that gun availability does not affect the robbery and aggravated assault rates but does marginally affect the percentage of guns used in those crimes.

Yet community life is not poisoned because people commit crimes with guns; it is poisoned because people commit crimes. Being robbed at the point of an ice pick is not much less terrifying than being robbed at the point of a "Saturday Night Special." From the victim's point of view, the handgun robbery might not be the worst alternative. Victims of handgun-related robbery are more likely to submit than are the victims of other types of robberies; partly for that reason, the injury rate for handgun rob-beries is low. If the victim resists (usually a foolish move at the point of a loaded gun), a handgun wound, especially a wound from a small handgun, is about as survivable as a serious knife wound.[26] Robbers who use hand-guns, having a more efficient instrument, are more likely to attack "hard" targets such as stores, and less likely to go after low-payoff easy targets like the elderly.[27]

Most proposed gun policies, and most foreign gun laws, emphasize handguns. Deciding whether encouraging robbers to substitute other weapons—such as knives, ice picks, or sawed-off shotguns, for handguns—would be an appropriate social policy involves a complex calculus about which weapons would be substituted in what situations, and what their impact would be. If the switch is made from small handguns to ice picks and knives, the criminal has not become significantly less lethal. If the switch is from cheap handguns to good ones, or from handguns to long guns (including sawed-off shotguns), the risk of victim death is much greater. In the only thorough study of the gun habits of felons, 74 percent of "handgun predators" said they would convert to sawed-off shoulder weapons if handguns were unavailable.[28] Fatalities will also increase if criminals are encouraged to change from relatively low-power rifles (such as the Ruger Mini 14, Kalashnikov variants, or the Colt AR-15 Sporter) and to use big-game rifles or hunting shotguns instead.[29]

Changing gun deaths into knife deaths hardly seems a meaningful social goal. Turning handgun-related crime into knife- and/or long-gun–related crime may seem more plausible, but could increase the death rate. Attempting to change the tool of determined criminals is likely an unproductive and dangerous enterprise.

Notably, the anti-gun lobby, in its calmer moments, does not assert that gun controls will affect criminals. States Michael Beard, director of the National Coalition to Ban Handguns (now the Coalition to Stop Gun Violence): "I would agree that clearly no law's going to prevent criminals from getting handguns or any kind of weapon they want. . . . You can't take guns away from criminals."[30] As Josh Sugarmann, former communications director for the coalition, wrote in the *Washington Monthly:* "Handgun controls do little to stop criminals from obtaining handguns."[31] The theory of gun control is that disarming ordinary citizens is good in itself, because, as the coalition's political affairs director, Eric Ellman, asserts: "the majority of gun owners are not responsible."

What kinds of killings by ordinary citizens would gun control help prevent? Gun control likely would reduce the number of firearms-related suicides, but the data from other nations suggest that other, equally deadly methods of suicide would be substituted.[32]

Would gun control reduce accidental death? Most of the 1,700 people involved in a typical year's fatal gun accidents are not normal gun owners but self-destructive individuals who are also "disproportionately involved in other accidents, violent crime and heavy drinking."[33] Without guns, they would likely find some other way to kill themselves accidentally.

As for the accidental deaths of children, the number of children under five years old who die in any type of firearms-related accident in a typical year is thirty-four. Any child's death is tragic, but outlawing private swimming pools or cigarette lighters would save far more young children from accidental death than would a gun ban.[34]

The context of domestic homicide is the one for which many advocates of gun control believe a reduction in firearms would lead to a reduction in death. Cook believes that gun availability affects the homicide rate because many shootings are not intentional murders (for which alternative weapons could be easily substituted), but instead drunken, semi-intentional acts in which the perpetrator, without a homicidal intent, merely reaches for the first available weapon.[35] Cook's thesis is supported by Zimring's study of Chicago handgun-related homicide, which shows a large number of deaths where only one or two shots were fired. Zimring reasons that in some of those homicides, the killer might not have formed a clear intent to kill, but might simply have acted in a rage. Had a less lethal weapon been available, death might not have resulted.[36]

Some research questioning the Cook-Zimring conclusion argues that the one/two-shot gun killers really did have homicidal intent; that is why they picked up a gun. That only one or two shots were fired simply means that the killer did not bother pumping lead into a dead body. Had there been no gun, the killer would have used a different weapon instead.[37]

Another response to Zimring has been to argue that substituted weapons would be equally deadly if not more deadly. Indeed, if half the prospective handgun killers used knives instead, and if they inflicted not a single fatality; and if the other half of prospective handgun killers used long guns instead, the overall fatality rate would double or triple.[38]

The counter-response is that long guns, being more cumbersome, are less likely to be used impulsively. This counter-response does not seem fully satisfactory, since most domestic homicides take place after a long history of violent physical abuse.[39] People who are accustomed to violent attacks may not care as much about the different feel of a long gun as a nonviolent academic researcher might imagine.

Disarming the perpetrators of domestic homicides may be almost as difficult as disarming criminals. Many domestic homicides occur in dwellings where drugs are not unknown.[40] Most perpetrators of such homicides already have violent felony arrests and convictions.[41] It is therefore reasonable to infer that most perpetrators of domestic homicides have some access to the underground economy. Hence, the typical perpetrator might find it easy to buy a black market gun, even if all legal channels of acquisition were closed.

Nevertheless, assume that Zimring and Cook are right: reducing the availability of handguns, or all guns, would reduce the number of deaths in situations of domestic violence. It is not clear that pursuing a lower number of domestic killings through gun control is worth the cost. A great many domestic homicides involve some self-defense. As was noted in chapter 7, 75 percent of Detroit wives who shot and killed their husbands were not prosecuted, because the wives were legally defending themselves or their children against criminal assault. The rate is comparable in other major cities.[42] Indeed, abused wives commit roughly 50 percent of interspousal homicides, and the huge majority of interspousal homicides involving a firearm are perpetrated by wives.[43] When a gun is fired (or brandished) for legal self-defense in a home, the criminal attacker may well be a relative or acquaintance perpetrating aggravated assault, rather than a total stranger committing a burglary.

Even when a gun is fired unlawfully in a domestic situation, the victim may well be a criminal. According to the Southern California Coalition on Battered Women, 63 percent of the boys aged twelve to sixteen who are incarcerated for homicide in California killed a man who was or had been violently abusing them, their siblings, or their mothers. Feminist attorney Cynthia Gillespie suggests that many cases where women shoot husbands or ex-boyfriends and are convicted of a crime are really genuine self-defense. She contends that the legal rules for self-defense, which were written for a context of a fist-fight between men of equal strength, are inappropriately applied to battered women.[44] She also observes that while women are often blamed for failing to leave an abusive relationship, an attempt to leave often precipitates a homicidal act by the male.[45]

Gun control to disarm domestic killers would need to be enforced severely for a long time to have even a chance of a significant effect on the criminal fringe of society that perpetrates and suffers most domestic homicides. If successful, the controls would further the victimization of women. Men do not need firearms to abuse and kill their wives.[46] Wives who defend themselves often do need guns.

In sum, what benefits could strict gun control yield? The experience of other nations shows that a black market pool of illegal guns will remain available to criminals who want one. In no nation except Japan was obtaining a gun more than a little inconvenient for a criminal. Controls at best might turn some gun-related murders into knife-related murders, or some gun-related robberies into knife-related robberies, a rather trivial social benefit.[47] Some researchers suggest that control might reduce domestic homicide, but the main beneficiaries of the policy would be abusive husbands, and the main victims of the policy would be battered wives. Gun control would likely reduce gun suicide, but the evidence from Japan, Britain, and Canada suggests that gun-related suicide would simply be replaced by other methods of self-destruction.

Firearms restrictions in other countries play some role in reducing crime, but not because they make it harder for criminals to obtain guns. The Japanese and British Commonwealth gun controls reinforce the shared social assumption that the government possesses a rightful monopoly of force, that subjects are subordinate to the government, and that individuals are subordinate to society. Gun control in the United States cannot play a similar role in reinforcing social controls, because Americans do not share the values of subordination which most citizens in other democracies do. As one scholar observes, "The specific property of symbolic power is that it can be exercised only through the complicity of those who are dominated by it."[48]

Many Americans who support gun control concede that it may not have much of an effect. But perhaps it might have at least a small marginal effect. Since the need to "do something" about gun crime is so clear, why not adopt strict control? If gun control did not work, no harm would be done. If it did work, things would be at least marginally better.

The problem with the "do something" approach is that it fails to consider the risk that gun control might actually increase crime. The home burglary statistics of other countries give some reason to fear that gun control facilitates burglary in general and sharply raises the rate at which burglars attack occupied residences.[49] Burglary, and especially burglary of an occupied residence, occurs far less often in America than in countries with stricter gun control. While the American violent crime rate, for both gun-related crime and nongun-related crime, is higher than in the other Commonwealth nations studied (except Jamaica), the burglary rate is lower. The burglary of occupied residences is far lower.

A significant reduction in the number of Americans keeping loaded guns in the home would, if the experience of other countries is a guide, lead to a large increase in the burglary rate, and to many more burglaries being perpetrated while potential victims are present in the home. Because, for violent criminals as a whole, the risk of being shot by an armed victim is at least equal to the risk of being sent to prison, any gun-control policy that further reduces the frequency with which Americans keep or bear loaded firearms would remove an important deterrent to crime. If America adopted "sane" and "civilized" foreign gun policies, the deterrent anti-burglary effect of widespread gun ownership would be diminished.

There is another sense in which strict gun control would be criminogenic in the United States. Tens of millions of otherwise law-abiding American citizens will actively and passively resist.[50] Even well-entrenched cultural patterns can be reversed, of course. In the last four decades, the United States has made important progress in weakening its three-century-old tradition of racism and slavery. The benefits of attacking racism are clear, and, benefits aside, racism was inconsistent with the principles of equality that America always considered as its ideals. The attack on racism took an enormous investment of national energy and caused, for a time, tremendous disruption. Effective gun control might take just as much effort. The plausible benefits of gun control—e.g., felons running a lesser risk of being shot by their girlfriends—are not so clear-cut. Unlike racism, firearms ownership has been a point of pride in America's past and present definition of itself. Getting rid of, or even greatly diminishing, America's gun culture is likely to be difficult indeed.

THE PERMANENCE OF GUNS IN AMERICAN CULTURE

"British law is predicated on the simple principle that possession of a weapon is a privilege rather than a right," says Handgun Control, Inc.[51] They are right about Britain. The American republic explicitly chose a different path: that the militia—the whole armed citizenry—possess "the right to keep and bear arms." The Second Amendment was written in part to keep America from the fate of Britain, where monarchs had attempted civil disarmament to protect their regimes.[52] The early republic's leading constitutional commentators pointedly contrasted the robust American right to bear arms with what they thought was a withered British right.[53] Supreme Court Justice Story's famed *Commentaries on the Constitution* also contrasted the vigorous American right to bear arms with its feeble British cousin.[54]

As a deliberate and sharp change from British policies, the Second Amendment was very much like the religious freedom clauses of the First Amendment, the Third Amendment ban on quartering of soldiers in the home, and the Eighth Amendment provision against cruel and unusual punishments. The concept of a federal government possessing only the limited powers explicitly granted by the people was also a radical change from the British system.[55] Indeed, the Declaration of Independence was a conscious rejection of the theory of "rights of Englishmen"—rights that were granted by government or tradition—in favor of the "rights of man"— rights that are universal, are granted by the Creator, and which governments recognize, but do not create.[56]

Whether the framers chose wisely or not, their choice cannot be undone. Indeed, the Second Amendment simply reflected the social reality that Americans were already extremely well armed. Gun culture is too deeply embedded in the American soul to change now. Even anti-gun polemicist Robert Sherrill understands:

We have a trashy society. But if we are trashy, at least we are trashy in the grand and gloriously anarchistic-qua-democratic manner that no other part of the world has ever been able to develop or enjoy. . . . "God made man, but Colonel Colt made him equal." It's a cheap simplistic, wahoo strutty way to view life. It's the kind of sloganeering that has made us the most violent major nation in the history of the modern world. That's what I tell myself, but those genes that came over to supply labor for Oglethorpe's debtor colony keep responding the wrong way.[57]

Sherrill thus traces America's affair with the gun back to the disreputable character of American immigrants—such were the British debtors who chose "transportation" to Georgia over debt imprisonment. In contrast, the leaders of the early republic thought Americans uniquely virtuous and capable of bearing arms responsibly. James Madison spoke of "the advantage of being armed, which the Americans possess over the people of almost every other nation," and contrasted America with the kingdoms of Europe, whose "governments are afraid to trust the people with arms."[58] Joel Barlow, a leading diplomat and author of the 1780s and 1790s, noted that in Europe, an armed populace would be regarded "as a mark of an uncivilized people, extremely dangerous to a well-ordered society." Barlow contended that because the American system was built on popular sovereignty, which brought out the best in man's character, the people could be trusted with guns: "It is *because the people are civilized that they are with safety armed.*"[59] Timothy Dwight, a future president of Yale, explained: "[I]f proper attention be paid to the education of the children in knowledge and religion, few men will be disposed to use arms, unless for their amusement, and for the defense of themselves and their country."[60]

Conversely, thought Revolutionary-era Americans, an unarmed populace was a sign of ethical decay. The revolutionaries had read Sir Thomas More's *Utopia,* which stated that when people relied on uniformed forces for their protection, rather than defending themselves and their nation, the people's character was corrupted. More thought that the introduction of a standing army had caused moral decline in France, Rome, Carthage, and Syria.[61] The Continental Congress distinguished Americans "trained to arms from their infancy and animated by love of liberty," to the "debauched," "dissipated," and "disarmed" British.[62]

In the cities with severe gun control—New York, Washington, Chicago, or London—citizens have retreated into a personal security shell. They rarely come to the aid of their fellow citizens who are being attacked by criminals. The predictions of More and the rest seem vindicated; when people cannot protect themselves, civic virtue declines. Psychologists have noted the phenomenon of "diffusion of responsibility." If several bystanders witness an emergency, they are less likely to respond than if only one person witnesses it.[63] If the police are official monopolists of public safety, if citizens are told that they are too clumsy and unstable to be trusted with guns, citizens will naturally develop a "don't get involved" attitude toward public safety.

Some anti-gun theorists believe that, regardless of the situation in 1787, Americans today are no longer capable of bearing guns. Columnist Max Lerner, for example, made the startling argument that Americans in Jefferson's time "did not have the kinds of mental illnesses that have become widespread today, perhaps even among those who so fiercely want the freedom of guns."[64]

But how could modern Americans be less fit to bear arms than their ancestors? It is not intuitively obvious that post-1787 immigrants or blacks (now allowed to own guns) are any less fit as citizens than were the Anglo-Saxons who dominated two centuries ago. Society may be more crowded and stressful, but it hardly seems likely that there is *more* mental illness today than two centuries ago, considering the development of modern medicine in the last century, the introduction of therapeutic techniques of psychoanalysis, and the availability of anti-psychotic medicine. It would be historically shortsighted to confuse the eighteenth century's dim awareness of mental illness for the nonexistence of mental illness during that period.

It might be argued that the tension of urban life make the modern urbanite less fit to use guns than the eighteenth-century Jeffersonian yeoman. Since crime and gun-related crime is so much higher in cities than in rural areas, the argument is not implausible. On the other hand, it might be noted that modern urbanites are considerably better educated and much less afflicted by racial, gender, and religious prejudice than Jefferson's yeoman. Further, it should be remembered that only a tiny fraction of urban gun owners ever carry out any gun-related crime. The people who perpetrate urban crime using guns are the last people who would be affected by gun controls.

If modern Americans are supposedly less fit because their government has neglected to promote the teaching of responsible gun use through "a well-regulated militia," the problem can begin to be remedied immediately, as the next section details.

Ultimately, it is not necessary to answer the question of whether today's urbanized, ethnically diverse society is less fit to bear arms than the America of two centuries ago. Whether or not urban Americans should own guns, they do, and in huge numbers, even in cities such as New York or Chicago, where gun ownership is legally difficult. The pervasive ownership of guns in America had its roots in the unique conditions of the conquest of the frontier, one farm at a time. But once the gun had arrived in America, it was quickly adapted to urban situations. The tradition of urban gun-carrying and urban vigilantism, which dates from the 1840s to the present, results from conditions of urban crime and disorder at least as pervasive or threatening as frontier crime.

In both urban and rural contexts, the gun acquired a symbolic role that it never achieved elsewhere, except in Switzerland. American attachment to individual gun ownership is further magnified by other conditions that have nothing to do with a rural/urban distinction, such as a strong distrust of the police and government and a pervasive individualism rivaled by no other nation.

The American gun is here to stay. Robert Sherrill and James Madison define the policy alternatives: a trashy, wahoo, randomly violent, gun-toting society. Or a virtuous, responsible, well-armed society. A gunless American society is not possible.

AMERICA'S ONLY REALISTIC OPTION: PROMOTING RESPONSIBLE GUN OWNERSHIP

The prevalence of the American gun does not condemn the nation to a high violent crime rate. America's high crime level has much more to do with the absence of internal social controls than with the absence of statutory gun controls. An appropriate gun policy for America, therefore, is to encourage social control and civic virtue in gun ownership. Instead of a futile attempt to erase gun culture, there must be a conscientious effort to mold gun culture for the better.

Shaping a positive gun culture does not mean America can imitate Switzerland. Americans are harder to motivate with patriotic cries for the fatherland, especially when danger seems far away. Contrast the attitudes of the two nations' gun lobbies: Switzerland's Pro-Tell insists on mandatory citizen soldier duty and mandatory home ownership of firearms. The American NRA touts the notion of "choice" that roots a right (but not a duty) to bear arms in the American tradition of individualism.

In earlier times, America explicitly linked firearms ownership and civic responsibility. The framers of the Second Amendment envisioned a polity in which gun ownership—like voting, jury duty, and paying taxes—was one of the basic components of responsible citizenship.

The decay of the link to civic responsibility was inevitable. A society as dedicated to individualism as America could never achieve or maintain the disciplined militia culture of Switzerland. Neither Britain nor pre-Revolutionary America kept up the militia well when times were safe. While American citizen militias sometimes held their own against foreign armies, no foreign empire would have squandered its money by hiring the American militia into imperial service. Although the well-disciplined Swiss Guards were always in demand, renting the American militias would have been impossible and a waste of money anyway. And whatever the value of an armed citizenry two hundred years ago, the militia seems to have little relevance to the problems of today. Two of the purposes for gun ownership envisioned by the framers—protection against foreign invasion and overthrow of domestic tyranny—may one day be important, but appear remote now. As Supreme Court Justice Story predicted a century and a half ago, the abolition of militia training has meant that some people have no familiarity with arms. "There is certainly no small danger, that indifference may lead to disgust, and disgust to contempt; and thus gradually undermine all the protection intended by this clause of our national bill of rights."[65]

Historian Joe B. Frantz advances the case for the irrelevance of the gun culture to modern problems. He acknowledges that the frontier experience promoted important American values: individualism, mobility (both physical and social), and nationalism. These frontier virtues, including the attachment to firearms, Frantz continues, are no longer appropriate, for "direct action does not befit a nation whose problems are corporate, community, and complex."[66] Frantz is partly right. Unlike in former times, when American foreign policy consisted mostly of taking and holding as much frontier as possible, armed citizens cannot play a role in modern foreign policy. Likewise, direct action does not address acid rain control or space exploration.

Direct action can, however, make a significant contribution to the crime problem—by deterring and stopping criminals. One of the original purposes of gun ownership—defense of self and the community against crime—is as necessary as ever. On the American frontier, the law was not something in a statute book owned by the government. Law was mostly the coercive power of ordinary citizens carrying firearms and making criminal activity difficult. Today, there is a good body of scholarship to suggest that citizen gun ownership does deter crime. The subjects of burglary by strangers and physical abuse by intimates have been discussed above. In polls conducted by both anti- and pro-gun firms, large numbers of Americans say they or someone in their households have actually used (i.e., fired or brandished) a gun for self-defense. The number of defensive handgun uses annually that can be derived from such totals, using conservative assumptions, is 645,000 defensive handgun uses every year.[67]

Michael Beard of the Coalition to Stop Gun Violence argues that reports of handgun-related self-defense may not be accurate. A person might hear a car backfire, jump out of bed, grab his gun, discover no danger, and report that he used a gun for self-defense. Perhaps there are many flawed reports. Still, the polling of civilians on the handgun issue is consistent with the polling of criminals. In the Wright and Rossi survey of felony offenders, three-fifths of the prisoners said that a criminal would not attack a potential victim who was known to be armed. Two-fifths of them had personally decided not to commit a crime because they thought the victim might have a gun. Criminals in states with higher civilian gun-ownership rates worried the most about armed victims.[68]

Guns in civilian hands pose a risk to criminals at least as large as the risk they face from the government. Criminologist Gary Kleck writes: "gun use by private citizens against violent criminals and burglars is common and about as frequent as arrest, is a more prompt negative consequence of crime than legal punishment, and is more severe, at its most serious, than legal punishment. . . . Serious predatory criminals say they perceive a risk from victim gun use which is roughly comparable to that of criminal justice system actions. . . ."[69] As noted above, the National Institute of Justice study found an American burglar's chance of being sent to jail is about the same as his chance of being shot by a victim.[70]

If an armed citizenry would make even a small difference, then an armed citizenry might be a "frontier" response well suited to modern life. The rough sections of most American big cities, where the police have given up trying, are more dangerous than the nineteenth-century frontier. Law-abiding frontier folk who did not brawl in saloons had no reason to fear homicide or any other violent crime. Armed, they were secure.[71]

As discussed in the previous chapter, the American vigilante tradition has changed, but never died, because the conditions that necessitated it have continued. Legal protection against violent crime is scarce in many American cities. In the real world of the inner cities, it is the armed citizen, not the 911 caller, who can protect the victim of a crack addict brought to a psychotic rage by desperation for money for a hit.

Attempting to erase the "frontier virtue" of gun ownership, urban policy makers may be tearing at the fabric of social cohesion. By devolving citizens of community responsibility in the use of guns, gun control and overemphasis on the police have reduced citizens' sense of responsibility for community well-being. After the Sullivan Law was passed in 1911, New Yorkers became more apathetic toward crime.[72]

Conversely, firearms owners are more inclined to assist crime victims—just as George Washington or Thomas Jefferson might have predicted. Of the "good Samaritans" who come to the aid of victims of violent crime, 81 percent are gun owners. Those gun owners are "familiar with violence, feel competent to handle it, and don't believe they will get hurt if they get involved."[73]

There is some reason, then, to consider the possibility that encouraging gun ownership might be a partial solution to the crime problem. Citizen anti-crime efforts might be especially successful if the government encouraged citizens to possess arms and offered them safety training, and the media publicized the citizens' armament.[74]

There is also an extended range of lesser possibilities for using an armed citizenry to reduce crime. A police leader might simply state that citizens are encouraged to buy arms for self-defense, doing so through proper channels, and also encouraged to undergo safety training. The statement, if publicized, might itself deter some crime.

Unarmed neighborhood watch patrols are more and more common. Armed patrols have arisen in dangerous circumstances. As noted, government encouragement can help ensure that all kinds of patrols are racially integrated, and thus help to unite diverse communities rather than dividing them.

Along with armed citizens, and (usually unarmed) citizen patrols, the police have their own role in restoring order to the cities. In recent years there has been a trend back to community-based policing. Some police forces have even experimented with police mini-stations similar to the Japanese *kōban*.[75] Community policing may prove itself to be a cost-effective idea. But more fundamentally, community control of crime must come from within the community. Fine-tuning of external anti-crime measures from government employees is useful, but will not decide the issue.

Would an armed citizenry produce blood in the streets? Carnage was predicted in Florida after the legislature enacted a law mandating that citizens be granted "carry" licenses after a background check. In fact, the permit-holders have proven themselves highly law-abiding, as might be expected of any group of citizens who voluntarily submitted to government screening.[76] Oregon enacted a similar law in 1989. As a result, 2,200 carry permits were issued in Portland in the first seven months of 1990, compared with only 17 the previous year. Homicide fell 33 percent, the second-largest drop of any major city.[77]

A citizenry that is armed to deter and resist crime is a controversial idea that involves trusting ordinary people to possess and use deadly weapons. To favor other, less controversial, elements of a responsible gun-ownership policy, it is not necessary that one share Adam Smith's or Thomas Jefferson's favorable view of guns or people. It is simply necessary to recognize that guns cannot be eradicated from American culture; hence, a policy that promotes responsible gun use is more likely to prevent gun misuse than is a futile effort at prohibition (or semi-prohibition through bureaucratic controls).

The prospects for promoting responsible gun use are bright. America has a three-century-old tradition of gun use—in large part responsible gun use—on which to draw. Only in a few large cities has visible, responsible gun ownership by ordinary citizens been drive underground.

It is these quasi-prohibitionist cities—where the only persons seen with a gun are criminals, policemen, or television characters—that have the most to gain from responsible firearms ownership.[78]

New York City's government, after nearly a century of trying to eradicate gun culture, has succeeded instead in creating a gun culture where teenagers have no models of responsible gun users such as target match competitors. Since almost all of the one-half million to two million New Yorkers who own guns for self-defense must do so illegally and surreptitiously, they can hardly act as role models of responsible use. In a world where the only public role models are supplied by drug dealers, children learn from what they see. Far from being eradicated from New York City's culture, guns are now a must-have status symbol for many street teenagers. New York City would be better off if it had laws like modern Dodge City, Kansas, where guns may be readily purchased and used for sports and self-protection—where, perhaps partly as a result, young people are exposed to models of responsible gun ownership.

A more subtle benefit of promoting responsible gun ownership would be that the anti-gun segment of society (a more educated, urban, and pacifist group) might at least come to better understand people who own guns. A diminution in the intensity of the symbolic crusade against "demon" guns and their "sick" owners will leave the American polity more united and better able to concentrate on all social problems.[79]

Whatever the legal controls on the acquisition and handling of guns, as long as America does not choose a total prohibition, it seems that encouraging people who do own guns to handle them safely and skillfully should be agreeable to both sides of the gun debate. If guns are part of American culture, and will be for many more generations, the government should encourage responsible use.

Marksmanship

The simplest component of a "civic virtue" gun policy is marksmanship programs. People who practice shooting with their friends at target ranges are the most likely to be influenced by social models of responsible gun use. City dwellers, who may buy a gun for self-protection and never learn how to fire it safely, could particularly benefit from such a program.[80]

To require school districts to offer marksmanship programs would be an intrusion on local prerogative. On the other hand, there seems to be no downside to letting the decision about school programs remain under local control. State laws taking away such local authority should be lifted. In Illinois, the laws make it difficult or impossible even for colleges to offer target shooting as an option for student athletes.[81] Laws such as Illinois's should be reformed.

Marksmanship has a number of benefits in the context of character development in a city or school. The mental discipline leads some students to report improved ability to concentrate. Target shooting is nonsexist. Females play on the same teams as males, and regularly defeat them. The only facility needed can fit into a twenty-by-fifty-foot room. Students who have been the worst players on the junior high football team can take up marksmanship for the first time in high school and win awards. And while high school or college football players do not learn an activity that they can enjoy for the rest of their lives, target shooting, like golf, is a lifetime sport; a number of national champions have been nearly seventy years old.

Target shooting has a lower injury rate than any other sport, and fights between competitors are nonexistent. In baseball, spiked soles and beanballs are used to threaten, and sometimes inflict, serious bodily harm. Hockey, boxing, and football all involve the deliberate imposition of physical suffering on the opponent.

Thomas Jefferson advised his nephew: "Games played with a bat and ball are too violent, and stamp no character on the mind. . . . [A]s to the species of exercise, I advise the gun."[82] Were Jefferson to visit a high school shooting competition, and then a high school football game where students cheered as a player was slammed to the ground, Jefferson might think his earlier view confirmed.

The surest argument against permitting schools to offer marksmanship classes is that doing so legitimizes gun ownership. So it does. Yet even America's gun-control lobbies insist that they have no quarrel with sporting use of long guns. If there is no campaign against sporting use, and some sporting uses would reduce the injury rate in school sports, why not allow schools the choice?

Other regulations that serve solely to harass adult target shooters have no place in a rational gun-control policy. The less target shooting, the less trained and more dangerous that gun owner will be. Zoning regulations which outlaw indoor target ranges within a particular distance of a school or a church are irrational. They simply make the statement that guns are bad and should not exist near good institutions.

Likewise, there is no social benefit from laws like the one in New York City, where, according to government interpretation of the gun laws, a licensed target shooter cannot even bring a guest to a shooting range to fire a single bullet; the prospective guest must obtain his own expensive gun permit and purchase his own gun. Such a law is not a rational policy of gun control. It is bureaucratic gun prohibition, done simply to make a statement that the government heartily disapproves of anyone but the government having guns.

While airguns can be safely fired inside an apartment, New York City makes it illegal for youths to even hold an airgun in their hands, even under direct parental supervision. Thus, the city closes off one more opportunity for the children to be taught controlled, responsible gun safety.

Another simple step to encourage responsible gun use is to better allocate funds the government already spends on civilian gun use. The Pittman-Robertson Act of 1937, initiated by sportsmen, levies a federal excise tax on firearms, ammunition, and archery gear. States receive the revenue as matching funds. Hunting and associated activities get the lion's share. Putting more funds into public shooting ranges, and less into hunting, would make responsible gun training available and convenient for large numbers of urban gun owners.

Police and military target ranges, now closed to the general public, should be available to all citizens as a public resource. The typical pretext for excluding the public—fear of liability in case of an accident (despite the very low accident rate in target shooting)—could be dealt with by making government-owned ranges immune from suit.

Lastly, ranges of all types need protection from suits claiming that the noise or traffic associated with the range is a nuisance. Such suits should not be allowed if the plaintiff "came to the nuisance" by knowingly moving near an already established target range.

In short, there are numerous ways for government to promote (or at least stop impeding) target shooting and marksmanship programs. None of the suggestions requires new taxes; all of the suggestions would foster responsible gun practices and attitudes.

Safety Training

Target ranges are the best place to practice responsible gun use. Learning the theory of responsible gun use can take place in the classroom, which can be the back room of the gun store or the front room of a school. The United States already has a great deal of voluntary safety education. The National Rifle Association has trained seventeen million Americans in mature firearms handling and use. Many Californians have taken private classes entitling them to carry defensive tear gas.[83]

After mandating that all residents keep operable guns at home, Kennesaw, Georgia, offered a voluntary firearms safety program; a high percentage of the town's citizens took the course, and since the law went into effect, the town has had no firearms accidents or homicides.[84] Nancy Pywell of the University of Florida argues that schools are a good forum for gun-safety education. She also believes that the opportunity to shoot guns is a leadership experience.[85] ·

The chapter on New Zealand discussed the fierce reaction of American gun controllers against the NRA's American gun-safety comic book for children, even though the comic did not endorse gun use and simply told children that if they found a gun, they should not touch it, but instead tell an adult. Such a reaction, based on a prohibitionist mentality, is inconsistent with what even the anti-gun lobby claims are its values, and is certainly inconsistent with the rest of America's values. It is disappointing to see anti-gun citizens throw themselves into legislative battles to defeat laws to allow junior and senior high schools to offer voluntary classes in the safe use of firearms.[86]

While a citizenry armed against crime is a controversial idea for some people, the simple promotion of gun safety and responsible use, through education and marksmanship training, can be objectionable only to the gun prohibitionist.

Objections to a Civic Virtue Policy

There are a number of objections to a "civic virtue" firearms policy. The objection that guns are too dangerous for the citizenry, and must belong only to the state, works in Japan, but not in America. America has guns, and they are not going to vanish. As long as guns exist, America should encourage responsible use instead of trying to wish them out of existence. While some people would prefer a gunless society, the more realistic goal is a society that is safely armed.

A more serious problem with the government getting into the business of "responsible" or "safe" gun ownership is the possibility that the slogans can be hijacked by anti-gun administrators. The Canadian government, for example, instituted its nationwide gun-licensing program while claiming to "encourage the responsible use of guns."[87] In practice, the new law did nothing to promote responsible gun use or to reduce crime, and simply turned into a bureaucratic tool sometimes used for harassment. In the United States, groups such as Handgun Control, Inc., tout mandatory safety exams with the same enthusiasm that Jim Crow election officials touted literacy tests. A literacy requirement for voters made sense in the abstract, but racist Southern election officials turned it into a tool to prevent blacks from voting. Likewise, safety training run by police administrators who receive personal financial donations from Handgun Control, Inc., would likely be perverted into bureaucratic prohibition.[88] The Japanese police already abuse their authority to require safety training by making the training as inconvenient as possible.[89]

Firearms owners are justifiably skeptical about any proposal propounded by the extremist groups whose members have never foregone any opportunity to eliminate as much of the American gun culture as can be destroyed at any given moment.[90] As a result, proposals that might seem innocuous in the abstract (such as registration, licensing, or waiting periods) are fiercely resisted because the lobbies behind them usually intend them as a first step toward drastically reducing the numbers of guns in American life.[91] In the political context created by the anti-gun lobbies, mandatory government firearms training is correctly rejected by those who want to keep gun control off the slippery slope that most of the British Commonwealth is descending.

Even for a friend of responsible gun ownership, it is not clear whether a larger government role would be desirable. The New Zealand Mountain Safety Council gladly takes government checks. Yet the council's chairman cautions against making his volunteers into government workers.[92]

Yet some kind of promotion of responsible gun ownership is especially important because of the undeniable presence of irresponsible elements in the gun culture. Some of the most American traits are the most awful. The custom of shooting off guns at midnight on New Year's Eve is several centuries old,[93] and utterly indefensible in an urban society. The American image of the frontier West is the image of "Buffalo Bill" Cody. In real life, Cody slaughtered tens of thousands of bison with high-powered rifles. His "Wild West" stage show became the image of the West that America accepted as its true past. That image was grossly distorted, and so over-emphasized frontier violence that it might have been a parody. But instead of being a parody, Buffalo Bill's Wild West became the American archetype.[94]

Important parts of America's memory of its violent past are violent fiction: the always brave and virtuous militiaman who could defeat any professional army; the bloodthirsty and uncontrolled vigilante mobs; the feuding and savage Hatfields and McCoys; the Wild West. The misconnection with historical experience is indicative of a culture that in some ways is immature and irresponsible in its approach to guns and violence.

The tendency of America's affair with the gun to turn to the imaginary and the lurid is a continuing obstacle in fashioning responsible gun policy. Memory of a shoot-em-up West that never was may encourage improper and unnecessary use of deadly force in self-defense. The mistaken memory of the West may also lead policy analysts to the incorrect conclusion that more guns correlated with more violent crime, when just the opposite was true.

Yet for all the immaturity and irresponsibility in America's past, there are other examples of responsible gun use. Jim Bridger, the frontiersman who was the first white man to see the Great Salt Lake, also witnessed the wanton shooting of the bison. He was disgusted.[95] To the limited extent that government can influence popular culture, government can encourage Jim Bridger and discourage Bill Cody.

Voluntary private training has little against it, and will yield at least some benefits in safety and responsibility. In the prohibitionist strongholds, such as Washington, D.C., safety training can be a step toward a rational gun policy. Instead of prohibiting handguns, the cities should make purchases legal upon completion of safety training. Even gun carry permits should be allowed for citizens who pass both a safety test and a marksmanship test. In cities with the most extreme gun controls and worst gun crime, government support for (or at least not active hostility toward) responsible gun ownership would undo some of the damage of prohibition, which has prevented the development of a publicly visible culture of responsible gun use.

CONCLUSION

The details of a responsible gun policy can be decided by each state and city for itself. The examination of guns and gun culture in America and abroad seems to indicate the some type of civic virtue policy is desirable. There is little evidence that foreign gun statutes, with at best a mixed record in their own countries, would succeed in the United States. Contrary to the claims of the American gun-control movement, gun control does not deserve credit for the low crime rates in Britain, Japan, or other nations. Despite strict and sometimes draconian gun controls in other nations, guns remain readily available on the criminal black market. Gun control has not reduced crime; in fact, it has encouraged burglary. Gun registration has proven itself valueless in solving or preventing crime. Gun control has in some instances reduced gun suicide, only to see other equally deadly methods of suicide substituted.

The experiences of all the countries described in this book, including the United States, point to social control as far more important than gun control. Gun control works superbly in Japan and fairly well in most of the English-speaking British Commonwealth not because gun control directly reduces gun misuse, but because gun control validates other authoritarian features of the society. Exaltation of the police and submission to authority are values, which, when internally adopted by the citizenry, keep people out of the trouble with the law. The most important effect of gun control in Japan and the Commonwealth is that it reinforces the message that citizens must be obedient to the government. To the extent that citizens internalize that message (and everywhere except Australia and Jamaica they do), crime of all types (including gun-related crimes) is reduced.

Foreign-style gun control is doomed to failure in America. Foreign gun control comes along with searches and seizures, and with many other restrictions on civil liberties that are too intrusive for America. Gun control had done little to mature the body politic of other English-speaking nations; in the British Commonwealth and in the United States gun control is often hysterical, and often directed at already persecuted classes and races.

Foreign gun control—whether England's severe legal controls or Switzerland's strict social controls—postulates an authoritarian philosophy of government and society fundamentally at odds with the individualist and egalitarian American ethos. In the United States, the people give the law to government, not, as in almost every other country, the other way around. Even if some Americans want their nation to be more like other countries, America cannot be more like them. There are too many guns in America, and too much of an individualist gun culture in the American psyche, for imported gun control to stand a chance. Instead of transplanting foreign gun control and culture to America, a realistic American gun policy must accept the permanence of guns in American life. The encouragement of mature, responsible gun use is the policy best suited to the United States.

NOTES

1. International Association of Chiefs of Police, *Position of the International Association of Chiefs of Police on Firearms Management* (Washington: I.A.C.P., no date), pp. 8–9.

2. Ibid.

3. Handgun Control, Inc., "Handgun Facts" (brochure, n.d., unpaginated). The comparative international statistic is the statistic most widely quoted by Handgun Control, Inc.'s supporters. See, for example, Carl T. Bogus, "An Attempt to Weaken Gun Laws," *Pittsburgh Post-Gazette,* November 10, 1988; "Delaying Gun Sales Will Stop Criminals," *USA Today,* May 26, 1987, p. 12A.

4. National Coalition to Ban Handguns [now Coalition to Stop Gun Violence], "20 Questions and Answers" (brochure, n.d.), question 4 (comparing handgun murder rates in Japan, Britain, and United States).

5. Crime rates are for 1984, using Interpol statistics, and reported in Carol Kalish, *International Crime Rates,* Bureau of Justice Statistics Special Report (Washington, D.C.: Department of Justice, May 1988). When 1984 data are not available, the most recent preceding year is used. Accordingly, the Australian homicide rate is for 1981; England and Wales is 1983. For rape, Canada's data are from 1983, England and Wales from 1983 also. For robbery and burglary, England and Wales are 1983. The homicide rate for Britain does not include "political" homicides.

Suicides are for the year 1985, and recorded in *Statistical Abstract of the United States, 1989,* p. 820 and in *United Nations Demographics Yearbook 1985* (1987).

The Scottish homicide and suicide rates are based on figures supplied by British Information Office (communication with author) April 7, 1992. Owing to Scotland's earlier independence from Great Britain, Scottish criminal justice statistics have always been reported separately.

The two nations with the very highest suicide rates had (until Communist rule ended) severe gun control: Rumania, at 66.2, and Hungary, at 45.9. *United Nations 1985.*

6. Even if homicide is the only measure, with no regard paid to suicide, the United

States homicide rate is below that of half the other nations in the world (although above the rate of most of the nations discussed in this book).

7. Kleck suggests that the reason official government reports do not indicate such a high figure is that FBI statistics are based exclusively on incidents reported to the police, and that if a killing is initially labeled a criminal homicide, but later determined to be self-defense, the killing is still counted by the FBI as a criminal homicide. Gary Kleck, "Crime Control Through the Private Use of Armed Force," *Social Problems* 35 (February 1988), pp. 4–7. An example of mistaken gathering of statistics: A Bronx man was held up at gunpoint by two robbers. Refusing to submit, the man bit a robber's arm, forcing the robber to drop a handgun. A scuffle ensued, and the victim picked up the handgun and shot the robber dead. The man was arrested and charged with murder "although a police spokesman said investigators thought the man had acted in self-defense." "Man Shoots Assailant; Murder is Charged," *New York Times*, July 22, 1990, p. 20, col. 1. Because of the arrest, the death of the robber will be recorded by the FBI as a murder by a person unknown to the victim, rather than as an act of self-defense.

The FBI estimates that civilians justifiably kill 300 criminals annually; Lawrence Sherman of the pro-control Police Foundation puts the figure at 600.

See also Paul Blackman, *Firearms and Violence, 1938/84,* monograph (Washington, D.C.: NRA/ILA, July 1985); Paul Blackman and Richard Gardiner, "Flaws in the Current and Proposed Uniform Crime Reporting Programs Regarding Homicide and Weapons Use in Violent Crime," paper presented at the annual meeting of the American Society of Criminology, Atlanta, October 29–November 1, 1986.

8. Martin Gold, "Suicide, Homicide, and the Socialization of Aggression," *American Journal of Sociology* 62 (May 1958): 651–61.

9. "U.S. Says Violent Crime Dropped from '80 to '84," *New York Times*, May 9, 1988, p. A15.

10. See chapter 8, notes 31–50 and accompanying text for Swiss gun laws.

11. Robert Sherrill, *The Saturday Night Special* (New York: Penguin, 1975), pp. 159–60; Hugh Graham and Ted Robert Gurr, "Conclusion," in Hugh Graham and Ted Robert Gurr, eds., *Violence in America,* Report of the National Commission on the Causes and Prevention of Violence (Washington, D.C.: Government Printing Office, 1969), pp. 791–92.

The one exception to America's relative freedom from assassination is that frequency of assassination attempts against presidents. A foreign observer suggests to columnist Flora Lewis that presidents might be such tempting assassination targets because, unlike other foreign leaders, they are both head of state and head of government, virtually embodying the whole state. Flora Lewis, "The Crazy Americans," *New York Times*, April 6, 1981, p. A-5.

12. James Q. Wilson and Richard Hernstein, *Crime and Human Nature* (New York: Basic Books), p. 430.

Other academics make the same point. James Fox, a criminologist at Northeastern, attributes high homicide rates to the decline in socializing institutions such as the church, the neighborhood, and the family. Andrew H. Malcolm, "More Americans Are Killing Each Other," *New York Times*, December 31, 1989, p. 20.

As the Dalai Lama put it: "[T]he source of peace is within us; so also is the source of war, and the real enemy is within us, and not outside. The source of war is not the existence of nuclear weapons or other arms. It is the minds of human beings who decide to push the button and to use those arms out of hatred, anger, or greed."

See chapters 2, 3, and 8 for discussion of the social control issues in the context of Japan, Britain, and Switzerland.

13. Freda Adler, *Nations Not Obsessed with Crime* (Littleton, Colo.: Fred B. Rothman, 1983), p. 130. The nations were Ireland, Switzerland, Saudi Arabia, Japan, East Germany, Bulgaria, Costa Rica, Peru, and Nepal.

14. Wilson, pp. 408–409; Ted Robert Gurr, "Historical Trends in Violent Crime," *Crime & Justice* 3 (1981), p. 339.

15. Wilson, *Crime and Human Nature,* p. 409.

16. Wilson, *Thinking About Crime,* p. 240 (Japan); Gurr, "Historical Trends in Violent Crime," pp. 339–40 (Japan, Israel, and Switzerland).

17. Charles Silberman, *Criminal Violence, Criminal Justice* (New York: Random House, 1978), p. 36. Historian John William Ward writes:

A society such as ours, which increasingly rejects the sanctions of tradition, the family, the church, and the power of the state, necessarily must create the kind of personality who is self-governing, self-restraining, self-repressive. The founding fathers, following the Roman model, defined the essential quality as virtue; Emerson called it character, the Protestant evangelical tradition named it benevolence. The tradition is a long one, and we may respond warmly to some of its phrases, but we should not in our self-congratulation ignore the enormous psychic burden such an ideal places upon the individual. Until we reach the millennium of American democratic hopes, we must accept the probable instability of our society, especially when it denies the opportunity and self-respect which its ideology constantly celebrates.

John William Ward, "Violence, Anarchy, and Alexander Berkman," *New York Review of Books,* November 5, 1970, p. 29.

18. America has 54 births per 1,000 teenage women; Britain has 31; Canada 28; France 25; Sweden 14; and Holland 14. "Teen-age Pregnancy and Birth Rates Drop," *New York Times,* October 20, 1987, p. A29. Twenty-one percent of American children live below the poverty line, a figure approached among major industrial nations only by Australia. Torrey, review of J. Kozol's *Rachel and Her Children, Washington Monthly* (March 1988), p. 60. Likewise, the U.S. ranks nineteenth among industrialized nations in infant mortality. *Hunger Action Forum* 1, no. 14 (October 1988) (Washington, D.C.: The Hunger Project).

19. Bradley Chapin, *Criminal Justice in Colonial America, 1606–1660* (Athens: University of Georgia Press, 1983), pp. 139–41.

20. See chapter 10, notes 101–103 and accompanying text, and the next section of chapter 11.

For drug prohibition as a very large cause of violent crime see Daniel K. Benjamin and Roger Leroy Miller, *Undoing Drugs: Beyond Legalization* (New York: Basic Books, 1991) (federal government should force uniform drug policy on the states); David Boaz, ed., *The Crisis in Drug Prohibition* (Washington, D.C.: Cato Institute, 1990); Ronald Hamowy, ed., *Dealing with Drugs: Consequences of Government Control* (Lexington, Mass.: Lexington Books, 1987).

21. The two best surveys of available research are: Gary Kleck, *Point Blank: Gun and Violence in America* (New York: Aldine de Gruyter, 1991); James D. Wright, Peter Rossi, and Kathleen Daly, *Under the Gun: Weapons, Crime, and Violence in America* (New York: Aldine de Gruyter, 1983).

22. Only a small percent of cases are not prosecuted or are reduced to lesser charges because of the rules against illegally seized physical evidence and coerced confessions. Peter F. Nardulli, "The Societal Cost of the Exclusionary Rule: An Empirical Assessment," *American Bar Foundation Research Journal* 1983 (1983): 585–610; Thomas Y. Davies, "A Hard Look at What We Know (and Still Need to Learn) about the 'Costs' of the Exclusionary Rule: The NIJ Study and Other Studies of 'Lost' Arrests," *American Bar Foundation Research*

Journal 1983 (1983): 611–90; "Legal Safeguards Don't Hamper Crime-Fighting," *National Law Journal,* December 12, 1988, p. 5: Six-tenths of one percent to 2.35 percent of cases are dismissed because of bad searches; in a survey of prosecutors, 87 percent said that 5 percent or less of their cases were dismissed because of Miranda problems.

As discussed in chapter 2, Japan's coercive interrogation techniques and causeless searches probably have something to do with the low crime rate. Japanese practice, however, is far beyond permissible American criminal procedure even in the pre-Warren era. Bringing American police practices into line with Japanese practices would mean not only the repeal of *Mapp* and *Miranda,* but of most constitutional law in the twentieth century. Not only would the effort conflict with longstanding legal American doctrine, it would likely fail because American citizens are less tolerant of police intrusions than are the Japanese.

23. Brandon Centerwall, "Exposure to Television as a Risk Factor for Violence," *American Journal of Epidemiology* 129 (April 1989): 643–52. See also D. Pearl, L. Bouthilet, and J. Lazar, eds., *Television and Behavior: Ten Years of Scientific Progress and Implications for the Eighties* (Rockville, Md.: National Institute of Mental Health, 1982) ("overwhelming" evidence said to link television violance to aggression in youth).

24. George Newton and Franklin Zimring, *Firearms and Violence in American Life* (Washington, D.C.: Government Printing Office, 1969), p. 123.

25. Pete Shields, *Guns Don't Die—People Do* (New York: Arbor House, 1981), pp. 63–64. Shields quotes a newspaper report of a 1981 speech by a British police official. The official states that only 1 in 6 British murders are committed with a gun, but 7 in 10 American murders are.

26. Gary Kleck, *Point Blank: Guns and Violence in America* (New York: Aldine de Gruyter, 1991), p. 165; James D. Wright, Peter Rossi, and Kathleen Daly, *Under the Gun: Weapons, Crimes, and Violence in America* (New York: Aldine de Gruyter, 1983), p. 199 n.9; H. Wilson and R. Sherman, "Civilian Penetrating Wounds of the Abdomen," *Annals of Surgery* 153 (1961), p. 642.

27. Kleck, *Point Blank,* p. 172.

28. James Wright and Peter Rossi, *Armed and Considered Dangerous: A Survey of Felons and Their Firearms* (Hawthorne, N.Y.: Aldine, 1986), p. 220. See generally, Kleck, *Point Blank,* pp. 91–94.

29. See the discussion in chapter 3 at notes 151–52 and accompanying text regarding the comparative lethality of rifles and hunting shotguns.

30. Michael Beard, press conference, January 23, 1979, quoted in *Reports from Washington* 6, no. 3 (February 13, 1979), p. 1.

31. Josh Sugarman, "The NRA Is Right: But We Still Need to Ban Handguns," *Washington Monthly* (June 1987): 11–15. Sugarman authored the November 1988 strategy memo suggesting that the press and the public had lost interest in handgun control. He counseled the anti-gun lobby to switch to the "assault weapon" issue, which the lobby did with spectacular success in 1989.

32. See chapters 2 at notes 210–14 and accompanying text, 3 at notes 250–51 and accompanying text, and 4 at notes 145–50 and accompanying text.

33. Philip Cook, "The Role of Firearms in Violent Crime: An Interpretive Review of the Literature," in Marvin Wolfgang and Neil Weiler, eds., *Criminal Violence* (Beverly Hills, Calif.: Sage, 1982), p. 269. See also Kleck, *Point Blank,* pp. 282–87.

34. The figure for thirty-four accidental deaths from both handguns and long guns for children under the age of five is from Centers for Disease Control, "Mortality and Morbidity Weekly Report," March 11, 1988, p. 145 (1984 statistics). The number of children

under age five who die in fires started by playing with cigarette lighters is ninety. *Consumer's Research,* May 1988, p. 34.

The chances that a child between the ages of one and nine will die from a firearms-related injury are about 1 in 10,000. (Based on Maryland data for 1980-86 contained in the article "Firearms Fatalities: A Leading Cause of Death in Maryland," and prepared by the Johns Hopkins School of Hygiene and Public Health.)

The total number of accidental fatalities from all types of firearms, for all age groups was 1,695 in 1986, about 2 percent of all accidental deaths. For comparison, the number of accidental deaths from "electric current" was 872; from "fires and flames," 5,028. National Safety Council, *Accident Facts,* 1986 edition, pp. 12-13. The majority of the accidental gun deaths were hunting accidents.

35. Philip Cook, "Gun Availability and Violent Crime," *Crime & Justice* 4 (1982), p. 84.

36. Franklin Zimring, "Is Gun Control Likely To Reduce Violent Killings?" *Journal of Legal Studies* 1 (1971): 721-37.

37. For detailed critiques of the Zimring study, see James D. Wright, Peter Rossi, and Kathleen Daly, *Under the Gun: Weapons, Crime, and Violence in America* (Hawthorne, N.Y.: Aldine, 1983), pp. 193-202; David T. Hardy and John Stompoly, "Of Arms and the Law," *Chicago-Kent Law Review* 51 (Summer 1974), pp. 42-49.

38. Alan Lizotte, "The Costs of Using Gun Control to Reduce Homicide," *Bulletin of the New York Academy of Medicine* 62 (1986), p. 541; Donald B. Kates, Jr., "Some Remarks on the Prohibition of Handguns," *St. Louis University Law Journal* 23 (1979), p. 20. The particularly high lethality of shotguns is discussed in chapter 3 at notes 146-47 and accompanying text.

39. A study by the Police Foundation of domestic homicides in Kansas City in 1977 revealed that in 85 percent of homicides among family members, the police had been called in before to break up violence. In half the cases, the police had been called in five or more times. M. Wilt, G. Marie, J. Bannon, R. K. Breedlove, J. W. Kennish, D. M. Snadker, and R. K. Satwell, *Domestic Violence and the Police: Studies in Detroit and Kansas City* (Washington, D.C.: Government Printing Office, 1977), quoted in Wright, Rossi, and Daly, p. 193, n.3.

40. In a study of the victims of near-fatal domestic shootings and stabbings, 78 percent of the victims volunteered a history of hard drug use, and 16 percent admitted using heroin the day of the incident. Kirkpatrick and Walt, "The High Cost of Gunshot and Stab Wounds," *Journal of Surgical Research* 14 (1973), pp. 261-62.

41. About 70 to 75 percent of domestic homicide offenders have a previous arrest, and about half have a previous conviction. Kleck, "Policy Lessons," pp. 40-41.

42. The figure for Miami was 60 percent, and for Houston, 85.7 percent. Martin Daly and Margo Wilson, *Homicide* (New York: Aldine, 1988), pp. 15, 200.

See generally Lenore E. Walker, *Terrifying Love: Why Battered Women Kill and How Society Responds* (New York: Harper and Row, 1989).

43. Saunders, "When Battered Women Use Violence: Husband Abuse or Self-Defense," *Violence and Victims* 1 (1986), p. 49; Barnard et al., "Till Death Do Us Part: A Study of Spouse Murder," *Bulletin of the American Academy of Psychology and the Law* 10 (1982): 271; Donald T. Lunde, *Murder and Madness* (San Francisco: San Francisco Book Co., 1976), p. 10 (in 85 percent of decedent-precipitated interspousal homicides, the wife kills an abusing husband); Daly and Wilson, p. 278 ("when women kill, their victims are . . . most typically men who have assaulted them"); E. Benedek, "Women and Homicide," in Bruce Danto, ed., *The Human Side of Homicide* (New York: Columbia, 1982); Kates, *Guns, Murders, and the Constitution,* p. 25.

44. In particular:

• The law requires that force be only met with equal force. It is legitimate to require a man who is punched in the nose to respond with no more than a punch in the nose. A woman who is being pummelled with a man's fists does not have realistic option of punching back at her larger assailant. Her realistic choices are to endure the beating, or to grab an "equalizer" and threaten to shoot the man if he continues.

• As a general rule, the attack for which self-defense is invoked must be "imminent." For a man who is exchanging harsh words in a bar with a stranger, it makes sense not to allow force to legally be used until an attack actually begins. A verbal threat is not enough. But when a man tells a woman that he is going to beat her to a pulp, or perhaps kill her, the woman cannot wait until the attack is in progress. By that point, her chances of successful resistance will be much lower.

• About half of all American states impose a duty to retreat before self-defense is allowed. To require a person to leave a bar to avoid the need to use deadly force in self-defense is appropriate. Pursuant to the "castle doctrine," most states do not demand that a person retreat from his own home. But many states create an exception to the castle doctrine, requiring that a woman leave her own home rather than use force in self-defense against a husband or boyfriend. Since abandoning the home will often mean abandoning children to abuse by the husband/boyfriend, and since the husband/boyfriend often tracks down the woman to kill her or harm her after she does leave, the exception to the castle doctrine is improper.

• The test of reasonableness for self-defense is usually an objective test for what a reasonable person under the circumstances would do. The "reasonable person" who is the norm for the test, is, in essence, the reasonable white male whose norms dominate society. What might seem reasonable to a white male who has, perhaps, been mugged once or twice, would not be reasonable to a woman who has been battered over and over. Gillespie asserts that the test for reasonableness should be a subjective one, based on what a reasonable person in the woman's circumstances (including the history of abuse) would do.

Cynthia K. Gillespie, *Justifiable Homicide: Battered Women, Self-Defense, and the Law* (Columbus: Ohio State University Press, 1989).

45. Gillespie, pp. 151, 164. See also chapter 5, note 173 and accompanying text.

46. "Analysis of family homicide data reveals an interesting pattern. When women kill men, they often use a gun. When men kill women, they usually do it in some more degrading or brutalizing way—such as strangulation or knifing." James D. Wright, "Second Thoughts About Gun Control," *The Public Interest* 91 (1988), p. 32.

47. During one debate on the Canadian gun law, Member of Parliament Stuart Leggatt praised the benefits of strict gun laws: "New York, which has a fairly respectable Sullivan law, has a 25 percent murder rate by firearms, whereas Dallas, where unrestricted use of firearms is allowed, has a rate of 72 percent of murder by firearms." M.P. Otto Lang replied: "The honourable member has made an interesting case which, if read carefully, shows that murder by knife is a nicer game than murder by gun. I cannot see the point of that." F. Paul Fromm, "Canada Faces Gun Confiscation," *Review of the News,* January 22, 1975, pp. 35–37.

48. Pierre Bourdieu, "The Force of Law: Toward Sociology of the Judicial Field," *Hastings Law Journal* 38 (1987), p. 237.

49. See chapters 3 at notes 252–54 and accompanying text, and 4 at notes 139–43 and accompanying text.

50. See chapter 5, note 210; and chapter 10 at notes 116–18 and accompanying text for resistance to current gun laws.

51. Shields, p. 63.

52. *State* v. *Dawson,* 272 N.C. 535, 159 S.E.2d 1, 14 (1968) (Lake, J., concurring and dissenting) ("It was the very fact that the right to bear arms had been infringed in England, and that this is a step frequently taken by a despotic government, which caused the adoption of the provision in the North Carolina Declaration of Rights in 1776 and the insertion in the Federal Bill of Rights of the Second Amendment.")

See also William Marina, "Weapons, Technology, Legitimacy," in Donald B. Kates, Jr., ed., *Firearms and Violence: Issues of Public Policy* (Cambridge, Mass.: Ballinger, 1984), p. 431.

53. St. George Tucker, author of the American version of Blackstone, was for a quarter of a century the legal commentator most often cited by the U.S. Supreme Court. [Tucker's role as the first major American commentator is noted in *New York Times* v. *Sullivan,* 376 U.S. 254, 296–97 (1964).] He served as law professor at William and Mary, a justice of Virginia's highest court, and a federal district judge. Tucker's edition of Blackstone noted that the American people enjoyed a right to bear arms that applied "without qualification as to their condition or degree, as in the case in the British government." Tucker further noted:

Whoever examines the forest and game laws in the British code, will readily see that the right of keeping arms is effectually taken away from the people of England.

William Blackstone, *Blackstone's Commentaries, With Notes of Reference to the Constitution and Laws* *143 n.40 (St. George Tucker edition, 1803). Tucker described the right to bear arms

as the true palladium of liberty. In England, the people have been disarmed, generally under the specious pretext of preserving the game. . . . True it is, their bill of rights seems at first view to counteract this policy, but the right of bearing arms is limited to protestants, and the words suitable to their condition and degree, have been interpreted so that not one man in five hundred can keep a gun in his house without being subject to a penalty.

Ibid., 300. Tucker was, of course, wrong. Even the most draconian gun laws under James II and Charles II had not disarmed 499/500th of the population. When Tucker wrote in 1803, there were virtually no restrictions on Englishmen's keeping and bearing arms. (See chapter 3, notes 74–76 and accompanying text.) Although Tucker is not a reliable guide to British gun policy, his commentary does express the widely held American view that American gun policy was based on a conscious rejection of Britain's limited "right."

William Rawle declined President Washington's offer to become the first attorney general of the United States. Instead, he served as United States attorney for Pennsylvania. Rawle's Constitutional law textbook was the standard in American law schools in the first half of the nineteenth century; it was used at Harvard until 1845. Rawle viewed the Second Amendment a bar to the disarming of individual citizens by either Congress or a state legislature, such attempted disarmament being a "blind pursuit of inordinate power." But

In England, a country which boasts so much of its freedom, the right was assured to protestant subjects only, and it is cautiously described to be that of bearing arms for their defense "suitable to their conditions, and as allowed by law." An arbitrary code for the preservation of game in that country has long disgraced them.

William A. Rawle, *A View of the Constitution* (2d ed., 1829), p. 125.

At the Constitutional convention of the new Republic of Texas in 1845, judge and delegate William B. Ochiltree explained that the legislature's power to regulate concealed carrying of weapons should not be extended to allow regulation of unconcealed carrying, for such regulation might become a prohibition, and "We might be placed in the condition of the people of Ireland, and large portion of England, who are denied the right of having firearms about their houses." *Debates of the Texas Convention* (Houston: 1846), p. 311, quoted in Stephen Halbrook, "The Right to Bear Arms in Texas: The Intent of the Framers of the Bill of Rights," *Baylor Law Review* 41 (1989), p. 642.

54. Joseph Story, *Commentaries on the Constitution of the United States,* Vol. III (1833), pp. 746–77. See chapter 3, note 18.

Thomas Cooley, the most influential legal commentator of the second latter part of the nineteenth century, noted that the Second Amendment was a "modification and enlargement" of the English Bill of Rights of 1688. Thomas Cooley, *General Principles of Constitutional Law* 3d ed. (Boston: Little, Brown, 1898), pp. 298–99.

55. Howard Owen Hunter, "Problems in Search of Principles: The First Amendment in the Supreme Court from 1791–1930," *Emory Law Journal* 39 (Winter 1986), p. 85:

But the religion clauses, the second amendment provisions on arms, the third amendment provisions on quartering soldiers, and the eighth amendment prohibition of cruel and unusual punishment were patent breaks with the English practice. There may have been some common law antecedents, but these amendments indicated a desire to shift away from English common law in certain fundamental areas. In addition, the two major structural components of the American system—the federalism which dispersed power, and the concept of a government of limited powers delegated by the people—were radical departures from English government in both fact and theory.

See generally chapter 3, notes 311–75 and accompanying text.

56. Dan Himmelfarb, "The Constitutional Relevance of the Second Sentence of the Declaration of Independence," *Yale Law Journal* 100 (October 1990), pp. 171–73.

57. Sherrill, p. 324.

58. The Federalist, No. 46 (James Madison), Clinton Rossiter, ed. (New York: Mentor, 1961). Madison predicted that if the European peasantry were armed, and rebellious local governments (like American states) existed, "the throne of every tyranny in Europe would be speedily overturned." For more, see chapter 9, notes 94–96 and accompanying text.

59. Joel Barlow, *Advice to the Privileged Orders in the Several States of Europe: Resulting From the Necessity and Propriety of a General Revolution in the Principle of Government* (Ithaca, N.Y.: Cornell University Press, 1956; reprinting London: 1792), p. 16 (emphasis in original). *Advice to the Privileged Orders,* written at the suggestion of Barlow's friend Tom Paine, argued that if the state represented the people as a whole, not just one class, society would be more stable.

60. Timothy Dwight, *Travels in New England and New York,* quoted in Donald B. Kates, Jr., "Handgun Prohibition and the Original Meaning of the Second Amendment," *Michigan Law Review* 82 (1983), pp. 233–34, n.131.

61. Sir Thomas More, *Utopia,* J. H. Lupton, ed. (Oxford: Clarendon, 1845; 1st ed. 1516), pp. 47–51; Lois Schwoerer, *"No Standing Armies!": The Antiarmy Ideology in Seventeenth-Century England* (Baltimore: Johns Hopkins University Press, 1974), p. 16.

62. Quoted in Donald B. Kates, Jr., "Handgun Prohibition and the Original Meaning of the Second Amendment," *Michigan Law Review* 82 (1983), p. 237 n.144.

63. John Howard Society of Alberta, *Bystander Intervention,* February 19, 1986, pp. 3–8.

64. Quoted in Carl Bakal, *The Right to Bear Arms* (New York: McGraw-Hill, 1966), p. 308.

65. Joseph Story, *Commentaries on the Constitution* (abridged) § 709. Story had exalted the right to bear arms as "the palladium of the liberties of a republic; since it offers a strong moral check against the usurpation and arbitary power of rulers; and will generally, if these are successful in the first instance, enable the people to resist and triumph over them." Ibid.

66. Joe B. Frantz, "The Frontier Tradition," in *Violence in America: Historical and Comparative Perspectives* (New York: Praeger, 1969), pp. 152–53.

67. Kleck, "Crime Control," pp. 2–4.

Kleck analyzed data collected by pollster Peter Hart for the no longer active National Alliance Against. Six percent of the Hart respondents had replied "yes" to the question "Within the past five years, have you yourself or another member of your household used a handgun, even if it was not fired, for self-protection or for the protection of property at home, work, or elsewhere, excluding military service or police work?" Taking into account the number of U.S. households, and assuming that each "yes" response only related to one defensive handgun use, Kleck calculated at least 645,000 defensive handgun uses per year.

68. Wright and Rossi, pp. 146, 155. Paul Blackman, "The Armed Criminal," *American Rifleman,* August 1985, p. 35 (using the cross-tabulations from the unpublished Wright-Rossi data).

69. Kleck, pp. 16–17.

70. James D. Wright, Peter Rossi, and Kathleen Daly, *Under the Gun: Weapons, Crime, and Violence in America* (Hawthorne, N.Y.: Aldine, 1983), pp. 139–40.

Anecdotal real-world experiences seem consistent with NIJ findings. In 1966 the police in Orlando, Florida, responded to a rape epidemic by embarking on a highly publicized program to train 2,500 women in firearm use. In the next year rape fell by 88 percent in Orlando (the only major city to experience a decrease that year); burglary fell by 25 percent. Not one of the 2,500 women actually ended up firing her weapon; the deterrent effect of the publicity sufficed. Five years later Orlando's rape rate was still 13 percent below the preprogram level, whereas the surrounding standard metropolitan area had suffered a 308 percent increase. Gary Kleck, "Policy Lessons from Recent Gun Control Research," *Journal of Law and Contemporary Problems* 49 (Winter 1986): 35–47; Alan S. Krug, "The Relationship Between Firearms Ownership and Crime Rates: A Statistical Analysis," *Congressional Record,* January 30, 1968, pp. H570–2.

The pattern has been repeated elsewhere, although the type of citizen arming was not on so broad and constant a scale as Orlando. During a 1974 police strike in Albuquerque armed citizens patrolled their neighborhoods and shop owners publicly armed themselves; felonies dropped significantly. Carol Ruth Silver and Donald B. Kates, Jr., "Self-Defense, Handgun Ownership, and the Independence of Women in a Violent, Sexist Society," in Donald B. Kates, Jr., ed., *Restricting Handguns: The Liberal Skeptics Speak Out* (Croton-on-Hudson, North River Press, 1979), p. 152.

In March 1982 Kennesaw, Georgia, enacted a law requiring householders to keep a gun at home; house burglaries fell from 65 per year to 26, and to 11 the following year. "Town to Celebrate Mandatory Arms," *New York Times,* April 11, 1987, p. 6.

Similar publicized training programs for gun-toting merchants sharply reduced robberies in stores in Highland Park, Michigan, and in New Orleans; a grocers organization's gun clinics produced the same result in Detroit. Gary Kleck and David Bordua, "The Factual Foundation for Certain Key Assumptions of Gun Control," *Law and Police Quarterly* 5 (1983): 271–98.

It should be noted, however, that when the Orlando and Kennesaw crime rates were studied in the context of long-term patterns, researchers did not find a statistically significant correlation between the change in gun policy and the crime declines. David McDowall, Alan Lizotte, and Brian Wiersman, "Deterrence Effects of Civilian Gun Ownership: An Assessment of the Quasi-Experimental Evidence," *Criminology* 29, no. 4 (November 1991): 541–59.

71. See chapter 9.

72. Edward F. Chandler, Member Kings County Grand Jury, letter to the Editor, "Urges Arms Law Repeal," *New York Times,* August 25, 1923, p. 6, col. 7 (if Sullivan law repealed and New Yorkers rearmed, "there would be no such thing as a daylight payroll holdup with a crowd looking on.")

73. Ted L. Huston, Gilbert Geis, and Richard Wright, "The Angry Samaritans," *Psychology Today* (June 1976), p. 64.

Adam Smith found "a man incapable of defending or of revenging himself evidently wants one of the most essential parts of the character of a man." Even if a society had no fear of external invasion, Smith favored widespread training in the use of weapons "to prevent that sort of mental mutilation, deformity and wretchedness, which cowardice necessarily involves in it, from spreading themselves throughout the great body of the people." Adam Smith, *The Wealth of Nations* (New York: Random House, 1937; 1st pub. 1776), Book V, chapter I, part III, article II, p. 739.

74. The best summary of the relevant research is Donald B. Kates, Jr., "The Value of Civilian Handgun Possession as a Deterrent to Crime or a Defense Against Crime," *American Journal of Criminal Law* 18, no. 2 (1991): 113–67.

75. Norval Morris, *Judicature* 72 (August–September 1988), p. 113; John F. Personos, "The Return of Officer Friendly," *Governing,* August 1989: 56–61.

76. Kleck, *Point Blank,* pp. 411–14.

77. "Portland Concealed Weapons Permits Credited with Reducing Homicide Rates," *Women & Guns,* September 1990, p. 7. Despite the headline of the cited article, it is not necessarily clear that the increase in carry permits caused the reduced homicide rate; the point is simply that more carry permits did not lead to more murders.

78. Franklin Fisher and Don Gentile, "List of Young Victims Grows," *Daily News,* September 26, 1990, p. 11.

79. One legal theorist suggests that one of the major benefits of the First Amendment's protection of almost all types of speech, no matter how repulsive, is that society is strengthened by the exercise of tolerance. Lee C. Bollinger, *The Tolerant Society* (New York: Oxford University Press, 1986).

80. Roy Innis, National Chairman of the Congress on Racial Equality, writes: "Another irony of oppressive gun control laws is that as decent citizens are forced to arm themselves illegally, they are less likely to practice and gain proficiency with the weapon." Roy Innis, "Bearing Arms for Self-Defense—A Human and Civil Right," speech, May 15, 1990, transcript, p. 3.

81. Ill. Ann. Stat, Chapter 38, § 87-2 (Smith-Hurd, 1977) (prohibition on possessing handguns without a license, with no exception for school sports).

82. John Foley, *The Jefferson Cyclopedia* (New York: Russell & Russell, 1967), p. 318.

83. "Violence in Big Cities—Behind the Surge," *U.S. News & World Report,* February 23, 1981, pp. 63, 65. Successful use of tear gas requires a difficult pinpoint shot into an oncoming attacker's eyes.

84. Patrick Carr and George W. Gardner, *Gun People* (Garden City, N.Y.: Doubleday, 1985), p. 112, quoting Kennesaw Mayor Darvis Purdy.

85. "Orlando Sessions Educate," *American Rifleman,* July 1988, p. 57.

86. California Senate Bill no. 1130, March 7, 1985; Gale Cook, "Senator Wants Schools to Teach Gun Use, Hunting," *San Francisco Examiner,* June 9, 1985, p. B4.

87. Solicitor General of Canada, *Gun Control in Canada: Working Together to Save Lives* (1978), p. 1.

88. Mandatory safety courses in Detroit and East Lansing, Michigan, charged $60, a rather high amount for the exercise of a fundamental right. The Detroit courses were only given twice a year, thereby imposing a waiting period of up to six months on gun purchasers. In 1990, the Michigan legislature preempted the field of firearms control, and abolished local ordinances like those in Detroit.

89. See chapter 2, note 20 and accompanying text.

90. Chapter 3 note 224 discusses the prohibitionist efforts of American lobbies that assert they only want moderate "control" of firearms.

91. After the House of Representatives passed a bill for a national handgun waiting period, Representative William Clay (D-Missouri) stated: "The Brady Bill is the minimum step. . . . We need much stricter gun control and, eventually, we should bar the ownership of handguns, except in a few cases."

For more on waiting periods, see David B. Kopel, *Why Gun Waiting Periods Threaten Public Safety,* Independence Institute Issue Paper No. 4–91 (Golden, Colo.: Independence Institute, 1991), reprinted in *Congressional Record,* June 28, 1991: S9046-61 (Waiting periods and associated background checks so rarely prevent crime that the use of police resources for background checks diverts police from tasks more likely to enhance public safety. In states with waiting periods, police frequently abuse short waiting periods to turn them into lengthy waiting periods or near prohibition).

92. Bob Badland, "Firearm Safety Education in New Zealand," in *Proceedings of the International Shooting Sports Symposium* (Wellington, New Zealand: New Zealand Mountain Safety Council, 1981) (symposium held October 25, 1980).

93. Edward Countryman, *A People in Revolution: The American Revolution and Political Society in New York, 1760–1790* (New York: W. W. Norton, 1989), p. 178.

94. Joseph G. Rosa and Robin May, *Buffalo Bill and His Wild West* (Lawrence: University Press of Kansas, 1989).

95. Lee Kennett and James L. Anderson, *The Gun in America: The Origins of a National Dilemma* (New York: Westport Press, 1975), p. 119.

Index

443